MyMISLab™: Improves Student Engagement Before, During, and After Class

Prep and Engagement

- **NEW! VIDEO LIBRARY –** Robust video library with over 100 new book-specific videos that include easy-to-assign assessments, the ability for instructors to add YouTube or other sources, the ability for students to upload video submissions, and the ability for polling and teamwork.

- **Decision-making simulations – NEW and improved feedback for students.** Place your students in the role of a key decision-maker! Simulations branch based on the decisions students make, providing a variation of scenario paths. Upon completion students receive a grade, as well as a detailed report of the choices and the associated consequences of those decisions.

- **Video exercises – UPDATED with new exercises.** Engaging videos that bring business concepts to life and explore business topics related to the theory students are learning in class. Quizzes then assess students' comprehension of the concepts covered in each video.

- **Learning Catalytics –** A "bring your own device" student engagement, assessment, and classroom intelligence system helps instructors analyze students' critical-thinking skills during lecture.

- **Dynamic Study Modules (DSMs) – UPDATED with additional questions.** Through adaptive learning, students get personalized guidance where and when they need it most, creating greater engagement, improving knowledge retention, and supporting subject-matter mastery. Also available on mobile devices.

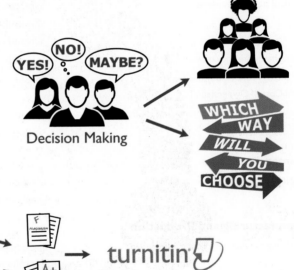

Decision Making

Critical Thinking

- **Writing Space – UPDATED with new commenting tabs, new prompts, and a new tool for students called Pearson Writer.** A single location to develop and assess concept mastery and critical thinking, the Writing Space offers assisted graded and create your own writing assignments, allowing you to exchange personalized feedback with students quickly and easily.

Writing Space can also check students' work for improper citation or plagiarism by comparing it against the world's most accurate text comparison database available from **Turnitin**.

- **Additional Features –** Included with the MyLab are a powerful homework and test manager, robust gradebook tracking, Reporting Dashboard, comprehensive online course content, and easily scalable and shareable content.

http://www.pearsonmylabandmastering.com

PEARSON

Integrating Business with Technology

By completing the projects in this text, students will be able to demonstrate business knowledge, application software proficiency, and Internet skills. These projects can be used by instructors as learning assessment tools and by students as demonstrations of business, software, and problem-solving skills to future employers. Here are some of the skills and competencies students using this text will be able to demonstrate:

Business Application skills: Use of both business and software skills in real-world business applications. Demonstrates both business knowledge and proficiency in spreadsheet, database, and Web page/blog creation tools.

Internet skills: Ability to use Internet tools to access information, conduct research, or perform online calculations and analysis.

Analytical, writing and presentation skills: Ability to research a specific topic, analyze a problem, think creatively, suggest a solution, and prepare a clear written or oral presentation of the solution, working either individually or with others in a group.

* Dirt Bikes Running Case in MyMISLab

Business Application Skills

Business Skills	Software Skills	Chapter
Finance and Accounting		
Financial statement analysis	Spreadsheet charts	Chapter 2*
	Spreadsheet formulas	Chapter 10
	Spreadsheet downloading and formatting	
Pricing hardware and software	Spreadsheet formulas	Chapter 5
Technology rent vs. buy decision	Spreadsheet formulas	Chapter 5*
Total Cost of Ownership (TCO) Analysis		
Analyzing telecommunications services and costs	Spreadsheet formulas	Chapter 7
Risk assessment	Spreadsheet charts and formulas	Chapter 8
Human Resources		
Employee training and skills tracking	Database design	Chapter 12*
	Database querying and reporting	
Manufacturing and Production		
Analyzing supplier performance and pricing	Spreadsheet date functions	Chapter 2
	Data filtering	
	Database functions	
Inventory management	Importing data into a database	Chapter 6
	Database querying and reporting	
Bill of materials cost sensitivity analysis	Spreadsheet data tables	Chapter 11*
	Spreadsheet formulas	
Sales and Marketing		
Sales trend analysis	Database querying and reporting	Chapter 1
Customer reservation system	Database querying and reporting	Chapter 3
Customer sales analysis	Database design	
Marketing decisions	Spreadsheet pivot tables	Chapter 11
Customer profiling	Database design	Chapter 6*
	Database querying and reporting	

Customer service analysis	Database design	Chapter 9
	Database querying and reporting	
Sales lead and customer analysis	Database design	Chapter 12
	Database querying and reporting	
Blog creation and design	Blog creation tool	Chapter 4

Internet Skills

Using online software tools for job hunting and career development	Chapter 1
Using online interactive mapping software to plan efficient transportation routes	Chapter 2
Researching product information	Chapter 3
Evaluating Web sites for auto sales	
Analyzing Web browser privacy protection	Chapter 4
Researching travel costs using online travel sites	Chapter 5
Searching online databases for products and services	Chapter 6
Using Web search engines for business research	Chapter 7
Researching and evaluating business outsourcing services	Chapter 8
Researching and evaluating supply chain management services	Chapter 9
Evaluating e-commerce hosting services	Chapter 10
Using shopping bots to compare product price, features, and availability	Chapter 11
Analyzing Web site design	Chapter 12

Analytical, Writing, and Presentation Skills*

Business Problem	Chapter
Management analysis of a business	Chapter 1
Value chain and competitive forces analysis	Chapter 3
Business strategy formulation	
Formulating a corporate privacy policy	Chapter 4
Employee productivity analysis	Chapter 7
Disaster recovery planning	Chapter 8
Locating and evaluating suppliers	Chapter 9
Developing an e-commerce strategy	Chapter 10

Essentials of Management Information Systems

Twelfth Edition

Global Edition

Kenneth C. Laudon
New York University

Jane P. Laudon
Azimuth Information Systems

PEARSON

Boston   Columbus   Indianapolis   New York   San Francisco
Amsterdam   Cape Town   Dubai   London   Madrid   Milan   Munich   Paris   Montréal   Toronto
Delhi   Mexico City   São Paulo   Sydney   Hong Kong   Seoul   Singapore   Taipei   Tokyo

Vice President, Business Publishing: Donna Battista
Editor-in-Chief: Stephanie Wall
Acquisitions Editor: Nicole Sam
Editorial Assistant: Olivia Vignone
Vice President, Product Marketing: Maggie Moylan
Director of Marketing, Digital Services and Products: Jeanette
    Koskinas
Executive Field Marketing Manager: Adam Goldstein
Field Marketing Manager: Lenny Ann Raper
Product Marketing Assistant: Jessica Quazza
Team Lead, Program Management: Ashley Santora
Program Manager: Denise Weiss
Team Lead, Project Management: Jeff Holcomb
Project Manager: Karalyn Holland
Managing Editor, Global Edition: Steven Jackson
Associate Project Editor: Amrita Kar
Senior Project Editor, Global Edition: Daniel Luiz
Manager, Media Production, Global Edition: M. Vikram
    Kumar

Senior Manufacturing Controller, Production, Global Edition:
    Trudy Kimber
Operations Specialist: Carol Melville
Creative Director: Blair Brown
Senior Art Director: Janet Slowik
Vice President, Director of Digital Strategy
    and Assessment: Paul Gentile
Manager of Learning Applications: Paul DeLuca
Digital Editor: Brian Surette
Director, Digital Studio: Sacha Laustsen
Digital Studio Manager: Diane Lombardo
Digital Studio Project Manager: Regina DaSilva
Digital Studio Project Manager: Alana Coles
Digital Studio Project Manager: Robin Lazrus
Full-Service Project Management and Composition:
Interior and Cover Design: Integra
Cover Image: Syda Productions/Shutterstock
Printer/Binder: Courier/Kendallville
Cover Printer: Phoenix Color/Hagerstown

Pearson Education Limited
Edinburgh Gate
Harlow
Essex CM20 2JE
England
and Associated Companies throughout the world

Visit us on the World Wide Web at:
www.pearson.com/uk

© Pearson Education Limited 2015

British Library Cataloguing-in-Publication Data
A catalogue record for this book is available from the British Library

10 9 8 7 6 5 4 3 2 1
19 18 17 16

Typeset in 10.5/12.5 Times LT Std, 9.5pt by Azimuth Interactive, Inc.
Printed and bound by Vivar in Malaysia

ISBN 10: 1-292-15377-6
ISBN 13: 978-1-292-15377-3

About the Authors

Kenneth C. Laudon is a Professor of Information Systems at New York University's Stern School of Business. He holds a B.A. in Economics from Stanford and a Ph.D. from Columbia University. He has authored twelve books dealing with electronic commerce, information systems, organizations, and society. Professor Laudon has also written over forty articles concerned with the social, organizational, and management impacts of information systems, privacy, ethics, and multimedia technology.

Professor Laudon's current research is on the planning and management of large-scale information systems and multimedia information technology. He has received grants from the National Science Foundation to study the evolution of national information systems at the Social Security Administration, the IRS, and the FBI. Ken's research focuses on enterprise system implementation, computer-related organizational and occupational changes in large organizations, changes in management ideology, changes in public policy, and understanding productivity change in the knowledge sector.

Ken Laudon has testified as an expert before the United States Congress. He has been a researcher and consultant to the Office of Technology Assessment (United States Congress), Department of Homeland Security, and to the Office of the President, several executive branch agencies, and Congressional Committees. Professor Laudon also acts as an in-house educator for several consulting firms and as a consultant on systems planning and strategy to several Fortune 500 firms.

At NYU's Stern School of Business, Ken Laudon teaches courses on Managing the Digital Firm, Information Technology and Corporate Strategy, Professional Responsibility (Ethics), and Electronic Commerce and Digital Markets. Ken Laudon's hobby is sailing.

Jane Price Laudon is a management consultant in the information systems area and the author of seven books. Her special interests include systems analysis, data management, MIS auditing, software evaluation, and teaching business professionals how to design and use information systems.

Jane received her Ph.D. from Columbia University, her M.A. from Harvard University, and her B.A. from Barnard College. She has taught at Columbia University and the New York University Stern School of Business. She maintains a lifelong interest in Oriental languages and civilizations.

The Laudons have two daughters, Erica and Elisabeth, to whom this book is dedicated.

Brief Contents

Complete Contents

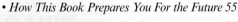

Preface

The Global Edition is written for business school students in Europe, the Middle East, South Africa, Australia, and the Pacific Asian region. Case studies and examples focus on how firms in these regions use information systems. We wrote this book for business school students who wanted an in-depth look at how today's business firms use information technologies and systems to achieve corporate objectives. Information systems are one of the major tools available to business managers for achieving operational excellence, developing new products and services, improving decision making, and achieving competitive advantage. Students will find here the most up-to-date and comprehensive overview of how business firms use information systems to achieve these objectives. After reading this book, we expect students will be able to participate in, and even lead, management discussions of information systems for their firms.

When interviewing potential employees, business firms often look for new hires who know how to use information systems and technologies for achieving bottom-line business results. Regardless of whether you are an accounting, finance, management, operations management, marketing, or information systems major, the knowledge and information you find in this book will be valuable throughout your business career.

What's New in This Edition

CURRENCY

The 12th edition features all new opening, closing, and Interactive Session cases. The text, figures, tables, and cases have been updated through December 2015 with the latest sources from industry and MIS research.

NEW FEATURES

- Assisted-graded Writing Questions at the end of each chapter with prebuilt grading rubrics and computerized essay scoring help instructors prepare, deliver, and grade writing assignments.
- A new Video Cases collection contains 31 video cases (2 or more per chapter) and 13 additional instructional videos covering key concepts and experiences in the MIS world.
- The text contains 47 Learning Tracks in MyMISLab for additional coverage of selected topics.
- Video Cases and Chapter Cases are listed at the beginning of each chapter.

NEW TOPICS

- **Big data and the Internet of Things:** In-depth coverage of big data, big data analytics, and the Internet of Things (IoT) are included in Chapters 1, 6, 7, and 11. Coverage includes big data analytics, analyzing IoT data streams, Hadoop, in-memory computing, nonrelational databases, and analytic platforms.
- **Cloud computing:** Updated and expanded coverage of cloud computing appears in Chapter 5 (IT Infrastructure) with more detail on types of cloud services, private and public clouds, hybrid clouds, managing cloud services, and a new Interactive Session on using cloud services. Cloud computing is also covered in Chapter 6 (databases in the cloud), Chapter 8 (cloud security), Chapter 9 (cloud-based CRM and ERP), Chapter 10 (e-commerce), and Chapter 12 (cloud-based systems development).
- **Social, mobile, local:** New e-commerce content in Chapter 10 describes how social tools, mobile technology, and location-based services are transforming marketing and advertising.

- **Social business:** Expanded coverage of social business is introduced in Chapter 2 and discussed throughout the text. Detailed discussions of enterprise (internal corporate) social networking as well as social networking in e-commerce are included.
- BYOD and mobile device management
- Wearable computers
- Smart products
- Internet of Things (IoT)
- Mobile application development, mobile and native apps
- Operational intelligence
- Expanded coverage of business analytics, including big data analytics
- On-demand business
- Windows 10
- Microsoft Office 365
- Zero-day vulnerabilities
- Two-factor authentication
- Ransomware
- Chief data officer
- MOOCs in business firms

What's New in MIS?

Plenty. In fact, there's a whole new world of doing business using new technologies for managing and organizing. What makes the MIS field the most exciting area of study in schools of business is the continuous change in technology, management, and business processes. (Chapter 1 describes these changes in more detail.)

IT INNOVATIONS

A continuing stream of information technology innovations is transforming the traditional business world. Examples include the emergence of cloud computing, the growth of a mobile digital business platform based on smartphones and tablet computers, big data, and the use of social networks by managers to achieve business objectives. Most of these changes have occurred in the past few years. These innovations enable entrepreneurs and innovative traditional firms to create new products and services, develop new business models, and transform the day-to-day conduct of business. In the process, some old businesses, even industries, are being destroyed while new businesses are springing up.

NEW BUSINESS MODELS

For instance, the emergence of online video services such as Netflix for streaming, Apple iTunes, Amazon, and many others for downloading video, has forever changed how premium video is distributed and even created. Netflix in 2015 attracted 62 million subscribers worldwide to what it calls the Internet TV revolution. Netflix has moved into premium TV show production with nearly 30 original shows such as *House of Cards* and *Orange is the New Black* challenging cable and broadcast producers of TV shows and potentially disrupting cable network dominance of TV show production. Apple's iTunes now accounts for 67 percent of movie and TV show downloads and has struck deals with major Hollywood studios for recent movies and TV shows. A growing trickle of viewers are unplugging from cable and using only the Internet for entertainment.

E-COMMERCE EXPANDING

E-commerce generated about $531 billion in revenues in 2015 and is estimated to grow to nearly $800 billion by 2019. E-commerce is changing how firms design, produce, and deliver their products and services. E-commerce has reinvented itself again, disrupting the traditional marketing and advertising industry and putting major media and content firms in jeopardy. Facebook and other social networking sites such as YouTube, Twitter, and Tumblr, along with Netflix, Apple Beats music service, and many other media firms exemplify the new face of e-commerce in the 21st century. They sell services. When we think of e-commerce, we tend to think of selling physical products. Although this iconic vision of e-commerce is still very powerful and the fastest growing form of retail in the U.S., growing up alongside is a whole new value stream based on selling services, not goods. It's a services model of e-commerce. Growth in social commerce is spurred by powerful growth of the mobile platform; 80 percent of Facebook's users access the service from mobile phones and tablets. Information systems and technologies are the foundation of this new services-based e-commerce.

MANAGEMENT CHANGES

Likewise, the management of business firms has changed: With new mobile smartphones, high-speed wireless Wi-Fi networks, and wireless laptop computers, remote salespeople on the road are only seconds away from their managers' questions and oversight. Business is going mobile, along with consumers. Managers on the move are in direct, continuous contact with their employees. The growth of enterprise-wide information systems with extraordinarily rich data means that managers no longer operate in a fog of confusion but, instead, have online, nearly instant access to the really important information they need for accurate and timely decisions. In addition to their public uses on the web, wikis and blogs are becoming important corporate tools for communication, collaboration, and information sharing.

CHANGES IN FIRMS AND ORGANIZATIONS

Compared to industrial organizations of the previous century, new, fast-growing, 21st-century business firms put less emphasis on hierarchy and structure and more emphasis on employees taking on multiple roles and tasks. They put greater emphasis on competency and skills than on position in the hierarchy. They emphasize higher speed and more accurate decision making based on data and analysis. They are more aware of changes in technology, consumer attitudes, and culture. They use social media to enter into conversations with consumers and demonstrate a greater willingness to listen to consumers, in part because they have no choice. They show better understanding of the importance of information technology in creating and managing business firms and other organizations. To the extent that organizations and business firms demonstrate these characteristics, they are 21st-century digital firms.

The 12th Edition: The Comprehensive Solution for the MIS Curriculum

Since its inception, this text has helped define the MIS course around the globe. This edition continues to be authoritative but is also more customizable, flexible, and geared to meeting the needs of different colleges, universities, and individual instructors. Many of its learning tools are now available in digital form. This book is now part of a complete learning package that includes the core text, Video Case Study Package, and Learning Tracks.

The core text consists of 12 chapters with hands-on projects covering the most essential topics in MIS. An important part of the core text is the Video Case Study and Instructional Video Package: 31 video case studies (2 to 3 per chapter) plus 13 instructional videos that illustrate business uses of information systems, explain new technologies, and explore concepts. Videos are keyed to the topics of each chapter.

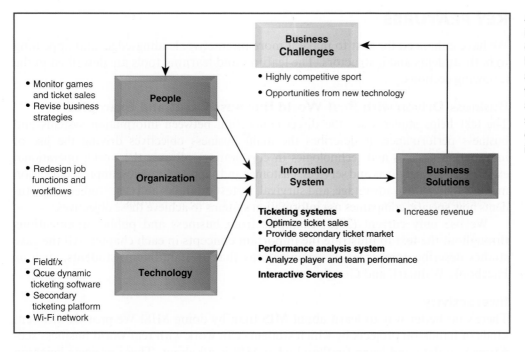

A diagram accompanying each chapter-opening case graphically illustrates how people, organization, and technology elements work together to create an information system solution to the business challenges discussed in the case.

In addition, for students and instructors who want to go deeper into selected topics, 47 Learning Tracks in MyMISLab cover a variety of MIS topics in greater depth.

THE CORE TEXT

The core text provides an overview of fundamental MIS concepts by using an integrated framework for describing and analyzing information systems. This framework shows information systems composed of people, organization, and technology elements and is reinforced in student projects and case studies.

CHAPTER ORGANIZATION

Each chapter contains the following elements:

- A Chapter Outline based on Learning Objectives
- Lists of all the Case Studies and Video Cases for each chapter
- A chapter-opening case describing a real-world organization to establish the theme and importance of the chapter
- A diagram analyzing the opening case in terms of the people, organization, and technology model used throughout the text
- Two Interactive Sessions with Case Study Questions
- A Review Summary keyed to the Student Learning Objectives
- A list of Key Terms that students can use to review concepts
- Review questions for students to test their comprehension of chapter material
- Discussion questions the broader themes of the chapter raise.
- A series of Hands-on MIS Projects consisting of two Management Decision Problems, a hands-on application software project, and a project to develop Internet skills
- A Collaboration and Teamwork Project to develop teamwork and presentation skills, with options for using open source collaboration tools
- A chapter-ending case study for students to apply chapter concepts
- Two assisted-graded writing questions with prebuilt grading rubrics
- Chapter references

KEY FEATURES

We have enhanced the text to make it more interactive, leading-edge, and appealing to both students and instructors. The features and learning tools are described in the following sections:

Business-Driven with Real-World Business Cases and Examples

The text helps students see the direct connection between information systems and business performance. It describes the main business objectives driving the use of information systems and technologies in corporations all over the world: operational excellence, new products and services, customer and supplier intimacy, improved decision making, competitive advantage, and survival. In-text examples and case studies show students how specific companies use information systems to achieve these objectives.

We use only current (2015) examples from business and public organizations throughout the text to illustrate the important concepts in each chapter. All the case studies describe companies or organizations that are familiar to students, such as Facebook, Walmart, and Google.

Interactivity

There's no better way to learn about MIS than by doing MIS! We provide different kinds of hands-on projects by which students can work with real-world business scenarios and data and learn firsthand what MIS is all about. These projects heighten student involvement in this exciting subject.

- **Online Video Case Package:** Students can watch short videos online, either in class or at home or work, and then apply the concepts of the book to the analysis of the video. Every chapter contains at least two business video cases that explain how business firms and managers are using information systems and explore concepts discussed in the chapter. Each video case consists of a video about a real-world company, a background text case, and case study questions. These video cases enhance students' understanding of MIS topics and the relevance of MIS to the business world. In addition, 13 Instructional Videos describe developments and concepts in MIS keyed to respective chapters.
- **Interactive Sessions:** Two short cases in each chapter have been redesigned as Interactive Sessions to be used in the classroom (or on Internet discussion boards) to stimulate student interest and active learning. Each case concludes with case study questions. The case study questions provide topics for class discussion, Internet discussion, or written assignments.

Each chapter contains two Interactive Sessions on People, Organizations, or Technology using real-world companies to illustrate chapter concepts and issues.

INTERACTIVE SESSION: PEOPLE   Getting Social with Customers

Businesses of all sizes are finding Facebook, Twitter, and other social media to be powerful tools for engaging customers, amplifying product messages, discovering trends and influencers, building brand awareness, and taking action on customer requests and recommendations. Half of all Twitter users recommend products in their tweets.

About 1.4 billion people use Facebook, and more than 30 million businesses have active brand pages enabling users to interact with the brand through blogs, comment pages, contests, and offerings on the brand page. The Like button gives users a chance to share with their social network their feelings about content and other objects they are viewing and websites they are visiting. With Like buttons on millions of websites, Facebook can

In addition to monitoring people's chatter on Twitter, Facebook, and other social media, some companies are using sentiment analysis (see Chapter 6) to probe more deeply into their likes and dislikes. For example, during the 2014 Golden Globe Awards, thousands of women watching the ceremony tweeted detailed comments about Hayden Panettiere and Kelly Osborne's slicked-back hairdos. Almost instantaneously, the Twitter feeds of these women received instructions from L'Oréal Paris showing them how to capture various red-carpet looks at home, along with promotions and special deals for L'Oréal products. L'Oreal had worked with Poptip, a real-time market research company to analyze what conversations about hairstyling connected to Golden Globe

1. Assess the people, organization, and technology issues for using social media to engage with customers.

2. What are the advantages and disadvantages of using social media for advertising, brand building, market research, and customer service?

3. Give some examples of business decisions in this case study that were facilitated by using social media to interact with customers.

4. Should all companies use Facebook and Twitter for customer service and marketing? Why or why not? What kinds of companies are best suited to use these platforms?

Case Study Questions encourage students to apply chapter concepts to real-world companies in class discussions, student presentations, or writing assignments.

- **Hands-on MIS Projects:** Every chapter concludes with a Hands-on MIS Projects section containing three types of projects: two Management Decision problems; a hands-on application software exercise using Microsoft Excel, Access, or web page and blog creation tools; and a project that develops Internet business skills. A Dirt Bikes USA running case in MyMISLab provides additional hands-on projects for each chapter.

II-9 Applebee's is the largest casual dining chain in the world, with more than 1800 locations throughout the United States and 20 other countries. The menu features beef, chicken, and pork items as well as burgers, pasta, and seafood. Applebee's CEO wants to make the restaurant more profitable by developing menus that are tastier and contain more items that customers want and are willing to pay for despite rising costs for gasoline and agricultural products. How might business intelligence help management implement this strategy? What pieces of data would Applebee's need to collect? What kinds of reports would be useful to help management make decisions about how to improve menus and profitability?

Two real-world business scenarios per chapter provide opportunities for students to apply chapter concepts and practice management decision making.

Store & Region Sales Database

I ▾	Store N ▾	Sales Regic ▾	Item I ▾	Item Descripti ▾	Unit Pri ▾	Units So ▾	Week Ending ▾	Click to Add ▾
1	1	South	2005	17" Monitor	$229.00	28	10/27/2015	
2	1	South	2005	17" Monitor	$229.00	30	11/24/2015	
3	1	South	2005	17" Monitor	$229.00	9	12/29/2015	
4	1	South	3006	101 Keyboard	$19.95	30	10/27/2015	
5	1	South	3006	101 Keyboard	$19.95	35	11/24/2015	
6	1	South	3006	101 Keyboard	$19.95	39	12/29/2015	
7	1	South	6050	PC Mouse	$8.95	28	10/27/2015	
8	1	South	6050	PC Mouse	$8.95	3	11/24/2015	
9	1	South	6050	PC Mouse	$8.95	38	12/29/2015	
10	1	South	8500	Desktop CPU	$849.95	25	10/27/2015	
11	1	South	8500	Desktop CPU	$849.95	27	11/24/2015	
12	1	South	8500	Desktop CPU	$849.95	33	12/29/2015	
13	2	South	2005	17" Monitor	$229.00	8	10/27/2015	
14	2	South	2005	17" Monitor	$229.00	8	11/24/2015	
15	2	South	2005	17" Monitor	$229.00	10	12/29/2015	
16	2	South	3006	101 Keyboard	$19.95	8	10/27/2015	
17	2	South	3006	101 Keyboard	$19.95	8	11/24/2015	
18	2	South	3006	101 Keyboard	$19.95	8	12/29/2015	
19	2	South	6050	PC Mouse	$8.95	9	10/27/2015	
20	2	South	6050	PC Mouse	$8.95	9	11/24/2015	
21	2	South	6050	PC Mouse	$8.95	8	12/29/2015	
22	2	South	8500	Desktop CPU	$849.95	18	10/27/2015	

Students practice using software in real-world settings for achieving operational excellence and enhancing decision making.

IMPROVING DECISION MAKING: USING WEB TOOLS TO CONFIGURE AND PRICE AN AUTOMOBILE

Software skills: Internet-based software
Business skills: Researching product information and pricing

3-11 In this exercise, you will use software at car-selling websites to find product information about a car of your choice and use that information to make an important purchase decision. You will also evaluate two of these sites as selling tools.

You are interested in purchasing a new Ford Escape (or some other car of your choice). Go to the website of CarsDirect (www.carsdirect.com) and begin your investigation. Locate the Ford Escape. Research the various Escape models; choose one you prefer in terms of price, features, and safety ratings. Locate and read at least two reviews. Surf the website of the manufacturer, in this case Ford (www.ford.com). Compare the information available on Ford's website with that of CarsDirect for the Ford Escape. Try to locate the lowest price for the car you want in a local dealer's inventory. Suggest improvements for CarsDirect.com and Ford.com.

• **Collaboration and Teamwork Projects:** Each chapter features a collaborative project that encourages students working in teams to use Google Drive, Google Docs, or other open-source collaboration tools. The first team project in Chapter 1 asks students to build a collaborative Google site.

Assessment and AACSB Assessment Guidelines

The Association to Advance Collegiate Schools of Business (AACSB) is a not-for-profit corporation of educational institutions, corporations and other organizations that seek to improve business education primarily by accrediting university business programs. As part of its accreditation activities, the AACSB has developed an Assurance of Learning Program designed to ensure that schools do in fact teach students what they promise. Schools are required to state a clear mission, develop a coherent business program, identify student learning objectives, and then prove that students do in fact achieve the objectives.

We have attempted in this book to support AACSB efforts to encourage assessment-based education. The front end papers of this edition identify student learning objectives and anticipated outcomes for our Hands-on MIS projects. The authors will provide custom advice on how to use this text in their colleges with different missions and assessment needs. Please email the authors or contact your local Pearson representative for contact information.

For more information on the AACSB Assurance of Learning Program, and how this text supports assessment-based learning, please visit the website for this book.

Customization and Flexibility: New Learning Track Modules

Our Learning Tracks feature gives instructors the flexibility to provide in-depth coverage of the topics they choose. Forty-seven Learning Tracks in MyMISLab are available to instructors and students. This supplementary content takes students deeper into MIS topics, concepts, and debates; reviews basic technology concepts in hardware, software, database design, telecommunications, and other areas; and provides additional hands-on software instruction. The 12th edition includes new Learning Tracks on e-commerce payment systems, including Bitcoin, and Occupational and Career Outlook for Information Systems Majors 2012–2020.

Author-certified test bank and supplements

• **Author-certified test bank:** The authors have worked closely with skilled test item writers to ensure that higher-level cognitive skills are tested. Test bank multiple choice questions include questions on content but also include many questions that require analysis, synthesis, and evaluation skills.

- **Annotated slides:** The authors have prepared a comprehensive collection of 50 PowerPoint slides to be used in your lectures. Many of these slides are the same as Ken Laudon uses in his MIS classes and executive education presentations. Each of the slides is annotated with teaching suggestions for asking students questions, developing in-class lists that illustrate key concepts, and recommending other firms as examples in addition to those provided in the text. The annotations are like an instructor's manual built into the slides and make it easier to teach the course effectively.

Student Learning Focused

Student Learning Objectives are organized around a set of study questions to focus student attention. Each chapter concludes with a Review Summary and Review Questions organized around these study questions, and each major chapter section is based on a Learning Objective.

Career Resources

The instructor resources for this text include extensive career resources, including job-hunting guides and instructions on how to build a digital portfolio demonstrating the business knowledge, application software proficiency, and Internet skills acquired from using the text. The portfolio can be included in a résumé or job application or used as a learning assessment tool for instructors.

INSTRUCTOR RESOURCES

At the Instructor Resource Center, www.pearsonhighered.com/irc, instructors can easily register to gain access to a variety of instructor resources available with this text in downloadable format.

If assistance is needed, our dedicated technical support team is ready to help with the media supplements that accompany this text. Visit http://247.pearsoned.com for answers to frequently asked questions and toll-free user support phone numbers.

The following supplements are available with this text:

- Instructor's Resource Manual
- Test Bank
- TestGen® Computerized Test Bank
- PowerPoint Presentation
- Image Library
- Lecture Notes

Video Cases and Instructional Videos

Instructors can download step-by-step instructions for accessing the video cases from the Instructor Resources Center. All Video Cases and Instructional Videos are listed at the beginning of each chapter as well as in the Preface.

Learning Tracks Modules

Forty-seven Learning Tracks in MyMISLab provide additional coverage topics for students and instructors. See page 25 for a list of the Learning Tracks available for this edition.

Video Cases and Instructional Videos

Chapter	Video
Chapter 1: Business Information Systems in Your Career	Case 1: UPS Global Operations with the DIAD Case 2: Google Data Center Efficiency Best Practices Instructional Video 1: Green Energy Efficiency in a Data Center Using Tivoli Architecture (IBM) Instructional Video 2: Tour IBM's Raleigh Data Center
Chapter 2: Global E-Business and Collaboration	Case 1: Walmart's Retail Link Supply Chain Case 2: CEMEX - Becoming a Social Business Instructional Video 1: US Foodservice Grows Market with Oracle CRM on Demand
Chapter 3: Achieving Competitive Advantage with Information Systems	Case 1: National Basketball Association: Competing on Global Delivery with Akamai OS Streaming Case 2: IT and Geo-Mapping Help a Small Business Succeed Case 3: Materials Handling Equipment Corp: Enterprise Systems Drive Corporate Strategy for a Small Business Instructional Video 1: SAP BusinessOne ERP: From Orders to Final Delivery and Payment
Chapter 4: Ethical and Social Issues in Information Systems	Case 1: What Net Neutrality Means for You Case 2: Facebook Privacy: Social Network Data Mining Case 3: Data Mining for Terrorists and Innocents Instructional Video 1: Viktor Mayer Schönberger on the Right to Be Forgotten
Chapter 5: IT Infrastructure: Hardware and Software	Case 1: Rockwell Automation Fuels the Oil and Gas Industry with the Internet of Things Case 2: ESPN.com: Getting to eXtreme Scale on the Web Instructional Video 1: IBM Blue Cloud Is Ready-to-Use Computing
Chapter 6: Foundations of Business Intelligence: Databases and Information Management	Case 1: Dubuque Uses Cloud Computing and Sensors to Build a Smarter City Case 2: Brooks Brothers Closes in on Omnichannel Retail Case 3: Maruti Suzuki Business Intelligence and Enterprise Databases
Chapter 7: Telecommunications, the Internet, and Wireless Technology	Case 1: Telepresence Moves Out of the Boardroom and into the Field Case 2: Virtual Collaboration with IBM Sametime
Chapter 8: Securing Information Systems	Case 1: Stuxnet and Cyberwarfare Case 2: Cyberespionage: The Chinese Threat Case 3: IBM Zone Trusted Information Channel Instructional Video 1: Sony PlayStation Hacked; Data Stolen from 77 Million Users Instructional Video 2: Zappos Working to Correct Online Security Breach Instructional Video 3: Meet the Hackers: Anonymous Statement on Hacking Sony
Chapter 9: Achieving Operational Excellence and Customer Intimacy: Enterprise Applications	Case 1: Workday: Enterprise Cloud Software-as-a-Service (SaaS) Case 2: Evolution Homecare Manages Patients with Microsoft Dynamics CRM Instructional Video 1: GSMS Protects Patients by Serializing Every Bottle of Drugs
Chapter 10: E-Commerce: Digital Markets, Digital Goods	Case 1: Groupon: Deals Galore Case 2: Etsy: A Marketplace and Community Case 3: Ford Manufacturing Supply Chain: B2B Marketplace
Chapter 11: Improving Decision Making and Managing Knowledge	Case 1: How IBM's Watson Became a Jeopardy Champion Case 2: Alfresco: Open Source Document Management and Collaboration Case 3: FreshDirect Uses Business Intelligence to Manage Its Online Grocery Case 4: Business Intelligence Helps the Cincinnati Zoo Instructional Video 1: Analyzing Big Data: IBM Watson: After Jeopardy
Chapter 12: Building Information Systems and Managing Projects	Case 1: IBM: BPM in a Service-Oriented Architecture Case 2: IBM Helps the City of Madrid with Real-Time BPM Software Instructional Video 1: BPM: Business Process Management Customer Story Instructional Video 2: Workflow Management Visualized

Learning Tracks

Chapter	Learning Tracks
Chapter 1: Business Information Systems in Your Career	How Much Does IT Matter? The Changing Business Environment for IT The Business Information Value Chain The Mobile Digital Platform Occupational and Career Outlook for Information Systems Majors 2012–2020
Chapter 2: Global E-Business and Collaboration	Systems from a Functional Perspective IT Enables Collaboration and Teamwork Challenges of Using Business Information Systems Organizing the Information Systems Function
Chapter 3: Achieving Competitive Advantage with Information Systems	Challenges of Using Information Systems for Competitive Advantage Primer on Business Process Design and Documentation Primer on Business Process Management
Chapter 4: Ethical and Social Issues in Information Systems	Developing a Corporate Code of Ethics for IT
Chapter 5: IT Infrastructure: Hardware and Software	How Computer Hardware and Software Work Service Level Agreements Cloud Computing The Open Source Software Initiative The Evolution of IT Infrastructure Technology Drivers of IT Infrastructure Fourth Generation Languages
Chapter 6: Foundations of Business Intelligence: Databases and Information Management	Database Design, Normalization, and Entity-Relationship Diagramming Introduction to SQL Hierarchical and Network Data Models
Chapter 7: Telecommunications, the Internet, and Wireless Technology	Broadband Network Services and Technologies Cellular System Generations Wireless Applications for Customer Relationship Management, Supply Chain Management, and Health Care Introduction to Web 2.0 LAN Topologies
Chapter 8: Securing Information Systems	The Booming Job Market in IT Security The Sarbanes-Oxley Act Computer Forensics General and Application Controls for Information Systems Management Challenges of Security and Control Software Vulnerability and Reliability
Chapter 9: Achieving Operational Excellence and Customer Intimacy: Enterprise Applications	SAP Business Process Map Business Processes in Supply Chain Management and Supply Chain Metrics Best-Practice Business Processes in CRM Software
Chapter 10: E-Commerce: Digital Markets, Digital Goods	E-Commerce Challenges: The Story of Online Groceries Build an E-Commerce Business Plan Hot New Careers in E-Commerce E-Commerce Payment Systems Building an E-Commerce Website
Chapter 11: Improving Decision Making and Managing Knowledge	Building and Using Pivot Tables The Expert System Inference Engine Challenges of Knowledge Management Systems
Chapter 12: Building Information Systems and Managing Projects	Capital Budgeting Methods for Information Systems Investments Enterprise Analysis: Business Systems Planning and Critical Success Factors Unified Modeling Language Information Technology Investments and Productivity

Acknowledgements

The production of any book involves valued contributions from a number of persons. We would like to thank all of our editors for encouragement, insight, and strong support for many years. We thank our editor Nicole Sam, Program Manager Denise Weiss, and Project Manager Karalyn Holland for their role in managing the project. We remain grateful to Bob Horan for all his years of editorial guidance.

Our special thanks go to our supplement authors for their work, including the following MyLab content contributors: John Hupp, Columbus State University; Robert J. Mills, Utah State University; J.K. Sinclaire, Arkansas State University; and Michael L. Smith, SUNY Oswego. We are indebted to Robin Pickering for her assistance with writing and to William Anderson and Megan Miller for their help during production. We thank Diana R. Craig for her assistance with database and software topics.

Special thanks to colleagues at the Stern School of Business at New York University; to Professor Werner Schenk, Simon School of Business, University of Rochester; to Professor Mark Gillenson, Fogelman College of Business and Economics, University of Memphis; to Robert Kostrubanic, CIO and Director of Information Technology Services Indiana-Purdue University Fort Wayne; to Professor Lawrence Andrew of Western Illinois University; to Professor Detlef Schoder of the University of Cologne; to Professor Walter Brenner of the University of St. Gallen; to Professor Lutz Kolbe of the University of Gottingen; to Professor Donald Marchand of the International Institute for Management Development; and to Professor Daniel Botha of Stellenbosch University who provided additional suggestions for improvement. Thank you to Professor Ken Kraemer, University of California at Irvine, and Professor John King, University of Michigan, for more than a decade's long discussion of information systems and organizations. And a special remembrance and dedication to Professor Rob Kling, University of Indiana, for being my friend and colleague over so many years.

We also want especially to thank all our reviewers whose suggestions helped improve our texts. Reviewers for this edition include the following:

Brad Allen, Plymouth State University

Dawit Demissie, University of Albany

Anne Formalarie, Plymouth State University

Bin Gu, University of Texas–Austin

Essia Hamouda, University of California–Riverside

Linda Lau, Longwood University

Kimberly L. Merritt, Oklahoma Christian University

James W. Miller, Dominican University

Fiona Nah, University of Nebraska–Lincoln

M. K. Raja, University of Texas Arlington

Thomas Schambach, Illinois State University

Shawn Weisfeld, Florida Institute of Technology

Pearson gratefully acknowledges and thanks the following people for their work on the Global Edition:

International Contributors

Ahmed Elragal, German University in Cairo

Niveen Ezzat, Cairo University

Bee Hua Goh, National University of Singapore

Jonas Hedman, Copenhagen Business School

Ari Heiskanen, University of Oulu

Stefan Henningsson, Copenhagen Business School

Andy Jones, Staffordshire University

Faouzi Kamoun, Zayed University

Patricia Lago, VU University Amsterdam

Lesley Land, University of New South Wales

Robert Manderson, University of Roehampton Business School

Roehampton Business School

Daniel Ortiz-Arroyo, Aalborg University

Sahil Raj, Punjabi University

Neerja Sethi, Nanyang Technological University

Vijay Sethi, Nanyang Technological University

Upasana Singh, University of KwaZulu-Natal

Damian A. Tamburri, VU University Amsterdam

International Reviewers

Indriyati Atmosukarto, Singapore Institute of Technology

V.V. Moorthy, SIM University

Neerja Sethi, Nanyang Technological University

K.C.L.
J.P.L.

Information Systems in the Digital Age

Part I introduces the major themes and the problem-solving approaches that are used throughout this book. While surveying the role of information systems in today's businesses, this part raises a series of major questions: What is an information system? Why are information systems so essential in businesses today? How can information systems help businesses become more competitive? What do I need to know about information systems to succeed in my business career? What ethical and social issues do widespread use of information systems raise?

PART I

Business Information Systems in Your Career

CHAPTER 1

LEARNING OBJECTIVES

After reading this chapter, you will be able to answer the following questions:

1-1 Why are information systems so essential for running and managing a business today?

1-2 What exactly is an information system? How does it work? What are its people, organizational, and technology components?

1-3 How will a four-step method for business problem solving help you solve information system-related problems?

1-4 How will information systems affect business careers, and what information systems skills and knowledge are essential?

CHAPTER CASES

Rugby Football Union Tries Big Data

The Mobile Pocket Office

UPS Competes Globally with Information Technology

Mashaweer: On-Demand Personal Services in the Gulf

VIDEO CASES

Case 1: UPS Global Operations with the DIAD

Case 2: Google Data Center Efficiency Best Practices

Instructional Videos

Green Energy Efficiency in a Data Center, Using Tivoli Architecture (IBM)

Tour IBM's Raleigh Data Center

RUGBY FOOTBALL UNION TRIES BIG DATA

In 1871, twenty-one English clubs decided that their sport, officially called rugby union but commonly referred to simply as rugby, needed an administrative body. The clubs formed The Rugby Football Union (RFU), which today manages the English national team (England Rugby) in partnership with Premier Rugby Limited. Responsible for the promotion of rugby at all levels, the RFU organizes the Six Nations Championship, the unofficial northern hemisphere championship featuring teams from England, Scotland, Wales, Italy, Ireland, and France, and the Heineken Cup, its club-level counterpart. Owned by its member clubs, the RFU's mission is to maximize profits from international ticket sales and vending so that it can support the more than 60,000 volunteers who organize matches and seminars, help secure loans and insurance policies, fundraise, write grant proposals, provide medical advice and support, and perform the clerical duties that keep the lower-level clubs operating.

To succeed in this complicated mission, the RFU entered into a five-year deal with IBM to capture and analyze Big Data that will be useful to both fans, and later—it is hoped—the players themselves. The system is called TryTracker. In rugby, a try, worth five points, is the highest scoring opportunity. Teams get possession of the ball through a scrum, a contest for the ball where eight players bind together and push against eight players from the other team. The outcome determines who can control the ball. To score a try, a team must break through the opposition's defenses, move into their in-goal area, and "ground" the ball. This is done in one of two ways. A player can either hold the ball in one or both hands or

© Fabrique/Fotolia

arms and then touch it to the ground in the in-goal area, or exert downward pressure on a ball already on the ground using one or both hands or arms or the upper front of the body (from the neck to the waistline).

The IBM TryTracker does not just track tries, however. It uses predictive analytics to track three categories of data: keys to the game, momentum, and key players. TryTracker uses over 8,000 measures of performance. Traditional rugby statistics on team and individual performance as well as live text commentary complement the TryTracker data. The keys to the game are determined ahead of a specific contest by analyzing a historical database of past matchups between a pair. For example, in 2015 England's key was to average at least 3.2 meters per carry in the forwards; attempt an offload from 10 percent of opposition tackles; and make more than 66 percent of total line-breaks in the match. Fans can use their mobile devices to keep track of how their favorite team is faring, concentrating on game elements that will increase its winning chances. Key players for each team are selected after the game by comparing a single score compiled using different criteria for each position. Goal scoring is currently excluded so as not to overvalue kickers and undervalue players who contribute to creating scoring opportunities.

Like the IBM SlamTracker used at the Grand Slam tennis tournaments, the goal of TryTracker is to provide data visualization and real-time statistics to draw in fans. To compete with more popular sports such as Premier League football, the RFU hopes that enhanced communication will increase fan engagement. In 2015, IBM TryTracker was an ever-present fixture of EnglandRugby.com's extensive match coverage. As their understanding of game mechanics and emotional investment in what their team needs to do in order to prevail grows, casual fans will become dedicated fans who return again and again. Beyond marketing strategy, the long-term potential of predictive analysis is that it may provide tactical insights to players and coaches that will improve match play and thus the overall product offered to fans.

Sources: "About Us," rfu.com, accessed December, 14, 2015; "TryTracker: Rugby Data Analysis," *Telegraph*, November 19, 2015; Oliver Pickup, "How Does TryTracker Work," *Telegraph*, November 19, 2015; Simon Creasey, "Rugby Football Union Uses IBM Predictive Analytics for Six Nations," *ComputerWeek*, September 2015; "IBM Rugby Insight Summer 2015," MSN.com/sports, September 3, 2015; "Live England vs. Scotland with IBM TryTracker," www.englandrugby.com, March 15, 2015; "IBM TryTracker Confirms Performance," www.englandrugby.com/ibmtrytracker/, November 29, 2014; IBM UK, "IBM TryTracker Rugby Insight: QBE Internationals 2014 England vs. Australia," *IBM Rugby Insight,* November 27, 2014; Oliver Pickup, "IBM TryTracker: How Does It Work?" *Telegraph*, October 31, 2013; "IBM's Live 'TryTracker' Is New RFU Online Insights Tool," activative.co.uk, February 5, 2013; Simon Creasey, "Rugby Football Union Uses IBM Predictive Analytics for Six Nations," computerweekly.com, February, 2013; Steve McCaskill, "IBM TryTracker Brings Big Data To Rugby," techweekeurope.co.uk, February 11, 2013; Caroline Baldwin, "Rugby Football Union Uses Analytics to Educate and Engage with Users," computerweekly.com, October 8, 2013; "Rugby Tries," rugby-sidestep-central.com, accessed December 13, 2013.

The challenges facing the RFU demonstrate why information systems are so essential today. The RFU is classified as a "Friendly Society," somewhere between a true company and a charity. It receives both government support and corporate sponsorship money. But it must maximize revenues from ticket sales, hospitality and catering, television rights, and its travel company in order to support both grassroots and elite rugby in England.

The chapter-opening diagram calls attention to important points raised by this case and this chapter. The RFU entered into a strategic partnership with IBM to educate and engage fans. Using the data collected by sports data company Opta and the analytics developed by IBM, it may also be able to improve coaching and game performance as an additional way of cultivating customers. IBM is also helping the RFU to develop a customer relationship management (CRM) system integrated with its Web site.

Here are some questions to think about: What role does technology play in the RFU's success as the administrative head of rugby union in England? Assess the contributions which these systems make to the future of RFU.

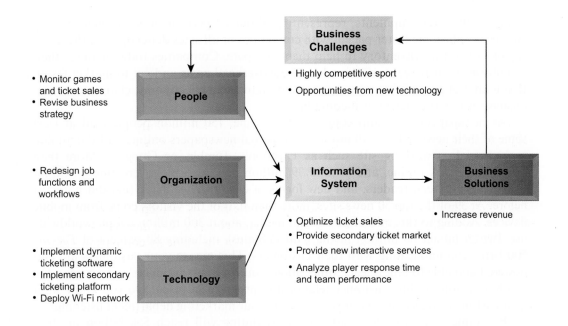

1-1 Why are information systems so essential for running and managing a business today?

It's not business as usual in America, or the rest of the global economy, any more. In 2015, American businesses will invest nearly $600 billion in information systems hardware, software, and telecommunications equipment—about one quarter of all capital investment in the United States. In addition, they will spend another $400 billion on business and management consulting and information technology services, much of which involves redesigning firms' business operations to take advantage of these new technologies. Together, investments in technology and management consulting added up to more than $1 trillion being invested in information systems in 2014. These expenditures grew at around 4 percent in 2014, far faster than the economy as a whole (BEA, 2014). Worldwide, expenditures for information technology exceeded €3.8 trillion (Gartner, 2015).

HOW INFORMATION SYSTEMS ARE TRANSFORMING BUSINESS

You can see the results of this spending around you every day by observing how people conduct business. Cell phones, smartphones, tablet computers, email, and online conferencing over the Internet have all become essential tools of business. In 2015, more than 118 million businesses had registered dot-com Internet sites. Approximately 227 million adult Americans are online, 170 million people buy something online, 205 million research a product, and 220 million use a search engine. What this means is that if you and your business aren't connected to the Internet and wireless networks, chances are you are not being as effective as you could be (Pew Internet and American Life, 2015; eMarketer, 2015).

Despite the economic downturn, in 2014 FedEx moved more than one billion packages in the United States, mostly overnight, and United Parcel Service (UPS) moved more than 4 billion packages, as businesses sought to sense and respond to rapidly changing customer demand, reduce inventories to the lowest possible levels, and achieve higher levels of operational efficiency. The growth of e-commerce has had a significant impact on UPS's shipping volume; UPS delivers about 42 percent of all e-commerce shipments, representing about 22 percent of its revenue. Supply chains have become faster paced, with companies of all sizes depending on the delivery of just-in-time inventory to help them compete. Companies today manage their inventories in near real time to reduce their overhead costs and get to market faster. If you are not part of this new supply chain management economy, chances are your business is not as efficient as it could be.

As newspaper readership continues to decline, 150 million people read at least some of their news online, 110 million read actual newspapers online, and 180 million use a social networking site such as Facebook, Tumblr, or Google+. More than 135 million bank online, and around 79 million now read blogs, creating an explosion of new writers, readers, and new forms of customer feedback that did not exist before. At 39 of the top 50 news sites, more than half of the visitors come from mobile devices. Adding to this mix of new social media, about 300 million people worldwide use Twitter (about 60 million in the United States), including 80 percent of *Fortune* 500 firms communicating with their customers. This means your customers are empowered and able to talk to each other about your business products and services. Do you have a solid online customer relationship program in place? Do you know what your customers are saying about your firm? Is your marketing department listening?

E-commerce and Internet advertising spending will reach $58 billion in 2015, growing at around 15 percent at a time when traditional advertising and commerce have been flat. Facebook's ad revenue hit $12 billion in 2014, and Google's online ad revenues surpassed $60 billion in 2014. Is your advertising department reaching this new web-based customer?

New federal security and accounting laws require many businesses to keep email messages for 5 years. Coupled with existing occupational and health laws requiring firms to store employee chemical exposure data for up to 60 years, these laws are spurring the growth of digital information now estimated to be 1.8 zettabytes (1.8 trillion gigabytes), equivalent to more than 50,000 Libraries of Congress. This trove of information is doubling every year thanks in part to more than 200 billion Internet sensors and data generators. Does your compliance department meet the minimal requirements for storing financial, health, and occupational information? If they don't, your entire business may be at risk.

Briefly, it's a new world of doing business, one that will greatly affect your future business career. Along with the changes in business come changes in jobs and careers. No matter whether you are a finance, accounting, management, marketing, operations management, or information systems major, how you work, where you work, and how well you are compensated will all be affected by business information systems. The purpose of this book is to help you understand and benefit from these new business realities and opportunities.

WHAT'S NEW IN MANAGEMENT INFORMATION SYSTEMS?

Lots! What makes management information systems the most exciting topic in business is the continual change in technology, management use of the technology, and the impact on business success. New businesses and industries appear, old ones decline, and successful firms are those that learn how to use the new technologies. Table 1.1 summarizes the major new themes in business uses of information systems. These themes will appear throughout the book in all the chapters, so it might be a good idea to take some time now to discuss these with your professor and other students.

In the technology area are three interrelated changes: (1) the mobile digital platform composed of smartphones and tablet devices, (2) the growing business use of big data, including the Internet of Things (IoT) driven by billions of data-producing sensors, and (3) the growth in cloud computing, by which more and more business software runs over the Internet.

Change	Business Impact
TECHNOLOGY	
Cloud computing platform emerges as a major business area of innovation	A flexible collection of computers on the Internet begins to perform tasks traditionally performed on corporate computers. Major business applications are delivered online as an Internet service (software as a service [SaaS]).
Big data and the Internet of Things (IoT)	Businesses look for insights in huge volumes of data from web traffic, email messages, social media content, and Internet-connected machines (sensors).
A mobile digital platform emerges to compete with the PC as a business system	The Apple iPhone and Android mobile devices can download hundreds of thousands of applications to support collaboration, location-based services, and communication with colleagues. Small tablet computers, including the iPad, Samsung Galaxy, and Kindle Fire, challenge conventional laptops as platforms for consumer and corporate computing.
MANAGEMENT	
Managers adopt online collaboration and social networking software to improve coordination, collaboration, and knowledge sharing.	More than 100 million business professionals worldwide use Google Apps, Google Drive, Microsoft SharePoint, and IBM Connections to support blogs, project management, online meetings, personal profiles, and online communities.
Business intelligence applications accelerate.	More powerful data analytics and interactive dashboards provide real-time performance information to managers to enhance decision making.
Virtual meetings proliferate.	Managers adopt telepresence, video conferencing, and web conferencing technologies to reduce travel time and cost, improving collaboration and decision making.
ORGANIZATIONS	
Social business	Businesses use social networking platforms, including Facebook, Twitter, Instagram, and internal corporate social tools, to deepen interactions with employees, customers, and suppliers. Employees use blogs, wikis, email, texting, and messaging to interact in online communities.
Telework gains momentum in the workplace.	The Internet, wireless laptops, smartphones, and tablet computers make it possible for growing numbers of people to work away from the traditional office. Fifty-five percent of U.S. businesses have some form of remote work program.
Co-creation of business value	Sources of business value shift from products to solutions and experiences and from internal sources to networks of suppliers and collaboration with customers. Supply chains and product development become more global and collaborative; customer interactions help firms define new products and services.

TABLE 1.1

What's New in MIS

IPhones, Android phones, and high-definition tablet computers are not just gadgets or entertainment outlets. They represent new emerging computing and media platforms based on an array of new hardware and software technologies. More and more business computing is moving from PCs and desktop machines to these mobile devices. Managers are increasingly using these devices to coordinate work, communicate with employees, and provide information for decision making. In 2015, more than 60 percent of Internet users will access the web through mobile devices. To a large extent, these devices change the character of corporate computing.

iPhone and iPad Applications for Business
1. *Salesforce1*
2. *Cisco WebEx*
3. *SAP Business ByDesign*
4. *iWork*
5. *Evernote*
6. *Adobe Reader*
7. *Oracle Business Intelligence*
8. *Dropbox*

Whether it's attending an online meeting, checking orders, working with files and documents, or obtaining business intelligence, Apple's iPhone and iPad offer unlimited possibilities for business users. A stunning multitouch display, full Internet browsing, and capabilities for messaging, video and audio transmission, and document management make each an all-purpose platform for mobile computing.

© STANCA SANDA/Alamy

Managers routinely use online collaboration and social technologies to make better, faster decisions. As management behavior changes, how work is organized, coordinated, and measured also changes. By connecting employees working on teams and projects, the social network is where work is done, where plans are executed, and where managers manage. Collaboration spaces are where employees meet one another—even when they are separated by continents and time zones.

The strength of cloud computing, and the growth of the mobile digital platform, mean that organizations can rely more on telework, remote work, and distributed decision making. This same platform means firms can outsource more work and rely on markets (rather than employees) to build value. It also means that firms can collaborate with suppliers and customers to create new products or make existing products more efficiently.

You can see some of these trends at work in the Interactive Session on People. Millions of managers and employees rely heavily on the mobile digital platform to coordinate suppliers and shipments, satisfy customers, and organize work activities. A business day without these mobile devices or Internet access would be unthinkable. As you read the case on the next page note how the mobile platform has changed the way people do their work and make decisions.

GLOBALIZATION CHALLENGES AND OPPORTUNITIES: A FLATTENED WORLD

Prior to AD 1500, there was no truly global economic system of trade that connected all the continents on earth. After the sixteenth century, a global trading system began to emerge based on global shipping and voyages of discovery and regular trade. The world trade that ensued after these voyages has brought the peoples and cultures of the world much closer together. The industrial revolution was really a worldwide phenomenon energized by expansion of trade among nations, and since that period, nations have been both competitors and collaborators in business. The Internet has greatly heightened both the competitive tensions among nations as global trade expands and strengthened the benefits that flow from trade.

By 2005, journalist Thomas Friedman wrote an influential book declaring the world was now flat, by which he meant that the Internet and global communications had greatly expanded the opportunities for people to communicate with one another and reduced the economic and cultural advantages of developed countries. U.S. and

INTERACTIVE SESSION: PEOPLE   The Mobile Pocket Office

Can you run your company out of your pocket? Perhaps not entirely, but many business functions today can be performed using an iPhone, iPad, or Android mobile handheld device. The smartphone has been called the Swiss Army knife of the digital age. A flick of the finger turns it into a web browser, a telephone, a camera, a music or video player, an email and messaging machine, and, increasingly, a gateway into corporate systems. New software applications for document sharing, collaboration, sales, order processing, inventory management, and production monitoring make these devices even more versatile business tools. Mobile pocket offices that fit into a purse or coat pocket are helping to run companies large and small.

Sonic Automotive is one of the largest automotive retailers in the United States, with more than 100 dealerships in 14 states. Every year, Sonic sells 250,000 new and used cars from approximately 25 automotive brands; it also sells auto parts and maintenance, warranty, collision, and vehicle financing services. Sonic Automotive managers and employees do much of their work on the iPhone and iPad.

Sonic developed several custom iPhone and iPad applications to speed up sales and service. Virtual Lot, a dealer inventory app, enables sales associates to search quickly for vehicles held in inventory at all Sonic dealerships. They have immediate access to vehicle information, pricing, trade-in values, interest rates, special promotions, financing, and what competitors are charging for identical vehicles. The associates can quickly find the best selection for each customer and, often, offer far many more choices than the competition. Dealers are not limited to selling only their own inventory.

A mobile app called the Sonic Inventory Management System (SIMS) has speeded up and simplified trade-in appraisals and pricing. Sonic staff members use their iPhones or iPads to take photos of a car, input the VIN (vehicle identification number) and mileage, and note any issues. The data are transmitted to corporate headquarters, which can quickly appraise the car. A Service Pad app simplifies the steps in repair and warranty work. In the past, customers with cars requiring repairs had to go inside the dealership and sit at a desk with a Sonic staff member who wrote up the repair order by hand. Now the Sonic staff

members go outside to the customer's vehicle and enter the repair order on an iPad on the spot.

SKF is a global engineering company headquartered in Gothenburg, Sweden, with 148 manufacturing sites in 28 countries and 40,000 employees worldwide. SKF produces bearings, seals, lubrication systems, and services used in more than 40 industries, including mining, transportation, and manufacturing. SKF has developed more than 30 custom iPhone and iPad applications for streamlining workflows and accessing critical corporate data from anywhere in the world.

For example, a virtual reality app uses the iPhone or iPad camera to identify a factory machine and produce a 3-D overlay of the SKF parts it contains. SKF service teams and customers in the field use a sensor-driven app called Shaft Align, which connects by wireless Bluetooth sensors to a piece of machinery such as a motor-driven fan to ensure that the drive shaft is running in proper alignment. If not, the app generates step-by-step instructions and a 3-D rendering to show how to align the motor manually. Then it checks the work and produces a report.

A mobile app called MOST enables factory operators to monitor some SKF factory production lines. MOST links to the back-end systems running the machinery and provides operators with key pieces of data. Operators using this mobile app use secure instant messaging to communicate with managers and each other, update maintenance logs, and track products in real time as they move through the factory line.

SKF's Shelf mobile app allows sales engineers and customers to access, on demand, more than 5000 pieces of product literature, catalogs, product specifications, and interactive marketing materials. Sales teams can use Shelf to create custom shelves to organize, annotate, and share materials with customers right from their iPhones or iPads. The iPhone, iPad, and Shelf app save company sales engineers as much as 25 minutes per day on processes and paperwork, freeing them up to spend more time in the field supporting customers. This increase in productivity is equivalent to putting 200 more sales engineers in the field.

SKF auditors perform about 60 audits per year, each audit taking more than one month to complete. With the SKF Data Collect app, auditors use their iPads to collect data and present customers with detailed reports instantly.

SKF Seals offers specifications and information about SKF's machined and injection-molded seals and plastic parts; the Seal Select app helps users select seals and accessories by using several input parameters to find the right solution for their needs.

Sources: "Sonic Automotive: Driving Growth with iPhone and iPad," and "SKF Sets the World in Motion with IOS," *iPhone in Business*, www.apple.com, accessed March 5, 2015; www.skf.com, accessed March 5, 2015; www.sonicautomotive.com, accessed March 5, 2015; "Why the Mobile Pocket Office Is Good for Business," ITBusinesEdge.com, accessed March 6, 2015; and Robert Bamforth, "Do You Need Tablets in Your Workplace? ComputerWeekly.com, January 27, 2014.

CASE STUDY QUESTIONS

1. What kinds of applications are described here? What business functions do they support? How do they improve operational efficiency and decision making?

2. Identify the problems that businesses in this case study solved by using mobile digital devices.

3. What kinds of businesses are most likely to benefit from equipping their employees with mobile digital devices such as iPhones and iPads?

4. One company deploying iPhones has said, "The iPhone is not a game changer, it's an industry changer. It changes the way that you can interact with your customers [and] with your suppliers." Discuss the implications of this statement.

European countries were in a fight for their economic lives, competing for jobs, markets, resources, and even ideas with highly educated, motivated populations in low-wage areas in the less developed world (Friedman, 2007). This globalization presents you and your business with both challenges and opportunities.

A growing percentage of the economy of the United States and other advanced industrial countries in Europe and Asia depends on imports and exports. In 2014, more than 30 percent of the U.S. economy resulted from foreign trade of goods and services, both imports and exports. In Europe and Asia, the number exceeds 50 percent. Half of the *Fortune* 500 U.S. firms derive at least half their revenues from foreign operations. For instance, more than 50 percent of Intel's revenues in 2014 came from overseas sales of its microprocessors, and the same is true for General Electric, Ford Motor Company, IBM, Dow Chemical, and McDonald's. Toys for chips: 80 percent of the toys sold in the United States are manufactured in China; about 90 percent of the PCs manufactured in China use American-made Intel or Advanced Micro Design (AMD) chips.

It's not just goods that move across borders. So too do jobs, some of them high-level jobs that pay well and require a college degree. In the past decade, the United States lost several million manufacturing jobs to offshore, low-wage producers, but manufacturing is now a very small part of U.S. employment (less than 12 percent). In a normal year, about 300,000 service jobs move offshore to lower-wage countries, many of them in less-skilled information system occupations, but also include tradable service jobs in architecture, financial services, customer call centers, consulting, engineering, and even radiology.

On the plus side, the U.S. economy creates more than 3 million new jobs in a normal year (3.2 million in 2014, the best year since 1999 for new jobs). Employment in information systems and the other service occupations listed previously have expanded in sheer numbers, wages, productivity, and quality of work. Outsourcing has actually accelerated the development of new systems in the United States and worldwide. In the midst of an economic recession, jobs in information systems are among the most in demand.

The challenge for you as a business student is to develop high-level skills through education and on-the-job experience that cannot be outsourced. The challenge for your business is to avoid markets for goods and services that can be produced offshore much less expensively. The opportunities are equally immense. You can learn how to profit from the lower costs available in world markets and the chance to serve a marketplace with billions of customers. You have the opportunity to develop higher-level and more profitable products and services. Throughout this book, you will find examples of companies and individuals who either failed or succeeded in using information systems to adapt to this new global environment.

What does globalization have to do with management information systems? The answer is simple: everything. The emergence of the Internet into a full-blown international communications system has drastically reduced the costs of operating and transacting on a global scale. Communication between a factory floor in Shanghai and a distribution center in Sioux Falls, South Dakota, is now instant and virtually free. Customers now can shop in a worldwide marketplace, obtaining price and quality information reliably 24 hours a day. Firms producing goods and services on a global scale achieve extraordinary cost reductions by finding low-cost suppliers and managing production facilities in other countries. Internet service firms, such as Google and eBay, can replicate their business models and services in multiple countries without having to redesign their expensive, fixed-cost information systems infrastructure.

BUSINESS DRIVERS OF INFORMATION SYSTEMS

What makes information systems so essential today? Why are businesses investing so much in information systems and technologies? They do so to achieve six important business objectives: operational excellence; new products, services, and business models; customer and supplier intimacy; improved decision making; competitive advantage; and survival.

Operational Excellence

Businesses continuously seek to improve the efficiency of their operations to achieve higher profitability. Information systems and technologies are some of the most important tools available to managers for achieving higher levels of efficiency and productivity in business operations, especially when coupled with changes in business practices and management behavior.

Walmart, the largest retailer on earth, exemplifies the power of information systems coupled with brilliant business practices and supportive management to achieve world-class operational efficiency. In fiscal year 2014, Walmart achieved more than $473 billion in sales—nearly one-tenth of retail sales in the United States—in large part because of its Retail Link system, which digitally links its suppliers to every one of Walmart's 9,600 stores worldwide. As soon as a customer purchases an item, the supplier monitoring the item knows to ship a replacement to the shelf. Walmart is the most efficient retail store in the industry, achieving sales of more than $600 per square foot compared to its closest competitor, Target, at $425 a square foot, with other large general merchandise retail firms producing less than $200 a square foot.

Amazon, the largest online retailer on earth, generating $89 billion in sales in 2014, invested $2.1 billion in information systems so that when one of its estimated 170 million customers searches for a product, Amazon can respond in milliseconds with the correct product displayed (and recommendations for other products).

New Products, Services, and Business Models

Information systems and technologies are a major enabling tool for firms to create new products and services, as well as entirely new business models. A **business model** describes how a company produces, delivers, and sells a product or service to create wealth. Today's music industry is vastly different from the industry a decade ago. Apple Inc. transformed an old business model of music distribution based on vinyl records, tapes, and CDs into an online, legal download distribution model based on its own operating system and iTunes store. Apple has prospered from a continuing stream of innovations, including the original iPod, iPod nano, iTunes music service, iPhone, and iPad.

Customer and Supplier Intimacy

When a business really knows its customers and serves them well, the way they want to be served, the customers generally respond by returning and purchasing more. This raises revenues and profits. Likewise with suppliers: the more a business engages its suppliers, the better the suppliers can provide vital inputs. This lowers costs. How really to know your customers, or suppliers, is a central problem for businesses with millions of offline and online customers.

The Mandarin Oriental in Manhattan and other high-end hotels exemplify the use of information systems and technologies to achieve customer intimacy. These hotels use information systems to keep track of guests' preferences, such as their preferred room temperature, check-in time, frequently dialed telephone numbers, and television programs, and store these data in a giant data repository. Individual rooms in the hotels are networked to a central network server so that they can be remotely monitored or controlled. When a customer arrives at one of these hotels, the system automatically changes the room conditions, such as dimming the lights, setting the room temperature, or selecting appropriate music, based on the customer's digital profile. The hotels also analyze their customer data to identify their best customers and develop individualized marketing campaigns based on customers' preferences.

JCPenney exemplifies the benefits of information systems-enabled supplier intimacy. Every time a dress shirt is bought at a JCPenney store in the United States, the record of the sale appears immediately on computers in Hong Kong at TAL Apparel Ltd., a giant contract manufacturer that produces one in eight dress shirts sold in the United States. TAL runs the numbers through a computer model it developed and decides how many replacement shirts to make and in what styles, colors, and sizes. TAL then sends the shirts to each JCPenney store, completely bypassing the retailer's warehouses. In other words, JCPenney's surplus shirt inventory is near zero, as is the cost of storing it.

Improved Decision Making

Many business managers operate in an information fog bank, never really having the right information at the right time to make an informed decision. Instead, managers rely on forecasts, best guesses, and luck. The result is over- or underproduction of goods and services, misallocation of resources, and poor response times. These poor outcomes raise costs and lose customers. In the past 10 years, information systems and technologies have made it possible for managers to use real-time data from the marketplace when making decisions.

For instance, Verizon Corporation, one of the largest regional Bell operating companies in the United States, uses a web-based digital dashboard to provide managers with precise real-time information on customer complaints, network performance for each locality served, and line outages or storm-damaged lines. Using this information, managers can immediately allocate repair resources to affected areas, inform consumers of repair efforts, and restore service fast.

Competitive Advantage

When firms achieve one or more of these business objectives—operational excellence; new products, services, and business models; customer/supplier intimacy; and improved decision making—chances are they have already achieved a competitive advantage. Doing things better than your competitors, charging less for superior products, and responding to customers and suppliers in real time all add up to higher sales and higher profits that your competitors cannot match. Apple Inc., Walmart, and UPS are industry leaders because they know how to use information systems for this purpose.

Survival

Business firms also invest in information systems and technologies because they are necessities of doing business. Sometimes these necessities are driven by industry-level changes. For instance, after Citibank introduced the first automated teller machines (ATMs) in the New York region to attract customers through higher service levels, its competitors rushed to provide ATMs to their customers to keep up with Citibank. Today, virtually all banks in the United States have regional ATMs and link to national and international ATM networks, such as CIRRUS. Providing ATM services to retail banking customers is simply a requirement of being in and surviving in the retail banking business.

Many federal and state statutes and regulations create a legal duty for companies and their employees to retain records, including digital records. For instance, the Toxic Substances Control Act (1976), which regulates the exposure of U.S. workers to more than 75,000 toxic chemicals, requires firms to retain records on employee exposure for 30 years. The Sarbanes-Oxley Act (2002), which was intended to improve the accountability of public firms and their auditors, requires public companies to retain audit working papers and records, including all email messages, for five years. Firms turn to information systems and technologies to provide the capability to respond to these information retention and reporting requirements. The Dodd–Frank Act (2010) requires financial service firms to expand their public reporting greatly on derivatives and other financial instruments.

1-2 What exactly is an information system? How does it work? What are its people, organizational, and technology components?

So far we've used *information systems and technologies* informally without defining the terms. **Information technology (IT)** consists of all the hardware and software that a firm needs to use to achieve its business objectives. This includes not only computers, disk drives, and mobile handheld devices but also software, such as the Windows or Linux operating systems, the Microsoft Office desktop productivity suite, and the many thousands of computer programs that can be found in a typical large firm. Information systems are more complex and can be understood best by looking at them from both a technology and a business perspective.

WHAT IS AN INFORMATION SYSTEM?

An **information system (IS)** can be defined technically as a set of interrelated components that collect (or retrieve), process, store, and distribute information to support decision making, coordinating, and control in an organization. In addition, information systems may also help managers and workers analyze problems, visualize complex subjects, and create new products.

Information systems contain information about significant people, places, and things within the organization or in the environment surrounding it. By **information**, we mean data that have been shaped into a form that is meaningful and useful to human beings. **Data**, in contrast, are streams of raw facts representing events occurring in organizations or the physical environment before they have been organized and arranged into a form that people can understand and use.

A brief example contrasting information and data may prove useful. Supermarket checkout counters scan millions of pieces of data, such as bar codes, that describe the product. Such pieces of data can be totaled and analyzed to provide meaningful

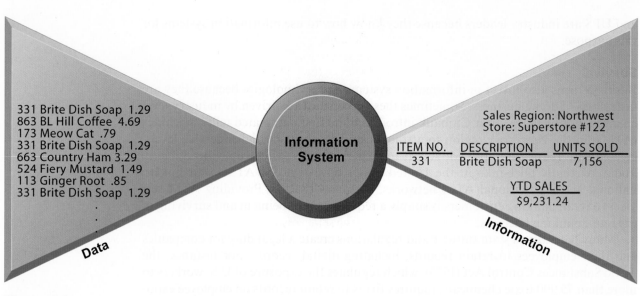

Figure 1.1
Data and Information
Raw data from a supermarket checkout counter can be processed and organized to produce meaningful information, such as the total unit sales of dish detergent or the total sales revenue from dish detergent for a specific store or sales territory.

information, such as the total number of bottles of dish detergent sold at a particular store, which brands of dish detergent were selling the most rapidly at that store or sales territory, or the total amount spent on that brand of dish detergent at that store or sales region (see Figure 1.1).

Three activities in an information system produce the information that organizations need to make decisions, control operations, analyze problems, and create new products or services. These activities are input, processing, and output (see Figure 1.2). **Input** captures or collects raw data from within the organization or from its external environment. **Processing** converts this raw input into a meaningful form. **Output** transfers the processed information to the people who will use it or to the activities for which it will be used. Information systems also require **feedback**, which is output that is returned to appropriate members of the organization to help them evaluate or correct the input stage.

Figure 1.2
Functions of an
Information System
An information system contains information about an organization and its surrounding environment. Three basic activities— input, processing, and output—produce the information organizations need. Feedback is output returned to appropriate people or activities in the organization to evaluate and refine the input. Environmental actors, such as customers, suppliers, competitors, stockholders, and regulatory agencies, interact with the organization and its information systems.

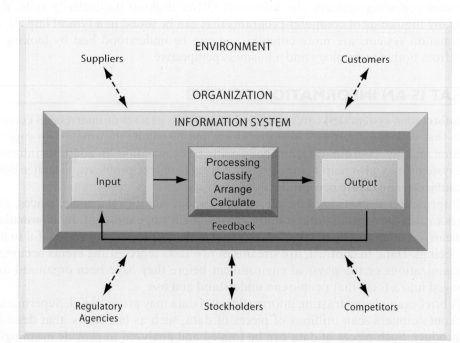

In a professional sports team's system for selling tickets, the raw input consists of order data for tickets, such as the purchaser's name, address, credit card number, number of tickets ordered, and the date of the game for which the ticket is being purchased. Another input would be the ticket price, which would fluctuate based on computer analysis of how much could optimally be charged for a ticket for a particular game. Computers store these data and process them to calculate order totals, to track ticket purchases, and to send requests for payment to credit card companies. The output consists of tickets to print out, receipts for orders, and reports on online ticket orders. The system provides meaningful information, such as the number of tickets sold for a particular game or at a particular price, the total number of tickets sold each year, and frequent customers.

Although computer-based information systems use computer technology to process raw data into meaningful information, there is a sharp distinction between a computer and a computer program and an information system. Computers and related software programs are the technical foundation, the tools and materials, of modern information systems. Computers provide the equipment for storing and processing information. Computer programs, or software, are sets of operating instructions that direct and control computer processing. Knowing how computers and computer programs work is important in designing solutions to organizational problems, but computers are only part of an information system.

A house is an appropriate analogy. Houses are built with hammers, nails, and wood, but these alone do not make a house. The architecture, design, setting, landscaping, and all of the decisions that lead to the creation of these features are part of the house and are crucial for solving the problem of putting a roof over one's head. Computers and programs are the hammer, nails, and lumber of computer-based information systems, but alone they cannot produce the information a particular organization needs. To understand information systems, you must understand the problems they are designed to solve, their architectural and design elements, and the organizational processes that lead to these solutions.

IT ISN'T SIMPLY TECHNOLOGY: THE ROLE OF PEOPLE AND ORGANIZATIONS

To understand information systems fully, you will need to be aware of the broader organization, people, and information technology dimensions of systems (see Figure 1.3) and their power to provide solutions to challenges and problems in the business environment. We refer to this broader understanding of information

Figure 1.3
Information Systems Are More Than Computers
Using information systems effectively requires an understanding of the organization, people, and information technology shaping the systems. An information system provides a solution to important business problems or challenges facing the firm.

systems, which encompasses an understanding of the people and organizational dimensions of systems as well as the technical dimensions of systems, as **information systems literacy**. Information systems literacy includes a behavioral as well as a technical approach to studying information systems. **Computer literacy**, in contrast, focuses primarily on knowledge of information technology.

The field of **management information systems (MIS)** tries to achieve this broader information systems literacy. MIS deals with behavioral issues as well as technical issues surrounding the development, use, and impact of information systems that managers and employees in the firm use.

DIMENSIONS OF INFORMATION SYSTEMS

Let's examine each of the dimensions of information systems—organizations, people, and information technology.

Organizations

Information systems are an integral part of organizations and, although we tend to think about information technology changing organizations and business firms, it is, in fact, a two-way street. The history and culture of business firms also affects how the technology is used and how it should be used. To understand how a specific business firm uses information systems, you need to know something about the structure, history, and culture of the company.

Organizations have a structure that is composed of different levels and specialties. Their structures reveal a clear-cut division of labor. A business firm is organized as a hierarchy, or a pyramid structure, of rising authority and responsibility. The upper levels of the hierarchy consist of managerial, professional, and technical employees, whereas the lower levels consist of operational personnel. Experts are employed and trained for different business functions, such as sales and marketing, manufacturing and production, finance and accounting, and human resources. The firm builds information systems to serve these different specialties and levels of the firm. Chapter 2 provides more detail on these business functions and organizational levels and the ways in which information systems support them.

An organization accomplishes and coordinates work through this structured hierarchy and through its **business processes**, which are logically related tasks and behaviors for accomplishing work. Developing a new product, fulfilling an order, and hiring a new employee are examples of business processes.

Most organizations' business processes include formal rules that it has developed over a long time for accomplishing tasks. These rules guide employees in a variety of procedures, from writing an invoice to responding to customer complaints. Some of these business processes have been written down, but others are informal work practices, such as a requirement to return telephone calls from coworkers or customers, that are not formally documented. Information systems automate many business processes. For instance, how a customer receives credit or how a customer is billed is often determined by an information system that incorporates a set of formal business processes.

Each organization has a unique **culture**, or fundamental set of assumptions, values, and ways of doing things, that has been accepted by most of its members. Parts of an organization's culture can always be found embedded in its information systems. For instance, the United Parcel Service's concern with placing service to the customer first is an aspect of its organizational culture that can be found in the company's package tracking systems.

Different levels and specialties in an organization create different interests and points of view. These views often conflict. Conflict is the basis for organizational politics. Information systems come out of this cauldron of differing perspectives, conflicts, compromises, and agreements that are a natural part of all organizations.

People

A business is only as good as the people who work there and run it. Likewise with information systems, they are useless without skilled people to build and maintain them or people who can understand how to use the information in a system to achieve business objectives.

For instance, a call center that provides help to customers by using an advanced customer relationship management system (described in later chapters) is useless if employees are not adequately trained to deal with customers, find solutions to their problems, and leave the customer feeling that the company cares for them. Likewise, employee attitudes about their jobs, employers, or technology can have a powerful effect on their abilities to use information systems productively.

Business firms require many kinds of skills and people, including managers as well as rank-and-file employees. The job of managers is to make sense out of the many situations organizations face, make decisions, and formulate action plans to solve organizational problems. Managers perceive business challenges in the environment, they set the organizational strategy for responding to those challenges, and they allocate the human and financial resources to coordinate the work and achieve success. Throughout, they must exercise responsible leadership.

However, managers must do more than manage what already exists. They must also create new products and services and even re-create the organization from time to time. A substantial part of management responsibility is creative work driven by new knowledge and information. Information technology can play a powerful role in helping managers develop novel solutions to a broad range of problems.

As you will learn throughout this text, technology is relatively inexpensive today, but people are very expensive. Because people are the only ones capable of business problem solving and converting information technology into useful business solutions, we spend considerable effort in this text looking at the people dimension of information systems.

Technology

Information technology is one of many tools managers use to cope with change and complexity. **Computer hardware** is the physical equipment used for input, processing, and output activities in an information system. It consists of the following: computers of various sizes and shapes; various input, output, and storage devices; and telecommunications devices that link computers.

Computer software consists of the detailed, preprogrammed instructions that control and coordinate the computer hardware components in an information system. Chapter 5 describes the contemporary software and hardware platforms firms use today in greater detail.

Data management technology consists of the software governing the organization of data on physical storage media. More detail on data organization and access methods can be found in Chapter 6.

Networking and telecommunications technology, consisting of both physical devices and software, links the various pieces of hardware and transfers data from one physical location to another. Computers and communications equipment can be connected in networks for sharing voice, data, images, sound, and video. A **network** links two or more computers to share data or resources such as a printer.

The world's largest and most widely used network is the **Internet**, a global network of networks that uses universal standards (described in Chapter 7) to connect millions of networks in more than 230 countries around the world.

The Internet has created a new, universal technology platform on which to build new products, services, strategies, and business models. This same technology platform has internal uses, providing the connectivity to link different systems and networks within the firm. Internal corporate networks based on Internet technology are called **intranets**. Private intranets extended to authorized users outside the organization are called **extranets**, and firms use such networks to coordinate their activities with other firms for making purchases, collaborating on design, and performing other interorganizational work. For most business firms today, using Internet technology is a business necessity and a competitive advantage.

The **World Wide Web** is a service the Internet provides that uses universally accepted standards for storing, retrieving, formatting, and displaying information in a page format on the Internet. Web pages contain text, graphics, animations, sound, and video and are linked to other web pages. By clicking highlighted words or buttons on a web page, you can link to related pages to find additional information and links to other locations on the web. The web can serve as the foundation for new kinds of information systems such as UPS's web-based package tracking system.

All these technologies, along with the people required to run and manage them, represent resources that can be shared throughout the organization and constitute the firm's **information technology (IT) infrastructure**. The IT infrastructure provides the foundation, or *platform*, on which the firm can build its specific information systems. Each organization must carefully design and manage its information technology infrastructure so that it has the set of technology services it needs for the work it wants to accomplish with information systems. Chapters 5, 6, 7, and 8 of this text examine each major technology component of information technology infrastructure and show how they all work together to create the technology platform for the organization.

The Interactive Session on Technology on the next page describes some of the typical technologies used in computer-based information systems today. UPS invests heavily in information systems technology to make its business more efficient and customer oriented. It uses an array of information technologies, including bar code scanning systems, wireless networks, large mainframe computers, handheld computers, the Internet, and many pieces of software for tracking packages, calculating fees, maintaining customer accounts, and managing logistics. As you read this case, try to identify the problem this company was facing, what alternative solutions were available to management, and how well the chosen solution worked.

Let's identify the organization, people, and technology elements in the UPS package tracking system we have just described. The organization element anchors the package tracking system in UPS's sales and production functions (the main product of UPS is a service—package delivery). It specifies the required procedures for identifying packages with both sender and recipient information, taking inventory, tracking the packages en route, and providing package status reports for UPS customers and customer service representatives.

The system must also provide information to satisfy the needs of managers and workers. UPS drivers need to be trained in both package pickup and delivery procedures and in how to use the package tracking system so that they can work efficiently and effectively. UPS customers may need some training to use UPS in-house package tracking software or the UPS website.

UPS's management is responsible for monitoring service levels and costs and for promoting the company's strategy of combining low cost and superior service. Management decided to use automation to increase the ease of sending a package via UPS and of checking its delivery status, thereby reducing delivery costs and increasing sales revenues.

The technology supporting this system consists of handheld computers, bar code scanners, wired and wireless communications networks, desktop computers, UPS's central computer, storage technology for the package delivery data, UPS in-house package tracking software, and software to access the World Wide Web. The result is an information system solution to the business challenge of providing a high level of service with low prices in the face of mounting competition.

INTERACTIVE SESSION: TECHNOLOGY   UPS Competes Globally with Information Technology

United Parcel Service (UPS) started out in 1907 in a closet-sized basement office. Jim Casey and Claude Ryan—two teenagers from Seattle with two bicycles and one phone—promised the "best service and lowest rates." UPS has used this formula successfully for more than a century to become the world's largest ground and air package–delivery company. It's a global enterprise with nearly 400,000 employees; 96,000 vehicles; and the world's ninth largest airline.

Today, UPS delivers 16.9 million packages and documents each day in the United States and more than 220 other countries and territories. The firm has been able to maintain leadership in small-package delivery services despite stiff competition from FedEx and the United States Postal Service by investing heavily in advanced information technology. UPS spends more than $1 billion each year to maintain a high level of customer service while keeping costs low and streamlining its overall operations.

It all starts with the scannable barcoded label attached to a package, which contains detailed information about the sender, the destination, and when the package should arrive. Customers can download and print their own labels by using special software UPS provides or by accessing the UPS website. Before the package is even picked up, information from the smart label is transmitted to one of UPS's computer centers in Mahwah, New Jersey, or Alpharetta, Georgia, and sent to the distribution center nearest its final destination.

Dispatchers at this center download the label data and use special routing software called ORION to create the most efficient delivery route for each driver that considers traffic, weather conditions, and the location of each stop. Each UPS driver makes an average of 120 stops per day. In a network with 55,000 routes in the U.S. alone, shaving even one mile off each driver's daily route translates into big savings—$50 million per year. These savings are critical because UPS tries to boost earnings growth as more of its business shifts to less-profitable e-commerce deliveries. UPS drivers who used to drop off several heavy packages a day at one retailer now make several stops scattered across residential neighborhoods, delivering one lightweight package per household. The shift requires more fuel and more time, increasing the cost to deliver each package

The first thing a UPS driver picks up each day is a handheld computer called a Delivery Information Acquisition Device (DIAD), which can access a cell phone network. As soon as the driver logs on, his or her day's route is downloaded onto the handheld. The DIAD also automatically captures customers' signatures along with pickup and delivery information. Package tracking information is then transmitted to UPS's computer network for storage and processing. From there, the information can be accessed worldwide to provide proof of delivery to customers or to respond to customer queries. It usually takes less than 60 seconds from the time a driver presses Complete on the DIAD for the new information to be available on the web.

Through its automated package tracking system, UPS can monitor and even reroute packages throughout the delivery process. At various points along the route from sender to receiver, bar code devices scan shipping information on the package label and feed data about the progress of the package into the central computer. Customer service representatives can check the status of any package from desktop computers linked to the central computers and respond immediately to inquiries from customers. UPS customers can also access this information from the company's website, using their own computers or mobile phones. UPS now has mobile apps and a mobile website for iPhone, BlackBerry, and Android smartphone users.

Anyone with a package to ship can access the UPS website to track packages, check delivery routes, calculate shipping rates, determine time in transit, print labels, and schedule a pickup. The data collected at the UPS website are transmitted to the UPS central computer and then back to the customer after processing. UPS also provides tools that enable customers, such Cisco Systems, to embed UPS functions, such as tracking and cost calculations, into their own websites so that they can track shipments without visiting the UPS site.

A web-based Post Sales Order Management System (OMS) manages global service orders and inventory for critical parts fulfillment. The system enables high-tech electronics, aerospace, medical equipment, and other companies anywhere in the world that ship critical parts to assess their critical parts inventory quickly, determine the optimal routing strategy to meet customer needs, place orders online, and track parts from the warehouse to the end user. An automated email or fax feature keeps customers informed of each shipping milestone and can provide notification of any changes to flight schedules for commercial airlines carrying their parts.

UPS is now leveraging its decades of expertise managing its own global delivery network to manage logistics and supply chain activities for other companies. It created a UPS Supply Chain Solutions division that provides a complete bundle of standardized services to subscribing companies at a fraction of what it would cost to build their own systems and infrastructure. These services include supply-chain design and management, freight forwarding, customs brokerage, mail services, multimodal transportation, and financial services in addition to logistics services.

For example, UPS handles fulfillment and distribution for Plasticard Locktech International (PLI), the world's largest manufacturer of key cards, including hotel key cards, gift cards, and customer loyalty program cards. PLI's customers require quick delivery. Although PLI had no problem fulfilling orders, shipping internationally from its Asheville, North Carolina, manufacturing and distribution location was too costly. PLI now stores inventory at UPS locations in Canada, the United Arab Emirates, and the Netherlands and will soon ship from a Hong Kong facility as well. It would have cost PLI millions to provide its own services for opening a warehouse, hiring staffing, buying insurance, and developing logistics. In addition to reducing international shipping costs, PLI realized savings of $200,000 per year by switching to UPS Customs Brokerage Services.

Sources: Steven Rosenbush and Laura Stevens, "At UPS, Algorithm Is the Driver," *Wall Street Journal*, February 16, 2015; "Keys to Success," *UPS Compass*, Winter 2015; www.ups.com, accessed March 7, 2015; and Laura Stevens, "For UPS, E-Commerce Brings Big Business and Big Problems," *Wall Street Journal*, September 11, 2014.

CASE STUDY QUESTIONS

1. What are the inputs, processing, and outputs of UPS's package tracking system?

2. What technologies does UPS use? How are these technologies related to UPS's business strategy?

3. What strategic business objectives do UPS's information systems address?

4. What would happen if UPS's information systems were not available?

Using a handheld computer called a Delivery Information Acquisition Device (DIAD), UPS drivers automatically capture customers' signatures along with pickup, delivery, and time card information. UPS information systems use these data to track packages while they are being transported.

© Bill Aron/PhotoEdit.

1-3 How will a four-step method for business problem solving help you solve information system–related problems?

Our approach to understanding information systems is to consider information systems and technologies as solutions to a variety of business challenges and problems. We refer to this as a problem-solving approach. Businesses face many challenges and problems, and information systems are one major way of solving these problems. All the cases in this book illustrate how a company used information systems to solve a specific problem.

The problem-solving approach has direct relevance to your future career. Your future employers will hire you because you can solve business problems and achieve business objectives. Your knowledge of how information systems contribute to problem solving will be very helpful to both you and your employers.

THE PROBLEM-SOLVING APPROACH

At first glance, problem solving in daily life seems to be perfectly straightforward; a machine breaks down, parts and oil spill all over the floor, and, obviously, somebody has to do something about it. So, of course, you find a tool around the shop and start repairing the machine. After a cleanup and proper inspection of other parts, you start the machine, and production resumes.

No doubt, some problems in business are this straightforward, but few problems are this simple in the real world of business. In real-world business firms, a number of major factors are simultaneously involved in problems. These major factors can usefully be grouped into three categories: *organization, technology,* and *people.* In other words, a whole set of problems is usually involved.

A MODEL OF THE PROBLEM-SOLVING PROCESS

There is a simple model of problem solving that you can use to help you understand and solve business problems by using information systems. You can think of business problem-solving as a four-step process (see Figure 1.4). Most problem solvers

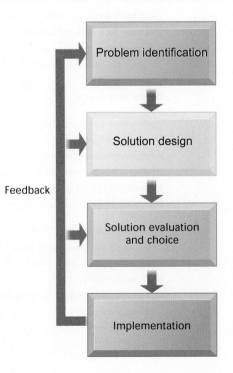

Figure 1.4
Problem Solving Is a Continuous Four-Step Process
During implementation and thereafter, the outcome must be continually measured, and the information about how well the solution is working is fed back to the problem solvers. In this way, the identification of the problem can change over time, solutions can be changed, and new choices made, all based on experience.

Feedback

Problem identification

Solution design

Solution evaluation and choice

Implementation

work through this model on their way to finding a solution. Let's take a brief look at each step.

Problem Identification

The first step in the problem-solving process is to understand what kind of problem exists. Contrary to popular beliefs, problems are not like basketballs on a court simply waiting to be picked up by some objective problem solver. Before problems can be solved, there must be agreement in a business that a problem exists, about what the problem is, about its causes, and about what can be done about it, given the limited resources of the organization. Problems have to be properly defined by people in an organization before they can be solved.

For instance, what at first glance what might seem like a problem with employees not adequately responding to customers in a timely and accurate manner might in reality be a result of an older, out-of-date information system for keeping track of customers; or it might be a combination of both poor employee incentives for treating customers well and an outdated system. Once you understand this critical fact, you can start to solve problems creatively. Finding answers to these questions will require fact gathering, interviews with people involved in the problem, and analysis of documents.

In this text, we emphasize three different and typical dimensions of business problems: organizations, technology, and people (see Table 1.2). Typical organizational problems include poor business processes (usually inherited from the past), unsupportive culture, political in-fighting, and changes in the organization's surrounding environment. Typical technology problems include insufficient or aging hardware, outdated software, inadequate database capacity, insufficient telecommunications capacity, and the incompatibility of old systems with new technology. Typical people problems include employee training, difficulties of evaluating performance, legal and regulatory compliance, ergonomics, poor or indecisive management, and employee support and participation. When you begin to analyze a business problem, you will find these dimensions are helpful guides to understanding the kind of problem with which you are working.

TABLE 1.2

Dimensions of Business
Problems

Dimension	Description
Organizational dimensions	Outdated business processes
	Unsupportive culture and attitudes
	Political conflict
	Turbulent business environment, change
	Complexity of task
	Inadequate resources
Technology dimensions	Insufficient or aging hardware
	Outdated software
	Inadequate database capacity
	Insufficient telecommunications capacity
	Incompatibility of old systems with new technology
	Rapid technological change and failure to adopt new technology
People dimensions	Lack of employee training
	Difficulties of evaluating performance
	Legal and regulatory compliance
	Work environment
	Lack of employee support and participation
	Indecisive management
	Poor management
	Wrong incentives

Solution Design

The second step is to design solutions to the problem(s) you have identified. As it turns out, there are usually a great many solutions to any given problem, and the choice of solution often reflects the differing perspectives of people in an organization. You should try to consider as many solutions as possible so that you can understand the range of possible solutions. Some solutions emphasize technology; others focus on change in the organization and people aspects of the problem. As you will find throughout the text, most successful solutions result from an integrated approach in which changes in organization and people accompany new technologies.

Solution Evaluation and Choice

Choosing the best solution for your business firm is the next step in the process. Some of the factors to consider when trying to find the best single solution are the cost of the solution, the feasibility of the solution for your business given existing resources and skills, and the length of time required to build and implement the solution. Also very important at this point are the attitudes and support of your employees and managers. A solution that does not have the support of all the major interests in the business can quickly turn into a disaster.

Implementation

The best solution is one that can be implemented. Implementation of an information system solution involves building the solution and introducing it into the organization. This includes purchasing or building the software and hardware—the technology part of the equation. The software must be tested in a realistic business setting; then employees need to be trained, and documentation about how to use the new system needs to be written.

You will definitely need to think about change management. **Change management** refers to the many techniques used to bring about successful change in a business. Nearly all information systems require changes in the firm's business processes and, therefore, changes in what hundreds or even thousands of employees do every day. You will have to design new, more efficient business processes and then figure out how to encourage employees to adapt to these new ways of doing business. This may require meeting sessions to introduce the change to groups of employees, new training modules to bring employees quickly up to speed on the new information systems and processes, and, finally, some kind of rewards or incentives to encourage people to support the changes enthusiastically.

Implementation also includes the measurement of outcomes. After a solution has been implemented, it must be evaluated to determine how well it is working and whether any additional changes are required to meet the original objectives. This information is fed back to the problem solvers. In this way, the identification of the problem can change over time, solutions can be changed, and new choices made, all based on experience.

Problem Solving: A Process, Not an Event

It is often assumed that once a problem is solved, it goes away and can be forgotten about. It is easy to fall into the trap of thinking about problem solving as an event that is over at some point, like a relay race or a baseball game. Often in the real world, this does not happen. Sometimes the chosen solution does not work, and new solutions are required.

For instance, the U.S. National Aeronautics and Space Administration (NASA) spent more than $1 billion to fix a problem with shedding foam on the space shuttle. Experience proved the initial solution did not work. More often, the chosen solution partially works but needs a lot of continuous changes to fit the situation well. Initial solutions are often rough approximations at first of what ultimately works. Sometimes, the nature of the problem changes in a way that makes the initial solution ineffective. For instance, hackers create new variations on computer viruses that require continually evolving antivirus programs to hold them in check. For all these reasons, problem solving is a continuous process rather than a single event.

THE ROLE OF CRITICAL THINKING IN PROBLEM SOLVING

It is amazingly easy to accept someone else's definition of a problem or to adopt the opinions of some authoritative group that has objectively analyzed the problem and offers quick solutions. You should try to resist this tendency to accept existing definitions of any problem. It is essential for you to try to maintain some distance from any specific solution until you are sure you have properly identified the problem, developed understanding, and analyzed alternatives. Otherwise, you may leap off in the wrong direction, solve the wrong problem, and waste resources. You will have to engage in some critical-thinking exercises.

Critical thinking can be briefly defined as the sustained suspension of judgment with an awareness of multiple perspectives and alternatives. It involves at least four elements.
- Maintaining doubt and suspending judgment
- Being aware of different perspectives
- Testing alternatives and letting experience guide
- Being aware of organizational and personal limitations

Simply following a rote pattern of decision making, or a model, does not guarantee a correct solution. The best protection against incorrect results is to engage in critical thinking throughout the problem-solving process.

First, maintain doubt and suspend judgment. Perhaps the most frequent error in problem solving is to arrive prematurely at a judgment about the nature of the problem. By doubting all solutions at first and refusing to rush to a judgment, you create the necessary mental conditions to take a fresh, creative look at problems, and you keep open the chance to make a creative contribution.

Second, recognize that all interesting business problems have many dimensions and that the same problem can be viewed from different perspectives. In this text, we have emphasized the usefulness of three perspectives on business problems: technology, organizations, and people. Within each of these very broad perspectives are many subperspectives, or views. The *technology perspective*, for instance, includes a consideration of all the components in the firm's IT infrastructure and the way they work together. The *organization perspective* includes a consideration of a firm's business processes, structure, culture, and politics. The *people perspective* includes consideration of the firm's management as well as employees as individuals and their interrelationships in workgroups.

You will have to decide for yourself which major perspectives are useful for viewing a given problem. The ultimate criterion here is usefulness: Does adopting a certain perspective tell you something more about the problem that is useful for solving the problem? If not, reject that perspective as not meaningful in this situation and look for other perspectives.

The third element of critical thinking involves testing alternatives, or modeling solutions to problems, letting experience be the guide. Not all contingencies can be known in advance, and much can be learned through experience. Therefore, experiment, gather data, and reassess the problem periodically.

THE CONNECTIONS AMONG BUSINESS OBJECTIVES, PROBLEMS, AND SOLUTIONS

Now let's make the connection between business information systems and the problem-solving approach. At the beginning of this chapter, we identified six business objectives of information systems: operational excellence; new products, services, and business models; customer/supplier intimacy; improved decision making; strategic advantage; and survival. When firms cannot achieve these objectives, they become challenges or problems that receive attention. Managers and employees who are aware of these challenges often turn to information systems as one of the solutions or the entire solution.

Review the diagram at the beginning of this chapter. The diagram shows how the Rugby Football Union's systems solved the business problem presented by the need to generate revenue in a highly competitive industry. These systems created a solution that takes advantage of opportunities that new digital technology and the Internet provided. They opened up new channels for selling tickets and interacting with customers, optimized ticket pricing, and used new tools to analyze player performance. These systems were essential in improving the rugby teams' overall business performance. The diagram also illustrates how people, technology, and organizational elements work together to create the systems.

Each chapter of this text begins with a diagram similar to this one to help you analyze the chapter-opening case. You can use this diagram as a starting point for analyzing any information system or information system problem you encounter.

1-4 How will information systems affect business careers, and what information systems skills and knowledge are essential?

Looking out to 2022, the U.S. economy will create 16 million new jobs, and 32 million existing jobs will open up as their occupants retire. More than 95 percent of the new jobs will be created in the service sector. The vast majority of these new jobs and replacement jobs will require a college degree to perform (U.S. Bureau of Labor Statistics, 2015; Dubina, 2015).

What this means is that U.S. business firms are looking for candidates who have a broad range of problem-solving skills—the ability to read, write, and present ideas—as well as the technical skills required for specific tasks. Regardless of your business school major, or your future occupation, information systems and technologies will play a major and expanding role in your day-to-day work and your career. Your career opportunities, and your compensation, will in part depend on your ability to help business firms use information systems to achieve their objectives.

HOW INFORMATION SYSTEMS WILL AFFECT BUSINESS CAREERS

In the following sections, we describe how specific occupations will be affected by information systems and what skills you should be building in order to benefit from this emerging labor market based on the research of the Bureau of Labor Statistics (Bureau of Labor Statistics, 2015).

Accounting

There are about 1.2 million accountants in the U.S. labor force today, and the field is expected to expand by 13 percent by the year 2022, adding 170,000 new jobs and twice as many to replace retirees. This above-average growth in accounting is driven in part by new accounting laws for public companies, greater scrutiny of public and private firms by government tax auditors, and a growing demand for management and operational advice.

Accountants rely heavily on information systems to summarize transactions, create financial records, organize data, and perform financial analysis. Because of new public laws, accountants require an intimate knowledge of databases, reporting systems, and networks to trace financial transactions. Because so many transactions are occurring over the Internet, accountants need to understand online transaction and reporting systems and how systems are used to achieve management accounting functions in an online, and mobile business environment.

Finance

If you include financial analysts, stock analysts, insurance underwriters, and related financial service occupations, there are currently about 2.2 million managers and employees in finance. Financial managers develop financial reports, direct investment activities, and implement cash management strategies. These financial occupations are expected to grow by about 20 percent by the year 2022 and add more than 500,000 new jobs.

Financial managers play important roles in planning, organizing, and implementing information system strategies for their firms. Financial managers work directly with a firm's board of directors and senior management to ensure that investments in information systems help achieve corporate goals and high returns. The relationship between information systems and the practice of modern financial management and services is so strong that many advise finance majors to co-major in information systems (and vice versa).

Marketing

No field has undergone more technology-driven change in the past five years than marketing and advertising. The explosion in e-commerce activity described earlier means that eyeballs are moving rapidly to the Internet. As a result, Internet advertising is the fastest growing form of advertising, reaching $40 billion in 2014. Product branding and customer communication are moving online at a fast pace.

There are about 1.5 million public relations, marketing analysts, and marketing and sales managers in the U.S. labor force. This field is growing faster than average, at about 16 percent, and is expected to add more than 300,000 jobs by 2022. There is a much larger group of 2.6 million nonmanagerial employees in marketing-related occupations (art, design, entertainment, sports, and media) and more than 15.9 million employees in sales. These occupations together are expected to create an additional 3.1 million jobs by 2022. Marketing and advertising managers deal with large databases of customer behavior both online and offline in the process of creating brands and selling products and services. They develop reports on product performance, retrieve feedback from customers, and manage product development. These managers need an understanding of how enterprise-wide systems for product management, sales force management, and customer relationship management are used to develop products that consumers want, to manage the customer relationship, and to manage an increasingly mobile sales force.

Operations Management in Services and Manufacturing

The growing size and complexity of modern industrial production and the emergence of huge global service companies have created a growing demand for employees who can coordinate and optimize the resources required to produce goods and services. Operations management as a discipline is directly relevant to three occupational categories: industrial production managers, administrative service managers, and operations analysts.

Production managers, administrative service managers, and operations analysts will be employing information systems and technologies every day to accomplish their jobs, with extensive use of database and analytical software.

Management

Management is the largest single group in the U.S. business labor force with more than 16 million members, not including an additional 627,000 management consultants. Overall, the management corps in the United States is expected to expand at an

The job of management requires extensive use of information systems to support decision making and monitor the performance of the firm.

© Konstantin Chagin/123RF

average pace of 15 percent, adding about 2.4 million new jobs by 2022. The Bureau of Labor Statistics tracks more than 20 types of managers, all the way from chief executive officer to human resource managers, production managers, project managers, lodging managers, medical managers, and community service managers.

Information systems have transformed the job of management. Arguably, it would be impossible to manage business firms today, even very small firms, without the extensive use of information systems. Nearly all U.S. managers use information systems and technologies every day to accomplish their jobs, from desktop productivity tools to applications coordinating the entire enterprise. Managers today manage through a variety of information technologies without which it would be impossible to control and lead the firm.

Information Systems

The information systems field is one of the fastest-changing and dynamic of all the business professions because information technologies are among the most important tools for achieving business firms' key objectives. The explosive growth of business information systems has generated a growing demand for information systems employees and managers who work with other business professionals to design and develop new hardware and software systems to serve the needs of business. Of the top 20 fastest-growing occupations through 2022, 5 are information systems occupations.

There are about 332,000 information system managers in the United States, with an estimated growth rate of 15 percent through 2022, expanding the number of new jobs by more than 51,000 new positions. As businesses and government agencies increasingly rely on the Internet for communication and computing resources, system and network security management positions are growing very rapidly. One of the fastest growing U.S. occupational groups is network and computer systems administrators, with a projected growth rate of 12 percent.

Outsourcing and Offshoring

The Internet has created new opportunities for outsourcing many information systems jobs, along with many other service sector and manufacturing jobs. There are two kinds of outsourcing: outsourcing to domestic U.S. firms and offshore outsourcing to low-wage countries such as India, China, and eastern European countries. Even this distinction blurs as domestic service providers, such as IBM, develop global outsourcing centers in India.

The most common and successful offshore outsourcing projects involve production programming and system maintenance programming work, along with call center work related to customer relationship management systems. However, inflation in Indian and Chinese wages for technology work, coupled with the additional management costs incurred in outsourcing projects, is leading to a counter movement of some IT jobs back to the United States. Moreover, although routine technical information systems (IS) jobs such as software maintenance can be outsourced easily, all those management and organizational tasks required in systems development—including business process design, customer interface, and supply chain management—often remain in the United States.

Innovative new products, services, and systems are rarely outsourced either domestically or globally. The advantage of low-wage countries is their low wages, not their keen sense of new products, services, and technologies for the United States market. Software design and new programming efforts are rarely outsourced because of their strategic importance to firms and because domestic software designers are much closer to the American marketplace and customer base. Software outsourcing of routine IS work to low-wage countries lowers the cost of building and maintaining systems in the United States. As systems become less expensive, more are built. The net result is that offshore outsourcing may increase demand in the United States for managerial IS positions as well as for many of the IS occupations previously described.

Given all these factors in the IT labor market, on what kinds of skills should information system majors focus? Following is a list of general skills we believe will optimize employment opportunities.

- An in-depth knowledge of how business firms can use new and emerging hardware and software to make them more efficient and effective, enhance customer and supplier intimacy, improve decision making, achieve competitive advantage, and ensure firm survival. This includes an in-depth understanding of databases, database design, implementation, and management
- An ability to take a leadership role in the design and implementation of new information systems, work with other business professionals to ensure systems meet business objectives, and work with software packages providing new system solutions

INFORMATION SYSTEMS AND YOUR CAREER: WRAP-UP

Looking back at the information system skills required for specific majors, there are some common themes that affect all business majors. Following is a list of these common requirements for information system skills and knowledge.

- All business students, regardless of major, should understand how information systems and technologies can help firms achieve business objectives such as attaining operational efficiency, developing new products and services, and maintaining customer intimacy.
- Perhaps the most dominant theme that pervades this review of necessary job skills is the central role of databases in a modern firm. Each of the careers we have just described relies heavily on practice in databases.
- With the pervasive growth in databases comes inevitably an exponential growth in digital information and a resulting challenge to managers trying to understand all this information. Regardless of major, business students need to develop skills in analysis of information and helping firms understand and make sense of their environments. Business analytics and intelligence are important skill sets to analyze the mountains of big data the online environment of business firms produces.
- All business majors need to be able to work with specialists and system designers who build and implement information systems. This is necessary to ensure that the systems that are built actually service business purposes and provide the information and understanding managers and employees require.
- Each of the business majors will be affected by changes in the ethical, social, and legal environment of business. Business school students need to understand how

information systems can be used to meet business requirements for reporting to government regulators and the public and how information systems affect the ethical issues in their fields.

HOW THIS BOOK PREPARES YOU FOR THE FUTURE

This book is explicitly designed to prepare you for your future business career. It provides you with the necessary knowledge and foundational concepts for understanding the role of information systems in business organizations. You will be able to use this knowledge to identify opportunities for increasing the effectiveness of your business. You will learn how to use information systems to improve operations, create new products and services, improve decision making, increase customer intimacy, and promote competitive advantage.

Equally important, this book develops your ability to use information systems to solve problems that you will encounter on the job. You will learn how to analyze and define a business problem and how to design an appropriate information system solution. You will deepen your critical-thinking and problem-solving skills. The following features of the text and the accompanying learning package reinforce this problem-solving and career orientation.

A Framework for Describing and Analyzing Information Systems

The text provides you with a framework for analyzing and solving problems by examining the people, organizational, and technology components of information systems. This framework is used repeatedly throughout the text to help you understand information systems in business and analyze information systems problems.

A Four-Step Model for Problem Solving

The text provides you with a four-step method for solving business problems, which we introduced in this chapter. You will learn how to identify a business problem, design alternative solutions, choose the correct solution, and implement the solution. You will be asked to use this problem-solving method to solve the case studies in each chapter. Chapter 12 will show you how to use this approach to design and build new information systems.

Hands-On MIS Projects for Stimulating Critical Thinking and Problem Solving

Each chapter concludes with a series of hands-on MIS projects to sharpen your critical-thinking and problem-solving skills. These projects include two Management Decision Problems, hands-on application software problems, and projects for building Internet skills. For each of these projects, we identify both the business skills and the software skills required for the solution.

Career Resources

To make sure you know how the text is directly useful in your future business career, we've added a full set of Career Resources to help you with career development and job hunting.

Digital Portfolio MyMISLab™ includes a template for preparing a structured digital portfolio to demonstrate the business knowledge, application software skills, Internet skills, and analytical skills you have acquired in this course. You can include this portfolio in your resume or job applications. Your professors can also use the portfolio to assess the skills you have learned.

Career Resources A Career Resources section in MyMISLab shows you how to integrate what you have learned in this course in your résumé, cover letter, and job interview to improve your chances for success in the job market.

Review Summary

1-1 **Why are information systems so essential for running and managing a business today?** Information systems are a foundation for conducting business today. In many industries, survival and even existence is difficult without extensive use of information technology. Businesses use information systems to achieve six major objectives: operational excellence; new products, services, and business models; customer/supplier intimacy; improved decision making; competitive advantage; and day-to-day survival.

1-2 **What exactly is an information system? How does it work? What are its people, organization, and technology components?** From a technical perspective, an information system collects, stores, and disseminates information from an organization's environment and internal operations to support organizational functions and decision making, communication, coordination, control, analysis, and visualization. Information systems transform raw data into useful information through three basic activities: input, processing, and output. From a business perspective, an information system provides a solution to a problem or challenge facing a firm and represents a combination of people, organization, and technology elements.

The people dimension of information systems involves issues such as training, job attitudes, and management behavior. The technology dimension consists of computer hardware, software, data management technology, and networking/telecommunications technology, including the Internet. The organization dimension of information systems involves issues such as the organization's hierarchy, functional specialties, business processes, culture, and political interest groups.

1-3 **How will a four-step method for business problem solving help you solve information system–related problems?** Problem identification involves understanding what kind of problem is being presented and identifying people, organizational, and technology factors. Solution design involves designing several alternative solutions to the problem that has been identified. Evaluation and choice entail selecting the best solution, taking into account its cost and the available resources and skills in the business. Implementation of an information system solution entails purchasing or building hardware and software, testing the software, providing employees with training and documentation, managing change as the system is introduced into the organization, and measuring the outcome. Problem solving requires critical thinking in which one suspends judgment to consider multiple perspectives and alternatives.

1-4 **How will information systems affect business careers, and what information system skills and knowledge are essential?** Business careers in accounting, finance, marketing, operations management, management and human resources, and information systems all will need an understanding of how information systems help firms achieve major business objectives; an appreciation of the central role of databases; skills in information analysis and business intelligence; sensitivity to the ethical, social, and legal issues systems raise; and the ability to work with technology specialists and other business professionals in designing and building systems.

Key Terms

Business model, 37	Computer	Data management
Business processes, 42	software, 43	technology, 43
Change management, 49	Critical thinking, 50	Extranets, 44
Computer hardware, 43	Culture, 42	Feedback, 40
Computer literacy, 42	Data, 39	Information, 39

MyMISLab™
To complete the problems with the ⭐, go to EOC Discussion Questions in the MyLab.

Review Questions

1-1 Why are information systems so essential for running and managing a business today?
  • List and describe the six reasons information systems are so important for business today.
  • Explain what globalization has to do with information systems.

1-2 What exactly is an information system? How does it work? What are its people, organization, and technology components?
  • List and describe the organizational, people, and technology dimensions of information systems.
  • Define an information system and describe the activities it performs.
  • Distinguish between data and information and between information technology and and information system.
  • Explain how the Internet and the World Wide Web are related to the other technology components of information systems.

1-3 How will a four-step method for business problem solving help you solve information system–related problems?
  • List and describe each of the four steps for solving business problems.
  • Give some examples of people, organizational, and technology problems found in businesses.
  • Define critical thinking and list four elements that are involved in critical thinking.
  • Describe the role of information systems in business problem solving.

1-4 How will information systems affect business careers, and what information system skills and knowledge are essential?
  • Describe the role of information systems in careers in accounting, finance, marketing, management, and operations management and explain how careers in information systems have been affected by new technologies and outsourcing.
  • List and describe the information system skills and knowledge that are essential for all business careers.

Discussion Questions

⭐1-5 Information systems are too important to be left to computer specialists. Do you agree? Why or why not?

⭐1-6 If you were setting up the Web site for a rugby team, what management, organization, and technology issues might you encounter?

⭐1-7 How have federal and state statutes and regulations impacted the use of information systems?

Hands-On MIS Projects

The projects in this section give you hands-on experience in analyzing financial reporting and inventory management problems, using data management software to improve management decision making about increasing sales, and using Internet software for researching job requirements. Visit MyMISLab's Multimedia Library to access this chapter's Hands-On MIS Projects

MANAGEMENT DECISION PROBLEMS

1-8   Warbenton Snack Foods is a manufacturer of potato crisps and savoury snacks in the U.K. Warbenton's financial department uses spreadsheets and manual processes for much of its data gathering and reporting. Their financial analyst would spend the entire final week of every month collecting spreadsheets from the heads of more than 50 departments worldwide. She would then consolidate and reenter all the data into another spreadsheet, which would serve as the company's monthly profit-and-loss statement. If a department needed to update its data after submitting the spreadsheet to the main office, the analyst had to return the original spreadsheet and wait for the department to resubmit its data before finally submitting the updated data in the consolidated document. Assess the impact of this situation on business performance and management decision making.

1-9   Rabatt operates deep-discount stores offering housewares, cleaning supplies, clothing, health and beauty aids, and packaged food throughout Germany, with most items selling for €1. Its business model calls for keeping costs as low as possible. The company has no automated method for keeping track of inventory at each store. Managers know approximately how many cases of a particular product the store is supposed to receive when a delivery truck arrives, but the stores lack technology for scanning the cases or verifying the item count inside the cases. Merchandise losses from theft or other mishaps have been rising and now represent more than 3 percent of total sales. What decisions have to be made before investing in an information system solution?

IMPROVING DECISION MAKING: USING DATABASES TO ANALYZE SALES TRENDS

Software skills: Database querying and reporting
Business skills: Sales trend analysis

1-10   In this project, you will start out with raw transactional sales data and use Microsoft Access database software to develop queries and reports that help managers make better decisions about product pricing, sales promotions, and inventory replenishment. In MyMISLab, you can find a Store and Regional Sales Database developed in Microsoft Access. The database contains raw data on weekly store sales of computer equipment in various sales regions. The database includes fields for store identification number, sales region, item number, item description, unit price, units sold, and the weekly sales period when the sales were made. Use Access to develop some reports and queries to make this information more useful for running the business. Sales and production managers want answers to the following questions:
- Which products should be restocked?
- Which stores and sales regions would benefit from a promotional campaign and additional marketing?
- When (what time of year) should products be offered at full price, and when should discounts be used?

You can easily modify the database table to find and report your answers. Print your reports and results of queries.

IMPROVING DECISION MAKING: USING THE INTERNET TO LOCATE JOBS REQUIRING INFORMATION SYSTEMS KNOWLEDGE

Software skills: Internet-based software
Business skills: Job searching

1-11   Visit a job-posting website such as Monster.com. Spend some time at the site examining jobs for accounting, finance, sales, marketing, and human resources. Find two or three descriptions of jobs that require some information systems knowledge. What information systems knowledge do these jobs require? What do you need to do to prepare for these jobs? Write a one- to two-page report summarizing your findings.

Collaboration and Teamwork Project

Selecting Team Collaboration Tools

1-12   Form a team with three or four classmates and review the capabilities of Google Drive and Google Sites for your team collaboration work. Compare the capabilities of these two tools for storing team documents, project announcements, source materials, work assignments, illustrations, presentations, and web pages of interest. Learn how each works with Google Docs. Explain why Google Drive or Google Sites is more appropriate for your team. If possible, use Google Docs to brainstorm and develop a presentation of your findings for the class. Organize and store your presentation by using the Google tool you have selected.

BUSINESS PROBLEM-SOLVING CASE

Mashaweer: On-Demand Personal Services in the Gulf

Mashaweer is the first personal service company in Egypt. It's purely dedicated to saving its clients' time and effort by offering a personal assistant 24 hours a day. The personal assistant is a rider with a motorcycle who runs any errands for individual clients or corporations at any given time. The most common service they provide is buying groceries or other goods from stores, paying bills, and acting as a courier. Mashaweer's success relies heavily on their flexibility, and they have often received unusual requests that they have fulfilled in order to gain customer loyalty, including going to the gym to tell someone to turn on the phone as someone is trying to reach them, delivering presents to a client's fiancée every 15 minutes, and carrying a client's shopping bags from the car to the house. Before Uber and Airbnb became popular in the United States and elsewhere, Mashaweer was pioneering an on-demand form of e-commerce.

Mashaweer is an essential service for Egyptians because traffic is a problem that everyone in Egypt faces, making it difficult for an individual to get a couple of errands done on the same day. Mashaweer's service has achieved great success in Alexandria and Cairo, where traffic is an issue, saving people one of the most valuable commodities out there: time. The service is able to give people more quality time to spend with family or friends, instead of taking care of the daily errands that usually take up half of one's day. They also act as a security or safety measure as they perform people's errands in unsafe times, such as the period after the revolution or simply late at night. Most individuals cannot afford having a full-time assistant to perform their errands whenever needed. Mashaweer's agents act as full-time assistants for every individual at a part-time cost.

Since it was founded in Alexandria in 2010, Mashaweer has expanded to Cairo and operates around 600 orders per day. They have since expanded into Dubai with an on-demand taxi-based errand service providing errand fulfillment as well as transportation.

The idea of Mashaweer was created by Mohamed Wahid (24 years old) and then co-founded with his partners, Ahmed El Kordy (25 years old) and Aly El Shazly (27 years old). They were all born and raised in Alexandria. Ahmed El Kordy and Mohamed Wahid met when they both transferred from different

schools to IGCSE Academy (AAST) for high school. Ahmed El Kordy finished high school in 2 years and went on to achieve his bachelor's degree in industrial engineering from the Arab Academy of Science and Technology (AAST), graduating in 2008. Part of his undergraduate degree was spent doing a year abroad in Carleton University in Ottawa, Canada. During the summers of his undergraduate years, Ahmed completed several internships in the United Kingdom and Ireland. Mohamed Wahid also went to AAST, graduating in 2009 with a bachelor's degree in construction engineering. Aly El Shazly attended St. Marks School for his entire school career; he then went to Alexandria University, where he studied business and graduated in 2007. After college, Ahmed El Kordy went on to work at his father's import/export business. Mohamed Wahid went on to establish a company called X-trade for trade and contracting, followed by a marketing and advertising company called Green Media. Currently, he's a main shareholder in both, in addition to being the vice-chairman of Green Towers, a real estate company with a net worth of about $16 million.

Wahid thought of the idea of establishing Mashaweer while he was preparing for his wedding. His bride-to-be was overwhelmed with errands that she had to get done within a few days, and he started wondering what she would have done if she couldn't afford a full-time driver who did all of her errands for her. While on his honeymoon, he kept thinking about this idea and how much time people could save and what a valuable service it could be. He decided to call his friends to start transforming the idea into an actual business plan. After developing the plan, the three entrepreneurs decided to go into the implementation phase and actually build this business. They started small and grew organically as the demand for the service increased. Each of the three entrepreneurs invested $5,000 into the project to total a starting capital of $15,000. They started with only 3 motorcycles, 6 riders, and a hotline.

When the three friends realized they had actually succeeded in Alexandria, they decided they wanted to move to the next phase by establishing Mashaweer in Cairo. When they decided to expand to Cairo they chose to adopt a completely different strategy. They wanted to be able to cover all of Greater Cairo, as a whole, and not just specific areas, from the very beginning. During the Revolution in January 2011 they started gathering market research to expand in Cairo and started investing heavily. Since business all over the country had come to a standstill, they made several large purchases such as motorcycles and advertising space for fractions of the price. When others saw it as a time to slow down, the entrepreneurs saw it as an opportunity to start marketing for their business. By March they realized that they needed to increase the original investment so that they could grow large enough to capture the market in Cairo. To do so, they brought in other investors, mainly from their friends and family, to raise the capital investment up to $1.67 million. They planned to enter Cairo in full force so that there would be a high barrier of entry for any competitor. They decided that their competitive advantage would have to be in investing in technology. They wanted to get an enterprise resource planning (ERP) system but found quotations to be too high. To fix this they started their own information technology company, Innov8 ("innovate"), through which they created a customized ERP system that they then connected to their customized personal digital assistants (PDAs) through a cloud computing system made by LinkDotNet and Mobinil. Each rider receives tasks one at a time on the PDA, which also includes a GPS to provide detailed directions. The GPS monitors the rider's location. By 2015, these early PDA devices were replaced with smartphones.

To reduce cost and ensure quality, Mashaweer does not rely on outsourcing in any of its stages as long as it can do the work with the same or better quality. This was why Mashaweer founded Innov8—in order to build its system and manage its technical work. Now, Mashaweer only owns part of this company and is one of its numerous clients. One further example of Mashaweer's in-house capabilities is its call center. The company preferred to have an internal call center after rejecting a number of offers for an outsourced one. They wanted to be able to monitor the performance of the agents and always work on improving the quality of their customer service. Investing in an innovative contact center and using CISCO, which supports up to 300IP smartphones, a reporting module, and a recording system, made it much easier for Mashaweer to track its received calls and work on any problems that its customer service agents might face.

Software components developed by Innov8 include the Mashaweer Server, Mashaweer application programmers' interface (API), and Mashaweer app client.

The Mashaweer Server is a centralized application that manages the following elements:
- Orders (placement, editing, pricing, review, tracking, and reports)
- Routes management and optimization
- Clients (management, reports, discounts)
- Packages tracking
- Contracts
- The call center
- Satellite offices
- Representatives
- Cash transactions and expenses tracking for representatives and satellite offices
- Asset tracking of vehicles, PDAs, and mobile printers
- Management reports

The API is a method of integrating Mashaweer's ordering system with third parties. This allows the latter to automate their delivery system and integrate Mashaweer into their existing CRM/dispatching systems, opening a wide opportunity for business expansion.

The Mashaweer application is installed on each representative's smartphone and manages the following elements:
- Order items progress tracking
- Collection of order fees and other costs against a printed invoice
- Package handling (barcode scanning and destinations)
- Messaging
- Cash and expenses tracking
- Synchronizing data periodically and at the beginning of each shift

When Mashaweer was first introduced in Egypt, it captured 100 percent of market share for such a service because it was the first and only company of its nature. However, the market was not aware or used to such a service, so it started growing slowly in Alexandria until people grasped the idea and got accustomed to the fact that there was a company that can take over your errands. In contrast, when the company started operating in Cairo, it grew at a surprisingly fast pace. There are several factors that are expected to affect the target market and make it easier for Mashaweer to penetrate it aggressively.

At the beginning, people's assumption is that using Mashaweer is too luxurious and costly. When they use it for the first few times, this perception changes and they begin to rely on this convenient service. As more and more people get accustomed to the service, it creates a cultural change that significantly affects the demand on the service.

Another factor that is expected to facilitate working conditions and reduce costs is the technological advances that occur every day. Mashaweer heavily depends on technological tools, and will benefit from the advancements and price reductions that continuously take place. As a result, Mashaweer's total costs will decrease, enabling it to decrease its prices and further improve its quality to become even more convenient for a larger number of people.

Mashaweer is the only company of its kind in Egypt that operates on this scale. However, there is a company called Wassaly that was established in Cairo after Mashaweer's success in Alexandria. This company operates on a much smaller scale. Their indirect competitors include other courier services (e.g. DHL, UPS, TNT, and FedEx). However, they have positioned themselves as the flexible courier in contrast to the others available in the market today; they offer same-day delivery rather than next-day delivery.

Mashaweer has several advantages that make it very hard for others to compete:

- A database of thousands of loyal clients
- Manageable self-investment
- Highly qualified and carefully selected riders due to the high salaries compared to the delivery sector in Egypt
- Various revenue streams
- Ownership of Innov8, which fosters technology integration in Mashaweer

Mashaweer has several unique selling propositions. The main aspects are being the first in the market, and being the only company of its kind. The most important differentiator is the flexibility of their service, which addresses all of their customer's needs and requests.

Using the technology they have invested in building their infrastructure, Mashaweer now has the potential to easily enter and penetrate other markets in different regions at a very low initiation cost. They plan to expand to other regions within Egypt in addition to expanding to other countries within the Middle East. In October 2013 they opened their first franchise in Beirut, Lebanon. In 2014 they opened up for business in Dubai, and have plans for expanding to several countries in the Gulf. In February 2015 Mashaweer was one of the winners of the E-Services Excellence Award (ESEA) from Dubai Trade, primarily for its adoption of e-Services on the Dubai Trade Portal (www.dubaitrade.ae) during 2014, measuring transactions for key services as well as the number and volume of transactions.

Sources: "Dubai Trade Honours 7th ESEA Award Winners," ArabianSupplyChain.com, February 11, 2015; Pamella de Leon, "Startup Mashaweer Wants to Do Your Errands In Dubai," entrepreneurmiddleeast.com, November 19, 2014; Mohammad Osmangoni, "Case 1: Mashaweer," mohammadosmangoni.wordpress.com/2014/10/17/case-1, October 17, 2014; Nivriti Butalia, "Errand Services in Dubai Are Thriving and Ready to Assist," *Khaleej Times*, September 13, 2014; Neil King, "The Business of Errands," by Neil King, ArabianBusiness.com, May 7, 2014; "Brands Speak Digital: Mahsaweer's Social Media Strategy," http://www.digibuzzme.com, November 22, 2012.

Case Study Questions

1-13 What kinds of applications are described in this case? What business functions do they support?

1-14 What are the benefits from equipping their riders with PDAs?

1-15 Was it a good decision to expand the business to Cairo? What are the implications of information systems?

1-16 Do you think that Mashaweer will be able to accomplish its future strategy and sustain its market share?

Case contributed by Niveen Ezzat, Cairo University.

MyMISLab

Go to the Assignments section of your MyLab to complete these writing exercises.

1-17 What are the strategic objectives that firms try to achieve by using information systems? For each strategic objective, give an example of how a firm could use information systems to achieve the objective.

1-18 Describe three ways in which information systems are transforming how business is conducted.

Chapter I References

Brynjolfsson, Erik. "VII Pillars of IT Productivity." *Optimize* (May 2005).

Bureau of Economic Analysis. *National Income and Product Accounts*, www.bea.gov, accessed August 19, 2014.

Chae, Ho-Chang, Chang E. Koh, and Victor Prybutok. "Information Technology Capability and Firm Performance: Contradictory Findings and Their Possible Causes," *MIS Quarterly* 38, No. 1 (March 2014).

Dubina, Kevin. "*Job Openings Reach a New High, Hires and Quits Also Increase*," Bureau of Labor Statistics Monthly Labor Review (June 2015).

eMarketer. "Chart: U.S. Digital Shoppers and Buyers, 2013–2019 (Millions and % of Internet Users), (June 2015).

FedEx Corporation. "SEC Form 10-K for the Fiscal Year Ended 2015."

Friedman, Thomas. *The World is* Flat. New York: Picador, 2007.

"Gartner Says Worldwide IT Spending to Decline 1.3 Percent in 2015. Press Release. Garnter Research, Stamford, Connecticut (April 9, 2015).

IBM Corporation. "The Individual Enterprise: How Mobility Redefines Business," (2014).

Laudon, Kenneth C. *Computers and Bureaucratic Reform.* New York: Wiley, 1974.

Pew Internet and American Life. "Internet Use Over Time," (June 2015).

Ross, Jeanne W., and Peter Weill. "Four Questions Every CEO Should Ask About IT," *Wall Street Journal* (April 25, 2011).

Sampler, Jeffrey L., and Michael J. Earl. "What's Your Information Footprint?" *MIT Sloan Management Review* (Winter 2014).

U.S. Bureau of Labor Statistics. *Occupational Outlook Handbook, 2014–2015,* (April 15, 2014).

Weill, Peter, and Jeanne Ross. *IT Savvy: What Top Executives Must Know to Go from Pain to Gain,* Boston: Harvard Business School Press, 2009.

Global E-Business and Collaboration

CHAPTER 2

LEARNING OBJECTIVES

After reading this chapter, you will be able to answer the following questions:

2-1 What major features of a business are important for understanding the role of information systems?

2-2 How do systems serve different management groups in a business and how do systems that link the enterprise improve organizational performance?

2-3 Why are systems for collaboration and social business so important and what technologies do they use?

2-4 What is the role of the information systems function in a business?

CHAPTER CASES

Social Business at BASF

Schiphol International Hub to Become Faultless: Truth or Dare?

Is Social Business Working Out?

Modernization of NTUC Income

VIDEO CASES

Case 1: Walmart's Retail Link Supply Chain

Case 2: CEMEX—Becoming a Social Business

Instructional Video

US Foodservice Grows Market with Oracle CRM on Demand

SOCIAL BUSINESS AT BASF

BASF is the largest chemical company in the world, generating over €73.3 billion in 2013, about .5 percent higher than 2013, still an achievement during a European and Asian recession. BASF is a German company with headquarters in Ludwigshaven. It has nearly 400 production sites around the world, operates in 200 countries, and has just over 100,000 employees. As a diversified chemical company, BASF supplies chemicals, plastics, catalysts, industrial coatings, crop technology, and crude oil and gas exploration for a wide variety of industries. The very size and scope of BASF's operations provide obvious advantages of scale, but also raise difficult management and organizational issues. With existing information technologies it was difficult to create a single global BASF culture, to coordinate initiatives and employees across so many time zones, to collaborate in real time, and to allow employees to participate in decision making.

BASF managers believed one potential solution to the challenges of managing a far-flung global enterprise was to use social technology as a platform to solve the challenges. Exactly how to do this, what technology to use, and how to implement this across the globe for its 100,000 employees was not initially clear. Older stand-alone solutions such as forums, blogs, wikis, and corporate Web sites provided only partial solutions.

Instead, management implemented a social business platform called connect.BASF. The platform is based on the IBM Connections enterprise social network platform, which operates in the IBM Cloud environment. According to IDC, enterprise social network platforms provided by several firms have been adopted rapidly by global firms in the last few years to drive greater collaboration, coordination, and innovation throughout their firms. Connect.BASF includes many of the same functions that can be found on popular consumer social sites like Facebook, LinkedIn, Tumblr, cloud storage sites like Dropbox, and Web-based community knowledge sites like Wikipedia, inclduing user profiles, status updates, news feeds, notifications, bookmarks, and file sharing. The purpose is to share knowledge, col-

laborate, and encourage employees and managers to have conversations about their work.

To implement connect.BASF, managers decided that employees should not be required to participate, but instead should be attracted to participate based on the benefits and capabilities of the platform as they perceived them. Implementation was carried out by two global community managers, and three regional community managers. They in turn recruited advocates, the early adopters who volunteer their time to spread awareness of the social network and document best practices. Users are encouraged to build communities of practice, online spaces where employees with similar professional backgrounds can share ideas. The implementation team used a multifaceted set of tools such as webinars, learning events, demonstrations, and internal consulting to attract employees.

In the first two years of operation, connect.BASF gathered over 33,000 users. The network supports more than 3,100 active work communities, and 84 percent of the users understand the business objectives of connect.BASF. Management believes the enterprise social network provides faster access to company experts, higher employee productivity, and better flow of knowledge throughout the firm. Younger workers in particular are attracted to the network and more comfortable with using it. The use of email and the extensive overhead in systems and employee distraction has been greatly reduced. Managers have also had to learn new styles of management suitable to an online social environment as opposed to relying solely on traditional face-to-face interactions with employees. In Brazil BASF created a single social hub using connect.BASF for the agricultural community. The hub enables messaging, alerts, and up-to-date information on weather and agriculture to be tailored to the customer's region and specialization.

Sources: Ricardo Rossi Neto, and Brenda Shu, "BASF a Social Business in the Agricultural B2B Business," IBM Connect 2014 Wiki, accessed December 5, 2015; "Worldwide Enterprise Social Networks and Online Communities 2015–2019 Forecast and 2014 Vendor Shares," International Data Corporation, July 2015; BASF, Annual Report 2014, http://report.basf.com/2014, March 16, 2015; MIT Sloan Management Review and Deloitte, "Findings From the 2014 Social Business Global Executive Study," MIT Sloan Management Review, 2014; "The Growth of an Enterprise Social Network at BASF," simply-communicate.com, November 26, 2014; "Worldwide Enterprise Social Networks 2014–2018 Forecast and 2013 Vendor Shares," International Data Corporation, July 2014; BASF, Annual Report 2013, http://report.basf.com/2013/en/notes/policies-and-scope-of-consolidation/accounting-policies/general-information.html, March 16, 2014.

The chapter-opening diagram calls attention to important points raised by this case and this chapter. BASF is very much a knowledge-intensive company, but it was hampered by the absence of an information system that enabled efficient global management decision making, collaboration among professional employees, and convenient sharing of knowledge. This impacted the company's ability to create and deliver leading-edge chemical products and services. It was very difficult to manage the firm on a global basis, or to bring together teams located in distant time zones. BASF management decided that the best solution was to deploy recently developed social network technologies to move from a static corporate knowledge and work environment to one in which actively engaged employees and enabled them to obtain more knowledge from colleagues. The company implemented IBM's Enterprise Social Network platform as an enterprise-wide platform for collaboration, management, knowledge acquisition, and knowledge transfer. It took advantage of the software's new "social" tools to increase employee collaboration and engagement. BASF now relies on its internal enterprise social network for much of employee learning and problem solving.

Much more than technology was involved in the transformation of BASF's work culture. BASF managers developed a management philosophy of voluntary participation in the network. It created an implementation team at the top and middle of the

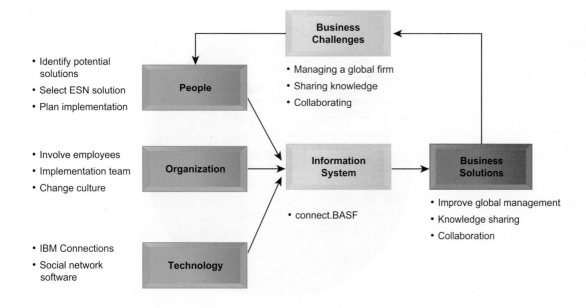

form, and slowly spread the word to corporate entities around the globe through webinars, learning events, and internal consulting.

Here are some questions to think about: How are collaboration and employee engagement keeping BASF competitive? How did using a single enterprise social network platform change the way work was performed at BASF?

2-1 What major features of a business are important for understanding the role of information systems?

A **business** is a formal organization whose aim is to produce products or provide services for a profit—that is, to sell products or services at a price greater than the costs of production. Customers are willing to pay this price because they believe they receive a value greater than or equal to the sale price. Business firms purchase inputs and resources from the larger environment (suppliers who are often other firms). Employees of the business firm transform these inputs by adding value to them in the production process.

There are, of course, nonprofit firms and government agencies that are complex formal organizations that produce services and products but do not operate to generate a profit. Nevertheless, even these organizations consume resources from their environments, add value to these inputs, and deliver their outputs to constituents and customers. In general, the information systems found in government and nonprofit organizations are remarkably similar to those found in private industry.

ORGANIZING A BUSINESS: BASIC BUSINESS FUNCTIONS

Imagine you want to set up your own business. Simply deciding to go into business is the most important decision, but next is the question of what product or service to produce (and hopefully sell). The decision of what to produce is called a *strategic choice* because it determines your likely customers, the kinds of employees you will need, the production methods and facilities needed, the marketing themes, and many other choices.

Once you decide what to produce, what kind of organization do you need? First, you need to develop a production division—an arrangement of people, machines, and business processes (procedures) that will produce the product. Second, you need

Figure 2.1
The Four Major
Functions of a Business
*Every business, regardless
of its size, must perform
four functions to succeed.
It must produce the prod-
uct or service; market and
sell the product or service;
keep track of accounting
and financial transactions;
and perform basic human
resources tasks such
as hiring and retaining
employees.*

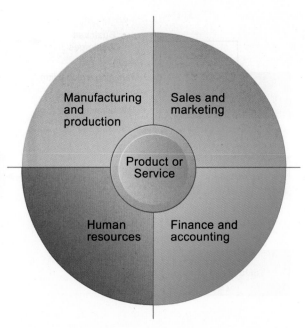

a sales and marketing group who will attract customers, sell the product, and keep track of after-sales issues, such as warranties and maintenance. Third, once you generate sales, you will need a finance and accounting group to keep track of financial transactions, such as orders, invoices, disbursements, and payroll. In addition, this group will seek out sources of credit and finance. Finally, you will need a group of people to focus on recruiting, hiring, training, and retaining employees. Figure 2.1 summarizes the four basic functions found in every business.

If you were an entrepreneur or your business was very small with only a few employees, you would not need, and probably could not afford, all these separate groups of people. Instead, in small firms, you would be performing all these functions yourself or with a few others. In any event, even in small firms, the four basic functions of a firm are required. Larger firms often will have separate departments for each function: production and manufacturing, sales and marketing, finance and accounting, and human resources.

Figure 2.1 is also useful for thinking about the basic entities that make up a business. The five basic entities in a business with which it must deal are: suppliers, customers, employees, invoices/payments, and, of course, products and services. A business must manage and monitor many other components, but these are the basic ones at the foundation of any business.

BUSINESS PROCESSES

Once you identify the basic business functions and entities for your business, your next job is to describe exactly how you want your employees to perform these functions. What specific tasks do you want your sales personnel to perform, in what order, and on what schedule? What steps do you want production employees to follow as they transform raw resources into finished products? How will customer orders be fulfilled? How will vendor bills be paid?

The actual steps and tasks that describe how work is organized in a business are called **business processes**. A business process is a logically related set of activities that defines how specific business tasks are performed. Business processes also refer to the unique ways in which work, information, and knowledge are coordinated in a specific organization.

Every business can be seen as a collection of business processes. Some of these processes are part of larger, encompassing processes. Many business processes are tied to a specific functional area. For example, the sales and marketing function

TABLE 2.1

Examples of Functional
Business Processes

Functional Area	Business Process
Manufacturing and production	Assembling the product
	Checking for quality
	Producing bills of materials
Sales and marketing	Identifying customers
	Making customers aware of the product
	Selling the product
Finance and accounting	Paying creditors
	Creating financial statements
	Managing cash accounts
Human resources	Hiring employees
	Evaluating employees' job performance
	Enrolling employees in benefits plans

would be responsible for identifying customers, and the human resources function would be responsible for hiring employees. Table 2.1 describes some typical business processes for each of the functional areas of business.

Other business processes cross many functional areas and require coordination across departments. Consider the seemingly simple business process of fulfilling a customer order (see Figure 2.2). Initially, the sales department receives a sales order. The order goes to accounting to ensure that the customer can pay for the order either by a credit verification or request for immediate payment prior to shipping. Once the customer credit is established, the production department has to pull the product from inventory or produce the product. Next, the product needs to be shipped (which may require working with a logistics firm such as UPS or FedEx). The accounting department then generates a bill or invoice and sends a notice to the customer, indicating that the product has shipped. Sales has to be notified of the shipment and prepare to support the customer by answering calls or fulfilling warranty claims.

What at first appears to be a simple process—fulfilling an order—turns out to be a very complicated series of business processes that require the close coordination of major functional groups in a firm. Moreover, to perform all these steps efficiently in the order fulfillment process requires the rapid flow of a great deal of information within the firm, with business partners such as delivery firms, and with the customer. The particular order fulfillment process we have just described is not only *cross-functional*,

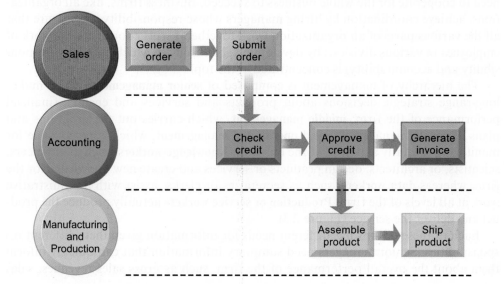

Figure 2.2
The Order Fulfillment Process
Fulfilling a customer order involves a complex set of steps that requires the close coordination of the sales, accounting, and manufacturing functions.

it is also *interorganizational* because it includes interactions with delivery firms and customers who are outside the boundaries of the organization. Ordering raw materials or components from suppliers would be another interorganizational business process.

To a large extent, the efficiency of a business firm depends on how well its internal and interorganizational business processes are designed and coordinated. A company's business processes can be a source of competitive strength if they enable the company to innovate or to execute better than its rivals. Business processes can also be liabilities if they are based on outdated ways of working that impede organizational responsiveness and efficiency.

How Information Technology Enhances Business Processes

Exactly how do information systems enhance business processes? Information systems automate many steps in business processes that were formerly performed manually, such as checking a client's credit or generating an invoice and shipping order. Today, however, information technology can do much more. New technology can actually change the flow of information, making it possible for many more people to access and share information, replacing sequential steps with tasks that can be performed simultaneously and eliminating delays in decision making. It can even transform the way the business works and drive new business models. Ordering a book online from Amazon.com and downloading a music track from iTunes are new business processes based on new business models that are inconceivable without information technology.

That's why it's so important to pay close attention to business processes, both in your information systems course and in your future career. By analyzing business processes, you can achieve a very clear understanding of how a business actually works. Moreover, by conducting a business process analysis, you will also begin to understand how to change the business to make it more efficient or effective. Throughout this book, we examine business processes with a view to understanding how they might be changed, or replaced, by using information technology to achieve greater efficiency, innovation, and customer service. Chapter 3 discusses the business impact of using information technology to redesign business processes, and MyMISLab™ has a Learning Track with more detailed coverage of this topic.

MANAGING A BUSINESS AND FIRM HIERARCHIES

What is missing from Figures 2.1 and 2.2 is any notion of how to coordinate and control the four major functions, their departments, and their business processes. Each of these functional departments has its own goals and processes, and they obviously need to cooperate for the whole business to succeed. Business firms, like all organizations, achieve coordination by hiring managers whose responsibility is to ensure that all the various parts of an organization work together. Firms coordinate the work of employees in various divisions by developing a hierarchy in which authority (responsibility and accountability) is concentrated at the top.

The hierarchy of management is composed of **senior management**, which makes long-range strategic decisions about products and services and ensures financial performance of the firm; **middle management**, which carries out the programs and plans of senior management; and **operational management**, which is responsible for monitoring the daily activities of the business. **Knowledge workers**, such as engineers, scientists, or architects, design products or services and create new knowledge for the firm, whereas **data workers**, such as secretaries or clerks, assist with administrative work at all levels of the firm. **Production or service workers** actually produce the product and deliver the service (Figure 2.3).

Each of these groups has different needs for information given their different responsibilities. Senior managers need summary information that can quickly inform them about the overall performance of the firm, such as gross sales revenues, sales

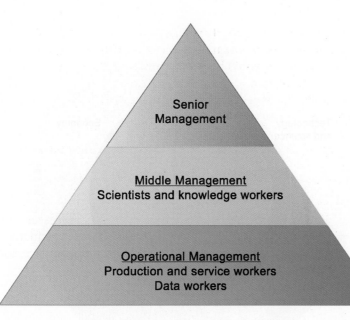

Figure 2.3
Levels in a Firm
Business organizations are hierarchies consisting of three principal levels: senior management, middle management, and operational management. Information systems serve each of these levels. Scientists and knowledge workers often work with middle management.

by product group and region, and overall profitability. Middle managers need more specific information about the results of specific functional areas and departments of the firm such as sales contacts by the sales force, production statistics for specific factories or product lines, employment levels and costs, and sales revenues for each month or even each day. Operational managers need transaction-level information such as the number of parts in inventory each day or the number of hours logged on Tuesday by each employee. Knowledge workers may need access to external scientific databases or internal databases with organizational knowledge. Finally, production workers need access to information from production machines, and service workers need access to customer records to take orders and answer questions from customers.

THE BUSINESS ENVIRONMENT

So far, we have talked about business as if it operated in a vacuum, but nothing could be further from the truth. In fact, business firms depend heavily on their environments to supply capital, labor, customers, new technology, services and products, stable markets and legal systems, and general educational resources. Even a pizza parlor cannot survive long without a supportive environment that delivers the cheese, tomato sauce, and flour!

Figure 2.4 summarizes the key actors in the environment of every business. To stay in business, a firm must monitor changes in its environment and share information with the key entities in that environment. For instance, a firm must respond to political shifts, respond to changes in the overall economy (such as changes in labor rates and price inflation), keep track of new technologies, and respond to changes in the global business environment (such as foreign exchange rates). In their immediate environment, firms need to track and share information with suppliers, customers, stockholders, regulators, and logistic partners (such as shipping firms).

Business environments are constantly changing; new developments in technology, politics, customer preferences, and regulations happen all the time. In general, when businesses fail, it is often because they failed to respond adequately to changes in their environments.

Changes in technology, such as the Internet, are forcing entire industries and leading firms to change their business models or suffer failure. Apple's iTunes and other online music services have made the music industry's traditional business model based on distributing music on CDs obsolete. Traditional cameras with film have been largely supplanted by digital photography, and digital cameras themselves are losing ground to iPhones and other mobile devices with cameras.

Figure 2.4
The Business
Environment
*To be successful, an orga-
nization must constantly
monitor and respond
to—or even anticipate—
developments in its environment. A firm's environment
includes specific groups
with which the business
must deal directly, such
as customers, suppliers,
and competitors, as well
as the broader general
environment, including
socioeconomic trends,
political conditions, technological innovations, and
global events.*

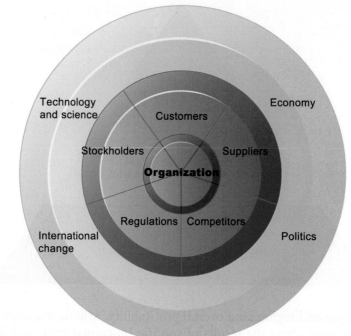

THE ROLE OF INFORMATION SYSTEMS IN A BUSINESS

Until now, we have not mentioned information systems, but from the brief review of business functions, entities, and environments, you can see the critical role that information plays in the life of a business. Up until the mid-1950s, firms managed all this information and information flow with paper records. During the past 50 years, more and more business information, and the flow of information among key business actors in the environment, has been moved from manual to digital systems.

Businesses invest in information systems as a way to cope with and manage their internal production functions and cope with the demands of key actors in their environments. Specifically, as we noted in Chapter 1, firms invest in information systems for the following business objectives:

• To achieve operational excellence (productivity, efficiency, agility)
• To develop new products and services
• To attain customer intimacy and service (continuous marketing, sales, and service; customization and personalization)
• To improve decision making (accuracy and speed)
• To achieve competitive advantage
• To ensure survival

2-2 How do systems serve different management groups in a business and how do systems that link the enterprise improve organizational performance?

Now it is time to look more closely at how businesses use information systems to achieve these goals. Because there are different interests, specialties, and levels in an organization, there are different kinds of systems. No single system can provide all the information an organization needs.

A typical business organization will have systems supporting processes for each of the major business functions—sales and marketing, manufacturing and production, finance and accounting, and human resources. You can find examples of systems for each of these business functions in the Learning Tracks for this chapter. Functional systems that operated independently of each other are becoming outdated because they cannot easily share information to support cross-functional business processes. They are being replaced with large-scale cross-functional systems that integrate the activities of related business processes and organizational units. We describe these integrated cross-functional applications later in this section.

A typical firm will also have different systems supporting the decision-making needs of each of the main management groups described earlier. Operational management, middle management, and senior management each use a specific type of system to support the decisions they must make to run the company. Let's look at these systems and the types of decisions they support.

SYSTEMS FOR DIFFERENT MANAGEMENT GROUPS

A business firm has systems to support decision making and work activities at different levels of the organization. They include transaction processing systems and systems for business intelligence.

Transaction Processing Systems

Operational managers need systems that keep track of the elementary activities and transactions of the organization such as sales, receipts, cash deposits, payroll, credit decisions, and the flow of materials in a factory. **Transaction processing systems (TPS)** provide this kind of information. A transaction processing system is a computerized system that performs and records the daily routine transactions necessary to conduct business, such as sales order entry, hotel reservations, payroll, employee record keeping, and shipping.

The principal purpose of systems at this level is to answer routine questions and to track the flow of transactions through the organization. How many parts are in inventory? What happened to Mr. Williams's payment? To answer these kinds of questions, information generally must be easily available, current, and accurate.

At the operational level, tasks, resources, and goals are predefined and highly structured. The decision to grant credit to a customer, for instance, is made by a lower-level supervisor according to predefined criteria. All that must be determined is whether the customer meets the criteria.

Figure 2.5 illustrates a TPS for payroll processing. A payroll system keeps track of money paid to employees. An employee time sheet with the employee's name, social security number, and number of hours worked per week represents a single transaction for this system. Once this transaction is input in the system, it updates the system's file (or database—see Chapter 6) that permanently maintains employee information for the organization. The data in the system are combined in different ways to create reports of interest to management and government agencies and to send paychecks to employees.

Managers need TPS to monitor the status of internal operations and the firm's relations with the external environment. TPS are also major producers of information for the other systems and business functions. For example, the payroll system illustrated in Figure 2.5, along with other accounting TPS, supplies data to the company's general ledger system, which is responsible for maintaining records of the firm's income and expenses and for producing reports such as income statements and balance sheets. It also supplies employee payment history data for insurance, pension, and other benefits calculations to the firm's human resources function, and employee payment data to government agencies such as the U.S. Internal Revenue Service and Social Security Administration.

Transaction processing systems are often so central to a business that TPS failure for a few hours can lead to a firm's demise and perhaps that of other firms linked to it. Imagine what would happen to UPS if its package tracking system were not working! What would the airlines do without their computerized reservation systems?

Figure 2.5
A Payroll TPS

A TPS for payroll processing captures employee payment transaction data (such as a timecard). System outputs include online and hard copy reports for management and employee paychecks.

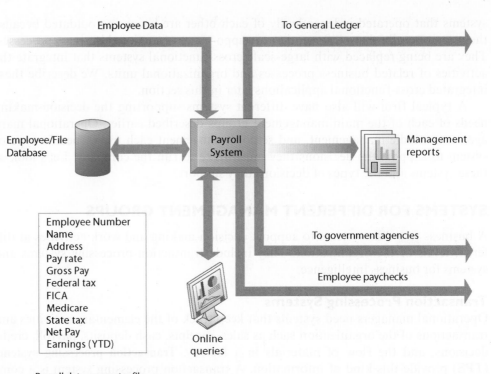

Payroll data on master file

Systems for Business Intelligence

Firms also have business intelligence systems that focus on delivering information to support management decision making. **Business intelligence** is a contemporary term for data and software tools for organizing, analyzing, and providing access to data to help managers and other enterprise users make more informed decisions. Business intelligence addresses the decision-making needs of all levels of management. This section provides a brief introduction to business intelligence. You'll learn more about this topic in Chapters 6 and 11.

Business intelligence systems for middle management help with monitoring, controlling, decision-making, and administrative activities. In Chapter 1, we defined management information systems as the study of information systems in business and management. The term **management information systems (MIS)** also designates a specific category of information systems serving middle management. MIS provide middle managers with reports about the organization's current performance. Managers use this information to monitor and control the business and predict future performance.

MIS summarize and report on the company's basic operations using data supplied by transaction processing systems. The basic transaction data from TPS are compressed and usually presented in reports that are produced on a regular schedule. Today, many of these reports are delivered online. Figure 2.6 shows how a typical MIS transforms transaction-level data from inventory, production, and accounting into MIS files that provide managers with reports. Figure 2.7 shows a sample report from this system.

MIS typically provide answers to routine questions that have been specified in advance and have a predefined procedure for answering them. For instance, MIS reports might list the total pounds of lettuce used this quarter by a fast-food chain or, as illustrated in Figure 2.7, compare total annual sales figures for specific products to planned targets. These systems generally are not flexible and have little analytical capability. Most MIS use simple routines, such as summaries and comparisons, as opposed to sophisticated mathematical models or statistical techniques.

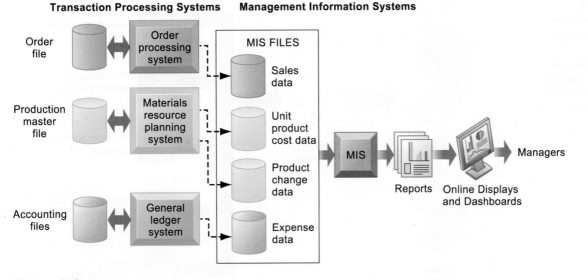

Figure 2.6
How Management Information Systems Obtain Their Data from the Organization's TPS
In the system illustrated by this diagram, three TPS supply summarized transaction data to the MIS reporting system at the end of the time period. Managers gain access to the organizational data through the MIS, which provides them with the appropriate reports.

Other types of business intelligence systems support more nonroutine decision making. **Decision-support systems (DSS)** focus on problems that are unique and rapidly changing, for which the procedure for arriving at a solution may not be fully predefined in advance. They try to answer questions such as these: What would be the impact on production schedules if we were to double sales in the month of December? What would happen to our return on investment if a factory schedule were delayed for six months?

Although DSS use internal information from TPS and MIS, they often bring in information from external sources, such as current stock prices or product prices of competitors. Super-user managers and business analysts who want to use sophisticated analytics and models to analyze data employ these systems.

An interesting, small but powerful DSS is the voyage-estimating system of a large global shipping company that exists primarily to carry bulk cargoes of coal, oil, ores, and finished products for its parent company. The firm owns some vessels, charters

Figure 2.7
Sample MIS Report
This report, showing summarized annual sales data, was produced by the MIS in Figure 2.6.

Consolidated Consumer Products Corporation Sales by Product and Sales Region: 2016					
PRODUCT CODE	PRODUCT DESCRIPTION	SALES REGION	ACTUAL SALES	PLANNED	ACTUAL versus PLANNED
4469	Carpet Cleaner	Northeast	4,066,700	4,800,000	0.85
		South	3,778,112	3,750,000	1.01
		Midwest	4,867,001	4,600,000	1.06
		West	4,003,440	4,400,000	0.91
	TOTAL		16,715,253	17,550,000	0.95
5674	Room Freshener	Northeast	3,676,700	3,900,000	0.94
		South	5,608,112	4,700,000	1.19
		Midwest	4,711,001	4,200,000	1.12
		West	4,563,440	4,900,000	0.93
	TOTAL		18,559,253	17,700,000	1.05

Figure 2.8
Voyage-Estimating
Decision-Support
System
This DSS operates on a
powerful PC. Managers
who must develop bids
on shipping contracts use
it daily.

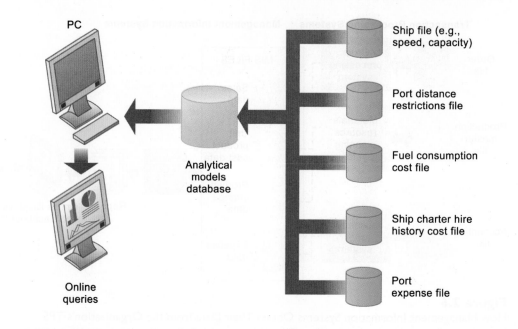

others, and bids for shipping contracts in the open market to carry general cargo. A voyage-estimating system calculates financial and technical voyage details. Financial calculations include ship/time costs (fuel, labor, capital), freight rates for various types of cargo, and port expenses. Technical details include a myriad of factors, such as ship cargo capacity, speed, port distances, fuel and water consumption, and loading patterns (location of cargo for different ports).

The system can answer questions such as the following: Given a customer delivery schedule and an offered freight rate, which vessel should be assigned at what rate to maximize profits? What is the optimal speed at which a particular vessel can optimize its profit and still meet its delivery schedule? What is the optimal loading pattern for a ship bound for the U.S. West Coast from Malaysia? Figure 2.8 illustrates the DSS built for this company. The system operates on a powerful desktop personal computer, providing a system of menus that makes it easy for users to enter data or obtain information.

The voyage-estimating DSS we have just described draws heavily on models. Other business intelligence systems are more data-driven, focusing instead on extracting useful information from massive quantities of data. For example, large ski resort companies such as Intrawest and Vail Resorts collect and store large amounts of customer data from call centers, lift tickets, lodging and dining reservations, ski schools, and ski equipment rental stores. They use special software to analyze these data to determine the value, revenue potential, and loyalty of each customer to help managers make better decisions about how to target their marketing programs.

Business intelligence systems also address the decision-making needs of senior management. Senior managers need systems that focus on strategic issues and long-term trends, both in the firm and in the external environment. They are concerned with questions such as: What will employment levels be in five years? What are the long-term industry cost trends? What products should we be making in five years?

Executive support systems (ESS) help senior management make these decisions. They address nonroutine decisions requiring judgment, evaluation, and insight because there is no agreed-on procedure for arriving at a solution. ESS present graphs and data from many sources through an interface that is easy for senior managers to use. Often the information is delivered to senior executives through a **portal**, which uses a web interface to present integrated personalized business content.

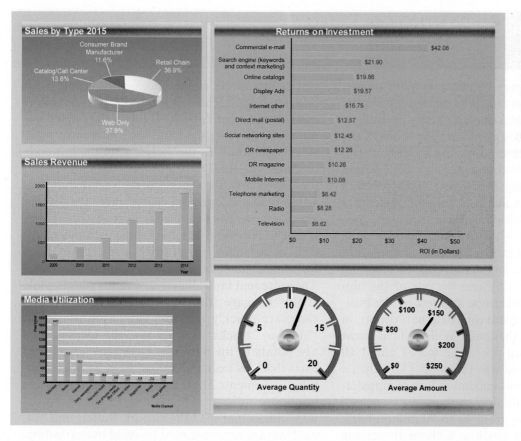

A digital dashboard delivers comprehensive and accurate information for decision making, often using a single screen. The graphical overview of key performance indicators helps managers quickly spot areas that need attention.

ESS are designed to incorporate data about external events such as new tax laws or competitors, but they also draw summarized information from internal MIS and DSS. They filter, compress, and track critical data, displaying the data of greatest importance to senior managers. Increasingly, such systems include business intelligence analytics for analyzing trends, forecasting, and drilling down to data at greater levels of detail.

For example, the CEO of Leiner Health Products, the largest manufacturer of private-label vitamins and supplements in the United States, has an ESS that provides on his desktop a minute-to-minute view of the firm's financial performance as measured by working capital, accounts receivable, accounts payable, cash flow, and inventory. The information is presented in the form of a **digital dashboard**, which displays on a single screen graphs and charts of key performance indicators for managing a company. Digital dashboards are becoming an increasingly popular tool for management decision makers.

The Interactive Session on Technology illustrates how Schiphol International Airport uses data to power its new baggage handling system and improve the customer experience. As you read this case, identify the problems solved by Schiphol's information systems and how the systems improve operations and decision making.

SYSTEMS FOR LINKING THE ENTERPRISE

Reviewing all the types of systems we have just described, you might wonder how a business can manage all the information in these differing systems. You might also wonder how costly it is to maintain so many systems. You might also wonder how all these systems can share information and how managers and employees can coordinate their work. In fact, these are all important questions for businesses today.

Enterprise Applications

Conceptually, baggage handling is quite simple. Baggage input is connected to merely two events: an airplane lands or a person checks in. In fact, it's risky business. Baggage handling is one of the most important factors in having a pleasant trip. Moreover, mishandled baggage is a $2.5 billion problem for industry every year. This problem may annually affect about 51 million passengers traveling through Schiphol alone.

In 2004, IBM Corporation, Vanderlande Industries, and later Grenzebach Automation Systems jointly took up the challenge of renewing the Baggage Control System for one of the biggest airport hubs in Europe and one of the busiest in the world: Schiphol International Airport, in Amsterdam, the Netherlands. With an investment of around $1 billion over a period of about 10 years, Schiphol's goal was threefold: (a) realize a monumental 1 percent maximum loss of transfer-bags (against the initial 22 million lost baggage); (b) increase capacity from 40 to 70 million bags; and (c) reduce cost per bag without increasing wait-times.

Most of the job involved Schiphol's gigantic baggage conveyors network: 21 kilometers of transport tracks, 6 robotic units, and 9,000 storage capacitors all behaving as one system. Also, extending it with more surfaces is not possible, given the land conditions surrounding the airport. The Schiphol baggage conveyor networks have a very simple goal: the right bag must be at the right place at the right time. To pursue this goal, the network must perform several key roles: move bags from the check-in area to the departure gate, move bags from gate to gate, move bags from the arrival gate to the baggage claim, and plan and control peripheral hardware and software. In addition, these roles involve a wide variety of sensors, actuators, mechanical devices, and computers. The network uses over 3 million lines of source code. Some of the advanced technology used in baggage-handling systems includes destination-coded vehicles (DCVs), automatic bar code scanners, radio-frequency identification (RFID) tags, and high-tech conveyors equipped with sorting machines. In addition, all of this must be available and robust; that is, operate 99.99 percent of the time while being able to minimize loss or damage in that 0.01 percent of the time it doesn't.

The following simple scenario summarizes the operations of the Schiphol baggage conveyors net-work. You arrive at the check-in desk and your bags are tagged. The tags contain your flight information and a bar-code/RFID that all of the computers in the baggage-handling system can read. When computers in the system scan the bar code or detect the RFID, they process the information it contains and determine where to send your bag. After being scanned (at least) once, the system always knows where your bag is at any point, and is able to redirect it based on three parameters: (a) time of its flight, (b) priority, and (c) size. Bags for immediate embarkation are considered "hot." These are sent immediately to aircraft stands while "cold" baggage (i.e., low priority, distant flight time) are quickly rerouted away from the main "highway" tracks, directed towards various storage points in the network. DCVs are unmanned carts that can load and unload bags without stopping movement. These carts move on tracks like miniature roller coasters along the main "highway" tracks that span the airport. Buffers and hot/cold storage areas are used to avoid overcrowding. Computers throughout the system keep track of the location of each bag, its destination, and the time it is needed at that destination. The system can optimize the routes taken by the carts to get the bags needed most urgently to their destinations fastest. Because DCVs move at high speed and do not come to a full stop to receive baggage, the conveyors must be extremely precise, depositing bags where they are needed at just the right time for maximum efficiency. Once bags reach the gate, they enter a sorting station where airline employees use computer terminals to send bags to the correct plane. To make even surer that baggage is not lost, the system "reconciles" baggage with its owner; it checks if the baggage and the owner are actually on the same plane.

However beautiful and harmonious this process may seem, there are still many things that can go wrong. For example, what if baggage is mistagged? What if the tag is unreadable? What about schedule changes? Although baggage handling is a complex process and baggage handling systems can be extremely expensive, if implemented successfully, they pay for themselves. Imagine saving around 0.1 percent of 2.5 billion. That's a lot of money!

The new baggage system at Schiphol is not flawless. In November 2012, a special warrant by local police was issued that required stopping the tracks at Schiphol as part of a cocaine-smuggling investigation. Some of the 140,000 passengers that were being served by the international hub suffered baggage losses. In 2014, many of the baggage handlers involved in the investigation went on trial, and other drug-related arrests were announced. But these sorts of incidents aren't confined to Schiphol; other regional airports are also affected by drug-related activities. On a brighter note, Schiphol launched a fleet of 167 Tesla electrically powered taxis in 2014, further cementing its status as one of the greenest airports in the world.

Schiphol continues to make multi-billion dollar improvements to its baggage handling. In 2015 Schiphol received a Top Ten Baggage Handling designation for replacing its 130 security lanes with a centralized baggage and passenger clearance system in five large central checkpoints. Schiphol managers call this "security as a service," and without its prior investments in IT, this service could not be provided.

Sources: "Schiphol's Baggage Handling Film Premier," *Airport Professional Focus International*, September 13, 2015; Ana Swanson, "Where Your Luggage Goes After You Check It," *Washington Post*, August 21, 2015; "The Top 10 Airport Innovations of 2015 So Far...", AirportBusiness.com, June 4, 2015; "Airports In The News—Winter 2014," Airportbusiness.com, November 18, 2014; "Baggage Handlers Go on Trial over Cocaine Smuggling Ring at Schiphol Airport," *Amsterdam Herald*, January 6, 2014; Ciara Byrne, "Robots, Dutchmen and IBM Create Supersmart Baggage Handling System," Venturebeat.com, March 18, 2011; "Schiphol Introduces Innovative Unloading System for Baggage Containers," Schiphol.nl, accessed December 2014.

Case Contributed by Damian A. Tamburri and Patricia Lago, VU University Amsterdam

CASE STUDY QUESTIONS

1. How many levels of complexity can you identify in Schiphol's baggage conveyors network?

2. What are the management, organization, and technology components of Schiphol's baggage conveyors network?

3. What is the problem that Schiphol is trying to solve? Discuss the business impact of this problem

4. Think of the data that the network uses. What kinds of management reports can be generated from that data?

Getting the different kinds of systems in a company to work together has proven a major challenge. Typically, corporations are put together both through normal organic growth and through acquisition of smaller firms. Over time, corporations end up with a collection of systems, most of them older, and face the challenge of getting them all to talk with one another and work together as one corporate system. There are several solutions to this problem.

One solution is to implement **enterprise applications**, which are systems that span functional areas, focus on executing business processes across the business firm, and include all levels of management. Enterprise applications help businesses become more flexible and productive by coordinating their business processes more closely and integrating groups of processes so they focus on efficient management of resources and customer service.

There are four major enterprise applications: enterprise systems, supply chain management systems, customer relationship management systems, and knowledge management systems. Each of these enterprise applications integrates a related set

Figure 2.9
Enterprise Application
Architecture
*Enterprise applications
automate processes that
span multiple business
functions and organi-
zational levels and may
extend outside the
organization.*

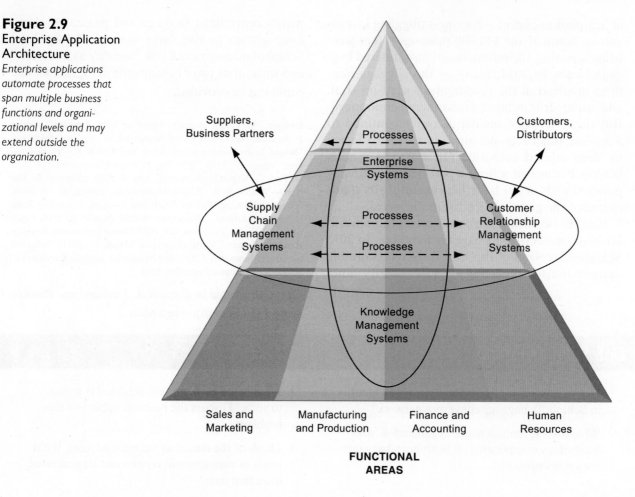

FUNCTIONAL
AREAS

of functions and business processes to enhance the performance of the organization as a whole. Figure 2.9 shows that the architecture for these enterprise applications encompasses processes spanning the entire organization and, in some cases, extending beyond the organization to customers, suppliers, and other key business partners.

Enterprise Systems Firms use **enterprise systems**, also known as *enterprise resource planning (ERP)* systems, to integrate business processes in manufacturing and production, finance and accounting, sales and marketing, and human resources into a single software system. Information that was previously fragmented in many systems is stored in a single comprehensive data repository where it can be used by many parts of the business.

For example, when a customer places an order, the order data flow automatically to other parts of the company that they affect. The order transaction triggers the warehouse to pick the ordered products and schedule shipment. The warehouse informs the factory to replenish whatever has been depleted. The accounting department is notified to send the customer an invoice. Customer service representatives track the progress of the order through every step to inform customers about the status of their orders. Managers can use firm-wide information to make more precise and timely decisions about daily operations and longer-term planning.

Supply Chain Management Systems Firms use **supply chain management (SCM) systems** to help manage relationships with their suppliers. These systems help suppliers, purchasing firms, distributors, and logistics companies share information about orders, production, inventory levels, and delivery of products and services so that they can source, produce, and deliver goods and services efficiently. The ultimate objective is to get the right number of their products from their source to their point of consumption in the shortest time and at the lowest cost. These systems increase firm profitability by lowering the costs of moving and making products and by enabling managers to make better decisions about how to organize and schedule sourcing, production, and distribution.

Supply chain management systems are one type of **interorganizational system** because they automate the flow of information across organizational boundaries. You will find examples of other types of interorganizational information systems throughout this text because such systems make it possible for firms to link firms to customers and to outsource their work to other companies.

Customer Relationship Management Systems Firms use **customer relationship management (CRM) systems** to help manage their relationships with their customers. CRM systems provide information to coordinate all the business processes that deal with customers in sales, marketing, and service to optimize revenue, customer satisfaction, and customer retention. This information helps firms identify, attract, and retain the most profitable customers; provide better service to existing customers; and increase sales.

Knowledge Management Systems Some firms perform better than others do because they have better knowledge about how to create, produce, and deliver products and services. This firm knowledge is unique, difficult to imitate, and can be leveraged into long-term strategic benefits. **Knowledge management systems (KMS)** enable organizations to manage processes better for capturing and applying knowledge and expertise. These systems collect all relevant knowledge and experience in the firm and make it available wherever and whenever it is needed to improve business processes and management decisions. They also link the firm to external sources of knowledge.

We examine enterprise systems and systems for supply chain management and customer relationship management in greater detail in Chapter 9. We discuss collaboration systems that support knowledge management in this chapter and cover other types of knowledge management applications in Chapter 11.

Intranets and Extranets

Enterprise applications create deep-seated changes in the way the firm conducts its business, offering many opportunities to integrate important business data into a single system. They are often costly and difficult to implement. Intranets and extranets deserve mention here as alternative tools for increasing integration and expediting the flow of information within the firm and with customers and suppliers.

Intranets are simply internal company websites that are accessible only by employees. The term *intranet* refers to an internal network in contrast to the Internet, which is a public network linking organizations and other external networks. Intranets use the same technologies and techniques as the larger Internet, and they often are simply a private access area in a larger company website. Extranets are company websites that are accessible to authorized vendors and suppliers and often used to coordinate the movement of supplies to the firm's production apparatus.

For example, Six Flags, which operates 19 theme parks throughout North America, maintains an intranet for its 2,500 full-time employees that provides company-related news and information on each park's day-to-day operations, including weather forecasts, performance schedules, and details about groups and celebrities visiting the parks. We describe the technology for intranets and extranets in more detail in Chapter 7.

E-BUSINESS, E-COMMERCE, AND E-GOVERNMENT

The systems and technologies we have just described are transforming firms' relationships with customers, employees, suppliers, and logistic partners into digital relationships by using networks and the Internet. So much business is now enabled by or based on digital networks that we use the terms *e-business* and *e-commerce* frequently throughout this text.

E-business, or **electronic business**, refers to the use of digital technology and the Internet to execute the major business processes in the enterprise. E-business includes activities for the internal management of the firm and for coordination with suppliers and other business partners. It also includes **e-commerce**, or **electronic commerce**. E-commerce is the part of e-business that deals with buying and selling goods and services over the Internet. It also encompasses activities supporting those market transactions, such as advertising, marketing, customer support, security, delivery, and payment.

The technologies associated with e-business have also brought about similar changes in the public sector. Governments on all levels are using Internet technology to deliver information and services to citizens, employees, and businesses with which they work. **E-government** refers to the application of the Internet and networking technologies to enable government and public sector agencies' relationships with citizens, businesses, and other arms of government digitally. In addition to improving delivery of government services, e-government can make government operations more efficient and empower citizens by giving them easier access to information and the ability to network with other citizens. For example, citizens in some states can renew their driver's licenses or apply for unemployment benefits online, and the Internet has become a powerful tool for instantly mobilizing interest groups for political action and fund-raising.

2-3 Why are systems for collaboration and social business so important and what technologies do they use?

With all these systems and information, you might wonder how is it possible to make sense of them. How do people working in firms pull it all together, work toward common goals, and coordinate plans and actions? In addition to the types of systems we have just described, businesses need special systems to support collaboration and teamwork.

WHAT IS COLLABORATION?

Collaboration is working with others to achieve shared and explicit goals. Collaboration focuses on task or mission accomplishment and usually takes place within a business or other organization and between businesses. You collaborate with a colleague in Tokyo who has expertise in a topic about which you know nothing. You collaborate with many colleagues in publishing a company blog. If you're in a law firm, you collaborate with accountants in an accounting firm in servicing the needs of a client with tax problems.

Collaboration can be short-lived, lasting a few minutes, or longer term, depending on the nature of the task and the relationship among participants. Collaboration can be one-to-one or many-to-many.

Employees may collaborate in informal groups that are not a formal part of the business firm's organizational structure, or they may be organized into formal teams. **Teams** have a specific mission that someone in the business assigned to them. Team members need to collaborate on the accomplishment of specific tasks and collectively achieve the team mission. The team mission might be to win the game or increase online sales by 10 percent. Teams are often short-lived, depending on the problems they tackle and the length of time needed to find a solution and accomplish the mission.

Collaboration and teamwork are more important today than ever for a variety of reasons.

- *Changing nature of work*. The nature of work has changed from factory manufacturing and pre-computer office work, when each stage in the production process occurred independently of one another and was coordinated by supervisors. Work was organized into silos. Within a silo, work passed from one machine tool station to another, from one desktop to another, until the finished product was completed. Today, the kinds of jobs we have require much closer coordination and interaction among the parties involved in producing the service or product. A recent report from the consulting firm McKinsey and Company argued that 41 percent of the U.S. labor force is now composed of jobs in which interaction (talking, emailing, presenting, and persuading) is the primary value-adding activity. Even in factories, workers today often work in production groups, or pods.

- *Growth of professional work.* Interaction jobs tend to be professional jobs in the service sector that require close coordination and collaboration. Professional jobs require substantial education and sharing information and opinions to get work done. Each actor on the job brings specialized expertise to the problem, and all the actors need to consider one another to accomplish the job.
- *Changing organization of the firm.* For most of the industrial age, managers organized work in a hierarchical fashion. Orders came down the hierarchy, and responses moved back up the hierarchy. Today, work is organized into groups and teams, which are expected to develop their own methods for accomplishing the task. Senior managers observe and measure results but are much less likely to issue detailed orders or operating procedures. In part this is because expertise and decision making power have been pushed down in organizations.
- *Changing scope of the firm.* The work of the firm has spread from a single location to occupying multiple locations—offices or factories throughout a region, a nation, or even around the globe. For instance, Henry Ford developed the first mass-production automobile plant at a single Dearborn, Michigan, factory. In 2014, Ford employed 187,000 people at 62 plants and facilities worldwide. With this kind of global presence, the need for close coordination of design, production, marketing, distribution, and service obviously takes on new importance and scale. Large global companies need teams to work on a global basis.
- *Emphasis on innovation.* Although we tend to attribute innovations in business and science to great individuals, these great individuals are most likely working with a team of brilliant colleagues. Think of Bill Gates and Steve Jobs (founders of Microsoft and Apple, respectively), both of whom are highly regarded innovators, and both of whom built strong collaborative teams to nurture and support innovation in their firms. Their initial innovations derived from close collaboration with colleagues and partners. Innovation, in other words, is a group and social process, and most innovations derive from collaboration among individuals in a lab, a business, or government agencies. Strong collaborative practices and technologies are believed to increase the rate and quality of innovation.
- *Changing culture of work and business.* Most research on collaboration supports the notion that diverse teams produce better outputs faster than individuals working on their own. Popular notions of the crowd (crowdsourcing and the wisdom of crowds) also provide cultural support for collaboration and teamwork.

WHAT IS SOCIAL BUSINESS?

Today, many firms are enhancing collaboration by embracing **social business**, the use of social networking platforms, including Facebook, Twitter, and internal corporate social tools, to engage their employees, customers, and suppliers. These tools enable workers to set up profiles, form groups, and follow each other's status updates. The goal of social business is to deepen interactions with groups inside and outside the firm to expedite and enhance information sharing, innovation, and decision making.

A key word in social business is *conversations*. Customers, suppliers, employees, managers, and even oversight agencies continually have conversations about firms, often without the knowledge of the firm or its key actors (employees and managers). Supporters of social business argue that if firms could tune into these conversations,

TABLE 2.2

Applications of Social Business

Business Application	Description
Social networks	Connect through personal and business profiles
Crowdsourcing	Harness collective knowledge to generate new ideas and solutions
Shared workspaces	Coordinate projects and tasks, co-create content
Blogs and wikis	Publish and rapidly access knowledge; discuss opinions and experiences
Social commerce	Share opinions about purchasing or purchase on social platforms
File sharing	Upload, share, and comment on photos, videos, audio, text documents
Social marketing	Use social media to interact with customers, derive customer insights
Communities	Discuss topics in open forums, share expertise

they will strengthen their bonds with consumers, suppliers, and employees, increasing their emotional involvement in the firm.

All of this requires a great deal of information transparency. People need to share opinions and facts with others quite directly, without intervention from executives or others. Employees get to know directly what customers and other employees think; suppliers will learn very directly the opinions of supply chain partners; and even managers presumably will learn more directly from their employees how well they are doing. Nearly everyone involved in the creation of value will know much more about everyone else.

If such an environment could be created, it is likely to drive operational efficiencies, spur innovation, and accelerate decision making. If product designers can learn directly about how their products are doing in the market in real-time, based on consumer feedback, they can speed up the redesign process. If employees can use social connections inside and outside the company to capture new knowledge and insights, they will be able to work more efficiently and solve more business problems.

Table 2.2 describes important applications of social business inside and outside the firm. This chapter focuses on enterprise social business: its internal corporate uses. Chapter 10 will describe social business applications relating to customers and suppliers outside the company.

BUSINESS BENEFITS OF COLLABORATION AND SOCIAL BUSINESS

Although many articles and books have been written about collaboration, nearly all the research on this topic is anecdotal. Nevertheless, among both business and academic communities, there is a general belief that the more collaborative a business firm is, the more successful it will be and that collaboration within and among firms is more essential than in the past. A global survey of business and information systems managers found that investments in collaboration technology produced organizational improvements that returned more than four times the amount of the investment, with the greatest benefits for sales, marketing, and research and development functions (Frost and White, 2009). McKinsey & Company consultants

TABLE 2.3

Business Benefits
of Collaboration
and Social Business

Benefit	Rationale
Productivity	People interacting and working together can capture expert knowledge and solve problems more rapidly than the same number of people working in isolation from one another. There will be fewer errors.
Quality	People working collaboratively can communicate errors and correct actions faster than if they work in isolation. Collaborative and social technologies help reduce time delays in design and production.
Innovation	People working collaboratively can come up with more innovative ideas for products, services, and administration than the same number working in isolation from one another. Advantages to diversity and the wisdom of crowds.
Customer service	People working together using collaboration and social tools can solve customer complaints and issues faster and more effectively than if they were working in isolation from one another.
Financial performance (profitability, sales, and sales growth)	As a result of all these factors, collaborative firms have superior sales, sales growth, and financial performance.

predicted that social technologies used within and across enterprises could raise the productivity of interaction workers by 20 to 25 percent (McKinsey, 2012).

Table 2.3 summarizes some of the benefits of collaboration and social business that have been identified. Figure 2.10 graphically illustrates how collaboration is believed to affect business performance.

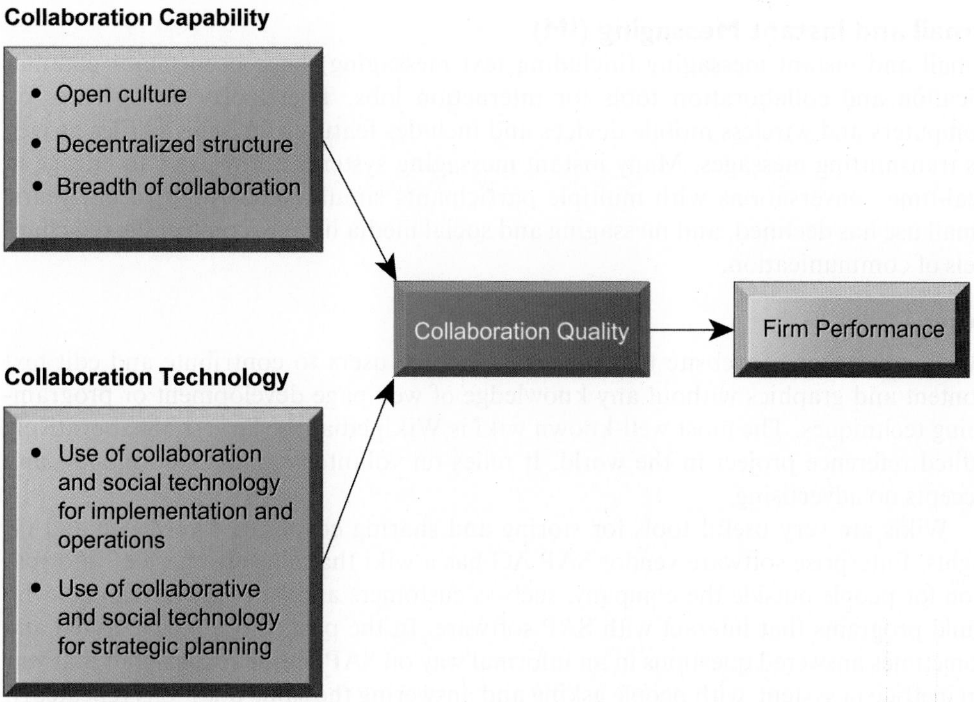

Collaboration Capability

- Open culture
- Decentralized structure
- Breadth of collaboration

Collaboration Technology

- Use of collaboration and social technology for implementation and operations
- Use of collaborative and social technology for strategic planning

Collaboration Quality → Firm Performance

Figure 2.10
Requirements for
Collaboration
*Successful collaboration
requires an appropriate
organizational structure
and culture along with
appropriate collaboration
technology.*

BUILDING A COLLABORATIVE CULTURE AND BUSINESS PROCESSES

Collaboration won't take place spontaneously in a business firm, especially if there is no supportive culture or business processes. Business firms, especially large firms, had in the past a reputation for being command-and-control organizations in which the top leaders thought up all the really important matters and then ordered lower-level employees to execute senior management plans. The job of middle management supposedly was to pass messages back and forth up and down the hierarchy.

Command-and-control firms required lower-level employees to carry out orders without asking too many questions, with no responsibility to improve processes, and with no rewards for teamwork or team performance. If your workgroup needed help from another work group, that was something for the bosses to figure out. You never communicated horizontally, always vertically, so management could control the process. Many business firms still operate this way.

A collaborative business culture and business processes are very different. Senior managers are responsible for achieving results but rely on teams of employees to achieve and implement the results. Policies, products, designs, processes, and systems are much more dependent on teams at all levels of the organization to devise, to create, and to build. Teams are rewarded for their performance, and individuals are rewarded for their performance in a team. The function of middle managers is to build the teams, coordinate their work, and monitor their performance. The business culture and business processes are more social. In a collaborative culture, senior management establishes collaboration and teamwork as vital to the organization, and it actually implements collaboration for the senior ranks of the business as well.

TOOLS AND TECHNOLOGIES FOR COLLABORATION AND SOCIAL BUSINESS

A collaborative, team-oriented culture won't produce benefits without information systems in place to enable collaboration and social business. Currently, hundreds of tools are designed for this purpose. Some of these tools are expensive, but others are available online for free (or with premium versions for a modest fee) and are suitable for small businesses. Let's look more closely at some of these tools.

Email and Instant Messaging (IM)

Email and instant messaging (including text messaging) have been major communication and collaboration tools for interaction jobs. Their software operates on computers and wireless mobile devices and includes features for sharing files as well as transmitting messages. Many instant messaging systems allow users to engage in real-time conversations with multiple participants simultaneously. In recent years, email use has declined, and messaging and social media have become preferred channels of communication.

Wikis

Wikis are a type of website that makes it easy for users to contribute and edit text content and graphics without any knowledge of web page development or programming techniques. The most well-known wiki is Wikipedia, the largest collaboratively edited reference project in the world. It relies on volunteers, makes no money, and accepts no advertising.

Wikis are very useful tools for storing and sharing corporate knowledge and insights. Enterprise software vendor SAP AG has a wiki that acts as a base of information for people outside the company, such as customers and software developers who build programs that interact with SAP software. In the past, those people asked and sometimes answered questions in an informal way on SAP online forums, but that was an inefficient system, with people asking and answering the same questions repeatedly.

Virtual Worlds

Virtual worlds, such as Second Life, are online 3-D environments populated by residents who have built graphical representations of themselves known as avatars. Companies such as IBM, Cisco, and Intel Corporation use this virtual world for on-line meetings, interviews, guest speaker events, and employee training. Real-world people represented by avatars meet, interact, and exchange ideas at these virtual locations using gestures, chat box conversations, and voice communication.

Collaboration and Social Business Platforms

There are now suites of software products providing multifunction platforms for collaboration and social business among teams of employees who work together from many locations. The most widely used are Internet-based audioconferencing and videoconferencing systems, cloud collaboration services such as Google's online tools and cyberlockers, corporate collaboration systems such as IBM Notes and Microsoft SharePoint, and enterprise social networking tools such as Salesforce Chatter, Microsoft Yammer, Jive, Facebook at Work, and IBM Connections.

Virtual Meeting Systems In an effort to reduce travel expenses, many companies, both large and small, are adopting videoconferencing and web conferencing technologies. Companies such as Heinz, General Electric, and PepsiCo are using virtual meeting systems for product briefings, training courses, strategy sessions, and even inspirational chats.

A videoconference allows individuals at two or more locations to communicate simultaneously through two-way video and audio transmissions. High-end videoconferencing systems feature **telepresence** technology, an integrated audio and visual environment that allows a person to give the appearance of being present at a location other than his or her true physical location. Free or low-cost Internet-based systems such as Skype group videoconferencing, Google+ Hangouts, Zoom, and ooVoo are lower quality but still useful for smaller companies. Apple's FaceTime is useful for one-to-one videoconferencing.

Companies of all sizes are finding web-based online meeting tools such as Cisco WebEx, Skype for Business, and Adobe Connect especially helpful for training and sales presentations. These products enable participants to share documents and presentations in conjunction with audioconferencing and live video by webcam.

Cloud Collaboration Services: Google Tools and Cyberlockers Google offers many online tools and services, and some are suitable for collaboration. They include Google Drive, Google Docs, Google Apps, Google Sites, and Google+. Most are free of charge.

Google Drive is a file storage and synchronization service for cloud storage, file sharing, and collaborative editing. Google Drive is an example of a cloud-based cyberlocker. **Cyberlockers** are online file-sharing services that allow users to upload files to secure online storage sites from which the files can be shared with others. Microsoft OneDrive and Dropbox are other leading cyberlocker services. They feature both free and paid services, depending on the amount of storage space required. Users can synchronize their files stored online with their local PCs and other kinds of devices, with options for making the files private or public and for sharing them with designated contacts.

Google Drive and Microsoft OneDrive are integrated with tools for document creation and sharing. OneDrive provides online storage for Microsoft Office documents and other files and works with Microsoft Office apps, both installed and on the web. It can share to Facebook as well. Google Drive is integrated with Google Docs, a suite of productivity applications that offer collaborative editing on documents, spreadsheets, and presentations. Google's cloud-based productivity suite for businesses (word processing, spreadsheets, presentations, calendars, and mail) called Google Apps for Business also works with Google Drive.

Google Sites allows users to create online team-oriented sites quickly, where multiple people can collaborate and share files. Google+ is Google's effort to make these tools and other products and services it offers more social for both consumer and business use. Google+ users can create a profile as well as Circles for organizing people into specific groups for sharing and collaborating. Hangouts enable people to engage in group video chat with a maximum of 10 people participating at any point in time.

Microsoft SharePoint and IBM Notes Microsoft SharePoint is a browser-based collaboration and document management platform combined with a powerful search engine that is installed on corporate servers. SharePoint has a web-based interface and close integration with everyday tools such as Microsoft Office desktop software products. SharePoint software makes it possible for employees to share their documents and collaborate on projects by using Office documents as the foundation.

SharePoint can be used to host internal websites that organize and store information in one central workspace to enable teams to coordinate work activities, collaborate on and publish documents, maintain task lists, implement workflows, and share information through wikis and blogs. Users can control versions of documents and document security. Because SharePoint stores and organizes information in one place, users can find relevant information quickly and efficiently while working together closely on tasks, projects, and documents. Enterprise search tools help locate people, expertise, and content. SharePoint now features social tools.

The Fair Work Ombudsman (FWO) is an independent office of the Australian federal government that provides advice and related services to employers and employees on workplace relations and entitlements. FWO has about 800 full-time staff in offices in all Australian capital cities and 18 regional locations. FWO had been overwhelmed with the details of project management and compliance, with staff having to draw information from many systems and piece it together manually. FWO implemented Microsoft SharePoint to create a single, organization-wide, secure, and reliable platform for managing and reporting on projects, programs, and portfolios that would also facilitate collaboration. The SharePoint system captures all project types that FWO undertakes; supports built-in user roles, views, and security; provides storage and access to data, including project documentation; and automates workflows, including approvals, alerts, and communication (Microsoft, 2014).

IBM Notes (formerly Lotus Notes) is a collaborative software system with capabilities for sharing calendars, email, messaging, collective writing and editing, shared database access, and online meetings. Notes software installed on desktop or laptop computers obtains applications stored on an IBM Domino server. Notes is web-enabled and offers an application development environment so that users can build custom applications to suit their unique needs. Notes has also added capabilities for blogs, microblogs, wikis, online content aggregators, help desk systems, voice and video conferencing, and online meetings. IBM Notes promises high levels of security and reliability and the ability to retain control over sensitive corporate information.

Enterprise Social Networking Tools The tools we have just described include capabilities for supporting social business, but there are also more specialized social tools for this purpose, such as Salesforce Chatter, Microsoft Yammer, Jive, Facebook for Business, and IBM Connections. Enterprise social networking tools create business value by connecting the members of an organization through profiles, updates, and notifications, similar to Facebook features but tailored to internal corporate uses. Table 2.4 provides more detail about these internal social capabilities.

Although companies have benefited from enterprise social networking, internal social networking has not caught on as quickly as consumer uses of Facebook, Twitter, and other public social networking products. The Interactive Session on People on page 90 addresses this topic.

Social Software Capability	Description
Profiles	Ability to set up member profiles describing who individuals are, educational background, interests. Includes work-related associations and expertise (skills, projects, teams).
Content sharing	Share, store, and manage content, including documents, presentations, images, and videos.
Feeds and notifications	Real-time information streams, status updates, and announcements from designated individuals and groups.
Groups and team workspaces	Establish groups to share information, collaborate on documents, and work on projects, with the ability to set up private and public groups and to archive conversations to preserve team knowledge.
Tagging and social bookmarking	Indicate preferences for specific pieces of content, similar to the Facebook Like button. Tagging lets people add keywords to identify content they like.
Permissions and privacy	Ability to make sure private information stays within the right circles as determined by the nature of relationships. In enterprise social networks, there is a need to establish who in the company has permission to see what information.

TABLE 2.4

Enterprise Social Networking Software Capabilities

Checklist for Managers: Evaluating and Selecting Collaboration Software Tools

With so many collaboration tools and services available, how do you choose the right collaboration technology for your firm? You need a framework for understanding just what problems these tools are designed to solve. One framework that has been helpful for us in talking about collaboration tools is the time/space collaboration and social tool matrix developed by a number of collaborative-work scholars (Figure 2.11).

The time/space matrix focuses on two dimensions of the collaboration problem: time and space. For instance, you need to collaborate with people in different time zones and you cannot all meet at the same time. Midnight in New York is noon in

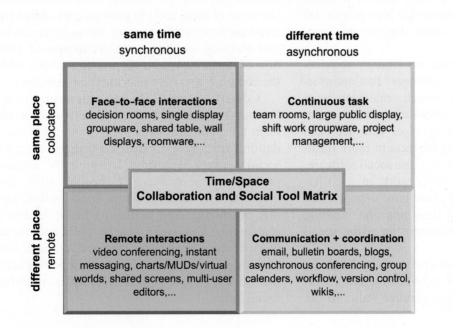

Figure 2.11
The Time/Space Collaboration and Social Tool Matrix
Collaboration technologies can be classified in terms of whether they support interactions at the same or different time or place and whether these interactions are remote or colocated.

INTERACTIVE SESSION: PEOPLE   Is Social Business Working Out?

Many of today's employees are already well versed in the basics of public social networking, using tools such as Facebook, Twitter, and Instagram. Larry Ellison, head of the giant software firm Oracle, even went so far as to declare that social networking should be the backbone of business applications and that Facebook is a good model for how users should interact with software.

According to Gartner, Inc., by 2016, 50 percent of large organizations will have internal Facebook-like social networks, and 30 percent of these will be considered as essential as email and telephones are today. Enterprise social networks will become the primary communications channels for noticing, deciding, or acting on information relevant to carrying out work. However, Gartner also notes that through 2015, 80 percent of social business efforts will not achieve the intended benefits due to inadequate leadership and an overemphasis on technology.

Social initiatives in a business are different from other technology deployments. For example, implementations of enterprise resource planning or customer relationship management systems are top-down; workers are trained in the application and expected to use it. In contrast, social business tools require a more of a pull approach, one that engages workers and offers them a significantly better way to work. In most cases, they can't be forced to use social apps.

This means that instead of focusing on the technology, businesses should first identify how social initiatives will improve work practices for employees and managers. They need a detailed understanding of social networks: how people are currently working, with whom they are working, and what their needs are.

A successful social business strategy requires leadership and behavioral changes. Just sponsoring a social project is not enough—managers need to demonstrate their commitment to a more open, transparent work style. Employees who are used to collaborating and doing business in more traditional ways need an incentive to use social software. Changing an organization to work in a different way requires enlisting those most engaged and interested in helping and designing and building the right workplace environment for using social technologies.

Management needs to ensure that the internal and external social networking efforts of the company are providing genuine value to the business. Content on the networks needs to be relevant, up to date, and easy to access; users need to be able to connect to people who have the information they need and would otherwise be out of reach or difficult to reach. Social business tools should be appropriate for the tasks on hand and the organization's business processes, and users need to understand how and why to use them.

In summer 2009, NASA's Goddard Space Flight Center launched a custom-built enterprise social network called Spacebook to help small teams collaborate without emailing larger groups. Spacebook featured user profiles, group workspaces (wikis, file sharing, discussion forums, groups), and social bookmarks. Very few users adopted it, and Spacebook was decommissioned on June 1, 2012. According to Kevin Jones, a consulting social and organizational strategist at NASA's Marshall and Goddard Space Flight Centers, Spacebook failed because it didn't focus enough on people. It had been designed and developed without taking into consideration the organization's culture and politics. No one knew how Spacebook would help them do their jobs, as opposed to an existing method of collaboration such as email.

Despite the challenges associated with launching an internal social network, some companies are using these networks successfully. For example, Covestro, formerly Bayer Material Science, the U.S. $11.8 billion material sciences division of Bayer, made social collaboration a success by making the tools more accessible, demonstrating the value of these tools in pilot projects, employing a reverse mentoring program for senior executives, and training employee experts to spread know-how of the new social tools and approaches within the company and demonstrate their usefulness.

Covestro chose IBM Connections for its social business toolset. IBM Connections is a social platform for collaboration, cooperation, and consolidation typically used in a centralized enterprise social network. Featured are tools for employee profiles; communities of people with common interests and expertise; blogs, wikis, viewing, organizing, and managing tasks; forums for exchanging ideas with others; polls and surveys of customers and fellow employees; and a home page for each user to see what is happening across that person's social network and access important social data.

A year after the new collaboration tools were introduced, adoption had plateaued. Working with company information technology and business leaders, management established an ambitious set of goals for growing social business along with seven key performance indicators (KPIs) to measure success. The goals included fostering global collaboration, creating stronger networks across regions and departments, creating a less hierarchical culture of sharing, and reducing the confusion about which tools are intended for which job.

These efforts are now paying off; 50 percent of employees are now routinely active in the company's enterprise social network. Although ROI on social business initiatives has been difficult to measure, Covestro has benefited from faster knowledge flows, increased efficiency, and lower operating costs.

Sources: Dion Hinchcliffe, "In Europe's Biggest Firms, Social Business Is All Grown Up," *Enterprise Web 2.0*, February 12, 2015; Margaret Jones, "Top Four Social Collaboration Software Fails," SearchConsumerization.com, accessed March 17, 2015; www.ibm.com, accessed March 16, 2015; www.nasa.gov, accessed March 16, 2015; James Niccolai, "Ellison: Facebook, the New Model for Business Applications," IDG News Service, January 30, 2014; Gartner Inc., "Gartner Says 80 Percent of Social Business Efforts Will Not Achieve Intended Benefits Through 2015," January 29, 2013; and Michael Healey, "Why Enterprise Social Networking Falls Short," *Information Week*, March 4, 2013.

CASE STUDY QUESTIONS

1. Identify the people, organization, and technology factors responsible for impeding adoption of internal corporate social networks.

2. Compare the experiences implementing internal social networks of the two organizations Why was one more successful than the other? What role did management play in this process?

3. Should all companies implement internal enterprise social networks? Why or why not?

Bombay, so this makes it difficult to have a video conference. Time is clearly an obstacle to collaboration on a global scale.

Place (location) also inhibits collaboration in large global or even national and regional firms. Assembling people for a physical meeting is made difficult by the physical dispersion of distributed firms (firms with more than one location), the cost of travel, and the time limitations of managers.

The collaboration technologies described previously are ways of overcoming the limitations of time and space. Using this time/space framework will help you choose the most appropriate collaboration and teamwork tools for your firm. Note that some tools are applicable in more than one time/place scenario. For example, Internet collaboration suites such as IBM Notes have capabilities for both synchronous (instant messaging, meeting tools) and asynchronous (email, wikis, document editing) interactions.

Here's a to-do list to get started. If you follow these six steps, you should be led to investing in the correct collaboration software for your firm at a price you can afford and within your risk tolerance.

1. What are the collaboration challenges facing the firm in terms of time and space? Locate your firm in the time/space matrix. Your firm can occupy more than one cell in the matrix. Different collaboration tools will be needed for each situation.

2. Within each cell of the matrix where your firm faces challenges, exactly what kinds of solutions are available? Make a list of vendor products.

3. Analyze each of the products in terms of their cost and benefits to your firm. Be sure to include the costs of training and the costs of involving the information systems department in your cost estimates if needed.

4. Identify the risks to security and vulnerability involved with each of the products. Is your firm willing to put proprietary information into the hands of external service providers over the Internet? Is your firm willing to risk its important operations in systems other firms control? What are the financial risks facing your vendors? Will they be here in three to five years? What would be the cost of making a switch to another vendor in the event the vendor firm fails?

5. Seek the help of potential users to identify implementation and training issues. Some of these tools are easier to use than others are.
6. Make your selection of candidate tools, and invite the vendors to make presentations.

2-4 What is the role of the information systems function in a business?

We've seen that businesses need information systems to operate today and that they use many kinds of systems, but who is responsible for running these systems? Who is responsible for making sure the hardware, software, and other technologies these systems use are running properly and up to date? End users manage their systems from a business standpoint, but managing the technology requires a special information systems function.

In all but the smallest of firms, the **information systems department** is the formal organizational unit responsible for information technology services. The information systems department is responsible for maintaining the hardware, software, data storage, and networks that comprise the firm's IT infrastructure. We describe IT infrastructure in detail in Chapter 5.

THE INFORMATION SYSTEMS DEPARTMENT

The information systems department consists of specialists such as programmers, systems analysts, project leaders, and information systems managers. **Programmers** are highly trained technical specialists who write the software instructions for computers. **Systems analysts** constitute the principal liaisons between the information systems groups and the rest of the organization. It is the systems analyst's job to translate business problems and requirements into information requirements and systems. **Information systems managers** are leaders of teams of programmers and analysts, project managers, physical facility managers, telecommunications managers, or database specialists. They are also managers of computer operations and data entry staff. External specialists, such as hardware vendors and manufacturers, software firms, and consultants, also frequently participate in the day-to-day operations and long-term planning of information systems.

In many companies, the information systems department is headed by a **chief information officer (CIO)**. The CIO is a senior manager who oversees the use of information technology in the firm. Today's CIOs are expected to have a strong business background, as well as information systems expertise, and to play a leadership role in integrating technology with the firm's business strategy. Large firms today also have positions for a chief security officer, chief knowledge officer, chief data officer, and chief privacy officer, all of whom work closely with the CIO.

The **chief security officer (CSO)** is in charge of information systems security for the firm and is responsible for enforcing the firm's information security policy (see Chapter 8). (Where information systems security is separated from physical security, this position is sometimes called the chief information security officer [CISO]). The CSO is responsible for educating and training users and information systems specialists about security, keeping management aware of security threats and breakdowns, and maintaining the tools and policies chosen to implement security.

Information systems security and the need to safeguard personal data have become so important that corporations collecting vast quantities of personal data have established positions for a **chief privacy officer (CPO)**. The CPO is responsible for ensuring that the company complies with existing data privacy laws.

The **chief knowledge officer (CKO)** is responsible for the firm's knowledge management program. The CKO helps design programs and systems to find new sources of knowledge or to make better use of existing knowledge in organizational and management processes.

The **chief data officer (CDO)** is responsible for enterprise-wide governance and usage of information to maximize the value of the organization's data. The CDO ensures that the firm is collecting appropriate data to serve its needs, deploying appropriate technologies for analyzing the data, and using the results to support business decisions. This position arose to deal with the massive amounts of data organizations are now generating and collecting (see Chapter 6).

End users are representatives of departments outside of the information systems group for whom applications are developed. These users are playing an increasingly large role in the design and development of information systems.

In the early years of computing, the information systems group was composed mostly of programmers who performed highly specialized but limited technical functions. Today, a growing proportion of staff members are systems analysts and network specialists, with the information systems department acting as a powerful change agent in the organization. The information systems department suggests new business strategies and new information-based products and services and coordinates both the development of the technology and the planned changes in the organization.

INFORMATION SYSTEMS SERVICES

Services the information systems department provides include the following:

- Computing platforms provide computing services that connect employees, customers, and suppliers into a coherent digital environment, including large mainframes, desktop and laptop computers, and mobile handheld devices.
- Telecommunications services provide data, voice, and video connectivity to employees, customers, and suppliers.
- Data management services store and manage corporate data and provide capabilities for analyzing the data.
- Application software services provide development and support services for the firm's business systems, including enterprise-wide capabilities such as enterprise resource planning, customer relationship management, supply chain management, and knowledge management systems, that all business units share.
- Physical facilities management services develop and manage the physical installations required for computing, telecommunications, and data management services.
- IT management services plan and develop the infrastructure, coordinate with the business units for IT services, manage accounting for the IT expenditure, and provide project management services.
- IT standards services provide the firm and its business units with policies that determine not only which information technology will be used but when and how they are used.
- IT educational services provide training in system use to employees and offer managers training in how to plan for and manage IT investments.
- IT research and development services provide the firm with research on potential future information systems projects and investments that could help the firm differentiate itself in the marketplace.

In the past, firms generally built their own software and managed their own computing facilities. As our discussion of collaboration systems has shown, many firms are turning to external vendors and Internet-based services to provide these services (see also Chapters 5 and 12) and are using their information systems departments to manage these service providers.

Review Summary

2-1 **What major features of a business are important for understanding the role of information systems?** A business is a formal, complex organization producing products or services for a profit. Businesses have specialized functions such as finance and accounting, human resources, manufacturing and production, and sales and marketing. Business organizations are arranged hierarchically into levels of management. A business process is a logically related set of activities that define how specific business tasks are performed. Business firms must monitor and respond to their surrounding environments.

2-2 **How do systems serve different management groups in a business and how do systems that link the enterprise improve organizational performance?** Systems serving operational management are transaction processing systems (TPS), such as payroll or order processing, that track the flow of the daily routine transactions necessary to conduct business. Business intelligence systems serve multiple levels of management and help employees make more informed decisions. Management information systems (MIS) and decision-support systems (DSS) support middle management. Most MIS reports condense information from TPS and are not highly analytical. DSS support management decisions that are unique and rapidly changing, using advanced analytical models and data analysis capabilities. Executive support systems (ESS) support senior management by providing data that are often in the form of graphs and charts delivered in portals and dashboards using many sources of internal and external information.

Enterprise applications are designed to coordinate multiple functions and business processes. Enterprise systems integrate the key internal business processes of a firm into a single software system to improve coordination and decision making. Supply chain management (SCM) systems help the firm manage its relationship with suppliers to optimize the planning, sourcing, manufacturing, and delivery of products and services. Customer relationship management (CRM) systems coordinate the business processes surrounding the firm's customers. Knowledge management systems enable firms to optimize the creation, sharing, and distribution of knowledge. Intranets and extranets are private corporate networks based on Internet technology. Extranets make portions of private corporate intranets available to outsiders.

2-3 **Why are systems for collaboration and social business so important and what technologies do they use?** Collaboration means working with others to achieve shared and explicit goals. Social business is the use of internal and external social networking platforms to engage employees, customers, and suppliers, and it can enhance collaborative work. Collaboration and social business have become increasingly important in business because of globalization, the decentralization of decision making, and growth in jobs where interaction is the primary value-adding activity. Collaboration and social business enhance innovation, productivity, quality, and customer service. Tools for collaboration and social business include email and instant messaging, wikis, virtual meeting systems, virtual worlds, cloud-based services and cyberlockers, corporate collaboration platforms such Microsoft SharePoint and IBM Notes, and enterprise social networking tools such as Chatter, Yammer, Jive, and IBM Connections.

2-4 **What is the role of the information systems function in a business?** The information systems department is the formal organizational unit responsible for information technology services. It is responsible for maintaining the hardware, software, data storage, and networks that comprise the firm's IT infrastructure. The department consists of specialists, such as programmers, systems analysts, project leaders, and information systems managers, and is often headed by a chief information officer (CIO).

Key Terms

Business, 67
Business intelligence, 74
Business processes, 68
Chief data officer (CDO), 93
Chief information officer
 (CIO), 92
Chief knowledge officer
 (CKO), 93
Chief privacy officer
 (CPO), 92
Chief security officer
 (CSO), 92
Collaboration, 82
Customer relationship
 management (CRM)
 systems, 81
Cyberlocker, 87
Data workers, 70
Decision-support systems
 (DSS), 75

Digital dashboard, 77
E-government, 82
Electronic business
 (e-business), 82
Electronic commerce
 (e-commerce), 82
End users, 93
Enterprise applications, 79
Enterprise systems, 80
Executive support systems
 (ESS), 76
Information systems
 department, 92
Information systems
 managers, 92
Interorganizational
 system, 81
Knowledge management
 systems (KMS), 81
Knowledge workers, 70

Management
 information systems
 (MIS), 74
Middle management, 70
Operational
 management, 70
Portal, 77
Production or service
 workers, 70
Programmers, 92
Senior management, 70
Social business, 83
Supply chain management
 (SCM) systems, 80
Systems analysts, 92
Teams, 82
Telepresence, 87
Transaction processing
 systems (TPS), 73

MyMISLab™

To complete the problems with the ⭐, go to EOC Discussion Questions in the MyLab.

Review Questions

2-1 What major features of a business are important for understanding the role of information systems?
- Define a business and describe the major business functions.
- Define business processes and describe the role they play in organizations.
- Explain how information technology and information systems enhance business processes.
- Explain why environments are important for understanding a business.

2-2 How do systems serve different management groups in a business and how do systems that link the enterprise improve organizational performance?
- Identify the principal levels of management in a business and describe the different needs for information for each level.
- Describe the characteristics of transaction processing systems (TPS) and the role they play in a business.
- Describe the characteristics of management information systems (MIS), decision support systems (DSS), and executive support systems (ESS) and explain how each type of system helps managers make decisions.
- Explain how enterprise applications improve organizational performance.
- Define enterprise systems, supply chain management systems, customer relationship management systems, and knowledge management systems and describe their business benefits.
- Explain how intranets and extranets help firms improve business performance.

2-3 Why are systems for collaboration and social business so important and what technologies do they use?
- Define collaboration and social business and explain why they have become so important in business today.

- List and describe the business benefits of collaboration and social business.
- Explain how you can evaluate and select collaboration software tools.
- List and describe the various types of collaboration and social business tools.

2-4 What is the role of the information systems function in a business?
- Describe the services provided by information systems departments.
- Compare the roles programmers, systems analysts, information systems managers, the chief information officer (CIO), chief security officer (CSO), chief data officer (CDO), chief privacy officer (CPO), and chief knowledge officer (CKO) play.

Discussion Questions

✪ 2-5 How could information systems be used to support the order fulfillment process illustrated in Figure 2.2? What are the most important pieces of information these systems should capture? Explain your answer.

✪ 2-6 Identify the steps that are performed in the process of selecting and checking out a book from your college library and the information that flows among these activities. Diagram the process. Are there any ways this process could be adjusted to improve the performance of your library or your school? Diagram the improved process.

✪ 2-7 Why do you think digital dashboards have become an increasingly popular tool for management decision makers?.

Hands-On MIS Projects

The projects in this section give you hands-on experience analyzing opportunities to improve business processes with new information system applications, using a spreadsheet to improve decision making about suppliers and using Internet software to plan efficient transportation routes. Visit MyMISLab's Multimedia Library to access this chapter's Hands-On MIS Projects.

MANAGEMENT DECISION PROBLEMS

2-8 Fulbert Timber Merchants in Brixton, UK features a large selection of building supplies, including timber, fencing and decking, mouldings, hardwood flooring, sheet materials, windows, doors, ironmongery, and other materials. The prices of building materials are constantly changing. Both the customer and the sales representatives use manual price sheets. Often, the supplier must call back Fulbert's sales reps because the company does not have the newest pricing information immediately on hand. Assess the business impact of this situation, describe how this process could be improved with information technology, and identify the decisions that would have to be made to implement a solution.

2-9 Quincaillerie is a small family hardware store in Paris, France. The owners must use every square foot of store space as profitably as possible. They have never kept detailed inventory or sales records. As soon as a shipment of goods arrives, the items are immediately placed on store shelves. Invoices from suppliers are only kept for tax purposes. When an item is sold, the item number and price are rung up at the cash register. The owners use their own judgment in identifying items that need to be reordered. What is the business impact of this situation? How could information systems help the owners run their business? What data should these systems capture? What decisions could the systems improve?

IMPROVING DECISION MAKING: USE A SPREADSHEET TO SELECT SUPPLIERS

Software skills: Spreadsheet date functions, data filtering, DAVERAGE function
Business skills: Analyzing supplier performance and pricing

2-10 In this exercise, you will learn how to use spreadsheet software to improve management decisions about selecting suppliers. You will filter transactional data about suppliers based on several criteria to select the best suppliers for your company.

You run a company that manufactures aircraft components. You have many competitors who are trying to offer lower prices and better service to customers, and you are trying to determine whether you can benefit from better supply chain management. In MyMISLab, you will find a spreadsheet file that contains a list of all the items your firm has ordered from its suppliers during the past three months. The fields in the spreadsheet file include vendor name, vendor identification number, purchaser's order number, item identification number and item description (for each item ordered from the vendor), cost per item, number of units of the item ordered (quantity), total cost of each order, vendor's accounts payable terms, order date, and actual arrival date for each order.

Prepare a recommendation of how you can use the data in this spreadsheet database to improve your decisions about selecting suppliers. Some criteria to consider for identifying preferred suppliers include the supplier's track record for on-time deliveries, suppliers offering the best accounts payable terms, and suppliers offering lower pricing when the same item can be provided by multiple suppliers. Use your spreadsheet software to prepare reports to support your recommendations.

ACHIEVING OPERATIONAL EXCELLENCE: USING INTERNET SOFTWARE TO PLAN EFFICIENT TRANSPORTATION ROUTES

2-11 In this exercise, you will use Google Maps to map out transportation routes for a business and select the most efficient route.

You have just started working as a dispatcher for Trans-Europe Transport, a trucking and delivery service based in Brussels, Belgium. Your first assignment is to plan a shipment of paintings from the Museum Aan de Stroom in Antwerp, Belgium to the Royal Museums of Fine Arts of Belgium in Brussels. To guide your trucker, you need to know the most efficient route between the two cities. Use Google Maps to determine the route that is the shortest distance between the two cities, the route that takes the least time, and the estimated fuel cost for both routes Compare the results. Which route should Trans-Europe Transport use?

Collaboration and Teamwork Project

Identifying Management Decisions and Systems

2-12 With a team of three or four other students, find a description of a manager in a corporation in *Business Week, Forbes, Fortune, Wall Street Journal,* or another business publication or do your research on the web. Gather information about what the manager does and the role he or she plays in the company. Identify the organizational level and business function where this manager works. Make a list of the kinds of decisions this manager has to make and the kind of information that manager would need for those decisions. Suggest how information systems could supply this information. If possible, use Google Docs and Google Drive or Google Sites to brainstorm, organize, and develop a presentation of your findings for the class.

BUSINESS PROBLEM-SOLVING CASE

Modernization of NTUC Income

NTUC Income (Income), one of Singapore's largest insurers, has over 2 million policy holders with total assets of S$31.3 billion. As of 2015, the insurer employs about 3,400 insurance advisors and 1,200 office staff, with the majority located across an eight-branch network. In 2015, the company solidified its status as a market leader in Singapore, generating €2.5 billion in revenue, and earning €309 million, but its modernization began years ago with a critical information systems upgrade.

On June 1, 2003, Income succeeded in the migration of its legacy insurance systems to a digital Web-based system. The Herculean task required not only the upgrading of hardware and applications, it also required Income to streamline its decade-old business processes and IT practices.

Up until a few years prior to the revamp, Income's insurance processes were very tedious and paper-based. The entire insurance process started with customers meeting an agent, filling in forms, and submitting documents. The agent would then submit the forms at branches, from where they were sent by couriers to the office services department. The collection schedule could introduce delays of two to three days. Office services would log documents, sort them, and then send them to departments for underwriting. Proposals were allocated to underwriting staff, mostly randomly. Accepted proposals were sent for printing at the computer services department and then redistributed. For storage, all original documents were packed and sent to warehouses where, over two to three days, a total of seven staff would log and store the documents. In all, paper policies comprising 45 million documents were stored in over 16,000 cartons at three warehouses. Whenever a document needed to be retrieved, it would take about two days to locate and ship it by courier. Refiling would again take about two days.

In 2002, despite periodic investments to upgrade the HP 3000 mainframe that hosted the core insurance applications as well as the accounting and management information systems, it still frequently broke down. According to James Kang, then CIO at Income, "The system breakdowns were a real nightmare. Work would stop and the staff had to choose either data reconciliation or backup. However, the HP 3000 backup system allowed restoration only up to the previous day's backup data. If the daily backup was not completed at the end of the day, the affected day's data would be lost and costly and tedious reconciliation would be needed to bring the data up to date." In one of the hardware crashes, reconciliation took several months to restore the data loss. In all, the HP 3000 system experienced a total of three major hardware failures, resulting in a total of six days of complete downtime.

That was not enough. The COBOL programs that were developed in the early 1980s and maintained by Income's in-house IT team also broke multiple times, halted the systems, and caused temporary interruptions. In addition, the IT team found developing new products in COBOL to be quite cumbersome and the time taken to launch new products ranged from a few weeks to months.

At the same time, transaction processing for policy underwriting was still a batch process and information was not available to agents and advisors in real-time. As a result, when staff processed a new customer application for motor insurance, they did not know if the applicant was an existing customer of Income, which led to the loss of opportunities for cross-product sales. Commenting on the problems faced by the agents, Kang said, "When the agents tried to submit the documents using notebooks, they ran into a lot of problems. HP 3000 was a terrible machine to connect to such devices. And with more of the advisors telecommuting, availability became an issue too." In addition, various departments did not have up-to-date information and had to pass physical documents among each other.

All this changed in June 2003, when Income switched to the Java-based eBao LifeSystem from eBao Technology. The software comprised three subsystems: Policy Administration, Sales Management, and Supplementary Resources. Commenting on its features, Kang said, "It has everything we are looking for—a customer-centric design, seamless integration with imaging and bar code technology, a product definition module that supports new products, new channels, and changes in business processes."

Implementation work started in September 2002 and the project was completed in 9 months. By May 2003, all the customization, data migration of Income's individual and group life insurance businesses, and training were completed.

The new system was immediately operational on a high-availability platform. All applications resided on two or more servers, each connected by two or more communication lines, all of which were "load balanced." This robust architecture minimized downtime occurrence due to hardware or operating system failures.

As part of eBao implementation, Income decided to replace its entire IT infrastructure with a more robust, scalable architecture. For example, all servicing branches were equipped with scanners; monitors were changed to 20 inches; PC RAM size was upgraded to 128 MB; and new hardware and software for application servers, database servers, Web servers, and disk storage systems were installed. Furthermore, the LAN cables were replaced with faster cables, a fiber-optic backbone, and wireless capability.

In addition, Income also revamped its business continuity and disaster-recovery plans. A real-time hot backup disaster-recovery center, where the machines were always running and fully operational, was implemented. Data was transmitted immediately on the fly from the primary data center to the backup machines' data storage. In the event of the data center site becoming unavailable, the operations could be switched quickly to the disaster-recovery site without the need to rely on restoration of the previous day's data.

Moving to a paperless environment, however, was not easy. Income had to throw away all paper records, including legal paper documents. Under the new system, all documents were scanned and stored on 'trusted' storage devices—secured, reliable digital vaults that enabled strict compliance with stringent statutory requirements. Income had to train employees who had been accustomed to working with paper to use the eBao system and change the way they worked.

As a result of adopting eBao Life System, about 500 office staff and 3,400 insurance advisors could access the system anytime, anywhere. Staff members who would telecommute enjoyed faster access to information, almost as fast as those who accessed the information in the office.

According to Kang, "We got a singular view of every customer—across products and channels and even better life and general insurance business lines. That allowed us opportunities to cross-sell and improve customer service. In addition, because of the straight through processing workflow capabilities, we had 50 percent savings on both the time and cost needed to process policies. We had also cut the time needed to design and launch new products which was reduced from weeks to just days using the table-driven rule-based product-definition module."

Commenting on the benefits of eBao system, former CEO Tan Kin Lian remarked, "…eBaoTech LifeSystem has the best straight through processing workflow and it is very flexible. It cuts our new product launch time from months to days. It also allows us to support agents, brokers, and customers to do online services easily. I got a fantastic deal: the best system with much lower cost and much shorter implementation time. I have to say that this is a revolution!"

Although the eBao system has undergone improvements since its initial rollout, Income's culture of innovation and modernization continues. In 2011, Income announced plans to invest $4 million annually to improve its customer service as part of its "Orange Revolution" campaign. The broader goal of the campaign was to establish Income as a friendlier, more honest insurance company known for superlative customer service. The subgoals include Orange Speak, to standardize usage of simple-to-understand English across the firm, and Orange Force, to create a more visible presence of Income insurance advisors in the public eye.

For example, as part of Orange Speak, the company released a series of television advertisements and videos poking fun at the insurance industry's complicated verbiage, casting themselves as a simpler, more straightforward alternative. As part of Orange Force, the company created a task force of 30 motorcyclists with a distinctive orange NTUC Income color palette with the objective of being able to ride to traffic accidents in the surrounding areas within 20 minutes.

In 2014, the campaign was finally completed and has been a resounding success, resulting in multiple national awards for exemplary service; a reduction of average monthly complaints from 274 before the launch of the campaign to approximately 70 midway through the campaign's completion; and improving the company's bottom line, boosting profits slightly over the course of the campaign.

Technologically, the company continues to keep pace. In 2013, Income adopted Singapore's national two-factor authentication system, becoming the first local insurer to do so. The system uses a physical token that resembles a credit card and links to individual Income accounts, generating one-use passwords for online transactions. The system will help NTUC policyholders to stay safe online while sharing sensitive personal information. The company also continues to bolster its policy offerings, announcing plans to extend insurance to children with special needs such as Downs syndrome and autism, insurance for low-income families with young children, and more comprehensive motorcycle insurance. In 2015 NTUC launched a new Web-based service called Advisor Connect, which allows people to chat with NTUC financial planners while not revealing their names or personal information. Visitors to the Web site can get answers to questions, and they can choose a financial advisor for more in-depth discussion in follow-up meetings. The legacy of modernization established in the 2000s continues at NTUC Income to the present day.

Sources: "NTUC Income Creates Platform to Connect Customers and Agents," MarketingInteractive.com, October 4, 2015; "NTUC Income Launches Online Service That Lets Public Chat With Financial Planners," StraitsTimes.com, April 14, 2015; "NTUC Income Launches Adviser Connect to Provide Better Access to Financial Advice," press release, Income.com, April 9, 2015; "2015 Consolidated Financial Statements for the Fiscal Year Ended December 31, 2014," Income.com.sg, filed March 30, 2015; Giles Simon, "Membership Campaign Case Study: NTUC Income," www.thenews.coop, April 9, 2014; Eileen Yu, "NTUC Income Adopts S'pore 2FA," Zdnet.com, March 6, 2013; "2013 Consolidated Financial Statements," income.com.sg, accessed 2014; "Media Releases—2014," income.com.sg, accessed 2014; Melina Chan, "Singapore's NTUC Income Simplifies Contracts, Parodies the Industry's Legalese," Anxietyindex.com, April 8, 2013.

Case Study Questions

2-13 What were the problems faced by Income in this case? How were the problems resolved by the new digital system?

2-14 What types of information systems and business processes were used by Income before migrating to the fully digital system?

2-15 Describe the information systems and IT infrastructure at Income after migrating to the fully digital system. What benefits did Income reap from the new system?

2-16 How well is Income prepared for the future? Are the problems described in the case likely to be repeated?

Case contributed by Neerja Sethi and Vijay Sethi, Nanyang Technological University.

MyMISLab

Go to the Assignments section of your MyLab to complete these writing exercises.

2-17 Identify and describe the capabilities of enterprise social networking software.

2-18 Describe the systems various management groups use within the firm in terms of the information they use, their outputs, and groups served.

Chapter 2 References

Aral, Sinan, Erik Brynjolfsson, and Marshall Van Alstyne. "Productivity Effects of Information Diffusion in Networks," MIT Center for Digital Business (July 2007).

Banker, Rajiv D., Nan Hu, Paul A. Pavlou, and Jerry Luftman. "CIO Reporting Structure, Strategic Positioning, and Firm Performance," *MIS Quarterly* 35, No. 2 (June 2011).

Bughin, Jacques, Angela Hung Byers, and Michael Chui. "How Social Technologies Are Extending the Organization," *McKinsey Quarterly* (November 2011).

Forrester Consulting. "Total Economic Impact of IBM Social Collaboration Tools," (September 2010).

Forrester Research. "Social Business: Delivering Critical Business Value," (April 2012).

Frenkel, Karen A. "How the CIO's Role Will Change by 2018," *CIO Insight* (January 31, 2014).

Drakos, Nikos, Jeffrey Mann, and Mike Gotta. "Magic Quadrant for Social Software in the Workplace." Gartner Inc. (September 3, 2014).

Dwoskin, Elizabeth. "Big Data's High-Priests of Algorithms." *Wall Street Journal* (August 8, 2014).

Frost & White. "Meetings Around the World II: Charting the Course of Advanced Collaboration," (October 14, 2009).

Gast, Arne, and Raul Lansink. "Digital Hives: Creating a Surge Around Change." *McKinsey Quarterly* (April 2015).

Greengard, Samuel. "Collaboration: At the Center of Effective Business," *Baseline* (January 24, 2014).

_____. "The CIO's Evolving Role in the Digital Enterprise," *Baseline* (June 17, 2014).

_____. "The Social Business Gets Results," *Baseline* (June 19, 2014).

Guillemette, Manon G., and Guy Pare. "Toward a New Theory of the Contribution of the IT Function in Organizations." *MIS Quarterly* 36, No. 2 (June 2012).

Kane, Gerald C. "Enterprise Social Media: Current Capabilities and Future Possibilities," *MIS Quarterly Executive* 14, No. 1 (2015).

Kane, Gerald C., Doug Palmer, Anh Nguyen Phillips, and David Kiron. "Finding the Value in Social Business, *MIT Sloan Management Review* 55, No. 3 (Spring 2014).

Kiron, David, Doug Palmer, Anh Nguyen Phillips, and Nina Kruschwitz. "What Managers Really Think About Social Business," *MIT Sloan Management Review* 53, No. 4 (Summer 2012).

Kolfschoten, Gwendolyn L., Fred Niederman, Robert O. Briggs, and Gert-Jan DeVreede. "Facilitation Roles and Responsibilities for Sustained Collaboration Support in Organizations," *Journal of Management Information Systems* 28, No. 4 (Spring 2012).

Li, Charlene. "Making the Business Case for Enterprise Social Networks," Altimeter Group (February 22, 2012).

Maruping, Likoebe M., and Massimo Magni. "Motivating Employees to Explore Collaboration Technology in Team Contexts," *MIS Quarterly* 39, No.1 (March 2015).

McKinsey& Company. "Transforming the Business Through Social Tools," (2015).

McKinsey Global Institute. "The Social Economy: Unlocking Value and Productivity Through Social Technologies," McKinsey & Company (July 2012).

Microsoft Corporation. "Fair Work Ombudsman Australian Government Body Increases Compliance through LOB Connection," (February 2, 2014).

Reisinger, Don. "10 Social Networks Aimed at Improving Enterprise Collaboration," *eWeek* (January 15, 2015).

Saunders, Carol, A. F. Rutkowski, Michiel van Genuchten, Doug Vogel, and Julio Molina Orrego. "Virtual Space and Place: Theory and Test," *MIS Quarterly* 35, No. 4 (December 2011).

Tallon, Paul P., Ronald V. Ramirez, and James E. Short. "The Information Artifact in IT Governance: Toward a Theory of Information Governance," *Journal of Management Information Systems* 30, No. 3 (Winter 2014).

Violino, Bob. "What Is Driving the Need for Chief Data Officers?" *Information Management* (February 3, 2014).

Achieving Competitive Advantage with Information Systems

CHAPTER 3

LEARNING OBJECTIVES

After reading this chapter, you will be able to answer the following questions:

3-1 How do Porter's competitive forces model, the value chain model, synergies, core competencies, and network-based strategies help companies use information systems for competitive advantage?

3-2 How do information systems help businesses compete globally?

3-3 How do information systems help businesses compete using quality and design?

3-4 What is the role of business process management (BPM) in enhancing competitiveness?

CHAPTER CASES

Should T.J. Maxx Sell Online?

Automakers Become Software Companies

Identifying Market Niches in the Age of Big Data

Will Technology Save Sears?

VIDEO CASES

Case 1: National Basketball Association: Competing on Global Delivery with Akamai OS Streaming

Case 2: IT and Geo-Mapping Help a Small Business Succeed

Case 3: Materials Handling Equipment Corp: Enterprise Systems Drive Corporate Strategy for a Small Business

Instructional Video:

SAP BusinessOne ERP: From Orders to Final Delivery and Payment

SHOULD T.J. MAXX SELL ONLINE?

If he giant off-price clothing retailer with more than 1000 stores across the United States, has been a relative latecomer to online selling. It didn't launch its e-commerce platform until September 2013, many years after rivals such as Target and Kohl's did so. (The company made a feeble effort to sell online in 2004 but quickly pulled back after a year of lower than expected sales and too much time and money spent on updating inventory.) So why did T.J. Maxx wait so long to try again?

There are several reasons. First, it is difficult for an off-price store like T.J. Maxx to provide a stable and predictable inventory for online purchases. It buys excess inventory and off-season fashions from a vast network of department stores and manufacturers (more than 16,000 vendors in more than 75 countries), 15 percent of which are merchandise left over from the year before. However, it buys these items in much smaller lots than traditional retailers such as Nordstrom or Macy's do, with much of its inventory consisting of one-time items in small quantities. Macy's might order 1000 blue, zippered, long-sleeve Under Armour tops for all sizes small through extra-large, whereas T.J. Maxx might have 20 blue, zippered, long-sleeve Under Armour tops, 30 pairs of purple Nike basketball shoes in assorted sizes, and 3 pairs of Adidas soccer socks in extra-small size. Whereas traditional department stores tend to buy seasonally, T.J. Maxx has new brand-name and designer fashions arriving every week. The inventory varies a great deal from one store to the next, and you never knew what you'll find when you visit a T.J. Maxx store. Shoppers are lured into the stores in the hope that they might find a hot bargain that might be available for only a few days. High-end clothing brands such as Polo Ralph Lauren or Nicole Miller do not want to see their merchandise deeply discounted online. In addition, an online storefront can cannibalize in-store sales, and management was worried about that as well.

© Photolink/Photodisc

On the other hand, ignoring e-commerce can mean losing market share to competitors. E-commerce has opened the doors to many more competitors for T.J. Maxx. Today's budget shopper is bombarded with bargains and discount shopping opportunities from many more sources. These include web-only off-price stores such as Overstock.com and sites such as Rue LaLa and Gilt Groupe with short-term deals known as flash sales. Brick-and-mortar outlet stores have also expanded, occupying 68 million square feet of retail space, compared to 56 million in 2006, according to Value Retail News. Even high-end retailers such as Neiman Marcus and Bloomingdales have set up discount outlets. T.J. Maxx management felt it had to take the online leap.

In 2012, T.J. Maxx's parent company, TJX, purchased off-price Internet retailer Sierra Trading Post to learn about selling online. The new T.J. Maxx site tries to preserve the feel of its stores. You can't just search Nanette Lepore—you must comb through all women's dresses or shoes. Online shoppers may or may not like that. The retailer is also experimenting with its own flash sale site called Maxx Flash. Unlike other flash sites, this one can accept returns at stores and resell items there.

T.J. Maxx has not yet furnished performance metrics for the site, so analysts still don't have a precise idea of how much value is being created, but it is possible to estimate the platform's potential contribution to profit roughly once it ramps up after three or four years. Profit margins from online sales tend to be higher by 7 percentage points on average than those from brick-and-mortar stores. If T.J. Maxx's operating margin was 12 percent (as occurred in fiscal 2012), and it obtained 10 percent of its revenue from e-commerce, an operating margin of 18 percent would add about 45 cents, or 13.6 percent, to fiscal 2014 earnings per share, according to financial services firm Sterne Agee estimates. A more conservative estimate, with e-commerce making up only 6 percent of sales, and margins coming in at 16, would still add 24 cents to earnings per share.

Carol Meyrowitz, CEO of T.J. Maxx's parent company TJX, stated that the company does not want e-commerce growth to be at the expense of its brick-and-mortar stores and is therefore not pouring too much into online selling. At this point, company management feels that its foray into e-commerce is measured, focused, and beneficial to the business as a whole.

Sources: www.tjx.com, accessed January 26, 2015; Hilary Burns, "Carol Meyrowitz Reports TJX Companies' Q3 Earnings and Talks E-commerce," Bizjournal.com, November 18, 2014; Miriam Gottfried, "Get Caught Up in T.J.Maxx's Web," *Wall Street Journal*, December 1, 2013; and "T.J.Maxx Revisits Online Strategy," *Seeking Alpha*, Oct. 7, 2013.

T.J. Maxx's story illustrates some of the ways that information systems help businesses compete as well as the challenges of finding the right business strategy and how to use technology in that strategy. Retailing today is an extremely crowded playing field, both online and in physical brick-and-mortar stores. Even though T.J. Maxx is a leading off-price retailer, it has many competitors, and it is searching for a way to use the Internet that will work with its particular business model.

The chapter-opening diagram calls attention to important points this case and this chapter raise. T.J. Maxx, part of the TJX group of retail stores, including Marshall's and Home Goods, has been a highly successful off-price retailer, with more than 1000 stores in the United States alone. Its business model depends on picking up department store and designer excess inventory or last year's fashions and selling at low prices to appeal to opportunistic shoppers. That business model is being challenged by more off-price competitors, both physical stores and off-price and flash sale sites on the Internet. T.J. Maxx would like to do more selling online because profit margins are higher, but its inability to provide a reliable and stable inventory has impeded this effort. The company is making one more big push into online retailing, learning from the experience of Sierra Trading Post, but it is still unclear whether an online business strategy will work.

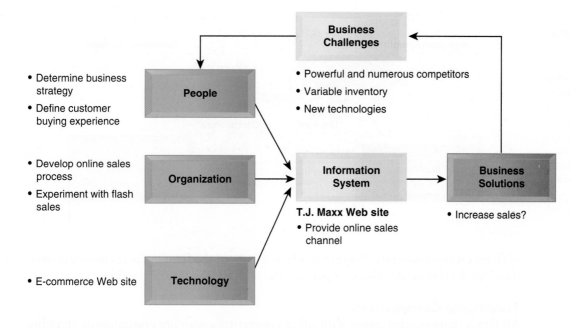

Here are some questions to think about: How do the competitive forces and value chain models apply to T.J. Maxx? Visit the T.J. Maxx website and examine its offerings and ease of use. Do you think selling on the Internet will work for T.J. Maxx? Why or why not?

3-1 How do Porter's competitive forces model, the value chain model, synergies, core competencies, and network-based strategies help companies use information systems for competitive advantage?

In almost every industry you examine, you will find that some firms do better than most others do. There's almost always a standout firm. In pure online retail, Amazon is the leader; in offline retail, Walmart, the largest retailer on earth, has been the leader.

In online music, Apple's iTunes is considered the leader with more than 60 percent of the downloaded music market, and in the related industry of digital music players, the iPod is the leader. In web search, Google is considered the leader.

Firms that do better than others are said to have a competitive advantage. They either have access to special resources that others do not, or they use commonly available resources more efficiently—usually because of superior knowledge and information assets. In any event, they do better in terms of revenue growth, profitability, or productivity growth (efficiency), all of which ultimately translate into higher stock market valuations than their competitors.

But why do some firms do better than others and how do they achieve competitive advantage? How can you analyze a business and identify its strategic advantages? How can you develop a strategic advantage for your own business? How do information systems contribute to strategic advantages? One answer to these questions is Michael Porter's competitive forces model.

PORTER'S COMPETITIVE FORCES MODEL

Arguably, the most widely used model for understanding competitive advantage is Michael Porter's **competitive forces model** (see Figure 3.1). This model provides a general view of the firm, its competitors, and the firm's environment. Recall that in Chapter 2 we described the importance of a firm's environment and the dependence

Figure 3.1
Porter's Competitive
Forces Model
*In Porter's competitive
forces model, the strategic
position of the firm and its
strategies are determined
not only by competition
with its traditional direct
competitors but also by
four forces in the industry's
environment: new market
entrants, substitute
products, customers, and
suppliers.*

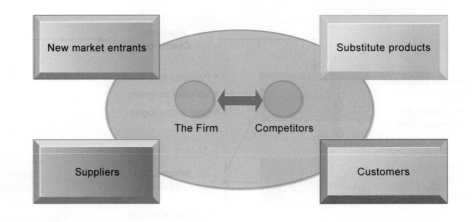

of firms on environments. Porter's model is all about the firm's general business environment. In this model, five competitive forces shape the fate of the firm.

Traditional Competitors

All firms share market space with other competitors who are continuously devising new, more efficient ways to produce by introducing new products and services and attempting to attract customers by developing their brands and imposing switching costs on their customers.

New Market Entrants

In a free economy with mobile labor and financial resources, new companies are always entering the marketplace. In some industries, there are very low barriers to entry, whereas in other industries, entry is very difficult. For instance, it is fairly easy to start a pizza business or just about any small retail business, but it is much more expensive and difficult to enter the computer chip business, which has very high capital costs and requires significant expertise and knowledge that is hard to obtain. New companies have several possible advantages. They are not locked into old plants and equipment, they often hire younger workers who are less expensive and perhaps more innovative, they are not encumbered by old worn-out brand names, and they are more hungry (more highly motivated) than traditional occupants of an industry. These advantages are also their weaknesses. They depend on outside financing for new plants and equipment, which can be expensive; they have a less-experienced workforce; and they have little brand recognition.

Substitute Products and Services

In just about every industry, there are substitutes that your customers might use if your prices become too high. New technologies create new substitutes all the time. Even oil has substitutes. Ethanol can substitute for gasoline in cars; vegetable oil for diesel fuel in trucks; and wind, solar, and hydropower for coal, oil, and gas electricity generation. Likewise, Internet telephone service has substituted for traditional telephone service, and fiber-optic telephone lines to the home substitute for cable TV lines. Streaming Internet music services substitute for CDs, music stores, and digital download sites like iTunes. The more substitute products and services in your industry, the less you can control pricing and the lower your profit margins.

Customers

A profitable company depends in large measure on its ability to attract and retain customers (while denying them to competitors) and charge high prices. The power of customers grows if they can easily switch to a competitor's products and services or if they can force a business and its competitors to compete on price alone in a transparent marketplace where there is little product differentiation, and all prices are known instantly (such as on the Internet). For instance, in the used–college textbook market on the Internet, students (customers) can find multiple suppliers of just about any current college textbook. In this case, online customers have extraordinary power over used-book firms.

Suppliers

The market power of suppliers can have a significant impact on firm profits, especially when the firm cannot raise prices as fast as suppliers can. The more suppliers a firm has, the greater control it can exercise over those suppliers in terms of price, quality, and delivery schedules. For instance, manufacturers of laptop PCs usually have multiple competing suppliers of key components, such as keyboards, hard drives, and display screens.

INFORMATION SYSTEM STRATEGIES FOR DEALING WITH COMPETITIVE FORCES

What is a firm to do when faced with all these competitive forces? How can the firm use information systems to counteract some of these forces? How do you prevent substitutes and inhibit new market entrants? How do you become the most successful firm in an industry in terms of profit and share price (two measures of success)?

Basic Strategy 101: Align the IT with the Business Objectives

The basic principle of IT strategy for a business is to ensure that the technology serves the business and not the other way around. The research on IT and business performance has found that (a) the more successfully a firm can align its IT with its business goals, the more profitable it will be, and (b) only about one-quarter of firms achieve alignment of IT with business. About half of a business firm's profits can be explained by alignment of IT with business (Luftman, 2003). Most businesses get it wrong; IT takes on a life of its own and does not serve management and shareholder interests very well. Instead of business people taking an active role in shaping IT to the enterprise, they ignore it, claim not to understand IT, and tolerate failure in the IT area as just a nuisance to work around. Such firms pay a hefty price in poor performance. Successful firms and managers understand what IT can do and how it works, take an active role in shaping its use, and measure its impact on revenues and profits.

So how do you as a manager achieve this alignment of IT with business? In the following sections, we discuss some basic ways to do this, but here's a summary:

- Identify your business strategy and goals.
- Break these strategic goals down into concrete activities and processes.
- Identify how you will measure progress toward the business goals (e.g., by using metrics).
- Ask yourself, "How can information technology help me achieve progress toward our business goals, and how will it improve our business processes and activities?"
- Measure actual performance. Let the numbers speak.

Let's see how this works out in practice. There are four generic strategies, each of which often is enabled by using information technology and systems: low-cost leadership, product differentiation, focus on market niche, and strengthening customer and supplier intimacy.

Low-Cost Leadership

Use information systems to achieve the lowest operational costs and the lowest prices. The classic example is Walmart. By keeping prices low and shelves well stocked using a legendary inventory replenishment system, Walmart became the leading retail business in the United States. Point-of-sale terminals record the bar code of each

Supermarkets and large retail stores such as Walmart use sales data captured at the checkout counter to determine which items have sold and need to be reordered. Walmart's continuous replenishment system transmits orders to restock directly to its suppliers. The system enables Walmart to keep costs low while fine-tuning its merchandise availability to meet customer demands.

© Betty LaRue/Alamy

item passing the checkout counter and send a purchase transaction directly to a central computer at Walmart headquarters. The computer collects the orders from all Walmart stores and transmits them to suppliers. Suppliers can also access Walmart's sales and inventory data by using web technology.

Because the system replenishes inventory with lightning speed, Walmart does not need to spend much money on maintaining large inventories of goods in its own warehouses. The system also enables Walmart to adjust the items stocked in its stores to meet customer demands. By using systems to keep operating costs low, Walmart can charge less for its products than competitors yet reap higher profits.

Walmart's continuous replenishment system is also an example of an **efficient customer response system**. An efficient customer response system directly links consumer behavior to distribution and production and supply chains. Walmart's continuous replenishment system provides such an efficient customer response.

Product Differentiation

Use information systems to provide new products and services or greatly change the customer convenience in using your existing products and services. For instance, Google continuously introduces new and unique search services, such as Google Pay peer payments in 2014, and improvements in Google Docs and Google Drive. Apple has continued to differentiate its hand held computing products with nearly annual introductions of new iPhone and iPad models.

Manufacturers and retailers are using information systems to create products and services that are customized and personalized to fit the precise specifications of individual customers. For example, Nike sells customized sneakers through its Nike iD program on its website. Customers can select the type of shoe, colors, material, outsoles, and even a logo of up to eight characters. Nike transmits the orders by computers to specially equipped plants in China and Korea. The sneakers cost only about $10 extra and take about three weeks to reach the customer. This ability to offer individually tailored products or services using the same production resources as mass production is called **mass customization**.

INTERACTIVE SESSION: TECHNOLOGY Automakers Become Software Companies

As the smartphone market continues to expand, another industry has begun getting "smarter" with software and apps: the automobile industry. Ford, BMW, and other automobile companies are enhancing their vehicles with on-board software that improves the customer experience, and the auto industry is working on technology that will allow cars to be managed via the cloud.

Automakers are finding that software is a way of adding more "value" and freshness to their products without having to invest so heavily in new vehicle production. It takes Ford Motor Company, for example, about two and a half years to plan, design, and build a new car. Design and production, including metal stamping equipment and assembly line setup, must be finalized long before the car rolls off the line. But the auto makers can create a new software interface for a car within months and update it again and again over the life of the car without much lead time. This enables Ford and other auto makers to significantly improve the driving experience and add new features to cars years after they are built.

Ford is perhaps the automaker doing the most to innovate with software and apps. Its MyFord Touch interface is an in-dash touchscreen available for select vehicles with controls for navigation, music, phone integration, and temperature. Ford has upgraded this interface and the Sync software behind the interface, adding tablet and smartphone integration and better voice response. In 2010 Ford added support for the online music streaming service Pandora, which is very popular among young potential buyers. This update enables drivers to connect their tablets and smartphones to the Sync system to access music and other apps using voice commands.

Chairman Bill Ford, Jr., has championed the use of software to alleviate urban congestion by investing in technology that responds to the problems created by traffic in the biggest cities. Theoretically, technology might help cars to avoid traffic jams, reserve parking spaces in advance, and even drive themselves.

To manage vehicles in this way, cars need to be connected to some kind of central system that would coordinate with public transit and other transportation methods, and to do this, cars need to be equipped with software that can monitor and enhance vehicle function at the most basic levels. The eventual system would require that cars feed increasing amounts of information to systems whose purpose would be to minimize highway congestion. The system would also require an industry standard, which does not exist yet. Ford has doubled its investment in vehicle-to-vehicle communication technologies and BMW is also continuing to develop ways for vehicles to communicate with one another on the road to avoid collisions.

With the inclusion of software in their cars, automakers are entering uncharted territory. They must now devote resources to updating and testing their software as well as establishing ways to provide the updated software to their customers. Car companies need to coordinate their car development cycles more closely with their software development cycles. Also, many of the technologies included in automobile software packages raise the same privacy concerns surrounding location tracking that have often plagued smartphone manufacturers and app developers.

Ford is grappling with the best way to roll out software upgrades to its customers. The company has been mailing USB sticks to 250,000 customers whose cars have an advanced touchscreen control panel running the MyFord Touch interface. The stick contains a software upgrade that will improve navigation controls, the music and phone features, as well as the ability to control car temperature. The upgrade also contains code that will upgrade system speed and improve the interface based on common criticisms from Ford owners.

Although Ford says it plans to continue issuing software upgrades this way, the company hopes that customers will get into the habit of checking the Ford Web site for software upgrades on their own. Though most car owners are used to the technology in their cars remaining constant throughout the life of the car, newer cars are poised to change all of that.

Ford has hired "human–machine interface engineers," whose job is to analyze how their customers interact with the software in their cars. Often, these engineers use customer feedback to make changes to the software. Customers complained that too much information was available on each screen of the interface, so Ford moved the most commonly used features to more prominent positions on screen and increased their font size, relegating the rest to submenus. Feedback has been positive. Ford has also asked dealers to dedicate more time and personnel to hands-on technology training to help customers master its interface.

GM, Daimler, and other companies are all developing new features for their cars that operate online in the cloud. Users will be able to remotely track their cars (you'll never forget where you parked again) and diagnose problems with the car, such as low tire pressure or the need for an oil change. Corporations will be able to track employee use of company cars by interpreting car sensors and engine readouts. Manufacturers will be able to aggregate and analyze the data from customers' cars to identify quality problems and, if necessary, quickly issue recalls. Just as with apps, the possibilities are limited only by the imagination of automakers.

GM will allow its app developers to access its computer systems to improve app function, which raises a familiar set of privacy concerns. Auto analysts believe that automakers will make mistakes as they learn how to properly handle sensitive customer data and to provide robust privacy options. On the other hand, automakers are hoping that younger customers who have grown up using Facebook are less likely to care about privacy and

features that collect highly targeted information about a car's location and driving habits.

BMW is also investing a whopping $100 million in mobile apps, hoping to market them to their customers as "premium services." Some analysts are skeptical of the decision to invest that much money, but BMW believes that mobile apps will become an increasingly attractive selling point for customers of its BMWi electric and hybrid cars. Although the future of cars sharing information with other nearby cars is still years away, automakers are excited by the possibilities afforded by smart software and apps.

Sources: Jaclyn Trop, "Tired of Silicon Valley? Try Motor City," *New York Times*, July 1, 2013; Ian Scherr and Mike Ramsey, "Drive into the Future," *Wall Street Journal*, March 11, 2013; Michelle Maisto, "Ford, Google, Facebook Team Up to Reconsider Mobility," *eWeek*, March 28, 2013; Ian Sherr, "Cars Pump Up IQ To Get Edge," *Wall Street Journal*, January 13, 2012; Chris Murphy, "4 Ways Ford Is Exploring Next-Gen Car Tech," *Information Week*, July 27, 2012; Mike Ramsey, "Avoiding Gridlock with Smart Autos," *Wall Street Journal*, February 27, 2012.

CASE STUDY QUESTIONS

1. How is software adding value to automakers' products?

2. How are the automakers benefiting from software-enhanced cars? How are customers benefiting?

3. What value chain activities are involved in enhancing cars with software?

4. How much of a competitive advantage is software providing for automakers? Explain your answer.

Table 3.1 lists a number of companies that have developed IS-based products and services that other firms have found difficult to copy.

Focus on Market Niche

Use information systems to enable a specific market focus and serve this narrow target market better than competitors. Information systems support this strategy

TABLE 3.1		
IS-Enabled New Products and Services Providing Competitive Advantage	Amazon: One-click shopping	Amazon holds a patent on one-click shopping that it licenses to other online retailers.
	Online music: Apple iPod and iTunes	Apple's integrated, handheld player is backed up with an online library of more than 30 million songs.
	Golf club customization: Ping	Customers can select from more than 1 million golf club options; a build-to-order system ships their customized clubs within 48 hours.
	Online person-to-person payment: PayPal.com	PayPal enables transfer of money between individual bank accounts and between bank accounts and credit card accounts.

by producing and analyzing data for finely tuned sales and marketing techniques. Information systems enable companies to analyze customer buying patterns, tastes, and preferences closely so that they efficiently pitch advertising and marketing campaigns to smaller and smaller target markets.

The data come from a range of sources—credit card transactions, demographic data, purchase data from checkout counter scanners at supermarkets and retail stores, and data collected when people access and interact with websites. Sophisticated software tools find patterns in these large pools of data and infer rules from them that can be used to guide decision making. Analysis of such data drives one-to-one marketing by which personal messages can be created based on individualized preferences. For example, Hilton Hotels' OnQ system analyzes detailed data collected on active guests in all of its properties to determine the preferences of each guest and each guest's profitability. Hilton uses this information to give its most profitable customers additional privileges, such as late checkouts. Contemporary customer relationship management (CRM) systems feature analytical capabilities for this type of intensive data analysis (see Chapters 2 and 9).

Strengthen Customer and Supplier Intimacy

Use information systems to tighten linkages with suppliers and develop intimacy with customers. Toyota, Ford, and other automobile manufacturers have information systems that give their suppliers direct access to their production schedules, enabling suppliers to decide how and when to ship supplies to the plants where cars are assembled. This allows suppliers more lead time in producing goods. On the customer side, Amazon.com keeps track of user preferences for book and music purchases and can recommend titles purchased by others to its customers. Strong linkages to customers and suppliers increase **switching costs** (the cost of switching from one product or service to a competitor) and loyalty to your firm.

Table 3.2 summarizes the competitive strategies we have just described. Some companies focus on one of these strategies, but you will often see firms pursuing several of them simultaneously. For example, Starbucks, the world's largest specialty coffee retailer, offers unique high-end specialty coffees and beverages, but it is also trying to compete by lowering costs.

Implementing any of these strategies is no simple matter, but it is possible, as evidenced by the many firms that obviously dominate their markets and that have used information systems to enable their strategies. As shown by the cases throughout this book, successfully using information systems to achieve a competitive advantage requires a precise coordination of technology, organizations, and people. Indeed, as many have noted with regard to Walmart, Apple, and Amazon, the ability to implement information systems successfully is not equally distributed, and some firms are much better at it than others are.

TABLE 3.2 Four Basic Competitive Strategies

Strategy	Description	Example
Low-cost leadership	Use information systems to produce products and services at a lower price than competitors while enhancing quality and level of service.	Walmart
Product differentiation	Use information systems to differentiate products and provide new services and products.	Uber, Nike, Apple, Starbucks
Focus on market niche	Use information systems to enable a focused strategy on a single market niche; specialize.	Hilton Hotels, Harrah's
Customer and supplier intimacy	Use information systems to develop strong ties and loyalty with customers and suppliers.	Toyota Corporation, Amazon

THE INTERNET'S IMPACT ON COMPETITIVE ADVANTAGE

Because of the Internet, the traditional competitive forces are still at work, but competitive rivalry has become much more intense (Porter, 2001). Internet technology is based on universal standards that any company can use, making it easier for rivals to compete on price alone and for new competitors to enter the market. Because information is available to everyone, the Internet raises the bargaining power of customers, who can quickly find the lowest-cost provider on the web. Profits have often been dampened as a result of increased competition. Table 3.3 summarizes some of the potentially negative impacts of the Internet on business firms Porter has identified.

The Internet has nearly destroyed some industries and has severely threatened others. For instance, the printed encyclopedia industry and the travel agency industry have been nearly decimated by the availability of substitutes over the Internet. Likewise, the Internet has had a significant impact on the retail, music, book, retail brokerage, software, and telecommunications industries. However, the Internet has also created entirely new markets, formed the basis for thousands of new products, services, and business models, and provided new opportunities for building brands with very large and loyal customer bases. Amazon, eBay, iTunes, YouTube, Facebook, Travelocity, and Google are examples. In this sense, the Internet is transforming entire industries, forcing firms to change how they do business.

Smart Products and the Internet of Things

The growing use of sensors in industrial and consumer products, often called the Internet of Things, is an excellent example of how the Internet is changing competition within industries and creating new products and services. In 2015, Nike and Under Armour, along with many other sports apparel companies, are pouring money into their wearable health trackers, which use sensors to report activities of users to a cloud database. John Deere tractors are loaded with field radar, GPS transceivers, and hundreds of sensors to keep track of the equipment. GE is renowned for its use of 10,000 sensors in its aircraft turbines and uses 20,000 sensors in its wind turbines! The result is what's referred to as smart products—products that are part of a larger set of services firms sell (Porter and Heppelmann, 2014; Iansiti and Lakhani, 2014).

The impact of smart, Internet-connected products is just now being understood. Smart products offer new functionality, greater reliability, and more intense use of

TABLE 3.3

Impact of the Internet on Competitive Forces and Industry Structure

Competitive Force	Impact of the Internet
Substitute products or services	Enables new substitutes to emerge with new approaches to meeting needs and performing functions
Customers' bargaining power	Shifts bargaining power to customers due to the availability of global price and product information
Suppliers' bargaining power	Tends to raise bargaining power over suppliers in procuring products and services; however, suppliers can benefit from reduced barriers to entry and from the elimination of distributors and other intermediaries standing between them and their users
Threat of new entrants	Reduces barriers to entry, such as the need for a sales force, access to channels, and physical assets; provides a technology for driving business processes that makes other things easier to do
Positioning and rivalry among existing competitors	Widens the geographic market, increasing the number of competitors and reducing differences among competitors; makes it more difficult to sustain operational advantages; puts pressure to compete on price

products. They expand opportunities for product and service differentiation. When you buy a wearable digital health product, you not only get the product itself, you also get a host of services available from the manufacturer's cloud servers. Smart products increase rivalry among firms that will either innovate or lose customers to competitors. Smart products generally inhibit new entrants to a market simply because existing customers are trapped in the dominant firm's software environment. Finally, smart products may decrease the power of suppliers of industrial components if, as many believe, the physical product becomes less important than the software and hardware that makes it run.

THE BUSINESS VALUE CHAIN MODEL

Although the Porter model is very helpful for identifying competitive forces and suggesting generic strategies, it is not very specific about what exactly to do, and it does not provide a methodology to follow for achieving competitive advantages. If your goal is to achieve operational excellence, where do you start? Here's where the business value chain model is helpful.

The **value chain model** highlights specific activities in the business where competitive strategies can best be applied (Porter, 1985) and where information systems are most likely to have a strategic impact. This model identifies specific, critical advantage points at which a firm can use information technology most effectively to enhance its competitive position. The value chain model views the firm as a series or chain of basic activities that add a margin of value to a firm's products or services. These activities can be categorized as either primary activities or support activities (see Figure 3.2).

Primary activities are most directly related to the production and distribution of the firm's products and services, which create value for the customer. Primary activities include inbound logistics, operations, outbound logistics, sales and marketing, and service. Inbound logistics includes receiving and storing materials for distribution to production. Operations transforms inputs into finished products. Outbound logistics entails storing and distributing finished products. Sales and marketing

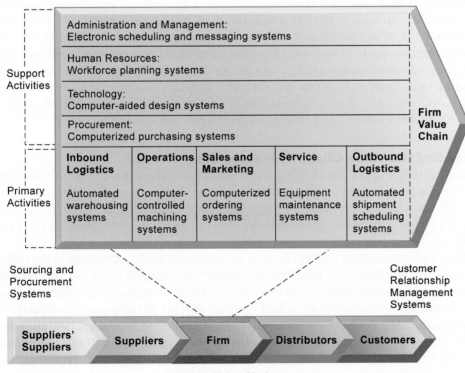

Figure 3.2
The Value Chain Model
This figure provides examples of systems for both primary and support activities of a firm and of its value partners that would add a margin of value to a firm's products or services.

includes promoting and selling the firm's products. The service activity includes maintenance and repair of the firm's goods and services.

Support activities make the delivery of the primary activities possible and consist of organization infrastructure (administration and management), human resources (employee recruiting, hiring, and training), technology (improving products and the production process), and procurement (purchasing input).

You can ask at each stage of the value chain, "How can we use information systems to improve operational efficiency and improve customer and supplier intimacy?" This will force you to examine critically how you perform value-adding activities at each stage and how the business processes might be improved. For example, value chain analysis would indicate that Nike has improved its processes for using technology and for sales and marketing. Value chain analysis helped Nike embrace its current strategy of trying to differentiate its products using technology. Nike created technology-based products that provide additional value to customers because they take advantage of complementary existing technologies (such as the Internet and the iPhone) that customers already own and are familiar with.

You can also begin to ask how information systems can be used to improve the relationship with customers and with suppliers who lie outside the firm's value chain but belong to the firm's extended value chain where they are absolutely critical to your success. Here, supply chain management systems that coordinate the flow of resources into your firm, and customer relationship management systems that coordinate your sales and support employees with customers, are two of the most common system applications that result from a business value chain analysis. We discuss these enterprise applications in detail in Chapter 9.

Using the business value chain model will also encourage you to consider benchmarking your business processes against your competitors or others in related industries and identifying industry best practices. **Benchmarking** involves comparing the efficiency and effectiveness of your business processes against strict standards and then measuring performance against those standards. Industry **best practices** are usually identified by consulting companies, research organizations, government agencies, and industry associations as the most successful solutions or problem-solving methods for consistently and effectively achieving a business objective.

Once you have analyzed the various stages in the value chain at your business, you can come up with candidate applications of information systems. Then, when you have a list of candidate applications, you can decide which to develop first. By making improvements in your own business value chain that your competitors might miss, you can achieve competitive advantage by attaining operational excellence, lowering costs, improving profit margins, and forging a closer relationship with customers and suppliers. If your competitors are making similar improvements, then at least you will not be at a competitive disadvantage—the worst of all cases!

Extending the Value Chain: The Value Web

Figure 3.2 shows that a firm's value chain is linked to the value chains of its suppliers, distributors, and customers. After all, the performance of most firms depends not only on what goes on inside a firm but also on how well the firm coordinates with direct and indirect suppliers, delivery firms (logistics partners, such as FedEx or UPS), and, of course, customers.

How can information systems be used to achieve strategic advantage at the industry level? By working with other firms, industry participants can use information technology to develop industry-wide standards for exchanging information or business transactions electronically, which force all market participants to subscribe to similar standards. Such efforts increase efficiency, making product substitution less likely and perhaps raising entry costs—thus discouraging new entrants. Moreover, industry members can build industry-wide, IT-supported consortia, symposia, and communications networks to coordinate activities concerning government agencies, foreign competition, and competing industries.

Looking at the industry value chain encourages you to think about how to use information systems to link up more efficiently with your suppliers, strategic partners, and customers. Strategic advantage derives from your ability to relate your value chain to the value chains of other partners in the process. For instance, if you were Amazon.com, you would want to build systems that

- Make it easy for suppliers to display goods and open stores on the Amazon site.
- Make it easy for customers to pay for goods.
- Develop systems that coordinate the shipment of goods to customers.
- Develop shipment tracking systems for customers.

In fact, this is exactly what Amazon has done to make it one of the web's most satisfying online retail shopping sites.

Internet technology has made it possible to create highly synchronized industry value chains called value webs. A **value web** is a collection of independent firms that use information technology to coordinate their value chains to produce a product or service for a market collectively. It is more customer driven and operates in a less linear fashion than the traditional value chain.

Figure 3.3 shows that this value web synchronizes the business processes of customers, suppliers, and trading partners among different companies in an industry or in related industries. These value webs are flexible and adaptive to changes in supply and demand. Relationships can be bundled or unbundled in response to changing market conditions. Firms will accelerate time to market and to customers by optimizing their value web relationships to make quick decisions on who can deliver the required products or services at the right price and location.

SYNERGIES, CORE COMPETENCIES, AND NETWORK-BASED STRATEGIES

A large corporation is typically a collection of businesses. Often, the firm is organized financially as a collection of strategic business units, and the returns to the firm are directly tied to the performance of all the units. For instance, General Electric—one

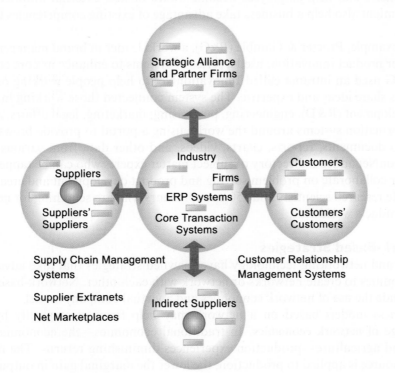

Figure 3.3
The Value Web
The value web is a networked system that can synchronize the value chains of business partners within an industry to respond rapidly to changes in supply and demand.

of the largest industrial firms in the world—is a collection of aerospace, heavy manufacturing, electrical appliance, medical imaging, electronics, and financial services firms called *business units*. Information systems can improve the overall performance of these business units by promoting communication, synergies, and core competencies among the units.

Synergies

Synergies develop when the output of some units can be used as inputs to other units, or two organizations can pool markets and expertise, and these relationships lower costs and generate profits. Bank and financial firm mergers, such as the merger of Bank of America and Countrywide Financial as well as of JPMorgan Chase and Washington Mutual, occurred precisely for this purpose.

One use of information technology in these synergy situations is to tie together the operations of disparate business units so that they can act as a whole. For example, acquiring Countrywide Financial enabled Bank of America to expand its mortgage lending business and acquire a large pool of new customers that might be interested in its credit cards, consumer banking, and other financial products. Information systems would help the merged companies consolidate operations, lower retailing costs, and increase cross-marketing of financial products.

Enhancing Core Competencies

Another use of information systems for competitive advantage is to think about ways that systems can enhance core competencies. The argument is that the performance of all business units can increase insofar as these business units develop, or create, a central core of competencies. A **core competency** is an activity for which a firm is an industry leader, best in class leader. Core competencies may involve being the best miniature parts designer, the best package delivery service, or the best thin-film manufacturer. In general, a core competency relies on knowledge that is gained over many years of experience and a first-class research organization or, simply, key people who follow the literature and stay abreast of new external knowledge.

Any information system that encourages the sharing of knowledge across business units enhances competency. Such systems might encourage or enhance existing competencies and help employees become aware of new external knowledge; such systems might also help a business take advantage of existing competencies to related markets.

For example, Procter & Gamble (P&G), a world leader in brand management and consumer product innovation, used a series of systems to enhance its core competencies. P&G used an intranet called InnovationNet to help people working on similar problems share ideas and expertise. The system connected those working in research and development (R&D), engineering, purchasing, marketing, legal affairs, and business information systems around the world, using a portal to provide browser-based access to documents, reports, charts, videos, and other data from various sources. InnovationNet added a directory of subject matter experts who can be tapped to give advice or collaborate on problem solving and product development and created links to outside research scientists and 150 entrepreneurs who are searching for new, innovative products worldwide.

Network-Based Strategies

Internet and networking technology have spawned strategies that take advantage of firms' abilities to create networks or network with each other. Network-based strategies include the use of network economics and a virtual company model.

Business models based on a network may help firms strategically by taking advantage of **network economics**. In traditional economics—the economics of factories and agriculture—production experiences diminishing returns. The more any given resource is applied to production, the lower the marginal gain in output, until a point is reached when the additional inputs produce no additional outputs. This is the law of diminishing returns, and it is one foundation of modern economics.

In some situations, the law of diminishing returns does not work. For instance, in a network, the marginal costs of adding another participant are about zero, whereas the marginal gain is much larger. The larger the number of subscribers in a telephone system or the Internet, the greater the value to all participants because each user can interact with more people. It is no more expensive to operate a television station with 1,000 subscribers than with 10 million subscribers. The value of a community of people grows as the number of participants increases, whereas the cost of adding new members is inconsequential. This is referred to as a "network effect."

From this network economics perspective, information technology can be strategically useful. Firms can use Internet sites to build *communities of users*—like-minded customers who want to share their experiences. This can build customer loyalty and enjoyment and build unique ties to customers. EBay, the giant online auction and retail site is an example. This business is based on a network of millions of users and has built an online community by using the Internet. The more people offering products on eBay, the more valuable the eBay site is to everyone because more products are listed, and more competition among suppliers lowers prices. Network economics also provide strategic benefits to commercial software vendors. The value of their software and complementary software products increases as more people use them, and there is a larger installed base to justify continued use of the product and vendor support.

Another network-based strategy uses the model of a virtual company to create a competitive business. A **virtual company**, also known as a *virtual organization*, uses networks to link people, assets, and ideas, enabling it to ally with other companies to create and distribute products and services without being limited by traditional organizational boundaries or physical locations. The virtual company model is useful when a company finds it cheaper to acquire products, services, or capabilities from an external vendor or when it needs to move quickly to exploit new market opportunities and lacks the time and resources to respond on its own.

Fashion companies, such as GUESS, Ann Taylor, Levi Strauss, and Reebok, enlist Hong Kong–based Li & Fung to manage production and shipment of their garments. Li & Fung handles product development, raw material sourcing, production planning, quality assurance, and shipping. Li & Fung does not own any fabric, factories, or machines, outsourcing all of its work to a network of more than 15,000 suppliers in 37 countries all over the world. Customers place orders to Li & Fung over its private extranet. Li & Fung then sends instructions to appropriate raw material suppliers and factories where the clothing is produced. The Li & Fung extranet tracks the entire production process for each order. Working as a virtual company keeps Li & Fung flexible and adaptable so that it can design and produce quickly the products its clients order to keep pace with rapidly changing fashion trends.

DISRUPTIVE TECHNOLOGIES: RIDING THE WAVE

Sometimes a technology and resulting business innovation comes along to change the business landscape and environment radically. These innovations are loosely called *disruptive* (Christensen, 2003). In some cases, **disruptive technologies** are substitute products that perform as well or better than anything currently produced. The automobile substituted for the horse-drawn carriage, the Apple iPod for portable CD players, digital photography for process film photography. In these cases, entire industries are put out of business.

In other cases, disruptive technologies simply extend the market, usually with less functionality and much less cost, than existing products. Eventually they turn into low-cost competitors for whatever was sold before. Disk drives are an example. Small hard-disk drives used in PCs extended the market for computer disk drives by

TABLE 3.4

Disruptive Technologies: Winners and Losers

Technology	Description	Winners and Losers
Microprocessor chips (1971)	Thousands and eventually millions of transistors on a silicon chip	Microprocessor firms win (Intel, Texas Instruments); transistor firms (GE) decline
Personal computers (1975)	Small, inexpensive, but fully functional desktop computers	PC manufacturers (HP, Apple, IBM) and chip manufacturers prosper (Intel); mainframe (IBM) and minicomputer (DEC) firms lose
Digital photography 1975	Using charge-coupled device (CCD) image sensor chips to record images	CCD manufacturers and smartphone companies win, manufacturers of film products lose
World Wide Web (1989)	A global database of digital files and pages instantly available	E-commerce online stores benefit; small retailers and shopping malls lose
Internet music, video, TV services	Repositories of downloadable music, video, TV broadcasts on the web	Owners of Internet platforms, telecommunications providers owning Internet backbone (AT&T, Verizon), local Internet service providers win; content owners and physical retailers lose (Tower Records, Blockbuster)
PageRank algorithm	A method for ranking web pages in terms of their popularity to supplement web search by key terms	Google is the winner (it owns the patent); traditional keyword search engines (Alta Vista) lose
Software as web service	Using the Internet to provide remote access to online software	Online software services companies (Salesforce.com) win; traditional boxed software companies (Microsoft, SAP, Oracle) lose

offering cheap digital storage for small files on small computers. Eventually, small PC hard-disk drives became the largest segment of the disk drive marketplace.

Some firms can create these technologies and ride the wave to profits, whereas others learn quickly and adapt their business; still others are obliterated because their products, services, and business models become obsolete. There are also cases when no firms benefit, and all gains go to consumers (firms fail to capture any profits). Table 3.4 provides examples of some disruptive technologies.

Disruptive technologies are tricky. Firms that invent disruptive technologies as first movers do not always benefit if they lack the resources to exploit the technology or fail to see the opportunity. The MITS Altair 8800 is widely regarded as the first PC, but its inventors did not take advantage of their first-mover status. Second movers, so-called fast followers such as IBM and Microsoft, reaped the rewards. Citibank's ATMs revolutionized retail banking, but other banks copied them. Now all banks use ATMs, and the benefits go mostly to the consumers.

3-2 How do information systems help businesses compete globally?

Look closely at your jeans or sneakers. Even if they have a U.S. label, they were probably designed in California and stitched together in Hong Kong or Guatemala, using materials from China or India. Call Microsoft Support, or Verizon Support, and chances are good you will be speaking to a customer service representative located in India.

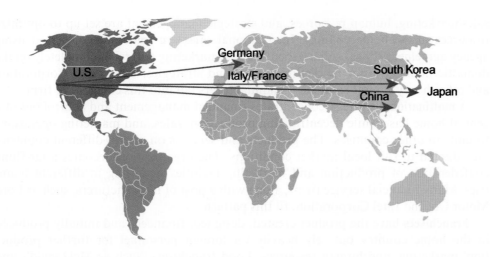

Figure 3.4
Apple iPhone's Global Supply Chain
Apple designs the iPhone in the United States and relies on suppliers in the United States, Germany, Italy, France, and South Korea for parts. Final assembly occurs in China.

Consider the path to market for an iPhone, which is illustrated in Figure 3.4. The iPhone was designed by Apple engineers in the United States, sourced with more than 100 high-tech components from around the world, and assembled in China. Companies in South Korea, Japan, France, Italy, Germany, and the United States provided components such as the applications processor, accelerator, gyroscope, electronic compass, power management chip, touch screen controller, and high-definition display screen. Foxconn, a Chinese division of Taiwan's Hon Hai Group, is in charge of manufacturing and assembly.

Firms pursuing a global strategy benefit from economies of scale and resource cost reduction (usually wage cost reduction). Apple spread design, sourcing, and production for its iPhone over multiple countries overseas to reduce tariffs, and labor costs. Digital content firms that produce Hollywood movies can sell millions more copies of DVDs of popular films by using foreign markets.

THE INTERNET AND GLOBALIZATION

Up until the mid-1990s, huge multinational firms, such as General Electric, General Motors, Toyota, and IBM, dominated competition on a global scale. These large firms could afford huge investments in factories, warehouses, and distribution centers in foreign countries and proprietary networks and systems that could operate on a global scale. The emergence of the Internet into a full-blown international communications system has drastically reduced the costs of operating on a global scale, deepening the possibilities for large companies but simultaneously creating many opportunities for small and medium-sized firms.

The global Internet, along with internal information systems, puts manufacturing firms in nearly instant contact with their suppliers. Internet telephony (see Chapter 7) permits millions of service calls to U.S. companies to be answered in India and Jamaica just as easily and cheaply as if the help desk were in New Jersey or California. Likewise, the Internet makes it possible to move very large computer files with hundreds of graphics, or complex industrial designs, across the globe in seconds.

GLOBAL BUSINESS AND SYSTEM STRATEGIES

There are four main ways of organizing businesses internationally: domestic exporter, multinational, franchiser, and transnational, each with different patterns of organizational structure or governance. In each type of global business organization, business functions may be centralized (in the home country), decentralized (to local foreign units), and coordinated (all units participate as equals).

The **domestic exporter** strategy is characterized by heavy centralization of corporate activities in the home country of origin. Production, finance/accounting, sales/marketing, human resources, and strategic management are set up to optimize resources in the home country. International sales are sometimes dispersed using agency agreements or subsidiaries, but foreign marketing still relies completely on the domestic home base for marketing themes and strategies. Caterpillar Corporation and other heavy capital equipment manufacturers fall into this category of firm.

A **multinational** strategy concentrates financial management and control out of a central home base while decentralizing production, sales, and marketing operations to units in other countries. The products and services on sale in different countries are adapted to suit local market conditions. The organization becomes a far-flung confederation of production and marketing facilities operating in different countries. Many financial service firms, along with a host of manufacturers, such as Ford Motor Co. and Intel Corporation, fit this pattern.

Franchisers have the product created, designed, financed, and initially produced in the home country but rely heavily on foreign personnel for further production, marketing, and human resources. Food franchisers, such as McDonald's and Starbucks, fit this pattern. McDonald's created a new form of fast-food chain in the United States and continues to rely largely on the United States for inspiration of new products, strategic management, and financing. Nevertheless, local production of some items, local marketing, and local recruitment of personnel are required.

Transnational firms have no single national headquarters but instead have many regional headquarters and perhaps a world headquarters. In a **transnational** strategy, nearly all the value-adding activities are managed from a global perspective without reference to national borders, optimizing sources of supply and demand wherever they appear and taking advantage of any local competitive advantages. There is a strong central management core of decision making but considerable dispersal of power and financial muscle throughout the global divisions. In 2015, many Fortune 500 companies are transnational.

Nestlé S.A., the largest food and beverage company in the world, is one of the world's most globalized companies, with 340,000 employees at 500 facilities in 197 countries. Nestlé launched a $2.4 billion initiative to adopt a single set of business processes and systems for procurement, distribution, and sales management using mySAP enterprise software. All of Nestlé's worldwide business units use the same processes and systems for making sales commitments, establishing factory production schedules, billing customers, compiling management reports, and reporting financial results. Nestlé has learned how to operate as a single unit on a global scale.

GLOBAL SYSTEM CONFIGURATION

Figure 3.5 depicts four types of systems configurations for global business organizations. *Centralized systems* are those in which systems development and operation occur totally at the domestic home base. *Duplicated systems* are those in which development occurs at the home base, but operations are handed over to autonomous units in foreign locations. *Decentralized systems* are those in which each foreign unit designs its own unique solutions and systems. *Networked systems* are those in which systems development and operations occur in an integrated and coordinated fashion across all units.

As can be seen in Figure 3.5, domestic exporters tend to have highly centralized systems in which a single domestic systems development staff develops worldwide applications. Multinationals allow foreign units to devise their own systems solutions based on local needs with few, if any, applications in common with headquarters (the exceptions being financial reporting and some telecommunications applications). Franchisers typically develop a single system, usually at the home base, and then replicate it around the world. Each unit, no matter where it is located, has identical applications. Firms such as Nestlé, organized along transnational lines, use networked systems that span multiple countries, using powerful telecommunications networks and a shared management culture that crosses cultural barriers.

SYSTEM CONFIGURATION	Strategy			
	Domestic Exporter	Multinational	Franchiser	Transnational
Centralized	X			
Duplicated			X	
Decentralized	x	X	x	
Networked		x		X

Figure 3.5
Global Business
Organization
and Systems
Configurations
*The large Xs show the
dominant patterns, and the
small Xs show the emerg-
ing patterns. For instance,
domestic exporters rely
predominantly on central-
ized systems, but there
is continual pressure and
some development of de-
centralized systems in local
marketing regions.*

3-3 How do information systems help businesses compete using quality and design?

Quality has developed from a business buzzword into a very serious goal for many companies. Quality is a form of differentiation. Companies with reputations for high quality, such as Lexus or Nordstrom, can charge premium prices for their products and services. Information systems have a major contribution to make in this drive for quality. In the services industries in particular, superior information systems and services generally enable quality strategies.

WHAT IS QUALITY?

Quality can be defined from both producer and customer perspectives. From the perspective of the producer, quality signifies conformance to specifications or the absence of variation from those specifications. The specifications for a telephone might include one that states the strength of the phone should not be weakened if the phone is dented or otherwise damaged by a drop from a four-foot height onto a wooden floor. A simple test can measure this specification.

A customer definition of quality is much broader. First, customers are concerned with the quality of the physical product—its durability, safety, ease of use, and instal-lation. Second, customers are concerned with the quality of service, by which they mean the accuracy and truthfulness of advertising, responsiveness to warranties, and ongoing product support. Finally, customer concepts of quality include psychological aspects: the company's knowledge of its products, the courtesy and sensitivity of sales and support staff, and the reputation of the product.

Today, as the quality movement in business progresses, the definition of quality is increasingly from the perspective of the customer. Customers are concerned with get-ting value for their dollar and product fitness, performance, durability, and support.

Many companies have embraced the concept of **total quality management (TQM)**. TQM makes quality the responsibility of all people and functions within an organiza-tion. TQM holds that the achievement of quality control is an end in itself. Everyone is expected to contribute to the overall improvement of quality—the engineer who avoids design errors, the production worker who spots defects, the sales representa-tive who presents the product properly to potential customers, and even the secretary who avoids typing mistakes. TQM derives from quality management concepts that American quality experts such as W. Edwards Deming and Joseph Juran developed, but the Japanese popularized it.

Another quality concept that is widely implemented today is six sigma, which Amazon.com used to reduce errors in order fulfillment. **Six sigma** is a specific mea-sure of quality, representing 3.4 defects per million opportunities. Most companies cannot achieve this level of quality but use six sigma as a goal to implement a set of methodologies and techniques for improving quality and reducing costs. Studies have repeatedly shown that the earlier in the business cycle a problem is eliminated, the less it costs the company. Thus, quality improvements not only raise the level of prod-uct and service quality but can also lower costs.

HOW INFORMATION SYSTEMS IMPROVE QUALITY

Let's examine some of the ways companies face the challenge of improving quality to see how information systems can be part of the process.

Reduce Cycle Time and Simplify the Production Process

Studies have shown that one of the best ways to reduce quality problems is to reduce **cycle time**, which refers to the total elapsed time from the beginning of a process to its end. Shorter cycle times mean that problems are caught earlier in the process, often before the production of a defective product is completed, saving some of the hidden production costs. Finally, finding ways to reduce cycle time often means finding ways to simplify production steps. The fewer steps in a process, the less time and opportunity for an error to occur. Information systems help eliminate steps in a process and critical time delays.

1-800-Flowers, a multimillion-dollar company selling flowers by telephone or over the web, used to be a much smaller company that had difficulty retaining its customers. It had poor service, inconsistent quality, and a cumbersome manual order-taking process. Telephone representatives had to write each order, obtain credit card approval, determine which participating florist was closest to the delivery location, select a floral arrangement, and forward the order to the florist. Each step in the manual process increased the chance of human error, and the whole process took at least a half hour. A new information system now downloads orders taken in telecenters or over the web to a central computer and electronically transmits them to local florists. Orders are more accurate and arrive at the florist within two minutes.

Benchmark

Companies achieve quality by using benchmarking to set standards for products, services, and other activities and then measuring performance against those standards. Companies may use external industry standards, standards other companies set, internally developed standards, or some combination of the three. L.L. Bean, the Freeport, Maine, clothing company, used benchmarking to achieve an order-shipping accuracy of 99.9 percent. Its old batch order fulfillment system could not handle the surging volume and variety of items to be shipped. After studying German and Scandinavian companies with leading-edge order fulfillment operations, L.L. Bean carefully redesigned its order fulfillment process and information systems so that orders could be processed as soon as they were received and shipped within 24 hours.

Use Customer Demands to Improve Products and Services

Improving customer service, and making customer service the number-one priority, will improve the quality of the product itself. Delta Airlines decided to focus on its customers, installing a customer care system at its airport gates. For each flight, the airplane seating chart, reservations, check-in information, and boarding data are linked in a central database. Airline personnel can track which passengers are on board regardless of where they checked in and use this information to help passengers reach their destination quickly, even if delays cause them to miss connecting flights.

Improve Design Quality and Precision

Computer-aided design software has made a major contribution to quality improvements in many companies, from producers of automobiles to producers of razor blades. A **computer-aided design (CAD) system** automates the creation and revision of designs, using computers and sophisticated graphics software. The software enables users to create a digital model of a part, a product, or a structure and make changes to the design on the computer without having to build physical prototypes.

For example, Ford Motor Company used a computer simulation that came up with the most efficient design possible for an engine cylinder. Engineers altered that design to account for manufacturing constraints and tested the revised design on the computer, using models with decades of data on material properties and engine performance. Ford then created the physical mold to make a real part that could be

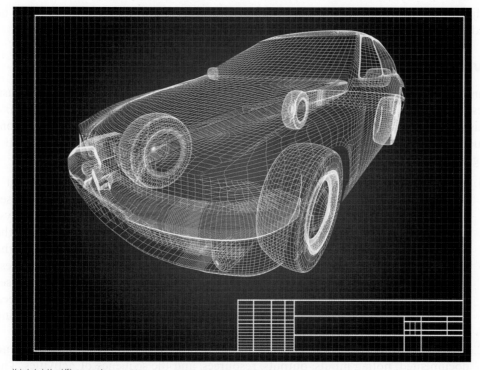

Yakobchuk Vasyl/Shutterstock

Computer-aided design (CAD) systems improve the quality and precision of product design by performing much of the design and testing work on the computer.

bolted onto an engine for further testing. The entire process took days instead of months and cost thousands of dollars instead of millions.

CAD systems can supply data for **3-D printing**, also known as additive manufacturing, which uses machines to make solid objects, layer by layer, from specifications in a digital file. Unlike traditional techniques, by which objects are cut or drilled from molds, resulting in some wasted materials, 3-D printing lets workers model an object on a computer and print it out with plastic, metal, or composite materials. 3-D printing is currently being used for prototyping, custom manufacturing, and fashioning items with small production runs.

GE Aviation has used 3-D printers to manufacture more than 85,000 fuel nozzles for its Leap jet engines. (There are 19 nozzles per engine.) Earlier fuel nozzles had 20 parts, whereas the 3-D printed version is a single piece optimized to spray fuel into engines, is 25 percent lighter than current models, and is capable of lasting five times longer before servicing. Nike made 3-D printed cleats for the 2014 Super Bowl. The featherweight Nike Vapor Laser Talon, which Nike designed for football players running the 40-yard dash on football turf, has a 3-D printed plate and cleats.

Improve Production Precision and Tighten Production Tolerances

For many products, quality can be enhanced by making the production process more precise, thereby decreasing the amount of variation from one part to another. CAD software often produces design specifications for tooling and manufacturing processes, saving additional time and money while producing a manufacturing process with far fewer problems. The user of this software can design a more precise production system, a system with tighter tolerances, than could ever be done manually.

3-4 What is the role of business process management (BPM) in enhancing competitiveness?

Technology alone is often not enough to make organizations more competitive, efficient, or quality-oriented. The organization itself needs to be changed to take advantage of the power of information technology. These changes may require minor adjustments in work activities, but, often, entire business processes will need to be redesigned. Business process management (BPM) addresses these needs.

WHAT IS BUSINESS PROCESS MANAGEMENT?

Business process management (BPM) is an approach to business that aims to improve business processes continuously. BPM uses a variety of tools and methodologies to understand existing processes, design new processes, and optimize those processes. BPM is never concluded because continuous improvement requires continual change. Companies practicing business process management need to go through the following steps.

1. **Identify processes for change:** One of the most important strategic decisions that a firm can make is not deciding how to use computers to improve business processes but, rather, understanding which business processes need improvement. When systems are used to strengthen the wrong business model or business processes, the business can become more efficient at doing what it should not do. As a result, the firm becomes vulnerable to competitors who may have discovered the right business model. Considerable time and cost may also be spent improving business processes that have little impact on overall firm performance and revenue. Managers need to determine which business processes are the most important and how improving these processes will help business performance.

2. **Analyze existing processes:** Existing business processes should be modeled and documented, noting inputs, outputs, resources, and the sequence of activities. The process design team identifies redundant steps, paper-intensive tasks, bottlenecks, and other inefficiencies.

Figure 3.6 illustrates the as-is process for purchasing a book from a physical bookstore. Consider what happens when a customer visits a physical bookstore and searches its shelves for a book. If he or she finds the book, that person takes it to the checkout counter and pays for it by credit card, cash, or check. If the customer cannot locate the book, he or she must ask a bookstore clerk to search the shelves or check the bookstore's inventory records to see whether it is in stock. If the clerk finds the book, the customer purchases it and leaves. If the book is not available locally, the clerk inquires about ordering it for the customer, either from the bookstore's warehouse or from the book's distributor or publisher. Once the ordered book arrives at the bookstore, a bookstore employee telephones the customer with this information. The customer would have to go to the bookstore again to pick up the book and pay for it. If the bookstore cannot order the book for the customer, the customer would have to try another bookstore. You can see that this process has many steps and might require the customer to make multiple trips to the bookstore.

3. **Design the new process:** Once the existing process is mapped and measured in terms of time and cost, the process design team will try to improve the process by designing a new one. A new, streamlined to-be process will be documented and modeled for comparison with the old process.

Figure 3.7 illustrates how the book purchasing process can be redesigned by taking advantage of the Internet. The customer accesses an online bookstore over the Internet from his or her computer. He or she searches the bookstore's online catalog for the book he or she wants. If the book is available, the customer orders the book online, supplying credit card and shipping address information, and the book is delivered to the customer's home. If the online bookstore does not carry the book, the customer selects another online bookstore and searches for the book again. This process has far fewer steps than that for purchasing the book in a physical bookstore, requires much less effort from the customer, and requires fewer sales staff for customer service. The new process is therefore much more efficient and timesaving.

The new process design needs to be justified by showing how much it reduces time and cost or enhances customer service and value. Management first measures the

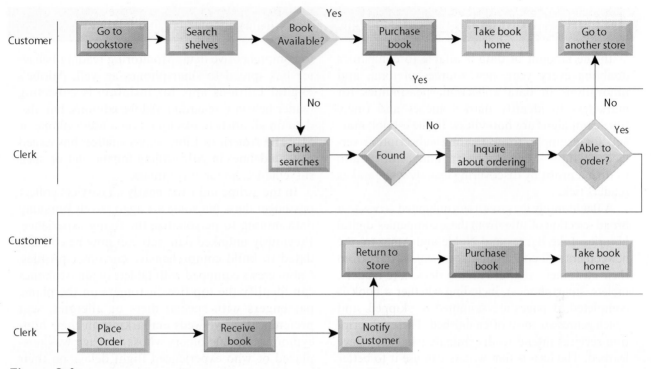

Figure 3.6
As-Is Business Process for Purchasing a Book from a Physical Bookstore
Purchasing a book from a physical bookstore requires both the seller and the customer to perform many steps.

time and cost of the existing process as a baseline. In our example, the time required for purchasing a book from a physical bookstore might range from 15 minutes (if the customer immediately finds what he or she wants) to 30 minutes if the book is in stock but sales staff has to locate it. If the book has to be ordered from another source, the process might take one or two weeks and another trip to the bookstore for the customer. If the customer lives far away from the bookstore, the time to travel to the bookstore would have to be factored in. The bookstore will have to pay the costs for maintaining a physical store and keeping the book in stock, for sales staff on site, and for shipment costs if the book has to be obtained from another location.

The new process for purchasing a book online might only take several minutes, although the customer might have to wait several days or weeks to receive the book in the mail and will have to pay a small shipping charge. Nevertheless, the customer saves time and money by not having to travel to the bookstore or make additional visits to pick up the book. Booksellers' costs are lower because they do not have to pay for a physical store location or for local inventory.

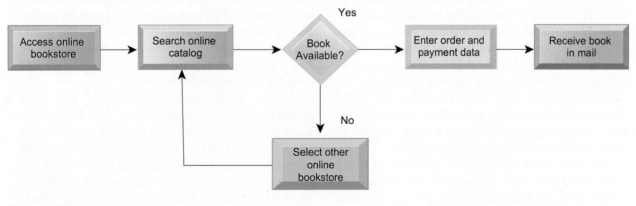

Figure 3.7
Redesigned Process for Purchasing a Book Online
Using Internet technology makes it possible to redesign the process for purchasing a book so that it only has a few steps and consumes fewer resources.

INTERACTIVE SESSION: PEOPLE | Identifying Market Niches in the Age of Big Data

With the amount of data available to companies doubling every year, new sources of data, and innovations in data collection, possibilities for marketers to identify market niches and finely tune campaigns are boundless. In the e-book market, for example, three reading subscription service startups—Scribd, Oyster, and Entitle—aim to turn a profit by discovering exactly what makes readers tick.

A flat monthly fee gives users unlimited access to a broad selection of titles from these companies' digital libraries. Like Barnes and Noble and Amazon, the newcomers will collect an assortment of data from their customers' digital reading devices (e-readers, tablets, smartphones), including whether a book is completed, if pages are skimmed or skipped, and which genres are most often finished. These subscription services intend to disseminate what they have learned. The idea is that writers can use it to better tailor their work to their readership, and book editors can use it to choose which manuscripts to publish.

When customers sign up with these services, they are informed that some of their data will be collected and used but assured that their identities will be protected. Large independent publisher Smashwords.com is enthusiastic about the value of such data to the authors who use its platform to self-publish and distribute their work. Many contemporary authors have already explored the feedback opportunities available through their own Web sites, social networking sites, and Goodreads, a user-populated database of books, annotations, and reviews now owned by Amazon. The subscription services will take this type of market research to a more quantifiable level.

Preliminary data analysis has already revealed that as the length of a mystery novel increases so does the likelihood that a reader will skip to the end to discover the resolution. Business books are less likely to be finished than biographies, most readers complete just a single chapter of a yoga book, and some of the quickest reading is recorded for romance novels, with erotica leading the pack. Shorter chapters entice readers on e-readers, tablets, and smartphones to finish a book 25 percent more often than books with long chapters.

But does book completion translate to book sales? And how will this knowledge impact the creative process? Will quality be negatively impacted to satisfy reader preferences? Before any of these questions can be answered, authors will need access to comprehensive data. Monitoring reading behavior has spread to smartphones as well. Adobe's Digital Editions app, for instance, is collecting reader behavior regarding Adobe editions, but also data on all other books found on a user's phone or PC. The American Library Association has issued new guidelines in 2015 calling for the end of such surveillance. So far, it continues.

In the airline industry, nearly all carriers collect passenger data, but some are aggressively pursuing data mining to personalize the flying experience. Previously unlinked data sets can now be consolidated to build comprehensive customer profiles. Cabin crews equipped with tablets or smartphones can identify the top five customers on the plane, passengers with special diets or allergies, seat preferences, newlyweds embarking on their honeymoon, and customers whose luggage was misplaced or who experienced flight delays on their previous flights. In-flight browsing history and Facebook likes are even used to fashion relevant marketing pitches.

This "captive audience" aspect of air travel in conjunction with the sheer volume of information airlines collect presents a unique opportunity to marketers. Allegiant Travel Company has already been able to sell show tickets, car rentals, and helicopter tours to Las Vegas travelers. United Airlines' revamp of its Web site, kiosks, and mobile app, along with its data integration initiative, have enabled it to target flyers predisposed to upgrading to an economy plus seat.

Not all customers are pleased. A user on Delta's FlyerTalk forum complained that a link from the new DL.com Web site led to a personal profile that included a lot more than her miles accumulated and home airport. Annual income, home value, and the age ranges of her children were included along with expected data such as amount spent on airfare, hotel preference, and type of credit card. The resulting negative publicity prompted Delta to apologize, but it defended its use of demographic data and data not covered under its privacy policy.

As car companies explore their Big Data opportunities, customer privacy will become an issue for them as well. Performance monitoring using vehicle Internet connections to collect fuel economy, mechanical failure, and other safety and performance metrics could soon be used to improve product engineering at many companies. What's more, onboard connections can be used to message drivers about potential breakdown issues, perhaps heading off an expensive recall. Since Ford estimates that by 2016, up to a third of all its consumer communication will occur inside vehicles, possibilities abound. Leased vehicle usage data could inform end-of-lease marketing pitches; driving pattern, schedule, and driving maneuver data could suggest routes most compatible to a driver's habits; car location data could be sent to traffic management systems to control stop lights; data from networked cars could alert other drivers to hazardous conditions and traffic jams, and current car value and payment data can advise drivers of their optimal trade-in date. According to the Government Accountability Office, all the top ten automakers in the world are now tracking and sharing driver location data.

It's not hard to foresee the privacy issues that could come into play as drivers realize that not only their location, but their every movement inside their vehicle is being tracked.

Sources: Michael Robinson, "New Privacy Guidelines for Ebooks," *American Libraries Magazine*, August 7, 2015; Rimon Christiani, "Making Summer Air Travel Less Stressful with Big Data and Mobile Technology," *Forbes*, July 15, 2015; Bob Tita, "Big Data Gives Manufacturers a New Revenue Source," *Wall Street Journal*, June 2, 2015; Rob Miller, "White House Report Sees Potential, Pitfalls of Big Data," Techcrunch.com, February 5, 2015; "E-books and Privacy Again," Chooseprivacyweek.com, October 13, 2014; Nate Hoffelder, "Adobe Is Spying on Users, Collecting Data on Their eBook Libraries," October 6, 2014; Mike Ramsey, "Auto Makers Face Questions over Privacy in Connected Cars," *Wall Street Journal*, January 16, 2014; Tim Winship, "Big Brother Unmasked as ... Delta Air Lines," smartertravel.com, January 28, 2013; Jack Nisas, "How Airlines Mine Personal Data In-Flight," *Wall Street Journal*, November 8, 2013; David Streitfeld, "As New Services Track Habits, the E-Books Are Reading You," *New York Times*, December 24, 2013.

CASE STUDY QUESTIONS

1. Describe the kinds of data being analyzed by the companies in this case.
2. How is this fine-grained data analysis improving operations and decision making in the companies described in this case? What business strategies are being supported?
3. Are there any disadvantages to mining customer data? Explain your answer.
4. How do you feel about airlines mining your in-flight data? Is this any different from companies mining your credit card purchases or Web surfing?

4. **Implement the new process:** After the new process has been thoroughly modeled and analyzed, it must be translated into a new set of procedures and work rules. New information systems or enhancements to existing systems may have to be implemented to support the redesigned process. The new process and supporting systems are rolled out into the business organization. As the business starts using this process, problems are uncovered and addressed. Employees working with the process may recommend improvements.

5. **Continuous measurement:** After a process has been implemented and optimized, it needs to be measured continually. Why? Processes may deteriorate over time as employees fall back on old methods, or they may lose their effectiveness if the business experiences other changes.

More than 100 software firms provide tools for various aspects of BPM, including IBM, Oracle, and Tibco. These tools help businesses identify and document processes requiring improvement, create models of improved processes, capture and enforce business rules for performing processes, and integrate existing systems to support new or redesigned processes. BPM software tools also provide analytics for verifying that process performance has been improved and for measuring the impact of process changes on key business performance indicators.

Business Process Reengineering

Many business process improvements are incremental and ongoing, but occasionally, more radical change is required. Our example of a physical bookstore redesigning the book purchasing process so that it can be carried out online is an example of this type of radical, far-reaching change. This radical rethinking and redesign of business processes is called **business process reengineering (BPR)**.

When properly implemented, BPR can lead to dramatic gains in productivity and efficiency, even changing the way the business is run. In some instances, it drives a paradigm shift that transforms the nature of the business itself. This actually happened in book retailing when Amazon challenged traditional physical bookstores with its online retail model. By radically rethinking the way a book can be purchased and sold, Amazon and other online bookstores have achieved remarkable efficiencies, cost reductions, and a whole new way of doing business.

BPM poses challenges. Executives report that the most significant barrier to successful business process change is organizational culture. Employees do not like unfamiliar routines and often resist change. This is especially true of business process reengineering projects because the organizational changes are so far-reaching. Managing change is neither simple nor intuitive, and companies committed to extensive process improvement need a good change management strategy (see Chapter 12).

Review Summary

3-1 **How do Porter's competitive forces model, the value chain model, synergies, core competencies, and network-based strategies help companies use information systems for competitive advantage?** In Porter's competitive forces model, the strategic position of the firm, and its strategies, are determined by competition with its traditional direct competitors. They are also greatly affected by new market entrants, substitute products and services, suppliers, and customers. Information systems help companies compete by maintaining low costs, differentiating products or services, focusing on market niche, strengthening ties with customers and suppliers, and increasing barriers to market entry with high levels of operational excellence. Information systems are most successful when the technology is aligned with business objectives.

The value chain model highlights specific activities in the business where competitive strategies and information systems will have the greatest impact. The model views the firm as a series of primary and support activities that add value to a firm's products or services. Primary activities are directly related to production and distribution, whereas support activities make the delivery of primary activities possible. A firm's value chain can be linked to the value chains of its suppliers, distributors, and customers. A value web consists of information systems that enhance competitiveness at the industry level by promoting the use of standards and industry-wide consortia and by enabling businesses to work more efficiently with their value partners.

Because firms consist of multiple business units, information systems achieve additional efficiencies or enhanced services by tying together the operations of disparate business units. Information systems help businesses use their core competencies by promoting the sharing of knowledge across business units. Information systems facilitate business models based on large networks of users or subscribers that take advantage of network economics. A virtual company strategy uses networks to link to other firms so that a company can use the capabilities of other companies to build, market, and distribute products and services. Disruptive technologies provide strategic opportunities, although first movers do not necessarily obtain long-term benefit.

3-2 **How do information systems help businesses compete globally?** Information systems and the Internet help companies operate internationally by facilitating coordination of geographically dispersed units of the company and communication with faraway customers and suppliers. There are four main strategies for organizing businesses internationally: domestic exporter, multinational, franchiser, and transnational.

3-3 **How do information systems help businesses compete using quality and design?** Information systems can enhance quality by simplifying a product or service, facilitating benchmarking, reducing product development cycle time, and increasing quality and precision in design and production.

3-4 **What is the role of business process management (BPM) in enhancing competitiveness?** Organizations often have to change their business processes to execute their business strategies successfully. If these business processes use technology, they can be redesigned to make the technology more effective. BPM combines and streamlines the steps in a business process to eliminate repetitive and redundant work and to achieve dramatic improvements in quality, service, and speed. BPM is most effective when it is used to strengthen a good business model and when it strengthens processes that have a major impact on firm performance.

Key Terms

3-D printing, 123	Core competency, 116	Primary activities, 113
Benchmarking, 114	Cycle time, 122	Quality, 121
Best practices, 114	Disruptive technologies,	Six sigma, 121
Business process	117	Support activities, 114
management (BPM), 124	Domestic exporter, 119	Switching costs, 111
Business process	Efficient customer	Total quality management
reengineering (BPR), 128	response system, 108	(TQM), 121
Competitive forces	Franchiser, 120	Transnational, 120
model, 105	Mass customization, 108	Value chain model, 113
Computer-aided design	Multinational, 120	Value web, 115
(CAD) system, 122	Network economics, 116	Virtual company, 117

MyMISLab™

To complete the problems with the ★, go to EOC Discussion Questions in the MyLab.

Review Questions

3-1 How do Porter's competitive forces model, the value chain model, synergies, core competencies, and network-based strategies help companies use information systems for competitive advantage?

- Define Porter's competitive forces model and explain how it works.
- Describe some situations in which a firm's customers have market power.
- List and describe four competitive strategies enabled by information systems that firms can pursue.
- Describe how information systems can support each of these competitive strategies and give examples.
- Explain how management of a firm can achieve alignment of IT with business objectives.
- Define and describe the value chain model.
- Explain how the value chain model can be used to identify opportunities for information systems.
- Define the value web and show how it is related to the value chain.
- Describe how the Internet has changed competitive forces and competitive advantage.

- Explain how information systems promote synergies and core competencies that enhance competitive advantage.
- Explain how businesses benefit by using network economics.
- Define the law of diminishing returns and describe some situations in which the law does not work
- Explain how disruptive technologies create strategic opportunities.

3-2 How do information systems help businesses compete globally?
- Describe how globalization has increased opportunities for businesses.
- List and describe the four main ways of organizing a business internationally and the types of systems configuration for global business organizations.

3-3 How do information systems help businesses compete using quality and design?
- Define quality and compare the producer and consumer definitions of quality.
- Define the concepts of total quality management (TQM) and six sigma.

3-4 What is the role of business process management (BPM) in enhancing competitiveness?
- Define BPM and explain how it helps firms become more competitive.
- Distinguish between BPM and business process reengineering (BPR).
- List and describe the steps companies should take to make sure BPM is successful.

Discussion Questions

✪ **3-5** Why are disruptive technologies tricky?

✪ **3-6** What are some of the issues to consider in determining whether the Internet would provide your business with a competitive advantage?

✪ **3-7** It has been said that the advantage that leading-edge retailers such as Walmart have over competitors isn't technology—it's their management. Do you agree? Why or why not?

Hands-On MIS Projects

The projects in this section give you hands-on experience identifying information systems to support a business strategy and solve a customer retention problem, using a database to improve decision making about business strategy, and using web tools to configure and price an automobile. Visit MyMISLab's Multimedia Library to access this chapter's Hands-On MIS Projects.

MANAGEMENT DECISION PROBLEMS

3-8 Marks & Spencer Group is a leading department store chain in the United Kingdom. Its retail stores sell a range of merchandise Senior management has decided that Marks & Spencer needs to tailor merchandise more to local tastes and that the colors, sizes, brands, and styles of clothing and other merchandise should be based on the sales patterns in each store. How could information systems help Marks & Spencer's management implement this new strategy? What pieces of data should these systems collect to help management make merchandising decisions that support this strategy?

3-9 Despite aggressive campaigns to attract customers with lower mobile phone prices, T-Mobile has been losing large numbers of monthly contract subscribers. Management wants to know why so many customers are leaving T-Mobile and what can be done to entice them back. Are customers deserting because of poor customer service, uneven network coverage, or wireless service charges? How can the company use information systems to help find the answer? What management decisions could be made using information from these systems?

IMPROVING DECISION MAKING: USING A DATABASE TO CLARIFY BUSINESS STRATEGY

Software skills: Database querying and reporting; database design
Business skills: Reservation systems; customer analysis

3-10 In this exercise, you'll use database software to analyze the reservation transactions for a hotel and use that information to fine-tune the hotel's business strategy and marketing activities.

In MyMISLab™, you'll find a database for hotel reservation transactions developed in Microsoft Access with information about The Waterfront Inn in Brighton, UK. At the Inn, 10 rooms overlook side streets, 10 rooms have bay windows with limited views of the ocean, and the remaining 10 rooms in the front of the hotel face the ocean. Room rates are based on room choice, length of stay, and number of guests per room. Room rates are the same for one to four guests. Fifth and sixth guests must pay an additional £20 per person per day. Guests staying for seven days or more receive a 10 percent discount on their daily room rates.

The owners currently use a manual reservation and bookkeeping system, which cannot provide management with immediate data about the hotel's daily operations and revenue. Use the database to develop reports on average length of stay per room type, average visitors per room type, base revenue per room (i.e., length of visit multiplied by the daily rate) during a specified period of time, and strongest customer base. After answering these questions, write a brief report about the Inn's current business situation and suggest future strategies.

IMPROVING DECISION MAKING: USING WEB TOOLS TO CONFIGURE AND PRICE AN AUTOMOBILE

Software skills: Internet-based software
Business skills: Researching product information and pricing

3-11 In this exercise, you will use software at car-selling websites to find product information about a car of your choice and use that information to make an important purchase decision. You will also evaluate two of these sites as selling tools.

You are interested in purchasing a new Vauxhall Corsa (or some other car of your choice). Go to the website of AutoTrader (www.autotrader.co.uk) and begin your investigation. Locate the Vauxhall Corsa. Research the various Escape models; choose one you prefer in terms of price, features, and safety ratings. Locate and read at least two reviews. Surf the website of the manufacturer, in this case Vauxhall (www.vauxhall.co.uk). Compare the information available on Vauxhall's website with that of AutoTrader for the Corsa. Try to locate the lowest price for the car you want in a local dealer's inventory. Suggest improvements for both sites.

Collaboration and Teamwork Project

Identifying Opportunities for Strategic Information Systems

3-12 With your team of three or four students, select a company described in the *Wall Street Journal, Fortune, Forbes,* or another business publication. Visit the company's website to find additional information about that company and to see how the firm is using the web. On the basis of this information, analyze the business. Include a description of the organization's features, such as important business processes, culture, structure, and environment, as well as its business strategy. Suggest strategic information systems appropriate for that particular business, including those based on Internet technology, if appropriate. If possible, use Google Docs and Google Drive or Google Sites to brainstorm, organize, and develop a presentation of your findings for the class.

BUSINESS PROBLEM-SOLVING CASE

Will Technology Save Sears?

Sears, Roebuck used to be the largest retailer in the United States, with sales representing 1 to 2 percent of the U.S. gross national product for almost 40 years after World War II. Since then, Sears has steadily lost ground to discounters such as Walmart and Target and to competitively priced specialty retailers such as Home Depot and Lowe's. Even the merger with Kmart in 2005 to create Sears Holding Company failed to stop the downward spiral in sales and market share.

Over the years, Sears had invested heavily in information technology. At one time, it spent more on information technology and networking than all other noncomputer firms in the United States except the Boeing Corporation. The company was noted for its extensive customer databases of 60 million past and present Sears credit card holders, which it used to target groups such as tool buyers, appliance buyers, and gardening enthusiasts with special promotions. For example, Sears would mail customers who purchased a washer and dryer an offer for a maintenance contract and follow up with annual contract renewal forms. These efforts did not translate into competitive advantage because Sears's cost structure was one of the highest in its industry.

In 1993, under the leadership of Arthur Martinez, Sears embarked on a $4 billion five-year store renovation program to make stores more efficient, attractive, and convenient by bringing all transactions closer to the sales floor and centralizing every store's general offices, cashiers, customer services, and credit functions. New point-of-sale (POS) terminals allowed sales staff to issue new credit cards, accept charge card payments, issue gift certificates, and report account information to card holders. The POS devices provided information such as the status of orders and availability of products, allowing associates to order out-of-stock goods directly from the sales floor. Some stores installed ATM machines to give customers cash advances against their Sears credit cards. Sears also moved its suppliers to an electronic ordering system. By linking its computerized ordering system directly to that of each supplier, Sears hoped to eliminate paper throughout the order process and expedite the flow of goods into its stores.

Sears was among the first major retailers to change the way it sold based on shifting consumer habits. For example, in 2001, Sears began testing a service that lets shoppers buy online and pick up their goods in stores—well ahead of competitors Walmart in 2007 and Target Corp. in 2013. Sears has also been out front with the introduction in 2011 of a service that lets shoppers reserve goods online and pay cash for them in store; in 2012, it launched online layaway.

Despite these improvements, Sears has lagged in reducing operating costs, keeping pace with current merchandising trends, and remodeling its 2429 stores, many of which are run down and in undesirable locations. It is still struggling to find a viable business strategy that will pull it out of its rut. The Sears company continued to use technology strategies to revive flagging sales: online shopping, mobile apps, and an Amazon.com-like marketplace with other vendors for 18 million products, along with heavy in-store promotions. So far, these efforts have not paid off, and sales have declined since the 2005 merger with Kmart. The company posted a loss of nearly $1.4 billion for 2013. Total losses between early 2011 and November 2014 amounted to almost $7 billion.

Sears continued to pin its hopes on technology, aiming for even more intensive use of technology and mining of customer data. The expectation was that deeper knowledge of customer preferences and buying patterns would make promotions, merchandising, and selling much more effective. Customers would flock to Sears stores because they would be carrying exactly what customers want.

A customer loyalty program called Shop Your Way Rewards promised customers generous free deals for repeat purchases if they agreed to share their personal shopping data with the company. Sears would not disclose how many customers signed up for Shop Your Way Rewards, but loyalty-marketing firm Colloquy estimated around 50 million people are members.

The data Sears is collecting are changing how its sales floors are arranged and how promotions are designed to attract shoppers. For example, work wear has been moved closer to where tools are sold. After data analysis showed that many jewelry customers were men who bought tools, the company created a special Valentine's Day offer for Shop Your Way Rewards members that offered $100 credit for $400 spent on jewelry.

Sears wanted to personalize marketing campaigns, coupons, and offers down to the individual customer, but its legacy systems were incapable of supporting that level of activity. To use complex analytic models on large data sets, Sears revamped its data management technology. It used to take Sears six weeks to analyze marketing campaigns for loyalty club members, using a traditional large mainframe computer and Teradata data warehouse software. With new technology called Hadoop for managing very large datasets (see Chapter 6), the processing can be completed weekly. Certain online and mobile commerce analyses can be performed daily, and targeting is much more precise, in some cases down to the individual customer.

Sears's old models were able to use 10 percent of available data, but the new models can work with 100 percent. In the past, Sears could retain data from only 90 days to two years, but with the new big data management technology, it can keep everything, increasing its chances of finding more meaningful patterns in the data. Hadoop processing is about one-third the cost of conventional relational databases. With Hadoop's massively parallel processing power, processing 2 billion records takes Sears little more than one minute longer than processing 100 million records.

Sears spent several hundred million dollars improving its stores in 2011, including technological enhancements. Woodfield Mall Sears, one of several hundred that was recently remodeled, reflects the new approach. Outdoor clothing from Lands' End dominates the area near the main mall entrance, and pastel-colored women's tops from Covington line the main hall. (Sears owns both of these brands.) Workers use iPads and iPod Touches to access online reviews for customers and check whether items are in stock. Ron Boire, who oversees Sears merchandising and store formats, believes that with a little more time and customer information, he can make the store experience much better.

Working with McKinsey & Co. consultants, Sears opened a test store in 2009 called Mygofer in Joliet, Illinois. Mygofer was touted as a revolutionary combination that would meld the convenience of the Internet with the instant gratification of a bricks-and-mortar store. The company gutted an 80,000-square-foot Kmart, but the store did not stock items for sale. The idea was to have shoppers place their orders at computers in the front of the store, then pick up their goods at a delivery bay out back. Sears Holdings CEO Edward Lampert hoped to roll out hundreds of Mygofer stores if the experiment succeeded. However, some days, more people returned goods than bought them. Shoppers didn't like the fact that they couldn't see and touch things. Sears management had projected that over four years, Mygofer would eventually generate $8 million in annual sales. Annual sales struggled to top $1 million. Lampert stated that going to a store with no

products may have been weird for shoppers, but the idea was ahead of its time. Lampert continues in the Sears tradition of trying to solve problems by ramping up new technologies, at the same time curtailing some of the mundane investments needed to keep the giant retailer generating sales.

Experts believe that experiments like Mygofer are a diversion from Sears's overarching problems: a deteriorating store network and a brand image that doesn't resonate with today's consumers. Other retailers, such as Macy's and Nordstrom, are also struggling to keep relevant in a world where shopping is steadily moving to the web. However, Macy's and Nordstrom are still profitable. Sears Holdings spends nearly $1.90 a square foot on Sears stores and roughly 60 cents a square foot on Kmart stores, according to Matt McGinley, an analyst with Evercore ISI Institutional Equities. That compares with $9.70 a square foot spent by Wal-Mart and $5.75 by Macy's. Although Sears spent more than $1 million setting up the Mygofer store in Joliet, the company was starving a profitable crosstown Kmart.

Lampert still wants to focus on technology projects that he hopes will turn Sears around, acknowledging that that today's shoppers are less likely to browse and buy in stores. One new service lets Sears customers browse for shoes and apparel online and then reserve items to try on in physical stores. Sears is also creating digital displays for products that are more likely to engage customers with reviews, instructional videos, and Consumer Reports ratings.

A service called In-Vehicle Pickup lets customers order goods online and have them delivered to them while they wait in their cars. Sear's In-Vehicle Return/Exchange in Five enables customers to return or exchange purchases in the parking lot within a guaranteed time period of five minutes. Sears improved its online ordering system so that orders could be shipped more quickly and economically by using Sears's physical stores as well as distribution centers to fulfill them.

Sears is refashioning its consumer electronic departments as Connected Solutions shops that sell devices such as a Craftsman garage door that can be opened or closed remotely with a smartphone and baby monitors that can connect to the Internet. The Connected Solutions shops are being tested at three Chicago stores before being rolled out more widely.

Sears is also piloting radio-frequency tags in 15 stores in the hope of increasing sales and margins by giving a more accurate picture of the merchandise stores have in stock. Management said this fall that initiatives like digital signs and radio tags on inventory could bring in $500 million a year in savings and increased sales.

According to Don Ingham, a portfolio manager at Tenth Avenue Holdings, Sears Holdings is poised to benefit from its moves to cut its physical space and increase its e-commerce operations. Sear's poor financial position prompted it to start embracing e-commerce much earlier than other retailers to reduce its physical storefront presence. Sears' efforts should pay off in a few years.

Other experts disagree. Despite bold attempts to innovate with technology, execution is where Sears has stumbled, according to Credit Suisse analyst Gary Balter. Balter believes the company didn't invest enough in systems to make sure all its ideas worked properly, and it has not attracted younger, tech-savvy customers who want to shop that way. By all accounts, Sears remains a fading brand saddled with too many nonperforming physical stores in undesirable locations.

Even with better data analytics, knowledge of customers, loyalty programs, and e-commerce innovations, the question still lingers about whether Sears is using technology effectively to solve its enormous business problems. Is it truly able to offer customers personalized promotions and are they working? What is the business impact? Where are the numbers to show that Sears's big bet on technology is making the company more profitable? Will Sear's technological forays be able to halt its downward spiral?

Sources: "How Sears Holding Company Optimized Online Fulfillment," *SupplyChainBrain*, January 27, 2015; Mark Nacinovic, "Sears Is Poised for a Rebound: Tenth Avenue Portfolio Manager," thestreet.com, January 2, 2015; www.sears.com, accessed January 23, 2015; Suzanne Kapner, "Sears Bets Big on Technology," *Wall Street Journal*, December 16, 2014; Kate Kaye," How Sears Got into the Data-Services Game," *AdAge*, April1, 2013; and Miguel Bustillo, "The Plan to Rescue Sears," *Wall Street Journal*, March 12, 2012.

Case Study Questions

3-13 Analyze Sears, using the competitive forces and value chain models.

3-14 What was the problem facing Sears? What people, organization, and technology factors contributed to this problem?

3-15 What solution did Sears select? What was the role of technology in this solution?

3-16 How effective was the solution Sears selected? Explain your answer.

MyMISLab

Go to the Assignments section of your MyLab to complete these writing exercises.

3-17 Describe the impact of the Internet on each of the five competitive forces.

3-18 Describe how computer-aided design (CAD) systems improve quality and operational efficiency.

Chapter 3 References

Bell, David R., Santiago Galleno, and Antonio Moreno. "How to Win in an Omnichannel World," *MIT Sloan Management Review* (Fall 2014).

Chen, Daniel Q., Martin Mocker, David S. Preston, and Alexander Teubner. "Information Systems Strategy: Reconceptualization, Measurement, and Implications," *MIS Quarterly* 34, No. 2 (June 2010).

Christensen, Clayton. *Competitive Advantage: The Revolutionary Book That Will Change the Way You Do Business.* (New York: HarperCollins, 2003.)

D'Aveni, Richard. "The 3-D Printing Revolution," *Harvard Business Review* (May 2015).

Davenport, Thomas H., and Jeanne G. Harris. *Competing on Analytics: The New Science of Winning.* (Boston: Harvard Business School Press, 2007.)

De Jong, Jeroen P.J., and Erik de Bruijn. "Innovation Lessons from 3-D Printing," *MIT Sloan Management Review* 54, No. 2 (Winter 2013).

Dedrick, Jason, Kenneth L. Kraemer, and Eric Shih. "Information Technology and Productivity in Developed and Developing Countries," *Journal of Management Information Systems* 30, No. 1 (Summer 2013).

Downes, Larry, and Paul F.Nunes. "Big-Bang Disruption," *Harvard Business Review* (March 2013).

Drnevich, Paul L., and David C. Croson. "Information Technology and Business-Level Strategy: Toward an Integrated Theoretical Perspective," *MIS Quarterly* 37, No. 2 (June 2013).

El Sawy, Omar A. *Redesigning Enterprise Processes for E-Business*. (New York: McGraw-Hill, 2001.)

Gerow, Jennifer E., Varun Grover, Jason Thatcher, and Philip L. Roth. "Looking Toward the Future of IT–Business Strategic Alignment Through the Past: A Meta-Analysis," *MIS Quarterly* 38, No. 4 (December 2014).

Hammer, Michael, and James Champy. *Reengineering the Corporation*. (New York: HarperCollins, 1993.)

Hessman, Travis. "Rethink Everything: 3-D Printing and the Product Design Revolution," *Industry Week* (August 25, 2014).

Hirt, Martin, and Paul Willmott. "Strategic Principles for Competing in the Digital Age," *McKinsey Quarterly* (May 2014).

Iansiti, Marco, and Karim R. Lakhani. "Digital Ubiquity: How Connections, Sensors, and Data Are Revolutionizing Business," *Harvard Business Review* (November 2014).

Iansiti, Marco, and Roy Levien. "Strategy as Ecology," *Harvard Business Review* (March 2004).

Kauffman, Robert J., and Yu-Ming Wang. "The Network Externalities Hypothesis and Competitive Network Growth," *Journal of Organizational Computing and Electronic Commerce* 12, No. 1 (2002).

Luftman, Jerry. *Competing in the Information Age: Align in the Sand*, 2nd ed. (New York: Oxford University Press, 2003.)

McAfee, Andrew, and Erik Brynjolfsson. "Investing in the IT That Makes a Competitive Difference," *Harvard Business Review* (July/August 2008).

McLaren, Tim S., Milena M. Head, Yufei Yuan, and Yolande E. Chan. "A Multilevel Model for Measuring Fit Between a Firm's Competitive Strategies and Information Systems Capabilities," *MIS Quarterly* 35, No. 4 (December 2011).

Mithas, Sunil, Ali Tafti, and Will Mitchell. "How a Firm's Competitive Environment and Digital Strategic Posture Influence Digital Business Strategy," *MIS Quarterly* 37, No. 2 (June 2013).

Piccoli, Gabriele, and Blake Ives. "Review: IT-Dependent Strategic Initiatives and Sustained Competitive Advantage: A Review and Synthesis of the Literature," *MIS Quarterly* 29, No. 4 (December 2005).

Porter, Michael. *Competitive Advantage*. (New York: Free Press, 1985.)

_____ . "Strategy and the Internet," *Harvard Business Review* (March 2001).

Porter, Michael E., and James E. Heppelmann. "How Smart, Connected Products Are Transforming Competition," *Harvard Business Review* (November 2014).

Porter, Michael E., and Scott Stern. "Location Matters," *Sloan Management Review* 42, No. 4 (Summer 2001).

Rigby, Darrell. "Digital-Physical Mashups," *Harvard Business Review* (September 2014).

Shapiro, Carl, and Hal R. Varian. *Information Rules*. (Boston: Harvard Business School Press, 1999.)

Tallon, Paul P. "Value Chain Linkages and the Spillover Effects of Strategic Information Technology Alignment: A Process-Level View," *Journal of Management Information Systems* 28, No. 3 (Winter 2014).

Weill, Peter and Stephen L. Weorner. "Thriving in an Increasingly Digital Ecosystem." MIT Sloan Management Review 56 No. 4 (Summer 2014).

Ethical and Social Issues in Information Systems

LEARNING OBJECTIVES

After reading this chapter, you will be able to answer the following questions:

4-1   What ethical, social, and political issues are raised by information systems?

4-2   What specific principles for conduct can be used to guide ethical decisions?

4-3   Why do contemporary information systems technology and the Internet pose challenges to the protection of individual privacy and intellectual property?

4-4   How have information systems affected laws for establishing accountability and liability and the quality of everyday life?

CHAPTER CASES

Content Pirates Sail the Web

Monitoring in the Workplace

Big Data Gets Personal: Behavioral Targeting

Facebook Privacy: What Privacy?

VIDEO CASES

Case 1: What Net Neutrality Means for You

Case 2: Facebook Privacy: Social Network Data Mining

Case 3: Data Mining for Terrorists and Innocents

Instructional Video:

Viktor Mayer Schönberger on the Right to Be Forgotten

CONTENT PIRATES SAIL THE WEB

More than 11 million HBO subscribers watched each episode of *Game of Thrones* in 2014, but more than 4.5 million were able to watch the same shows without paying a cent. They were watching pirated versions of each episode that were made available by companies specializing in distributing digital content for free without paying the owners and creators of that content for using it. Television shows, music, movies, and videogames have all been plundered this way.

Such "content pirates" have sailed the World Wide Web since its earliest days, but today they are bolder, faster and better equipped than ever. The antipiracy and security firm Irdeto detected over 21 billion instances of pirated online content in 2014, a 45 percent increase from 2013.

Pirated content threatens television industry profits, much of which comes from subscription fees on cable channels like HBO and USA. Viewers watching pirated versions of shows are less likely to pay for cable subscriptions or to buy movies or rent them from services such as Netflix. According to one industry estimate, pirated content costs the U.S. economy $30 billion a year, including theft of content, lost entertainment jobs and taxes lost to federal and state governments. Academic research puts the direct loss at only $3 billion, not including impacts on lost employment.

The explosion in pirated TV shows and movies has been made possible by faster Internet speeds. Longer videos can be downloaded within minutes from peer-to-peer networks and online cyberlockers. A great deal of illegal content, including live sports, is also available through instant streaming. Online ad networks also help finance piracy by placing ads on sites that traffic in unauthorized content. A study commissioned in part by Google found that 86 percent of peer-to-peer sharing sites depend on advertising for income.

One of the biggest content pirate sites was The Pirate Bay, based in Sweden, which offered free access to millions of copyrighted songs and thousands of copy-

© Eldeiv/Shutterstock

righted movies. The Pirate Bay used BitTorrent file-sharing technology, which breaks up large computer files into small pieces so they can zip across the Web. In April 2014, The Pirate Bay had over 6.5 million registered users and was the 87th most trafficked site in the world. There have been many legal efforts to shut it down, and to a large extent, The Pirate Bay has been shut down, its owners and creators either in jail, or hiding. A pirate competitor, cyberlocker site MegaUpload, has also been disrupted. But the technology of piracy keeps evolving: in 2015 millions of people can use smartphone apps like Periscope and Meerkat to stream live TV shows and movies to millions of Twitter, Facebook, and YouTube viewers. Anyone can be a pirate today, no special training is needed.

What can be done to stop this pirating? Google adjusted its search algorithm to obscure search results for sites with pirated content. NBCUniversal uses armies of automated "crawlers" to scour the Web for unauthorized videos and also applies "content recognition" technology to its programming, which it then passes on to video sites like YouTube to help block illegal uploads. NBC sends out digital snapshots of its shows to YouTube and other video sites to prevent users from putting up copyrighted shows. The five major Internet service providers, including NBC's parent company, Comcast, initiated an alert system which notifies users suspected of piracy and results in progressive penalties, including slowed Web access in some cases. Digital content owners are taking much harder stance with advertising networks and payment platforms supporting piracy to encourage them to close down ad-funded pirate sites. Stopping thousands of smartphone users from streaming live TV shows is much harder.

On a positive note, new technologies and services have made pirated content less attractive. High-quality content now can be streamed for a small fee to both home televisions and mobile devices. Apple's iTunes made buying individual songs inexpensive and easy, while new subscription-based services such as Spotify, Pandora, and Apple Music have attracted 40 million paying subscribers. Netflix and other video services offer access to movies and television shows at low prices. Right now content pirates are still sailing, but new and better ways to listen to music and view videos may eventually put them out of business or at least stem their growth. Technology cuts both ways.

Sources: Nick Wingfield and Emily Steel, "With Boxing Match, Video Piracy Battle Enters Latest Round: Mobile Apps," New York Times May 4, 2015; Caitlin Dewey, "The Future of Online Piracy Is Easy, Free and Already in Your Pocket," Washington Post, April 15, 2015; "Irdeto Reveals 385% Spike in Piracy Worldwide," Irdeto Inc., Press Release, February 19, 2015; Josh Peter, "Digital Pirates Steal Signals, Money From Leagues," USA TODAY, October 8, 2014; Jack Marshall, "More Ad Dollars Flow to Pirated Video," Wall Street Journal, May 7, 2014; Adam Nightingale, "Will 2014 Be the Year of IPTV Streaming Piracy? RapidTVNews.com, accessed April 11, 2014; www.alexa.com, accessed April 10, 2014; Christopher S. Stuart, "As TV Pirates Run Rampant, TV Studios Dial Up Pursuit," The Wall Street Journal, March 3, 2013; "Pirate Bay Sails to the Caribbean," I4U News, May 2, 2013; and L. Gordon Crovitz, "A Six-Strike Rule for Internet Privacy," The Wall Street Journal, March 3, 2013..

The prevalence and brazen activities of "content pirates" described in the chapter-opening case show that technology can be a double-edged sword. It can be the source of many benefits, including the ability to share and transmit legitimate photos, music, videos, and information over the Internet at high speeds. But, at the same time, digital technology creates new opportunities for breaking the law or taking benefits away from others, including owners of valuable intellectual property, such as music, videos, and television shows that are protected by copyright law.

The chapter-opening diagram calls attention to important points raised by this case and this chapter. Content pirating has become rampant because of opportunities created by broadband communications technology and the global nature of the Internet. Various policies and technology solutions have been put in place to put a stop to content piracy, but the practice still prevails. New technology-based products and services that make online content purchase and downloads very quick and inexpensive may eventually provide a solution.

This case illustrates an ethical dilemma because it shows two sets of interests at work— the interests of people and organizations that have worked to develop intellectual property and need to be rewarded versus those of groups who fervently believe the Internet should foster the free exchange of content and ideas. As a manager, you will need to be sensitive to both the positive and negative impacts of information systems for your firm, employees and customers. You will need to learn how to resolve ethical dilemmas involving information systems.

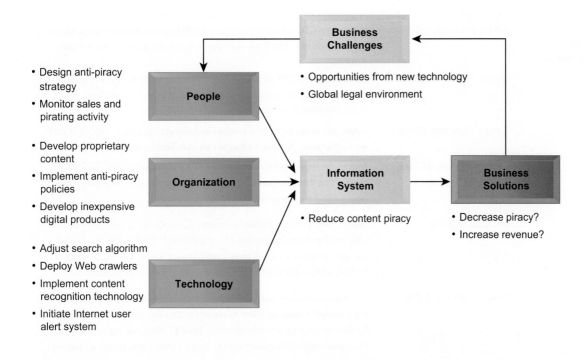

- Design anti-piracy strategy
- Monitor sales and pirating activity

- Develop proprietary content
- Implement anti-piracy policies
- Develop inexpensive digital products

- Adjust search algorithm
- Deploy Web crawlers
- Implement content recognition technology
- Initiate Internet user alert system

Business Challenges
- Opportunities from new technology
- Global legal environment

People

Organization

Technology

Information System
- Reduce content piracy

Business Solutions
- Decrease piracy?
- Increase revenue?

Here are some questions to think about: Does analyzing big data about people create an ethical dilemma? Why or why not? Should there be new privacy laws to protect individuals from being targeted by companies analyzing big data? Why or why not?

4-1 What ethical, social, and political issues are raised by information systems?

In the past 10 years, we have witnessed, arguably, one of the most ethically challenging periods for U.S. and global business. Table 4.1 provides a small sample of recent cases demonstrating failed ethical judgment by senior and middle managers. These lapses in ethical and business judgment occurred across a broad spectrum of industries.

In today's new legal environment, managers who violate the law and are convicted will most likely spend time in prison. U.S. federal sentencing guidelines adopted in 1987 mandate that federal judges impose stiff sentences on business executives based on the monetary value of the crime, the presence of a conspiracy to prevent discovery of the crime, the use of structured financial transactions to hide the crime, and failure to cooperate with prosecutors (U.S. Sentencing Commission, 2004).

Although business firms would, in the past, often pay for the legal defense of their employees enmeshed in civil charges and criminal investigations, firms are now encouraged to cooperate with prosecutors to reduce charges against the entire firm for obstructing investigations. These developments mean that, more than ever, as a manager or an employee, you will have to decide for yourself what constitutes proper legal and ethical conduct.

Although these major instances of failed ethical and legal judgment were not masterminded by information systems departments, information systems were instrumental in many of these frauds. In many cases, the perpetrators of these crimes artfully used financial reporting information systems to bury their decisions from public scrutiny in the vain hope they would never be caught.

We deal with the issue of control in information systems in Chapter 8. In this chapter, we will talk about the ethical dimensions of these and other actions based on the use of information systems.

TABLE 4.1

Recent Examples of
Failed Ethical Judgment by
Senior Managers

Volkswagen Group (2015)	Volkswagen CEO admits the company has lied to regulators and the public on nitrous oxide emissions levels in its diesel engines for a period of ten years.
General Motors Inc. (2015)	General Motors CEO admits the firm covered up faulty ignition switches for more than a decade, resulting in the deaths of at least 114 customers. The firm has recalled 8.4 million cars in North America.
Takata Corporation (2015)	Takata executives admit they covered up faulty airbags used in millions of cars over many years. To date, 34 million cars have been recalled.
Citigroup, JPMorgan Chase, Barclays, UBS (2012)	Four of the largest money center banks in the world plead guilty to criminal charges that they manipulated the LIBOR interest rate used to establish loan rates throughout the world.
SAC Capital (2013)	SAC Capital, a hedge fund led by founder Steven Cohen, pleads guilty to insider trading charges and agrees to pay a record $1.2 billion penalty. The firm was also forced to leave the money management business. Individual traders for SAC were found guilty of criminal charges and were sentenced to prison.
GlaxoSmithKline LLC (2012)	The global health care giant admitted to unlawful and criminal promotion of certain prescription drugs, its failure to report certain safety data, and its civil liability for alleged false price reporting practices. Fined $3 billion, the largest health care fraud settlement in U.S. history and the largest payment ever by a drug company.
McKinsey & Company (2012)	CEO Rajat Gupta heard on tapes leaking insider information; found guilty in 2012 and sentenced to two years in prison.
Bank of America (2012)	Federal prosecutors accused Bank of America and its affiliate, Countrywide Financial, of defrauding government-backed mortgage agencies by rapidly issuing loans without proper controls. Prosecutors sought $1 billion in penalties.

Ethics refers to the principles of right and wrong that individuals, acting as free moral agents, use to make choices to guide their behaviors. Information systems raise new ethical questions for both individuals and societies because they create opportunities for intense social change and, thus, threaten existing distributions of power, money, rights, and obligations. Like other technologies, such as steam engines, electricity, the telephone, and the radio, information technology can be used to achieve social progress, but it can also be used to commit crimes and threaten cherished social values. The development of information technology will produce benefits for many and costs for others.

Ethical issues in information systems have been given new urgency by the rise of the Internet and e-commerce. Internet and digital firm technologies make it easier than ever to assemble, integrate, and distribute information, unleashing new concerns about the appropriate use of customer information, the protection of personal privacy, and the protection of intellectual property.

Other pressing ethical issues that information systems raise include establishing accountability for the consequences of information systems, setting standards to safeguard system quality that protects the safety of the individual and society, and preserving values and institutions considered essential to the quality of life in an information society. When using information systems, it is essential to ask, "What is the ethical and socially responsible course of action?"

A MODEL FOR THINKING ABOUT ETHICAL, SOCIAL, AND POLITICAL ISSUES

Ethical, social, and political issues are closely linked. The ethical dilemma you may face as a manager of information systems typically is reflected in social and political debate. One way to think about these relationships is shown in Figure 4.1. Imagine society as

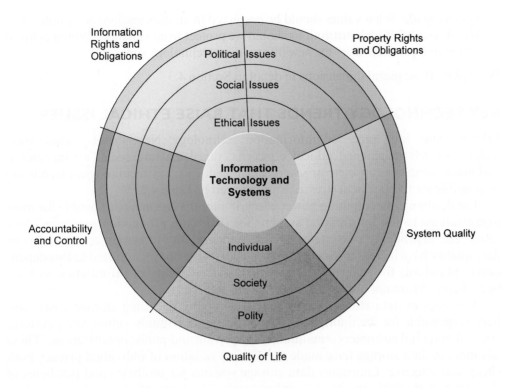

Figure 4.1
The Relationship Between Ethical, Social, And Political Issues in An Information Society
The introduction of new information technology has a ripple effect, raising new ethical, social, and political issues that must be dealt with on the individual, social, and political levels. These issues have five moral dimensions: information rights and obligations, property rights and obligations, system quality, quality of life, and accountability and control.

a more or less calm pond on a summer day, a delicate ecosystem in partial equilibrium with individuals and with social and political institutions. Individuals know how to act in this pond because social institutions (family, education, organizations) have developed well-honed rules of behavior, and these are supported by laws developed in the political sector that prescribe behavior and promise sanctions for violations. Now toss a rock into the center of the pond. What happens? Ripples, of course.

Imagine instead that the disturbing force is a powerful shock of new information technology and systems hitting a society more or less at rest. Suddenly, individual actors are confronted with new situations often not covered by the old rules. Social institutions cannot respond overnight to these ripples—it may take years to develop etiquette, expectations, social responsibility, politically correct attitudes, or approved rules. Political institutions also require time before developing new laws and often require the demonstration of real harm before they act. In the meantime, you may have to act. You may be forced to act in a legal gray area.

We can use this model to illustrate the dynamics that connect ethical, social, and political issues. This model is also useful for identifying the main moral dimensions of the information society, which cut across various levels of action—individual, social, and political.

FIVE MORAL DIMENSIONS OF THE INFORMATION AGE

The major ethical, social, and political issues that information systems raise include the following moral dimensions.

- *Information rights and obligations* What **information rights** do individuals and organizations possess with respect to themselves? What can they protect?
- *Property rights and obligations* How will traditional intellectual property rights be protected in a digital society in which tracing and accounting for ownership are difficult and ignoring such property rights is so easy?
- *Accountability and control* Who can and will be held accountable and liable for the harm done to individual and collective information and property rights?
- *System quality* What standards of data and system quality should we demand to protect individual rights and the safety of society?

- *Quality of life* What values should be preserved in an information- and knowledge-based society? Which institutions should we protect from violation? Which cultural values and practices does the new information technology support?

We explore these moral dimensions in detail in Section 4.3.

KEY TECHNOLOGY TRENDS THAT RAISE ETHICAL ISSUES

Ethical issues long preceded information technology. Nevertheless, information technology has heightened ethical concerns, taxed existing social arrangements, and made some laws obsolete or severely crippled. Five key technological trends are responsible for these ethical stresses, summarized in Table 4.2.

The doubling of computing power every 18 months has made it possible for most organizations to use information systems for their core production processes. As a result, our dependence on systems and our vulnerability to system errors and poor data quality have increased. Social rules and laws have not yet adjusted to this dependence. Standards for ensuring the accuracy and reliability of information systems (see Chapter 8) are not universally accepted or enforced.

Advances in data storage techniques and rapidly declining storage costs have been responsible for the multiplying databases on individuals—employees, customers, and potential customers—maintained by private and public organizations. These advances in data storage have made the routine violation of individual privacy both cheap and effective. Enormous data storage systems for terabytes and petabytes of data are now available on-site or as online services for firms of all sizes to use in identifying customers.

Advances in data analysis techniques for large pools of data are another technological trend that heightens ethical concerns because companies and government agencies can find out highly detailed personal information about individuals. With contemporary data management tools (see Chapter 6), companies can assemble and combine the myriad pieces of information about you stored on computers much more easily than in the past.

Think of all the ways you generate digital information about yourself—credit card purchases; telephone calls; magazine subscriptions; video rentals; mail-order purchases; banking records; local, state, and federal government records (including court and police records); and visits to websites. Put together and mined properly, this information could reveal not only your credit information but also your driving habits, your tastes, your associations, what you read and watch, and your political interests.

Companies purchase relevant personal information from these sources to help them more finely target their marketing campaigns. Chapters 6 and 11 describe how companies can analyze large pools of data from multiple sources to identify buying

---

TABLE 4.2

Technology Trends That
Raise Ethical Issues

Trend	Impact
Computing power doubles every 18 months	More organizations depend on computer systems for critical operations and become more vulnerable to system failures.
Data storage costs rapidly decline	Organizations can easily maintain detailed databases on individuals. There are no limits on the data collected about you.
Data analysis advances	Companies can analyze vast quantities of data gathered on individuals to develop detailed profiles of individual behavior. Large-scale population surveillance is enabled.
Networking advances	The cost of moving data and making it accessible from anywhere falls exponentially. Access to data becomes more difficult to control.
Mobile device growth impact	Individual cell phones may be tracked without user consent or knowledge. The always-on device becomes a tether.

© Andriy Popov/123RF

Credit card purchases can make personal information available to market researchers, telemarketers, and direct mail companies. Advances in information technology facilitate the invasion of privacy.

patterns of customers rapidly and suggest individual responses. The use of computers to combine data from multiple sources and create digital dossiers of detailed information on individuals is called **profiling**.

For example, several thousand of the most popular websites allow DoubleClick (owned by Google), an Internet advertising broker, to track the activities of their visitors in exchange for revenue from advertisements based on visitor information DoubleClick gathers. DoubleClick uses this information to create a profile of each online visitor, adding more detail to the profile as the visitor accesses an associated DoubleClick site. Over time, DoubleClick can create a detailed dossier of a person's spending and computing habits on the web that is sold to companies to help them target their web ads more precisely. The top 50 websites in the United States contain on average more than 100 tracking programs advertising firms install to track your online behavior.

LexisNexis Risk Solutions (formerly ChoicePoint) gathers data from police, criminal, and motor vehicle records, credit and employment histories, current and previous addresses, professional licenses, and insurance claims to assemble and maintain dossiers on almost every adult in the United States. The company sells this personal information to businesses and government agencies. Demand for personal data is so enormous that data broker businesses such as Risk Solutions are flourishing. The two largest credit card networks, Visa Inc. and MasterCard Inc., have agreed to link credit card purchase information with consumer social network and other information to create customer profiles that could be sold to advertising firms. In 2014, Visa processed more than 53 billion transactions a year, and MasterCard processed more than 36 billion transactions. Currently, this transactional information is not linked with consumer Internet activities.

A data analysis technology called **nonobvious relationship awareness (NORA)** has given both the government and the private sector even more powerful profiling capabilities. NORA can take information about people from many disparate sources, such as employment applications, telephone records, customer listings, and wanted lists, and correlate relationships to find obscure connections that might help identify criminals or terrorists (see Figure 4.2).

NORA technology scans data and extracts information as the data are being generated so that it could, for example, instantly discover a man at an airline ticket counter who shares a phone number with a known terrorist before that person boards an airplane. The technology is considered a valuable tool for homeland security but does have privacy implications because it can provide such a detailed picture of the activities and associations of a single individual.

An example of how digital government and private industry not only use the same data mining techniques to identify and track individuals but, in cases of national

Figure 4.2
Nonobvious
Relationship
Awareness (NORA)
*NORA technology can take
information about people
from disparate sources and
find obscure, nonobvious
relationships. It might
discover, for example, that
an applicant for a job at a
casino shares a telephone
number with a known
criminal and issue an alert
to the hiring manager.*

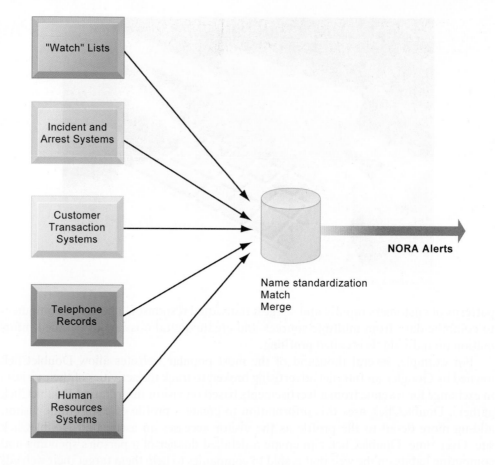

security, closely cooperate with one another in gathering data was provided by the unauthorized release of documents describing the digital surveillance activities of the U.S. National Security Agency (NSA).

Finally, advances in networking, including the Internet, promise to reduce greatly the costs of moving and accessing large quantities of data and open the possibility of mining large pools of data remotely by using small desktop machines, mobile devices, and cloud servers, permitting an invasion of privacy on a scale and with a precision heretofore unimaginable.

4-2 What specific principles for conduct can be used to guide ethical decisions?

Ethics is a concern of humans who have freedom of choice. Ethics is about individual choice: When faced with alternative courses of action, what is the correct moral choice? What are the main features of ethical choice?

BASIC CONCEPTS: RESPONSIBILITY, ACCOUNTABILITY, AND LIABILITY

Ethical choices are decisions made by individuals who are responsible for the consequences of their actions. **Responsibility** is a key element of ethical action. Responsibility means that you accept the potential costs, duties, and obligations for the decisions you make. **Accountability** is a feature of systems and social institutions; it means that mechanisms are in place to determine who took action, and who is responsible. Systems and institutions in which it is impossible to find out who took what action are inherently incapable of ethical analysis or ethical action. **Liability**

INTERACTIVE SESSION: PEOPLE   Monitoring in the Workplace

There may be only 11 players on the pitch during a match, but the Blackburn Rovers Football Club in the United Kingdom employs more than 800 people. As with any modern organization, computers are at the heart of running an efficient business. Most of the club's computers are housed with the administration department at the Ewood Park office, but others can be found at the club's training center and soccer academy.

The club decided to install a software product called Spector 360, which it obtained from the Manchester-based company Snapguard. According to Snapguard's sales literature, the product enables company-wide monitoring of employee PC and Internet usage. Previously, the club had tried to introduce an acceptable use policy (AUP), but initial discussions with employees stalled, and the policy was never implemented. Early trials of Spector 360 showed that some employees were abusing the easygoing nature of the workplace to spend most of their day surfing the Web, using social networking sites, and taking up a huge amount of bandwidth for downloads.

Before officially implementing the monitoring software, the AUP was resurrected. The policy was also made part of the terms and conditions of employment. Understandably, some employees were annoyed at the concept of being watched, but the software was installed anyway. According to Ben Hayler, Senior Systems Administrator at Blackburn Rovers, Spector 360 has definitely restored order, increasing productivity and reducing activity on non-business apps.

Reports provided by Spector 360 can show managers the following: excessive use of Facebook, Twitter, and other social networking sites; visits to adult sites or shopping sites; use of chat services; the printing or saving of confidential information; and staff login and logout times. Managers can also use the software to drill down to look at patterns of usage, generate screen snapshots, or even log individual keystrokes.

The software can also be used to benefit employees. For example, because it can log exactly what an employee is doing, the system can help in staff training and troubleshooting, because it is easy to track exactly what caused a particular problem to occur.

In the United States there is also very little limitation on employee monitoring as long as the monitoring is related to job performance. Employee knowledge is desirable, but not necessary, especially if criminal behavior is involved. With portable cameras and an explosion of sensors that employees may be asked to wear, so-called "sociometric" badges are being introduced in some locations. These badges are equipped with microphones, GPS location sensors, and accelerometers to measure the detailed behavior of employees and their conversations. Among the more recent findings are that employees are more productive and far less likely to quit when they have more time to interact with other employees. More coffee breaks were recommended! A recent research paper found that workplace monitoring with video cameras in restaurants had very strong positive impacts on revenues, not by reducing suspected theft, but by increasing the motivation of wait staff to sell more drinks and special foods. On average, restaurant revenues expanded by nearly $3,000 per month. Employee tips also grew with the greater sales effort.

However, what is the wider view of the monitoring of employees in the workplace? According to the Citizens Advice Bureau (a free information and advice service for UK residents), the following are some of the ways that employers monitor their employees in the workplace: recording the workplace on CCTV cameras, opening mail or e-mail, using automated software to check e-mail, checking telephone logs or recording telephone calls, checking logs of Web sites visited, videoing outside the workplace, getting information from credit reference agencies, and collecting information from point-of-sale terminals.

Although this list may look formidable, there is no argument that the employer has a right to ensure that his or her employees are behaving in a manner that is not illegal or harmful to the company. However, under UK data protection law, the employer must ensure that the monitoring is justified and take into account any negative effects the monitoring may have on staff. Monitoring for the sake of it is not allowed. Secret monitoring without employees' knowledge is usually illegal.

In a case that went before the European Court of Human Rights in 2007 (*Copeland v. the United Kingdom*), Ms. Copeland, who was an employee of Carmarthenshire College, claimed that her privacy had been violated. She was a personal assistant to the principal and also worked closely with the deputy principal, who instigated monitoring and analysis of her telephone bills, Web sites visited, and e-mail communication. The deputy principal wanted to determine whether Copeland was making excessive use of the college's services. The European Court ruled in her favor, stating that her personal Internet usage was deemed to be under the definitions of the Convention for the Protection of Rights, covered as "private life."

The major fault of Carmarthenshire College was in not having a usage policy in place. Employers and employees should have an agreed-upon policy as part of the contract of employment that clarifies what is and is not acceptable computer usage in the workplace. The employer can then follow normal disciplinary procedures if an employee is using workplace equipment in a manner that is not permitted in the contract of employment.

Whatever the legal situation, it is clear where potential problems can occur in the workplace regarding information technology use. An e-mail, once sent, becomes a legally published document that can be produced as evidence in court cases involving issues of libel, breach of contract, and so on. Most businesses rely on their company data to keep ahead of the competition. Therefore, the loss, theft, or sabotage of data is potentially more dangerous than similar problems with hardware. If a USB memory stick is lost in a bar parking lot, replacing the hardware will cost a few dollars, but if it contains the company's confidential data, then its loss could put the company out of business!

Sources: Gov.UK, "Data Protection and Your Business," gov.uk, February 23, 2015; Ethan Bernstein, "How Being Filmed Changes Employee Behavior," *Harvard Business Review*, September 12, 2014; Steve Lohr, "Unblinking Eyes Track Employees," *New York Times*, June 21, 2014; Lamar Pierce, et al., "Cleaning House: The Impact of Information Technology Monitoring on Employee Theft and Productivity, Olin School of Business, Washington University, 2014. Spencer E. Ante and Lauren Weber, "Memo to Workers: The Boss Is Watching," *Wall Street Journal*, October 22, 2014; Steve Lohr, "Unblinking Eyes Track Employees," *New York Times*, June 21, 2014; Information Commissioners Office, "Employment Practices Data Protection Code-Supplementary Guidance," www.ico.gov.uk, accessed October 25, 2010; "Spector 360 Helps Blackburn Rovers Show Red Card to PC and Internet Abuse," Snapguard, www.snapguard.co.uk/blackburn_fc.html, accessed October 25, 2010; "Citizens Advice Bureau Advice Guide, Basic Rights at Work," Adviceguide, accessed October 25, 2010.

Case contributed by Andy Jones, Staffordshire University.

CASE STUDY QUESTIONS

1. How does information technology affect socioeconomic disparities? Explain your answer.

2. Why is access to technology insufficient to eliminate the digital divide?

3. How serious a problem is the "new" digital divide? Explain your answer.

4. Why is the digital divide problem an ethical dilemma?

extends the concept of responsibility further to the area of laws. Liability is a feature of political systems in which a body of laws is in place that permits individuals to recover the damages done to them by other actors, systems, or organizations. **Due process** is a related feature of law-governed societies and is a process in which laws are known and understood, and ability exists to appeal to higher authorities to ensure that the laws are applied correctly.

These basic concepts form the underpinning of an ethical analysis of information systems and those who manage them. First, information technologies are filtered through social institutions, organizations, and individuals. Systems do not have impacts by themselves. Whatever information system effects exist are products of institutional, organizational, and individual actions and behaviors. Second, responsibility for the consequences of technology falls clearly on the institutions, organizations, and individual managers who choose to use the technology. Using information technology in a socially responsible manner means that you can and will be held accountable for the consequences of your actions. Third, in an ethical, political society, individuals and others can recover damages done to them through a set of laws characterized by due process.

ETHICAL ANALYSIS

When confronted with a situation that seems to present ethical issues, how should you analyze it? The following five-step process should help.

1. *Identify and describe the facts clearly* Find out who did what to whom and where, when, and how. In many instances, you will be surprised at the errors in the initially

reported facts, and often you will find that simply getting the facts straight helps define the solution. It also helps to get the opposing parties involved in an ethical dilemma to agree on the facts.

2. *Define the conflict or dilemma and identify the higher-order values involved* Ethical, social, and political issues always reference higher values. The parties to a dispute all claim to be pursuing higher values (e.g., freedom, privacy, protection of property, and the free enterprise system). Typically, an ethical issue involves a dilemma: two diametrically opposed courses of action that support worthwhile values. For example, the chapter-opening case study illustrates two competing values: the need to make organizations more efficient and cost-effective and the need to respect individual privacy.

3. *Identify the stakeholders* Every ethical, social, and political issue has stakeholders: players in the game who have an interest in the outcome, who have invested in the situation, and usually who have vocal opinions. Find out the identity of these groups and what they want. This will be useful later when designing a solution.

4. *Identify the options that you can reasonably take* You may find that none of the options satisfy all the interests involved but that some options do a better job than others. Sometimes arriving at a good or ethical solution may not always be a balancing of consequences to stakeholders.

5. *Identify the potential consequences of your options* Some options may be ethically correct but disastrous from other points of view. Other options may work in one instance but not in similar instances. Always ask yourself, "What if I choose this option consistently over time?"

CANDIDATE ETHICAL PRINCIPLES

Once your analysis is complete, what ethical principles or rules should you use to make a decision? What higher-order values should inform your judgment? Although you are the only one who can decide which among many ethical principles you will follow, and how you will prioritize them, it is helpful to consider some ethical principles with deep roots in many cultures that have survived throughout recorded history.

1. Do unto others as you would have them do unto you (the **Golden Rule**). Putting yourself in the place of others, and thinking of yourself as the object of the decision, can help you think about fairness in decision making.

2. If an action is not right for everyone to take, it is not right for anyone (**Immanuel Kant's categorical imperative**). Ask yourself, "If everyone did this, could the organization, or society, survive?"

3. If an action cannot be taken repeatedly, it is not right to take at all. This is the **Slippery Slope Rule**: An action may bring about a small change now that is acceptable, but if it is repeated, it would bring unacceptable changes in the long run. In the vernacular, it might be stated as "once started down a slippery path, you may not be able to stop."

4. Take the action that achieves the higher or greater value (**utilitarian principle**). This rule assumes you can prioritize values in a rank order and understand the consequences of various courses of action.

5. Take the action that produces the least harm or the least potential cost (**risk aversion principle**). Some actions have extremely high failure costs of very low probability (e.g., building a nuclear generating facility in an urban area) or extremely high failure costs of moderate probability (speeding and automobile accidents). Avoid taking actions when the consequences of failure are catastrophic or even just severe.

6. Assume that virtually all tangible and intangible objects are owned by someone else unless there is a specific declaration otherwise. (This is the **ethical "no free lunch" rule**.) If something someone else has created is useful to you, it has value, and you should assume the creator wants compensation for this work.

Actions that do not easily pass these rules deserve close attention and a great deal of caution. The appearance of unethical behavior may do as much harm to you and your company as actual unethical behavior.

PROFESSIONAL CODES OF CONDUCT

When groups of people claim to be professionals, they take on special rights and obligations because of their special claims to knowledge, wisdom, and respect. Professional codes of conduct are promulgated by associations of professionals such as the American Medical Association (AMA), the American Bar Association (ABA), the Association of Information Technology Professionals (AITP), and the Association for Computing Machinery (ACM). These professional groups take responsibility for the partial regulation of their professions by determining entrance qualifications and competence. Codes of ethics are promises by professions to regulate themselves in the general interest of society. For example, avoiding harm to others, honoring property rights (including intellectual property), and respecting privacy are among the General Moral Imperatives of the ACM's Code of Ethics and Professional Conduct.

SOME REAL-WORLD ETHICAL DILEMMAS

Information systems have created new ethical dilemmas in which one set of interests is pitted against another. For example, many of the large telecommunications companies are using information technology to reduce the sizes of their workforces. Voice recognition software reduces the need for human operators by enabling computers to recognize a customer's responses to a series of computerized questions. Many companies monitor what their employees are doing on the Internet to prevent them from wasting company resources on nonbusiness activities. Facebook monitors its subscribers and then sells the information to advertisers and app developers (see the chapter-ending case study).

In each instance, you can find competing values at work, with groups lined up on either side of a debate. A company may argue, for example, that it has a right to use information systems to increase productivity and reduce the size of its workforce to lower costs and stay in business. Employees displaced by information systems may argue that employers have some responsibility for their welfare. Business owners might feel obligated to monitor employee email and Internet use to minimize drains on productivity. Employees might believe they should be able to use the Internet for short personal tasks in place of the telephone. A close analysis of the facts can sometimes produce compromised solutions that give each side half a loaf. Try to apply some of the principles of ethical analysis described to each of these cases. What is the right thing to do?

4-3 Why do contemporary information systems technology and the Internet pose challenges to the protection of individual privacy and intellectual property?

In this section, we take a closer look at the five moral dimensions of information systems first described in Figure 4.1. In each dimension, we identify the ethical, social, and political levels of analysis and use real-world examples to illustrate the values involved, the stakeholders, and the options chosen.

INFORMATION RIGHTS: PRIVACY AND FREEDOM IN THE INTERNET AGE

Privacy is the claim of individuals to be left alone, free from surveillance or interference from other individuals or organizations, including the state. Claims to privacy are also involved at the workplace. Millions of employees are subject to digital and other forms of high-tech surveillance. Information technology and systems threaten individual claims to privacy by making the invasion of privacy cheap, profitable, and effective.

General Federal Privacy Laws	Privacy Laws Affecting Private Institutions
Freedom of Information Act of 1966 as Amended (5 USC 552)	Fair Credit Reporting Act of 1970
Privacy Act of 1974 as Amended (5 USC 552a)	Family Educational Rights and Privacy Act of 1974
Electronic Communications Privacy Act of 1986	Right to Financial Privacy Act of 1978
Computer Matching and Privacy Protection Act of 1988	Privacy Protection Act of 1980
Computer Security Act of 1987	Cable Communications Policy Act of 1984
Federal Managers Financial Integrity Act of 1982	Electronic Communications Privacy Act of 1986
Driver's Privacy Protection Act of 1994	Video Privacy Protection Act of 1988
E-Government Act of 2002	The Health Insurance Portability and Accountability Act (HIPAA) of 1996
	Children's Online Privacy Protection Act (COPPA) of 1998
	Financial Modernization Act (Gramm-Leach-Bliley Act) of 1999

TABLE 4.3

Federal Privacy Laws In The United States

The claim to privacy is protected in the U.S., Canadian, and German constitutions in a variety of ways and in other countries through various statutes. In the United States, the claim to privacy is protected primarily by the First Amendment guarantees of freedom of speech and association, the Fourth Amendment protections against unreasonable search and seizure of one's personal documents or home, and the guarantee of due process.

Table 4.3 describes the major U.S. federal statutes that set forth the conditions for handling information about individuals in such areas as credit reporting, education, financial records, newspaper records, and electronic and digital communications. The Privacy Act of 1974 has been the most important of these laws, regulating the federal government's collection, use, and disclosure of information. At present, most U.S. federal privacy laws apply only to the federal government and regulate very few areas of the private sector. There were 20 major privacy bills before Congress in 2015, although few of them are likely to be passed in the near future (Kosseff, 2014).

Most American and European privacy law is based on a regime called **Fair Information Practices (FIP)** first set forth in a report written in 1973 by a federal government advisory committee and updated most recently in 2010 to take into account new privacy-invading technology (Federal Trade Commission [FTC], 2010; U.S. Department of Health, Education, and Welfare, 1973). FIP is a set of principles governing the collection and use of information about individuals. FIP principles are based on the notion of a mutuality of interest between the record holder and the individual. The individual has an interest in engaging in a transaction, and the record keeper—usually a business or government agency—requires information about the individual to support the transaction. After information is gathered, the individual maintains an interest in the record, and the record may not be used to support other activities without the individual's consent. In 1998, the Federal Trade Commission (FTC) restated and extended the original FIP to provide guidelines for protecting online privacy. Table 4.4 describes the FTC's Fair Information Practice principles.

The FTC's FIP principles are being used as guidelines to drive changes in privacy legislation. In July 1998, the U.S. Congress passed the Children's Online Privacy Protection Act (COPPA), requiring websites to obtain parental permission before

TABLE 4.4

Federal Trade
Commission Fair
Information Practice
Principles

Notice/awareness (core principle). Websites must disclose their information practices before collecting data. Includes identification of collector; uses of data; other recipients of data; nature of collection (active/inactive); voluntary or required status; consequences of refusal; and steps taken to protect confidentiality, integrity, and quality of the data.

Choice/consent (core principle). A choice regime must be in place allowing consumers to choose how their information will be used for secondary purposes other than supporting the transaction, including internal use and transfer to third parties.

Access/participation. Consumers should be able to review and contest the accuracy and completeness of data collected about them in a timely, inexpensive process.

Security. Data collectors must take responsible steps to ensure that consumer information is accurate and secure from unauthorized use.

Enforcement. A mechanism must be in place to enforce FIP principles. This can involve self-regulation, legislation giving consumers legal remedies for violations, or federal statutes and regulations.

collecting information on children under the age of 13. The FTC has recommended additional legislation to protect online consumer privacy in advertising networks that collect records of consumer web activity to develop detailed profiles, which other companies then use to target online ads. In 2010, the FTC added three practices to its framework for privacy. Firms should adopt privacy by design, building products and services that protect privacy, firms should increase the transparency of their data practices, and firms should require consumer consent and provide clear options to opt out of data collection schemes (FTC, 2012). Other proposed Internet privacy legislation focuses on protecting the online use of personal identification numbers, such as social security numbers; protecting personal information collected on the Internet that deals with individuals not covered by COPPA; and limiting the use of data mining for homeland security.

In 2012, the FTC extended its FIP doctrine to address the issue of behavioral targeting. The FTC held hearings to discuss its program for voluntary industry principles for regulating behavioral targeting. The online advertising trade group Network Advertising Initiative (discussed later in this section), published its own self-regulatory principles that largely agreed with the FTC. Nevertheless, the government, privacy groups, and the online ad industry are still at loggerheads over two issues. Privacy advocates want both an opt-in policy at all sites and a national Do Not Track list. The industry opposes these moves and continues to insist that an opt-out capability is the only way to avoid tracking. Nevertheless, there is an emerging consensus among all parties that greater transparency and user control (especially making opting out of tracking the default option) is required to deal with behavioral tracking. Public opinion polls show an ongoing distrust of online marketers. Although there are many studies of privacy issues at the federal level, there has been no significant legislation in recent years.

Privacy protections have also been added to recent laws deregulating financial services and safeguarding the maintenance and transmission of health information about individuals. The Gramm-Leach-Bliley Act of 1999, which repeals earlier restrictions on affiliations among banks, securities firms, and insurance companies, includes some privacy protection for consumers of financial services. All financial institutions are required to disclose their policies and practices for protecting the privacy of nonpublic personal information and to allow customers to opt out of information-sharing arrangements with nonaffiliated third parties.

The Health Insurance Portability and Accountability Act (HIPAA) of 1996, which took effect on April 14, 2003, includes privacy protection for medical records. The law gives patients access to their personal medical records that health care providers, hospitals, and health insurers maintain and the right to authorize how protected information about themselves can be used or disclosed. Doctors, hospitals, and other health care providers must limit the disclosure of personal information about patients to the minimum amount necessary to achieve a given purpose.

The European Directive on Data Protection

In Europe, privacy protection is much more stringent than in the United States. Unlike the United States, European countries do not allow businesses to use personally identifiable information without consumers' prior consent. On October 25, 1998, the European Commission's Directive on Data Protection went into effect, broadening privacy protection in the European Union (EU) nations. The directive requires companies to inform people when they collect information about them and disclose how it will be stored and used. Customers must provide their **informed consent** before any company can legally use data about them, and they have the right to access that information, correct it, and request that no further data be collected. Informed consent can be defined as consent given with knowledge of all the facts needed to make a rational decision. EU member nations must translate these principles into their own laws and cannot transfer personal data to countries, such as the United States, that do not have similar privacy protection regulations. In 2009, the European Parliament passed new rules governing the use of third-party cookies for behavioral tracking purposes. These new rules were implemented in May 2011 and require website visitors to give explicit consent to be tracked by cookies. Websites will be required to have highly visible warnings on their pages if third-party cookies are being used (European Parliament, 2009).

In January 2012, the EU issued significant proposed changes to its data protection rules, the first overhaul since 1995 (European Commission, 2012). The new rules would apply to all companies providing services in Europe and require Internet companies such as Amazon, Facebook, Apple, Google, and others to obtain explicit consent from consumers about the use of their personal data, delete information at the user's request (based on the right to be forgotten), and retain information only as long as absolutely necessary. In 2014, the European Parliament gave strong support to significant changes in privacy policies by extending greater control to users of the Internet. Although the privacy policies of United States firms (in contrast to the government's) are largely voluntary, in Europe, corporate privacy policies are mandated and more consistent across jurisdictions.

Among the changes being discussed are a requirement for firms to inform users before collecting data, every time they collect data, and how it will be used. Users would have to give consent to any data collection. Other proposals call for users to have a right of access to personal data, and the right to be forgotten. The right to be forgotten was upheld by a European Union court in 2014, and since then, Google has had to respond to more than 200,000 requests to remove personal information from its search engine.

Working with the European Commission, the U.S. Department of Commerce developed a safe harbor framework for U.S. firms. A **safe harbor** is a private, self-regulating policy and enforcement mechanism that meets the objectives of government regulators and legislation but does not involve government regulation or enforcement. U.S. businesses would be allowed to use personal data from EU countries if they develop privacy protection policies that meet EU standards. Enforcement would occur in the United States by using self-policing, regulation, and government enforcement of fair trade statutes. In October 2015, the European Court of Justice found that the Safe Harbor program was not effective, and therefore invalid. Talks are underway to devise a new program.

Internet Challenges to Privacy

Internet technology has posed new challenges for the protection of individual privacy. Information sent over this vast network of networks may pass through many computer systems before it reaches its final destination. Each of these systems is capable of monitoring, capturing, and storing communications that pass through it.

Websites track searches that have been conducted, the websites and web pages visited, the online content a person has accessed, and what items that person has inspected or purchased over the web. This monitoring and tracking of website visitors occurs in the background without the visitor's knowledge. It is conducted not just by individual websites but by advertising networks such as Microsoft Advertising, Yahoo, and Google's DoubleClick that are capable of tracking personal browsing behavior across thousands of websites. Both website publishers and the advertising industry defend tracking of individuals across the web because doing so allows more relevant ads to be targeted to users, and it pays for the cost of publishing websites. In this sense, it's like broadcast television: advertiser-supported content that is free to the user. The commercial demand for this personal information is virtually insatiable. However, these practices also impinge on individual privacy. **Cookies** are small text files deposited on a computer hard drive when a user visits websites. Cookies identify the visitor's web browser software and track visits to the website. When the visitor returns to a site that has stored a cookie, the website software searches the visitor's computer, finds the cookie, and knows what that person has done in the past. It may also update the cookie, depending on the activity during the visit. In this way, the site can customize its content for each visitor's interests. For example, if you purchase a book on Amazon.com and return later from the same browser, the site will welcome you by name and recommend other books of interest based on your past purchases. DoubleClick, described earlier in this chapter, uses cookies to build its dossiers with details of online purchases and examine the behavior of website visitors. Figure 4.3 illustrates how cookies work.

Websites using cookie technology cannot directly obtain visitors' names and addresses. However, if a person has registered at a site, that information can be combined with cookie data to identify the visitor. Website owners can also combine the data they have gathered from cookies and other website monitoring tools with personal data from other sources, such as offline data collected from surveys or paper catalog purchases, to develop very detailed profiles of their visitors.

There are now even more subtle and surreptitious tools for surveillance of Internet users. So-called super cookies or Flash cookies cannot be easily deleted and can be installed whenever a person clicks a Flash video. Flash uses these so-called local shared object files to play videos and puts them on the user's computer without his or her consent. Marketers use web beacons as another tool to monitor online behavior. **Web beacons**, also called *web bugs* (or simply tracking files), are tiny software programs that keep a record of users' online clickstreams. They report this data back to whomever owns the tracking file invisibly embedded in email messages and web

Figure 4.3

How Cookies Identify Web Visitors

Cookies are written by a website on a visitor's hard drive. When the visitor returns to that website, the web server requests the ID number from the cookie and uses it to access the data stored by that server on that visitor. The website can then use these data to display personalized information.

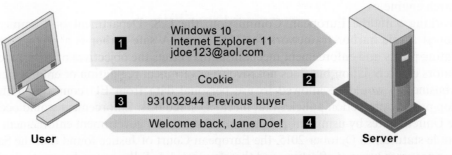

1. The Web server reads the user's Web browser and determines the operating system, browser name, version number, Internet address, and other information.
2. The server transmits a tiny text file with user identification information called a cookie, which the user's browser receives and stores on the user's computer hard drive.
3. When the user returns to the Web site, the server requests the contents of any cookie it deposited previously in the user's computer.
4. The Web server reads the cookie, identifies the visitor, and calls up data on the user.

pages that are designed to monitor the behavior of the user visiting a website or send-ing email. Web beacons are placed on popular websites by third-party firms who pay the websites a fee for access to their audience. So how common is web tracking? In a path-breaking series of articles in the *Wall Street Journal* in 2010 and 2011, research-ers examined the tracking files on 50 of the most popular U.S websites. What they found revealed a very widespread surveillance system. On the 50 sites, they discov-ered 3,180 tracking files installed on visitor computers. Only one site, Wikipedia, had no tracking files. Some popular sites such as Dictionary.com, MSN, and Comcast, installed more than 100 tracking files! Two-thirds of the tracking files came from 131 companies whose primary business is identifying and tracking Internet users to cre-ate consumer profiles that can be sold to advertising firms looking for specific types of customers. The biggest trackers were Google, Microsoft, and Quantcast, all of whom are in the business of selling ads to advertising firms and marketers. A follow-up study in 2012 found the situation had worsened; tracking on the 50 most popular sites had risen nearly fivefold! The cause: growth of online ad auctions where adver-tisers buy the data about users' web-browsing behavior.

Other **spyware** can secretly install itself on an Internet user's computer by pig-gybacking on larger applications. Once installed, the spyware calls out to websites to send banner ads and other unsolicited material to the user, and it can report the user's movements on the Internet to other computers. More information is available about intrusive software in Chapter 8.

Nearly 80 percent of global Internet users use Google Search and other Google services, making Google the world's largest collector of online user data. Whatever Google does with its data has an enormous impact on online privacy. Most experts believe that Google possesses the largest collection of personal information in the world—more data on more people than any government agency. The nearest com-petitor is Facebook.

After Google acquired advertising network DoubleClick in 2007, Google began using behavioral targeting to help it display more relevant ads based on users' search activities and to target individuals as they move from one site to another to show them display or banner ads. Google allows tracking software on its search pages, and using DoubleClick, it can track users across the Internet. One of its programs enables advertisers to target ads based on the search histories of Google users, along with any other information the user submits to Google such as age, demographics, region, and other web activities (such as blogging). Google's AdSense program enables Google to help advertisers select keywords and design ads for various market segments based on search histories such as helping a clothing website create and test ads targeted at teenage females. A recent study found that 88 percent of 400,000 websites had at least one Google tracking bug.

Google also scans the contents of messages users receive of its free web-based email service called Gmail. Ads that users see when they read their email are related to the subjects of these messages. Profiles are developed on individual users based on the content in their email. Google now displays targeted ads on YouTube and Google mobile applications, and its DoubleClick ad network serves up targeted banner ads.

The United States has allowed businesses to gather transaction information generated in the marketplace and then use that information for other marketing pur-poses without obtaining the informed consent of the individual whose information is being used, although these firms argue that when users agree to the sites' terms of service, they are also agreeing to allow the site to collect information about their online activities. An **opt-out** model of informed consent permits the collection of personal information until the consumer specifically requests the data not to be col-lected. Privacy advocates would like to see wider use of an **opt-in** model of informed consent in which a business is prohibited from collecting any personal information unless the consumer specifically takes action to approve information collection and use. Here, the default option is no collection of user information.

The online industry has preferred self-regulation to privacy legislation for protecting consumers. The online advertising industry formed the Online Privacy Alliance to encourage self-regulation to develop a set of privacy guidelines for its members. The group promotes the use of online seals, such as that of TRUSTe, certifying websites adhering to certain privacy principles. Members of the advertising network industry, including Google's DoubleClick, have created an additional industry association called the Network Advertising Initiative (NAI) to develop its own privacy policies to help consumers opt out of advertising network programs and provide consumers redress from abuses.

Individual firms such as Microsoft, Mozilla Foundation, Yahoo, and Google have recently adopted policies on their own in an effort to address public concern about tracking people online. Microsoft's Internet Explorer 11 web browser was released in 2015 with the opt-out option as the default. Other browsers have opt-out options, but users need to turn them on, and most users fail to do this. AOL established an opt-out policy that allows users of its site to choose not to be tracked. Yahoo follows NAI guidelines and allows opt-out for tracking and web beacons (web bugs). Google has reduced retention time for tracking data.

In general, most Internet businesses do little to protect the privacy of their customers, and consumers do not do as much as they should to protect themselves. For commercial websites that depend on advertising to support themselves, most revenue derives from selling customer information. Of the companies that do post privacy policies on their websites, about half do not monitor their sites to ensure that they adhere to these policies. The vast majority of online customers claim they are concerned about online privacy, but fewer than half read the privacy statements on websites. In general, website privacy policies require a law degree to understand and are ambiguous about key terms (Laudon and Traver, 2015). In 2014, what firms such as Facebook and Google call a privacy policy is in fact a data use policy. The concept of privacy is associated with consumer rights, which firms do not wish to recognize. A data use policy simply tells customers how the information will be used without any mention of rights.

In one of the more insightful studies of consumer attitudes toward Internet privacy, a group of Berkeley students conducted surveys of online users and of complaints filed with the FTC involving privacy issues. Some of their results show that people feel they have no control over the information collected about them, and they don't know who to complain to. Websites collect all this information but do not let users have access, the website policies are unclear, and they share data with affiliates but never identify who the affiliates are and how many there are. Web bug trackers are ubiquitous, and users are not informed of trackers on the pages they visit. The results of this study and others suggest that consumers are not saying, "Take my privacy, I don't care, send me the service for free." They are saying, "We want access to the information, we want some controls on what can be collected, what is done with the information, the ability to opt out of the entire tracking enterprise, and some clarity on what the policies really are, and we don't want those policies changed without our participation and permission." (The full report is available at knowprivacy.org.)

Technical Solutions

In addition to legislation, there are a few technologies that can protect user privacy during interactions with websites. Many of these tools are used for encrypting email, for making email or surfing activities appear anonymous, for preventing client computers from accepting cookies, or for detecting and eliminating spyware. For the most part, technical solutions have failed to protect users from being tracked as they move from one site to another.

Because of growing public criticism of behavioral tracking, targeting of ads, and the failure of industry to self-regulate, attention has shifted to browsers. Many browsers have Do Not Track options. For users who have selected the Do Not

Track browser option, their browser will send a request to websites requesting the user's behavior not be tracked, but websites are not obligated to honor their visitors' requests not to be tracked. There is no online advertising industry agreement on how to respond to Do Not Track requests nor, currently, any legislation requiring websites to stop tracking.

PROPERTY RIGHTS: INTELLECTUAL PROPERTY

Contemporary information systems have severely challenged existing laws and social practices that protect **intellectual property**. Intellectual property is considered to be tangible and intangible products of the mind created by individuals or corporations. Information technology has made it difficult to protect intellectual property because computerized information can be so easily copied or distributed on networks. Intellectual property is subject to a variety of protections under three legal traditions: trade secrets, copyright, and patent law.

Trade Secrets

Any intellectual work product—a formula, device, pattern, or compilation of data— used for a business purpose can be classified as a **trade secret**, provided it is not based on information in the public domain. Protections for trade secrets vary from state to state. In general, trade secret laws grant a monopoly on the ideas behind a work product, but it can be a very tenuous monopoly.

Software that contains novel or unique elements, procedures, or compilations can be included as a trade secret. Trade secret law protects the actual ideas in a work product, not only their manifestation. To make this claim, the creator or owner must take care to bind employees and customers with nondisclosure agreements and prevent the secret from falling into the public domain.

The limitation of trade secret protection is that, although virtually all software programs of any complexity contain unique elements of some sort, it is difficult to prevent the ideas in the work from falling into the public domain when the software is widely distributed.

Copyright

Copyright is a statutory grant that protects creators of intellectual property from having their work copied by others for any purpose during the life of the author plus an additional 70 years after the author's death. For corporate-owned works, copyright protection lasts for 95 years after their initial creation. Congress has extended copyright protection to books, periodicals, lectures, dramas, musical compositions, maps, drawings, artwork of any kind, and motion pictures. The intent behind copyright laws has been to encourage creativity and authorship by ensuring that creative people receive the financial and other benefits of their work. Most industrial nations have their own copyright laws, and there are several international conventions and bilateral agreements through which nations coordinate and enforce their laws.

In the mid-1960s, the Copyright Office began registering software programs, and in 1980, Congress passed the Computer Software Copyright Act, which clearly provides protection for software program code and copies of the original sold in commerce; it sets forth the rights of the purchaser to use the software while the creator retains legal title.

Copyright protects against copying entire programs or their parts. Damages and relief are readily obtained for infringement. The drawback to copyright protection is that the underlying ideas behind a work are not protected, only their manifestation in a work. A competitor can use your software, understand how it works, and build new software that follows the same concepts without infringing on a copyright.

Look-and-feel copyright infringement lawsuits are precisely about the distinction between an idea and its expression. For instance, in the early 1990s, Apple Computer sued Microsoft Corporation and Hewlett-Packard for infringement of the expression of Apple's Macintosh interface, claiming that the defendants copied the expression of overlapping windows. The defendants countered that the idea of overlapping windows can be expressed only in a single way and, therefore, was not protectable under the merger doctrine of copyright law. When ideas and their expression merge, the expression cannot be copyrighted.

In general, courts appear to be following the reasoning of a 1989 case—*Brown Bag Software v. Symantec Corp*—in which the court dissected the elements of software alleged to be infringing. The court found that similar concept, function, general functional features (e.g., drop-down menus), and colors are not protectable by copyright law (*Brown Bag Software v. Symantec Corp.*, 1992).

Patents

A **patent** grants the owner an exclusive monopoly on the ideas behind an invention for 20 years. The congressional intent behind patent law was to ensure that inventors of new machines, devices, or methods receive the full financial and other rewards of their labor and yet make widespread use of the invention possible by providing detailed diagrams for those wishing to use the idea under license from the patent's owner. The granting of a patent is determined by the United States Patent and Trademark Office and relies on court rulings.

The key concepts in patent law are originality, novelty, and invention. The Patent Office did not accept applications for software patents routinely until a 1981 Supreme Court decision that held that computer programs could be part of a patentable process. Since that time, hundreds of patents have been granted, and thousands await consideration.

The strength of patent protection is that it grants a monopoly on the underlying concepts and ideas of software. The difficulty is passing stringent criteria of nonobviousness (e.g., the work must reflect some special understanding and contribution), originality, and novelty as well as years of waiting to receive protection.

In what some call the patent trial of the century, in 2011, Apple sued Samsung for violating its patents for iPhones, iPads, and iPods. On August 24, 2012, a California jury in federal district court delivered a decisive victory to Apple and a stunning defeat to Samsung. The jury awarded Apple $1 billion in damages. The decision established criteria for determining just how close a competitor can come to an industry-leading and standard-setting product like Apple's iPhone before it violates the design and utility patents of the leading firm. The same court ruled that Samsung could not sell its new tablet computer (Galaxy 10.1) in the United States. In a later patent dispute, Samsung won an infringement case against Apple. In June 2013, the United States International Trade Commission issued a ban for a handful of older iPhone and iPad devices because they violated Samsung patents from years ago. In 2014, Apple sued Samsung again, claiming infringement of five patents. The patents cover hardware and software techniques for handling photos, videos, and lists used on the popular Galaxy 5. Apple sought $2 billion in damages. In 2015, the U.S. Court of Appeals reaffirmed that Samsung had copied specific design patents, but dropped the damages Apple was granted to $930 million.

To make matters more complicated, Apple has been one of Samsung's largest customers for flash memory processors, graphic chips, solid-state drives, and display parts that are used in Apple's iPhones, iPads, iPod Touch devices, and MacBooks. The Samsung and Apple patent cases are indicative of the complex relationships among the leading computer firms.

Challenges to Intellectual Property Rights

Contemporary information technologies, especially software, pose severe challenges to existing intellectual property regimes and, therefore, create significant ethical, social, and political issues. Digital media differ from books, periodicals, and other media in terms of ease of replication; ease of transmission; ease of alteration; compactness—making theft easy; and difficulties in establishing uniqueness.

The proliferation of digital networks, including the Internet, has made it even more difficult to protect intellectual property. Before widespread use of networks, copies of software, books, magazine articles, or films had to be stored on physical media, such as paper, computer disks, or videotape, creating some hurdles to distribution. Using networks, information can be more widely reproduced and distributed. The BSA Global Software Survey conducted by International Data Corporation and The Software Alliance (also known as BSA) reported that the rate of global software piracy climbed to 43 percent in 2014, representing $62.7 billion in global losses from software piracy (The Software Alliance, 2014).

The Internet was designed to transmit information freely around the world, including copyrighted information. With the World Wide Web in particular, you can easily copy and distribute virtually anything to thousands and even millions of people around the world, even if they are using different types of computer systems. Information can be illicitly copied from one place and distributed through other systems and networks even though these parties do not willingly participate in the infringement.

Individuals have been illegally copying and distributing digitized music files on the Internet for several decades. File-sharing services such as Napster and, later, Grokster, Kazaa, Morpheus, Megaupload, and The Pirate Bay sprang up to help users locate and swap digital music and video files, including those protected by copyright. Illegal file sharing became so widespread that it threatened the viability of the music recording industry and, at one point, consumed 20 percent of Internet bandwidth. The recording industry won several legal battles for shutting these services down, but it has not been able to halt illegal file sharing entirely. The motion picture and cable television industries are waging similar battles. Several European nations have worked with U.S. authorities to shut down illegal sharing sites, with mixed results. In France, illegal downloaders can lose access to the Internet for a year or more.

As legitimate online music stores such as the iTunes Store expanded, and more recently as Internet radio services such as Pandora expanded, some forms of illegal file sharing have declined. Technology has radically altered the prospects for intellectual property protection from theft, at least for music, videos, and television shows (less so for software). The Apple iTunes Store legitimated paying for music and entertainment and created a closed environment from which music and videos could not be easily copied and widely distributed unless played on Apple devices. Amazon's Kindle also protects the rights of publishers and writers because its books cannot be copied to the Internet and distributed. Streaming of Internet radio, on services such as Pandora and Spotify, and Hollywood movies (at sites such as Hulu and Netflix) also inhibits piracy because the streams cannot be easily recorded on separate devices, and videos can be downloaded so easily. Moreover, the large web distributors such as Apple, Google, and Amazon do not want to encourage piracy in music or videos simply because they need these properties to earn revenue. Despite these gains in legitimate online music platforms, Apple's iTunes based on downloads of singles, and streaming services' unwillingness to pay labels and artists a reasonable fee for playing, has resulted in a 50 percent decline in record industry revenues since 2000 and the loss of thousands of jobs.

The **Digital Millennium Copyright Act (DMCA)** of 1998 also provides some copyright protection. The DMCA implemented a World Intellectual Property Organization Treaty that makes it illegal to circumvent technology-based protections of copyrighted materials. Internet service providers (ISPs) are required to take down sites of copyright infringers they are hosting when the ISPs are notified of the problem. Microsoft and other major software and information content firms are represented by the Software and Information Industry Association (SIIA), which lobbies for new laws and enforcement of existing laws to protect intellectual property around the world. The SIIA runs an antipiracy hotline for individuals to report piracy activities, offers educational programs to help organizations combat software piracy, and has published guidelines for employee use of software.

4-4 How have information systems affected laws for establishing accountability and liability and the quality of everyday life?

Along with privacy and property laws, new information technologies are challenging existing liability laws and social practices for holding individuals and institutions accountable. If a person is injured by a machine controlled, in part, by software, who should be held accountable and, therefore, held liable? Should a social network site like Facebook or Twitter be held liable and accountable for the posting of pornographic material or racial insults, or should they be held harmless against any liability for what users post (as is true of common carriers, such as the telephone system)? What about the Internet? If you outsource your information processing to the cloud, and the cloud provider fails to provide adequate service, what can you do? Cloud providers often claim the software you are using is the problem, not the cloud servers. Some real-world examples may shed light on these questions.

COMPUTER-RELATED LIABILITY PROBLEMS

The Chapter 8 opening case describes how hackers in late 2013 obtained credit card, debit card, and additional personal information about 70 to 110 million customers of Target, one of the largest U.S. retailers. Target's sales took an immediate hit from which it has still not completely recovered. Target says it has spent over $60 million to strengthen its systems. In 2015, Target agreed to pay $10 million to customers and $19 million to MasterCard. It has paid an even greater price through the loss of sales and trust.

Who is liable for any economic harm caused to individuals or businesses whose credit cards were compromised? Is Target responsible for allowing the breach to occur despite efforts it did make to secure the information? Or is this just a cost of doing business in a credit card world where customers and businesses have insurance policies to protect them against losses? Customers, for instance, have a maximum liability of $50 for credit card theft under federal banking law.

Are information system managers responsible for the harm that corporate systems can do? Beyond IT managers, insofar as computer software is part of a machine, and the machine injures someone physically or economically, the producer of the software and the operator can be held liable for damages. Insofar as the software acts like a book, storing and displaying information, courts have been reluctant to hold authors, publishers, and booksellers liable for contents (the exception being instances of fraud or defamation); hence, courts have been wary of holding software authors liable for software.

In general, it is very difficult (if not impossible) to hold software producers liable for their software products that are considered to be like books, regardless of the physical or economic harm that results. Historically, print publishers of books and periodicals have not been held liable because of fears that liability claims would interfere with First Amendment rights guaranteeing freedom of expression. The kind of harm software failures causes is rarely fatal and typically inconveniences users but does not physically harm them (the exception being medical devices).

What about software as a service? ATM machines are a service provided to bank customers. If this service fails, customers will be inconvenienced and perhaps harmed economically if they cannot access their funds in a timely manner. Should liability protections be extended to software publishers and operators of defective financial, accounting, simulation, or marketing systems?

Software is very different from books. Software users may develop expectations of infallibility about software; software is less easily inspected than a book, and it is more difficult to compare with other software products for quality; software claims to perform a task rather than describe a task, as a book does; and people come to depend on services essentially based on software. Given the centrality of software to everyday life, the chances are excellent that liability law will extend its reach to include software even when the software merely provides an information service.

Telephone systems have not been held liable for the messages transmitted because they are regulated common carriers. In return for their right to provide telephone service, they must provide access to all, at reasonable rates, and achieve acceptable reliability. Likewise, cable networks are considered private networks not subject to regulation, but broadcasters using the public air waves are subject to a wide variety of federal and local constraints on content and facilities. In the United States, with few exceptions, websites are not held liable for content posted on their sites regardless of whether it was placed there by the website owners or users.

SYSTEM QUALITY: DATA QUALITY AND SYSTEM ERRORS

White Christmas turned into a black out for millions of Netflix customers and social network users on December 24, 2012. The blackout was caused by the failure of Amazon's cloud computing service, which provides storage and computing power for all kinds of websites and services, including Netflix. The loss of service lasted for a day. Amazon blamed it on elastic load balancing, a software program that balances the loads on all its cloud servers to prevent overload. Amazon's cloud computing services have had several subsequent outages, although not as long-lasting as the Christmas Eve outage. Outages at cloud computing services are rare but recurring. These outages have called into question the reliability and quality of cloud services. Are these outages acceptable?

The debate over liability and accountability for unintentional consequences of system use raises a related but independent moral dimension: What is an acceptable, technologically feasible level of system quality? At what point should system managers say, "Stop testing, we've done all we can to perfect this software. Ship it!" Individuals and organizations may be held responsible for avoidable and foreseeable consequences, which they have a duty to perceive and correct. The gray area is that some system errors are foreseeable and correctable only at very great expense, expense so great that pursuing this level of perfection is not feasible economically—no one could afford the product.

For example, although software companies try to debug their products before releasing them to the marketplace, they knowingly ship buggy products because the time and cost of fixing all minor errors would prevent these products from ever being released. What if the product was not offered on the marketplace? Would social welfare as a whole falter and perhaps even decline? Carrying this further, just what is the responsibility of a producer of computer services—should it withdraw the product that can never be perfect, warn the user, or forget about the risk (let the buyer beware)?

Three principal sources of poor system performance are (1) software bugs and errors, (2) hardware or facility failures caused by natural or other causes, and (3) poor input data quality. A Chapter 8 Learning Track discusses why zero defects in software code of any complexity cannot be achieved and why the seriousness of remaining bugs cannot be estimated. Hence, there is a technological barrier to perfect software, and users must be aware of the potential for catastrophic failure. The software industry has not yet arrived at testing standards for producing software of acceptable but imperfect performance.

Although software bugs and facility catastrophes are likely to be widely reported in the press, by far the most common source of business system failure is data quality. Few companies routinely measure the quality of their data, but individual organizations report data error rates ranging from 0.5 to 30 percent.

QUALITY OF LIFE: EQUITY, ACCESS, AND BOUNDARIES

The negative social costs of introducing information technologies and systems are beginning to mount along with the power of the technology. Many of these negative social consequences are not violations of individual rights or property crimes. Nevertheless, they can be extremely harmful to individuals, societies, and political institutions. Computers and information technologies potentially can destroy valuable elements of our culture and society even while they bring us benefits. If there is a balance of good and bad consequences of using information systems, who do we hold responsible for the bad consequences? Next, we briefly examine some of the negative social consequences of systems, considering individual, social, and political responses.

Balancing Power: Center Versus Periphery

An early fear of the computer age was that huge, centralized mainframe computers would centralize power in the nation's capital, resulting in a Big Brother society, as was suggested in George Orwell's novel *1984*. The shift toward highly decentralized client–server computing, coupled with an ideology of empowerment of Twitter and social media users, and the decentralization of decision making to lower organizational levels, up until recently reduced the fears of power centralization in government institutions. Yet much of the empowerment described in popular business magazines is trivial. Lower-level employees may be empowered to make minor decisions, but the key policy decisions may be as centralized as in the past. At the same time, corporate Internet behemoths such as Google, Apple, Yahoo, Amazon, and Microsoft have come to dominate the collection and analysis of personal private information of all citizens. Since the terrorist attacks against the United States on September 11, 2001, the federal government has greatly expanded its use of this private sector information under the authority of the Patriot Act of 2001 and subsequent and secret executive orders. In this sense, power has become more centralized in the hands of a few private oligopolies and large government agencies.

Rapidity of Change: Reduced Response Time to Competition

Information systems have helped to create much more efficient national and international markets. Today's more efficient global marketplace has reduced the normal social buffers that permitted businesses many years to adjust to competition. Time-based competition has an ugly side; the business you work for may not have enough time to respond to global competitors and may be wiped out in a year along with your job. We stand the risk of developing a just-in-time society with just-in-time jobs and just-in-time workplaces, families, and vacations. One impact of Uber (see Chapter 10) and other on-demand services firms is to create just-in-time jobs with no benefits or insurance for employees.

Maintaining Boundaries: Family, Work, and Leisure

Parts of this book were produced on trains and planes as well as on vacations and during what otherwise might have been family time. The danger to ubiquitous computing, telecommuting, nomad computing, mobile computing, and the do-anything-anywhere computing environment is that it is actually coming true. The traditional boundaries that separate work from family and just plain leisure have been weakened.

Although authors have traditionally worked just about anywhere, the advent of information systems, coupled with the growth of knowledge-work occupations,

© HONGQI ZHANG/123RF

Although some people enjoy the convenience of working at home, the do-anything-anywhere computing environment can blur the traditional boundaries between work and family time.

means that more and more people are working when traditionally they would have been playing or communicating with family and friends. The work umbrella now extends far beyond the eight-hour day into commuting time, vacation time, and leisure time. The explosive growth and use of smartphones has only heightened the sense of many employees that they are never away from work.

Even leisure time spent on the computer threatens these close social relationships. Extensive Internet and cell phone use, even for entertainment or recreational purposes, takes people away from their family and friends. Among middle school and teenage children, it can lead to harmful antisocial behavior, such as the recent upsurge in cyberbullying.

Weakening these institutions poses clear-cut risks. Family and friends historically have provided powerful support mechanisms for individuals, and they act as balance points in a society by preserving private life, providing a place for people to collect their thoughts, allowing people to think in ways contrary to their employer, and dream.

Dependence and Vulnerability

Today, our businesses, governments, schools, and private associations, such as churches, are incredibly dependent on information systems and are, therefore, highly vulnerable if these systems fail. Secondary schools, for instance, increasingly use and rely on educational software. Test results are often stored off campus. If these systems were to shut down, there is no backup educational structure or content that can make up for the loss of the system. With systems now as ubiquitous as the telephone system, it is startling to remember that there are no regulatory or standard-setting forces in place that are similar to telephone, electrical, radio, television, or other public utility technologies. The absence of standards and the criticality of some system applications will probably call forth demands for national standards and perhaps regulatory oversight.

Computer Crime and Abuse

New technologies, including computers, create new opportunities for committing crime by creating new, valuable items to steal, new ways to steal them, and new ways to harm others. **Computer crime** is the commission of illegal acts by using a computer or against a computer system. Simply accessing a computer system without authorization or with intent to do harm, even by accident, is now a federal crime. The most frequent types of incidents comprise a greatest hits list of cybercrime: malware, phishing, network interruption, spyware, and denial of service attacks. (PwC, 2014). The true cost of all computer crime is unknown, but it is estimated to be in the billions of dollars. You can find a more detailed discussion of computer crime in Chapter 8.

Computer abuse is the commission of acts involving a computer that may not be illegal but are considered unethical. The popularity of the Internet and email has turned one form of computer abuse—spamming—into a serious problem for both individuals and businesses. Originally, **spam** was junk email an organization or individual sent to a mass audience of Internet users who have expressed no interest in the product or service being marketed. However, as cell phone use has mushroomed, spam was certain to follow. Identity and financial-theft cybercriminals are turning their attention to smartphones as users check mail, do online banking, pay bills, and reveal personal information. Cell phone spam usually comes in the form of SMS text messages, but increasingly, users are receiving spam in their Facebook Newsfeed and messaging service as well. Spammers tend to market pornography, fraudulent deals and services, outright scams, and other products not widely approved in most civilized societies. Some countries have passed laws to outlaw spamming or restrict its use. In the United States, it is still legal if it does not involve fraud and the sender and subject of the email are properly identified.

Spamming has mushroomed because it costs only a few cents to send thousands of messages advertising wares to Internet users. The percentage of all email that is spam was estimated at around 70 percent in 2015 (Kaspersky, 2015). Most spam originates from bot networks, which consist of thousands of captured PCs that can initiate and relay spam messages. Spam volume has declined somewhat since authorities took down the Rustock botnet in 2011. Spam costs for businesses are very high (estimated at over $50 billion per year) because of the computing and network resources billions of unwanted email messages and the time required to deal with them consumes.

ISPs and individuals can combat spam by using spam filtering software to block suspicious email before it enters a recipient's email inbox. However, spam filters may block legitimate messages. Spammers know how to skirt filters by continually changing their email accounts, by incorporating spam messages in images, by embedding spam in email attachments and digital greeting cards, and by using other people's computers that have been hijacked by botnets (see Chapter 8). Many spam messages are sent from one country although another country hosts the spam website.

Spamming is more tightly regulated in Europe than in the United States. In 2002, the European Parliament passed a ban on unsolicited commercial messaging. Digital marketing can be targeted only to people who have given prior consent.

The U.S. CAN-SPAM Act of 2003, which went into effect in 2004, does not outlaw spamming but does ban deceptive email practices by requiring commercial email messages to display accurate subject lines, identify the true senders, and offer recipients an easy way to remove their names from email lists. It also prohibits the use of fake return addresses. A few people have been prosecuted under the law, but it has had a negligible impact on spamming in large part because of the Internet's exceptionally poor security and the use of offshore servers and botnets. Most large-scale spamming has moved offshore to Russia and Eastern Europe where hackers control global botnets capable of generating billions of spam messages. The largest spam network in recent years was the Russian network Festi based in St. Petersburg. Festi is best known as the spam generator behind the global Viagra-spam industry, which stretches from Russia to Indian pharmaceutical firms selling counterfeit Viagra. The spam industry in Russia generates an estimated $60 million for criminal groups (Kramer, 2013).

Employment: Trickle-Down Technology and Reengineering Job Loss

Reengineering work is typically hailed in the information systems community as a major benefit of new information technology. It is much less frequently noted that redesigning business processes has caused millions of mid-level factory managers and clerical workers to lose their jobs. In 2011, some economists sounded new alarms about information and computer technology threatening middle-class, white-collar jobs (in addition to blue-collar factory jobs). Erik Brynjolfsson and Andrew P. McAfee argue that the pace of automation has picked up in recent years because of a combination of technologies, including robotics, numerically controlled machines, computerized inventory control, pattern recognition, voice recognition, and online commerce. One result is that machines can now do a great many jobs heretofore reserved for humans, including tech support, call center work, X-ray examiners, and even legal document review (Brynjolfsson and McAfee, 2011). These views contrast with earlier assessments by economists that both labor and capital would receive stable shares of income and that new technologies created as many or more new jobs as they destroyed old ones. However, there is no guarantee this will happen in the future, and the income wealth share of labor may continue to fall relative to capital, resulting in a loss of high-paying jobs and further declines in wages.

Other economists are much more sanguine about the potential job losses. They believe relieving bright, educated workers from reengineered jobs will result in these workers moving to better jobs in fast-growth industries. Missing from this equation are unskilled, blue-collar workers and older, less well-educated middle managers. It is not clear that these groups can be retrained easily for high-quality (high-paying) jobs.

Equity and Access: Increasing Racial and Social Class Cleavages

Does everyone have an equal opportunity to participate in the digital age? Will the social, economic, and cultural gaps that exist in the United States and other societies be reduced by information systems technology? Or will the cleavages be increased, permitting the better off to become even more better off relative to others?

These questions have not yet been fully answered because the impact of systems technology on various groups in society has not been thoroughly studied. What is known is that information, knowledge, computers, and access to these resources through educational institutions and public libraries are inequitably distributed along ethnic and social class lines, as are many other information resources. Several studies have found that poor and minority groups in the United States are less likely to have computers or online Internet access even though computer ownership and Internet access have soared in the past five years. Although the gap in computer access is narrowing, higher-income families in each ethnic group are still more likely to have home computers and broadband Internet access than lower-income families in the same group. Moreover, the children of higher-income families are far more likely to use their Internet access to pursue educational goals, whereas lower-income children are much more likely to spend time on entertainment and games (Richtel, 2012).

Left uncorrected, this **digital divide** could lead to a society of information haves, computer literate and skilled, versus a large group of information have-nots, computer illiterate and unskilled. Public interest groups want to narrow this digital divide by making digital information services—including the Internet—available to virtually everyone, just as basic telephone service is now.

HEALTH RISKS: RSI, CVS, AND COGNITIVE DECLINE

A common occupational disease today is **repetitive stress injury (RSI)**. RSI occurs when muscle groups are forced through repetitive actions often with high-impact loads (such as tennis) or tens of thousands of repetitions under low-impact loads (such as working at a computer keyboard). The incidence of RSI is estimated to be as much as one-third of the labor force and accounts for one-third of all disability cases.

The single largest source of RSI is computer keyboards. The most common kind of computer-related RSI is **carpal tunnel syndrome (CTS)**, in which pressure on the median nerve through the wrist's bony structure, called a carpal tunnel, produces pain. The pressure is caused by constant repetition of keystrokes: in a single shift, a word processor may perform 23,000 keystrokes. Symptoms of CTS include numbness, shooting pain, inability to grasp objects, and tingling. Millions of workers have been diagnosed with CTS. It affects an estimated 3 percent to 6 percent of the workforce (LeBlanc and Cestia, 2011).

INTERACTIVE SESSION: TECHNOLOGY   Big Data Gets Personal: Behavioral Targeting

Ever get the feeling somebody is trailing you on the Web, watching your every click? Do you wonder why you start seeing display ads and pop-ups just after you've been searching the Web for a car, a dress, or cosmetic product? Well, you're right: your behavior is being tracked, and you are being targeted on the Web as you move from site to site in order to expose you to certain "targeted" ads. It's Big Data's dark side.

Individual Web sites and companies whose business is identifying and tracking Internet users for advertisers and marketers are collecting data on your every online move. Google, which handles more than 3.5 billion Web searches each day, knows more about you than your mother does. Many of the tracking tools gather incredibly personal information such as age, gender, race, income, marital status, health concerns (health topics you search for), TV shows and movies viewed, magazines and newspapers read, and books purchased. In 2015, a $50 billion dollar online ad industry drove this intense data collection. Facebook, which maintains detailed data on over 1.4 billion users, employs its Like button to follow users around the Web even if you log off, tracking what you and your friends like. Google's many different Web services know about your friendships on Gmail, the places you go on maps, and how you spend your time on the more than two million websites in Google's ad network. While millions of Web users are installing ad and cookie blocking software, new technologies like socalled canvas fingerprinting are able to track people online.

While tracking firms claim the information they gather is anonymous, this is true in name only. Scholars have shown that with just a few pieces of information, such as age, gender, zip code, and marital status, specific individuals can be easily identified. Moreover, tracking firms combine their online data with data they purchase from offline firms who track retail store purchases of virtually all Americans. Here, personal names and other identifiers are used.

Use of real identities across the Web is going mainstream at a rapid clip. A *Wall Street Journal* examination of nearly 1,000 top Web sites found that 75 percent now include code from social networks, such as Facebook's "Like" or Twitter's "Tweet" buttons. Such code can match people's identities with their Web-browsing activities on an unprecedented scale and can even track a user's arrival on a page if the button is never clicked.

In separate research, the *Journal* examined what happens when people logged in to roughly 70 popular Web sites that request a login and found that more than a quarter of the time, the sites passed along a user's real name, email address, or other personal details to third-party companies.

Online advertising titans like Google, Microsoft, and Facebook are all looking for ways to monetize their huge collections of online behavioral data. While search engine marketing is arguably the most effective form of advertising in history, untargeted banner display ad marketing is highly inefficient because it displays ads to everyone regardless of their interests. As a result, these firms cannot charge much for display ads. However, by tracking the online movements of 260 million U.S. Internet users, Web sites can develop a very clear picture of who you are, and use that information to show you ads that might be of interest to you. This would make the marketing process more efficient and more profitable for all the parties involved.

You're also being tracked closely when you use your mobile phone to access the Internet, visit your Facebook page, get Twitter feeds, watch videos, and listen to music. The mobile Web is working hard to keep track of your whereabouts, locations, habits, and friends in the hope of selling you even more products and services. Mobile advertising is less effective than Web-based marketing because advertisers cannot place cookies on your smartphone.

New technologies found on smartphones can identify where you are located within a few yards. Performing routine actions using your smart phone makes it possible to locate you throughout the day, to report this information to corporate databases, retain and analyze the information, and then sell it to advertisers. Most of the popular apps report your location. Law enforcement agencies certainly have an interest in knowing the whereabouts of criminals and suspects. There are, of course, many times when you would like to report your location either automatically or on your command. If you were injured, for instance, you might like your cell phone to be able to automatically report your location to the authorities, but what about occasions when you don't want anyone to know where you are, least of all advertisers and marketers?

Location data gathered from cell phones has extraordinary commercial value because advertising companies can send you highly targeted advertisements, coupons, and flash bargains, based on where you are located. This technology is the foundation for many location-based services, which include smartphone maps and charts, shopping apps, and social apps that you can use to let your friends know where you are and what you are doing. Revenues from the global location-based services market are projected to reach reach $10.3 billion in 2015, according to Gartner.

In 2014, Google earned $12 billion from its mobile ads. Smartphone apps that provide location-based services are also sources of personal, private location information based on the smartphone GPS capability.

New software is being developed to help advertisers track users across devices by establishing cross-screen identities. That means that companies will be able to serve ads to your mobile phone based on what they learned about you from surfing the Web on your PC, at the office or at home. Behavioral tracking and targeting of ads is about to get a boost from the Internet of Things, the connected set of billions of sensors on machines and worn by individuals. Google looks at your searches and mail, Facebook logs and tries to understand your social behavior, and iPhone and Androids track your physical location. Increasingly, cars, thermostats, and refrigerators will be tracking your movements as well.

Sources: Quentin Hardy, "Business Technology Starts to Get Personal", *New York Times*, October 4, 2015; Farhad Manjoo, "Ad Blockers and the Nuisance at the Heart of the Modern Web," *New York Times*, August 10, 2015; Michael McEnaney, "Canvas Fingerprinting: Meet Your New Online Behavior Tracker," *TechTimes*, July 23, 2014; Elizabeth Dwoskin, "Internet Users Tap Tech Tools That Protect Them From Prying Eyes," *Wall Street Journal*, March 23, 2014; Claire Cain Miller and Somni Sengupta, "Selling Secrets of Phone Users to Advertisers," *New York Times*, October 5, 2013; Spencer E. Ante, "Online Ads Can Now Follow Your Home," *Wall Street Journal*, April 29, 2013; Jennifer Valentino-Devries and Jeremy Singer, "They Know What You're Shopping for," *Wall Street Journal*, December 7 , 2013.

CASE STUDY QUESTIONS

1. Why is behavioral tracking such an important ethical dilemma today? Identify the stakeholders and interest groups in favor of and opposed to behavioral tracking.

2. How do businesses benefit from behavioral tracking? Do people benefit? Explain your answer.

3. What would happen if there were no behavioral tracking on the Internet?

RSI is avoidable. Designing workstations for a neutral wrist position (using a wrist rest to support the wrist), proper monitor stands, and footrests all contribute to proper posture and reduced RSI. Ergonomically correct keyboards are also an option. These measures should be supported by frequent rest breaks and rotation of employees to different jobs.

Repetitive stress injury (RSI) is the leading occupational disease today. The single largest cause of RSI is computer keyboard work.

RSI is not the only occupational illness computers cause. Back and neck pain, leg stress, and foot pain also result from poor ergonomic designs of workstations. **Computer vision syndrome (CVS)** refers to any eyestrain condition related to display screen use in desktop computers, laptops, e-readers, smartphones, and handheld video games. CVS affects about 90 percent of people who spend three hours or more per day at a computer (Beck, 2010). Its symptoms, which are usually temporary, include headaches, blurred vision, and dry and irritated eyes.

In addition to these maladies, computer technology may be harming our cognitive functions or at least changing how we think and solve problems. Although the Internet has made it much easier for people to access, create, and use information, some experts believe that it is also preventing people from focusing and thinking clearly. They argue that exposure to computers reduces intelligence and actually makes people dumb. One MIT scholar believes exposure to computers discourages drawing and encourages looking up answers rather than engaging in real problem solving. Students, in this view, don't learn much surfing the web or answering email when compared to listening, drawing, arguing, looking, and exploring (Henry, 2011). The Interactive Session on People describes a related concern: that automation is de-skilling people by removing opportunities to learn important tasks and impairing their ability to think on their own.

The computer has become part of our lives—personally as well as socially, culturally, and politically. It is unlikely that the issues and our choices will become easier as information technology continues to transform our world. The growth of the Internet and the information economy suggests that all the ethical and social issues we have described will be heightened further as we move further into the first digital century.

Review Summary

4-1 **What ethical, social, and political issues are raised by information systems?** Information technology is introducing changes for which laws and rules of acceptable conduct have not yet been developed. Increasing computing power, storage, and networking capabilities—including the Internet—expand the reach of individual and organizational actions and magnify their impacts. The ease and anonymity with which information is now communicated, copied, and manipulated in online environments pose new challenges to the protection of privacy and intellectual property. The main ethical, social, and political issues information systems raise center on information rights and obligations, property rights and obligations, accountability and control, system quality, and quality of life.

4-2 **What specific principles for conduct can be used to guide ethical decisions?** Six ethical principles for judging conduct include the Golden Rule, Immanuel Kant's categorical imperative, the slippery slope rule, the utilitarian principle, the risk aversion principle, and the ethical no-free-lunch rule. These principles should be used in conjunction with an ethical analysis.

4-3 **Why do contemporary information systems technology and the Internet pose challenges to the protection of individual privacy and intellectual property?** Contemporary data storage and data analysis technology enable companies to gather personal data from many sources easily about individuals and analyze these data to create detailed digital profiles about individuals and their behaviors. Data flowing over the Internet can be monitored at many points. Cookies and other web monitoring tools closely track the activities of website visitors. Not all websites have strong privacy protection policies, and they do not always allow for informed consent regarding the use of personal information. Traditional copyright laws are insufficient to protect against software piracy because digital material can be copied so easily and transmitted to many locations simultaneously over the Internet.

4-4 **How have information systems affected laws for establishing accountability and liability and the quality of everyday life?** New information technologies are challenging existing liability laws and social practices for holding individuals and institutions accountable for harm done to others. Although computer systems have been sources of efficiency and wealth, they have some negative impacts. Computer errors can cause serious harm to individuals and organizations. Poor data quality is also responsible for disruptions and losses for businesses. Jobs can be lost when computers replace workers or tasks become unnecessary in reengineered business processes. The ability to own and use a computer may be exacerbating socioeconomic disparities among different racial groups and social classes. Widespread use of computers increases opportunities for computer crime and computer abuse. Computers can also create health and cognitive problems such as repetitive stress injury, computer vision syndrome, and the inability to think clearly and perform complex tasks.

Key Terms

Accountability, 144
Carpal tunnel syndrome (CTS), 163
Computer abuse, 162
Computer crime, 161
Computer vision syndrome (CVS), 166
Cookies, 152
Copyright, 155
Digital divide, 163
Digital Millennium Copyright Act (DMCA), 157
Due process, 146

Ethical no-free-lunch rule, 147
Ethics, 140
Fair Information Practices (FIP), 149
Golden Rule, 147
Immanuel Kant's categorical imperative, 147
Information rights, 141
Informed consent, 151
Intellectual property, 155
Liability, 146
Nonobvious relationship awareness (NORA), 143

Opt-in, 153
Opt-out, 153
Patent, 156
Privacy, 148
Profiling, 143
Repetitive stress injury (RSI), 163
Responsibility, 144
Risk aversion principle, 147
Safe harbor, 151
Spam, 162
Spyware, 153
Trade secret, 155
Utilitarian principle, 147
web beacons, 152

MyMISLab™

To complete the problems with the ✪, go to EOC Discussion Questions in the MyLab.

Review Questions

4-1 What ethical, social, and political issues are raised by information systems?
- Define ethics and explain why information systems raise new ethical questions..
- List and describe the issues raised by the five moral dimensions of the information age.
- Differentiate between responsibility, accountability, and liability.

4-2 What specific principles for conduct can be used to guide ethical decisions?
- List and describe the five steps in an ethical analysis.
- Identify and describe six ethical principles.

4-3 Why do contemporary information systems technology and the Internet pose challenges to the protection of individual privacy and intellectual property?
- Define privacy and Fair Information Practices.
- Explain how the Internet challenges the protection of individual privacy and intellectual property.
- Explain how informed consent, legislation, industry self-regulation, and technology tools help protect the individual privacy of Internet users.
- Define intellectual property and explain how contemporary information technologies pose challenges to the protection of intellectual property..

4-4 How have information systems affected laws for establishing accountability and liability and the quality of everyday life?
- Explain why it is so difficult to hold software services liable for failure or injury.
- List and describe the principal causes of system quality problems.
- Name and describe four quality of life impacts of computers and information systems.
- Define and describe computer vision syndrome and repetitive stress injury (RSI) and explain their relationship to information technology.

Discussion Questions

✪ 4-5 Should producers of software-based services, such as ATMs, be held liable for economic injuries suffered when their systems fail?

✪ 4-6 Should companies be responsible for unemployment their information systems cause? Why or why not?

✪ 4-7 Is there a digital divide? If so, why does it matter?

Hands-On MIS Projects

The projects in this section give you hands-on experience in analyzing the privacy implications of using online data brokers, developing a corporate policy for employee web usage, using blog creation tools to create a simple blog, and analyzing Web browser privacy. Visit MyMISLab's Multimedia Library to access this chapter's Hands-On MIS Projects

MANAGEMENT DECISION PROBLEMS

4-8 InfoFree's website is linked to massive databases that consolidate personal data on millions of people. Users can purchase marketing lists of consumers broken down by location, age, income level, home value, and interests. One could use this capability to obtain a list, for example, of everyone in Lille, France, making €150,000 or more per year. Do data brokers such as InfoFree raise privacy issues? Why or why not? If your name and other personal information were in this database, what limitations on access would you want to preserve your privacy? Consider the following data users: government agencies, your employer, private business firms, other individuals.

4-9 As the head of a small insurance company with six employees, you are concerned about how effectively your company is using its networking and human resources. Budgets are tight, and you are struggling to meet payrolls because employees are reporting many overtime hours. You do not believe that the employees have a sufficiently heavy workload to warrant working longer hours and are looking into the amount of time they spend on the Internet.

Each employee uses a computer with Internet access on the job. Review a sample of your company's weekly report of employee web usage, which can be found in MyMISLab™.
- Calculate the total amount of time each employee spent on the web for the week and the total amount of time that company computers were used for this purpose. Rank the employees in the order of the amount of time each spent online.

- Do your findings and the contents of the report indicate any ethical problems employees are creating? Is the company creating an ethical problem by monitoring its employees' use of the Internet?
- Use the guidelines for ethical analysis presented in this chapter to develop a solution to the problems you have identified.

ACHIEVING OPERATIONAL EXCELLENCE: CREATING A SIMPLE BLOG

Software skills: Blog creation
Business skills: Blog and web page design

4-10 In this project, you'll learn how to build a simple blog of your own design using the online blog creation software available at Blogger.com. Pick a sport, hobby, or topic of interest as the theme for your blog. Name the blog, give it a title, and choose a template for the blog. Post at least four entries to the blog, adding a label for each posting. Edit your posts if necessary. Upload an image, such as a photo from your hard drive or the web, to your blog. Add capabilities for other registered users, such as team members, to comment on your blog. Briefly describe how your blog could be useful to a company selling products or services related to the theme of your blog. List the tools available to Blogger that would make your blog more useful for business and describe the business uses of each. Save your blog and show it to your instructor.

IMPROVING DECISION MAKING: USING SOCIAL MEDIA FOR ONLINE MARKET RESEARCH

Software Skills: Web browser software
Business Skills: Using social media to identify potential customers

4-11 This project will help develop your Internet skills in using social media for marketing. It will also ask you to think about the ethical implications of using information gleaned from social media for business purposes.

You are producing hiking boots that you sell through a few stores at this time. You would like to social media both to sell your boots and to make them well known. Visit a social network site of your choice (such as Facebook, Twitter, Pinterest or another of your choosing). Through the site you have chosen, search for posts that you think indicate the author might be interested in your products. Note all the information you can obtain, including information about the author.

- How could you use this information to market your boots?
- What ethical principles might you be violating if you use this information to sell your boots? Do you think there are ethical problems in using social media posts this way? Explain your answer.

Collaboration and Teamwork Project

Developing a Corporate Code of Ethics

4-12 With three or four of your classmates, develop a corporate ethics code on privacy that addresses both employee privacy and the privacy of customers and users of the corporate website. Be sure to consider email privacy and employer monitoring of worksites as well as corporate use of information about employees concerning their off-the-job behavior (e.g., lifestyle, marital arrangements, and so forth). If possible, use Google Docs and Google Drive or Google Sites to brainstorm, organize, and develop a presentation of your findings for the class.

BUSINESS PROBLEM-SOLVING CASE

Facebook Privacy: What Privacy?

In less than a decade, Facebook has morphed from a small, niche, networking site for mostly Ivy League college students into a publicly traded company with a market worth of $226 billion in 2015. Facebook boasts that it is free to join and always will be, so where's the money coming from to service 1.4 billion worldwide subscribers? Just like its fellow tech titan and rival Google, Facebook's revenue comes almost entirely from advertising. Facebook does not have a diverse array of hot new gadgets like Apple does, a global network of brick-and-mortar retail outlets like Walmart does, or a full inventory of software for sale. All Facebook has to sell is your personal information and the information of hundreds of millions of others with Facebook accounts.

Advertisers have long understood the value of Facebook's unprecedented trove of personal information. They can serve ads using highly specific details such as relationship status, location, employment status, favorite books, movies, or TV shows and a host of other categories. For example, an Atlanta woman who posts that she has become engaged might be offered an ad for a wedding photographer on her Facebook page. When advertisements are served to finely targeted subsets of users, the response is much more successful than traditional types of advertising.

A growing number of companies both big and small have taken notice. In 2014, Facebook generated $12.4 billion in revenue, 88 percent of which ($7 billion) was from selling ads and the remainder from selling games and virtual goods. Facebook's revenues in 2014 grew by 58 percent over the previous year, driven mostly by adding new users and showing 40 percent more ads than a year earlier.

That was good news for Facebook, which is expected to continue to increase its revenue in coming years, but is it good news for you, the Facebook user? More than ever, companies such as Facebook and Google, which made approximately $66 billion in advertising revenue in 2014, are using your online activity to develop a frighteningly accurate picture of your life. Facebook's goal is to serve advertisements that are more relevant to you than anywhere else on the web, but the personal information it gathers about you both with and without your consent can also be used against you in other ways.

Facebook has a diverse array of compelling and useful features. Facebook's partnership with the Department of Labor helps connect job seekers and employers; Facebook has helped families find lost pets; Facebook allows active-duty soldiers to stay in touch with their families; it gives smaller companies a chance to further their e-commerce efforts and larger companies a chance to solidify their brands; and, perhaps most obviously, Facebook allows you to keep in touch with your friends, relatives, local restaurants, and in short, just about all things you are interested in more easily. These are the reasons so many people use Facebook—it provides value to users.

However, Facebook's goal is to get its users to share as much data as possible because the more Facebook knows about you, the more accurately it can serve relevant advertisements to you. Facebook CEO Mark Zuckerberg often says that people want the world to be more open and connected. It's unclear whether that is truly the case, but it is certainly true that Facebook wants the world to be more open and connected because it stands to make more money in that world. Critics of Facebook are concerned that the existence of a repository of personal data of the size that Facebook has amassed requires protections and privacy controls that extend far beyond those that Facebook currently offers.

Facebook wanting to make more money is understandable, but the company has a checkered past of privacy violations and missteps that raise doubts about whether it should be responsible for the personal data of hundreds of millions of people. There are no laws in the United States that give consumers the right to know what data companies like Facebook have compiled. You can challenge information in credit reports, but you can't even see what data Facebook has gathered about you, let alone try to change it. It's different in Europe: you can request Facebook to turn over a report of all the information it has about you.

More than ever, your every move, every click, on social networks is being used by outside entities to assess your interests and behavior and then pitch you an ad based on this knowledge. Law enforcement agencies use social networks to gather evidence on tax evaders and other criminals; employers use social networks to make decisions about prospective candidates for jobs; and data aggregators are gathering as much information about you as they can sell to the highest bidder. Facebook has admitted that it uses a software bug or code to track users across the Internet even if they are not using Facebook.

A recent Consumer Reports study found that of 150 million Americans on Facebook, ever day, at least 4.8 million are willingly sharing information that could be used against them in some way. That includes plans to travel on a particular day, which burglars could use to time robberies, or Liking a page about a particular health condition or treatment, which insurers could use to deny coverage. Thirteen million users have never adjusted Facebook's privacy controls, which allow friends using Facebook applications to transfer your data unwittingly to a third party without your knowledge.

Credit card companies and similar organizations have begun engaging in weblining, taken from the phrase redlining, by altering their treatment of you based on the actions of other people with profiles similar to yours. Employers can assess your personality and behavior by using your Facebook likes. In one survey, 93 percent of people polled believe that Internet companies should be forced to ask for permission before using your personal information, and 72 percent want the ability to opt out of online tracking.

Why, then, do so many people share sensitive details of their life on Facebook? Often it's because users do not realize that their data are being collected and transmitted in this way. A Facebook user's friends are not notified if information about them is collected by that user's applications. Many of Facebook's features and services are enabled by default when they are launched without notifying users, and a study by Siegel+Gale found that Facebook's privacy policy is more difficult to comprehend than government notices or typical bank credit card agreements, which are notoriously dense. Next time you visit Facebook, click Privacy Settings and see whether you can understand your options.

Facebook's value and growth potential is determined by how effectively it can leverage the personal data it aggregated about its users to attract advertisers. Facebook also stands to gain from managing and avoiding the privacy concerns its users and government regulators raise. For Facebook users who value the privacy of their personal data, this situation appears grim, but there are some signs that Facebook might become more responsible with its data collection processes, whether by its own volition or because it is forced to do so. As a publicly traded company, Facebook now invites more scrutiny from investors and regulators because, unlike in the past, its balance sheets, assets, and financial reporting documents are readily available.

In August 2012, Facebook settled a lawsuit with the Federal Trade Commission (FTC) in which it was barred from misrepresenting the privacy or security of users' personal information. Facebook was charged with deceiving its users by telling them they could keep their information on Facebook private but then repeatedly allowing it to be shared and made public. Facebook agreed to obtain user consent before making any change to that user's privacy preferences and to submit to biannual privacy audits by an independent firm for the next 20 years.

Privacy advocate groups such as the Electronic Privacy Information Center (EPIC) want Facebook to restore its more robust privacy settings from 2009 as well as to offer complete access to all data it keeps about its users. Facebook has also come under fire from EPIC for collecting information about users who are not even logged on to Facebook or may not even have accounts on Facebook. Facebook keeps track of activity on other sites that have Like buttons or recommendations widgets and records the time of your visit and your IP address when you visit a site with those features, regardless of whether you click them.

Although U.S. Facebook users have little recourse to access data that Facebook has collected on them, users from other countries have made inroads in this regard. In Europe, 40,000 Facebook users have already requested their data, and European law requires Facebook to respond to these requests within 40 days. Government privacy regulators from France, Spain, Italy, Germany, Belgium, and the Netherlands have been actively investigating Facebook's privacy controls as the European Union pursues more stringent privacy protection legislation, In June 2015, Belgium's data-protection watchdog sued Facebook over privacy practices such as how Facebook tracks users across the web through Like and Share buttons on external websites.

In January 2014, Facebook shut down its Sponsored Stories feature, which served advertisements in the user's news feed highlighting products and businesses that Facebook friends were using. Sponsored Stories had been one of the most effective forms of advertising on Facebook because they don't seem like advertisements at all to most users. However, this feature triggered many lawsuits, attempted settlements, and criticism from privacy groups, the FTC, and annoyed parents whose children's photos were being used throughout Facebook to sell products.

Although Facebook has shut down one of its more egregious privacy-invading features, the company's Data Use policies make it very clear that, as a condition of using the service, users grant the company wide latitude in using their information in advertising. This includes a person's name, photo, comments, and other information. Facebook's existing policies make clear that users are required to grant the company wide permission to use their personal information in advertising as a condition of using the service. This includes social advertising, by which your personal information is broadcast to your friends and, indeed, the entire Facebook service if the company sees fit. Although users can limit some uses, an advanced degree in Facebook data features is required.

Ad-based firms like Facebook, and hundreds of others, including Google, justify their collection of personal information by arguing that consumers, by virtue of using the service, implicitly know about the data collection efforts and the role of advertisers in paying for the service and must, therefore, believe they are receiving real economic value from ads. This line of reasoning received a blow when in June 2015, researchers at the Annenberg School of Communication at the University of Pennsylvania found that 65 percent of Americans feel they have lost control over their information to advertisers, 84 percent want to control their information, and 91 percent do not believe it is fair for companies to offer discounts or coupons in exchange for their personal information without their knowledge.

In June 2015, Facebook held its first ever privacy conference as part of a growing effort to convince users it really is concerned about privacy and aware of public criticism of the firm. It has hired more than 50 privacy experts focused on Facebook's privacy practices. Critics asked Facebook why it doesn't offer an ad-free service—like music streaming sites—for a monthly fee. Others wanted to know why Facebook does not allow users just to opt out of tracking. But these kinds of changes would be very difficult for Facebook because its business model

depends entirely on the unfettered use of its users' personal private information, just like it declares in its data use policy. That policy declares very openly that if you use Facebook, you don't have any privacy with respect to any data you provide to it.

Sources: Natasha Singer, "Sharing Data, but Not Happily," *New York Times*, June 4, 2015; Sam Schechner and Natalia Drozdiak, "Belgium Takes Facebook to Court over Privacy, User Tracking," *Wall Street Journal*, June 16, 2015; Deepa Seethharaman, "At Facebook Summit, Little Consensus on Privacy," *New York Times*, June 4, 2015; Zeynep Tufecki, "Let Me Pay for Facebook," *New York Times*, June, 4, 2015; IBM, "IBM and Facebook Team Up to Deliver Personalized Brand Experiences through People-Based Marketing," press release, May 6, 2015; Lisa Fleisher, "Admitting Tracking Bug, Facebook Defends European Privacy Practices," *Wall Street Journal*, April 9, 2015; Facebook, Inc., SEC Form 10K filed with the Securities and Exchange Commission for the fiscal year ending December 31, 2014, January 29, 2015; Anna North, "How Your Facebook Likes Could Cost You a Job," *New York Times*, January 20, 2015; Natasha Singer, "Didn't Read Those Terms of Service? Here's What You Agreed to Give Up," *New York Times*, April 28, 2014; Vindu Goel and Edward Wyatt, "Facebook Privacy Change Is Subject of F.T.C. Inquiry," *New York Times*, September 11, 2013; Sarah Perez, "Facebook Graph Search Didn't Break Your Privacy Settings, It Only Feels Like That," *TechCrunch*, February 4, 2013; Julia Angwin and Jeremy Singer-Vine, "Selling You on Facebook," *Wall Street Journal*, April 7, 2012; and Somini Sengupta and Evelyn M. Rusli, "Personal Data's Value? Facebook Set to Find Out," *New York Times*, January 31, 2012.

Case Study Questions

4-13 Perform an ethical analysis of Facebook. What is the ethical dilemma presented by this case?

4-14 What is the relationship of privacy to Facebook's business model?

4-15 Describe the weaknesses of Facebook's privacy policies and features. What people, organization, and technology factors have contributed to those weaknesses?

4-16 Will Facebook be able to have a successful business model without invading privacy? Explain your answer. Could Facebook take any measures to make this possible?

MyMISLab

Go to the Assignments section of your MyLab to complete these writing exercises.

4-17 What are the five principles of Fair Information Practices? For each principle, describe a business situation in which the principle comes into play and how you think managers should react.

4-18 What are five digital technology trends that characterize American business today that raise ethical issues for business firms and managers? Provide an example from business or personal experience when an ethical issue resulted from each of these trends.

Chapter 4 References

Aeppel, Timothy. "What Clever Robots Mean for Jobs." *Wall Street Journal* (February 24, 2015).

Belanger, France, and Robert E. Crossler. "Privacy in the Digital Age: A Review of Information Privacy Research in Information Systems," *MIS Quarterly* 35, No. 4 (December 2011).

Bernstein, Amy, and Anand Raman. "The Great Decoupling: An Interview with Erik Brynjolfsson and Andrew McAfee, *Harvard Business Review* (June 2015).

Bernstein, Ethan, Saravanan Kesavan, and Bradley Staats. "How to Manage Scheduling Software Fairly," *Harvard Business Review* (December 2014).

Bertolucci, Jeff. "Big Data Firm Chronicles Your Online, Offline Lives," *Information Week* (May 7, 2013).

Bilski v. Kappos, 561 US, (2010).

Brown Bag Software vs. Symantec Corp. 960 F2D 1465 (Ninth Circuit, 1992).

Brynjolfsson, Erik, and Andrew McAfee. *Race against the Machine* (Digital Frontier Press, 2011).

Culnan, Mary J., and Cynthia Clark Williams. "How Ethics Can Enhance Organizational Privacy," *MIS Quarterly* 33, No. 4 (December 2009).

Davenport, Thomas H., and Julia Kirby. "Beyond Automation," *Harvard Business Review* (June 2015).

European Parliament. "Directive 2009/136/EC of the European Parliament and of the Council of November 25, 2009," European Parliament (2009).

Federal Trade Commission. "Protecting Consumer Privacy in an Era of Rapid Change," Washington DC (2012).

Goldfarb, Avi, and Catherine Tucker. "Why Managing Consumer Privacy Can Be an Opportunity," *MIT Sloan Management Review* 54, No. 3 (Spring 2013).

Henry, Patrick. "Why Computers Make Us Stupid," *Slice of MIT* (March 6, 2011).

Hsieh, J. J. Po-An, Arun Rai, and Mark Keil. "Understanding Digital Inequality: Comparing Continued Use Behavioral Models of the Socio-Economically Advantaged and Disadvantaged," *MIS Quarterly* 32, No. 1 (March 2008).

Kaspersky Lab. "Spam and Phishing Statistics Report Q1-2015," (2015).

Kosseff, Joseph. "Twenty Privacy Bills to Watch in 2014." (January 15, 2014)

Laudon, Kenneth C., and Carol Guercio Traver. *E-Commerce: Business, Technology, Society* 11th ed. (Upper Saddle River, NJ: Prentice-Hall, 2015).

Laudon, Kenneth C. *Dossier Society: Value Choices in the Design of National Information Systems* (New York: Columbia University Press, 1986).

Leblanc, K. E., and W. Cestia. "Carpal Tunnel Syndrome," *American Family Physician* 83, No. 8 (2011).

Lee, Dong-Joo, Jae-Hyeon Ahn, and Youngsok Bang. "Managing Consumer Privacy Concerns in Personalization: A Strategic Analysis of Privacy Protection," *MIS Quarterly* 35, No. 2 (June 2011).

MacCrory, Frank, George Westerman, Erik Brynjolfsson, and Yousef Alhammadi. "Racing with and against the Machine: Changes in Occupational Skill Composition in an Era of Rapid Technological Advance," (2014).

PwC, "U.S. State of Cybercrime Survey 2014," (June 2014).

Richtel, Matt. "Wasting Time Is New Divide in Digital Era," *New York Times* (May 29, 2012).

Robinson, Francis. "EU Unveils Web-Privacy Rules," *Wall Street Journal* (January 26, 2012).

Smith, H. Jeff. "The Shareholders vs. Stakeholders Debate," *MIS Sloan Management Review* 44, No. 4 (Summer 2003).

Sojer, Manuel, Oliver Alexy, Sven Kleinknecht, and Joachim Henkel. "Understanding the Drivers of Unethical Programming Behavior: The Inappropriate Reuse of Internet-Accessible Code," *Journal of Management Information Systems* 31, No. 3 (Winter 2014).

Tarafdar, Monideepa, John D'Arcy, Ofir Turel, and Ashish Gupta. "The Dark Side of Information Technology," *MIT Sloan Management Review* 56, No. 2 (Winter 2015).

The Software Alliance, "BSA Global Software Survey," (June 24, 2014).

United States Department of Health, Education, and Welfare. *Records, Computers, and the Rights of Citizens* (Cambridge: MIT Press, 1973).

U.S. Senate. "Do-Not-Track Online Act of 2011," Senate 913 (May 9, 2011).

U.S. Sentencing Commission. "Sentencing Commission Toughens Requirements for Corporate Compliance Programs," (April 13, 2004).

Information Technology Infrastructure

II

Part II provides the technical knowledge foundation for understanding information systems by examining hardware, software, databases, networking technologies, and tools and techniques for security and control. This part answers questions such as these: What technologies and tools do businesses today need to accomplish their work? What do I need to know about these technologies to make sure they enhance the performance of my firm? How are these technologies likely to change in the future?

IT Infrastructure: Hardware and Software

LEARNING OBJECTIVES

After reading this chapter, you will be able to answer the following questions:

5-1   What are the components of IT infrastructure?

5-2   What are the major computer hardware, data storage, input, and output technologies used in business and the major hardware trends?

5-3   What are the major types of computer software used in business and the major software trends?

5-4   What are the principal issues in managing hardware and software technology?

CHAPTER CASES

Toyota Motor Europe Reaches for the Cloud
The Greening of the Data Center
Cloud Computing Is the Future
The Risks and Benefits of BYOD

VIDEO CASES

Case 1: Rockwell Automation Fuels the Oil and Gas Industry with the Internet of Things (IoT).
Case 2: ESPN.com: Getting to eXtreme Scale on the Web
Instructional Video:
IBM Blue Cloud Is Ready-to-Use Computing

TOYOTA MOTOR EUROPE REACHES FOR THE CLOUD

Toyota Motor Europe (TME) manages the sales, marketing, engineering, and dealership network for Toyota and Lexus vehicles in Europe. TME is based in Brussels, Belgium. Founded in 1963, TME sales peaked at 1.3 million units in 2007 and ran about 900,000 units in 2014. TME employs about 95,000 people. Thirty-one National Marketing and Sales Companies (NMSCs) coordinate 3,100 sales outlets or dealerships in Europe and nine manufacturing plants.

With millions of consumers in Europe who have purchased Toyota cars in the last 50 years, providing a consistent repair and maintenance service to customers was always a challenge. Repair and maintenance manuals had been replaced by personal computers in the 1990s and 2000s. These early computerization efforts simply automated the traditional printed manuals but had the advantage that they could be updated by distributing disks to sales outlets. One problem: some outlets did not update their PCs in a timely fashion, and there was no way for TME management to manage the upgrade process.

TME changed its approach to maintenance as onboard computers and sensors were introduced into Toyota vehicles. These onboard computers could gather and store information from vehicle sensors. The vehicle data could be analyzed by PCs at dealerships. TME provided dealerships with over 3,500 new PCs running up-to-date software that could immediately analyze a customer's car engine performance and provide critical maintenance and repair information as well as recommendations to local mechanics.

While this change in approach was a vast improvement, management did not have a solution for how to manage these 3,500 computers, or to know if local outlets were using the latest versions of the software. In fact, these PCs remained outside the TME firewall, and they were essentially stand-alone computers as in the past. Thus, it was impossible for headquarters to know if dealers were providing the same quality of service to customers or to know if dealers' PCs were free of

viruses and operating appropriately. One partial solution was to send TME IT staff to the dealerships to install software updates, check for viruses, and advise mechanics on new techniques. But this was wasteful and time-consuming.

Management decided to use a cloud-based solution from Microsoft called Windows Intune. Intune allows central IT staff to run PC management tasks remotely. New software can be installed, virus protection programs run, and the status updated. Each local PC needs an Internet connection and a standard browser. The local PC downloads a client version of the program. The client sends information on the PC to central IT staff. By 2015 Toyota expanded the role of Intune into a general purpose e-learning platform for the entire organization. The Windows Intune interface is easy to use and requires only a few hours of training.

Rather than spend on building their own IT infrastructure and software to manage its dealers' PCs, the Intune cloud-based model provides a far less expensive pay-as-you-go (demand computing) model, and there are no additional hardware or software costs, or maintenance costs. TME believes it saved over €1 million in infrastructure and management costs over a three-year period. By 2015 Intune supported mobile devices and Toyota had adopted a fully mobile platform of smartphones and tablets for its operations. Other management objectives were also achieved, including better security, customer service, and reduced operating costs.

Sources: "Enable Remote Device Support Without Added Infrastructure Costs," https://rjsystemsiow-public.share-point.com/Pages/microsoft (accessed December 17, 2015); "Intune: Simplify management of apps & devices," Microsoft Corporation, https://www.microsoft.com/en-us/server-cloud/products/microsoft-intune, accessed December 17, 2015; "What's New in Microsoft Intune 2015," Microsoft Corporation, https://technet.microsoft.com/en-us/library/dn292747.aspx, December 14, 2015; Toyota Motor Corporation, "Form 20F Annual Report," filed with Securities and Exchange Commission, June 24, 2015; Kate Cornelius, "How Toyota Motor Europe Manages a Large, International eLearning Program," OpenSesame.com, February 10, 2014; "Toyota Motor Europe Automotive Retailer Avoids 1.3 Million in IT Costs with Cloud-Based PC Management Tool," www.microsoft.com, November 12, 2014; Marcia Savage, "8 Cloud-based IT Management Tools," Networkcomputing.com, June 18, 2013.

The experience of Toyota Motor Europe illustrates the importance of information technology infrastructure in running a business today. The right technology at the right price can improve organizational performance. Toyota Europe was able to use contemporary cloud technology infrastructure to improve the quality of its service, enhance security, and reduce operating. But it wasn't just technology that needed updating. Toyota also changed its entire philosophy of how to maintain vehicles using embedded computers in vehicles. In addition, it needed to change how it supported its 3,100 dealers. Rather than sending expensive staff members to each dealer, they were able to rely instead on the cloud-based solution to provide support.

The chapter-opening case diagram calls attention to important points raised by this case and this chapter. In an effort to upgrade the dealer computer system, Toyota Motor Europe found that new computer infrastructure was needed in order to properly manage their 3,000 strong dealer network. Increasingly, dealer PCs were under attack from computer viruses, and dealers could often not upgrade their software in a coordinated fashion. Customers in turn were expecting dealers to provide the most current solutions for their cars in need of repair. The existing IT infrastructure would require significant additional investment to solve these challenges.

The solution to these challenges involved changes in management, organization, and technology. Management chose to use a new approach to coordinating dealer PCs by adopting a cloud-based solution from Microsoft called Intune. Management developed an implementation plan, and made organizational changes in training, and in the culture of the organization. Rather than rely on visits from headquarters IT staff, dealers were now expected to maintain their local PCs using the company's new management software. The solution is serving important management goals: lower cost, better security, and better management of the dealer PC network. Here are some questions to think about: How does information technology help Toyota Motor Europe solve its own business problems? How does the new cloud-based technology help the dealers solve their business problems?

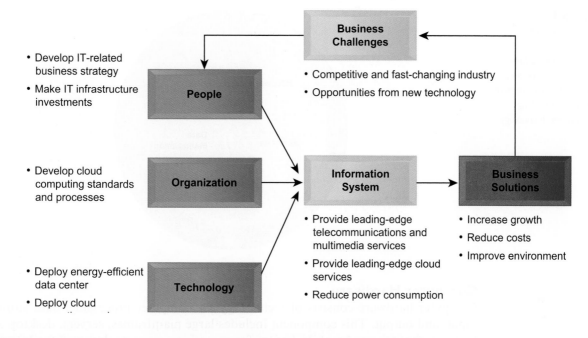

5-1 What are the components of IT infrastructure?

If you want to know why businesses worldwide spend about $3.8 trillion annually on computing and information systems, just consider what it would take for you personally to set up a business or manage a business today. Businesses require a wide variety of computing equipment, software, and communications capabilities simply to operate and solve basic business problems. Obviously, you need computers, and, as it turns out, a wide variety of computers are available, including desktops, laptops, and handhelds.

Do your employees travel or do some work from home? You will want to equip them with laptop computers (and perhaps tablets or smartphones). If you are employed by a medium or large business, you will also need larger server computers, perhaps an entire data center or server farm with hundreds or even thousands of servers. A **data center** is a facility housing computer systems and associated components such as telecommunications, storage, security systems, and backup power supplies.

You will also need plenty of software. Each computer will require an operating system and a wide range of application software capable of dealing with spreadsheets, documents, and data files. Unless you are a single-person business, you will most likely want to have a network to link all the people in your business and perhaps your customers and suppliers. In fact, you will probably want several networks: a local area network connecting employees in your office and remote access capabilities so employees can share email and computer files while they are out of the office. You will also want all your employees to have access to landline phone systems, cell phone networks, and the Internet. Finally, to make all this equipment and software work harmoniously, you will also need the services of trained people to help you run and manage this technology.

All the elements we have just described combine to make up the firm's *information technology (IT) infrastructure*, which we first defined in Chapter 1. A firm's IT infrastructure provides the foundation, or platform, for supporting all the information systems in the business.

IT INFRASTRUCTURE COMPONENTS

Today's IT infrastructure is composed of five major components: computer hardware, computer software, data management technology, networking and telecommunications technology, and technology services (see Figure 5.1). These components must be coordinated with each other.

Figure 5.1
IT Infrastructure
Components
*A firm's IT infrastructure
is composed of hardware,
software, data management
technology, networking
technology, and technology
services.*

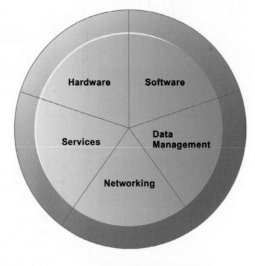

Computer Hardware

Computer hardware consists of technology for computer processing, data storage, input, and output. This component includes large mainframes, servers, desktop and laptop computers, and mobile devices for accessing corporate data and the Internet. It also includes equipment for gathering and inputting data, physical media for storing the data, and devices for delivering the processed information as output.

Computer Software

Computer software includes both system software and application software. **System software** manages the resources and activities of the computer. **Application software** applies the computer to a specific task for an end user, such as processing an order or generating a mailing list. Today, most system and application software is no longer custom programmed but rather is purchased from outside vendors. We describe these types of software in detail in Section 5.2.

Data Management Technology

In addition to physical media for storing the firm's data, businesses need specialized software to organize the data and make them available to business users. **Data management software** organizes, manages, and processes business data concerned with inventory, customers, and vendors. Chapter 6 describes data management software in detail.

Networking and Telecommunications Technology

Networking and telecommunications technology provides data, voice, and video connectivity to employees, customers, and suppliers. It includes technology for running a company's internal networks, services from telecommunications/telephone services companies, and technology for running websites and linking to other computer systems through the Internet. Chapter 7 provides an in-depth description of these technologies.

Technology Services

Businesses need people to run and manage the infrastructure components we have just described and to train employees in how to use these technologies for their work. Chapter 2 described the role of the information systems department, which is the firm's internal business unit set up for this purpose. Today, many businesses supplement their in-house information systems staff with external technology consultants to provide expertise that is not available internally. When businesses need to make major system changes or implement an entirely new IT infrastructure, they typically turn to external consultants to help them with systems integration.

Systems integration means ensuring that the new infrastructure works with the firm's legacy systems and that the new elements of the infrastructure work with one another. **Legacy systems** are generally older transaction-processing systems created for older computers that continue in use to avoid the high cost of replacing or redesigning them.

Thousands of technology vendors supply IT infrastructure components and services, and an equally large number of ways of putting them together exists. This chapter is about the hardware and software components of infrastructure you will need to run a business. Chapter 6 describes the data management component, and Chapter 7 is devoted to the networking and telecommunications technology component. Chapter 8 deals with hardware and software for ensuring that information systems are reliable and secure, and Chapter 9 discusses software for enterprise applications.

5-2 What are the major computer hardware, data storage, input, and output technologies used in business and the major hardware trends?

Business firms face many challenges and problems that computers and information systems can solve. To be efficient, firms need to match the right computer hardware to the nature of the business challenge, neither overspending nor underspending for the technology.

TYPES OF COMPUTERS

Computers come in an array of sizes with differing capabilities for processing information, from the smallest handheld devices to the largest mainframes and supercomputers. If you're working alone or with a few other people in a small business, you'll probably be using a desktop or laptop **personal computer (PC)**. You might carry around a mobile device with substantial computing capability, such as an iPhone, iPad, or Android mobile device. If you're doing advanced design or engineering work requiring powerful graphics or computational capabilities, you might use a **workstation**, which fits on a desktop but has more powerful mathematical and graphics-processing capabilities than a PC.

If your business has a number of networked computers or maintains a website, it will need a **server**. Server computers are specifically optimized to support a computer network, enabling users to share files, software, peripheral devices (such as printers), or other network resources.

Servers provide the hardware platform for electronic commerce. By adding special software, they can be customized to deliver web pages, process purchase and sale transactions, or exchange data with systems inside the company. You will sometimes find many servers linked to provide all the processing needs for large companies. If your company has to process millions of financial transactions or customer records, you will need multiple servers or a single large mainframe to solve these challenges.

Mainframe computers first appeared in the mid-1960s, and large banks, insurance companies, stock brokerages, airline reservation systems, and government agencies still use them to keep track of hundreds of thousands or even millions of records and transactions. A **mainframe** is a large-capacity, high-performance computer that can process large amounts of data very rapidly. Airlines, for instance, use mainframes to process upward of 3,000 reservation transactions per second.

IBM, the leading mainframe vendor, has repurposed its mainframe systems so they can be used as giant servers for large-scale enterprise networks and corporate websites. A single IBM mainframe can run enough instances of Linux or Windows server software to replace thousands of smaller Windows-based servers.

A **supercomputer** is a specially designed and more sophisticated computer that is used for tasks requiring extremely rapid and complex calculations with thousands of variables, millions of measurements, and thousands of equations. Supercomputers traditionally have been used in engineering analysis of structures, scientific exploration and simulations, and military work such as classified weapons research. Some private business firms also use supercomputers. For instance, Volvo and most other automobile manufacturers use supercomputers to simulate vehicle crash tests.

If you are a long-term weather forecaster, such as the National Oceanic and Atmospheric Administration (NOAA), or the National Hurricane Center, and your challenge is to predict the movement of weather systems based on hundreds of thousands of measurements and thousands of equations, you would want access to a supercomputer or a distributed network of computers called a grid.

Grid computing involves connecting geographically remote computers into a single network and combining the computational power of all computers on the grid. Grid computing takes advantage of the fact that most computers in the United States use their central processing units on average only 25 percent of the time, leaving 75 percent of their capacity available for other tasks. By using the combined power of thousands of PCs and other computers networked together, the grid can solve complicated problems at supercomputer speeds at far lower cost.

For example, Royal Dutch/Shell Group is using a scalable grid computing platform that improves the accuracy and speed of its scientific modeling applications to find the best oil reservoirs. This platform, which links 1024 IBM servers running Linux, in effect creates one of the largest commercial Linux supercomputers in the world. The grid adjusts to accommodate the fluctuating data volumes that are typical in this seasonal business.

Computer Networks and Client/Server Computing

Unless you are in a small business with a stand-alone computer, you'll be using networked computers for most processing tasks. The use of multiple computers linked by a communications network for processing is called **distributed processing**. **Centralized processing**, in which all processing is accomplished by one large central computer, is much less common.

One widely used form of distributed processing is **client/server computing**. Client/server computing splits processing between clients and servers. Both are on the network, but each machine is assigned functions it is best suited to perform. The **client** is the user point of entry for the required function and is normally a desktop or laptop computer. The user generally interacts directly only with the client portion of the application. The server provides the client with services. Servers store and process shared data and perform such functions as printer management and backup storage and network activities such as security, remote access, and user authentication. Figure 5.2 illustrates the client/server computing concept. Computing on the Internet uses the client/server model (see Chapter 7).

Figure 5.2
Client/Server
Computing

In client/server computing, computer processing is split between client machines and server machines linked by a network. Users interface with the client machines.

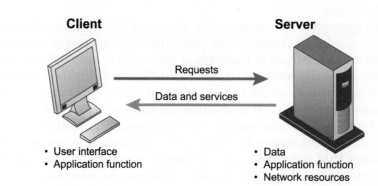

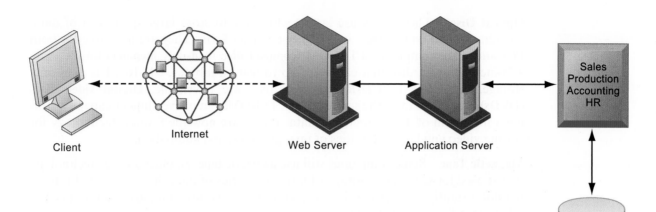

Figure 5.3
A Multitiered Client/Server Network (N-Tier)
In a multitiered client/server network, client requests for service are handled by different levels of servers.

Figure 5.2 illustrates the simplest client/server network, consisting of a client computer networked to a server computer, with processing split between the two types of machines. This is called a *two-tiered client/server architecture*. Whereas simple client/server networks can be found in small businesses, most corporations have more complex, multitiered (often called **N-tier) client/server architectures**, in which the work of the entire network is balanced over several levels of servers, depending on the kind of service being requested (see Figure 5.3).

For instance, at the first level a **web server** will serve a web page to a client in response to a request for service. Web server software is responsible for locating and managing stored web pages. If the client requests access to a corporate system (a product list or price information, for instance), the request is passed along to an **application server**. Application server software handles all application operations between a user and an organization's back-end business systems. The application server may reside on the same computer as the web server or on its own dedicated computer. Chapters 6 and 7 provide more detail about other pieces of software that are used in multitiered client/server architectures for e-commerce and e-business.

STORAGE, INPUT, AND OUTPUT TECHNOLOGY

In addition to hardware for processing data, you will need technologies for data storage and input and output. Storage and input and output devices are called *peripheral devices* because they are outside the main computer system unit.

Secondary Storage Technology
Electronic commerce and electronic business, and regulations such as the Sarbanes-Oxley Act of 2002, have made storage a strategic technology. The amount of data that companies now need to store is doubling every 12 to 18 months. The principal storage technologies are magnetic disks, optical disc, magnetic tape, and storage networks.

Magnetic Disks   The most widely used secondary storage medium today is the **magnetic disk**. Some PCs have *hard drives*, and large mainframe or midrange computer systems have multiple hard disk drives because they require immense disk storage capacity in the gigabyte and terabyte range. In lightweight PCs, such as the MacBook Air, smartphones, and tablets, hard drives have been replaced by **solid state drives (SSDs)**. SSDs use an array of semiconductors organized as an internal disk drive, whereas portable USB flash drives use similar technology for external storage.

Optical Discs   These discs use laser technology to store large quantities of data, including sound and images, in a highly compact form. They are available for both PCs and large computers. **CD-ROM (compact disc read-only memory)** for PCs is a 4.75-inch compact disc that can store up to 660 megabytes. CD-ROM is read-only storage, but *CD-RW (CD-ReWritable)* discs are rewritable. **Digital video discs (DVDs)** are optical discs the same size as CD-ROMs but of even higher capacity, storing a minimum of 4.7 gigabytes of data. DVDs are now the favored technology for storing video and large quantities of text, graphics, and audio data.

Magnetic Tape   Some companies still use **magnetic tape**, an older storage technology that is used for secondary storage of large quantities of data that are needed rapidly but not instantly. Tape stores data sequentially and is slow compared to the speed of other secondary storage media.

Storage Networking   Contemporary computer data storage technology can divide and replicate data among multiple linked physical drives or storage devices. **Storage area networks (SANs)** connect multiple storage devices on a separate high-speed network dedicated to storage. The SAN creates a large central pool of storage that multiple servers can rapidly access and share (see Figure 5.4).

Input and Output Devices

Human beings interact with computer systems largely through input and output devices. **Input devices** gather data and convert them into electronic form for use by the computer, whereas **output devices** display data after they have been processed. Table 5.1 describes the principal input and output devices.

CONTEMPORARY HARDWARE TRENDS

The exploding power of computer hardware and networking technology has dramatically changed how businesses organize their computing power, putting more of this power on networks and mobile handheld devices. Let's look at seven hardware trends: the mobile digital platform, consumerization of IT, nanotechnology and quantum

Figure 5.4
A Storage Area
Network (SAN)

A typical SAN consists of a server, storage devices, and networking devices and is used strictly for storage. The SAN stores data on many types of storage devices, providing data to the enterprise, and supports communication between any server and the storage unit as well as between different storage devices in the network.

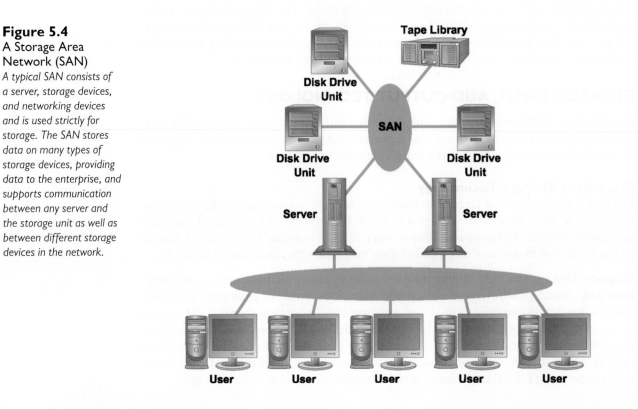

TABLE 5.1

Input and Output Devices

Input Device	Description
Keyboard	Principal method of data entry for text and numerical data.
Computer mouse	Handheld device with point-and-click capabilities for controlling a cursor's position on a computer display screen and selecting commands. Trackballs and touch pads often are used in place of the mouse as pointing devices on laptop PCs.
Touch screen	Device that allows users to interact with a computer by touching the surface of a sensitized display screen. Used in kiosks in airports, retail stores, and restaurants and in multitouch devices such as the iPhone, iPad, and multitouch PCs.
Optical character recognition	Device that can translate specially designed marks, characters, and codes into digital form. The most widely used optical code is the bar code.
Magnetic ink character recognition (MICR)	Technology used primarily in check processing for the banking industry. Characters on the bottom of a check identify the bank, checking account, and check number and are preprinted using special magnetic ink for translation into digital form for the computer.
Pen-based input	Handwriting-recognition devices that convert the motion made by an electronic stylus pressing on a touch-sensitive tablet screen into digital form.
Digital scanner	Device that translates images, such as pictures or documents, into digital form.
Audio input	Input devices that convert voice, music, or other sounds into digital form for processing by the computer.
Sensors	Devices that collect data directly from the environment for input into a computer system. For instance, farmers can use sensors to monitor the moisture of the soil in their fields.

Output Device	Description
Display	Often a flat-panel (LCD) display screen.
Printers	Devices that produce a printed hard copy of information output. They include impact printers (such as dot matrix printers) and nonimpact printers (such as laser, inkjet, and thermal transfer printers).
Audio output	Output devices that convert digital output data back into intelligible speech, music, or other sounds.

computers, virtualization, cloud computing, green computing, and high-performance/power-saving processors.

The Mobile Digital Platform

Chapter 1 pointed out that new mobile digital computing platforms have emerged as alternatives to PCs and larger computers. Mobile devices such as the iPhone and Android smartphones have taken on many functions of PCs, including transmitting data, surfing the web, transmitting email and instant messages, displaying digital content, and exchanging data with internal corporate systems. The new mobile platform also includes small, lightweight subnotebooks called *netbooks* optimized for wireless communication and Internet access, **tablet computers** such as the iPad, and digital e-book readers such as Amazon's Kindle with some web access capabilities.

Smartphones and tablet computers are becoming the primary means of accessing the Internet. These devices are increasingly used for business computing as well as for consumer applications. For example, senior executives at General Motors are using smartphone applications that drill down into vehicle sales information, financial performance, manufacturing metrics, and project management status.

INTERACTIVE SESSION: TECHNOLOGY   The Greening of the Data Center

What's too hot to handle? It might very well be your company's data center, which can easily consume more than 100 times more power than a standard office building. Data-hungry tasks such as video on demand, maintaining Web sites, or analyzing large pools of transactions or social media data require more and more power-hungry machines. Power and cooling costs for data centers have skyrocketed, with cooling a server requiring roughly the same number of kilowatts of energy as running one. All this additional power consumption has a negative impact on the environment as well as corporate operating costs.

Companies are now looking to green computing for solutions. The standard for measuring data center energy efficiency is power usage effectiveness (PUE). This metric is a ratio of the total annual power consumed by a data center divided by how much is used annually by IT equipment. The lower the ratio, the better, with a PUE of 1.0 representing a desirable target. The PUE of traditional data centers has hovered around 2.0. That means the data center is using twice the amount of electricity that's actually needed to do the computing. (The extra power is consumed by lighting, cooling, and other systems.) PUE is influenced by many factors, including hardware efficiency, data center size, the types of servers and their uses, the proficiency of monitoring software, building architecture, and the climate outside the facility. New data center designs with PUEs of 1.5 or better are emerging.

Virtualization is a highly effective tool for cost-effective green computing because it reduces the number of servers and storage resources in the firm's IT infrastructure. About five years ago, Acorda, a $210 million-per-year maker of drugs to treat nervous disorders such as multiple sclerosis found that it needed more servers and was outgrowing its data center. The company invested $100,000 in virtual servers running on technology from VMware. Using virtualization, Acorda avoided spending an additional $1.5 million on more physical servers and increasing energy consumption. Moreover, when the company moved to a new building in 2012, it was able to significantly shrink the size of its data center, further lowering cooling costs.

Acorda took additional steps to boost energy efficiency at the new facility. The company installed motion sensors that shut off lights after five minutes if no movement is detected, and it invested in a more intelligent cooling system that automatically changes settings as conditions change. Current plans include replacing all of Acorda's host servers and taking advantage of a VMware feature that moves virtual servers from one cluster to another, thereby reducing the number of clusters that require power at any given time. Acorda is also preparing to test virtualized desktops, which will greatly reduce the power required to run workstations and laptops.

Other tools and techniques are also available to make data centers more energy-efficient. Google and Microsoft have built data centers that take advantage of hydroelectric power. Facebook has publicly posted the specifications for the design of its data centers, including motherboards, power supplies, server chassis, server racks, and battery cabinets, as well as data center electrical and mechanical construction specifications. Facebook hardware engineers re-thought the electric design, power distribution, and thermal design of its servers to optimize energy efficiency, reducing power usage by 13 percent. The power supply, which converts alternating current into direct current consumed by the motherboard, operates at 94.5 percent efficiency. Instead of using air conditioning or air ducts, the servers are cooled by evaporative cooling and misting machines, which flow air through grill-covered walls. The server racks are taller to provide for bigger heat sinks, and the data center's large fans can move air through the servers more efficiently. Facebook's engineers modified the programming in the servers to work with these larger fans and reduce their reliance on small, individual fans that consume more power. This data center design, which has a 1.07 PUE rating, was implemented at Facebook's Prineville, Oregon, data center. All of these changes have reduced Facebook's energy consumption per unit of computing power by 38 percent and operating costs by nearly 25 percent. The Prineville data center reports that its PUE is 1.07, one of the lowest in the industry.

By using ambient air cooling techniques and running warmer than average, Google's newest data centers deliver a PUE rating of 1.16. Yahoo's new Lockport, New York, data center has a PUE of 1.08. Lockport's cool climate, prevailing winds, and hydropower help cool Yahoo's 120 foot by 60 foot server buildings. FedEx located its energy-efficient Colorado data center at an elevation of 6,000 feet so that the building can be cooled using outside air instead of internal air conditioning.

Financial services rely heavily on data centers, and improving efficiency in this sector can produce large returns. In Frankfurt, for instance, Siemens has built one of the most efficient data centers in the world for Citigroup (Frankfurt Data Center). When put into operation in 2008, the Center had a PUE rating of 2.8—quite high. By 2015, through optimization and "right sizing" cooling and electrical systems, the Center has achieved a PUE of 1.5. Web technology companies typically achieve very low PUE ratios. Intel has built a data center in Santa Clara with a PUE ratio of 1.06, and saves over 44 million gallons of cooling water a year by using large fans. In addition to lowering IT costs, using cloud computing services may save energy as well. Cloud computing centers pack in servers that have been optimized for virtualization and for supporting as many different subscribing companies as possible. A study by the Carbon Disclosure Project predicted that by 2020, large U.S. companies with revenues of more than $1 billion that used cloud computing would be able to achieve annual energy savings of $12.3 billion and annual carbon reduc-tions equivalent to 200 million barrels of oil—enough to power 5.7 million cars for one year.

In 2016 and beyond, electricity demands to power data centers will continue to grow rapidly, thanks to the continuing shift to the mobile platform. Experts predict there will be 7 billion mobile devices in use by year's end, and other estimates suggest there may be 50 billion by 2030. Meeting this considerable demand will require continued innovation in green computing to minimize environmental impact by any possible means.

Sources: National Renewable Energy Laboratory, "Chapter 20: Data Center IT Efficiency Measures," NREL U.S. Department of Energy, Office of Scientific and Technical Information, January 2015; Siemens, "Cool and Green: Frankfurt's Data Center," April 16, 2015; Rachael King, "Intel CIO Building Efficient Data Center to Rival Google, Facebook Efforts," *Wall Street Journal*, November 9, 2015; Robert Bryce, "Green Computing Can't Power the Cloud," economics21.org, May 22, 2014; Tony Kontzer, "Energy Management Revamps the Data Center," *Baseline*, January 30, 2013; Charles Babcock, "Facebook's Data Center: Where Likes Live," *Information Week*, March 6 , 2013; Doug Mohney, "The Little Guys: Survival vs. Green," *Green Data Center News*, May 15, 2013; Chris Murphy, "FedEx's Strategic Tech Shift," *Information Week*, May 20, 2013; "How Facebook's Data Center Leads by Example," *CIO Insight*, August 20, 2012; Sam Greengard, "IT Gets Greener," *Baseline*, April 11, 2012.

CASE STUDY QUESTIONS

1. What business and social problems does data center power consumption cause?

2. What solutions are available for these problems? Are they management, organizational, or technology solutions? Explain your answer.

3. What are the business benefits and costs of these solutions?

4. Should all firms move toward green computing? Why or why not?

Wearable computing devices are a recent addition to the mobile digital platform. These include smartwatches, smart glasses, smart badges, and activity trackers. Wearable computing technology is still in its infancy, but it already has business uses.

Consumerization of IT and BYOD

The popularity, ease of use, and rich array of useful applications for smartphones and tablet computers have created a groundswell of interest in allowing employees to use their personal mobile devices in the workplace, a phenomenon popularly called *bring your own device* (*BYOD*). **BYOD** is one aspect of the **consumerization of IT**, in which new information technology that first emerges in the consumer market spreads into business organizations. Consumerization of IT includes not only mobile personal devices but also business uses of software services that originated in the consumer marketplace as well, such as Google and Yahoo search, Gmail, Google Apps, Dropbox (see Chapter 2), and even Facebook and Twitter.

Consumerization of IT is forcing businesses to rethink the way they obtain and manage information technology equipment and services. Historically, at least in large firms, the IT department controlled selection and management of the firm's hardware and software. This ensured that information systems were protected and served the purposes of the firm. Today, employees and business departments are playing a much larger role in technology selection, in many cases demanding that workers be able to use their own personal mobile devices to access the corporate network. Although consumer technologies provide new tools to foster creativity, collaboration, and productivity, they are more difficult for firms to manage and control. We provide more detail on this topic in Section 5.3 and in the chapter-ending case study.

Nanotechnology and Quantum Computing

Over the years, microprocessor manufacturers have been able to increase processing power exponentially while shrinking chip size by finding ways to pack more transistors into less space. They are now turning to nanotechnology to shrink the size of transistors to the width of several atoms. **Nanotechnology** uses individual atoms and molecules to create computer chips and other devices that are thousands of times smaller than current technologies permit. IBM and other research labs have created transistors from nanotubes.

Another new way of enhancing computer processing power is to use quantum computing. **Quantum computing** uses the principles of quantum physics to represent data and perform operations on these data. A quantum computer would gain enormous processing power through the ability to be in many states at once, allowing it to perform multiple operations simultaneously and solve some scientific and business problems millions of times faster than can be done today. Researchers at IBM, MIT, and the Los Alamos National Laboratory have been working on quantum computing, and Lockheed Martin and Google have purchased quantum computers for business use.

Virtualization

Virtualization is the process of presenting a set of computing resources (such as computing power or data storage) so that they can all be accessed in ways that are not restricted by physical configuration or geographic location. Virtualization enables

Nanotubes are tiny tubes about 10,000 times thinner than a human hair. They consist of rolled-up sheets of carbon hexagons and have potential uses as minuscule wires or in ultrasmall electronic devices and are very powerful conductors of electrical current.

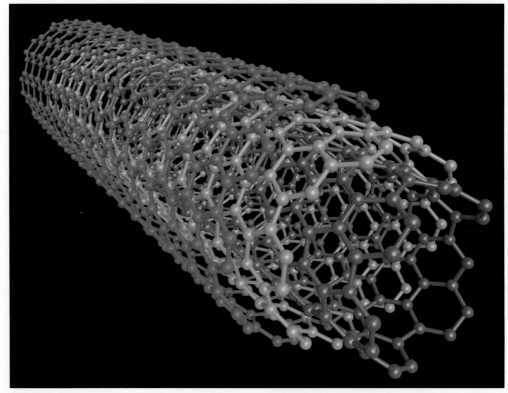

a single physical resource (such as a server or a storage device) to appear to the user as multiple logical resources. For example, a server or mainframe can be configured to run many instances of an operating system so that it acts like many machines. Virtualization also enables multiple physical resources (such as storage devices or servers) to appear as a single logical resource, as would be the case with storage area networks or grid computing. Virtualization makes it possible for a company to handle its computer processing and storage by using computing resources housed in remote locations. VMware is the leading virtualization software vendor for Windows and Linux servers.

By providing the ability to host multiple systems on a single physical machine, virtualization helps organizations increase equipment usage rates, conserving data center space and energy usage. Most servers run at just 15–20 percent of capacity, and virtualization can boost server usage rates to 70 percent or higher. Higher usage rates translate into fewer computers required to process the same amount of work. Virtualization also facilitates centralization and consolidation of hardware administration. It is now possible for companies and individuals to perform all of their computing work by using a virtualized IT infrastructure, as is the case with cloud computing.

Cloud Computing

Cloud computing is a model of computing in which computer processing, storage, software, and other services are provided as a shared pool of virtualized resources over a network, primarily the Internet. These clouds of computing resources can be accessed on an as-needed basis from any connected device and location. Currently, cloud computing is the fastest-growing form of computing, with cloud computing expenditures growing from $46 billion to $150 billion between 2008 and 2014. Within five to ten years, 50 percent of information technology will be in the cloud (Walden, May 11, 2015). Figure 5.5 illustrates the cloud computing concept.

Consumers use cloud services such as Apple's iCloud or Google Drive to store documents, photos, videos, and email. Cloud-based software powers social networks,

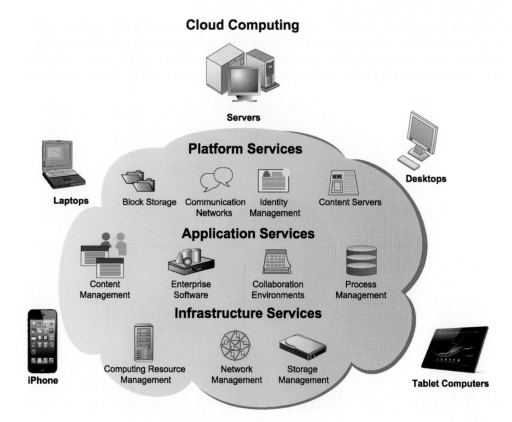

Figure 5.5
Cloud Computing Platform
In cloud computing, hardware and software capabilities are a pool of virtualized resources provided over a network, often the Internet. Businesses and employees have access to applications and IT infrastructure anywhere and at any time.

streamed video and music, and online games. Private and public organizations are turning to cloud services to replace internally run data centers and software applications. Amazon, Google, IBM, and Microsoft operate huge, scalable cloud computing centers offering computing power, data storage, and high-speed Internet connections to firms that want to maintain their IT infrastructures remotely. Google, Microsoft, SAP, Oracle, and Salesforce.com sell software applications as cloud services delivered over the Internet.

The U.S. National Institute of Standards and Technology (NIST) defines cloud computing as having the following essential characteristics.

- **On-demand self-service:** Consumers can obtain computing capabilities such as server time or network storage as needed automatically on their own.
- **Ubiquitous network access:** Cloud resources can be accessed using standard network and Internet devices, including mobile platforms.
- **Location-independent resource pooling:** Computing resources are pooled to serve multiple users, with different virtual resources dynamically assigned according to user demand. The user generally does not know where the computing resources are located.
- **Rapid elasticity:** Computing resources can be rapidly provisioned, increased, or decreased to meet changing user demand.
- **Measured service:** Charges for cloud resources are based on number of resources actually used.

Cloud computing consists of three types of services:

- **Infrastructure as a service (IaaS):** Customers use processing, storage, networking, and other computing resources from cloud service providers to run their information systems. For example, Amazon uses the spare capacity of its IT infrastructure to provide a broadly based cloud environment selling IT infrastructure services. These include its Simple Storage Service (S3) for storing customers' data and its Elastic Compute Cloud (EC2) service for running their applications. Users pay only for the amount of computing and storage capacity they actually use. (See the Interactive Session on Organizations.) Figure 5.6 shows the range of services Amazon Web Services offers.
- **Software as a service (SaaS):** Customers use software hosted by the vendor on the vendor's cloud infrastructure and delivered as a service over a network. Leading **software as a service (SaaS)** examples are Google Apps, which provides common business applications online, and Salesforce.com, which leases customer

Figure 5.6
Amazon Web Services
Amazon Web Services (AWS) is a collection of web services that Amazon provides to users of its cloud platform. AWS is the largest provider of cloud-based services in the United States.

INTERACTIVE SESSION: ORGANIZATIONS   Cloud Computing Is the Future

Cloud computing is taking off. The biggest players in the cloud computing marketplace include Amazon Web Services division (AWS), Microsoft, and Google. These companies have streamlined cloud computing and made it an affordable and sensible option for companies ranging from tiny Internet startups to established companies like FedEx. Cloud infrastructure spending in 2015 worldwide is expected to grow at 24 percent annually and exceed $32 billion in 2015 according to IDC Research.

For example, AWS provides subscribing companies with flexible computing power and data storage as well as data management, messaging, payment, and other services that can be used together or individually as the business requires. Anyone with an Internet connection and a little bit of money can harness the same computing systems that Amazon itself uses to run its retail business. If customers provide the amount of server space, bandwidth, storage, and any other services they require, AWS can automatically allocate those resources. Amazon's sales pitch is that you pay for exactly what you use instead of monthly or annual fees.

This appeals to many businesses because it allows Amazon to handle all of the maintenance and upkeep of IT infrastructures, leaving businesses to spend more time on higher-value work. For example, using AWS helped Merrifield Garden Center reduce costs, improve the stability and security of its applications and data, and eliminate the burden of managing IT infrastructure hardware so it can focus on new customer-facing initiatives to grow the business.

Startup companies and smaller companies are finding that they no longer need to build their own data center. With cloud infrastructures like Amazon's readily available, they have access to technical capability that was formerly available to only much larger businesses. San Francisco-based Socialcam provides a popular mobile social video application currently installed on over 20 million iPhone and Android smartphones. The Socialcam application makes it easy to take a video of any size, post it online, and share it with friends. Socialcam became so popular that the company's engineers couldn't install hardware fast enough to keep up with demand. By moving to the AWS Cloud, Socialcam can quickly add or remove capacity to meet demand. Netco Sports produces the Canal+ Football app that enables viewers to replay any move from any camera angle, on any device, within

3 minutes after it happens. By using AWS, Netco Sports can scale 100 servers in under 10 minutes to support streaming for 500,000 viewers.

Until recently, banks have been reluctant to use public cloud services due to security and regulatory concerns, but shrinking profits are encouraging them to take a second look. In the meantime, some banks are using private clouds for their sensitive financial transactions. National Australia Bank (NAB), with over $793 billion in assets in 2015, uses an internal private cloud based on IBM's infrastructure on demand. The private cloud hosts the bank's main production environment, including a new Oracle banking system, and will support short-term computing-intense projects such as marketing campaigns. NAB pays only for what it uses so that it doesn't have to make large IT capital expenditures. The equipment is all hosted in NAB's data centers, which is unusual for on-demand environments.

Although low overhead and infrastructure management costs make public cloud computing especially attractive to startups, the financial benefits of cloud computing for large and midsized organizations are less apparent. Cliff Olson, director of infrastructure systems at FP International, Inc., a Fremont, California-based packaging company, notes that paying a public cloud provider a monthly service fee for 10,000 or more employees will probably be more expensive than having the company maintain its own IT infrastructure and staff. Companies also worry about unexpected "runaway costs" from using a pay-per-use model. Integrating cloud services with existing IT infrastructures, errors, mismanagement, or unusually high volumes of Web traffic will run up the bill for cloud service users.

Gartner Inc. technology consultants advises clients contemplating public cloud services to take into account the number of machines an organization will run; the number of hours per day or per week they'll run; and the amount of storage their data will require. Additional costs include licenses that need to be paid for on a recurring basis, the rate of change for the data, and how much new data the business is expected to generate. A very large company may find it cheaper to own and manage its own data center or private cloud. But as public clouds become more efficient and secure and the technology grows cheaper, large companies will start using more cloud resources.

A major barrier to widespread cloud adoption is concern about cloud reliability and security. AWS cloud service has experienced several short duration outages in 2015. However, in August 2015 the AWS servers in Virginia went down for a period of nearly four hours, taking with it a large number of Web sites in the United States. Normally, cloud networks are very reliable, and often more so than private networks operated by individual companies. But when a cloud of significant size like Amazon's goes down, it sends ripples across the entire Web. A previous outage led to spiraling problems at a host of well-trafficked online services, including Instagram, Vine, AirBnB, and the mobile magazine app Flipboard. Nevertheless, AWS is the most reliable public cloud service with an average annual downtime of 2.3 hours, the best in the industry. Microsoft's Azure service is down 40 hours a year, one of the worst.

The outages have been proof that the vision of a cloud with 100 percent uptime is still far from reality. Nevertheless, some large cloud users such as Netflix believe that overall cloud service availability and reliability have steadily improved. A number of experts recommend that companies for whom an outage would be a major risk consider using another computing service as a backup.

Most midsized and large companies will gravitate toward a hybrid approach. For example, InterContinental Hotels revamped its IT infrastructure to include both private and public cloud usage. To improve response time for customers, InterContinental moved its core room reservation transaction system onto a private cloud within its own data center, but it moved room availability and pricing Web site applications onto public cloud data centers on the East and West coasts. Customers receive data faster if the data are located on a server that is physically close to them, and cloud computing helps InterContinental to take advantage of this.

Sources: "IDC Forecasts Worldwide Cloud IT Infrastructure Market to Grow 24% Year Over Year in 2015, Driven by Public Cloud Datacenter Expansion," IDC, October 5, 2015; Joseph Tsidulko, "Overnight AWS Outage Reminds World How Important AWS Stability Really Is," CRN News, August 10, 2015; "Annual Review 2015 National Australia Bank Limited," NAB Group, April 2, 2015; Beth Pariseau and Trevor Jones, "Cloud Outage Audit 2014 Reveals AWS on Top, Azure Down," search-cloudcomputing.techtarget.com/news, December 24, 2014; Beth Pariseau, "Enterprises Hit Tipping Point in AWS Cloud vs. Private Cloud Costs," searchAWS.com, April 17, 2014; Penny Crosman, "Banks Pushed Toward Cloud Computing by Cost Pressures," Information Management, March 11, 2014; "Customer Success. Powered by the AWS Cloud," www.aws.com, accessed April 1, 2014; Brad Stone, "Another Amazon Outage Exposes the Cloud's Dark Lining," *Bloomberg Business Week*, August 26, 2013.

CASE STUDY QUESTIONS

1. What business benefits do cloud computing services provide? What problems do they solve?

2. What are the disadvantages of cloud computing?

3. How do the concepts of capacity planning, scalability, and TCO apply to this case? Apply these concepts both to Amazon and to subscribers of its services.

4. What kinds of businesses are most likely to benefit from using cloud computing? Why?

relationship management and related software services over the Internet. Both charge users an annual subscription fee, although Google Apps also has a pared-down free version. Users access these applications from a web browser, and the data and software are maintained on the providers' remote servers.

- *Platform as a service (PaaS):* Customers use infrastructure and programming tools supported by the cloud service provider to develop their own applications. For example, IBM offers Bluemix for software development and testing on its cloud infrastructure. Another example is Salesforce.com's Force.com, which allows developers to build applications that are hosted on its servers as a service.

Chapter 2 discussed Google Docs, Google Apps, and related software services for desktop productivity and collaboration. These are among the most popular software services for consumers, although they are increasingly used in business. Salesforce .com is a leading software service for business, providing customer relationship management (CRM) and other application software solutions as software services leased over the Internet. Its Sales Cloud and Service Cloud offer applications for improving sales and customer service. A Marketing Cloud enables companies to engage in digital marketing interactions with customers through email, mobile, social, web, and connected products. Salesforce.com also provides a Community Cloud platform for online collaboration and engagement and an Analytics Cloud platform to deploy sales, service, marketing, and custom analytics apps.

Salesforce.com is also a leading example of PaaS. Its Force.com is an application development platform on which customers can develop their own applications for use within the broader Salesforce network. Force.com provides a set of development tools and IT services that enable users to customize their Salesforce.com CRM applications or build entirely new applications and run them in the cloud on Salesforce.com's data center infrastructure. Salesforce opened up Force.com to other independent software developers and listed their programs on its AppExchange, an online marketplace for third-party applications that run on the Force.com platform.

A cloud can be private or public. A **public cloud** is owned and maintained by a cloud service provider, such as Amazon Web Services, and made available to the general public or industry group. Public cloud services are often used for websites with public information and product descriptions, one-time large computing projects, new application development and testing, and consumer services such as online storage of data, music, and photos. Google Drive, Dropbox, and Apple iCloud are leading examples of these consumer cloud services.

A **private cloud** is operated solely for an organization. It might be managed by the organization or a third party and hosted either internally or externally. Like public clouds, private clouds can allocate storage, computing power, or other resources seamlessly to provide computing resources on an as-needed basis. Companies that want flexible IT resources and a cloud service model while retaining control over their own IT infrastructure are gravitating toward these private clouds. (Review the chapter opening case on EasyJet and the Interactive Session on Organizations.)

Because organizations using public clouds do not own the infrastructure, they do not have to make large investments in their own hardware and software. Instead, they purchase their computing services from remote providers and pay only for the amount of computing power they actually use (utility computing) or are billed on a monthly or annual subscription basis. The term **on-demand computing** has also been used to describe such services.

Cloud computing has some drawbacks. Unless users make provisions for storing their data locally, the responsibility for data storage and control is in the hands of the provider. Some companies worry about the security risks related to entrusting their critical data and systems to an outside vendor that also works with other companies. Companies expect their systems to be available 24/7 and do not want to suffer any loss of business capability if cloud infrastructures malfunction. Nevertheless, the trend is for companies to shift more of their computer processing and storage to some form of cloud infrastructure. Startups and small companies that do not have ample IT resources or budgets will find public cloud services especially helpful.

Large firms are most likely to adopt a **hybrid cloud** computing model, in which they use their own infrastructure for their most essential core activities and adopt public cloud computing for less-critical systems or for additional processing capacity during peak business periods. Table 5.2 compares the three cloud computing models. Cloud computing will gradually shift firms from having a fixed infrastructure capacity toward a more flexible infrastructure, some of it owned by the firm, and some of it rented from giant computer centers owned by cloud vendors. You can find out more about cloud computing in the Learning Tracks for this chapter.

Green Computing

By curbing hardware proliferation and power consumption, virtualization has become one of the principal technologies for promoting green computing. **Green**

TABLE 5.2

Cloud Computing Models Compared

Type of Cloud	Description	Managed By	Uses
Public cloud	Third-party service offering computing, storage, and software services to multiple customers and that is available to the public	Third-party service providers	Companies without major privacy concerns Companies seeking pay-as-you-go IT services Companies lacking IT resources and expertise
Private cloud	Cloud infrastructure operated solely for a single organization and hosted either internally or externally	In-house IT or private third-party host	Companies with stringent privacy and security requirements Companies that must have control over data sovereignty
Hybrid cloud	Combination of private and public cloud services that remain separate entities	In-house IT, private host, third-party providers	Companies requiring some in-house control of IT that are also willing to assign part of their IT infrastructures to a public cloud

computing or **green IT** refers to practices and technologies for designing, manufacturing, using, and disposing of computers, servers, and associated devices such as monitors, printers, storage devices, and networking and communications systems to minimize impact on the environment.

According to Green House Data, the world's data centers use as much energy as the output of 30 nuclear power plants, which is about 1.5 percent of all energy use in the world. Data center traffic is expected to quadruple by 2016. Reducing computer power consumption has been a very high green priority. A corporate data center can easily consume more than 100 times more power than a standard office building. All this additional power consumption has a negative impact on the environment and corporate operating costs. Data centers are now being designed with energy efficiency in mind, using state-of-the-art air-cooling techniques, energy-efficient equipment, virtualization, and other energy-saving practices. Big companies such as Microsoft, Google, Facebook, and Apple are starting to reduce their carbon footprint with clean energy–powered data centers, with extensive use of wind and hydropower.

High-Performance and Power-Saving Processors

Another way to reduce power requirements and hardware sprawl is to use more efficient and power-saving processors. Contemporary microprocessors now feature multiple processor cores (which perform the reading and execution of computer instructions) on a single chip. A **multicore processor** is an integrated circuit to which two or more processor cores have been attached for enhanced performance, reduced power consumption, and more efficient simultaneous processing of multiple tasks. This technology enables two or more processing engines with reduced power requirements and heat dissipation to perform tasks faster than a resource-hungry chip with a single processing core. Today, you'll find PCs with dual-core, quad-core, six-core, and eight-core processors and servers with 16-core processors.

Intel and other chip manufacturers are working on microprocessors that minimize power consumption, which is essential for prolonging battery life in small mobile digital devices. Highly power-efficient microprocessors, such as the A8 and A9 processors used in Apple's iPhone and iPad, and Intel's Atom processor, are used in lightweight smartphones and tablets, intelligent cars, and health care devices.

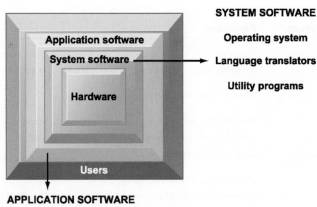

SYSTEM SOFTWARE

Operating system

Language translators

Utility programs

APPLICATION SOFTWARE
Programming languages
Apps
Software packages and desktop productivity tools

Figure 5.7
The Major Types of Software
The relationship between the system software, application software, and users can be illustrated by a series of nested boxes. System software—consisting of operating systems, language translators, and utility programs—controls access to the hardware. Application software, including programming languages and software packages, must work through the system software to operate. The user interacts primarily with the application software.

The Apple processors have about one-fiftieth of the power consumption of a laptop dual-core processor. Intel recently unveiled a line of ultrasmall, low-power microprocessors called Quark that can be used in wearable devices and skin patches or even swallowed to gather medical data.

5-3 What are the major types of computer software used in business and the major software trends?

To use computer hardware, you need software, which provides the detailed instructions that direct the computer's work. System software and application software are interrelated and can be thought of as a set of nested boxes, each of which must interact closely with the other boxes surrounding it. Figure 5.7 illustrates this relationship. The system software surrounds and controls access to the hardware. Application software must work through the system software to operate. End users work primarily with application software. Each type of software must be designed for a specific machine to ensure its compatibility.

OPERATING SYSTEM SOFTWARE

The system software that manages and controls the computer's activities is called the **operating system**. Other system software consists of computer language translation programs that convert programming languages into machine language that can be understood by the computer and utility programs that perform common processing tasks, such as copying, sorting, or computing a square root.

   The operating system is the computer system's chief manager, enabling the system to handle many tasks and users at the same time. The operating system allocates and assigns system resources, schedules the use of computer resources and computer jobs, and monitors computer system activities. The operating system provides locations in primary memory for data and programs and controls the input and output devices, such as printers, terminals, and telecommunication links. The operating system also coordinates the scheduling of work in various areas of the computer so that different parts of different jobs can be worked on simultaneously.

PC, Server, and Mobile Operating Systems
The operating system controls the way users interact with the computer. Contemporary PC operating systems and many types of contemporary application software use a **graphical user interface**, often called a **GUI**, which makes extensive use of icons, buttons, bars, and boxes to perform tasks.

TABLE 5.3

Leading PC and Server
Operating Systems

Operating System	Features
Windows 10	Most recent Windows client operating system, which supports multitouch and mobile devices as well as traditional PCs and includes voice search capabilities.
Windows Server	Windows operating system for servers.
UNIX	Used for PCs, workstations, and network servers. Supports multitasking, multiuser processing, and networking. Is portable to different models of computer hardware.
Linux	Open source, reliable alternative to UNIX and Windows operating systems that runs on many types of computer hardware and can be modified by software developers.
OS X	Operating system for the Macintosh computer that is highly visual and user-friendly, with support for multitouch. Most recent version is OS X El Capitan. The iPhone's iOS operating system is derived from OS X.

Conventional client operating system software was designed around the mouse and keyboard, but it is increasingly becoming more natural and intuitive by using **multitouch** technology. The multitouch interface on the iPhone and other smartphones and tablet computers as well as on newer PC models allows you to use one or more fingers to perform special gestures to manipulate lists or objects on a screen without using a mouse or a keyboard.

Table 5.3 compares leading PC and server operating systems. These include the Windows family of operating systems (Windows 10, Windows 8, Windows 7, and Windows Server), UNIX, Linux, and OS X, the operating system for the Macintosh computer.

The Microsoft Windows family of operating systems has both client and server versions and a streamlined GUI which now works with touch screens and mobile devices as well as with keyboards and traditional PCs. Windows systems can perform multiple programming tasks simultaneously and have powerful networking capabilities, including the ability to access information from the Internet. At the client level, 90 percent of PCs use some form of the Microsoft Windows operating system. The latest Windows client version is **Windows 10**.

Windows operating systems for servers provide network management functions, including support for virtualization and cloud computing. Windows Server has multiple versions for small, medium, and large businesses.

Today there is a much greater variety of operating systems than in the past, with new operating systems for computing on handheld mobile digital devices or cloud-connected computers. Google's **Chrome OS** provides a lightweight operating system for cloud computing using a web-connected computer or mobile device. Programs are not stored on the user's computing device but are used over the Internet and accessed through the Chrome web browser. User data reside on servers across the Internet. **Android** is an open source operating system for mobile devices such as smartphones and tablet computers developed by the Open Handset Alliance led by Google. It has become the most popular smartphone platform worldwide, competing with **iOS**, Apple's mobile operating system for the iPhone, iPad, and iPod Touch. Many Android devices have multitouch capabilities.

UNIX is a multiuser, multitasking operating system developed by Bell Laboratories in 1969 to connect various machines and is highly supportive of communications and networking. UNIX is often used on workstations and servers and provides the reliability and scalability for running large systems on high-end servers. UNIX can run on many kinds of computers and can be easily customized. Application programs that run under UNIX can be ported from one computer to run on a different computer with little modification. Graphical user interfaces have been developed for UNIX. Vendors have developed different versions of UNIX that are incompatible, thereby limiting software portability.

Linux is a UNIX-like operating system that can be downloaded from the Internet free of charge or purchased for a small fee from companies that provide additional tools for the software. It is free, reliable, compactly designed, and capable of running on many hardware platforms, including servers, handheld computers, and consumer electronics.

Linux has become popular as a robust, low-cost alternative to UNIX and the Windows operating systems. For example, E*Trade Financial saves $13 million annually with improved computer performance by running Linux on a series of small inexpensive IBM servers instead of large expensive Oracle Sun servers running a proprietary version of UNIX.

Linux plays a major role in the back office, running web servers and local area networks in about 35 percent of the worldwide server market. IBM, HP, Dell, and Oracle have made Linux part of their offerings to corporations, and major software vendors are starting to provide versions of their products that can run on Linux.

Linux is an example of **open source software**, which provides all computer users with free access to its program code, so they can modify the code to fix errors or to make improvements. Open source software is not owned by any company or individual. A global network of programmers and users manages and modifies the software, usually without being paid to do so. Other popular open source software tools include the Apache HTTP web server, the Mozilla Firefox web browser, and the Apache OpenOffice desktop productivity suite.

APPLICATION SOFTWARE AND DESKTOP PRODUCTIVITY TOOLS

Today, businesses have access to an array of tools for developing their application software. These include traditional programming languages, application software packages, and desktop productivity tools; software for developing Internet applications; and software for enterprise integration. It is important to know which software tools and programming languages are appropriate for the work your business wants to accomplish.

Programming Languages for Business

Popular programming languages for business applications include C, C++, Visual Basic, and Java. C is a powerful and efficient language developed in the early 1970s that combines machine portability with tight control and efficient use of computer resources. It is used primarily by professional programmers to create operating systems and application software, especially for PCs. C++ is a newer version of C that has all the capabilities of C plus additional features for working with software objects. Unlike traditional programs, which separate data from the actions to be taken on the data, a software **object** combines data and procedures. Chapter 12 describes object-oriented software development in detail. **Visual Basic** is a widely used visual programming tool and environment for creating applications that run on Microsoft Windows operating systems. A **visual programming language** allows users to manipulate graphic or iconic elements to create programs. COBOL (COmmon Business Oriented Language), was developed in the early 1960s for business processing and can still be found in large legacy systems in banking, insurance, and retail.

Java is an operating system–independent, processor-independent, object-oriented programming language created by Sun Microsystems that has become the leading interactive programming environment for the web. The Java platform has migrated into mobile phones, smartphones, automobiles, music players, game machines, and finally, into set-top cable television systems serving interactive content and pay-per-view services. Java software is designed to run on any computer or computing device, regardless of the specific microprocessor or operating system the device uses. For each of the computing environments in which Java is used, a Java Virtual Machine interprets Java programming code for that machine. In this manner, the code is written once and can be used on any machine for which there exists a Java Virtual Machine.

Other popular programming tools for web applications include Ruby, Python, and PHP. Ruby is an object-oriented programming language known for speed and ease of use in building web applications, and Python (praised for its clarity) is being used for building cloud computing applications.

Software Packages and Desktop Productivity Tools

Much of the software used in businesses today is not custom programmed but consists of application software packages and desktop productivity tools. A software package is a prewritten, precoded, commercially available set of programs that eliminates the need for individuals or organizations to write their own software programs for certain functions. There are software packages for system software, but most package software is application software. Software packages that run on mainframes and larger computers usually require professional programmers for their installation and support, but desktop productivity software packages for consumer users can easily be installed and run by the users themselves. Table 5.4 describes the major desktop productivity software tools.

Software Suites   The major desktop productivity tools are bundled together as a software suite. Microsoft Office is an example. There are a number of versions of Office for home and business users, but the core office tools include Word processing software, Excel **spreadsheet software** (see Figure 5.8), Access database software, PowerPoint presentation graphics software, and Outlook, a set of tools for email, scheduling, and contact management. Microsoft is promoting a hosted cloud version of its productivity and collaboration tools as a subscription service called **Office 365**. Competing with Microsoft Office are low-cost office productivity suites such as the open source

TABLE 5.4

Desktop Productivity Software.

Software Tool	Capabilities	Example
Word processing	Allows the user to make changes in a document electronically, with various formatting options.	Microsoft Word WordPerfect
Spreadsheet	Organizes data into a grid of columns and rows. When the user changes a value or values, all other related values on the spreadsheet are automatically recalculated. Used for modeling and what-if analysis (see Figure 5.8) and can also present numeric data graphically.	Microsoft Excel iWork Numbers
Data management	Creates files and databases in which users can store, manipulate, and retrieve related data. Suitable for building small information systems.	Microsoft Access
Presentation graphics	Creates professional-quality electronic graphics presentations and computerized slide shows; can include multimedia displays of sound, animation, photos, and video clips.	Microsoft PowerPoint iWork Keynote
Personal information management	Creates and maintains appointments, calendars, to-do lists, and business contact information; also used for email.	Microsoft Outlook
Desktop publishing	Creates professional-looking documents, brochures, or books	Adobe InDesign

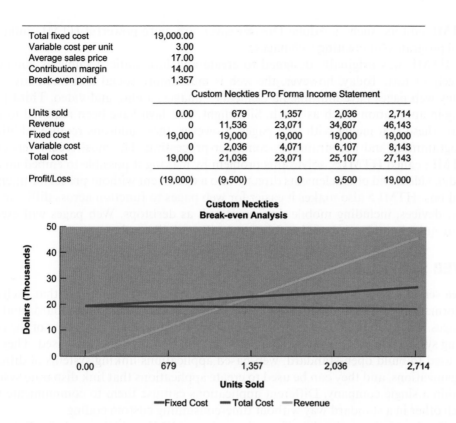

Total fixed cost	19,000.00				
Variable cost per unit	3.00				
Average sales price	17.00				
Contribution margin	14.00				
Break-even point	1,357				

Custom Neckties Pro Forma Income Statement

Units sold	0.00	679	1,357	2,036	2,714
Revenue	0	11,536	23,071	34,607	46,143
Fixed cost	19,000	19,000	19,000	19,000	19,000
Variable cost	0	2,036	4,071	6,107	8,143
Total cost	19,000	21,036	23,071	25,107	27,143
Profit/Loss	(19,000)	(9,500)	0	9,500	19,000

Custom Neckties Break-even Analysis

Figure 5.8
Spreadsheet Software
Spreadsheet software organizes data into columns and rows for analysis and manipulation. Contemporary spreadsheet software provides graphing abilities for a clear, visual representation of the data in the spreadsheets. This sample break-even analysis is represented as numbers in a spreadsheet as well as a line graph for easy interpretation.

OpenOffice (downloadable free over the Internet) and cloud-based Google Docs and Google Apps (see Chapter 2).

Web Browsers Easy-to-use software tools called **web browsers** are used for displaying web pages and for accessing the web and other Internet resources. Browsers can display or present graphics, audio, and video information as well as traditional text, and they allow you to click (or touch) on-screen buttons or highlighted words to link to related websites. Web browsers have become the primary interface for accessing the Internet or for using networked systems based on Internet technology. The leading web browsers today are Microsoft Internet Explorer, Mozilla Firefox, Apple Safari, and Google Chrome.

HTML AND HTML5

Hypertext Markup Language (HTML) is a page description language for specifying how text, graphics, video, and sound are placed on a web page and for creating dynamic links to other web pages and objects. Using these links, a user need only point at a highlighted keyword or graphic, click it, and immediately be transported to another document. Table 5.5 illustrates some sample HTML statements.

HTML programs can be custom written, but they also can be created using the HTML authoring capabilities of web browsers or of popular word processing, spreadsheet, data management, and presentation graphics software packages.

Plain English	HTML
Subcompact	<TITLE>Subcompact</TITLE>
4 passenger	<LI>4 passenger</LI>
$16,800	<LI>$16,800</LI>

TABLE 5.5

Examples of HTML

HTML editors, such as Adobe Dreamweaver, are more powerful HTML authoring tool programs for creating web pages.

HTML was originally designed to create and link static documents composed largely of text. Today, however, the web is much more social and interactive, and many web pages have multimedia elements—images, audio, and video. Third-party plug-in applications such as Flash, Silverlight, and Java have been required to integrate these rich media with web pages. However, these add-ons require additional programming and put strains on computer processing. The most recent version of HTML, called **HTML5**, solves this problem by making it possible to embed images, audio, video, and other elements directly into a document without processor-intensive add-ons. HTML5 also makes it easier for web pages to function across different display devices, including mobile devices as well as desktops. Web pages will execute more quickly, and web-based mobile apps will work like web pages.

WEB SERVICES

Web services refer to a set of loosely coupled software components that exchange information with each other using universal web communication standards and languages. They can exchange information between two systems regardless of the operating systems or programming languages on which the systems are based. They can be used to build open-standard, web-based applications linking systems of different organizations, and they can be used to create applications that link disparate systems within a single company. Different applications can use them to communicate with each other in a standard way without time-consuming custom coding.

The foundation technology for web services is **XML**, which stands for **Extensible Markup Language**. This language was developed in 1996 by the World Wide Web Consortium (W3C, the international body that oversees the development of the web) as a more powerful and flexible markup language than HTML for web pages. Whereas HTML is limited to describing how data should be presented in the form of web pages, XML can perform presentation, communication, and storage of data. In XML, a number is not simply a number; the XML tag specifies whether the number represents a price, a date, or a zip code. Table 5.6 illustrates some sample XML statements.

By tagging selected elements of the content of documents for their meanings, XML makes it possible for computers to manipulate and interpret their data automatically and perform operations on the data without human intervention. XML provides a standard format for data exchange, enabling web services to pass data from one process to another.

Web services communicate through XML messages over standard web protocols. Companies discover and locate web services through a directory much as they would locate services in the Yellow Pages of a telephone book. Using web protocols, a software application can connect freely to other applications without custom programming for each application with which it wants to communicate. Everyone shares the same standards.

The collection of web services that are used to build a firm's software systems constitutes what is known as a service-oriented architecture. A **service-oriented architecture (SOA)** is set of self-contained services that communicate with each other to create a

TABLE 5.6

Examples of XML

Plain English	XML
Subcompact	<AUTOMOBILETYPE="Subcompact">
4 passenger	<PASSENGERUNIT="PASS">4</PASSENGER>
$16,800	<PRICE CURRENCY="USD">$16,800</PRICE>

working software application. Software developers reuse these services in other combinations to assemble other applications as needed.

Virtually all major software vendors, such as IBM, Microsoft, Oracle, and HP, provide tools and entire platforms for building and integrating software applications using web services. IBM includes web service tools in its WebSphere e-business software platform, and Microsoft has incorporated web services tools in its Microsoft. NET platform.

Dollar Rent-A-Car's systems use web services to link its online booking system with the Southwest Airlines website. Although both companies' systems are based on different technology platforms, a person booking a flight on Southwest.com can reserve a car from Dollar without leaving the airline's website. Instead of struggling to get Dollar's reservation system to share data with Southwest's information systems, Dollar used Microsoft.NET web services technology as an intermediary. Reservations from Southwest are translated into web services protocols, which are then translated into formats that Dollar's computers can understand.

Other car rental companies have linked their information systems to airline companies' websites before, but without web services, these connections had to be built one at a time. Web services provide a standard way for Dollar's computers to talk to other companies' information systems without having to build special links to each one. Dollar is now expanding its use of web services to link directly to the systems of a small tour operator and a large travel reservation system as well as a wireless website for mobile phones. It does not have to write new software code for each new partner's information systems or each new wireless device (see Figure 5.9).

SOFTWARE TRENDS

Today there are many more sources for obtaining software and many more capabilities for users to create their own customized software applications. Expanding use of open source software and cloud-based software tools and services exemplify this trend.

Open Source Software
As noted earlier, open source software is developed by a community of programmers around the world, who make their programs available to users under one of several

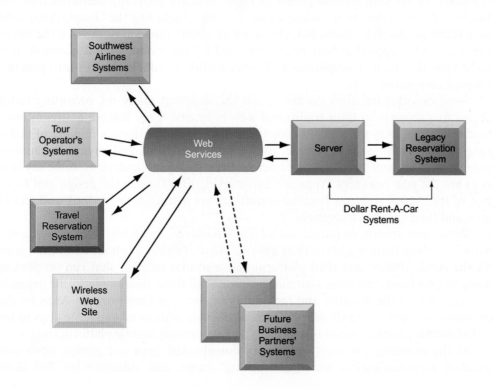

Figure 5.9
How Dollar Rent-A-Car Uses Web Services

Dollar Rent-A-Car uses web services to provide a standard intermediate layer of software to talk to other companies' information systems. Dollar Rent-A-Car can use this set of web services to link to other companies' information systems without having to build a separate link to each firm's systems.

licensing schemes. Essentially, users of the software can use the software as is, modify it at will, and even include it in for-profit software applications.

The open source movement started out small in 1983, but it has since grown to be a major part of corporate computing infrastructure, as the foundation for programs such as Linux and Apache, the most widely used web server software. Today you can find thousands of open source computer programs to accomplish everything from e-commerce shopping carts and funds clearance to sales force management. Google's Android mobile operating system and Chrome web browser are based on open source code.

Cloud-Based Software Services and Tools

In the past, software such as Microsoft Word or Adobe Illustrator came in a box and was designed to operate on a single machine. Today, you're more likely to download the software from the vendor's website or use the software as a cloud service delivered over the Internet. (Review our discussion of SaaS in Section 5-2.) Increasingly important are software tools for mobile devices, which can be downloaded or accessed from the cloud.

Mashups and Apps   The software you use for both personal and business tasks may consist of large self-contained programs, or it may be composed of interchangeable components that integrate freely with other applications on the Internet. Individual users and entire companies mix and match these software components to create their own customized applications and to share information with others. The resulting software applications are called **mashups**. The idea is to produce from different sources a new work that is greater than the sum of its parts. You have performed a mashup if you've ever personalized your Facebook profile or your blog with a capability to display videos or slide shows.

Web mashups combine the capabilities of two or more online applications to create a kind of hybrid that provides more customer value than the original sources alone. For instance, ZipRealty uses Google Maps and data provided by online real estate database Zillow.com to display a complete list of multiple listing service (MLS) real estate listings for any zip code the user specifies.

Apps are small specialized software programs that run on the Internet, on your computer, or on your mobile phone or tablet and are generally delivered over the Internet. Google refers to its online services as apps, including the Google Apps suite of desktop productivity tools, but when we talk about apps today, most of the attention goes to the apps that have been developed for the mobile digital platform. It is these apps that turn smartphones and other mobile handheld devices into general-purpose computing tools.

Some downloaded apps do not access the web, but many do, providing faster access to web content than traditional web browsers. They feature a streamlined, nonbrowser pathway for users to experience the web and perform a number of tasks, ranging from reading the newspaper to shopping, searching, and buying. Because so many people are now accessing the Internet from their mobile devices, some say that apps are the new browsers. Apps are also starting to influence the design and function of traditional websites because consumers are attracted to the look and feel of apps and their speed of operation.

Many apps are free or purchased for a small charge, much less than conventional software, which further adds to their appeal. There are already about 1.5 million apps for the Apple iPhone and iPad platform and a similar number that run on devices using the Android operating system. The success of these mobile platforms depends in large part on the quantity and the quality of the apps they provide. Apps tie the customer to a specific hardware platform; as the user adds more and more apps to his or her mobile phone, the cost of switching to a competing mobile platform rises.

At the moment, the most commonly downloaded apps are games, news and weather, maps/navigation, social networking, music, and video/movies. But there are also serious apps for business users that make it possible to create and edit documents, connect to corporate systems, schedule and participate in meetings, track shipments, and dictate voice messages (see the Chapter 1 Interactive Session on People). There are also a huge number of e-commerce apps for researching and buying goods and services online.

5-4 What are the principal issues in managing hardware and software technology?

Selection and use of computer hardware and software technology has a profound impact on business performance. We now describe the most important issues you will face when managing hardware and software technology: capacity planning and scalability; determining the total cost of technology assets; determining whether to own and maintain your own hardware, software, and other infrastructure components or lease them from an external technology service provider; and managing mobile platforms and software localization.

CAPACITY PLANNING AND SCALABILITY

E-commerce and e-business need much larger processing and storage resources to handle the surging digital transactions flowing between different parts of the firm and between the firm and its customers and suppliers. Many people using a website simultaneously place great strains on a computer system, as does hosting large numbers of interactive web pages with data-intensive graphics or video.

Managers and information systems specialists now need to pay more attention to hardware capacity planning and scalability than before. From an IT perspective, **capacity planning** is the process of predicting when a computer hardware system becomes saturated. It considers factors such as the maximum number of users that the system can accommodate at one time, the impact of existing and future software applications, and performance measures, such as minimum response time for processing business transactions. Capacity planning ensures that the firm has enough computing power for its current and future needs. For example, the NASDAQ stock market performs ongoing capacity planning to identify peaks in the volume of stock trading transactions and to ensure that it has enough computing capacity to handle large surges in volume when trading is very heavy.

Scalability refers to the ability of a computer, product, or system to expand to serve a large number of users without breaking down. Electronic commerce and electronic business both call for scalable IT infrastructures that have the capacity to grow with the business as the size of a website and number of visitors increase. Organizations must make sure they have sufficient computer processing, storage, and network resources to handle surging volumes of digital transactions and to make such data immediately available online.

TOTAL COST OF OWNERSHIP (TCO) OF TECHNOLOGY ASSETS

When you calculate how much your hardware and software cost, their purchase price is only the beginning. You must also consider ongoing administration costs for hardware and software upgrades, maintenance, technical support, training, and even utility and real estate costs for running and housing the technology. The **total cost of ownership (TCO)** model can be used to analyze these direct and indirect costs to help determine the actual cost of owning a specific technology. Table 5.7 describes the most important TCO components to consider in a TCO analysis.

TABLE 5.7

TCO Components

Hardware acquisition	Purchase price of computer hardware equipment, including computers, displays, storage, and printers
Software acquisition	Purchase or license of software for each user
Installation	Cost to install computers and software
Training	Cost to provide training to information systems specialists and end users
Support	Cost to provide ongoing technical support, help desks, and so forth
Maintenance	Cost to upgrade the hardware and software
Infrastructure	Cost to acquire, maintain, and support related infrastructure, such as networks and specialized equipment (including storage backup units)
Downtime	Lost productivity if hardware or software failures cause the system to be unavailable for processing and user tasks
Space and energy	Real estate and utility costs for housing and providing power for the technology

When all these cost components are considered, the hidden costs for support staff, downtime, and additional network management can make distributed client/ server architectures—especially those incorporating handheld computers and wireless devices—more expensive than centralized mainframe architectures.

Many large firms are saddled with redundant, incompatible hardware and software because of poor planning. These firms could reduce their TCO through greater centralization and standardization of their hardware and software resources. Companies could reduce the size of the information systems staff required to support their infrastructure if the firm minimized the number of computer models and pieces of software that employees are allowed to use.

USING TECHNOLOGY SERVICE PROVIDERS

Some of the most important questions facing managers are, "How should we acquire and maintain our technology assets?" "Should we build software applications ourselves or outsource them to an external contractor?" "Should we purchase and run them ourselves or rent them from external service providers?" In the past, most companies ran their own computer facilities and developed their own software. Today, more and more companies are obtaining their hardware and software technology from external service vendors.

Outsourcing

A number of firms are **outsourcing** the maintenance of their IT infrastructures and the development of new systems to external vendors. They may contract with an external service provider to run their computer center and networks, to develop new software, or to manage all the components of their IT infrastructures. For example, FedEx outsourced 30 percent of its IT system operations and software development to external IT service providers.

Specialized web hosting services are available for companies that lack the financial or technical resources to operate their own websites. A **web hosting service** maintains a large web server, or a series of servers, and provides fee-paying subscribers with space to maintain their websites. The subscribing companies may create their own web pages or have the hosting service, or a web design firm, create them. Some services offer *colocation*, in which the firm actually purchases and owns the server computer housing its website but locates the server in the physical facility of the hosting service.

Firms often retain control over their hardware resources but outsource custom software development or maintenance to outside firms, frequently firms that operate offshore in low-wage areas of the world. When firms outsource software work outside their national borders, the practice is called **offshore software outsourcing**. Until recently, this type of software development involved lower-level maintenance, data entry, and call center operations, but with the growing sophistication and experience of offshore firms, particularly in India, more and more new program development is taking place offshore. Chapter 12 discusses offshore software outsourcing in greater detail.

To manage their relationship with an outsourcer or technology service provider, firms will need a contract that includes a **service level agreement (SLA)**. The SLA is a formal contract between customers and their service providers that defines the specific responsibilities of the service provider and the level of service the customer expects. SLAs typically specify the nature and level of services provided, criteria for performance measurement, support options, provisions for security and disaster recovery, hardware and software ownership and upgrades, customer support, billing, and conditions for terminating the agreement.

Using Cloud Services

Firms now have the option of maintaining their own IT infrastructures or using cloud-based hardware and software services. Companies considering the cloud computing model need to assess the costs and benefits of external services carefully, weighing all management, organizational, and technology issues, including the level of service and performance that is acceptable for the business.

Cloud computing is more immediately appealing to small and medium-sized businesses that lack resources to purchase and own their own hardware and software. However, large corporations have huge investments in complex proprietary systems supporting unique business processes, some of which give them strategic advantages. Moreover, the cost savings from switching to cloud services are not always easy to determine for large companies that already have their own IT infrastructures in place.

Pricing for cloud services is usually based on a per-hour or other per-use charge. Even if a company can approximate the hardware and software costs to run a specific computing task on premises, it still needs to figure in how much of the firm's network management, storage management, system administration, electricity, and real estate costs should be allocated to a specific, individual, on-premises IT service. An information systems department might not have the right information to analyze those factors on a service-by-service basis.

MANAGING MOBILE PLATFORMS

Gains in productivity from equipping employees with mobile computing devices must be balanced against increased costs from integrating these devices into the firm's IT infrastructure and providing technical support. This is especially true when the organization allows employees to use their own personal devices for their jobs (BYOD).

In the past, companies tried to limit business smartphone use to a single platform. This made it easier to keep track of each mobile device and roll out software upgrades or fixes, because all employees were using the same devices or, at the very least, the same operating system. Today, employees want to be able to use a variety of personally owned mobile devices, including the iPad, iPhone, and Android handhelds, to access corporate systems such as email, databases, and applications.

For personal mobile devices to access company information, the company's networks must be configured to receive connections from that device. Firms need an efficient inventory management system that keeps track of which devices employees are using, where each device is, and what software is installed on it. They also need to know what pieces of corporate data are on those personal devices, and this is not always easy to determine. It is more difficult to protect the company's network and data when employees access them from their privately owned devices.

If a device is stolen or compromised, companies need to ensure that sensitive or confidential company information isn't exposed. Companies often use technologies that allow them to wipe data from devices remotely or encrypt data so that, if stolen, they cannot be used. You'll find a detailed discussion of mobile security issues in Chapter 8.

Many companies only allow employee mobile devices access to a limited set of applications and noncritical corporate data. For more critical business systems, more company control is required, and firms often turn to **mobile device management (MDM)** software, which monitors, manages, and secures mobile devices that are deployed across multiple mobile service providers and across multiple mobile operating systems being used in the organization. MDM tools enable the IT department to monitor mobile usage, install or update mobile software, back up and restore mobile devices, and remove software and data from devices that are stolen or lost.

MANAGING SOFTWARE LOCALIZATION FOR GLOBAL BUSINESS

If you are operating a global company, all the management issues we have just described will be affected by the need to create systems that can be realistically used by multiple business units in different countries. Although English has become a kind of standard business language, this is truer at higher levels of companies and not throughout the middle and lower ranks. Software may have to be built with local language interfaces before a new information system can be successfully implemented worldwide.

These interfaces can be costly and messy to build. Menu bars, commands, error messages, reports, queries, online data entry forms, and system documentation may need to be translated into all the languages of the countries where the system will be used. To be truly useful for enhancing productivity of a global workforce, the software interfaces must be easily understood and mastered quickly. The entire process of converting software to operate in a second language is called *software localization*.

Global systems must also consider differences in local cultures and business processes. Cross-functional systems such as enterprise and supply chain management systems are not always compatible with differences in languages, cultural heritages, and business processes in other countries. In a global systems environment, all these factors add to the TCO and will influence decisions about whether to outsource or use technology service providers.

Review Summary

5-1 **What are the components of IT infrastructure?** IT infrastructure consists of the shared technology resources that provide the platform for the firm's specific information system applications. Major IT infrastructure components include computer hardware, software, data management technology, networking and telecommunications technology, and technology services.

5-2 **What are the major computer hardware, data storage, input, and output technologies used in business and the major hardware trends?** Computers are categorized as mainframes, midrange computers, PCs, workstations, or supercomputers. Mainframes are the largest computers, midrange computers are servers, PCs are desktop or laptop machines, workstations are desktop machines with powerful mathematical and graphic capabilities, and supercomputers are sophisticated, powerful computers that can perform massive and complex computations rapidly. Computing power can be further increased by creating a computational grid that combines the computing power of all the computers on a network. In the client/server model of computing, computer processing is split between clients and servers connected by a network. The exact division of tasks between client and server depends on the application.

The principal secondary storage technologies are magnetic disk, optical disc, and magnetic tape. Optical CD-ROM and DVD discs can store vast amounts of data compactly, and some types are rewritable. Storage area networks (SANs) connect multiple storage devices on a separate high-speed network dedicated to storage. The principal input devices are keyboards, computer mice, touch screens (including those with multitouch), magnetic ink and optical character recognition devices, pen-based instruments, digital scanners, sensors, audio input devices, and radio-frequency identification devices. The principal output devices are display screens, printers, and audio output devices.

Major hardware trends include the mobile digital platform, nanotechnology, quantum computers, consumerization of IT, virtualization, cloud computing, green computing, and high-performance/power-saving processors. Cloud computing provides computer processing, storage, software, and other services as virtualized resources over a network, primarily the Internet, on an as-needed basis.

5-3 **What are the major types of computer software used in business and the major software trends?** The two major types of software are system software and application software. System software coordinates the various parts of the computer system and mediates between application software and computer hardware. Application software is used to develop specific business applications.

The system software that manages and controls the activities of the computer is called the operating system. Leading PC and server operating systems include Windows 10, Windows Server, UNIX, Linux, and the Macintosh operating system OS X. Linux is a powerful, resilient, open source operating system that can run on multiple hardware platforms and is used widely to run web servers.

The principal programming languages used in business application software include Java, C, C++, and Visual Basic. PC and cloud-based productivity tools include word processing, spreadsheet, data management, presentation graphics, and web browser software. Java is an operating system–independent and hardware-independent programming language that is the leading interactive programming environment for the web. Ruby and Python are used in web and cloud computing applications. HTML is a page description language for creating web pages.

Web services are loosely coupled software components based on XML and open web standards that can work with any application software and operating system. They can be used as components of applications to link the systems of two organizations or to link disparate systems of a single company.

Software trends include the expanding use of open source software and cloud-based software tools and services (including SaaS, mashups, and apps).

5-4 **What are the principal issues in managing hardware and software technology?** Managers and information systems specialists need to pay special attention to hardware capacity planning and scalability to ensure that the firm has enough computing power for its current and future needs. Businesses also need to balance the costs and benefits of building and maintaining their own hardware and software versus outsourcing or using an on-demand computing model. The total cost of ownership (TCO) of the organization's technology assets includes not only the original cost of computer hardware and software but also costs for hardware and software upgrades, maintenance, technical support, and training, including the costs for managing and maintaining mobile devices. Companies with global operations need to manage software localization.

Key Terms

Android, 196
Application server, 183
Application software, 180
Apps, 202
BYOD, 187
C, 197
C++, 197
Capacity planning, 203
CD-ROM (compact disc read-only memory), 184
Centralized processing, 182
Chrome OS, 196
Client, 182
Client/server computing, 182
Cloud computing, 189
Consumerization of IT, 187
Data center, 179
Data management software, 180
Digital video disc (DVD), 184
Distributed processing, 182
Extensible Markup Language (XML), 200
Graphical user interface (GUI), 195
Green computing (green IT), 193
Grid computing, 182
HTML5, 200

Hybrid cloud, 193
Hypertext Markup Language (HTML), 199
Input devices, 184
iOS, 196
Java, 197
Legacy systems, 181
Linux, 197
Magnetic disk, 183
Magnetic tape, 184
Mainframe, 181
Mashups, 202
Mobile device management (MDM), 206
Multicore processor, 194
Multitouch, 196
Nanotechnology, 188
N-tier client/server architectures, 183
Object, 197
Office 365, 198
Offshore software outsourcing, 205
On-demand computing, 193
Open source software, 197
Operating system, 195
Output devices, 184
Outsourcing, 204
Personal computer (PC), 181
Private cloud, 193

Public cloud, 193
Quantum computing, 188
Scalability, 203
Server, 181
Service level agreement (SLA), 205
Service-oriented architecture (SOA), 200
Software as a service (SaaS), 190
Software package, 198
Solid state drive (SSD), 183
Spreadsheet software, 198
Storage area networks (SANs), 184
Supercomputer, 182
System software, 180
Tablet computer, 185
Total cost of ownership (TCO), 203
UNIX, 196
Virtualization, 188
Visual Basic, 197
Visual programming language, 197
Web browsers, 199
Web hosting service, 204
Web server, 183
Web services, 200
Windows 10, 196
Workstation, 181

MyMISLab™

To complete the problems with the ⭐, go to EOC Discussion Questions in the MyLab.

Review Questions

5-1 What are the components of IT infrastructure?
• Define information technology (IT) infrastructure and describe each of its components.

5-2 What are the major computer hardware, data storage, input, and output technologies used in business and the major hardware trends?
• List and describe the various type of computers available to businesses today.
• Define the client/server model of computing and describe the difference between two-tiered and n-tier client/server architecture.
• List the most important secondary storage media and the strengths and limitations of each.
• List and describe the major computer input and output devices.
• Define and describe the mobile digital platform, BYOD, nanotechnology, grid computing, cloud computing, virtualization, green computing, and multicore processing.
• List the essential characteristics of cloud computing and distinguish between a public cloud and a private cloud.

5-3 What are the major types of computer software used in business and the major software trends?

- Distinguish between application software and system software and explain the role the operating system of a computer plays.
- List and describe the major PC and server operating systems.
- List and describe some popular programming languages for business applications.
- Define HTML and explain how HTML5 provides additional functionality.
- Define web services, describe the technologies they use, and explain how web services benefit businesses.
- Explain why open source software is so important today and its benefits for business.
- Define and describe cloud computing software services, mashups, and apps and explain how they benefit individuals and businesses.

5-4 What are the principal issues in managing hardware and software technology?
- Explain why managers need to pay attention to capacity planning and scalability of technology resources.
- Describe some methods that firms can use to reduce TCO of technology assets.
- Identify the benefits and challenges of using outsourcing, cloud computing services, and mobile platforms.
- Explain why software localization has become an important management issue for global companies.

Discussion Questions

✪ 5-5 Why is selecting computer hardware and software for the organization an important business decision? What people, organization, and technology issues should be considered when selecting computer hardware and software?

✪ 5-6 Should organizations use software service providers (including cloud services) for all their software needs? Why or why not? What people, organization, and technology factors should be considered when making this decision?

✪ 5-7 What are the advantages and disadvantages of BYOD?

Hands-On MIS Projects

The projects in this section give you hands-on experience in developing solutions for managing IT infrastructures and IT outsourcing, using spreadsheet software to evaluate alternative desktop systems, and using web research to budget for a sales conference. Visit MyMISLab's Multimedia Library to access this chapter's Hands-On MIS Projects.

MANAGEMENT DECISION PROBLEMS

5-8 Hischornklinik Group is a leading private medical clinic group in Germany. It relies on information systems to operate 14 hospitals, as well as hundreds of specialist institutes. Demand for additional servers and storage technology iswas growing by 20 percent each year. Hischornklinik was setting up a separate server for every application, and its servers and other computers were running a number of different operating systems, including several versions of UNIX and Windows. Hischornklinik had to manage technologies from many different vendors, including Hewlett-Packard (HP), Sun Microsystems, Microsoft, and IBM. Assess the impact of this situation on business performance. What factors and management decisions must be considered when developing a solution to this problem?

5-9 Qantas Airways, Australia's leading airline, faces cost pressures from high fuel prices and lower levels of global airline traffic. To remain competitive, the airline must find ways to keep costs low while providing a high level of customer service. Qantas had a 30-year-old data center. Management had to decide whether to replace its IT infrastructure with newer technology or outsource it. What factors should Qantas management consider when deciding whether to outsource? If Qantas decides to outsource, list and describe points that should be addressed in a service level agreement.

IMPROVING DECISION MAKING: USING A SPREADSHEET TO EVALUATE HARDWARE AND SOFTWARE OPTIONS

Software skills: Spreadsheet formulas
Business skills: Technology pricing

5-10 In this exercise, you will use spreadsheet software to calculate the cost of desktop systems, printers, and software.

Use the Internet to obtain pricing information on hardware and software for an office of 30 people. You will need to price 30 PC desktop systems (monitors, computers, and keyboards) manufactured by Lenovo, Dell, and HP. (For the purposes of this exercise, ignore the fact that desktop systems usually come with preloaded software packages.) Obtain pricing on 15 desktop printers manufactured by HP, Canon, and Dell. Each desktop system must satisfy the minimum specifications shown in tables that you can find in MyMISLab™. Also, obtain pricing on 30 copies of the most recent versions of Microsoft Office and OpenOffice. Each desktop productivity package should contain programs for word processing, spreadsheets, database, and presentations. Prepare a spreadsheet showing your research results for the software and the desktop system, printer, and software combination offering the best performance and pricing per worker. Because every two workers share one printer (15 printers/30 systems), your calculations should assume only half a printer cost per worker.

IMPROVING DECISION MAKING: USING WEB RESEARCH TO BUDGET FOR A SALES CONFERENCE

Software skills: Internet-based software
Business skills: Researching transportation and lodging costs

5-11 In this exercise, you'll use software at various online travel sites to obtain pricing for total travel and lodging costs for a sales conference.

EuroPlastiques is a leading EU plastics company. EuroPlastiques is planning a two-day sales conference for June 19–20, starting with a reception on the evening of June 18. The conference consists of all-day meetings that the entire sales force, numbering 100 sales representatives and their 15 managers, must attend. Each sales representative requires his or her own room, and the company needs two common meeting rooms, one large enough to hold the entire sales force plus a few visitors (150 total) and the other able to hold half the force.. The company would like to hold the conference in either Zurich Switzerland or Milan, Italy, at a Marriott - or Novotel-owned hotel. Use the Marriott and Novotel Web sites to select a hotel in whichever of these cities would enable the company to hold its sales conference within its budget and meet its sales conference requirements. Then locate flights arriving the afternoon prior to the conference.

Your attendees will be coming from Paris (44), London (22), Amsterdam (20),Stockholm (18), and Dublin (11). Determine costs of each airline ticket from these cities. When you are finished, create a budget for the conference. The budget will include the cost of each airline ticket, the room cost, and 60 euros per attendee per day for food.

Collaboration and Teamwork Project

Evaluating Server and Mobile Operating Systems

5-12 Form a group with three or four of your classmates. Choose two server or mobile operating systems to evaluate. You might research and compare the capabilities and costs of Linux versus UNIX or the most recent version of the Windows operating system for servers. Alternatively, you could compare the capabilities of the Android mobile operating system with iOS for the iPhone. If possible, use Google Docs and Google Drive or Google Sites to brainstorm; organize and develop a presentation of your findings for the class.

BUSINESS PROBLEM-SOLVING CASE

The Risks and Benefits of BYOD

Just about everyone who has a smartphone wants to be able to bring it to work and use it on the job. And why not? Employees using their own smartphones would allow companies to enjoy all the same benefits of a mobile workforce without spending their own money to purchase these devices. Smaller companies could go mobile without making large investments in devices and mobile services. One IBM-sponsored study by Forrester Consulting found that a BYOD program using IBM mobile enterprise services increased workplace productivity and raised effective employee work time by 45–60 minutes per week. By 2016, over 50 percent of companies will allow or require employees to bring their own mobile devices to work. BYOD is becoming the new normal.

But wait a minute. Half of all enterprises believe that BYOD represents a growing problem for their organizations, according to a number of studies. Although BYOD can improve employee job satisfaction and productivity, it also can cause a number of problems if not managed properly. Support for personally owned devices is more difficult than it is for company-supplied devices, the cost of managing mobile devices can increase, and protecting corporate data and networks becomes more difficult. Research conducted by the Aberdeen Group found that on average, an enterprise with 1,000 mobile devices spends an extra $170,000 per year when it allows BYOD. So it's not that simple.

BYOD requires a significant portion of corporate IT resources dedicated to managing and maintaining a large number of devices within the organization. In the past, companies tried to limit business smartphone use to a single platform. This made it easier to keep track of each mobile device and to roll out software upgrades or fixes because all employees were using the same devices or, at the very least, the same operating system. The most popular employer-issued smartphone used to be Research in Motion's BlackBerry because it was considered the most secure mobile platform available. (BlackBerry mobile devices access corporate email and data by using a proprietary software and networking platform that is company-controlled and protected from outsiders.)

Today, the mobile digital landscape is much more complicated, with a variety of devices and operating systems on the market that do not have well-developed tools for administration and security. Android has more than 79 percent of the worldwide smartphone market, but it is more difficult to use for corporate work than Apple mobile devices using the iOS operating system. iOS is considered a closed system and runs only on a limited number of different Apple mobile devices. In contrast, Android's fragmentation and multiple versions make it more difficult and costly for corporate IT to manage. As of August 2015, at least 24,000 Android-based devices were available, according to a report by OpenSignal, which researches wireless networks and devices. Android's huge consumer market share attracts many hackers. Android is also vulnerable because it has an open source architecture.

If employees are allowed to work with more than one type of mobile device and operating system, companies need an effective way to keep track of all the devices employees are using. When employees make changes to their personal phone, such as switching cellular carriers, changing their phone number, or buying a new mobile device altogether, companies will need to ensure, quickly and flexibly, that their employees can remain productive. Firms need a system that keeps track of which devices employees are using, where the device is located, whether it is being used, and what software it is equipped with. For unprepared companies, keeping track of who gets access to what data could be a nightmare.

With the large variety of phones and operating systems available, providing adequate technical support for every employee could be difficult. When employees cannot access critical data, or encounter other problems with their mobile devices, they will need assistance from the information systems department. Companies that rely on desktop computers tend to have many of the same computers with the same specs and operating systems, making tech support that much easier. Mobility introduces a new layer of variety and complexity to tech support that companies need to be prepared to handle.

There are significant concerns with securing company information accessed with mobile devices. If a device is stolen or compromised, companies need ways to ensure that sensitive or confidential information isn't freely available to anyone. Mobility puts assets and data at greater risk than if they were only located within company walls and on company machines. Marble Security Labs analyzed 1.2 million Android and iOS apps and found that the consumer apps on mobile devices did not adequately protect business information. Companies often use technologies that allow them to wipe data from devices remotely or encrypt data so that if it is stolen, it cannot be used. You'll find a detailed discussion of mobile security issues in Chapter 8.

Management at Michelin North America believes BYOD will make the business more flexible and productive. Initially, all 4000 mobile devices the company used were company-owned and obsolete, with a large number of traditional cell phones that could be used only for voice transmission and messaging. Only 90 employees were allowed access to email on mobile devices, and fewer than 400 were allowed access to calendars on these devices. Service costs were high, and the business received little value from its mobility program. Management had identified significant business benefits from increasing mobility in sales, customer support, and operations.

In mid-2011, the company created a team composed of executives and representatives from the IT, human resources, finance, and legal departments as well as the business units to share in the development, rollout, and management of a new mobile strategy for corporate-owned and personal mobile devices. The team decided to transition the mobility business model from corporate-owned to personally liable.

According to Gartner Inc. consultants, about half of organizations with a formal BYOD program compensate their employees for the time they use their personal devices on their jobs, using stipends, reimbursements, or allowances. Handling employee reimbursement for using personal devices for corporate purposes has proved to be one of the most problematic aspects of BYOD mobile programs. Although most companies use expense reports or payroll stipends to reimburse employees for BYOD, these methods have drawbacks. Expense reports are an administrative burden for both employee and employer, and payroll stipends can have tax consequences for both the employer and employee.

For some companies, the best option is to make direct payments to wireless carriers to reimburse employees for the expense they incur when they use their own wireless devices for company business. The employer reimburses funds to the wireless carrier, which then applies a credit to the employee's account. When the employee's bill arrives, the employee pays the amount owed, less the credit amount that the employer funded.

Michelin opted for a managed service from Cass Information Systems that enables the company to make payments directly to wireless carriers. Cass Information Systems is a leading provider of transportation, utility, waste, and telecom expense management and related business intelligence services. A single employee portal handles enrollment of corporate and BYOD devices and provides tracking and reporting of all ongoing mobile and related inventory and expenses. The portal can automatically register employees, verify user eligibility, ensure policy acknowledgement, and distribute credits directly to employees' wireless accounts for the service they used for their jobs.

Since implementing its version of BYOD, Michelin North America increased the number of mobile-enabled employees to 7000. Employee efficiency, productivity, and satisfaction have improved from updating the mobile technology and functionality available to employees and giving them choices in mobile devices and wireless carrier plans. The program is cost-neutral. Michelin has obtained new vendor discounts across all wireless vendors in the Unites States and Canada and has reduced the cost of deploying each mobile device by more than 30 percent.

Management at Rosendin Electric, a Silicon Valley electrical contractor, worried that BYOD would become a big headache. Rosendin has thousands of employees and deploys hundreds of smartphones, more than 400 iPads, and a few Microsoft Surface tablets. These mobile devices have greatly enhanced the company's productivity by enabling employees to order equipment and supplies on the spot at a job site or check on-site to see whether ordered items have arrived. However, CIO Sam Lamonica does not believe BYOD would work for this company. He worries employees would be too careless using apps, cloud, technology devices. (An Aruba Networks study of 11,500 workers in 23 countries found that 60 percent share their work and personal devices with others regularly, nearly 20 percent don't have passwords on devices, and 31 percent have lost data due to misuse of a mobile device.)

Lamonica feels more confident about equipping employees with company-owned devices because they can be more easily managed and secured. Rosendin uses MobileIron mobile device management (MDM) software for its smartphones and tablets. If a device is lost or stolen, the MDM software can wipe the devices remotely. Because MobileIron allows Rosendin to separate and isolate business apps and data from personal apps and data, the company allows employees to use certain consumer apps and store personal photos on company-owned tablets. Rosendin has found that employees of companies that can personalize company-owned iPads are more likely to treat them as prized possessions, and this has helped lower the number of devices that become broken or lost. The company has the right to wipe the devices if they are lost.

Rosendin's mobile security is not ironclad. An employee might be able to put company data in his or her personal Dropbox account instead of the company-authorized Box account. However, MobileIron can encrypt data before it gets into a Dropbox account, and this lowers the risk.

With company-owned and managed devices, Rosendin still benefits from volume discounts from wireless carriers and does not have to do the extra work involved in reimbursing employees when they use their own devices for work.

Sources: Aruba Networks, "Enterprise Security Threat Level Directly Linked to User Demographics, Industry and Geography," *Business Wire*, April 14, 2015; "5 BYOD Management Case Studies," Sunviewsoftware.com, accessed May 22, 2015; Tom Kaneshige, "Why One CIO Is Saying 'No' to BYOD," *CIO*, June 24, 2014, and "CIO Meets Mobile Challenges Head-On," *CIO*, July 7, 2014; OpenSignal, "Android Fragmentation Visualized," August 2015; Dennis McCafferty, "Surprising Facts About Mobility and BYOD," *Baseline*, January 29, 2014; "Cass BYOD: How Michelin Became a Mobile-First Enterprise,"

Cass Information Systems Inc., 2014; Beatrice Piquer-Durand, "BYOD and BYOA: Dangers and Complications," *Techradar Pro*, March 24, 2014; and Fred Donovan, "The Growing BYOD Problem," *FierceMobileIT*, February 13, 2013.

Case Study Questions

5-13 What are the advantages and disadvantages of allowing employees to use their personal smartphones for work?

5-14 What people, organization, and technology factors should be addressed when deciding whether to allow employees to use their personal smartphones for work?

5-15 Compare the BYOD experiences of Michelin North America and Rosendin Electric. Why did BYOD at Michelin work so well?

5-16 Allowing employees use their own smartphones for work will save the company money. Do you agree? Why or why not?

MyMISLab

Go to the Assignments section of your MyLab to complete these writing exercises.

5-17 What are the distinguishing characteristics of cloud computing and what are the three types of cloud services?

5-18 What is the total cost of ownership of technology assets and what are its cost components?

Chapter 5 References

Andersson, Henrik, James Kaplan, and Brent Smolinski. "Capturing Value from IT Infrastructure Innovation," *McKinsey Quarterly* (October 2012).

Babcock, Charles. "Cloud's Thorniest Question: Does It Pay Off?" *Information Week* (June 4, 2012).

Benlian, Alexander, Marios Koufaris, and Thomas Hess. "Service Quality in Software-as-a-Service: Developing the SaaS-Qual Measure and Examining Its Role in Usage Continuance," *Journal of Management Information Systems* 28, No. 3 (Winter 2012).

Carr, Nicholas. *The Big Switch.* (New York: Norton, 2008.)

Clark, Don. "Intel Unveils Tiny Quark Chips for Wearable Devices," *Wall Street Journal* (September 10, 2013).

Choi, Jae, Derek L. Nazareth, and Hemant K. Jain. "Implementing Service-Oriented Architecture in Organizations," *Journal of Management Information Systems* 26, No. 4 (Spring 2010).

EMarketer. "Smartphone Users Worldwide Will Total 1.75 Billion in 2014," (Jan 16, 2014).

Fitzgerald, Brian. "The Transformation of Open Source Software," *MIS Quarterly* 30, No. 3 (September 2006).

Gartner Inc. "Gartner Worldwide IT Spending Forecast, 2015," www.gartner.com (January 7, 2015.

Gartner, Inc. "Gartner Says Worldwide Traditional PC, Tablet, Ultramobile and Mobile Phone Shipments to Grow 4.2 Percent in 2014," (July 7, 2014).

Greengard, Samuel. "The Challenges and Rewards of Enterprise SaaS," *CIO Insight* (February 10, 2015).

Grossman, Lev. "Quantum Leap," *Time* (February 17, 2014).

Hamilton, David. "Enterprise Cloud IT Spending to Grow 20% in 2014, Reaching $174.2B: IHS Research," The Whir.com (February 19, 2014).

International Data Corporation. "Strategies for Effectively Implementing a Mobile Device Management Solution," (July 2014).

Hardy, Quentin. "The Era of Cloud Computing," *New York Times* (June 11, 2014).

McAfee, Andrew. "What Every CEO Needs to Know About the Cloud," *Harvard Business Review* (November 2011).

McCafferty, Dennis. "Eight Interesting Facts About Java," *CIO Insight* (June 16, 2014).

Mell, Peter, and Tim Grance. "The NIST Definition of Cloud Computing, Version 15," NIST (October 17, 2009).

Mueller, Benjamin, Goetz Viering, Christine Legner, and Gerold Riempp. "Understanding the Economic Potential of Service-Oriented Architecture," *Journal of Management Information Systems* 26, No. 4 (Spring 2010).

Schuff, David, and Robert St. Louis. "Centralization vs. Decentralization of Application Software," *Communications of the ACM* 44, No. 6 (June 2001).

Streitfeld, David, and Nick Wingfield. "With Amazon Atop the Cloud, Big Tech Rivals Are Giving Chase," *New York Times* (April 23, 2015).

Torode, Christine, Linda Tucci, and Karen Goulart. "Managing the Next-Generation Data Center," *Modern Infrastructure CIO Edition* (January 2013).

Varia, Jinesh, and Sajee Mathew. "Overview of Amazon Web Services." Amazon Web Services (January 2014).

Walden, Stephanie. "Cloud Computing by the Numbers: The Rise of the Private and Hybrid Cloud," *Mashable* (May 11, 2015).

Walden, Stephanie. "The Pros and Cons of Public, Private, and Hybrid Clouds," *Mashable* (April 2, 2015).

Foundations of Business Intelligence: Databases and Information Management

LEARNING OBJECTIVES

After reading this chapter, you will be able to answer the following questions:

6-1   What is a database and how does a relational database organize data?

6-2   What are the principles of a database management system?

6-3   What are the principal tools and technologies for accessing information from databases to improve business performance and decision making?

6-4   Why are information policy, data administration, and data quality assurance essential for managing the firm's data resources?

CHAPTER CASES

BAE Systems

American Water Keeps Data Flowing

Driving ARI Fleet Management with Real-Time Analytics

Lego's Enterprise Software Spurs Growth

VIDEO CASES

Case 1: Dubuque Uses Cloud Computing and Sensors to Build a Smarter City

Case 2: Brooks Brothers Closes in on Omnichannel Retail

Case 3: Maruti Suzuki Business Intelligence and Enterprise Databases.

BAE SYSTEMS

BAE Systems (BAE) is the United Kingdom's largest manufacturing company and one of the largest commercial aerospace and defence organizations in Europe. Its high-technology, information-driven products and services range from one of the world's most capable multi-role combat fighters, the Eurofighter Typhoon, to the Jetstream family of commercial aircraft, to the provision of information technology (IT) and information systems (IS) for e-business to develop and implement logistics, IT, and e-capability services. With sales, manufacturing, and support sites throughout the world, including the United Kingdom, Europe, the United States, and Australia, BAE employs 83,000 people in 40 countries and generated more than €16.6 billion in annual revenue in 2014.

Although BAE has consolidated its competitive position in established markets, and continues to expand into new markets in the Middle East and Asia, its performance in the aircraft part of the business was being impeded by legacy information systems that support the computer-aided design (CAD) and computer-aided manufacturing (CAM) of its aircraft. The distributed nature of BAE's design and manufacturing sites meant that storing and analyzing accurate sets of operational data describing the complex components of the various aircraft types to produce aircraft assembly reports for the production lines became increasingly challenging and resource-consuming.

Accessing the data from the many systems was a complex task involving many technical challenges. As the aircraft business of BAE grew, so did the likelihood of delays in producing the aircraft assembly reports and other operations data sets necessary for aircraft production management decision-making. In the worst case, the production of aircraft on the assembly line would stop until accurate information was available, with consequent schedule and cost implications. BAE's CAD/CAM staff were storing and analyzing data sets sourced from five major aircraft design and

manufacturing sites spread throughout the United Kingdom, each host to thousands of staff involved in the design and manufacturing process, so that assembly reports and other operations data could be produced. There were numerous occasions when paper drawings with annotations containing component design and manufacturing information were used to reconcile ambiguities and inconsistencies in the assembly reports. These data ambiguities and inconsistencies gave rise to a sense of uncertainty in the assembly reports produced.

What BAE needed was a single repository for CAD/CAM data that would also facilitate the integration of data held in its legacy systems. The company decided to replace its legacy systems with an enterprise-wide knowledge management system that would bring the design and manufacturing data into a single database that could be concurrently accessed by the design and manufacturing engineers. BAE implemented Siemens' Teamcenter product lifecycle management software and Dassault Systemes' CATIA CAD/CAM software. Teamcenter can also be configured to take advantage of recent developments in cloud computing using Microsoft's Azure, IBM's SmartCloud Enterprise+, and Amazon Web Services.

Bringing together Siemens' Teamcenter and Dassault Systemes' CATIA has given BAE Systems powerful integrated data management tools. The Teamcenter database includes tools for component markup and rollup capabilities, allowing users to visualize the effect of component design changes and configuration selections in real-time.

The new solution has produced significant cost savings at BAE in terms of its design and manufacturing data management and storage while boosting performance. With fewer legacy systems and data files to manage, BAE has been able to meet quality, time, and cost requirements by being able to produce complete and accurate aircraft component definitions and configurations. BAE has used Teamcenter to enlarge its business model to include "through-life" maintenance and repair for aircraft.

Sources: "BAE Systems Annual Report 2014," baesystems.com, accessed December 21, 2015; "BAE Systems Military Air Solutions: Case Study: Teamcenter Supports Aircraft Through 50-year Lifecycle," 2015 Siemens Product Lifecycle Management Software Inc., 2015; "CMI-CATIA Teamcenter Integration," T-Systems, April 13, 2015, https://servicenet.t-systems.de/t-systems-plm-de; "BAE Systems Half-Yearly Report and Presentation 2015," www.baesystems.com, accessed December 21, 2015; "Teamcenter Supports Aircraft Through 50-year Cycle: BAE Systems Military Air Solutions," www.plm.automation.siemens.com, accessed November 8, 2012.

The experience of BAE Systems illustrates the importance of data management. Business performance depends on the accuracy and reliability of its data. The company has grown its business, but, both operational CAD/CAM efficiency and production management decision making were impeded by data stored in legacy systems that were difficult to access. How businesses store, organize, and manage their data has a huge impact on organizational effectiveness.

The chapter-opening diagram calls attention to important points raised by this case and this chapter. BAE Systems management decided that the firm needed to improve the management of its data. Pieces of data about design components, manufactured components, and their final assembly had been stored in many large legacy systems that made it extremely difficult for the data to be retrieved and correctly unified so that it could be used in the production line assembly of aircraft components. The data were often redundant and inconsistent, limiting their usefulness. Management was unable to obtain an enterprise-view of the company.

In the past, BAE Systems had used manual paper processes to reconcile its inconsistent and redundant data and to assemble data for management reporting. This solution was extremely time-consuming and costly, and prevented the company's information technology department from performing higher-value work. A more appropriate solution was to install new hardware and software to create an enterprise-wide repository for business information that would support a more streamlined set of business applications. The new software included enterprise software that was integrated with an up-to-date database management system that could supply data for enterprise-wide report-

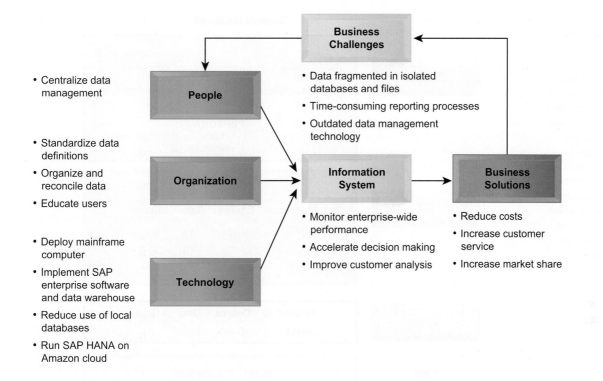

ing. The company had to reorganize its data into a standard company-wide format, eliminate redundancies, and establish rules, responsibilities, and procedures for updating and using the data.

A state-of-the-art database management system suite of software helps BAE Systems boost efficiency by making it easier to locate and assemble data for management reporting and for processing day-to-day CAD/CAM transactions for final aircraft component assembly. The data are more accurate and reliable, and costs for managing and storing the data have been considerably reduced.

Here are some questions to think about: What kinds of data management problems did BAE Systems experience in its legacy database environment? What work had to be done before the company could effectively take advantage of the new data management technology?

6-1 What is a database and how does a relational database organize data?

A computer system organizes data in a hierarchy that starts with bits and bytes and progresses to fields, records, files, and databases (see Figure 6.1). A **bit** represents the smallest unit of data a computer can handle. A group of bits, called a **byte**, represents a single character, which can be a letter, a number, or another symbol. A grouping of characters into a word, a group of words, or a complete number (such as a person's name or age) is called a **field**. A group of related fields, such as a student's identification number (ID), the course taken, the date, and the grade, comprises a **record**; a group of records of the same type is called a **file**. For example, the records in Figure 6.1 could constitute a student course file. A group of related files makes up a **database**. The student course file illustrated in Figure 6.1 could be grouped with files on students' personal histories and financial backgrounds to create a student database. Databases are at the heart of all information systems because they keep track of the people, places, and things that a business must deal with on a continuing, often instant basis.

Figure 6.1
The Data Hierarchy
*A computer system orga-
nizes data in a hierarchy
that starts with the bit,
which represents either a 0
or a 1. Bits can be grouped
to form a byte to represent
one character, number,
or symbol. Bytes can be
grouped to form a field,
and related fields can be
grouped to form a record.
Related records can be collected to form a file, and
related files can be organized into a database.*

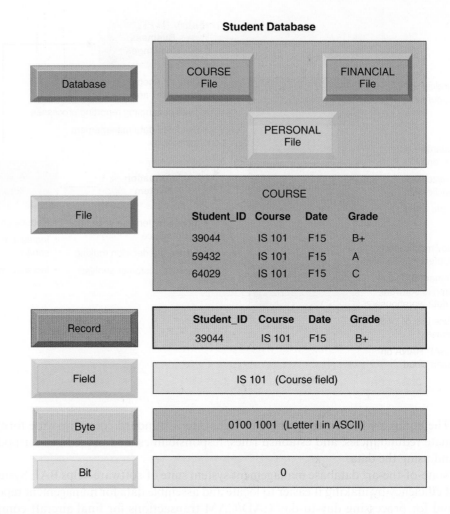

ENTITIES AND ATTRIBUTES

To run a business, you most likely will be using data about categories of information such as customers, suppliers, employees, orders, products, shippers, and perhaps parts. Each of these generalized categories representing a person, place, or thing on which we store information is called an **entity**. Each entity has specific characteristics called **attributes**. For example, in Figure 6.1, COURSE would be an entity, and Student_ID, Course, Date, and Grade would be its attributes. If you were a business keeping track of parts you used and their suppliers, the entity SUPPLIER would have attributes such as the supplier's name and address, which would most likely include the street, city, state, and zip code. The entity PART would typically have attributes such as part description, price of each part (unit price), and the supplier who produced the part.

ORGANIZING DATA IN A RELATIONAL DATABASE

If you stored this information in paper files, you would probably have a file on each entity and its attributes. In an information system, a database organizes the data much the same way, grouping related pieces of data. The **relational database** is the most common type of database today. Relational databases organize data into two-dimensional tables (called *relations*) with columns and rows. Each table contains data about an entity and its attributes. For the most part, there is one table for each business entity, so, at the most basic level, you will have one table for customers and a table each for suppliers, parts in inventory, employees, and sales transactions.

Let's look at how a relational database would organize data about suppliers and parts. Look at the SUPPLIER table illustrated in Figure 6.2. It consists of a grid of

SUPPLIER   **Columns (Attributes, Fields)**

Supplier_Number	Supplier_Name	Supplier_Street	Supplier_City	Supplier_State	Supplier_Zip
8259	CBM Inc.	74 5th Avenue	Dayton	OH	45220
8261	B. R. Molds	1277 Gandolly Street	Cleveland	OH	49345
8263	Jackson Composites	8233 Micklin Street	Lexington	KY	56723
8444	Bryant Corporation	4315 Mill Drive	Rochester	NY	11344

Rows (Records, Tuples)

Key Field (Primary Key)

Figure 6.2
A Relational Database Table

A relational database organizes data in the form of two-dimensional tables. Illustrated here is a table for the entity SUPPLIER showing how it represents the entity and its attributes. Supplier_Number is the key field.

columns and rows of data. Each element of data about a supplier, such as the supplier name, street, city, state, and zip code, is stored as a separate field within the SUPPLIER table. Each field represents an attribute for the entity SUPPLIER. Fields in a relational database are also called *columns*.

The actual information about a single supplier that resides in a table is called a *row*. Rows are commonly referred to as records, or, in very technical terms, as **tuples**.

Note that there is a field for Supplier_Number in this table. This field uniquely identifies each record so that the record can be retrieved, updated, or sorted, and it is called a **key field**. Each table in a relational database has one field designated as its **primary key**. This key field is the unique identifier for all the information in any row of the table, and this primary key cannot be duplicated.

We could use the supplier's name as a key field. However, if two suppliers had the same name (which does happen from time to time), supplier name would not uniquely identify each, so it is necessary to assign a special identifier field for this purpose. For example, if you had two suppliers, both named "CBM," but one was based in Dayton and the other in St. Louis, it would be easy to confuse them. However, if each has a unique supplier number, such confusion is prevented.

We also see that the address information has been separated into four fields: Supplier_Street, Supplier_City, Supplier_State, and Supplier_Zip. Data are separated into the smallest elements that one would want to access separately to make it easy to select only the rows in the table that match the contents of one field, such as all the suppliers in Ohio (OH). The rows of data can also be sorted by the contents of the Supplier_State field to get a list of suppliers by state regardless of their cities.

So far, the SUPPLIER table does not have any information about the parts that a particular supplier provides for your company. PART is a separate entity from SUPPLIER, and fields with information about parts should be stored in a separate PART table (see Figure 6.3).

Why not keep information on parts in the same table as suppliers? If we did that, each row of the table would contain the attributes of both PART and SUPPLIER. Because one supplier could supply more than one part, the table would need many extra rows for a single supplier to show all the parts that supplier provided. We would be maintaining a great deal of redundant data about suppliers, and it would be difficult to search for the information on any individual part because you would not know whether this part is the first or fiftieth part in this supplier's record. A separate table, PART, should be created to store these three fields and solve this problem.

Figure 6.3
The PART Table

Data for the entity PART have their own separate table. Part_Number is the primary key and Supplier_Number is the foreign key, enabling users to find related information from the SUPPLIER table about the supplier for each part.

PART

Part_Number	Part_Name	Unit_Price	Supplier_Number
137	Door latch	22.00	8259
145	Side mirror	12.00	8444
150	Door molding	6.00	8263
152	Door lock	31.00	8259
155	Compressor	54.00	8261
178	Door handle	10.00	8259

Primary Key   Foreign Key

The PART table would also have to contain another field, Supplier_Number, so that you would know the supplier for each part. It would not be necessary to keep repeating all the information about a supplier in each PART record because having a Supplier_ Number field in the PART table allows you to look up the data in the fields of the SUPPLIER table.

Notice that Supplier_Number appears in both the SUPPLIER and PART tables. In the SUPPLIER table, Supplier_Number is the primary key. When the field Supplier_Number appears in the PART table, it is called a **foreign key** and is essentially a look-up field to find data about the supplier of a specific part. Note that the PART table would itself have its own primary key field, Part_Number, to identify each part uniquely. This key is not used to link PART with SUPPLIER but could be used to link PART with a different entity.

As we organize data into tables, it is important to make sure that all the attributes for a particular entity apply only to that entity. If you were to keep the supplier's address with the PART record, that information would not really relate only to PART; it would relate to both PART and SUPPLIER. If the supplier's address were to change, it would be necessary to alter the data in every PART record rather than only once in the SUPPLIER record.

ESTABLISHING RELATIONSHIPS

Now that we've broken down our data into a SUPPLIER table and a PART table, we must make sure we understand the relationship between them. A schematic called an **entity-relationship diagram** clarifies table relationships in a relational database. The most important piece of information an entity-relationship diagram provides is the manner in which two tables are related to each other. Tables in a relational database may have one-to-one, one-to-many, and many-to-many relationships.

An example of a one-to-one relationship is a human resources system that stores confidential data about employees. The system stores data, such as the employee name, date of birth, address, and job position, in one table and confidential data about that employee, such as salary or pension benefits, in another table. These two tables pertaining to a single employee would have a one-to-one relationship because each record in the EMPLOYEE table with basic employee data has only one related record in the table storing confidential data.

The relationship between the SUPPLIER and PART entities in our database is a one-to-many relationship. Each supplier can supply more than one part, but each part has only one supplier. For every record in the SUPPLIER table, many related records might be in the PART table.

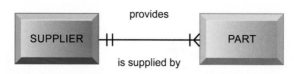

Figure 6.4
A Simple Entity-
Relationship Diagram
This diagram shows the relationship between the entities SUPPLIER and PART.

Figure 6.4 illustrates how an entity-relationship diagram would depict this one-to-many relationship. The boxes represent entities. The lines connecting the boxes represent relationships. A line connecting two entities that ends in two short marks designates a one-to-one relationship. A line connecting two entities that ends with a crow's foot preceded by a short mark indicates a one-to-many relationship. Figure 6.4 shows that each part has only one supplier, but the same supplier can provide many parts.

We would also see a one-to-many relationship if we wanted to add a table about orders to our database because one supplier services many orders. The ORDER table would contain only the Order_Number and Order_Date fields. Figure 6.5 illustrates a report showing an order of parts from a supplier. If you look at the report, you can see that the information on the top-right portion of the report comes from the ORDER table. The actual line items ordered are listed in the lower portion of the report.

Because one order can be for many parts from a supplier, and a single part can be ordered many times on different orders, this creates a many-to-many relationship between the PART and ORDER tables. Whenever a many-to-many relationship exists between two tables, it is necessary to link these two tables in a table that joins this information. Creating a separate table for a line item in the order would serve this purpose. This table is often called a *join table* or an *intersection relation*. This join table contains only three fields: Order_Number and Part_Number, which are used only to link the ORDER and PART tables, and Part_Quantity. If you look at the bottom-left part of the report, this is the information coming from the LINE_ITEM table.

We would thus wind up with a total of four tables in our database. Figure 6.6 illustrates the final set of tables, and Figure 6.7 shows what the entity-relationship diagram for this set of tables would look like. Note that the ORDER table does not contain data on the extended price because that value can be calculated by multiplying Unit_Price by Part_Quantity. This data element can be derived when needed, using information that already exists in the PART and LINE_ITEM tables. Order_Total is another derived field, calculated by totaling the extended prices for items ordered.

Order Number: 3502
Order Date: 1/15/2016

Supplier Number: 8259
Supplier Name: CBM Inc.
Supplier Address: 74 5th Avenue, Dayton, OH 45220

Order_Number	Part_Number	Part_Quantity	Part_Name	Unit_Price	Extended Price
3502	137	10	Door latch	22.00	$220.00
3502	152	20	Door lock	31.00	620.00
3502	178	5	Door handle	10.00	50.00
			Order Total:		$890.00

Figure 6.5
Sample Order Report
The shaded areas show which data came from the ORDER, SUPPLIER, and LINE_ITEM tables. The database does not maintain data on extended price or order total because they can be derived from other data in the tables.

PART

Part_Number	Part_Name	Unit_Price	Supplier_Number
137	Door latch	22.00	8259
145	Side mirror	12.00	8444
150	Door molding	6.00	8263
152	Door lock	31.00	8259
155	Compressor	54.00	8261
178	Door handle	10.00	8259

LINE_ITEM

Order_Number	Part_Number	Part_Quantity
3502	137	10
3502	152	20
3502	178	5

ORDER

Order_Number	Order_Date
3502	1/15/2016
3503	1/16/2016
3504	1/17/2016

SUPPLIER

Supplier_Number	Supplier_Name	Supplier_Street	Supplier_City	Supplier_State	Supplier_Zip
8259	CBM Inc.	74 5th Avenue	Dayton	OH	45220
8261	B. R. Molds	1277 Gandolly Street	Cleveland	OH	49345
8263	Jackson Components	8233 Micklin Street	Lexington	KY	56723
8444	Bryant Corporation	4315 Mill Drive	Rochester	NY	11344

Figure 6.6
The Final Database Design with Sample Records
The final design of the database for suppliers, parts, and orders has four tables. The LINE_ITEM table is a join table that eliminates the many-to-many relationship between ORDER and PART.

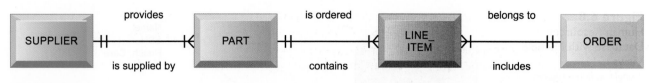

Figure 6.7
Entity-Relationship Diagram for the Database with Four Tables
This diagram shows the relationship between the SUPPLIER, PART, LINE_ITEM, and ORDER entities.

The process of streamlining complex groups of data to minimize redundant data elements and awkward many-to-many relationships and increase stability and flexibility is called **normalization**. A properly designed and normalized database is easy to maintain and minimizes duplicate data. The Learning Tracks for this chapter direct you to more-detailed discussions of database design, normalization, and entity-relationship diagramming.

Relational database systems enforce **referential integrity** rules to ensure that relationships between coupled tables remain consistent. When one table has a foreign key that points to another table, you may not add a record to the table with the foreign key unless there is a corresponding record in the linked table. In the database we have just created, the foreign key Supplier_Number links the PART table to the SUPPLIER table. We may not add a new record to the PART table for a part with supplier number 8266 unless there is a corresponding record in the SUPPLIER table for supplier number 8266. We must also delete the corresponding record in the PART table if we delete the record in the SUPPLIER table for supplier number 8266. In other words, we shouldn't have parts from nonexistent suppliers!

The example provided here for parts, orders, and suppliers is a simple one. Even in a very small business, you will have tables for other important entities such as customers, shippers, and employees. A very large corporation typically has databases with thousands of entities (tables) to maintain. What is important for any business, large or small, is to have a good data model that includes all its entities and the relationships among them, one that is organized to minimize redundancy, maximize accuracy, and make data easily accessible for reporting and analysis.

It cannot be emphasized enough: If the business does not get its data model right, the system will not be able to serve the business properly. The company's systems will not be as effective as they could be because they will have to work with data that may be inaccurate, incomplete, or difficult to retrieve. Understanding the organization's data and how they should be represented in a database is perhaps the most important lesson you can learn from this course.

For example, Famous Footwear, a shoe store chain with more than 1,100 locations in 49 states, could not achieve its goal of having the right style of shoe in the right store for sale at the right price because its database was not properly designed for a rapidly adjusting store inventory. The company had a database that was designed primarily for producing standard reports for management rather than for reacting to marketplace changes. Management could not obtain precise data on specific items in inventory in each of its stores. The company had to work around this problem by building a new database that organized the sales and inventory data better for analysis and inventory management.

6-2 What are the principles of a database management system?

Now that you have started creating the files and identifying the data your business requires, you will need a database management system to help you manage and use the data. A **database management system (DBMS)** is a specific type of software for creating, storing, organizing, and accessing data from a database. Microsoft Access

Figure 6.8
Human Resources
Database with Multiple
Views
*A single human resources
database provides many
views of data, depend-
ing on the information
requirements of the user.
Illustrated here are two
possible views, one of
interest to a benefits
specialist and one of
interest to a member of
the company's payroll
department*

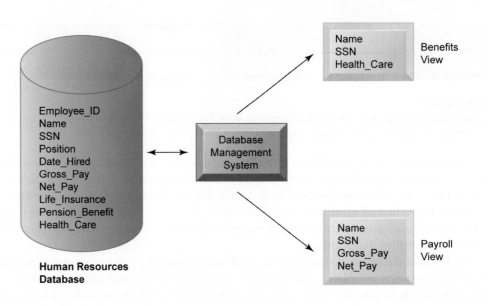

is a DBMS for desktop systems, whereas DB2, Oracle Database, and Microsoft SQL Server are DBMS for large mainframes and midrange computers. MySQL is a popular open-source DBMS. All these products are relational DBMS that support a relational database.

The DBMS relieves the end user or programmer from the task of understanding where and how the data are actually stored by separating the logical and physical views of the data. The *logical view* presents data as end users or business specialists would perceive them, whereas the *physical view* shows how data are actually organized and structured on physical storage media, such as a hard disk.

The database management software makes the physical database available for different logical views required by users. For example, for the human resources database illustrated in Figure 6.8, a benefits specialist typically will require a view consisting of the employee's name, social security number, and health insurance coverage. A payroll department member will need data such as the employee's name, social security number, gross pay, and net pay. The data for all of these views is stored in a single database, where the organization can managed it more easily.

OPERATIONS OF A RELATIONAL DBMS

In a relational database, tables can be easily combined to deliver data that users require, provided that any two tables share a common data element. Let's return to the database we set up earlier with PART and SUPPLIER tables illustrated in Figures 6.2 and 6.3.

Suppose we wanted to find in this database the names of suppliers who could provide us with part number 137 or part number 150. We would need information from two tables: the SUPPLIER table and the PART table. Note that these two tables have a shared data element: Supplier_Number.

In a relational database, three basic operations, as shown in Figure 6.9, are used to develop useful sets of data: select, project, and join. The *select* operation creates a subset consisting of all records in the file that meet stated criteria. Select creates, in other words, a subset of rows that meet certain criteria. In our example, we want to select records (rows) from the PART table where the Part_Number equals 137 or 150. The *join* operation combines relational tables to provide the user with more information than is available in individual tables. In our example, we want to join the now-shortened PART table (only parts 137 or 150 are presented) and the SUPPLIER table into a single new table.

PART

Part_Number	Part_Name	Unit_Price	Supplier_Number
137	Door latch	22.00	8259
145	Side mirror	12.00	8444
150	Door molding	6.00	8263
152	Door lock	31.00	8259
155	Compressor	54.00	8261
178	Door handle	10.00	8259

Select Part_Number = 137 or 150

SUPPLIER

Supplier_Number	Supplier_Name	Supplier_Street	Supplier_City	Supplier_State	Supplier_Zip
8259	CBM Inc.	74 5th Avenue	Dayton	OH	45220
8261	B. R. Molds	1277 Gandolly Street	Cleveland	OH	49345
8263	Jackson Components	8233 Micklin Street	Lexington	KY	56723
8444	Bryant Corporation	4315 Mill Drive	Rochester	NY	11344

Join by Supplier_Number

Part_Number	Part_Name	Supplier_Number	Supplier_Name
137	Door latch	8259	CBM Inc.
150	Door molding	8263	Jackson Components

Project selected columns

Figure 6.9
The Three Basic Operations of a Relational DBMS
The select, join, and project operations enable data from two tables to be combined and only selected attributes to be displayed.

Figure 6.10
Access Data
Dictionary Features
*Microsoft Access has a
rudimentary data diction-
ary capability that displays
information about the size,
format, and other charac-
teristics of each field in a
database. Displayed here is
the information maintained
in the SUPPLIER table. The
small key icon to the left of
Supplier_Number indicates
that it is a key field.*

Source: Microsoft Access,
Microsoft Corporation.
Used by permission.

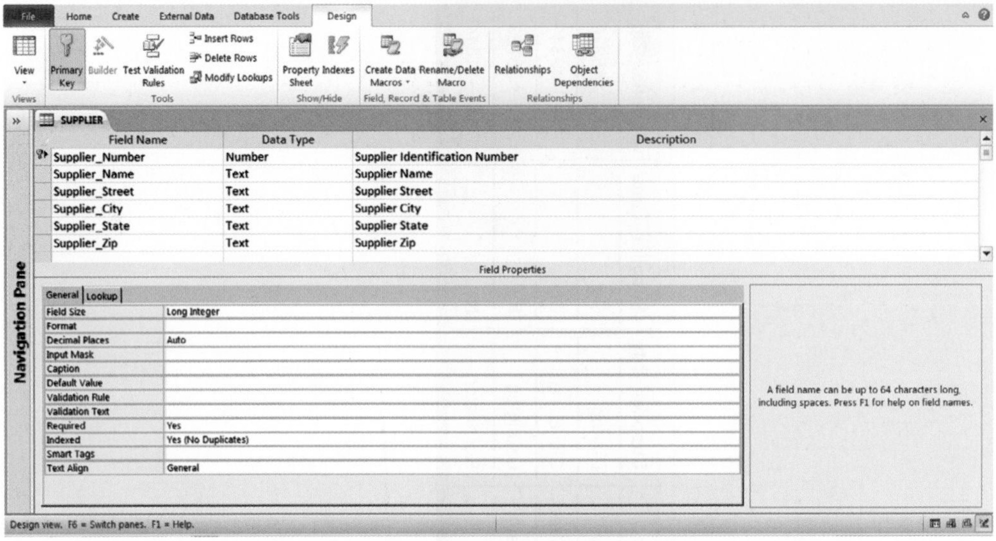

The *project* operation creates a subset consisting of columns in a table, permitting the user to create new tables that contain only the information required. In our example, we want to extract from the new table only the following columns: Part_Number, Part_Name, Supplier_Number, and Supplier_Name (see Figure 6.9).

CAPABILITIES OF DATABASE MANAGEMENT SYSTEMS

A DBMS includes capabilities and tools for organizing, managing, and accessing the data in the database. The most important are its data definition capability, data dictionary, and data manipulation language.

DBMS have a **data definition** capability to specify the structure of the content of the database. It would be used to create database tables and to define the characteristics of the fields in each table. This information about the database would be documented in a **data dictionary**. A data dictionary is an automated or manual file that stores definitions of data elements and their characteristics. Microsoft Access has a rudimentary data dictionary capability that displays information about the name, description, size, type, format, and other properties of each field in a table (see Figure 6.10). Data dictionaries for large corporate databases may capture additional information, such as usage, ownership (who in the organization is responsible for maintaining the data), authorization, security, and the individuals, business functions, programs, and reports that use each data element.

Querying and Reporting

DBMS include tools for accessing and manipulating information in databases. Most DBMS have a specialized language called a **data manipulation language** that is used to add, change, delete, and retrieve the data in the database. This language contains commands that permit end users and programming specialists to extract data from the database to satisfy information requests and develop applications. The most prominent data manipulation language today is **Structured Query Language**, or **SQL**. Figure 6.11

```
SELECT PART.Part_Number, PART.Part_Name, SUPPLIER.Supplier_Number,
SUPPLIER.Supplier_Name
FROM PART, SUPPLIER
WHERE PART.Supplier_Number = SUPPLIER.Supplier_Number AND
Part_Number = 137 OR Part_Number = 150;
```

Figure 6.11
Example of a SQL Query
Illustrated here are the SQL statements for a query to select suppliers for parts 137 or 150. They produce a list with the same results as Figure 6.9.

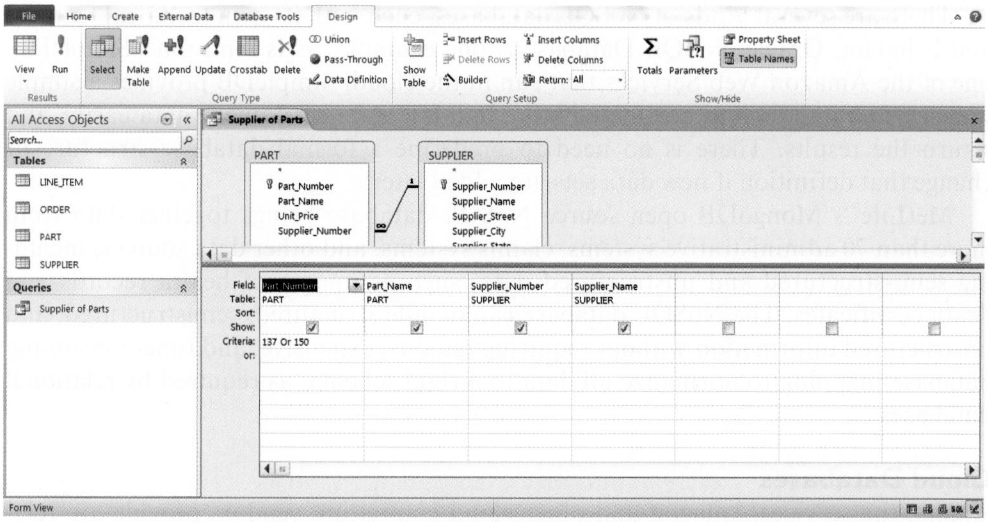

Figure 6.12
An Access Query
Illustrated here is how the query in Figure 6.11 would be constructed using Microsoft Access query-building tools. It shows the tables, fields, and selection criteria used for the query.

Source: Microsoft Access, Microsoft Corporation. Used by permission.

illustrates the SQL **query** that would produce the new resultant table in Figure 6.9. A query is a request for data from a database. You can find out more about how to perform SQL queries in our Learning Tracks for this chapter.

Users of DBMS for large and midrange computers, such as DB2, Oracle, or SQL Server, would employ SQL to retrieve information they needed from the database. Microsoft Access also uses SQL, but it provides its own set of user-friendly tools for querying databases and for organizing data from databases into more polished reports.

Microsoft Access has capabilities to help users create queries by identifying the tables and fields they want and the results and then selecting the rows from the database that meet particular criteria. These actions in turn are translated into SQL commands. Figure 6.12 illustrates how the SQL query to select parts and suppliers in Figure 6.11 would be constructed using Microsoft Access.

DBMS typically include capabilities for report generation so that the data of interest can be displayed in a more structured and polished format than would be possible just by querying. Crystal Reports is a popular **report generator** for large corporate DBMS, although it can also be used with Microsoft Access.

Microsoft Access also has capabilities for developing desktop system applications. These include tools for creating data entry screens and reports and developing the logic for processing transactions. Information systems specialists primarily use these capabilities.

NONRELATIONAL DATABASES AND DATABASES IN THE CLOUD

For more than three decades, relational database technology has been the gold standard. Cloud computing, unprecedented data volumes, massive workloads for web services, and the need to store new types of data require database alternatives to the traditional relational model of organizing data in the form of tables, columns, and rows. Companies are turning to *NoSQL* nonrelational-database technologies for this purpose. **Nonrelational database management systems** use a more flexible data model and are designed for managing large data sets across many distributed machines and for easily scaling up or down. They are useful for accelerating simple queries against large volumes of structured and unstructured data, including web, social media, graphics, and other forms of data that are difficult to analyze with traditional SQL-based tools.

There are several kinds of NoSQL databases, each with its own technical features and behavior. Oracle NoSQL Database is one example, as is Amazon's SimpleDB, one of the Amazon Web Services that run in the cloud. SimpleDB provides a simple web services interface to create and store multiple data sets, query data easily, and return the results. There is no need to predefine a formal database structure or change that definition if new data sets are added later.

MetLife 's MongoDB open source NoSQL database brings together data from more than 70 administrative systems, claims systems, and other data sources, including semi-structured and unstructured data, such as images of health records and death certificates. The NoSQL database can handle structured, semistructured, and unstructured information without requiring tedious, expensive, and time-consuming database-mapping to normalize all data to a rigid schema, as required by relational databases.

Cloud Databases

Among the services Amazon and other cloud computing vendors provide are relational database engines. Amazon Relational Database Service (Amazon RDS) offers MySQL, Microsoft SQL Server, Oracle Database, PostgreSQL, or Amazon Aurora as database engines. Pricing is based on usage. Oracle has its own Database Cloud Services using its relational Oracle Database, and Microsoft Windows Azure SQL Database is a cloud-based relational database service based on the Microsoft SQL Server DBMS. Cloud-based data management services have special appeal for web-focused start-ups or small to medium-sized businesses seeking database capabilities at a lower price than in-house database products.

In addition to public cloud-based data management services, companies now have the option of using databases in private clouds. For example, Sabre Holdings has a private database cloud that supports more than 100 projects and 700 users. A consolidated database spanning a pool of standardized servers running Oracle Database provides database services for multiple applications. Workload management tools ensure that sufficient resources are available to meet application needs even when the workload changes. The shared hardware and software platform reduces the number of servers, DBMS, and storage devices needed for Sabre's projects and work..

6-3 What are the principal tools and technologies for accessing information from databases to improve business performance and decision making?

Businesses use their databases to keep track of basic transactions, such as paying suppliers, processing orders, serving customers, and paying employees, but they also need databases to provide information that will help the company run the business more efficiently and help managers and employees make better decisions. If a company wants to know which product is the most popular or who is its most profitable customer, the answer lies in the data.

THE CHALLENGE OF BIG DATA

Most of the data that organizations collected was transaction data that could easily fit into rows and columns of relational database management systems. There has been an explosion of data from web traffic, email messages, and social media content (tweets, status messages) as well as machine-generated data from sensors. These data may be unstructured or semistructured and thus not suitable for relational database products that organize data in the form of columns and rows. We now use the term **big data** to describe these data sets with volumes so huge that they are beyond the ability of typical DBMS to capture, store, and analyze.

Big data doesn't designate any specific quantity but usually refers to data in the petabyte and exabyte range—in other words, billions to trillions of records, respectively, from different sources. Big data are produced in much larger quantities and much more rapidly than traditional data. For example, a single jet engine is capable of generating 10 terabytes of data in just 30 minutes, and there are more than 25,000 airline flights each day. Even though tweets are limited to 140 characters each, Twitter generates more than 8 terabytes of data daily. Digital information is growing exponentially, from 1.8 zettabytes in 2011 to an expected 35 zettabytes in 2020. According to a Cisco Systems report, if an 11-ounce cup of coffee represented one gigabyte, then one zettabyte would have the same volume as the Great Wall of China.

Businesses are interested in big data because they contain more patterns and interesting relationships than smaller data sets, with the potential to provide new insights into customer behavior, weather patterns, financial market activity, or other phenomena. For example, Shutterstock, the global online image marketplace, stores 24 million images and adds 10,000 more each day. To find ways to optimize the Shutterstock experience, it analyzes its big data to find out where its website visitors place their cursors and how long they hover over an image before making a purchase.

Big data is also finding many uses in the public sector. The chapter-opening case on the U.S. Postal Service is one example, as are city governments using big data to manage traffic flows and fight crime.

However, to derive business value from these data, organizations need new technologies and tools capable of managing and analyzing nontraditional data along with their traditional enterprise data. They also need to know what questions to ask of the data and the limitations of big data. Capturing, storing, and analyzing big data can be expensive, and information from big data may not necessarily help decision makers. It's important to have a clear understanding of the problems big data will solve for the business.

BUSINESS INTELLIGENCE INFRASTRUCTURE

Suppose you wanted concise, reliable information about current operations, trends, and changes across the entire company. If you worked in a large company, the data you need might have to be pieced together from separate systems, such as sales, manufacturing and accounting, and external sources such as demographic or competitor data. Increasingly, you might need to use big data. A contemporary infrastructure for business intelligence has an array of tools for obtaining useful information from all the types of data businesses use today, including semistructured and unstructured big data in vast quantities. These capabilities include data warehouses and data marts, Hadoop, in-memory computing, and analytical platforms. Some of these capabilities are now available as cloud services.

Data Warehouses and Data Marts

The traditional tool for analyzing corporate data for the past two decades has been the data warehouse. A **data warehouse** is a database that stores current and historical data of potential interest to decision makers throughout the company. The data originate in many core operational transaction systems, such as systems for sales, customer accounts, and manufacturing, and can include data from website transactions. The data warehouse extracts current and historical data from multiple operational systems inside the organization. These data are combined with data from external sources and transformed by correcting inaccurate and incomplete data and restructuring the data for management reporting and analysis before being loaded into the data warehouse.

INTERACTIVE SESSION: PEOPLE   American Water Keeps Data Flowing

American Water, founded in 1886, is the largest public water utility in the United States, generating over $3 billion in revenue in 2014. Headquartered in Voorhees, New Jersey, the company employs more than 6,400 dedicated professionals who provide drinking water, wastewater, and other related services to approximately 16 million people in 47 states, as well as Ontario and Manitoba, Canada. Most of American Water's services support locally-managed utility subsidiaries that are regulated by the U.S. state in which each operates as well as the federal government. American Water also owns subsidiaries that manage municipal drinking water and wastewater systems under contract and others that supply businesses and residential communities with water management products and services.

Until recently, American water's systems and business processes were very localized, and many of these processes were manual. Over time, this information environment became increasingly difficult to manage. Many systems were not integrated, so running any type of report that had to provide information about more than one region was a labor-intensive, manual process. Data had to be extracted from the systems supporting each region and then combined manually to create the desired output. When the company was preparing to hold an initial public offering of its stock in 2006, its software systems could not handle the required regulatory controls, so roughly 80 percent of this work had to be performed manually. It was close to a nightmare.

Management wanted to change the company from a decentralized group of independent regional businesses into a more centralized organization with standard company-wide business processes and enterprise-wide reporting. The first step toward achieving this goal was to implement an enterprise resource planning (ERP) system designed to replace disparate systems with a single integrated software platform. The company selected SAP as its ERP system vendor.

An important first step of this project was to migrate the data from American Water's old systems to the new platform. The company's data resided in many different systems in various formats. Each regional business maintained some of its own data in its own systems, and a portion of these data were redundant and inconsistent. For example, there were duplicate pieces of materials master data because a material might be called one thing in the

company's Missouri operation and another in its New Jersey business. These names had to be standardized so that the same name for a piece of data was used by every business unit. American Water's business users had to buy into this new company-wide view of data.

Data migration entails much more than just transferring data between old and new systems. Business users need to know that data are not just a responsibility of the information systems department: the business "owns" the data. It is business needs that determine the rules and standards for managing the data. Therefore, it is up to business users to inventory and review all the pieces of data in their systems to determine precisely which pieces of data from the old system will be used in the new system and which data do not need to be brought over. The data also need to be reviewed to make sure they are accurate and consistent, and that redundant data are eliminated.

Some type of data cleansing will likely be required. For example, American Water had data on more than 70,000 vendors in its vendor master data file, many of whom had not worked for the company in years. Andrew Clarkson, American Water's Business Intelligence Lead, asked business users to define an active vendor and to use that definition to identify which data to migrate. He also worked with various functional groups to standardize how to present address data.

One of the objectives of American Water's data management work was to support an enterprise-wide business intelligence program based on a single view of the business. An analytical system and data warehouse would be able to combine data from the SAP ERP System with data from other sources, including new customer information and enterprise asset management systems. That meant that American Water's business users had to do a lot of thinking about the kinds of reports they wanted. The company had originally planned to have the system provide 200 reports, but later reduced that number by half. Business users were trained to generate these reports and customize them. Most financial users initially tried to create their reports using Microsoft Excel spreadsheet software. Over time, however, they learned to do the same thing using SAP Business Objects Web Intelligence tools that came with the system. This set of tools enables business users to view, sort, and analyze business intelligence data. It includes tools for generating queries, reports, and interactive dashboards. In

2015 American Waterworks extended the functionality of its SAP systems with a customer management system (Torch Tolerance Optimizer) that reduced a large backlog of billing notices that were piling up using an older manual system to resolve errors and implausible bills.

At present, American Water is focusing on promoting the idea that data must be "clean" to be effective and has poured an incredible amount of effort into its data cleansing work—identifying incomplete, incorrect, inaccurate, and irrelevant pieces of data and then replacing, modifying, or deleting the "dirty" data.

Sources: American Water Works, "Form 10K," filed with the Securities and Exchange Commission, February 2, 2015; "American Water use BDi Apps- SAP for utilities," Basictechnologies.com, February 15, 2014; "Utilities Modernize Customer Experience With SAP," SAP News, February 20, 2014; "SAP to Deliver Software Solution to American Water," www.sap.com, accessed January 31, 2014; David Hannon, "Clean Smooth-Flowing Data at American Water," SAP Insider Profiles, January–March 2013 and www.amwater.com, accessed February 2, 2014.

CASE STUDY QUESTIONS

1. Discuss the role of information policy, data administration, and efforts to ensure data quality in improving data management at American Water.

2. Describe roles played by information systems specialists and end users in American Water's systems transformation project.

3. Why was the participation of business users so important? If they didn't play this role, what would have happened?

4. How did implementing a data warehouse help American Water move toward a more centralized organization?

5. Give some examples of problems that would have occurred at American Water if its data were not "clean."

6. How did American Water's data warehouse improve operations and management decision making?

The data warehouse makes the data available for anyone to access as needed, but it cannot be altered. A data warehouse system also provides a range of ad hoc and standardized query tools, analytical tools, and graphical reporting facilities.

Companies often build enterprise-wide central data warehouses that serve the entire organization, or they create smaller, decentralized warehouses called data marts. A **data mart** is a subset of a data warehouse, in which a summarized or highly focused portion of the organization's data is placed in a separate database for a specific population of users. For example, a company might develop marketing and sales data marts to deal with customer information. Bookseller Barnes & Noble used to maintain a series of data marts—one for point-of-sale data in retail stores, another for college bookstore sales, and a third for online sales.

Hadoop

Relational DBMS and data warehouse products are not well suited for organizing and analyzing big data or data that do not easily fit into columns and rows used in their data models. For handling unstructured and semistructured data in vast quantities, as well as structured data, organizations are starting to use **Hadoop**. Hadoop is an open-source software framework the Apache Software Foundation manages that enables distributed parallel processing of huge amounts of data across inexpensive computers. It breaks a big data problem down into subproblems, distributes them among up to thousands of inexpensive computer processing nodes, and then combines the result into a smaller data set that is easier to analyze. You've probably used Hadoop to find the best airfare on the Internet, get directions to a restaurant, or connect with a friend on Facebook.

Hadoop consists of several key services: the Hadoop Distributed File System (HDFS) for data storage and MapReduce for high-performance parallel data processing. HDFS links the file systems on the numerous nodes in a Hadoop cluster to turn them into one big file system. Hadoop's MapReduce was inspired by Google's MapReduce system for breaking down processing of huge data sets and assigning work to the various nodes in a cluster. HBase, Hadoop's nonrelational database, provides rapid access to the data stored on HDFS and a transactional platform for running high-scale real-time applications.

Hadoop can process large quantities of any kind of data, including structured transactional data, loosely structured data such as Facebook and Twitter feeds, complex data such as web server log files, and unstructured audio and video data. Hadoop runs on a cluster of inexpensive servers, and processors can be added or removed as needed. Companies use Hadoop for analyzing very large volumes of data as well as for a staging area for unstructured and semistructured data before they are loaded into a data warehouse. Yahoo! uses Hadoop to track user behavior so it can modify its home page to fit their interests. Life sciences research firm NextBio uses Hadoop and HBase to process data for pharmaceutical companies conducting genomic research. Top database vendors such as IBM, Hewlett-Packard, Oracle, and Microsoft have their own Hadoop software distributions. Other vendors offer tools for moving data into and out of Hadoop or for analyzing data within Hadoop.

In-Memory Computing

Another way of facilitating big data analysis is to use **in-memory computing**, which relies primarily on a computer's main memory (RAM) for data storage. (Conventional DBMS use disk storage systems.) Users access data stored in system primary memory, thereby eliminating bottlenecks from retrieving and reading data in a traditional, disk-based database and dramatically shortening query response times. In-memory processing makes it possible for very large sets of data, amounting to the size of a data mart or small data warehouse, to reside entirely in memory. Complex business calculations that used to take hours or days are able to be completed within seconds, and this can even be accomplished on handheld devices. The chapter-opening case shows how in-memory computing helps the U.S. Postal Service rapidly analyze the vast quantities of data it collects. The Interactive Session on Technology describes how other organizations are benefiting from this technology.

Chapter 5 details some of the advances in contemporary computer hardware technology that make in-memory processing possible, such as powerful high-speed processors, multicore processing, and falling computer memory prices. These technologies help companies optimize the use of memory and accelerate processing performance while lowering costs.

Leading commercial products for in-memory computing include SAP HANA and Oracle Exalytics. Each provides a set of integrated software components, including in-memory database software and specialized analytics software, that run on hardware optimized for in-memory computing work, including cloud platforms.

Analytic Platforms

Commercial database vendors have developed specialized high-speed **analytic platforms** using both relational and nonrelational technology that is optimized for analyzing large data sets. These analytic platforms, such as IBM PureData System for Analytics, feature preconfigured hardware-software systems that are specifically designed for query processing and analytics. For example, IBM PureData System for Analytics features tightly integrated database, server and storage components that can analyze up to 10 petabytes of data within minutes. Analytic platforms also include in-memory systems and NoSQL nonrelational database management systems, and some are available as cloud services.

INTERACTIVE SESSION: TECHNOLOGY   Driving ARI Fleet Management with Real-Time Analytics

Automotive Resources International®, better known as simply ARI®, is the world's largest privately held company for vehicle fleet management services. ARI is headquartered in Mt. Laurel, New Jersey, and has 2,500 employees and offices throughout North America, Europe, the United Kingdom, and Hong Kong. The company manages more than one million vehicles in the United States, Canada, Mexico, Puerto Rico, and Europe.

Businesses that need vehicles for shipments (trucks, vans, cars, ships, and rail cars) may choose to manage their own fleet of vehicles, or they may outsource fleet management to companies such as ARI, which specialize in these services. ARI manages the entire life cycle and operation of a fleet of vehicles for its customers, from up-front specification and acquisition through resale, including financing, maintenance, fuel management, and risk management services such as driver safety training and accident management. ARI also maintains six call centers in North America that operate around the clock 365 days a year to support customers' fleet operations by providing assistance regarding repairs, breakdowns, accident response, preventive maintenance, and other driver needs. These call centers handle about 3.5 million calls per year from customers, drivers, and suppliers who expect access to real-time actionable information.

Operating a single large commercial vehicle fleet generates high volumes of complex data such as data on fuel consumption, maintenance, licensing, and compliance. A fuel transaction, for example, requires data on state taxes paid, fuel grade, total sale, amount sold, and time and place of purchase. A simple brake job and preventive maintenance checkup generates dozens of records for each component that is serviced. Each part and service performed on a vehicle is tracked using American Trucking Association codes. ARI collects and analyzes more than 14,000 pieces of data per vehicle. Multiply the data by hundreds of fleets, some with up to 10,000 vehicles, all operating simultaneously throughout the globe, and you'll have an idea of the enormous volume of data ARI needs to manage, both for itself and for its customers.

ARI provided its customers with detailed information about their fleet operations, but the type of information it could deliver was very limited.

For example, ARI could generate detailed reports on line-item expenditures, vehicle purchases, maintenance records, and other operational information presented as simple spreadsheets, charts, or graphs, but it was not possible to analyze all the data to spot trends and make recommendations. ARI could analyze data customer by customer, but it couldn't aggregate data across its entire customer base. For instance, if ARI was managing a pharmaceutical company's vehicle fleet, its information systems could not benchmark that fleet's performance against others in the industry.

To create reports, ARI had to go through internal subject matter experts in various aspects of fleet operations, who were called reporting power users. A request for a report would take five days to fill. If the report was unsatisfactory, it would go back to the report writer to make changes. ARI's process for analyzing its data was extremely drawn out.

In mid-2011, ARI implemented SAP Business-Objects Explorer to give customers the capability to access data and run their own reports. SAP BusinessObjects Explorer enables business users to view, sort, and analyze business intelligence data. Users search through data sources by using an iTunes-like interface. They do not have to create queries to search the data, and results are shown with a chart that indicates the best information match. The graphical representation of results changes as the user asks further questions of the data.

In early 2012, ARI integrated SAP Business-Objects Explorer with HANA, SAP's in-memory computing platform that is deployable as an on-premise appliance (hardware and software) or in the cloud. HANA is optimized for performing real-time analytics and handling very high volumes of operational and transactional data in real time. HANA's in-memory analytics queries data stored in random access memory (RAM) instead of on a hard disk or flash storage.

Now, when ARI's controller wants an impact analysis of the company's top 10 customers, SAP HANA produces the result in 3 to 3½ seconds. In ARI's old systems environment, this task would have been assigned to a power user versed in using reporting tools, specifications would have to be drawn up, and a program designed for that specific query, a process that would have taken about 36 hours.

Using HANA, ARI can quickly mine its vast data resources and generate predictions based on the results. For example, the company can produce precise figures on what it costs to operate a fleet of a certain size over a particular route across specific industries during a certain type of weather and predict the impact of changes in any of these variables. It can do so nearly as easily as providing customers with a simple history of their expenditures on fuel. Such information helps ARI customers achieve greater operational efficiencies and lower costs.

HANA has also reduced by 5 percent the time required for each transaction ARI's call centers handle—from the time a call center staffer takes a call to retrieving and delivering the requested information. Because call center staff account for

40 percent of ARI's direct overhead, that time reduction translates into major cost savings.

ARI plans to make some of these real-time reporting and analytic capabilities available on mobile devices, which will enable customers to approve a variety of operational procedures instantly, such as authorizing maintenance repairs. Customers will also be able to use the mobile tools for instant insight into their fleet operations, down to a level of detail such as a specific vehicle's tire history.

Sources. "Customer Journey: Automotive Resources International," www.sap.com, accessed January 3, 2015; "ARI: Driving Results in Fleet Management on SAP HANA," www.sap.com, accessed January 3, 2015; www.arifleet.com, accessed February 1, 2015; and "ARI Fleet Management Drives Real-Time Analytics to Customers," SAP InsiderPROFILES, April 1, 2013.

CASE STUDY QUESTIONS

1. Why was data management so problematic at ARI?

2. Describe ARI's earlier capabilities for data analysis and reporting and their impact on the business.

3. Was SAP HANA a good solution for ARI? Why or why not?

4. Describe the changes in how ARI and its customers ran their businesses as a result of adopting HANA.

5. Describe two decisions that were improved by adopting HANA.

Figure 6.13 illustrates a contemporary business intelligence infrastructure using the technologies we have just described. Current and historical data are extracted from multiple operational systems along with web data, machine-generated data, unstructured audio/visual data, and data from external sources restructured and reorganized for reporting and analysis. Hadoop clusters preprocess big data for use in the data warehouse, data marts, or an analytic platform or for direct querying by power users. Outputs include reports and dashboards as well as query results. Chapter 11 discusses the various types of BI users and BI reporting in greater detail.

ANALYTICAL TOOLS: RELATIONSHIPS, PATTERNS, TRENDS

When data have been captured and organized using the business intelligence technologies we have just described, they are available for further analysis by using software for database querying and reporting, multidimensional data analysis (OLAP), and data mining. This section will introduce you to these tools, with more detail about business intelligence analytics and applications in Chapter 11.

Online Analytical Processing (OLAP)

Suppose your company sells four products—nuts, bolts, washers, and screws—in the East, West, and Central regions. If you wanted to ask a straightforward question, such as how many washers sold during the past quarter, you could easily find the answer by querying your sales database. However, what if you wanted to know

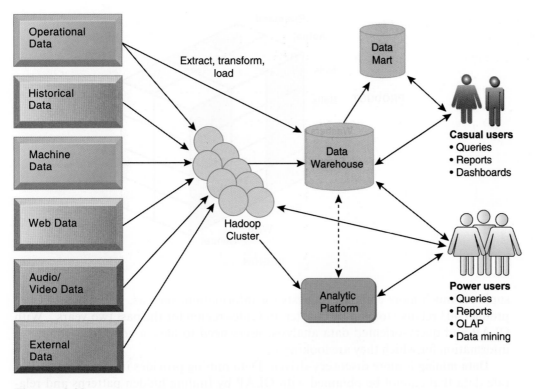

Figure 6.13
Contemporary Business Intelligence Infrastructure
A contemporary business intelligence infrastructure features capabilities and tools to manage and analyze large quantities and different types of data from multiple sources. Easy-to-use query and reporting tools for casual business users and more sophisticated analytical toolsets for power users are included.

how many washers sold in each of your sales regions and compare actual results with projected sales?

To obtain the answer, you would need **online analytical processing (OLAP)**. OLAP supports multidimensional data analysis, enabling users to view the same data in different ways using multiple dimensions. Each aspect of information—product, pricing, cost, region, or time period—represents a different dimension. A product manager could use a multidimensional data analysis tool to learn how many washers were sold in the East in June, how that compares with the previous month and the previous June, and how it compares with the sales forecast. OLAP enables users to obtain online answers to ad hoc questions such as these in rapid time, even when the data are stored in very large databases, such as sales figures for multiple years.

Figure 6.14 shows a multidimensional model that could be created to represent products, regions, actual sales, and projected sales. A matrix of actual sales can be stacked on top of a matrix of projected sales to form a cube with six faces. If you rotate the cube 90 degrees one way, the face showing will be product versus actual and projected sales. If you rotate the cube 90 degrees again, you will see region versus actual and projected sales. If you rotate 180 degrees from the original view, you will see projected sales and product versus region. Cubes can be nested within cubes to build complex views of data. A company would use either a specialized multidimensional database or a tool that creates multidimensional views of data in relational databases.

Data Mining
Traditional database queries answer such questions as, "How many units of product number 403 were shipped in February 2016?" OLAP, or multidimensional analysis,

Figure 6.14
Multidimensional Data
Model
*This view shows product
versus region. If you rotate
the cube 90 degrees,
the face that will show
is product versus actual
and projected sales. If you
rotate the cube 90 degrees
again, you will see region
versus actual and projected
sales. Other views are
possible.*

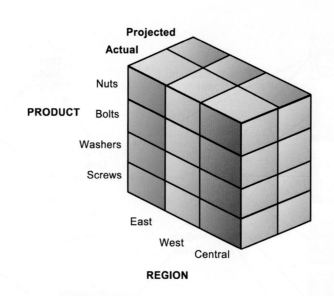

supports much more complex requests for information, such as, "Compare sales of product 403 relative to plan by quarter and sales region for the past two years." With OLAP and query-oriented data analysis, users need to have a good idea about the information for which they are looking.

Data mining is more discovery-driven. Data mining provides insights into corporate data that cannot be obtained with OLAP by finding hidden patterns and relationships in large databases and inferring rules from them to predict future behavior. The patterns and rules are used to guide decision making and forecast the effect of those decisions. The types of information obtainable from data mining include associations, sequences, classifications, clusters, and forecasts.

- *Associations* are occurrences linked to a single event. For instance, a study of supermarket purchasing patterns might reveal that, when corn chips are purchased, a cola drink is purchased 65 percent of the time, but when there is a promotion, cola is purchased 85 percent of the time. This information helps managers make better decisions because they have learned the profitability of a promotion.

- In *sequences*, events are linked over time. We might find, for example, that if a house is purchased, a new refrigerator will be purchased within two weeks 65 percent of the time, and an oven will be bought within one month of the home purchase 45 percent of the time.

- *Classification* recognizes patterns that describe the group to which an item belongs by examining existing items that have been classified and by inferring a set of rules. For example, businesses such as credit card or telephone companies worry about the loss of steady customers. Classification helps discover the characteristics of customers who are likely to leave and can provide a model to help managers predict who those customers are so that the managers can devise special campaigns to retain such customers.

- *Clustering* works in a manner similar to classification when no groups have yet been defined. A data mining tool can discover different groupings within data, such as finding affinity groups for bank cards or partitioning a database into groups of customers based on demographics and types of personal investments.

- Although these applications involve predictions, *forecasting* uses predictions in a different way. It uses a series of existing values to forecast what other values will be. For example, forecasting might find patterns in data to help managers estimate the future value of continuous variables, such as sales figures.

These systems perform high-level analyses of patterns or trends, but they can also drill down to provide more detail when needed. There are data mining applications for all the functional areas of business and for government and scientific work. One popular use for data mining is to provide detailed analyses of patterns in customer data for one-to-one marketing campaigns or for identifying profitable customers.

Caesars Entertainment, formerly known as Harrah's Entertainment, is the largest gaming company in the world. It continually analyzes data about its customers gathered when people play its slot machines or use its casinos and hotels. The corporate marketing department uses this information to build a detailed gambling profile, based on a particular customer's ongoing value to the company. For instance, data mining tells Caesars the favorite gaming experience of a regular customer at one of its riverboat casinos, along with that person's preferences for room accommodations, restaurants, and entertainment. This information guides management decisions about how to cultivate the most profitable customers, encourage those customers to spend more, and attract more customers with high revenue-generating potential. Business intelligence improved Caesar's profits so much that it became the centerpiece of the firm's business strategy, and customer data are Caesar's most valuable asset (O'Keefe, 2015).

Text Mining and Web Mining

Unstructured data, most in the form of text files, is believed to account for more than 80 percent of useful organizational information and is one of the major sources of big data that firms want to analyze. Email, memos, call center transcripts, survey responses, legal cases, patent descriptions, and service reports are all valuable for finding patterns and trends that will help employees make better business decisions. **Text mining** tools are now available to help businesses analyze these data. These tools can extract key elements from unstructured big data sets, discover patterns and relationships, and summarize the information.

Businesses might turn to text mining to analyze transcripts of calls to customer service centers to identify major service and repair issues or to measure customer sentiment about their company. **Sentiment analysis** software can mine text comments in an email message, blog, social media conversation, or survey form to detect favorable and unfavorable opinions about specific subjects.

For example, the discount broker Charles Schwab uses Attensity Analyze software to analyze hundreds of thousands of its customer interactions each month. The software analyzes Schwab's customer service notes, emails, survey responses, and online discussions to discover signs of dissatisfaction that might cause a customer to stop using the company's services. Attensity can automatically identify the various voices customers use to express their feedback (such as a positive, negative, or conditional voice) to pinpoint a person's intent to buy, intent to leave, or reaction to a specific product or marketing message. Schwab uses this information to take corrective actions such as stepping up direct broker communication with the customer and trying to resolve the problems quickly that are making the customer unhappy.

The web is another rich source of unstructured big data for revealing patterns, trends, and insights into customer behavior. The discovery and analysis of useful patterns and information from the World Wide Web is called **web mining**. Businesses might turn to web mining to help them understand customer behavior, evaluate the effectiveness of a particular website, or quantify the success of a marketing campaign. For instance, marketers use Google Trends and Insights for Search services, which track the popularity of various words and phrases used in Google search queries to learn what people are interested in and what they are interested in buying.

Web mining looks for patterns in data through content mining, structure mining, and usage mining. Web content mining is the process of extracting knowledge from the content of web pages, which may include text, image, audio, and video data. Web structure mining examines data related to the structure of a particular website. For example, links pointing to a document indicate the popularity of the document; links coming out of a document indicate the richness or perhaps the variety of topics covered in the document. Web usage mining examines user interaction data a web server records whenever requests for a website's resources are received. The usage data records the user's behavior when the user browses or makes transactions on the website and collects the data in a server log. Analyzing such data can help companies determine the value of particular customers, cross marketing strategies across products, and the effectiveness of promotional campaigns.

DATABASES AND THE WEB

Many companies are using the web to make some of the information in their internal databases available to customers and business partners. Prospective customers might use a company's website to view the company's product catalog or to place an order. The company in turn might use the web to check inventory availability for that product from its supplier.

These actions involve accessing and (in the case of ordering) updating corporate databases through the web. Suppose, for example, a customer with a web browser wants to search an online retailer's database for pricing information. Figure 6.15 illustrates how that customer might access the retailer's internal database over the web. The user would access the retailer's website over the Internet using web browser software on his or her client PC or mobile device. The user's web browser software would request data from the organization's database, using HTML commands to communicate with the web server.

Because many back-end databases cannot interpret commands written in HTML, the web server would pass these requests for data to software that translates HTML commands into SQL so the DBMS working with the database can process them. In a client/server environment, the DBMS resides on a dedicated computer called a **database server**. The DBMS receives the SQL requests and provides the required data. The information is transferred from the organization's internal database back to the web server for delivery in the form of a web page to the user.

Figure 6.15 shows that the software working between the web server and the DBMS could be on an application server running on its own dedicated computer (see Chapter 5). The application server takes requests from the web server, runs the business logic to process transactions based on those requests, and provides connectivity to the organization's back-end systems or databases. Alternatively, the software for handling these operations could be a custom program or a CGI script. A CGI script is a compact program using the *Common Gateway Interface (CGI)* specification for processing data on a web server.

There are a number of advantages to using the web to access an organization's internal databases. First, everyone knows how to use web browser software, and employees require much less training than if they used proprietary query tools. Second, the web interface requires few or no changes to the internal database. Companies leverage their investments in older systems because it costs much less to add a web interface in front of a legacy system than to redesign and rebuild the system to improve user access.

Accessing corporate databases through the web is creating new efficiencies and opportunities, and, in some cases, it is even changing the way business is being done. ThomasNet.com provides an up-to-date directory of information from more than 700,000 suppliers of industrial products such as chemicals, metals, plastics, rubber,

Figure 6.15
Linking Internal
Databases to the Web
Users access an organization's internal database through the web, using their desktop PCs or mobile devices and web browser software.

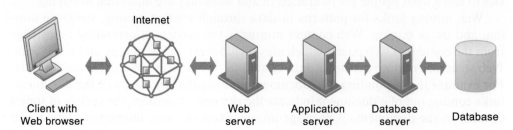

Client with   Internet   Web   Application   Database
Web browser   server   server   server   Database

and automotive equipment. Formerly called Thomas Register, the company used to send out huge paper catalogs with this information. Now, it provides this information to users on its website and has become a smaller, leaner company.

Other companies have created entirely new businesses based on access to large databases through the web. One is the social networking service Facebook, which helps users stay connected with each other and meet new people. Facebook features profiles with information about more than 1.4 billion active users with information about themselves, including interests, friends, photos, and groups with which they are affiliated. Facebook maintains a massive database to house and manage all this content.

6-4 Why are information policy, data administration, and data quality assurance essential for managing the firm's data resources?

Setting up a database is only a start. To make sure that the data for your business remain accurate, reliable, and readily available to those who need it, your business will need special policies and procedures for data management.

ESTABLISHING AN INFORMATION POLICY

Every business, large and small, needs an information policy. Your firm's data are an important resource, and you don't want people doing whatever they want with them. You need to have rules on how the data are to be organized and maintained and who is allowed to view the data or change them.

An **information policy** specifies the organization's rules for sharing, disseminating, acquiring, standardizing, classifying, and inventorying information. Information policies identify which users and organizational units can share information, where information can be distributed, and who is responsible for updating and maintaining the information. For example, a typical information policy would specify that only selected members of the payroll and human resources department would have the right to change and view sensitive employee data, such as an employee's salary or social security number, and that these departments are responsible for making sure that such employee data are accurate.

If you were in a small business, the owners or managers would establish and implement the information policy. In a large organization, managing and planning for information as a corporate resource often requires a formal data administration function. **Data administration** is responsible for the specific policies and procedures through which data can be managed as an organizational resource. These responsibilities include developing information policy, planning for data, overseeing logical database design and data dictionary development, and monitoring how information systems specialists and end-user groups use data.

A large organization will also have a database design and management group within the corporate information systems division that is responsible for defining and organizing the structure and content of the database and maintaining it. In close cooperation with users, the design group establishes the physical database, the logical relations among elements, and the access rules and security procedures. The functions it performs are called **database administration**.

ENSURING DATA QUALITY

What would happen if a customer's telephone number or account balance were incorrect? What would be the impact if the database had the wrong price for the product you sold? Data that are inaccurate, untimely, or inconsistent with other sources of information create serious operational and financial problems for businesses, even with a well-designed database and information policy. When faulty data go unnoticed, they often lead to incorrect decisions, product recalls, and even financial losses.

Gartner Inc. reported that more than 25 percent of the critical data in large Fortune 1000 companies' databases is inaccurate or incomplete, including bad product codes and product descriptions, faulty inventory descriptions, erroneous financial data, incorrect supplier information, and incorrect employee data.

Some of these data quality problems are caused by redundant and inconsistent data produced by multiple systems. For example, the sales ordering system and the inventory management system might both maintain data on the organization's products. However, the sales ordering system might use the term *Item Number*, and the inventory system might call the same attribute *Product Number*. The sales, inventory, or manufacturing systems of a clothing retailer might use different codes to represent values for an attribute. One system might represent clothing size as extra large, whereas the other system might use the code XL for the same purpose. During the design process for a database, data describing entities, such as a customer, product, or order, should be named and defined consistently for all business areas using the database.

If a database is properly designed and enterprise-wide data standards established, duplicate or inconsistent data elements should be minimal. Most data quality problems, however, such as misspelled names, transposed numbers, or incorrect or missing codes, stem from errors during data input. The incidence of such errors is rising as companies move their businesses to the web and allow customers and suppliers to enter data into their websites that directly update internal systems.

Think of all the times you have received several pieces of the same direct mail advertising on the same day. This is very likely the result of your name being maintained multiple times in a database. Your name may have been misspelled or you used your middle initial on one occasion and not on another or the information was initially entered on a paper form and not scanned properly into the system. Because of these inconsistencies, the database would treat you as different people! We often receive redundant mail addressed to Laudon, Lavdon, Lauden, or Landon.

Before a new database is in place, organizations need to identify and correct their faulty data and establish better routines for editing data once their database is in operation. Analysis of data quality often begins with a **data quality audit**, which is a structured survey of the accuracy and level of completeness of the data in an information system. Data quality audits can be performed by surveying entire data files, surveying samples from data files, or surveying end users for their perceptions of data quality.

Data cleansing, also known as *data scrubbing*, consists of activities for detecting and correcting data in a database that are incorrect, incomplete, improperly formatted, or redundant. Data cleansing not only corrects data but also enforces consistency among different sets of data that originated in separate information systems. Specialized data-cleansing software is available to survey data files automatically, correct errors in the data, and integrate the data in a consistent, company-wide format.

Review Summary

6-1 **What is a database and how does a relational database organize data?** A database is a group of related files that keeps track of people, places, and things (entities) about which organizations maintain information. The relational database is the primary method for organizing and maintaining data today in information systems. It organizes data in two-dimensional tables with rows and columns called relations. Each table contains data about an entity and its attributes. Each row represents a record and each column represents an attribute or field. Each table also contains a key field to identify each record uniquely for retrieval or manipulation. An entity-relationship diagram graphically depicts the relationship between entities (tables) in a relational database. The process of breaking down complex groupings of data and streamlining them to minimize redundancy and awkward many-to-many relationships is called normalization. Nonrelational databases are becoming popular for managing types of data that can't be handled easily by the relational data model.

6-2 **What are the principles of a database management system?** A DBMS consists of software that permits centralization of data and data management so that businesses have a single consistent source for all their data needs. A single database services multiple applications. The DBMS separates the logical and physical views of data so that the user does not have to be concerned with the data's physical location. The principal capabilities of a DBMS include a data definition capability, a data dictionary capability, and a data manipulation language.

6-3 **What are the principal tools and technologies for accessing information from databases to improve business performance and decision making?** Contemporary data management technology has an array of tools for obtaining useful information from all the types of data businesses use today, including semistructured and unstructured big data in vast quantities. These capabilities include data warehouses and data marts, Hadoop, in-memory computing, and analytical platforms. OLAP represents relationships among data as a multidimensional structure, which can be visualized as cubes of data and cubes within cubes of data. Data mining analyzes large pools of data, including the contents of data warehouses, to find patterns and rules that can be used to predict future behavior and guide decision making. Text mining tools help businesses analyze large unstructured data sets consisting of text. Web mining tools focus on analyzing useful patterns and information from the World Wide Web, examining the structure of websites, activities of website users, and the contents of web pages. Conventional databases can be linked to the web or a web interface to facilitate user access to an organization's internal data.

6-4 **Why are information policy, data administration, and data quality assurance essential for managing the firm's data resources?** Developing a database environment requires policies and procedures for managing organizational data as well as a good data model and database technology. A formal information policy governs the maintenance, distribution, and use of information in the organization. In large corporations, a formal data administration function is responsible for information policy as well as for data planning, data dictionary development, and monitoring data usage in the firm. Data that are inaccurate, incomplete, or inconsistent create serious operational and financial problems for businesses if they lead to bad decisions about the actions the firm should take. Assuring data quality involves using enterprise-wide data standards, databases designed to minimize inconsistent and redundant data, data quality audits, and data cleansing software.

Key Terms

Analytic platform, 234
Attributes, 220
Big data, 230
Bit, 219
Byte, 219
Data administration, 241
Data cleansing, 242
Data definition, 228
Data dictionary, 228

Data manipulation language, 228
Data mart, 233
Data mining, 238
Data quality audit, 242
Data warehouse, 231
Database, 219
Database administration, 241

Database management system (DBMS), 225
Database server, 240
Entity, 220
Entity-relationship diagram, 222
Field, 219
File, 219
Foreign key, 222

Hadoop, 233
Information policy, 241
In-memory computing, 234
Key field, 221
Nonrelational database
  management systems, 229
Normalization, 225

Online analytical process-
  ing (OLAP), 237
Primary key, 221
Query, 229
Record, 219
Referential integrity, 225
Relational database, 220

Report generator, 229
Sentiment analysis, 239
Structured Query
  Language (SQL), 228
Text mining, 239
Tuples, 221
Web mining, 239

MyMISLab™

To complete the problems with the ⭐, go to EOC Discussion Questions in the MyLab.

Review Questions

6-1 What is a database and how does a relational database organize data?
- Define a database.
- Define and explain the significance of entities, attributes, and key fields.
- Define a relational database and explain how it organizes and stores information.
- Explain the role of entity-relationship diagrams and normalization in database design.
- Define referential integrity and explain its role in relational database systems.
- Define a nonrelational database management system and explain how it differs from a relational DBMS.

6-2 What are the principles of a database management system?
- Define a database management system (DBMS), describe how it works, and explain how it benefits organizations.
- Define and compare the logical and physical views of data.
- Define and describe the three operations of a relational database management system.
- Name and describe the three major capabilities of a DBMS.
- Define nonrelational databases and describe their capabilities.

6-3 What are the principal tools and technologies for accessing information from databases to improve business performance and decision making?
- Define big data and describe the technologies for managing and analyzing big data.
- List and describe the components of a contemporary business intelligence infrastructure.
- Define data warehouse and explain how it differs from a data mart.
- Define data mining, describe what types of information can be obtained from it, and explain how it differs from OLAP.
- Explain how text mining and web mining differ from conventional data mining.
- Explain how users can access information from a company's internal databases through the web.

6-4 Why are information policy, data administration, and data quality assurance essential for managing the firm's data resources?
- Define information policy and data administration and explain how they help organizations manage their data.
- Explain why an organization needs an information policy.
- Explain how data quality problems arise.
- Explain how information policies are established in different-sized businesses.

Discussion Questions

✪ 6-5   It has been said that you do not need database management software to create a database environment. Discuss.

✪ 6-6   To what extent should end users be involved in the selection of a database management system and database design?

✪ 6-7   What are the consequences of an organization not having an information policy?

Hands-On MIS Projects

MANAGEMENT DECISION PROBLEMS

The projects in this section give you hands-on experience in analyzing data quality problems, establishing company-wide data standards, creating a database for inventory management, and using the web to search online databases for overseas business resources. Visit MyMISLab's Multimedia Library to access this chapter's Hands-On MIS Projects.

6-8   Iko Instrument Group, a global supplier of measurement, analytical, and monitoring instruments and services based in the Netherlands, had a new data warehouse designed to analyze customer activity to improve service and marketing. However, the data warehouse was full of inaccurate and redundant data. The data in the warehouse came from numerous transaction processing systems in the United States, Europe, Asia, and other locations around the world. The team that designed the warehouse had assumed that sales groups in all these areas would enter customer names, telephone numbers, and addresses the same way. In fact, companies in different countries were using multiple ways of entering quote, billing, shipping, contact information and other data. Assess the potential business impact of these data quality problems. What decisions have to be made and steps taken to reach a solution?

6-9   Your industrial supply company wants to create a data warehouse from which management can obtain a single corporate-wide view of critical sales information to identify bestselling products, key customers, and sales trends. Your sales and product information are stored in several systems: a divisional sales system running on a UNIX server and a corporate sales system running on an IBM mainframe. You would like to create a single standard format that consolidates these data from both systems. In MyMISLab, you can review the proposed format along with sample files from the two systems that would supply the data for the data warehouse. Then answer the following questions:

- What business problems are created by not having these data in a single standard format?
- How easy would it be to create a database with a single standard format that could store the data from both systems? Identify the problems that would have to be addressed.
- Should the problems be solved by database specialists or general business managers? Explain.
- Who should have the authority to finalize a single company-wide format for this information in the data warehouse?

ACHIEVING OPERATIONAL EXCELLENCE: BUILDING A RELATIONAL DATABASE FOR INVENTORY MANAGEMENT

Software skills: Database design, querying, and reporting
Business skills: Inventory management

6-10 In this exercise, you will use database software to design a database for managing inventory for a small business. Sylvester's Bike Shop, located in San Francisco, California, sells road, mountain, hybrid, leisure, and children's bicycles. Currently, Sylvester's purchases bikes from three suppliers but plans to add new suppliers in the near future. Using the information found in the tables in MyMISLab, build a simple relational database to manage information about Sylvester's suppliers and products. MyMISLab contains more details about the specifications for the database.

After you have built the database, perform the following activities.

- Prepare a report that identifies the five most expensive bicycles. The report should list the bicycles in descending order from most expensive to least expensive, the quantity on hand for each, and the markup percentage for each.
- Prepare a report that lists each supplier, its products, the quantities on hand, and associated reorder levels. The report should be sorted alphabetically by supplier. Within each supplier category, the products should be sorted alphabetically.
- Prepare a report listing only the bicycles that are low in stock and need to be reordered. The report should provide supplier information for the identified items.
- Write a brief description of how the database could be enhanced to improve management of the business further. What tables or fields should be added? What additional reports would be useful?

IMPROVING DECISION MAKING: SEARCHING ONLINE DATABASES FOR OVERSEAS BUSINESS RESOURCES

Software skills: Online databases
Business skills: Researching services for overseas operations

6-11 This project develops skills in searching online web-enabled databases with information about products and services in faraway locations.

Your company, Caledonian Furniture, is located in Cumbernauld, Scotland, and manufactures office furniture of various types. You are considering opening a facility to manufacture and sell your products in Australia. You would like to contact organizations that offer many services necessary for you to open your Australian office and manufacturing facility, including lawyers, accountants, import-export experts, and telecommunications equipment and support firms. Access the following online databases to locate companies that you would like to meet with during your upcoming trip: Australian Business Register, AustraliaTrade Now (australiatradenow.com), and the Nationwide Business Directory of Australia (www.nationwide.com.au). If necessary, use search engines such as Yahoo! and Google.

- List the companies you would contact on your trip to determine whether they can help you with these and any other functions you think are vital to establishing your office.
- Rate the databases you used for accuracy of name, completeness, ease of use, and general helpfulness.

Collaboration and Teamwork Project

Identifying Entities and Attributes in an Online Database

6-12 With your team of three or four students, select an online database to explore, such as AOL Music, iGo.com, or the Internet Movie Database. Explore one of these websites to see what information it provides. List the entities and attributes that the company running the website must keep track of in its databases. Diagram the relationships between the entities you have identified. If possible, use Google Docs and Google Drive or Google Sites to brainstorm, organize, and develop a presentation of your findings for the class.

BUSINESS PROBLEM-SOLVING CASE

Lego's Enterprise Software Spurs Growth

The Lego Group, which is headquartered in Billund, Denmark, is one of the largest toy manufacturers in the world. Lego's main products have been the bricks and figures that children have played with for generations. The Danish company has experienced sustained growth since its founding in 1932, and for most of its history its major manufacturing facilities were located in Denmark.

In 2003, Lego was facing tough competition from imitators and manufacturers of electronic toys. In an effort to reduce costs, the group decided to initiate a gradual restructuring process that continues today. In 2006, the company announced that a large part of its production would be outsourced to the electronics manufacturing service company Flextronics, which has plants in Mexico, Hungary, and the Czech Republic. The decision to outsource production came as a direct consequence of an analysis of Lego's total supply chain. To reduce labor costs, manually intensive processes were outsourced, keeping only the highly skilled workers in Billund. Lego's workforce was gradually reduced from 8,300 employees in 2003 to approximately 4,200 in 2010. Additionally, production had to be relocated to places closer to its natural markets. As a consequence of all these changes, Lego transformed itself from a manufacturing firm to a market-oriented company that is capable of reacting fast to changing global demand.

Lego's restructuring process, coupled with double-digit sales growth in the past few years, has led to the company's expansion abroad and made its workforce more international. These changes presented supply chain and human resources challenges to the company. The supply chain had to be reengineered to simplify production without reducing quality. Improved logistics planning allowed Lego to work more closely with retailers, suppliers, and the new outsourcing companies. At the same time, the human resources (HR) department needed to play a more strategic role inside the company. HR was now responsible for implementing effective policies aimed at retaining and recruiting the most qualified employees from a diversity of cultural backgrounds.

Adapting company operations to these changes required a flexible and robust IT infrastructure with business intelligence capabilities that could help management perform better forecasting and planning. As part of the solution, Lego chose to move to SAP business suite software. SAP AG, a German company that specializes in enterprise software solutions, is one of the leading software companies in the world. SAP's software products include a variety of applications designed to efficiently support all of a company's essential functions and operations. Lego chose to implement SAP's Supply Chain Management (SCM), Product Lifecycle Management (PLM), and Enterprise Resources Planning (ERP) modules.

The SCM module includes essential features such as supply chain monitoring and analysis as well as forecasting, planning, and inventory optimization. The PLM module enables managers to optimize development processes and systems. The ERP module includes, among other applications, the Human Capital Management (HCM) application for personnel administration and development.

SAP's business suite is based on a flexible three-tier client–server architecture that can easily be adapted to the new service-oriented architecture (SOA) available in the latest versions of the software. In the first tier, a client interface—a browser-type graphical user interface (GUI) running on a laptop, desktop, or mobile device—submits users' requests to the application servers. The applications servers (the second tier in the system) receive and process clients' requests. In turn, these application servers send the processed requests to the database system (the third tier), which consists of one or more relational databases. SAP's business suite supports databases from different vendors, including those offered by Oracle, Microsoft, MySQL, and others. The relational databases contain tables that store data on Lego's products, daily operations, the supply chain, and thousands of employees. Managers can easily use the SAP query tool to obtain reports from the databases because it does not require any technical skill. Additionally, the distributed architecture enables authorized personnel to have direct access to the database system from the company's various locations, including those in Europe, North America, and Asia.

SAP's ERP-HCM module includes advanced features such as "Talent Manager" as well as those for handling employee administration, reporting, and travel and time management. These features allow Lego's HR personnel to select the best candidates, schedule their training, and create a stimulus plan to retain them. It is also possible to include performance measurements and get real-time insight into HR trends. Using these advanced features, together with tools from other software vendors, Lego's managers are able to track employees' leadership potential, develop their careers, and forecast the recruiting of new employees with certain skills.

The investments that The Lego Group has made in information systems and business re-design have paid off handsomely. In 2014 the Group increased sales by 13 percent to €3.8 billion against €3.3 billion the year before. Operating profit increased 15 percent to €1.26 billion. Full-time employees increased to 11,755 as the company expanded production in Asia. In the first half of 2015, revenue increased 23 percent compared with the same period last year measured.

Reflecting its growing emphasis on developing a global company and its substantial investment in global information systems both in the supply chain and the distribution chain, The Lego Group in 2014 showed strong, long-term growth in all regions. In Europe, America, and Asia, sales growth has been in the double digits for over five years despite the fact that the Global Great Recession (2008 to 2013) led to flat sales of toys worldwide. In the Asian region, growth in Lego sales varied from market to market. China's growth in consumer sales of more than 50 percent was the most significant in the region. This supports The Lego Group's ambitions to further globalize the company and make Asia a significant contributor to future growth.

In May 2014 The Lego Group opened its first factory in China, located in Jiaxing, and a new office in Shanghai, which is one of five main offices globally for The Lego Group. The executives at Lego believe there is huge potential in Asia, and have decided to learn more about the Asian market and build capabilities in the region. The new factory and office represent a significant expansion of the Lego physical presence in the region. According to executives, in combination with their existing office in Singapore, the Shanghai office and the new factory enable strategically important functions to be located close to their customers as well as children and parents in China and Asia.

The decision to place a Lego factory in China is a direct consequence of The Lego Group's ambition to have production placed close to core markets. This same philosophy has led to expansions of the Lego factory in the Czech Republic, and an entirely new factory was opened in Nyiregyhaza, Hungary, in March 2014. These factories, along with the parent factory in Denmark, serve the European markets. To serve the Americas faster and with customized products, the company expanded its Lego factory in Monterrey, Mexico.

Executives believe the global approach to information systems and production facilities enables the company to deliver Lego products to retailers and ultimately to children all over the world very fast, offering world-class service to consumers. In 2014, in addition to its growth across a variety of markets, *The LEGO Movie* was also released to overwhelmingly positive reviews, bolstering the company's brand and allowing it to develop a new array of products based on the movie's themes. The movie has led to shortages of Lego bricks for Christmas 2015.

The Lego Group is primed to continue its growth throughout 2016 and beyond using its organizational flexibility and the concepts it has honed for years. The company is responding to its customers and releasing new versions of some of its most popular sets of toys, including its Bionicle series of block sets. So far, Lego has built an impressive worldwide presence, block by block.

Sources: Mary O'Connor, "LEGO Puts the RFID Pieces Together," *RFID Journal*, http://www.rfidjournal.com/articles/view?2145/2 accessed December 21, 2015; Henrik Amsinck, "LEGO: Building Strong Customer Loyalty Through Personalized Engagements," http://events.sap.com/ accessed December 20, 2015; Gregory Schmidt, "Lego's Success Leads to Competitors and Spinoffs," *New York Times*, November 20, 2015; Niclas Rolander, "China Shock Can't Halt Lego Executive Chasing 'Fantastic' Growth," Bloombergbusiness.com, September 2, 2015; Rebecca Kanthor, "New Lego Facility in China to Start Production This Year," *Plastics News*, May 15, 2015; "Now Lego's Business Rules Are on the Table," *Economic Engineering*, 2015; "The Lego Group Annual Report 2014," The Lego Group, April 2015; Roar Trangbaek, "New London Office Supports Lego Group Strategy to Reach Children Globally, Newsroom, www.lego.com, November 2014; Roar Trangbaek, "Global Lego Sales Up 15 Percent in First Half of 2014," Newsroom, www. lego.com, 2014; Jens Hansegard, "Oh, Snap! Lego's Sales Surpass Mattel," *Wall Street Journal*, September 4, 2014; "How Lego Became World's Hottest Toy Company," *Economist*, March 9, 2013; "Lego Creates Model Business Success with SAP and IBM," IBM Global Financing, May 19, 2010, www-01.ibm.com/ software/success/cssdb.nsf/CS/STRD- 85KGS6?OpenDocument, October 20, 2010; "Lego, the Toy of the Century Had to Reinvent the Supply-Chain to Save the Company," *Supply Chain Digest*, September 25, 2007, www.scdigest.com/ assets/on_target/07-09-25- 7.php?cid=1237, accessed November 16, 2010.

Case Study Questions

6-13 Explain the role of the database in SAP's three-tier system.

6-14 Explain why distributed architectures are flexible.

6-15 Identify some of the business intelligence features included in SAP's business software suite.

6-16 What are the main advantages and disadvantages of having multiple databases in a distributed architecture? Explain.

Case contributed by Daniel Ortiz Arroyo, Aalborg University.

MyMISLab

Go to the Assignments section of your MyLab to complete these writing exercises.

6-17 Define web mining and describe the three ways that web mining looks for patterns in data.

6-18 Discuss how the following facilitate the management of big data: Hadoop, in-memory computing, analytic platforms.

Chapter 6 References

Aiken, Peter, Mark Gillenson, Xihui Zhang, and David Rafner. "Data Management and Data Administration: Assessing 25 Years of Practice." *Journal of Database Management* (July–September 2011).

Barth, Paul S. "Managing Big Data: What Every CIO Needs to Know," *CIO Insight* (January 12, 2012).

Barton, Dominic, and David Court. "Making Advanced Analytics Work for You," *Harvard Business Review* (October 2012).

Bean, Randy. "Big Data Fatigue?" *MIT Sloan Management Review* (June 23, 2014).

Beath, Cynthia, Irma Becerra-Fernandez, Jeanne Ross, and James Short. "Finding Value in the Information Explosion." *MIT Sloan Management Review* 53, No. 4 (Summer 2012).

Bughin, Jacques, John Livingston, and Sam Marwaha. "Seizing the Potential for Big Data." *McKinsey Quarterly* (October 2011).

Court, David. "Getting Big Impact from Big Data." McKinsey Quarterly 1 (2015).

Davenport, Thomas H., and D. J. Patil. "Data Scientist: The Sexiest Job of the 21st Century," *Harvard Business Review* (October 2012).

Davenport, Thomas H. *Big Data at Work: Dispelling the Myths, Uncovering the Opportunities.* (Boston: Harvard Business Press, 2014.)

Eckerson, Wayne W. "Analytics in the Era of Big Data: Exploring a Vast New Ecosystem," *TechTarget* (2012).

_____. "Data Quality and the Bottom Line." Data Warehousing Institute (2002).

Greengard, Samuel. "Big Data Unlocks Business Value," *Baseline* (January 2012).

Hayashi, Alden M. "Thriving in a Big Data World," *MIT Sloan Management Review* (Winter 2014).

Henschen, Doug. "MetLife Uses NoSQL for Customer Service Breakthrough," *Information Week* (May 13, 2013).

Hoffer, Jeffrey A., Ramesh Venkataraman, and Heikki Toppi. *Modern Database Management*, 12th ed. (Upper Saddle River, NJ: Prentice Hall, 2015.)

Jordan, John. "The Risks of Big Data for Companies," *Wall Street Journal* (October 20, 2013).

Kajepeeta, Sreedhar. "How Hadoop Tames Enterprises' Big Data." *Information Week* (February 2012).

Kroenke, David M., and David Auer. *Database Processing: Fundamentals, Design, and Implementation*, 14th ed. (Upper Saddle River, NJ: Prentic Hall, 2016.)

Lee, Yang W., and Diane M. Strong. "Knowing-Why about Data Processes and Data Quality." *Journal of Management Information Systems* 20, No. 3 (Winter 2004).

Loveman, Gary. "Diamonds in the Datamine," *Harvard Business Review* (May 2003).

Marcus, Gary, and Ernest Davis. "Eight (No, Nine!) Problems with Big Data." *New York Times* (April 6, 2014).

Martens, David, and Foster Provost. "Explaining Data-Driven Document Classifications," *MIS Quarterly* 38, No. 1 (March 2014).

McAfee, Andrew, and Erik Brynjolfsson. "Big Data: The Management Revolution." *Harvard Business Review* (October 2012).

McKinsey Global Institute. "Big Data: The Next Frontier for Innovation, Competition, and Productivity," *McKinsey & Company* (2011).

Merrill, Douglas. "Beware Big Data's Easy Answers," *Harvard Business Review* (August 2014).

Morrison, Todd, and Mark Fontecchio, "In-memory Technology Pushes Analytics Boundaries, Boosts BI Speeds," SearchBusinessAnalytics.techtarget.com, accessed May 17, 2013.

Morrow, Rich. "Apache Hadoop: The Swiss Army Knife of IT," *Global Knowledge* (2013).

Mulani, Narendra. "In-Memory Technology: Keeping Pace with Your Data," *Information Management* (February 27, 2013).

O'Keefe, Kate. "Real Prize in Caesars Fight: Data on Players." *Wall Street Journal* (March 19, 2015).

Redman, Thomas. *Data Driven: Profiting from Your Most Important Business Asset*. Boston: (Boston: Harvard Business Press, 2008.)

Redman, Thomas C. "Data's Credibility Problem," *Harvard Business Review* (December 2013).

Rosenbush, Steven, and Michael Totty. "How Big Data Is Transforming Business," *Wall Street Journal* (March 10, 2013).

Ross, Jeanne W., Cynthia M. Beath, and Anne Quaadgras. "You May Not Need Big Data After All," *Harvard Business Review* (December 2013).

Wallace, David J. "How Caesar's Entertainment Sustains a Data-Driven Culture," *DataInformed* (December 14, 2012).

Telecommunications, the Internet, and Wireless Technology

CHAPTER 7

LEARNING OBJECTIVES

After reading this chapter, you will be able to answer the following questions:

7-1 What are the principal components of telecommunications networks and key networking technologies?

7-2 What are the different types of networks?

7-3 How do the Internet and Internet technology work and how do they support communication and e-business?

7-4 What are the principal technologies and standards for wireless networking, communication, and Internet access?

CHAPTER CASES

RFID and Wireless Technology Speed Up Production at Continental Tires

The Battle over Net Neutrality

Monitoring Employees on Networks: Unethical or Good Business?

RFID Propels the Angkasa Library Management System

VIDEO CASES

Case 1: Telepresence Moves out of the Boardroom and into the Field

Case 2: Virtual Collaboration with IBM Sametime

RFID AND WIRELESS TECHNOLOGY SPEED UP PRODUCTION AT CONTINENTAL TIRES

Continental AG, headquartered in Hanover, Germany, is a global auto and truck parts manufacturing company, with 189,000 employees in 46 countries. It is also the world's fourth-largest tire manufacturer and one of the top five automotive suppliers in the world. In 2014 Continental generated revenues of €34.5 billion.

One of the factories for Continental's Tire Division is located in Sarreguemines, France. The tire division generated €9.7 billion in 2014. This facility produces 1,000 different kinds of tires and encompasses nearly 1.5 million square feet. The production process requires large wheeled carts loaded with sheets of rubber or other components to be transported from storage to workstations as tires are being built. Until recently, if a carrier was not in its expected location, a worker had to look for it manually. Manual tracking was time-consuming and inaccurate, and the plant often lost track of tire components altogether.

Missing materials created bottlenecks and production delays at a time when business was growing and the company needed to increase production capacity. Continental found a solution in a new real-time location system based on a Wi-Fi wireless network using radio frequency identification (RFID) tags, AeroScout MobileView software, mobile computers, and Global Data Sciences' material inventory tracking system software.

The Sarreguemines plant mounted AeroScout T2-EB Industrial RFID tags on the sides of 1,100 of its carriers. As the carriers move from one manufacturing or storage station to another, location information about the cart is transmitted to nearby nodes of a Cisco Wi-Fi wireless network. AeroScout's MobileView software picks up the location and represents the carrier as an icon on a map of the facility displayed on computer screens. Fifteen Honeywell Dolphin 6500 and

Motorola Solutions MC9190 handheld computers are used to confirm that a carrier has been loaded with components or has arrived at a specific workstation.

Seven of the plant's tuggers, which are small trucks for hauling the carriers around the plant, are equipped with DLOG mobile vehicle-mounted computers. When a tugger driver is looking for a specific component, he or she can use the mobile device to access the MobileView system, pull up a map of the facility, and see an icon indicating where that component's carrier is located. The location tracking system provides a real-time snapshot of all the components used in the factory.

A bar code label is attached to each component and carrier, and the system starts tracking that component as soon as it is placed in a carrier. Plant workers use one of the Motorola or Honeywell handhelds and the MobileView software to scan the bar code labels on both the component and its carrier, which is associated with the ID number transmitted by an RFID tag mounted on the carrier.

When components are needed for manufacturing, a tugger driver uses the DLOG mobile computer to identify the location of the carrier with those specific components, and then goes to that location.

By enabling tugger drivers to quickly locate components, the new system has increased productivity and ensures that materials are not overlooked or misplaced. Fewer materials are thrown away because they expired and were not used when they were needed. The system is able to send alerts of materials that have been sitting too long in one spot.

When AeroScout and the new material inventory tracking system were implemented, Continental made sure all production employees, including truckers, tire builders, and management, received training in the new system functions. The company also provided workers with instruction cards with detailed descriptions of system functions that they could use for reference.

By 2014 Continental had extended its RFID effort to include the tires themselves, and communicating with the consumer's automobile systems. Called eTIS (electronic-Tire Information System), RFID chips are integrated into the tire body and report tire pressure, tread depth, load, and other measures. This is a leap towards the future when automobile sensors will be integrated into the Internet, sending data to manufacturers as well as consumers.

Sources: "Tracking Assets: RFID Meets Industrial Wi-Fi," *Industrial Ethernet Book*, November 12, 2015; Rich Ashley, "RFID: Today, Tomorrow, Yesterday," *Tire Review*, July 30, 2014; "Clever Tires: How Tires, TPMS, and RFID Are Combining," http://www.tyrepress.com, March 7, 2014; Claire Swedberg, "Continental Tire Plant Increases Productivity, Reduces Waste," *RFID Journal*, April 25, 2012 and www.conti-online.com, accessed May 2, 2012.

Continental Tires's experience illustrates some of the powerful capabilities and opportunities provided by contemporary networking technology. The company uses wireless networking, radio frequency identification (RFID) technology, mobile computers, and materials inventory management software to automate tracking of components as they move through the production process.

The chapter-opening diagram calls attention to important points raised by this case and this chapter. Continental Tires' production environment extends over a very large area, and requires intensive oversight and coordination to make sure that components are available when and where they are needed in the production process. Tracking components manually was very slow and cumbersome, increasing the possibility that components would be overlooked or lost.

Management decided that wireless technology and RFID tagging provided a solution and arranged for the deployment of a wireless RFID network throughout the entire Sarreguemines production facility. The network made it much easier to track components and to optimize tugger truck movements. Continental Tires had to redesign its production and other work processes and train employees in the new system to take advantage of the new technology.

Here are some questions to think about: How did Continental's real-time location system transform operations? Why was training so important?

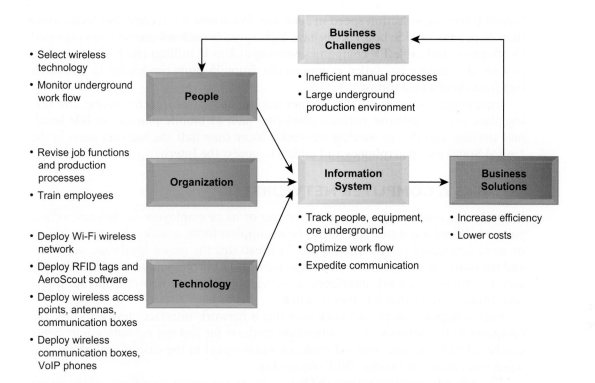

- Select wireless technology
- Monitor underground work flow

- Revise job functions and production processes
- Train employees

- Deploy Wi-Fi wireless network
- Deploy RFID tags and AeroScout software
- Deploy wireless access points, antennas, communication boxes
- Deploy wireless communication boxes, VoIP phones

Business Challenges
- Inefficient manual processes
- Large underground production environment

People

Organization

Technology

Information System
- Track people, equipment, ore underground
- Optimize work flow
- Expedite communication

Business Solutions
- Increase efficiency
- Lower costs

7-1 What are the principal components of telecommunications networks and key networking technologies?

If you run or work in a business, you can't do without networks. You need to communicate rapidly with your customers, suppliers, and employees. Until about 1990, businesses used the postal system or telephone system with voice or fax for communication. Today, however, you and your employees use computers, email, text messaging, the Internet, mobile phones, and mobile computers connected to wireless networks for this purpose. Networking and the Internet are now nearly synonymous with doing business.

NETWORKING AND COMMUNICATION TRENDS

Firms in the past used two fundamentally different types of networks: telephone networks and computer networks. Telephone networks historically handled voice communication, and computer networks handled data traffic. Telephone companies built telephone networks throughout the twentieth century by using voice transmission technologies (hardware and software), and these companies almost always operated as regulated monopolies throughout the world. Computer companies originally built computer networks to transmit data between computers in different locations.

Thanks to continuing telecommunications deregulation and information technology innovation, telephone and computer networks are converging into a single digital network using shared Internet-based standards and technology. Telecommunications providers today, such as AT&T and Verizon, offer data transmission, Internet access, mobile phone service, and television programming as well as voice service. Cable companies, such as Cablevision and Comcast, offer voice service and Internet access. Computer networks have expanded to include Internet telephone and video services.

Both voice and data communication networks have also become more powerful (faster), more portable (smaller and mobile), and less expensive. For instance, the typical Internet connection speed in 2000 was 56 kilobits per second, but today more than 74 percent of U.S. households have high-speed **broadband** connections provided by telephone and cable TV companies running at 1 to 15 million bits per second. The cost for this service has fallen exponentially, from 25 cents per kilobit in 2000 to a tiny fraction of a cent today.

Increasingly, voice and data communication, as well as Internet access, are taking place over broadband wireless platforms such as mobile phones, mobile handheld devices, and PCs in wireless networks. More than half the Internet users in the United States use smartphones and tablets to access the Internet.

WHAT IS A COMPUTER NETWORK?

If you had to connect the computers for two or more employees in the same office, you would need a computer network. In its simplest form, a network consists of two or more connected computers. Figure 7.1 illustrates the major hardware, software, and transmission components in a simple network: a client computer and a dedicated server computer, network interfaces, a connection medium, network operating system software, and either a hub or a switch.

Each computer on the network contains a network interface device to link the computer to the network. The connection medium for linking network components can be a telephone wire, coaxial cable, or radio signal in the case of cell phone and wireless local area networks (Wi-Fi networks).

The **network operating system (NOS)** routes and manages communications on the network and coordinates network resources. It can reside on every computer in the network or primarily on a dedicated server computer for all the applications on the network. A server is a computer on a network that performs important network functions for client computers, such as displaying web pages, storing data, and storing the network operating system (hence controlling the network). Microsoft Windows

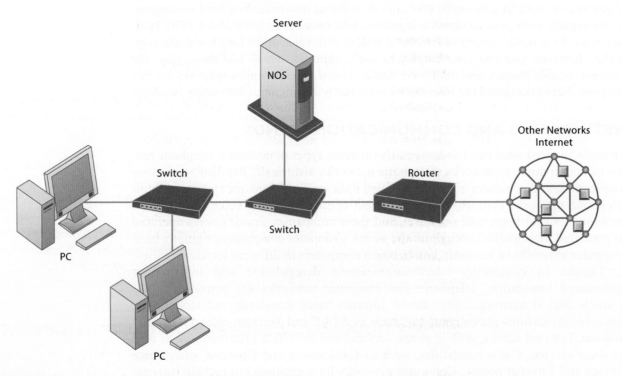

Figure 7.1
Components of a Simple Computer Network
Illustrated here is a simple computer network consisting of computers, a network operating system (NOS) residing on a dedicated server computer, cable (wiring) connecting the devices, switches, and a router.

Server, Linux, and Novell Open Enterprise Server are the most widely used network operating systems.

Most networks also contain a switch or a hub acting as a connection point between the computers. **Hubs** are simple devices that connect network components, sending a packet of data to all other connected devices. A **switch** has more intelligence than a hub and can filter and forward data to a specified destination on the network.

What if you want to communicate with another network, such as the Internet? You would need a router. A **router** is a communications processor that routes packets of data through different networks, ensuring that the data sent gets to the correct address.

Network switches and routers have proprietary software built into their hardware for directing the movement of data on the network. This can create network bottlenecks and makes the process of configuring a network more complicated and time-consuming. **Software-defined networking (SDN)** is a new networking approach in which many of these control functions are managed by one central program, which can run on inexpensive commodity servers that are separate from the network devices themselves. This is especially helpful in a cloud computing environment with many pieces of hardware because it allows a network administrator to manage traffic loads in a flexible and more efficient manner.

Networks in Large Companies

The network we've just described might be suitable for a small business, but what about large companies with many locations and thousands of employees? As a firm grows and collects hundreds of small local area networks, these networks can be tied together into a corporate-wide networking infrastructure. The network infrastructure for a large corporation consists of a large number of these small local area networks linked to other local area networks and to firmwide corporate networks. A number of powerful servers support a corporate website, a corporate intranet, and perhaps an extranet. Some of these servers link to other large computers supporting back-end systems.

Figure 7.2 provides an illustration of these more complex, larger scale corporate-wide networks. Here you can see that the corporate network infrastructure supports a mobile sales force using mobile phones and smartphones, mobile employees linking to the company website, and internal company networks using mobile wireless local area networks (Wi-Fi networks). In addition to these computer networks, the firm's infrastructure may include a separate telephone network that handles most voice data. Many firms are dispensing with their traditional telephone networks and using Internet telephones that run on their existing data networks (described later).

As you can see from this figure, a large corporate network infrastructure uses a wide variety of technologies—everything from ordinary telephone service and corporate data networks to Internet service, wireless Internet, and mobile phones. One of the major problems facing corporations today is how to integrate all the different communication networks and channels into a coherent system that enables information to flow from one part of the corporation to another and from one system to another. As more and more communication networks become digital, and based on Internet technologies, it will become easier to integrate them.

KEY DIGITAL NETWORKING TECHNOLOGIES

Contemporary digital networks and the Internet are based on three key technologies: client/server computing, the use of packet switching, and the development of widely used communications standards (the most important of which is Transmission Control Protocol/Internet Protocol, or TCP/IP) for linking disparate networks and computers.

Figure 7.2
Corporate Network
Infrastructure
*Today's corporate network
infrastructure is a collection
of many networks from the
public switched telephone
network, to the Internet, to
corporate local area net-
works linking workgroups,
departments, or office
floors.*

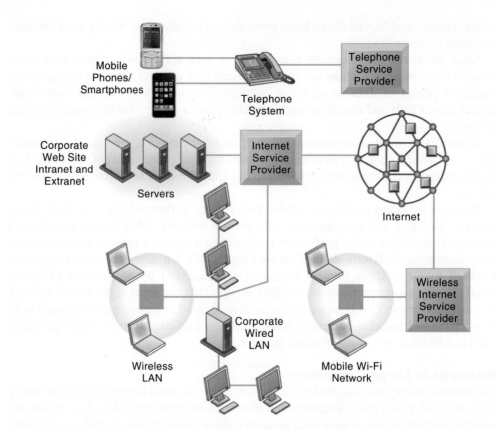

Client/Server Computing

Client/server computing, introduced in Chapter 5, is a distributed computing model in which some of the processing power is located within small, inexpensive client computers and resides literally on desktops or laptops or in handheld devices. These powerful clients are linked to one another through a network that is controlled by a network server computer. The server sets the rules of communication for the network and provides every client with an address so others can find it on the network.

Client/server computing has largely replaced centralized mainframe computing in which nearly all the processing takes place on a central large mainframe computer. Client/server computing has extended computing to departments, workgroups, factory floors, and other parts of the business that could not be served by a centralized architecture. It also makes it possible for personal computing devices such as PCs, laptops, and mobile phones to be connected to networks such as the Internet. The Internet is the largest implementation of client/server computing.

Packet Switching

Packet switching is a method of slicing digital messages into parcels called packets, sending the packets along different communication paths as they become available and then reassembling the packets once they arrive at their destinations (see Figure 7.3). Prior to the development of packet switching, computer networks used leased, dedicated telephone circuits to communicate with other computers in remote locations. In circuit-switched networks, such as the telephone system, a complete point-to-point circuit is assembled, and then communication can proceed. These dedicated circuit-switching techniques were expensive and wasted available communications capacity—the circuit was maintained regardless of whether any data were being sent.

Packet switching makes much more efficient use of the communications capacity of a network. In packet-switched networks, messages are first broken down into small fixed bundles of data called packets. The packets include information for directing

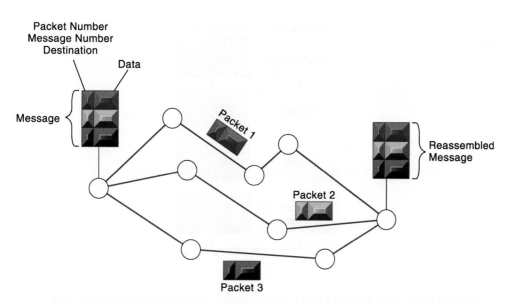

Figure 7.3
Packet-Switched Networks and Packet Communications
Data are grouped into small packets, which are transmitted independently over various communications channels and reassembled at their final destination.

the packet to the right address and for checking transmission errors along with the data. The packets are transmitted over various communications channels by using routers, each packet traveling independently. Packets of data originating at one source will be routed through many paths and networks before being reassembled into the original message when they reach their destinations.

TCP/IP and Connectivity

In a typical telecommunications network, diverse hardware and software components need to work together to transmit information. Different components in a network communicate with each other only by adhering to a common set of rules called protocols. A **protocol** is a set of rules and procedures governing transmission of information between two points in a network.

In the past, diverse proprietary and incompatible protocols often forced business firms to purchase computing and communications equipment from a single vendor. However, today, corporate networks are increasingly using a single, common, worldwide standard called **Transmission Control Protocol/Internet Protocol (TCP/IP)**. TCP/IP was developed during the early 1970s to support U.S. Department of Defense Advanced Research Projects Agency (DARPA) efforts to help scientists transmit data among different types of computers over long distances.

TCP/IP uses a suite of protocols, the main ones being TCP and IP. TCP refers to the Transmission Control Protocol, which handles the movement of data between computers. TCP establishes a connection between the computers, sequences the transfer of packets, and acknowledges the packets sent. IP refers to the Internet Protocol (IP), which is responsible for the delivery of packets and includes the disassembling and reassembling of packets during transmission. Figure 7.4 illustrates the four-layered Department of Defense reference model for TCP/IP, and the layers are described as follows.

1. **Application layer.** The Application layer enables client application programs to access the other layers and defines the protocols that applications use to exchange data. One of these application protocols is the Hypertext Transfer Protocol (HTTP), which is used to transfer web page files.
2. **Transport layer.** The Transport layer is responsible for providing the Application layer with communication and packet services. This layer includes TCP and other protocols.

Figure 7.4
The Transmission
Control Protocol/
Internet Protocol
(TCP/IP) Reference
Model
*This figure illustrates
the four layers of the
TCP/IP reference model
for communications.*

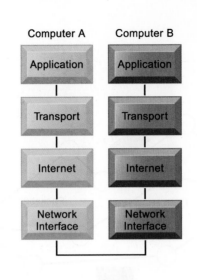

3. **Internet layer.** The Internet layer is responsible for addressing, routing, and packaging data packets called IP datagrams. The Internet Protocol is one of the protocols used in this layer.
4. **Network Interface layer.** At the bottom of the reference model, the Network Interface layer is responsible for placing packets on and receiving them from the network medium, which could be any networking technology.

Two computers using TCP/IP can communicate even if they are based on different hardware and software platforms. Data sent from one computer to the other passes downward through all four layers, starting with the sending computer's Application layer and passing through the Network Interface layer. After the data reach the recipient host computer, they travel up the layers and are reassembled into a format the receiving computer can use. If the receiving computer finds a damaged packet, it asks the sending computer to retransmit it. This process is reversed when the receiving computer responds.

7-2 What are the different types of networks?

Let's look more closely at alternative networking technologies available to businesses.

SIGNALS: DIGITAL VS. ANALOG

There are two ways to communicate a message in a network: an analog signal or a digital signal. An *analog signal* is represented by a continuous waveform that passes through a communications medium and has been used for voice communication. The most common analog devices are the telephone handset, the speaker on your computer, or your iPod earphone, all of which create analog waveforms that your ear can hear.

A *digital signal* is a discrete, binary waveform rather than a continuous waveform. Digital signals communicate information as strings of two discrete states: one bits and zero bits, which are represented as on-off electrical pulses. Computers use digital signals and require a modem to convert these digital signals into analog signals that can be sent over (or received from) telephone lines, cable lines, or wireless media that use analog signals (see Figure 7.5). **Modem** stands for modulator-demodulator. Cable modems connect your computer to the Internet by using a cable network. DSL modems connect your computer to the Internet using a telephone company's landline network. Wireless modems perform the same function as traditional modems, connecting your computer to a wireless network that could be a cell phone network or a Wi-Fi network.

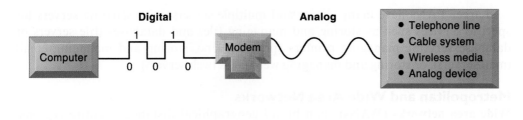

Figure 7.5
Functions of the Modem
A modem is a device that translates digital signals into analog form (and vice versa) so that computers can transmit data over analog networks such as telephone and cable networks.

TYPES OF NETWORKS

There are many kinds of networks and ways of classifying them. One way of looking at networks is in terms of their geographic scope (see Table 7.1).

Local Area Networks

If you work in a business that uses networking, you are probably connecting to other employees and groups via a local area network. A **local area network (LAN)** is designed to connect personal computers and other digital devices within a half-mile or 500-meter radius. LANs typically connect a few computers in a small office, all the computers in one building, or all the computers in several buildings in close proximity. LANs also are used to link to long-distance wide area networks (WANs, described later in this section) and other networks around the world, using the Internet.

Review Figure 7.1, which could serve as a model for a small LAN that might be used in an office. One computer is a dedicated network file server, providing users with access to shared computing resources in the network, including software programs and data files.

The server determines who gets access to what and in which sequence. The router connects the LAN to other networks, which could be the Internet, or another corporate network, so that the LAN can exchange information with networks external to it. The most common LAN operating systems are Windows, Linux, and Novell.

Ethernet is the dominant LAN standard at the physical network level, specifying the physical medium to carry signals between computers, access control rules, and a standardized set of bits that carry data over the system. Originally, Ethernet supported a data transfer rate of 10 megabits per second (Mbps). Newer versions, such as Gigabit Ethernet, support a data transfer rate of 1 gigabit per second (Gbps).

The LAN illustrated in Figure 7.1 uses a client/server architecture by which the network operating system resides primarily on a single file server, and the server provides much of the control and resources for the network. Alternatively, LANs may use a **peer-to-peer** architecture. A peer-to-peer network treats all processors equally and is used primarily in small networks with 10 or fewer users. The various computers on the network can exchange data by direct access and can share peripheral devices without going through a separate server.

TABLE 7.1

Types of Networks

Type	Area
Local area network (LAN)	Up to 500 meters (half a mile); an office or floor of a building
Campus area network (CAN)	Up to 1,000 meters (a mile); a college campus or corporate facility
Metropolitan area network (MAN)	A city or metropolitan area
Wide area network (WAN)	A regional, transcontinental, or global area

Larger LANs have many clients and multiple servers, with separate servers for specific services such as storing and managing files and databases (file servers or database servers), managing printers (print servers), storing and managing email (mail servers), or storing and managing web pages (web servers).

Metropolitan and Wide Area Networks

Wide area networks (WANs) span broad geographical distances—entire regions, states, continents, or the entire globe. The most universal and powerful WAN is the Internet. Computers connect to a WAN through public networks, such as the telephone system or private cable systems, or through leased lines or satellites. A **metropolitan area network (MAN)** is a network that spans a metropolitan area, usually a city and its major suburbs. Its geographic scope falls between a WAN and a LAN.

TRANSMISSION MEDIA AND TRANSMISSION SPEED

Networks use different kinds of physical transmission media, including twisted pair wire, coaxial cable, fiber-optic cable, and media for wireless transmission. Each has advantages and limitations. A wide range of speeds is possible for any given medium, depending on the software and hardware configuration. Table 7.2 compares these media.

Bandwidth: Transmission Speed

The total amount of digital information that can be transmitted through any telecommunications medium is measured in bits per second (bps). One signal change, or cycle, is required to transmit one or several bits; therefore, the transmission capacity of each type of telecommunications medium is a function of its frequency. The number of cycles per second that can be sent through that medium is measured in **hertz**—one hertz is equal to one cycle of the medium.

The range of frequencies that can be accommodated on a particular telecommunications channel is called its **bandwidth**. The bandwidth is the difference between the highest and lowest frequencies that can be accommodated on a single channel. The greater the range of frequencies, the greater the bandwidth and the greater the channel's transmission capacity.

7-3 How do the Internet and Internet technology work and how do they support communication and e-business?

The Internet has become an indispensable personal and business tool—but what exactly is the Internet? How does it work, and what does Internet technology have to offer for business? Let's look at the most important Internet features.

WHAT IS THE INTERNET?

The Internet is the world's most extensive public communication system. It's also the world's largest implementation of client/server computing and Internet working, linking millions of individual networks all over the world. This global network of networks began in the early 1970s as a U.S. Department of Defense network to link scientists and university professors around the world.

Most homes and small businesses connect to the Internet by subscribing to an Internet service provider. An **Internet service provider (ISP)** is a commercial organization with a permanent connection to the Internet that sells temporary connections to retail subscribers. EarthLink, NetZero, AT&T, and Time Warner are ISPs.

TABLE 7.2

Physical Transmission Media

Transmission medium	Description	Speed
Twisted pair wire (CAT 5)	Strands of copper wire twisted in pairs for voice and data communications. CAT 5 is the most common 10 Mbps LAN cable. Maximum recommended run of 100 meters.	10–100+ Mbps
Coaxial cable	Thickly insulated copper wire, which is capable of high-speed data transmission and less subject to interference than twisted wire. Currently used for cable TV and for networks with longer runs (more than 100 meters).	Up to 1 Gbps
Fiber-optic cable	Strands of clear glass fiber, transmitting data as pulses of light generated by lasers. Useful for high-speed transmission of large quantities of data. More expensive than other physical transmission media and harder to install; often used for network backbone.	15 Mbps to 6+ Tbps
Wireless transmission media	Based on radio signals of various frequencies and includes both terrestrial and satellite microwave systems and cellular networks. Used for long-distance, wireless communication and Internet access.	Up to 600+ Mbps

Individuals also connect to the Internet through their business firms, universities, or research centers that have designated Internet domains.

There is a variety of services for ISP Internet connections. Connecting via a traditional telephone line and modem, at a speed of 56.6 kilobits per second (Kbps), used to be the most common form of connection worldwide, but broadband connections have largely replaced it. Digital subscriber line, cable, satellite Internet connections, and T lines provide these broadband services.

Digital subscriber line (DSL) technologies operate over existing telephone lines to carry voice, data, and video at transmission rates ranging from 385 Kbps all the way up to 40 Mbps, depending on usage patterns and distance. **Cable Internet connections** provided by cable television vendors use digital cable coaxial lines to deliver high-speed Internet access to homes and businesses. They can provide high-speed access to the Internet of up to 50 Mbps, although most providers offer service ranging from 1 Mbps to 6 Mbps. Where DSL and cable services are unavailable, it is possible to access the Internet via satellite, although some satellite Internet connections have slower upload speeds than other broadband services.

T1 and T3 are international telephone standards for digital communication. They are leased, dedicated lines suitable for businesses or government agencies requiring high-speed guaranteed service levels. **T1 lines** offer guaranteed delivery at 1.54 Mbps, and T3 lines offer delivery at 45 Mbps. The Internet does not provide similar guaranteed service levels but, simply, best effort.

INTERNET ADDRESSING AND ARCHITECTURE

The Internet is based on the TCP/IP networking protocol suite described earlier in this chapter. Every computer on the Internet is assigned a unique **Internet Protocol (IP) address**, which currently is a 32-bit number represented by four strings of numbers ranging from 0 to 255 separated by periods. For instance, the IP address of www .microsoft.com is 207.46.250.119.

When a user sends a message to another user on the Internet, the message is first decomposed into packets using the TCP protocol. Each packet contains its destination address. The packets are then sent from the client to the network server and from there on to as many other servers as necessary to arrive at a specific computer with a known address. At the destination address, the packets are reassembled into the original message.

The Domain Name System

Because it would be incredibly difficult for Internet users to remember strings of 12 numbers, the **Domain Name System (DNS)** converts domain names to IP addresses. The **domain name** is the English-like name that corresponds to the unique 32-bit numeric IP address for each computer connected to the Internet. DNS servers maintain a database containing IP addresses mapped to their corresponding domain names. To access a computer on the Internet, users need only specify its domain name.

DNS has a hierarchical structure (see Figure 7.6). At the top of the DNS hierarchy is the root domain. The child domain of the root is called a top-level domain, and the child domain of a top-level domain is called a second-level domain. Top-level domains are two- and three-character names you are familiar with from surfing the web, for example, .com, .edu, .gov, and the various country codes such as .ca for Canada or .it for Italy. Second-level domains have two parts, designating a top-level name and a second-level name—such as buy.com, nyu.edu, or amazon.ca. A host name at the bottom of the hierarchy designates a specific computer on either the Internet or a private network.

The following list shows the most common domain extensions currently available and officially approved. Countries also have domain names such as .uk, .au, and .fr (United Kingdom, Australia, and France, respectively), and there is a new class of internationalized top-level domains that use non-English characters. In the future, this list will expand to include many more types of organizations and industries.

.com	Commercial organizations/businesses
.edu	Educational institutions
.gov	U.S. government agencies
.mil	U.S. military
.net	Network computers
.org	Nonprofit organizations and foundations
.biz	Business firms
.info	Information providers

Figure 7.6
The Domain Name System

Domain Name System is a hierarchical system with a root domain, top-level domains, second-level domains, and host computers at the third level.

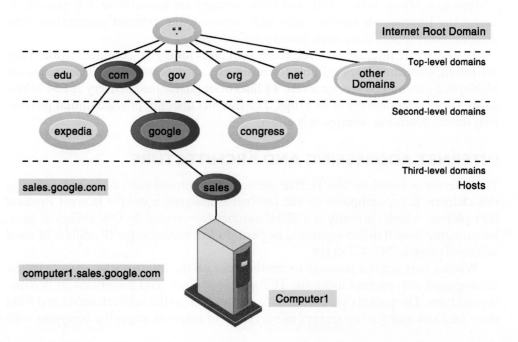

Internet Architecture and Governance

Internet data traffic is carried over transcontinental high-speed backbone networks that generally operate in the range of 155 Mbps to 2.5 Gbps (see Figure 7.7). These trunk lines are typically owned by long-distance telephone companies (called *network service providers*) or by national governments. Local connection lines are owned by regional telephone and cable television companies in the United States and in other countries that connect retail users in homes and businesses to the Internet. The regional networks lease access to ISPs, private companies, and government institutions.

Each organization pays for its own networks and its own local Internet connection services, a part of which is paid to the long-distance trunk line owners. Individual Internet users pay ISPs for using their service, and they generally pay a flat subscription fee, no matter how much or how little they use the Internet. A debate is now raging on whether this arrangement should continue or whether heavy Internet users who download large video and music files should pay more for the bandwidth they consume. The Interactive Session on Organizations explores this topic by examining the pros and cons of net neutrality.

No one owns the Internet, and it has no formal management. However, worldwide Internet policies are established by a number of professional organizations and government bodies, including the Internet Architecture Board (IAB), which helps define the overall structure of the Internet; the Internet Corporation for Assigned Names and Numbers (ICANN), which manages the domain name system; and the World Wide Web Consortium (W3C), which sets Hypertext Markup Language and other programming standards for the web.

These organizations influence government agencies, network owners, ISPs, and software developers with the goal of keeping the Internet operating as efficiently as possible. The Internet must also conform to the laws of the sovereign nation-states in which it operates as well as to the technical infrastructures that exist within the nation-states. Although in the early years of the Internet and the web there was very little legislative or executive interference, this situation is changing as the Internet plays a growing role in the distribution of information and knowledge, including content that some find objectionable.

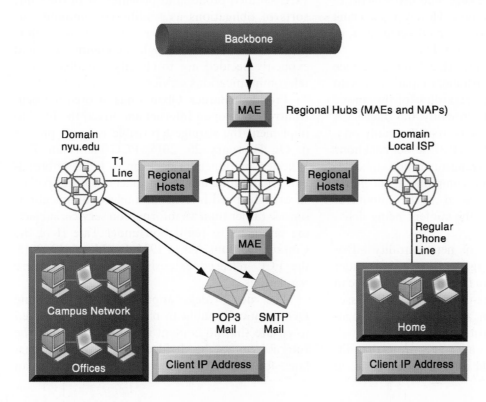

Figure 7.7
Internet Network Architecture
The Internet backbone connects to regional networks, which in turn provide access to Internet service providers, large firms, and government institutions. Network access points (NAPs) and metropolitan area exchanges (MAEs) are hubs where the backbone intersects regional and local networks and where backbone owners connect with one another.

INTERACTIVE SESSION: ORGANIZATIONS   The Battle over Net Neutrality

What kind of Internet user are you? Do you primarily use the Net to do a little email and online banking? Or are you online all day, watching YouTube videos, downloading music files, or playing online games? Do you use your iPhone to stream TV shows and movies on a regular basis? If you're a power Internet or smartphone user, you are consuming a great deal of bandwidth. Could hundreds of millions of people like you start to slow the Internet down?

Video streaming on Netflix has accounted for 32 percent of all bandwidth use in the United States and Google's YouTube for 19 percent of web traffic at peak hours. If user demand overwhelms network capacity, the Internet might not come to a screeching halt, but users could face sluggish download speeds and video transmission. Heavy use of iPhones in urban areas such as New York and San Francisco has degraded service on the AT&T wireless network. AT&T had reported that 3 percent of its subscriber base accounted for 40 percent of its data traffic.

Internet service providers (ISPs) assert that network congestion is a serious problem and that expanding their networks would require passing on burdensome costs to consumers. These companies believe differential pricing methods, which include data caps and metered use—charging based on the amount of bandwidth consumed—are the fairest way to finance necessary investments in their network infrastructures. However, metering Internet use is not widely accepted because of an ongoing debate about net neutrality.

Net neutrality is the idea that Internet service providers must allow customers equal access to content and applications, regardless of the source or nature of the content. Presently, the Internet is neutral; all Internet traffic is treated equally on a first-come, first-served basis by Internet backbone owners. However, this arrangement prevents telecommunications and cable companies from charging differentiated prices based on the amount of bandwidth consumed by the content being delivered over the Internet.

The strange alliance of net neutrality advocates includes MoveOn.org; the Electronic Frontier Foundation, the Christian Coalition; the American Library Association; data-intensive web businesses such as Netflix, Amazon, and Google; major consumer groups; and a host of bloggers and small businesses. Net neutrality advocates argue that differentiated pricing would impose heavy costs on heavy bandwidth users such as YouTube, Skype, and other innovative services, preventing high-bandwidth startup companies from gaining traction. Net neutrality supporters also argue that without net neutrality, ISPs that are also cable companies, such as Comcast, might block online streaming video from Netflix or Hulu to force customers to use the cable company's on-demand movie rental services.

Network owners believe regulation to enforce net neutrality will impede U.S. competitiveness by discouraging capital expenditure for new networks and curbing their networks' ability to cope with the exploding demand for Internet and wireless traffic. U.S. Internet service lags behind many other nations in overall speed, cost, and quality of service, adding credibility to this argument. Moreover, with enough options for Internet access, dissatisfied consumers could simply switch to providers who enforce net neutrality and allow unlimited Internet use.

On January 14, 2014, the U.S. Court of Appeals for the District of Columbia struck down the Federal Communication Commission (FCC) Open Internet rules that required equal treatment of Internet traffic and prevented broadband providers from blocking traffic favoring certain sites or charging special fees to companies that account for the most traffic. The court said the FCC saddled broadband providers with the same sorts of obligations as traditional common carrier telecommunications services, such as landline phone systems, even though the commission had explicitly decided not to classify broadband as a telecommunications service.

President Barack Obama has favored net neutrality and an open Internet and urged the FCC to implement the strongest possible rules to protect it. On February 26, 2015, FCC chairman Tom Wheeler announced a decision to regulate broadband as a public utility. The agency's order reclassifies high-speed Internet as a telecommunications service rather than an information service, subjecting providers to regulation under Title II of the Communications Act of 1934. On March 12, 2015, the FCC released extensive details about these regulations.

The new rules, approved 3 to 2 along Democratic–Republican party lines, are intended to ensure that no content is blocked and that the Internet cannot be divided into pay-to-play fast lanes for Internet and media companies that can afford it and slow lanes for everyone else. Outright blocking of content, slowing of transmissions, and the creation of so-called fast lanes were prohibited. The FCC stated that it favors a light touch rather than the heavy-handed regulations to which the old regulated telephone companies were subjected. One provision requiring "just and reasonable" conduct allows the FCC to decide what is acceptable on a case-by-case basis. The new rules apply to mobile data service for smartphones and tablets in addition to wired lines. The order also includes provisions to protect consumer privacy and ensure that Internet service is available to people with disabilities and in remote areas.

On April 13, 2015, United States Telecom Association, an industry trade group, filed a lawsuit to overturn the government's net neutrality rules. AT&T, the National Cable & Telecommunications Association, and CTIA, which represents wireless carriers, filed similar legal challenges. The battle over net neutrality is not yet over.

Sources: Rebecca Ruiz, "FCC Sets Net Neutrality Rules," *New York Times*, March 12, 2015; Rebecca Ruiz and Steve Lohr, "F.C.C. Approves Net Neutrality Rules, Classifying Broadband Internet Service as a Utility," *New York Times*, February. 26, 2015; Robert M. McDowell, "The Turning Point for Internet Freedom," *Wall Street Journal*, January 19, 2015; Ryan Knutson, "AT&T Sues to Overturn FCC's Net Neutrality Rules," *Wall Street Journal*, April 14, 2015; "Should the U.S. Regulate Broadband Internet Access as a Utility?" *Wall Street Journal*, May 11, 2014; Edward Wyatt, "F.C.C., in a Shift, Backs Fast Lane for web Traffic," *New York Times*, April 24, 2014; Gautham Nagesh, "FCC to Propose New 'Net Neutrality' Rules," *Wall Street Journal*, April 23, 2014; Shira Ovide, "Moving Beyond the Net Neutrality Debate," *Wall Street Journal*, January 14, 2014; and Gautham Nagesh and Amol Sharma, "Court Tosses Rules of Road for Internet," *Wall Street Journal*, January 4, 2014.

CASE STUDY QUESTIONS

1. What is net neutrality? Why has the Internet operated under net neutrality up to this point?

2. Who's in favor of net neutrality? Who's opposed? Why?

3. What would be the impact on individual users, businesses, and government if Internet providers switched to a tiered service model for transmission over landlines as well as wireless?

4. It has been said that net neutrality is the most important issue facing the Internet since the advent of the Internet. Discuss the implications of this statement.

5. Are you in favor of legislation enforcing network neutrality? Why or why not?

The Future Internet: IPv6 and Internet2

The Internet was not originally designed to handle the transmission of massive quantities of data and billions of users. Because of sheer Internet population growth, the world is about to run out of available IP addresses using the old addressing convention. The old addressing system is being replaced by a new version of the IP addressing schema called **IPv6** (Internet Protocol version 6), which contains 128-bit addresses (2 to the power of 128), or more than a quadrillion possible unique addresses. IPv6 is compatible with most modems and routers sold today, and IPv6 will fall back to the old addressing system if IPv6 is not available on local networks. The transition to IPv6 will take several years as systems replace older equipment.

Internet2 is an advanced networking consortium representing more than 500 U.S. universities, private businesses, and government agencies working with 66,000 institutions across the United States and international networking partners from more than 100 countries. To connect these communities, Internet2 developed a high-capacity, 100 Gbps network that serves as a test bed for leading-edge technologies that may eventually migrate to the public Internet, including large-scale network performance measurement and management tools, secure identity and access management tools, and capabilities such as scheduling high-bandwidth, high-performance circuits.

INTERNET SERVICES AND COMMUNICATION TOOLS

The Internet is based on client/server technology. Individuals using the Internet control what they do through client applications on their computers, such as web browser software. The data, including email messages and web pages, are stored on servers.

A client uses the Internet to request information from a particular web server on a distant computer, and the server sends the requested information back to the client over the Internet. Client platforms today include not only PCs and other computers but also smartphones and tablets.

Internet Services

A client computer connecting to the Internet has access to a variety of services. These services include email, chatting and instant messaging, electronic discussion groups, **Telnet**, **File Transfer Protocol (FTP)**, and the web. Table 7.3 provides a brief description of these services.

Each Internet service is implemented by one or more software programs. All the services may run on a single server computer, or different services may be allocated to different machines. Figure 7.8 illustrates one way these services can be arranged in a multitiered client/server architecture.

Email enables messages to be exchanged from computer to computer, with capabilities for routing messages to multiple recipients, forwarding messages, and attaching text documents or multimedia files to messages. Most email today is sent through the Internet. The cost of email is far lower than equivalent voice, postal, or overnight delivery costs, and email messages arrive anywhere in the world in a matter of seconds.

Chatting enables two or more people who are simultaneously connected to the Internet to hold live, interactive conversations. **Chat** systems now support voice and video chat as well as written conversations. Many online retail businesses offer chat services on their websites to attract visitors, to encourage repeat purchases, and to improve customer service.

Instant messaging is a type of chat service that enables participants to create their own private chat channels. The instant messaging system alerts the user whenever someone on his or her private list is online so that the user can initiate a chat session with other individuals. Instant messaging systems for consumers include Yahoo! Messenger, Google Hangouts, AOL Instant Messenger, and Facebook Chat. Companies concerned with security use proprietary communications and messaging systems such as IBM Sametime.

Newsgroups are worldwide discussion groups posted on Internet electronic bulletin boards on which people share information and ideas on a defined topic such as radiology or rock bands. Anyone can post messages on these bulletin boards for others to read.

Employee use of email, instant messaging, and the Internet is supposed to increase worker productivity, but the accompanying Interactive Session on People shows that this may not always be the case. Many company managers now believe they need

TABLE 7.3		
Major Internet Services		

Capability	Functions supported
Email	Person-to-person messaging; document sharing
Chatting and instant messaging	Interactive conversations
Newsgroups	Discussion groups on electronic bulletin boards
Telnet	Logging on to one computer system and doing work on another
File Transfer Protocol (FTP)	Transferring files from computer to computer
World Wide Web	Retrieving, formatting, and displaying information (including text, audio, graphics, and video) by using hypertext links

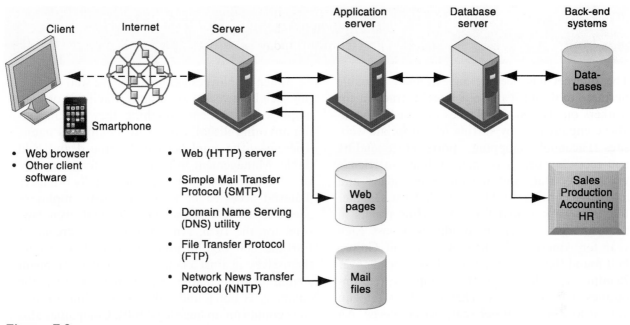

Figure 7.8
Client/Server Computing on the Internet
Client computers running web browsers and other software can access an array of services on servers over the Internet. These services may all run on a single server or on multiple specialized servers.

to monitor and even regulate their employees' online activity, but is this ethical? Although there are some strong business reasons companies may need to monitor their employees' email and web activities, what does this mean for employee privacy?

Voice over IP

The Internet has also become a popular platform for voice transmission and corporate networking. **Voice over IP (VoIP)** technology delivers voice information in digital form using packet switching, avoiding the tolls charged by local and long-distance telephone networks (see Figure 7.9). Calls that would ordinarily be transmitted over public telephone networks travel over the corporate network based on the Internet protocol, or the public Internet. Voice calls can be made and received with a computer equipped with a microphone and speakers or with a VoIP-enabled telephone.

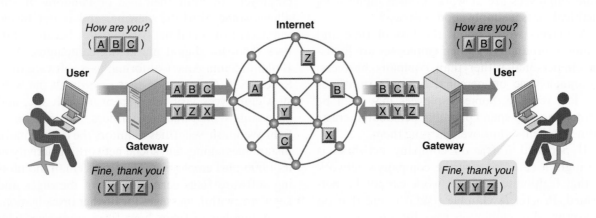

Figure 7.9
How Voice over IP Works
A VoIP phone call digitizes and breaks up a voice message into data packets that may travel along different routes before being reassembled at the final destination. A processor nearest the call's destination, called a gateway, arranges the packets in the proper order and directs them to the telephone number of the receiver or the IP address of the receiving computer.

The Internet has become an extremely valuable business tool, but it's also a huge distraction for workers on the job. Employees are wasting valuable company time by surfing inappropriate websites (Facebook, shopping, sports, etc.), sending and receiving personal email, talking to friends via online chat, and downloading videos and music. According to IT research firm Gartner Inc., non-work-related Internet surfing results in an estimated 40 percent productivity loss each year for American businesses. A recent Gallup Poll found that the average employee spends over 75 minutes per day using office computers for non-business-related activity. That translates into an annual loss of $6,250 per year, per employee. An average mid-size company of 500 employees could be expected to lose $3.25 million in lost productivity due to Internet misuse.

Many companies have begun monitoring employee use of email and the Internet, sometimes without employees' knowledge. Many tools are now available for this purpose, including SONAR, Spector CNE Investigator, iSafe, OsMonitor, IMonitor, Work Examiner, Activity Monitor, Mobistealth, and Spytech. These products enable companies to record online searches, monitor file downloads and uploads, record keystrokes, keep tabs on emails, create transcripts of chats, or take certain screen shots of images displayed on computer screens. Instant messaging, text messaging, and social media monitoring are also increasing. Although U.S. companies have the legal right to monitor employee Internet and email activity while employees are at work, is such monitoring unethical, or is it simply good business?

Managers worry about the loss of time and employee productivity when employees are focusing on personal rather than company business. Too much time on personal business translates into lost revenue. Some employees may even be billing time they spend pursuing personal interests online to clients, thus overcharging them.

If personal traffic on company networks is too high, it can also clog the company's network so that legitimate business work cannot be performed. Procter & Gamble (P&G) found that on an average day, employees were listening to 4,000 hours of music on Pandora and viewing 50,000 five-minute YouTube videos. These activities involved streaming huge quantities of data, which slowed down P&G's Internet connection.

When employees use email or the web (including social networks) at employer facilities or with employer equipment, anything they do, including anything illegal, carries the company's name. Therefore, the employer can be traced and held liable. Management in many firms fear that racist, sexually explicit, or other potentially offensive material accessed or traded by their employees could result in adverse publicity and even lawsuits for the firm. An estimated 27 percent of Fortune 500 organizations have had to defend themselves against claims of sexual harassment stemming from inappropriate email. Even if the company is not found liable, responding to lawsuits could run up huge legal bills. Companies also fear leakage of confidential information and trade secrets through email or social networks. Another survey conducted by the American Management Association and the ePolicy Institute found that 14 percent of the employees polled admitted they had sent confidential or potentially embarrassing company emails to outsiders.

U.S. companies have the legal right to monitor what employees are doing with company equipment during business hours. The question is whether electronic surveillance is an appropriate tool for maintaining an efficient and positive workplace. Some companies try to ban all personal activities on corporate networks—zero tolerance. Others block employee access to specific websites or social sites, closely monitor email messages, or limit personal time on the web.

For example, P&G blocks Netflix and has asked employees to limit their use of Pandora. It still allows some YouTube viewing, and is not blocking access to social networking sites because staff uses them for digital marketing campaigns. Ajax Boiler in Santa Ana, California, uses software from SpectorSoft Corporation that records all the websites employees visit, time spent at each site, and all emails sent. Financial services and investment firm Wedbush Securities monitors the daily emails, instant messaging, and social networking activity of its 1,000-plus employees. The firm's email monitoring software flags certain types of messages and keywords within messages for further investigation.

A number of firms have fired employees who have stepped out of bounds. A Proofpoint survey found that one in five large U.S. companies had fired an employee for violating email policies. Among managers who fired employees for

Internet misuse, the majority did so because the employees' email contained sensitive, confidential, or embarrassing information.

No solution is problem-free, but many consultants believe companies should write corporate policies on employee email, social media, and web use. The policies should include explicit ground rules that state, by position or level, under what circumstances employees can use company facilities for email, blogging, or web surfing. The policies should also inform employees whether these activities are monitored and explain why.

IBM now has social computing guidelines that cover employee activity on sites such as Facebook and Twitter. The guidelines urge employees not to conceal their identities, to remember that they are personally responsible for what they publish, and to refrain from discussing controversial topics that are not related to their IBM role.

The rules should be tailored to specific business needs and organizational cultures. For example, investment firms will need to allow many of their employees access to other investment sites. A company dependent on widespread information sharing, innovation, and independence could very well find that monitoring creates more problems than it solves.

Sources: "Could HR Be Snooping on Your Emails And Web Browsing? What Every Worker Should Know," www.Philly.com, March 30, 2015; "How Do Employers Monitor Internet Usage at Work?" www.wisegeek .org, accessed April 15, 2015; Dune Lawrence, "Companies Are Tracking Employees to Nab Traitors," *Bloomberg*, March 23, 2015; "Should Companies Monitor Their Employees' Social Media?" *Wall Street Journal*, May 11, 2014; Donna Iadipaolo, "Invading Your Privacy Is Now the Norm in the Workplace," www.Philly.com, April 28, 2014; "Office Slacker Stats," www.staffmonitoring.com, accessed May 1, 2014; "Office Productivity Loss," www.Staffmonitoring.com, accessed May 1, 2014; Samuel Greengard, "How Smartphone Addiction Hurts Productivity," *CIO Insight*, March 11, 2013; and Emily Glazer, "P&G Curbs Employees' Internet Use," *Wall Street Journal*, April 4, 2012.

CASE STUDY QUESTIONS

1. Should managers monitor employee email and Internet usage? Why or why not?

2. Describe an effective email and web use policy for a company.

3. Should managers inform employees that their web behavior is being monitored? Or should managers monitor secretly? Why or why not?

Cable firms such as Time Warner and Cablevision provide VoIP service bundled with their high-speed Internet and cable offerings. Skype offers free VoIP worldwide using a peer-to-peer network, and Google has its own free VoIP service.

Although up-front investments are required for an IP phone system, VoIP can reduce communication and network management costs by 20 to 30 percent. For example, VoIP saves Virgin Entertainment Group $700,000 per year in long-distance bills. In addition to lowering long-distance costs and eliminating monthly fees for private lines, an IP network provides a single voice-data infrastructure for both telecommunications and computing services. Companies no longer have to maintain separate networks or provide support services and personnel for each type of network.

Unified Communications

In the past, each of the firm's networks for wired and wireless data, voice communications, and videoconferencing operated independently of each other and had to be managed separately by the information systems department. Now, however, firms can merge disparate communications modes into a single universally accessible service using unified communications technology. **Unified communications** integrates disparate channels for voice communications, data communications, instant messaging, email, and electronic conferencing into a single experience by which users can seamlessly switch back and forth between different communication modes. Presence technology shows whether a person is available to receive a call.

CenterPoint Properties, a major Chicago area industrial real estate company, used unified communications technology to create collaborative websites for each of

Figure 7.10
A Virtual Private
Network Using the
Internet
This VPN is a private network of computers linked using a secure tunnel connection over the Internet. It protects data transmitted over the public Internet by encoding the data and wrapping them within the Internet protocol. By adding a wrapper around a network message to hide its content, organizations can create a private connection that travels through the public Internet.

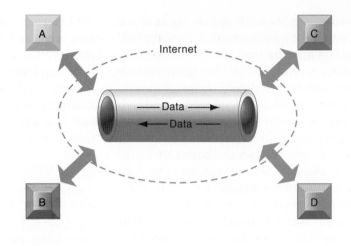

its real estate deals. Each website provides a single point for accessing structured and unstructured data. Integrated presence technology lets team members email, instant message, call, or videoconference with one click.

Virtual Private Networks

What if you had a marketing group charged with developing new products and services for your firm with members spread across the United States? You would want them to be able to email each other and communicate with the home office without any chance that outsiders could intercept the communications. In the past, one answer to this problem was to work with large private networking firms that offered secure, private, dedicated networks to customers, but this was an expensive solution. A much less expensive solution is to create a virtual private network within the public Internet.

A **virtual private network (VPN)** is a secure, encrypted, private network that has been configured within a public network to take advantage of the economies of scale and management facilities of large networks, such as the Internet (see Figure 7.10). A VPN provides your firm with secure, encrypted communications at a much lower cost than the same capabilities offered by traditional non-Internet providers that use their private networks to secure communications. VPNs also provide a network infrastructure for combining voice and data networks.

Several competing protocols are used to protect data transmitted over the public Internet, including Point-to-Point Tunneling Protocol (PPTP). In a process called *tunneling*, packets of data are encrypted and wrapped inside IP packets. By adding this wrapper around a network message to hide its content, business firms create a private connection that travels through the public Internet.

THE WEB

The web is the most popular Internet service. It's a system with universally accepted standards for storing, retrieving, formatting, and displaying information by using a client/server architecture. Web pages are formatted using hypertext with embedded links that connect documents to one another and that also link pages to other objects, such as sound, video, or animation files. When you click a graphic and a video clip plays, you have clicked a hyperlink. A typical **website** is a collection of web pages linked to a home page.

Hypertext

Web pages are based on a standard Hypertext Markup Language (HTML), which formats documents and incorporates dynamic links to other documents and pictures stored in the same or remote computers (see Chapter 5). Web pages are accessible through the Internet because web browser software operating your computer can request web pages stored on an Internet host server by using the **Hypertext Transfer Protocol (HTTP)**. HTTP is the communications standard that transfers pages on the web. For example, when you type a web address in your browser, such as http://www .sec.gov, your browser sends an HTTP request to the sec.gov server requesting the home page of sec.gov.

HTTP is the first set of letters at the start of every web address, followed by the domain name, which specifies the organization's server computer that is storing the document. Most companies have a domain name that is the same as or closely related to their official corporate name. The directory path and document name are two more pieces of information within the web address that help the browser track down the requested page. Together, the address is called a **uniform resource locator (URL)**. When typed into a browser, a URL tells the browser software exactly where to look for the information. For example, in the URL http://www.megacorp.com/content/ features/082610.html, *http* names the protocol that displays web pages, www.mega-corp.com is the domain name, content/features is the directory path that identifies where on the domain web server the page is stored, and 082610.html is the document name and the name of the format it is in. (It is an HTML page.)

Web Servers

A web server is software for locating and managing stored web pages. It locates the web pages a user requests on the computer where they are stored and delivers the web pages to the user's computer. Server applications usually run on dedicated computers, although they can all reside on a single computer in small organizations.

The most common web server in use today is Apache HTTP Server, followed by Microsoft Internet Information Services (IIS). Apache is an open source product that is free of charge and can be downloaded from the web.

Searching for Information on the Web

No one knows for sure how many web pages there really are. The surface web is the part of the web that search engines visit and about which information is recorded. For instance, Google visited an estimated 600 billion pages in 2014, and this reflects a large portion of the publicly accessible web page population. But there is a deep web that contains an estimated 1 trillion additional pages, many of them proprietary (such as the pages of *Wall Street Journal Online*, which cannot be visited without a subscription or access code) or that are stored in protected corporate databases. Searching for information on Facebook is another matter. With more than 1.4 billion members, each with pages of text, photos, and media, the population of web pages is larger than many estimates. However, Facebook is a closed web, and its pages are not searchable by Google or other search engines.

Search Engines Obviously, with so many web pages, finding specific ones that can help you or your business, nearly instantly, is an important problem. The question is, how can you find the one or two pages you really want and need out of billions of indexed web pages? **Search engines** attempt to solve the problem of finding useful information on the web nearly instantly and, arguably, they are the killer app of the Internet era. Today's search engines can sift through HTML files; files of Microsoft Office applications; PDF files; and audio, video, and image files. There are hundreds of search engines in the world, but the vast majority of search results come from Google, Yahoo!, and Microsoft's Bing (see Figure 7.11).

Web search engines started out in the early 1990s as relatively simple software programs that roamed the nascent web, visiting pages and gathering information about the content of each page. The first search engines were simple keyword indexes of all the pages they visited, leaving the user with lists of pages that may not have been truly relevant to their search.

In 1994, Stanford University computer science students David Filo and Jerry Yang created a hand-selected list of their favorite web pages and called it "Yet

Figure 7.11
Top Web Search
Engines in the United
States
*Google is the most popular
search engine, handling
more than 65 percent
of web searches in the
United States and around
90 percent in Europe.
Sources: Based on data
from comScore Inc.,
February 2015.*

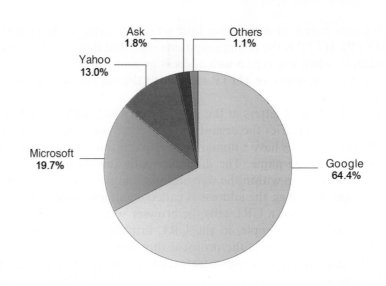

Another Hierarchical Officious Oracle," or Yahoo. Yahoo was not initially a search engine but rather an edited selection of websites organized by categories the editors found useful. Currently, Yahoo relies on Microsoft's Bing for search results.

In 1998, Larry Page and Sergey Brin, two other Stanford computer science students, released their first version of Google. This search engine was different. Not only did it index each web page's words but it also ranked search results based on the relevance of each page. Page patented the idea of a page ranking system (called *PageRank System*), which essentially measures the popularity of a web page by calculating the number of sites that link to that page as well as the number of pages to which it links. The premise is that popular web pages are more relevant to users. Brin contributed a unique web crawler program that indexed not only keywords on a page but also combinations of words (such as authors and the titles of their articles). These two ideas became the foundation for the Google search engine. Figure 7.12 illustrates how Google works.

Mobile Search   With the growth of mobile smartphones and tablet computers, and with about 167 million Americans accessing the Internet via mobile devices, the nature of e-commerce and search is changing. Mobile search from smartphones and tablets made up 50 percent of all searches in 2015 and will expand rapidly in the next few years. Both Google and Yahoo have developed new search interfaces to make searching and shopping from smartphones more convenient. Google revised its search algorithm to favor sites that look good on smartphone screens. Although smartphones are widely used to shop, actual purchases typically take place on laptops or desktops, followed by tablets.

Semantic Search   Another way for search engines to become more discriminating and helpful is to make search engines capable of understanding what we are really looking for. Called **semantic search**, the goal is to build a search engine that could really understand human language and behavior. Google and other search engine firms are attempting to refine search engine algorithms to capture more of what the user intended and the meaning of a search. In September 2013, Google introduced its Hummingbird search algorithm. Rather than evaluate each word separately in a search, Google's semantically informed Hummingbird tries to evaluate an entire sentence, focusing on the meaning behind the words. For instance, if your search is a long sentence like "Google annual report selected financial data 2015," Hummingbird should be able to figure out that you really want Google's SEC Form 10K report filed with the Securities and Exchange Commission on March 31, 2016.

Google searches also take advantage of Knowledge Graph, an effort of the search algorithm to anticipate what you might want to know more about as you search on a

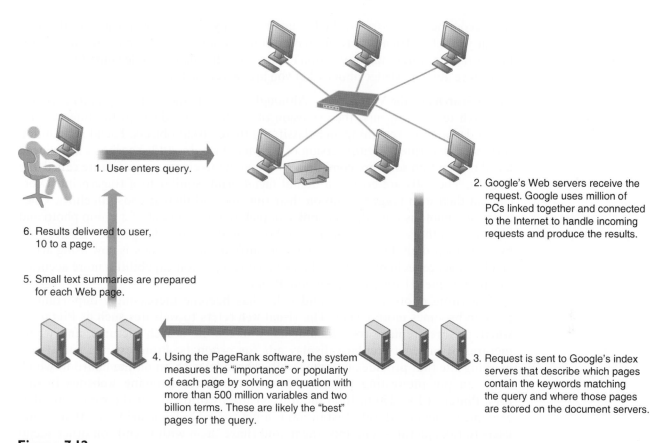

1. User enters query.

2. Google's Web servers receive the request. Google uses million of PCs linked together and connected to the Internet to handle incoming requests and produce the results.

6. Results delivered to user, 10 to a page.

5. Small text summaries are prepared for each Web page.

4. Using the PageRank software, the system measures the "importance" or popularity of each page by solving an equation with more than 500 million variables and two billion terms. These are likely the "best" pages for the query.

3. Request is sent to Google's index servers that describe which pages contain the keywords matching the query and where those pages are stored on the document servers.

Figure 7.12
How Google Works
The Google search engine is continuously crawling the web, indexing the content of each page, calculating its popularity, and storing the pages so that it can respond quickly to user requests to see a page. The entire process takes about one-half second.

topic. Results of the knowledge graph appear on the right of the screen and contain more information about the topic or person you are searching on. For example, if you search "Lake Tahoe," the search engine will return basic facts about Tahoe (altitude, average temperature, and local fish), a map, and hotel accommodations. Google has also made **predictive search** part of most search results. This part of the search algorithm guesses what you are looking for and suggests search terms as you type your search words.

Social Search   One problem with Google and mechanical search engines is that they are so thorough. Enter a search for "ultra computers" and, in 0.2 seconds, you will receive over 300 million responses! Search engines are not very discriminating. **Social search** is an effort to provide fewer, more relevant, and trustworthy search results based on a person's network of social contacts. In contrast to the top search engines that use a mathematical algorithm to find pages that satisfy your query, a social search website would review your friends' recommendations (and their friends'), their past web visits, and their use of Like buttons.

In January 2013, Facebook launched Graph Search (now called *Facebook Search*), a social network search engine that responds to user search queries with information from the user's social network of friends and connections. Facebook Search relies on the huge amount of data on Facebook that is, or can be, linked to individuals and organizations. You might use Facebook Search to search for Boston restaurants that your friends like, alumni from the University of South Carolina who like Lady Gaga, or pictures of your friends before 2012.

Google has developed Google +1 as a social layer on top of its existing search engine. Users can place a +1 next to the websites they found helpful, and their friends will be notified automatically. Subsequent searches by their friends would list the +1 sites recommended by friends higher up on the page. One problem with social search is that your close friends may not have intimate knowledge of topics you are exploring, or they may have tastes you don't appreciate. It's also possible your close friends don't have any knowledge about what you are searching for.

Visual Search and the Visual Web   Although search engines were originally designed to search text documents, the explosion of photos and videos on the Internet created a demand for searching and classifying these visual objects. Facial recognition software can create a digital version of a human face. In 2012, Facebook introduced facial recognition software combined with tagging to create a new feature called *Tag Suggest*. The software creates a digital facial print, similar to a fingerprint. Users can put their own tagged photo on their timeline and their friends' timelines. Once a person's photo is tagged, Facebook can pick that person out of a group photo and identify for others who is in the photo. You can also search for people on Facebook by using their digital image to find and identify them. Facebook is now using artificial intelligence technology to make its facial recognition capabilities more accurate (see the Chapter 11 Interactive Session, People).

Searching photos, images, and video has become increasingly important as the web becomes more visual. The **visual web** refers to websites such as Pinterest, where pictures replace text documents, where users search pictures, and where pictures of products replace display ads for products. Pinterest is a social networking site that provides users (as well as brands) with an online board to which they can pin interesting pictures. One of the fastest-growing websites in history, Pinterest has 250 million monthly visitors worldwide. Instagram is another example of the visual web. Instagram is a photo and video sharing site that allows users to take pictures, enhance them, and share them with friends on other social sites such as Facebook, Twitter, and Google+. In 2015, Instagram had 300 million monthly active users.

Intelligent Agent Shopping Bots   Chapter 11 describes the capabilities of software agents with built-in intelligence that can gather or filter information and perform other tasks to assist users. **Shopping bots** use intelligent agent software for searching the Internet for shopping information. Shopping bots such as MySimon or PriceGrabber can help people interested in making a purchase filter and retrieve information about products of interest, evaluate competing products according to criteria the users have established, and negotiate with vendors for price and delivery terms. Many of these shopping agents search the web for pricing and availability of products specified by the user and return a list of sites that sell the item along with pricing information and a purchase link.

Search Engine Marketing   Search engines have become major advertising platforms and shopping tools by offering what is now called **search engine marketing**. Searching for information is one of the web's most popular activities; 85 percent of American adult Internet users will use a search engine at least once a day in 2015, generating about 20 billion queries a month. In addition, 134 million smartphone users will generate another 8 billion monthly searches. With this huge audience, search engines are the foundation for the most lucrative form of online marketing and advertising, search engine marketing. When users enter a search term on Google, Bing, Yahoo, or any of the other sites serviced by these search engines, they receive two types of listings: sponsored links, for which advertisers have paid to be listed (usually at the top of the search results page), and unsponsored, organic search results. In addition, advertisers can purchase small text boxes on the side of search results pages. The paid, sponsored advertisements are the fastest growing form of Internet advertising and are powerful new marketing tools that precisely match consumer interests with advertising messages at the right moment. Search engine marketing monetizes the value of the search process. In 2015, search engine marketing is expected to generate $25 billion in revenue, nearly half of all online advertising ($52 billion). About 89 percent of Google's revenue of $66 billion in 2014 came from online advertising, and 90 percent of the ad revenue came from search engine marketing (Google, 2015).

Because search engine marketing is so effective (it has the highest click-through rate and the highest return on ad investment), companies seek to optimize their websites for search engine recognition. The better optimized the page is, the higher a ranking it will achieve in search engine result listings. **Search engine optimization (SEO)** is the process of improving the quality and volume of web traffic to a website by employing a series of techniques that help a website achieve a higher ranking with the major search engines when certain keywords and phrases are put into the search field. One technique is to make sure that the keywords used in the website description match the keywords likely to be used as search terms by prospective customers. For example, your website is more likely to be among the first ranked by search engines if it uses the keyword *lighting* rather than *lamps* if most prospective customers are searching for *lighting*. It is also advantageous to link your website to as many other websites as possible because search engines evaluate such links to determine the popularity of a web page and how it is linked to other content on the web.

Search engines can be gamed by scammers who create thousands of phony website pages and link them or link them to a single retailer's site in an attempt to fool Google's search engine. Firms can also pay so-called link farms to link to their site. Google changed its search algorithm in 2012. Codenamed *Penguin*, the revised algorithm examines the quality of links more carefully with the intent of down-ranking sites that have a suspicious pattern of sites linking to them. Penguin is updated annually.

In general, search engines have been very helpful to small businesses that cannot afford large marketing campaigns. Because shoppers are looking for a specific product or service when they use search engines, they are what marketers call hot prospects—people who are looking for information and often intending to buy. Moreover, search engines charge only for click-throughs to a site. Merchants do not have to pay for ads that don't work, only for ads that receive a click. Consumers benefit from search engine marketing because ads for merchants appear only when consumers are looking for a specific product. There are no pop-ups, Flash animations, videos, interstitials, emails, or other irrelevant communications to deal with. Thus, search engine marketing saves consumers cognitive energy and reduces search costs (including the cost of transportation needed to search for products physically). One study estimated the global value of search to both merchants and consumers to be more than $800 billion, with about 65 percent of the benefit going to consumers in the form of lower search costs and lower prices (McKinsey, 2011).

Web 2.0

Today's websites don't just contain static content—they enable people to collaborate, share information, and create new services and content online. These second-generation interactive Internet-based services are referred to as **Web 2.0**. If you have pinned a photo on Pinterest, posted a video to YouTube, created a blog, or added an app to your Facebook page, you've used some of these Web 2.0 services.

Web 2.0 has four defining features: interactivity, real-time user control, social participation (sharing), and user-generated content. The technologies and services behind these features include cloud computing, software mashups and apps, blogs, RSS, wikis, and social networks. We have already describd cloud computing, mashups, and apps in Chapter 5 and introduced social networks in Chapter 2.

A **blog**, the popular term for a weblog, is a personal website that typically contains a series of chronological entries (newest to oldest) by its author and links to related web pages. The blog may include a *blogroll* (a collection of links to other blogs) and *trackbacks* (a list of entries in other blogs that refer to a post on the first blog). Most blogs allow readers to post comments on the blog entries as well. The act of creating a blog is often referred to as blogging. Blogs can be hosted by a third-party service such as Blogger.com, TypePad.com, and Xanga.com, and blogging features have been incorporated into social networks such as Facebook and collaboration platforms such as Lotus Notes. WordPress is a leading open source blogging tool and content management system. **Microblogging**, used in Twitter, is a type of blogging that features short posts of 140 characters or fewer.

Blog pages are usually variations on templates provided by the blogging service or software. Therefore, millions of people without HTML skills of any kind can post their own web pages and share content with others. The totality of blog-related websites is often referred to as the **blogosphere**. Although blogs have become popular personal publishing tools, they also have business uses (see Chapters 2 and 10).

If you're an avid blog reader, you might use RSS to keep up with your favorite blogs without constantly checking them for updates. **RSS**, which stands for Really Simple Syndication or Rich Site Summary, pulls specified content from websites and feeds it automatically to users' computers. RSS reader software gathers material from the websites or blogs that you tell it to scan and brings new information from those sites to you. RSS readers are available through websites such as Google and Yahoo, and they have been incorporated into the major web browsers and email programs.

Blogs allow visitors to add comments to the original content, but they do not allow visitors to change the original posted material. **Wikis**, in contrast, are collaborative websites on which visitors can add, delete, or modify content, including the work of previous authors. Wiki comes from the Hawaiian word for *quick*.

Wiki software typically provides a template that defines layout and elements common to all pages, displays user-editable software program code, and then renders the content into an HTML-based page for display in a web browser. Some wiki software allows only basic text formatting, whereas other tools allow the use of tables, images, or even interactive elements, such as polls or games. Most wikis provide capabilities for monitoring the work of other users and correcting mistakes.

Because wikis make information sharing so easy, they have many business uses. The U.S. Department of Homeland Security's National Cyber Security Center (NCSC) deployed a wiki to facilitate collaboration among federal agencies on cybersecurity. NCSC and other agencies use the wiki for real-time information sharing on threats, attacks, and responses and as a repository for technical and standards information. Pixar Wiki is a collaborative community wiki for publicizing the work of Pixar Animation Studios. The wiki format allows anyone to create or edit an article about a Pixar film.

Social networking sites enable users to build communities of friends and professional colleagues. Members typically create a profile—a web page for posting photos, videos, audio files, and text—and then share these profiles with others on the service identified as their friends or contacts. Social networking sites are highly interactive, offer real-time user control, rely on user-generated content, and are broadly based on social participation and sharing of content and opinions. Leading social networking sites include Facebook, Twitter (with more than 1.4 billion and 290 million monthly active users, respectively, in 2015), and LinkedIn (for professional contacts).

For many, social networking sites are the defining Web 2.0 application and one that has radically changed how people spend their time online; how people communicate and with whom; how business people stay in touch with customers, suppliers, and employees; how providers of goods and services learn about their customers; and how advertisers reach potential customers. The large social networking sites are also morphing into application development platforms where members can create and sell software applications to other members of the community. Facebook alone has more than 1 million developers who created over 550,000 applications for gaming, video sharing, and communicating with friends and family. We talk more about business applications of social networking in Chapters 2 and 10, and you can find social networking discussions in many other chapters of this book. You can also find a more detailed discussion of Web 2.0 in our Learning Tracks.

Web 3.0 and the Future Web

The future of the Internet, so-called Web 3.0, is already visible. The key features of **Web 3.0** are more tools for individuals to make sense out of the 600 billion pages on the Internet, or the millions of apps available for smartphones and a visual, even three-dimensional (3D) Web where you can walk through pages in a 3D environment. (Review the discussion of semantic search and visual search earlier in this chapter.)

Even closer in time is a pervasive web that controls everything from a city's traffic lights and water usage, to the lights in your living room, to your car's rear view mirror, not to mention managing your calendar and appointments. This is referred to as the **Internet of Things** and is based on billions of Internet-connected sensors throughout our physical world. Objects, animals, or people are provided with unique identifiers and the ability to transfer data over a network without requiring human-to-human or human-to-computer interaction. Firms such as IBM, HP, and Oracle, and hundreds of smaller startups, are exploring how to build smart machines, factories, and cities through extensive use of remote sensors and fast cloud computing. We provide more detail on this topic in the following section.

The App Internet is another element in the future web. The growth of apps within the mobile platform is astounding. More than 80 percent of mobile minutes in the United States are generated through apps, only 20 percent using browsers. Apps give users direct access to content and are much faster than loading a browser and searching for content.

Other complementary trends leading toward a future Web 3.0 include more widespread use of cloud computing and software as a service (SaaS) business models, ubiquitous connectivity among mobile platforms and Internet access devices, and the transformation of the web from a network of separate siloed applications and content into a more seamless and interoperable whole. These more modest visions of the future Web 3.0 are more likely to be realized in the near term.

7-4 What are the principal technologies and standards for wireless networking, communication, and internet access?

Welcome to the wireless revolution! Cell phones, smartphones, tablets, and wireless-enabled personal computers have morphed into portable media and computing platforms that let you perform many of the computing tasks you used to do at your desk, and a whole lot more. We introduced smartphones in our discussions of the mobile digital platform in Chapters 1 and 5. **Smartphones** such as the iPhone, Android phones, and BlackBerry combine the functionality of a cell phone with that of a mobile laptop computer with Wi-Fi capability. This makes it possible to combine music, video, Internet access, and telephone service in one device. A large part of the Internet is becoming a mobile, access-anywhere, broadband service for the delivery of video, music, and web search.

CELLULAR SYSTEMS

In 2015, more than 1 billion cell phones were sold worldwide. In the United States, there are 252 million cell phone subscriptions, and 164 million people have smartphones. About 185 million people access the web by using their phone (eMarketer, 2015). Smartphones, not the desktop PC, are now responsible for more than half of all Internet searches.

Digital cellular service uses several competing standards. In Europe and much of the rest of the world outside the United Sates, the standard is Global System for Mobile Communications (GSM). GSM's strength is its international roaming capability. There are GSM cell phone systems in the United States, including T-Mobile and AT&T.

A competing standard in the United States is Code Division Multiple Access (CDMA), which is the system Verizon and Sprint use. CDMA was developed by the military during World War II. It transmits over several frequencies, occupies the entire spectrum, and randomly assigns users to a range of frequencies over time, making it more efficient than GSM.

Earlier generations of cellular systems were designed primarily for voice and limited data transmission in the form of short text messages. Today wireless carriers offer 3G and 4G networks. **3G networks**, with transmission speeds ranging from 144 Kbps for mobile users in, say, a car, to more than 2 Mbps for stationary users, offer fair transmission speeds for email, browsing the web, and online shopping but are too slow for videos. **4G networks** have much higher speeds: 100 megabits/second download and 50 megabits upload speed, with more than enough capacity for watching high-definition video on your smartphone. Long Term Evolution (LTE) and mobile Worldwide Interoperability for Microwave Access (WiMax—see the following section) are the current 4G standards.

WIRELESS COMPUTER NETWORKS AND INTERNET ACCESS

An array of technologies provides high-speed wireless access to the Internet for PCs and mobile devices. These new high-speed services have extended Internet access to numerous locations that could not be covered by traditional wired Internet services and have made ubiquitous computing, anywhere, anytime, a reality.

Bluetooth

Bluetooth is the popular name for the 802.15 wireless networking standard, which is useful for creating small **personal area networks (PANs)**. It links up to eight devices within a 10-meter area using low-power, radio-based communication and can transmit up to 722 Kbps in the 2.4-GHz band.

Wireless phones, pagers, computers, printers, and computing devices using Bluetooth communicate with each other and even operate each other without direct user intervention (see Figure 7.13). For example, a person could direct a notebook

Figure 7.13
A Bluetooth Network (PAN)
Bluetooth enables a variety of devices, including cell phones, smartphones, wireless keyboards and mice, PCs, and printers, to interact wirelessly with each other within a small, 30-foot (10-meter) area. In addition to the links shown, Bluetooth can be used to network similar devices to send data from one PC to another, for example.

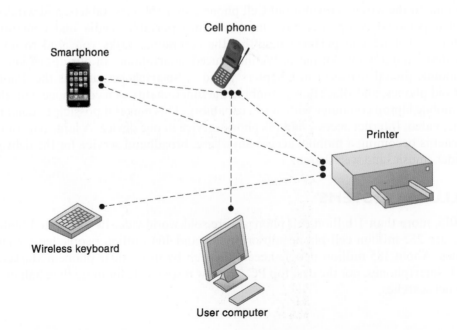

computer to send a document file wirelessly to a printer. Bluetooth connects wireless keyboards and mice to PCs or cell phones to earpieces without wires. Bluetooth has low power requirements, making it appropriate for battery-powered handheld computers or cell phones.

Although Bluetooth lends itself to personal networking, it has uses in large corporations. For example, FedEx drivers use Bluetooth to transmit the delivery data captured by their handheld computers to cellular transmitters, which forward the data to corporate computers. Drivers no longer need to spend time docking their handheld units physically in the transmitters, and Bluetooth has saved FedEx $20 million per year.

Wi-Fi and Wireless Internet Access

The 802.11 set of standards for wireless LANs and wireless Internet access is also known as **Wi-Fi**. The first of these standards to be widely adopted was 802.11b, which can transmit up to 11 Mbps in the unlicensed 2.4-GHz band and has an effective distance of 30 to 50 meters. The 802.11g standard can transmit up to 54 Mbps in the 2.4-GHz range. 802.11n is capable of transmitting over 100 Mbps. Today's PCs and netbooks have built-in support for Wi-Fi, as do the iPhone, iPad, and other smartphones.

In most Wi-Fi communication, wireless devices communicate with a wired LAN using access points. An access point is a box consisting of a radio receiver/transmitter and antennas that links to a wired network, router, or hub.

Figure 7.14 illustrates an 802.11 wireless LAN that connects a small number of mobile devices to a larger wired LAN and to the Internet. Most wireless devices are client machines. The servers that the mobile client stations need to use are on the wired LAN. The access point controls the wireless stations and acts as a bridge between the main wired LAN and the wireless LAN. The access point also controls the wireless stations.

The most popular use for Wi-Fi today is for high-speed wireless Internet service. In this instance, the access point plugs into an Internet connection, which could come from a cable service or DSL telephone service. Computers within range of the access point use it to link wirelessly to the Internet.

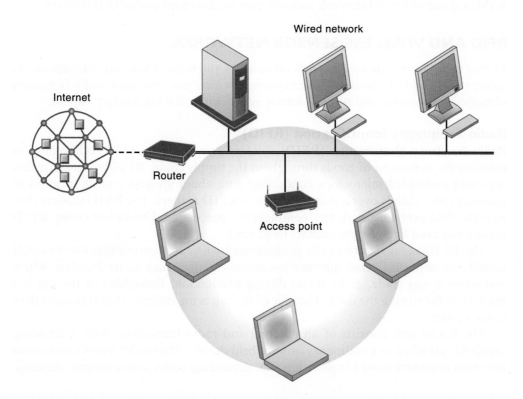

Figure 7.14

An 802.11 Wireless LAN

Mobile laptop computers equipped with network interface cards link to the wired LAN by communicating with the access point. The access point uses radio waves to transmit network signals from the wired network to the client adapters, which convert them to data that the mobile device can understand. The client adapter then transmits the data from the mobile device back to the access point, which forwards the data to the wired network.

Hotspots are locations with one or more access points providing wireless Internet access and are often in public places. Some hotspots are free or do not require any additional software to use; others may require activation and the establishment of a user account by providing a credit card number over the web.

Businesses of all sizes are using Wi-Fi networks to provide low-cost wireless LANs and Internet access. Wi-Fi hotspots can be found in hotels, airport lounges, libraries, cafes, and college campuses to provide mobile access to the Internet. Dartmouth College is one of many campuses where students now use Wi-Fi for research, course work, and entertainment.

Wi-Fi technology poses several challenges, however. One is Wi-Fi's security features, which make these wireless networks vulnerable to intruders. We provide more detail about Wi-Fi security issues in Chapter 8.

Another drawback of Wi-Fi networks is susceptibility to interference from nearby systems operating in the same spectrum, such as wireless phones, microwave ovens, or other wireless LANs. However, wireless networks based on the 802.11n standard solve this problem by using multiple wireless antennas in tandem to transmit and receive data and technology called MIMO (multiple input multiple output) to coordinate multiple simultaneous radio signals.

WiMax

A surprisingly large number of areas in the United States and throughout the world do not have access to Wi-Fi or fixed broadband connectivity. The range of Wi-Fi systems is no more than 300 feet from the base station, making it difficult for rural groups that don't have cable or DSL service to find wireless access to the Internet.

The Institute of Electrical and Electronics Engineers (IEEE) developed a new family of standards known as WiMax to deal with these problems. **WiMax**, which stands for Worldwide Interoperability for Microwave Access, is the popular term for IEEE Standard 802.16. It has a wireless access range of up to 31 miles and transmission speed of up to 75 Mbps.

WiMax antennas are powerful enough to beam high-speed Internet connections to rooftop antennas of homes and businesses that are miles away. Cellular handsets and laptops with WiMax capabilities are appearing in the marketplace. Mobile WiMax is one of the 4G network technologies we discussed earlier in this chapter.

RFID AND WIRELESS SENSOR NETWORKS

Mobile technologies are creating new efficiencies and ways of working throughout the enterprise. In addition to the wireless systems we have just described, radio frequency identification systems and wireless sensor networks are having a major impact.

Radio Frequency Identification (RFID)

Radio frequency identification (RFID) systems provide a powerful technology for tracking the movement of goods throughout the supply chain. RFID systems use tiny tags with embedded microchips containing data about an item and its location to transmit radio signals over a short distance to RFID readers. The RFID readers then pass the data over a network to a computer for processing. Unlike bar codes, RFID tags do not need line-of-sight contact to be read.

The RFID tag is electronically programmed with information that can uniquely identify an item plus other information about the item such as its location, where and when it was made, or its status during production. Embedded in the tag is a microchip for storing the data. The rest of the tag is an antenna that transmits data to the reader.

The reader unit consists of an antenna and radio transmitter with a decoding capability attached to a stationary or handheld device. The reader emits radio waves in ranges anywhere from 1 inch to 100 feet, depending on its power output, the radio

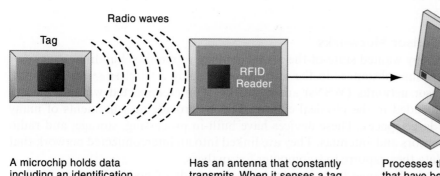

A microchip holds data including an identification number. The rest of the tag is an antenna that transmits data to a reader.

Has an antenna that constantly transmits. When it senses a tag, it wakes it up, interrogates it, and decodes the data. Then it transmits the data to a host system over wired or wireless connections.

Processes the data from the tag that have been transmitted by the reader.

Figure 7.15
How RFID Works
RFID uses low-powered radio transmitters to read data stored in a tag at distances ranging from 1 inch to 100 feet. The reader captures the data from the tag and sends them over a network to a host computer for processing.

frequency employed, and surrounding environmental conditions. When an RFID tag comes within the range of the reader, the tag is activated and starts sending data. The reader captures these data, decodes them, and sends them back over a wired or wireless network to a host computer for further processing (see Figure 7.15). Both RFID tags and antennas come in a variety of shapes and sizes.

In inventory control and supply chain management, RFID systems capture and manage more detailed information about items in warehouses or in production than bar coding systems. If a large number of items are shipped together, RFID systems track each pallet, lot, or even unit item in the shipment. This technology may help companies such as Walmart improve receiving and storage operations by improving their ability to see exactly what stock is stored in warehouses or on retail store shelves. Dundee Precious Metals, described in the chapter-opening case, uses RFID technology to track workers, equipment, and vehicles in its underground mine.

Walmart has installed RFID readers at store receiving docks to record the arrival of pallets and cases of goods shipped with RFID tags. The RFID reader reads the tags a second time just as the cases are brought onto the sales floor from backroom storage areas. Software combines sales data from Walmart's point-of-sale systems and the RFID data regarding the number of cases brought out to the sales floor. The program determines which items will soon be depleted and automatically generates a list of items to pick in the warehouse to replenish store shelves before they run out. This information helps Walmart reduce out-of-stock items, increase sales, and further shrink its costs.

The cost of RFID tags used to be too high for widespread use, but now it starts at around 7 cents per tag in the United States. As the price decreases, RFID is starting to become cost-effective for many applications.

In addition to installing RFID readers and tagging systems, companies may need to upgrade their hardware and software to process the massive amounts of data produced by RFID systems—transactions that could add up to tens or hundreds of terabytes.

Software is used to filter, aggregate, and prevent RFID data from overloading business networks and system applications. Applications often need to be redesigned to accept large volumes of frequently generated RFID data and to share those data with other applications. Major enterprise software vendors, including SAP and

Oracle PeopleSoft, now offer RFID-ready versions of their supply chain management applications.

Wireless Sensor Networks

If your company wanted state-of-the art technology to monitor building security or detect hazardous substances in the air, it might deploy a wireless sensor network. **Wireless sensor networks (WSNs)** are networks of interconnected wireless devices that are embedded in the physical environment to provide measurements of many points over large spaces. These devices have built-in processing, storage, and radio frequency sensors and antennas. They are linked into an interconnected network that routes the data they capture to a computer for analysis.

These networks range from hundreds to thousands of nodes. Because wireless sensor devices are placed in the field for years at a time without any maintenance or human intervention, they must have very low power requirements and batteries capable of lasting for years.

Figure 7.16 illustrates one type of wireless sensor network, with data from individual nodes flowing across the network to a server with greater processing power. The server acts as a gateway to a network based on Internet technology.

Wireless sensor networks are valuable for uses such as monitoring environmental changes; monitoring traffic or military activity; protecting property; efficiently operating and managing machinery and vehicles; establishing security perimeters; monitoring supply chain management; or detecting chemical, biological, or radiological material.

RFID systems and wireless sensor networks are major sources of big data that organizations are starting to analyze to improve their operations and decision making. Output from these systems is fueling what is called the *Industrial Internet*, also known as the Internet of Things, introduced earlier in this chapter, in which machines such as jet engines, power plant turbines, or agricultural sensors constantly gather data and send the data over the Internet for analysis. The data might signal the need to take action such as replacing a part that's close to wearing out, restocking a product on a store shelf, starting the watering system for a soybean field, or slowing down a turbine. Over time, more and more everyday physical objects will be connected to the Internet and will be able to identify themselves to other devices, creating networks that can sense and respond as data changes. You'll find more examples of the Internet of Things in Chapters 2 and 11.

Figure 7.16
A Wireless Sensor Network

The small circles represent lower-level nodes, and the larger circles represent high-end nodes. Lower-level nodes forward data to each other or to higher-level nodes, which transmit data more rapidly and speed up network performance.

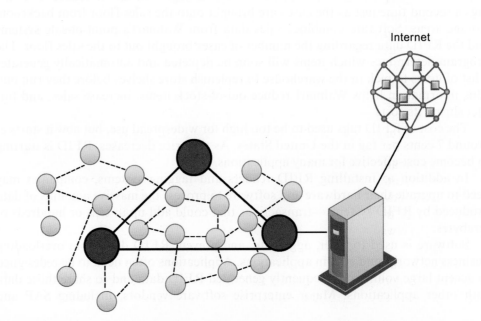

Internet

Review Summary

7-1 **What are the principal components of telecommunications networks and key networking technologies?** A simple network consists of two or more connected computers. Basic network components include computers, network interfaces, a connection medium, network operating system software, and either a hub or a switch. The networking infrastructure for a large company includes the traditional telephone system, mobile cellular communication, wireless local area networks, videoconferencing systems, a corporate website, intranets, extranets, and an array of local and wide area networks, including the Internet.

Contemporary networks have been shaped by the rise of client/server computing, the use of packet switching, and the adoption of Transmission Control Protocol/Internet Protocol (TCP/IP) as a universal communications standard for linking disparate networks and computers, including the Internet. Protocols provide a common set of rules that enable communication among diverse components in a telecommunications network.

7-2 **What are the different types of networks?** The principal physical transmission media are twisted copper telephone wire, coaxial copper cable, fiber-optic cable, and wireless transmission.

Local area networks (LANs) connect PCs and other digital devices within a 500-meter radius and are used today for many corporate computing tasks. Wide area networks (WANs) span broad geographical distances, ranging from several miles to continents and are often private networks that are independently managed. Metropolitan area networks (MANs) span a single urban area.

Digital subscriber line (DSL) technologies, cable Internet connections, and T1 lines are often used for high-capacity Internet connections.

7-3 **How do the Internet and Internet technology work, and how do they support communication and e-business?** The Internet is a worldwide network of networks that uses the client/server model of computing and the TCP/IP network reference model. Every computer on the Internet is assigned a unique numeric IP address. The Domain Name System (DNS) converts IP addresses to more user-friendly domain names. Worldwide Internet policies are established by organizations and government bodies such as the Internet Architecture Board (IAB) and the World Wide Web Consortium (W3C).

Major Internet services include email, newsgroups, chatting, instant messaging, Telnet, FTP, and the web. Web pages are based on Hypertext Markup Language (HTML) and can display text, graphics, video, and audio. Website directories, search engines, and RSS technology help users locate the information they need on the web. RSS, blogs, social networking, and wikis are features of Web 2.0. The future Web 3.0 will feature more semantic search, visual search, prevalence of apps, and interconnectedness of many different devices (Internet of Things).

Firms are also starting to realize economies by using VoIP technology for voice transmission and virtual private networks (VPNs) as low-cost alternatives to private WANs.

7-4 **What are the principal technologies and standards for wireless networking, communication, and Internet access?** Cellular networks are evolving toward high-speed, high-bandwidth, digital packet-switched transmission. Broadband 3G networks are capable of transmitting data at speeds ranging from 144 Kbps to more than 2 Mbps. 4G networks capable of transmission speeds of 100 Mbps are starting to be rolled out.

Major cellular standards include Code Division Multiple Access (CDMA), which is used primarily in the United States, and Global System for Mobile Communications (GSM), which is the standard in Europe and much of the rest of the world.

Standards for wireless computer networks include Bluetooth (802.15) for small personal area networks (PANs), Wi-Fi (802.11) for local area networks (LANs), and WiMax (802.16) for metropolitan area networks (MANs).

Radio frequency identification (RFID) systems provide a powerful technology for tracking the movement of goods by using tiny tags with embedded data about an item and its location. RFID readers read the radio signals transmitted by these tags and pass the data over a network to a computer for processing. Wireless sensor networks (WSNs) are networks of interconnected wireless sensing and transmitting devices that are embedded in the physical environment to provide measurements of many points over large spaces.

Key Terms

3G networks, 280
4G networks, 280
Bandwidth, 262
Blog, 277
Blogosphere, 278
Bluetooth, 280
Broadband, 256
Cable Internet
  connections, 263
Chat, 268
Digital subscriber line
  (DSL), 263
Domain name, 264
Domain Name System
  (DNS), 264
Email, 268
File Transfer Protocol
  (FTP), 268
Hertz, 262
Hotspots, 282
Hubs, 257
Hypertext Transfer
  Protocol (HTTP), 273
Instant messaging, 268
Internet of Things, 279
Internet Protocol (IP)
  address, 263
Internet service provider
  (ISP), 262

Internet2, 267
IPv6, 267
Local area network
  (LAN), 261
Metropolitan area network
  (MAN), 262
Microblogging, 278
Modem, 260
Network operating system
  (NOS), 256
Packet switching, 258
Peer-to-peer, 261
Personal area networks
  (PANs), 280
Predictive search, 275
Protocol, 259
Radio frequency
  identification
  (RFID), 282
Router, 257
RSS, 278
Search engine
  marketing, 276
Search engine optimization
  (SEO), 277
Search engines, 273
Semantic search, 274
Shopping bots, 276
Smartphones, 279

Social networking, 278
Social search, 275
Software-defined
  networking (SDN), 257
Switch, 257
T1 lines, 263
Telnet, 268
Transmission Control
  Protocol/Internet
  Protocol (TCP/IP), 259
Unified
  communications, 271
Uniform resource locator
  (URL), 273
Virtual private network
  (VPN), 272
Visual web, 276
Voice over IP (VoIP), 269
Web 2.0, 277
Web 3.0, 279
Website, 272
Wide area networks
  (WANs), 262
Wi-Fi, 281
Wiki, 278
WiMax, 282
Wireless sensor networks
  (WSNs), 284

MyMISLab ™

To complete the problems with the ⭐, go to EOC Discussion Questions in the MyLab.

Review Questions

7-1 What are the principal components of telecommunications networks and key networking technologies?

- Describe the features of a simple network and the network infrastructure for a large company.
- List and describe the four layers of the Department of Defense's reference model for TCP/IP.
- Describe one of the major problems facing corporations today with respect to telecommunications.

7-2 What are the different types of networks?
- List and describe the different types of physical transmission media.
- Distinguish between a LAN, MAN, and WAN.

7-3 How do the Internet and Internet technology work, and how do they support communication and e-business?
- Define the Internet, describe how it works, and explain how it provides business value.
- Explain how the Domain Name System (DNS) and IP addressing system work.
- List and describe the principal Internet services.
- Define and describe unified communications and explain how it provides value to businesses.
- List and describe alternative ways of locating information on the web.
- Describe how online search technologies are used for marketing.

7-4 What are the principal technologies and standards for wireless networking, communications, and Internet access?
- Define Bluetooth, Wi-Fi, WiMax, and 3G and 4G networks.
- Describe the capabilities of each and for which types of applications each is best suited.
- Define RFID, explain how it works, and describe how it provides value to businesses.
- Define WSNs, explain how they work, and describe the kinds of applications that use them.

Discussion Questions

✪ 7-5 It has been said that within the next few years, smartphones will become the single-most important digital device we own. Discuss the implications of this statement.

✪ 7-6 Does anyone own the Internet? Discuss how the Internet is currently governed and consider whether countries should be able to impose its own rules on the Internet within their own borders.

✪ 7-7 What are some of the issues to consider in determining whether the Internet would provide your business with a competitive advantage?

Hands-On MIS Projects

The projects in this section give you hands-on experience evaluating and selecting communications technology, using spreadsheet software to improve selection of telecommunications services, and using web search engines for business research. Visit MyMIS-Lab's Multimedia Library to access this chapter's Hands-On MIS Projects.

MANAGEMENT DECISION PROBLEMS

7-8 Your company supplies ceramic floor tiles to Leroy Merlin, Bricorama, and other home improvement stores in France. You have been asked to start using radio frequency identification tags on each case of tiles you ship to help your customers improve the management of your products and those of other suppliers in their warehouses. Use the web to identify the cost of hardware, software, and networking components for an RFID system for your company. What factors should be considered? What are the key decisions that have to be made in determining whether your firm should adopt this technology?

7-9 BD sells medical devices and instrument systems to hospitals, health clinics, medical offices, and laboratories in over 50 countries. The company employs over 30,000 people around the world, including account managers, customer service and support representatives, and warehouse staff. Management is considering adopting a system for unified communications. What factors should be considered? What are the key decisions that have to be made in determining whether to adopt this technology? Use the Web, if necessary, to find out more about unified communications and its costs.

IMPROVING DECISION MAKING: USING SPREADSHEET SOFTWARE TO EVALUATE WIRELESS SERVICES

Software skills: Spreadsheet formulas, formatting
Business skills: Analyzing telecommunications services and costs

7-10 In this project, you'll use the web to research alternative wireless services and use spreadsheet software to calculate wireless service costs for a sales force.

You would like to equip your sales force of 35, based in Dublin, Ireland, with mobile phones that have capabilities for voice transmission, text messaging, and taking and sending photos. Use the Web to select a wireless service provider that provides international service as well as good service in your home area. Examine the features of the mobile handsets offered by each of these vendors. Assume that each of the 35 salespeople will need to spend three hours per weekday between 8 a.m. and 6 p.m. on mobile voice communication, send 30 text messages per weekday, and send five photos per week. Use your spreadsheet software to determine the wireless service and handset that will offer the best pricing per user over a two-year period. For the purposes of this exercise, you do not need to consider corporate discounts.

ACHIEVING OPERATIONAL EXCELLENCE: USING WEB SEARCH ENGINES FOR BUSINESS RESEARCH

Software skills: Web search tools
Business skills: Researching new technologies

7-11 This project will help develop your Internet skills in using web search engines for business research.

Use Google and Bing to obtain information about the Internet of Things. If you wish, try some other search engines as well. Compare the volume and quality of information you find with each search tool. Which tool is the easiest to use? Which produced the best results for your research? Why?

Collaboration and Teamwork Project

Evaluating Smartphones

7-12 Form a group with three or four of your classmates. Compare the capabilities of Apple's iPhone with a smartphone handset from another vendor with similar features. Your analysis should consider the purchase cost of each device, the wireless networks where each device can operate, plan and handset costs, and the services available for each device. You should also consider other capabilities of each device, including available software, security features, and the ability to integrate with existing corporate or PC applications. Which device would you select? On what criteria would you base your selection? If possible, use Google Docs and Google Drive or Google Sites to brainstorm, organize, and develop a presentation of your findings for the class.

BUSINESS PROBLEM-SOLVING CASE

RFID Propels the Angkasa Library Management System

Radio-frequency identification (RFID) can play a key role in library management. The major advantage of using RFID is that it ensures traceability and security. In addition, RFID simplifies transactional processes at the library and can help to cut costs and save time. Across the globe, libraries are setting up the infrastructure for RFID as a replacement for manual management or barcodes. RFID tags can be embedded within a book, and unlike other forms of labeling, these tags can store additional information, like author and title. Using this system also speeds up the process of checking books in and out, prevents theft, and helps in inventory management. The Allianze University College of Medical Sciences (AUCMS) has successfully set up RFID tagging as part of its library management system.

AUCMS is a premier institute offering courses in medicine and applied health sciences in Penang, Malaysia. The institution has a vast array of resources, including books, journals, newspapers, and e-books, and the library caters to a large population of students and staff. AUCMS partnered with the Sains Group, which is a globally renowned software solutions and IT services provider, to install and implement the the company's Angkasa Library Management system. This system manages many of the core functions of the library, including acquisition, cataloguing, circulation, subscriptions to journals, and the management of an open-access catalog available to members on the Web.

The system is primarily useful as a repository of all library records. It enables the automatization of library processes that would earlier have been manual and paper-based. The Acquisition Module manages the process of acquiring the books, magazines, journals, and other materials for the library. This automates the entire process of acquisition, from the approval of orders to placing them, the recording of receipts and invoices to management of expenditure and maintenance of budgets. In a typical instance, lists of required reading material are sent over to the library heads, a final list is determined, and all of the important information is recorded on the system (invoice numbers, supplier names, and so on). The system provides a printable order form, which is then signed off on by the library head and sent to suppliers.

Information on newly acquired books is entered into the system through the Cataloguing Module, which assigns classification numbers to each book. Data is entered in the standard machine-readable format AACR2, which stands for Anglo-American Cataloguing Rules. Based on this standard format, the technical department enters details into the system, which then generates an index card in the same format. This card serves as an index for searching, and makes import/export of bibliographic data in standard exchange formats possible. The Circulation Module performs all the functions related to circulation, providing suitable checks at every stage. Since books may be circulated for multiple reasons such as book binding and display, in addition to being issued to members, this module records the current status of a circulated library item. The Serials Management Module controls the library's subscriptions to periodicals and monitors the scheduled arrival of individual issues in addition to recording budget information.

An important part of the library management system is the Online Public Access Catalog (OPAC), which provides online access to library resources. The OPAC module supports keyword searches in many languages, and page navigation is user-friendly. Since the catalog is Web-enabled, this makes it very easy to keep information on the availability of materials in the library up-to-date. Another member-centric module is the Member Management module, which stores profiles for all library members and includes a photograph and a registration number. This module sends reminders to members to return their books on time, and also records fines if items are not returned.

The first step toward setting this comprehensive system up at the AUCMS library was the tagging of the books. The RFID tag is the most important aspect of the system because the tag establishes a unique identity for each library asset, from books to magazines, and functions as the item's identity in the system. The tag contains electronically stored information that may be read from up to several meters. Unlike a bar code, the RFID tag does not need to be in the line of sight of a bar code reader. All library issuing and returns counters have a touch screen with an RFID glass sensor. A handheld reader is also required to scan membership cards.

Borrowers simply place books and other material they want to borrow on the touch screen, and hand over their cards to library staff. The screen reads RFID tags, while the card reader opens up a member's profile on the system. The staff member assigns material to the borrower in question, and an issuing receipt is generated, with the date of return clearly marked. This system eliminates the need for physical records, stamping, and other time-consuming activities involved in the process of checking a book out of a library. In addition, the system also minimizes human error.

Returning books is also much easier now, with members simply dropping their books at any time into a specially designed "drop box" machine in the library. Members drop the books to be returned in the box one at a time. A scanner within the drop box scans the RFID tag of the dropped book and marks it as returned in the system. Member accounts are updated accordingly and a proof-of-return slip is issued automatically. The whole process is accomplished through a link between the RFID system and the library's host computer. This eliminates the need for staff who would earlier have had to process all book returns, and is also convenient for members, since they can return their books even when the library is closed. The status of returned items is updated instantly, which means other members who are waiting for a particular item can acquire it at once.

Another major task that has always occupied library staff is shelf management. Since a large number of users access the library and do not put books back on shelves in the right order, shelves can become difficult to manage. Books that have been returned also have to be placed in specific shelves. The shelf management system in place at the AUCMS library consists of a portable scanner and a base station. The solution is designed to cover three main operations: searching for individual books, inventory checks of library stock, and locating and replacing books that have been shelved incorrectly. Each book has a shelf ID, which is the location identification code (this code enables section-wise and rack-wise identification of books). This information is saved in a central database against the book's information and RFID tag, as well as being linked to OPAC. The portable scanner fetches the information stored in a book's RFID tag, and using the shelving information also stored in the database, library staff can move books back into their places. Similarly, missing books can also be identified, with the portable scanner pulling up the records of all the books meant to be on a specific shelf. The collected information is compared against the library database to generate a report of missing books. This system has improved accuracy and enabled faster shelving (20 books per minute). It also

directs OPAC users to the exact physical locations of the books they are looking for. In total, the automatization of all of these library processes has resulted in a significant decrease in the amount of manpower required to staff the library.

Finally, one of the most pervasive problems in any library is theft. RFID tagging in concert with the installation of Electronic Article Surveillance (EAS) gates in libraries is extremely useful in preventing theft. Just like alarm systems in stores, a library member attempting to leave with an unissued item triggers an alarm because the gates can sense the book's RFID tag within a range of 1 meter without interference from magnetic items. The EAS gates are linked to the library's surveillance station. When someone passes through with an unissued item, an alarm is sounded and the gates are raised, an alarm is sounded, and the camera at the gates takes a photograph of the person and sends it to the surveillance station.

RFID systems are not without issues. RFID and associated databases develop a comprehensive record of what books people have read, and potentially, these systems can be used to invade the privacy of library users. RFID tags can fail, or be torn out of books. But for the most part RFID tags and data systems are the current best practices technology for library management.

Sources: Sally Eggloff, "Advantages and Disadvantages of Using RFID Technology in Libraries," University of Maryland, http://terpconnect.umd.edu, accessed December 28, 2015; Osborn James, "Bringing Libraries to Every Home: The Malaysia Scenario," Sarawak Information Systems Sdn. Bhd., December 18, 2015; Phil Morehart, "RFID to the Rescue," *American Libraries Magazine*, May 21, 2015; "Integrated Library Management Solution," SAINs Corporation, Sarawak, Malaysia, http://www.sains.com.my/solutions.php?id=47, February 11, 2015; http://www.allianzeunicollege.edu.my/; "Library Management Solution for Penang Allianze University College of Medical Sciences," Sarawak Information Systems Newsletter, 2012.

Case Study Questions

7-13 How can RFID technology simplify basic library processes like the lending and returns of books?

7-14 What kind of technology does your school or university library use? Does IT play a crucial role in managing operations?

7-15 How is RFID technology helping the Allianze University College of Medical Sciences library to detect and prevent the theft of books?

Case contributed by Sahil Raj, Punjabi University

MyMISLab

Go to the Assignments section of your MyLab to complete these writing exercises.

7-16 Compare Web 2.0 and Web 3.0.

7-17 How do social search, semantic search, and mobile search differ from searching for information on the web by using conventional search engines?

Chapter 7 References

Agresta, Tony. "Why Media Companies Organize Data with Semantic Search." DataInformed (April 28, 2015).

Bauer, Harald, Mark Patel, and Jan Veira."The Internet of Things: Sizing Up the Opportunity." McKinsey & Company (December 2014).

Boutin, Paul. "Search Tool on Facebook Puts Network to Work," *New York Times* (March 20, 2013).

Chiang, I. Robert, and Jhang-Li, Jhih-Hua. "Delivery Consolidation and Service Competition among Internet Service Providers," *Journal of Management Information Systems* 34, No. 3 (Winter 2014).

Efrati, Amir. "Google's Search Revamp: A Step Closer to AI," *Wall Street Journal* (March 14, 2012).

eMarketer, "It's 2015. What Does Mobile Mean Now?" (February 18, 2015).

Google, Inc. "SEC Form 10k for the Fiscal Year Ending December 31, 2014," (February 9, 2015).

Lahiri, Atanu I. "The Disruptive Effect of Open Platforms on Markets for Wireless Services," *Journal of Management Information Systems* 27, No. 3 (Winter 2011).

Manjoo, Farhad. "Google Mighty Now, but Not Forever," *New York Times* (February 11, 2015).

McBeath, Bill. "What Is This Thing Called 'Internet of Things'?" *Chain Link Research* (October 14, 2014).

McKinsey&Company. "The Impact of Internet Technologies: Search," (July 2011).

Mims, Christopher. "The Internet's Future Lies Up in the Skies," *Wall Street Journal* (December 12, 2014).

National Telecommunications and Information Agency. "NTIA Announces Intent to Transition Key Internet Domain Name Functions," (March 14, 2014).

Panko, Raymond R., and Julia Panko. *Business Data Networks and Security*, 10th ed. (Upper Saddle River, NJ: Prentice-Hall, 2015.)

SearchAgency.com. "Mobile Drives Increased Spend and Clicks on Both Google and Bing," (July 15, 2014).

Simonite, Tom. "Social Indexing," *Technology Review* (May/June 2011).

"Software Defined Networking," *Global Knowledge* (2014).

SupplyChainBrain. "RFID's Role in Today's Supply Chain," (November 4, 2013).

"The Internet of Things." *McKinsey Quarterly* (March 2010).

Winkler, Rolfe. "Getting More than Just Words in a Google Search Result," *Wall Street Journal* (August 18, 2014).

Wittman, Art. "Here Comes the Internet of Things," *Information Week* (July 22, 2013).

Wyatt, Edward. "U.S. to Cede Its Oversight of Addresses on Internet," *New York Times* (March 14, 2014).

Securing Information Systems

C H A P T E R 8

LEARNING OBJECTIVES

After reading this chapter, you will be able to answer the following questions:

8-1 Why are information systems vulnerable to destruction, error, and abuse?

8-2 What is the business value of security and control?

8-3 What are the components of an organizational framework for security and control?

8-4 What are the most important tools and technologies for safeguarding information resources?

CHAPTER CASES

MiniDuke Exposes EU Cybersecurity Gaps

Stuxnet and the Changing Face of Cyberwarfare

MWEB Business Hacked

Information Security Threats and Policies in Europe

VIDEO CASES

Case 1: Stuxnet and Cyberwarfare

Case 2: Cyberespionage: The Chinese Threat

Case 3: IBM Zone Trusted Information Channel (ZTIC)

Instructional Videos:

Sony PlayStation Hacked; Data Stolen from 77 Million Users

Zappos Working to Correct Online Security Breach

Meet the Hackers: Anonymous Statement on Hacking Sony

MINIDUKE EXPOSES EU CYBERSECURITY GAPS

When over 20 European countries, including Ukraine, Belgium, Portugal, Romania, the Czech Republic, and Ireland were infected with an unusual malware agent that combined malware writing techniques from the turn of the century with novel, new sandbox-evading techniques, security experts at Kaspersky Lab and CrySys Lab sounded the alarm. Dubbed MiniDuke, the social engineering exploit gained initial access by inducing targets to open infected PDF attachments that appeared legitimate and highly relevant to the recipient's work.

Sandboxing was developed as an alternative to traditional signature-based virus detection to find zero-day malware—unknown malware for which antivirus software signatures are not yet available. MiniDuke used a now patched Adobe Reader bug to avoid the sandbox, allowing it to install a dropper (small downloader) that provided the perpetrators with a customized backdoor unique to each system. Normal authentication procedures could then be bypassed and affected machines remotely accessed. What's more, the computer's unique fingerprint was then also used to encrypt communications back to the attackers. In hostile environments, MiniDuke goes dormant rather than proceeding to its next step—using Twitter to locate specific tweets from premade accounts created by its Command and Control (C2) operators. These tweets contain tags that identify encrypted URLs for the C2s. The C2s in turn transmit encrypted files containing commands and infected GIF files to create a bigger backdoor on the system. In the absence of Twitter, MiniDuke can use Google Search to locate the C2s.

By 2015 Miniduke has morphed into an entire family of malware tools called "the Dukes": CozyDuke, CosmicDuke, CloudDuke, SeaDuke, and HammerDuke. Each of these variants uses similar coding techniques and is believed to be the product of a Russian programming group with support from the government. One

research group found that the Ministry of Foreign Affairs in Europe was broken into, and documents referencing EU sanctions against Russia during the Ukraine crisis were stolen. Researchers believe that "the Dukes family of malware will not be defeated soon. When Dukes are discovered, the source group immediately repairs the software to avoid detection.

Duke attacks on European government agencies became a recurring theme. Trend Micro discovered that members of the diplomatic community in 16 European and several Asian countries had been targeted with malware-laden e-mail attachments suspected to have originated from China's defense ministry. Like MiniDuke, the malware exploited a vulnerability in widely-used business software (Microsoft Office 2003-2010), installed a dropper, and created a backdoor. It then collected e-mail user names and passwords from Outlook and Internet Explorer along with Web site login credentials and transmitted the data to two now-defunct URLs in Hong Kong. Throughout 2015, Duke variants continued to exert influence as law enforcement agencies reported its usage in attacks against governments and other organizations.

With the sophistication, efficacy, frequency, and geopolitical consequences of cyberattacks on the rise, ENISA, the European Union Agency for Network and Information Security, established in 2005, has urged implementation of a common cybersecurity strategy. However, the fledgling European Cybercrime Centre (EC3), created in January 2013, has not been able to stipulate a clear definition for cyber security, let alone persuade members to craft and implement coordinated policies.

The 28 members of the EU are simply not willing to cede any part of their national security policy to the EU, and the EC3 did not challenge this entrenched outlook. Lack of a centralized and cohesive approach to cybersecurity makes for disjointed and disparate policies and procedures and unequal levels of protection. While members whose economies depend on information and communications technology (ICT) stayed abreast of cybersecurity threats and defenses, others have not yet implemented the most basic protections. As MiniDuke demonstrated, having 28 different approaches to cybersecurity leaves all members vulnerable to national security breaches.

Sources: David Bisson, "Seven Years of Cyber Espionage: F-Secure Unveils 'The Dukes'," Tripwire. com, September 20, 2015; "The Duke Is Back: Kaspersky Lab Discovers New 'CozyDuke' Cyberthreat Related to Infamous Miniduke," Kapersky Labs, http://www.kaspersky.com/about/new, April 22, 2015; Eduard Kovacs, "CosmicDuke Variant Installs MiniDuke on Infected Systems: F-Secure," *Security Week*, January 8, 2015; "The Miniduke Attacks Are Back in Force," Kaspersky.com, July 3, 2014; "Kaspersky Lab Identifies 'MiniDuke', a New Malicious Program Designed for Spying on Multiple Government Entities and Institutions Across the World," Kaspersky.com, February 27, 2013; Josh Halliday, "Hackers Attack European Governments Using 'MiniDuke' Malware," theguardian.com, February 27, 2013; Mathew J. Schwartz, "MiniDuke Espionage Malware Uses Twitter to Infect PCs," informationweek.com, February 28, 2013.

The problems created by malware such as MiniDuke and DDoS attacks illustrate why the EU and businesses operating there need to pay special attention to information system security. The fragmented approach to cybersecurity in the EU does not allocate responsibility among the stakeholders, and with no cohesive strategy, members are not encouraged to work together. Neither governments nor businesses are adequately protected.

In November 2013, ENISA, recognizing the switch to cloud computing, urged adoption of a unified strategy for public sector cloud security. Standard procedures for security certification of both services and providers, a shared framework for service-level agreements (SLAs), and a common certification and accreditation process were recommended as well as cloud deployment security measures to protect the integrity of the cloud supply chain.

The chapter-opening diagram calls attention to important points raised by this case and this chapter. While Web servers can never be completely secure from hackers who can steal sensitive public and private sector data, the EU must clearly do more to protect its member nations and the businesses that serve its citizens. While establishment of the EC3 was a start, member nations must be convinced to participate in a consistent, common cybersecurity strategy. This strategy must include the expert knowledge collected by private sector security

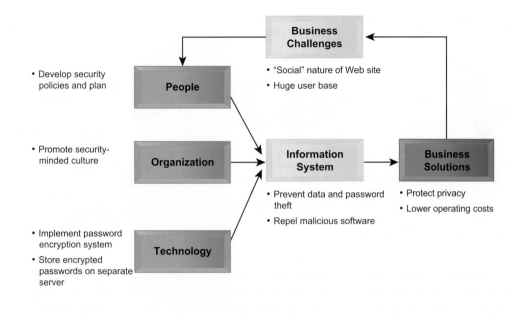

companies such as Kaspersky Lab McAfee, CrySys Lab, Trend Micro and others as well as input from large business entities which are at the greatest risk due to the greater sensitivity and value of their stored data.

8-1 Why are information systems vulnerable to destruction, error, and abuse?

Can you imagine what would happen if you tried to link to the Internet without a firewall or antivirus software? Your computer would be disabled in a few seconds, and it might take you many days to recover. If you used the computer to run your business, you might not be able to sell to your customers or place orders with your suppliers while it was down. And you might find that your computer system had been penetrated by outsiders, who perhaps stole or destroyed valuable data, including confidential payment data from your customers. If too much data were destroyed or divulged, your business might never be able to recover!

In short, if you operate a business today, you need to make security and control a top priority. **Security** refers to the policies, procedures, and technical measures used to prevent unauthorized access, alteration, theft, or physical damage to information systems. **Controls** are methods, policies, and organizational procedures that ensure the safety of the organization's assets, the accuracy and reliability of its records, and operational adherence to management standards.

WHY SYSTEMS ARE VULNERABLE

When large amounts of data are stored in electronic form, they are vulnerable to many kinds of threats. Through communications networks, information systems in different locations are interconnected. The potential for unauthorized access, abuse, or fraud is not limited to a single location but can occur at any access point in the network. Figure 8.1 illustrates the most common threats against contemporary information systems. They can stem from technical, organizational, and environmental factors compounded by poor management decisions. In the multitier client/ server computing environment illustrated here, vulnerabilities exist at each layer and in the communications between the layers. Users at the client layer can cause harm

Figure 8.1
Contemporary
Security Challenges
and Vulnerabilities
*The architecture of a
web-based application
typically includes a web
client, a server, and
corporate information
systems linked to data-
bases. Each of these
components presents
security challenges and
vulnerabilities. Floods, fires,
power failures, and other
electrical problems can
cause disruptions at any
point in the network.*

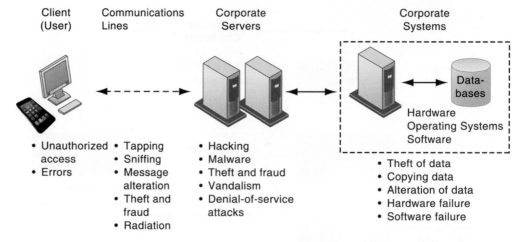

by introducing errors or by accessing systems without authorization. It is possible to access data flowing over networks, steal valuable data during transmission, or alter data without authorization. Radiation may disrupt a network at various points as well. Intruders can launch denial-of-service attacks or malicious software to disrupt the operation of websites. Those capable of penetrating corporate systems can steal, destroy, or alter corporate data stored in databases or files.

Systems malfunction if computer hardware breaks down, is not configured properly, or is damaged by improper use or criminal acts. Errors in programming, improper installation, or unauthorized changes cause computer software to fail. Power failures, floods, fires, or other natural disasters can also disrupt computer systems.

Domestic or offshore partnering with another company contribute s to system vulnerability if valuable information resides on networks and computers outside the organization's control. Without strong safeguards, valuable data could be lost, destroyed, or fall into the wrong hands, revealing important trade secrets or information that violates personal privacy.

The popularity of handheld mobile devices for business computing adds to these woes. Portability makes cell phones, smartphones, and tablet computers easy to lose or steal. Smartphones share the same security weaknesses as other Internet devices and are vulnerable to malicious software and penetration from outsiders. Smartphones that corporate employees use often contain sensitive data such as sales figures, customer names, phone numbers, and email addresses. Intruders may also be able to access internal corporate systems through these devices.

Internet Vulnerabilities

Large public networks, such as the Internet, are more vulnerable than internal networks because they are virtually open to anyone. The Internet is so huge that when abuses do occur, they can have an enormously widespread impact. When the Internet becomes part of the corporate network, the organization's information systems are even more vulnerable to actions from outsiders.

Telephone service based on Internet technology (see Chapter 7) is more vulnerable than the switched voice network if it does not run over a secure private network. Most Voice over IP (VoIP) traffic over the Internet is not encrypted, so anyone with a network can listen in on conversations. Hackers can intercept conversations or shut down voice service by flooding servers supporting VoIP with bogus traffic.

Vulnerability has also increased from widespread use of email, instant messaging (IM), and peer-to-peer (P2P) file-sharing programs. Email may contain attachments that serve as springboards for malicious software or unauthorized access to internal corporate systems. Employees may use email messages to transmit valuable trade secrets, financial data, or confidential customer information to unauthorized recipients. Popular IM applications for consumers do not use a secure layer for text messages, so they can be intercepted and read by outsiders during transmission over the Internet. Instant messaging activity over the Internet can in some cases be used as a back door to an otherwise secure network. Sharing files over P2P networks, such as those for illegal music sharing, may also transmit malicious software or expose information on either individual or corporate computers to outsiders.

Wireless Security Challenges

Is it safe to log on to a wireless network at an airport, library, or other public location? It depends on how vigilant you are. Even the wireless network in your home is vulnerable because radio frequency bands are easy to scan. Both Bluetooth and Wi-Fi networks are susceptible to hacking by eavesdroppers. Local area networks (LANs) using the 802.11 standard can be easily penetrated by outsiders armed with laptops, wireless cards, external antennae, and hacking software. Hackers use these tools to detect unprotected networks, monitor network traffic, and, in some cases, gain access to the Internet or to corporate networks.

Wi-Fi transmission technology was designed to make it easy for stations to find and hear one another. The service set identifiers (SSIDs) that identify the access points in a Wi-Fi network are broadcast multiple times and can be picked up fairly easily by intruders' sniffer programs (see Figure 8.2). Wireless networks in many locations do not have basic protections against **war driving**, in which eavesdroppers drive by buildings or park outside and try to intercept wireless network traffic.

An intruder who has associated with an access point by using the correct SSID is capable of accessing other resources on the network. For example, the intruder could use the Windows operating system to determine which other users are connected to the network, access their computer hard drives, and open or copy their files.

Intruders also use the information they have gleaned to set up rogue access points on a different radio channel in physical locations close to users to force a user's radio network interface controller (NIC) to associate with the rogue access point. Once this association occurs, hackers using the rogue access point can capture the names and passwords of unsuspecting users.

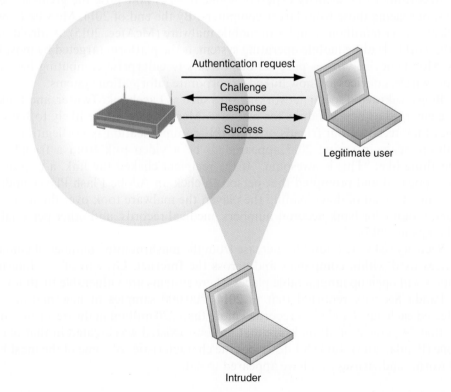

Figure 8.2
Wi-Fi Security Challenges
Many Wi-Fi networks can be penetrated easily by intruders using sniffer programs to obtain an address to access the resources of a network without authorization.

MALICIOUS SOFTWARE: VIRUSES, WORMS, TROJAN HORSES, AND SPYWARE

Malicious software programs are referred to as **malware** and include a variety of threats such as computer viruses, worms, and Trojan horses. A **computer virus** is a rogue software program that attaches itself to other software programs or data files to be executed, usually without user knowledge or permission. Most computer viruses deliver a payload. The payload may be relatively benign, such as instructions to display a message or image, or it may be highly destructive—destroying programs or data, clogging computer memory, reformatting a computer's hard drive, or causing programs to run improperly. Viruses typically spread from computer to computer when humans take an action, such as sending an email attachment or copying an infected file.

Most recent attacks have come from **worms**, which are independent computer programs that copy themselves from one computer to other computers over a network. Unlike viruses, worms can operate on their own without attaching to other computer program files and rely less on human behavior to spread from computer to computer. This explains why computer worms spread much more rapidly than computer viruses. Worms destroy data and programs as well as disrupt or even halt the operation of computer networks.

Worms and viruses are often spread over the Internet from files of downloaded software; from files attached to email transmissions; or from compromised email messages, online ads, or instant messaging. Viruses have also invaded computerized information systems from infected disks or infected machines. Especially prevalent today are **drive-by downloads**, consisting of malware that comes with a downloaded file that a user intentionally or unintentionally requests.

Hackers can do to a smartphone just about anything they can do to any Internet device: request malicious files without user intervention, delete files, transmit files, install programs running in the background to monitor user actions, and potentially convert the smartphone to a robot in a botnet to send email and text messages to anyone. With smartphones outselling PCs, and increasingly used as payment devices, they are becoming a major avenue for malware.

According to IT security experts, mobile devices now pose the greatest security risks, outpacing those from larger computers. By the end of 2014, McAfee Labs had collected over 6 million samples of mobile malware (McAfee, 2015). Android, which is the world's leading mobile operating system, is the platform targeted by most hackers. Mobile device viruses pose serious threats to enterprise computing because so many wireless devices are now linked to corporate information systems.

Blogs, wikis, and social networking sites such as Facebook, Twitter, and LinkedIn have emerged as new conduits for malware. Members are more likely to trust messages they receive from friends, even if this communication is not legitimate. One malware scam in spring 2015 appeared to be a video link from a friend saying something like, "This is awesome." If the recipient clicked the link. a pop-up window appeared and prompted that person to click an Adobe Flash Player update to continue. Instead of downloading the player, the malware took over the user's computer, looking for bank account numbers, medical records, and other personal data (Thompson, 2015).

Security risks are bound to increase from the mushrooming number of connected devices used within companies and across the Internet. Growth of the Internet of Things will open up innumerable places where systems are vulnerable to attack.

Panda Security reported that in 2014, 200,000 samples of new malware were detected each day. Panda has recorded more than 220 million malware strains, meaning that 34 percent of all malware that has ever existed was created in that one year alone (Panda, 2015). Table 8.1 describes the characteristics of some of the most harmful worms and viruses that have appeared to date.

TABLE 8.1

Examples of Malicious Code

Name	Type	Description
Conficker (aka Downadup, Downup)	Worm	First detected in November 2008 and still prevalent. Uses flaws in Windows software to take over machines and link them to a virtual computer that can be commanded remotely. Had more than 5 million computers worldwide under its control. Difficult to eradicate.
Sasser.ftp	Worm	First appeared in May 2004. Spread over the Internet by attacking random IP addresses. Causes computers continually to crash and reboot and infected computers to search for more victims. Affected millions of computers worldwide and caused an estimated $14.8 billion to $18.6 billion in damages.
MyDoom.A	Worm	First appeared on January 26, 2004. Spreads as an email attachment. Sends email to addresses harvested from infected machines, forging the sender's address. At its peak, this worm lowered global Internet performance by 10 percent and web page loading times by as much as 50 percent. Was programmed to stop spreading after February 12, 2004.
ILOVEYOU	Virus	First detected on May 3, 2000. Script virus written in Visual Basic script and transmitted as an attachment to email with the subject line ILOVEYOU. Overwrites music, image, and other files with a copy of itself and did an estimated $10 billion to $15 billion in damage.

More than 65 percent of the infections Panda found were Trojan horses. A **Trojan horse** is a software program that appears to be benign but then does something other than expected. The Trojan horse is not itself a virus because it does not replicate, but it is often a way for viruses or other malicious code to be introduced into a computer system. The term *Trojan horse* is based on the huge wooden horse the Greeks used to trick the Trojans into opening the gates to their fortified city during the Trojan War. Once inside the city walls, Greek soldiers hidden in the horse revealed themselves and captured the city.

An example of a modern-day Trojan horse is the Zeus Trojan. It is often used to steal login credentials for banking by surreptitiously capturing people's keystrokes as they use their computers. Zeus is spread mainly through drive-by downloads and phishing, and recent variants are hard for antimalware tools to detect.

SQL injection attacks have become a major malware threat. SQL injection attacks take advantage of vulnerabilities in poorly coded web application software to introduce malicious program code into a company's systems and networks. These vulnerabilities occur when a web application fails to validate properly or filter data a user enters on a web page, which might occur when ordering something online. An attacker uses this input validation error to send a rogue SQL query to the underlying database to access the database, plant malicious code, or access other systems on the network. Large web applications have hundreds of places for inputting user data, each of which creates an opportunity for an SQL injection attack.

Malware known as **ransomware** is proliferating on both desktop and mobile devices. Ransomware tries to extort money from users by taking control of their computers or displaying annoying pop-up messages. One nasty example, CryptoLocker, encrypts an infected computer's files, forcing users to pay hundreds of dollars to regain access. You can get ransomware from donwloading an infected attachment, clicking a link inside an email or by visiting the wrong website.

Some types of **spyware** also act as malicious software. These small programs install themselves surreptitiously on computers to monitor user web-surfing activity and serve up advertising. Thousands of forms of spyware have been documented.

Many users find such spyware annoying, and some critics worry about its infringement on computer users' privacy. Some forms of spyware are especially nefarious. **Keyloggers** record every keystroke made on a computer to steal serial numbers for software, to launch Internet attacks, to gain access to email accounts, to obtain passwords to protected computer systems, or to pick up personal information such as credit card and or bank account numbers. The Zeus Trojan described earlier uses keylogging. Other spyware programs reset web browser home pages, redirect search requests, or slow performance by taking up too much memory.

HACKERS AND COMPUTER CRIME

A **hacker** is an individual who intends to gain unauthorized access to a computer system. Within the hacking community, the term *cracker* is typically used to denote a hacker with criminal intent, although in the public press, the terms *hacker* and *cracker* are used interchangeably. Hackers gain unauthorized access by finding weaknesses in the security protections websites and computer systems employ, often taking advantage of various features of the Internet that make it an open system and easy to use.

Hacker activities have broadened beyond mere system intrusion to include theft of goods and information as well as system damage and **cybervandalism**, the intentional disruption, defacement, or even destruction of a website or corporate information system. For example, a group of pro-Syrian regime hackers called the Syrian Electronic Army hacked Skype's Twitter account, blog, and Facebook page in early January 2014, publishing a fake message that read, "Don't use Microsoft emails. . . . They are monitoring your accounts and selling the data to the governments" (Ribeiro, 2014).

Spoofing and Sniffing

Hackers attempting to hide their true identities often spoof, or misrepresent, themselves by using fake email addresses or masquerading as someone else. **Spoofing** may also involve redirecting a web link to an address different from the intended one, with the site masquerading as the intended destination. For example, if hackers redirect customers to a fake website that looks almost exactly like the true site, they can then collect and process orders, effectively stealing business as well as sensitive customer information from the true site. We will provide more detail about other forms of spoofing in our discussion of computer crime.

A **sniffer** is a type of eavesdropping program that monitors information traveling over a network. When used legitimately, sniffers help identify potential network trouble spots or criminal activity on networks, but when used for criminal purposes, they can be damaging and very difficult to detect. Sniffers enable hackers to steal proprietary information from anywhere on a network, including email messages, company files, and confidential reports.

Denial-of-Service Attacks

In a **denial-of-service (DoS) attack**, hackers flood a network server or web server with many thousands of false communications or requests for services to crash the network. The network receives so many queries that it cannot keep up with them and is thus unavailable to service legitimate requests. A **distributed denial-of-service (DDoS)** attack uses numerous computers to inundate and overwhelm the network from numerous launch points.

Although DoS attacks do not destroy information or access restricted areas of a company's information systems, they often cause a website to shut down, making it impossible for legitimate users to access the site. For example, on April 27, 2015, the state of Hawaii and the Thirty Meter Telescope (TMT) were hit with a DOS attack believed to have been launched by a group called Operation Green Rights. (The TMT organization is constructing one of the biggest telescopes in the world in

Hawaii.) Both organizations' websites were flooded with so much illicit traffic that they were not available until the following day (Wakida, 2015).

For busy e-commerce sites, these attacks are costly; while the site is shut down, customers cannot make purchases. Especially vulnerable are small and midsize businesses whose networks tend to be less protected than those of large corporations.

Perpetrators of DDoS attacks often use thousands of zombie PCs infected with malicious software without their owners' knowledge and organized into a **botnet**. Hackers create these botnets by infecting other people's computers with bot malware that opens a back door through which an attacker can give instructions. The infected computer then becomes a slave, or zombie, serving a master computer belonging to someone else. When hackers infect enough computers, they can use the amassed resources of the botnet to launch DDoS attacks, phishing campaigns, or unsolicited spam email.

Ninety percent of the world's spam and 80 percent of the world's malware are delivered by botnets. For example, a new version of the Pushdo spamming botnet was detected in spring 2015. Computers in more than 50 countries were infected. Pushdo has existed since 2007 despite numerous attempts to shut it down. The latest version has been pushing malware that steals login credentials and accesses online banking systems. At one time, Pushdo-infected computers sent as many as 7.7 billion spam messages per day (Kirk, 2015).

Computer Crime

Most hacker activities are criminal offenses, and the vulnerabilities of systems we have just described make them targets for other types of **computer crime** as well. Computer crime is defined by the U.S. Department of Justice as "any violations of criminal law that involve a knowledge of computer technology for their perpetration, investigation, or prosecution." Table 8.2 provides examples of the computer as both a target and an instrument of crime. The chapter-opening case describes one of the largest computer crime cases reported to date.

No one knows the magnitude of the computer crime problem—how many systems are invaded, how many people engage in the practice, or the total economic damage. According to the Ponemon Institute's 2014 Annual Cost of Cyber Crime Study sponsored by HP Enterprise Security, the average annualized cost of cybercrime for companies in the United States was $12.7 million per year (Ponemon Institute, 2014). Many companies are reluctant to report computer crimes because the crimes may involve employees, or the company fears that publicizing its vulnerability will hurt its reputation. The most economically damaging kinds of computer crime are DOS attacks, activities of malicious insiders, and web-based attacks.

Identity Theft

With the growth of the Internet and electronic commerce, identity theft has become especially troubling. **Identity theft** is a crime in which an imposter obtains key pieces of personal information, such as social security identification numbers, driver's license numbers, or credit card numbers, to impersonate someone else. The information may be used to obtain credit, merchandise, or services in the name of the victim or to provide the thief with false credentials.

Identity theft has flourished on the Internet, with credit card files a major target of website hackers. According to the 2015 Identity Fraud Study by Javelin Strategy & Research, 12.7 million consumers lost $16 billion to identity fraud in 2014 (Javelin, 2015). E-commerce sites are wonderful sources of customer personal information— name, address, and phone number. Armed with this information, criminals can assume new identities and establish new credit for their own purposes.

One increasingly popular tactic is a form of spoofing called **phishing**. Phishing involves setting up fake websites or sending email messages that look like those of legitimate businesses to ask users for confidential personal data. The email message instructs recipients to update or confirm records by providing social security numbers,

TABLE 8.2

Examples of Computer Crime

Computers as targets of crime

Breaching the confidentiality of protected computerized data

Accessing a computer system without authority

Knowingly accessing a protected computer to commit fraud

Intentionally accessing a protected computer and causing damage, negligently or deliberately

Knowingly transmitting a program, program code, or command that intentionally causes damage to a protected computer

Threatening to cause damage to a protected computer

Computers as instruments of crime

Theft of trade secrets

Unauthorized copying of software or copyrighted intellectual property, such as articles, books, music, and video

Schemes to defraud

Using email for threats or harassment

Intentionally attempting to intercept electronic communication

Illegally accessing stored electronic communications, including email and voice mail

Transmitting or possessing child pornography by using a computer

bank and credit card information, and other confidential data either by responding to the email message, by entering the information at a bogus website, or by calling a telephone number. EBay, PayPal, Amazon.com, Walmart, and a variety of banks are among the top spoofed companies. In a more targeted form of phishing called *spear phishing*, messages appear to come from a trusted source, such as an individual within the recipient's own company or a friend.

Phishing techniques called evil twins and pharming are harder to detect. **Evil twins** are wireless networks that pretend to offer trustworthy Wi-Fi connections to the Internet, such as those in airport lounges, hotels, or coffee shops. The bogus network looks identical to a legitimate public network. Fraudsters try to capture passwords or credit card numbers of unwitting users who log on to the network.

Pharming redirects users to a bogus web page, even when the individual types the correct web page address into his or her browser. This is possible if pharming perpetrators gain access to the Internet address information Internet service providers (ISPs) store to speed up web browsing and the ISP companies have flawed software on their servers that allows the fraudsters to hack in and change those addresses.

According to the Ponemon Institute's 2014 Cost of a Data Breach Study, the average cost of a breach to a company was $3.5 million (Ponemon, 2014). Moreover, brand damage can be significant, albeit hard to quantify. In addition to the data breaches described in the opening and ending case studies for this chapter, Table 8.3 describes other major data breaches.

The U.S. Congress addressed the threat of computer crime in 1986 with the Computer Fraud and Abuse Act, which makes it illegal to access a computer system without authorization. Most states have similar laws, and nations in Europe have comparable legislation. Congress passed the National Information Infrastructure Protection Act in 1996 to make malware distribution and hacker attacks to disable websites federal crimes.

U.S. legislation, such as the Wiretap Act, Wire Fraud Act, Economic Espionage Act, Electronic Communications Privacy Act, CAN-SPAM Act, and Protect Act of 2003 (prohibiting child pornograpy), covers computer crimes involving intercepting electronic communication, using electronic communication to defraud, stealing trade secrets, illegally accessing stored electronic communications, using email for threats

TABLE 8.3

Major Data Breaches

Data breach	Description
Home Depot	Hacked in 2014 with a malicious software program that plundered store registers while disguising itself as antivirus software. 56 million credit-card accounts were compromised, and 53 million customer email addresses were stolen.
eBay	Cyberattack on eBay servers during February and March 2014 compromised database containing customer names, encrypted passwords, email addresses, physical addresses, phone numbers, and birthdates. 145 million people were affected.
Heartland Payment Systems	In 2008, criminals led by Miami hacker Albert Gonzales installed spying software on the computer network of Heartland Payment Systems, a payment processor based in Princeton, NJ, and stole the numbers of as many as 100 million credit and debit cards. Gonzales was sentenced in 2010 to 20 years in federal prison, and Heartland paid about $140 million in fines and settlements.
TJX	A 2007 data breach at TJX, the retailer that owns national chains, including TJ Maxx and Marshalls, cost at least $250 million. Cyber criminals took more than 45 million credit and debit card numbers, some of which were used later to buy millions of dollars in electronics from Walmart and elsewhere. Albert Gonzales, who played a major role in the Heartland hack, was linked to this cyberattack as well.
Sony	In April 2011, hackers obtained personal information, including credit, debit, and bank account numbers, from more than 100 million PlayStation Network users and Sony Online Entertainment users. The breach could cost Sony and credit card issuers up to a total of $2 billion.

or harassment, and transmitting or possessing child pornography. A proposed federal Data Security and Breach Notification Act would mandate organizations that possess personal information to put in place "reasonable" security procedures to keep the data secure and notify anyone affected by a data breach, but it has not been enacted.

Click Fraud

When you click an ad displayed by a search engine, the advertiser typically pays a fee for each click, which is supposed to direct potential buyers to its products. **Click fraud** occurs when an individual or computer program fraudulently clicks an online ad without any intention of learning more about the advertiser or making a purchase. Click fraud has become a serious problem at Google and other websites that feature pay-per-click online advertising.

Some companies hire third parties (typically from low-wage countries) to click a competitor's ads fraudulently to weaken them by driving up their marketing costs. Click fraud can also be perpetrated with software programs doing the clicking, and botnets are often used for this purpose. Search engines such as Google attempt to monitor click fraud and have made some changes to curb it.

Global Threats: Cyberterrorism and Cyberwarfare

The cyber criminal activities we have described—launching malware, DOS attacks, and phishing probes—are borderless. Attack servers for malware are now hosted in more than 200 countries and territories. The most popular sources of malware attacks are the United States, India, Germany, South Korea, China, Netherlands, United Kingdom, and Russia. The global nature of the Internet makes it possible for cybercriminals to operate—and to do harm—anywhere in the world.

Internet vulnerabilities have also turned individuals and even entire nation-states into easy targets for politically motivated hacking to conduct sabotage and espionage.

Cyberwarfare is a state-sponsored activity designed to cripple and defeat another state or nation by penetrating its computers or networks to cause damage and disruption.

Cyberwarfare is more complex than conventional warfare. Although many potential targets are military, a country's power grids, financial systems, and communications networks can also be crippled. Non-state actors such as terrorists or criminal groups can mount attacks, and it is often difficult to tell who is responsible. Nations must constantly be on the alert for new malware and other technologies that could be used against them, and some of these technologies developed by skilled hacker groups are openly for sale to interested governments.

In general, cyberwarfare attacks have become much more widespread, sophisticated, and potentially devastating. There are 250,000 probes trying to find their way into the U.S. Department of Defense networks every hour, and cyberattacks on U.S. federal agencies have increased 150 percent since 2008. Over the years, hackers have stolen plans for missile tracking systems, satellite navigation devices, surveillance drones, and leading-edge jet fighters.

Cyberwarfare poses a serious threat to the infrastructure of modern societies, since their major financial, health, government, and industrial institutions rely on the Internet for daily operations. Cyberwarfare also involves defending against these types of attacks.

INTERNAL THREATS: EMPLOYEES

We tend to think the security threats to a business originate outside the organization. In fact, company insiders pose serious security problems. Employees have access to privileged information, and in the presence of sloppy internal security procedures, they are often able to roam throughout an organization's systems without leaving a trace.

Studies have found that user lack of knowledge is the single greatest cause of network security breaches. Many employees forget their passwords to access computer systems or allow co-workers to use them, which compromises the system. Malicious intruders seeking system access sometimes trick employees into revealing their passwords by pretending to be legitimate members of the company in need of information. This practice is called **social engineering**.

Both end users and information systems specialists are also a major source of errors introduced into information systems. End users introduce errors by entering faulty data or by not following the proper instructions for processing data and using computer equipment. Information systems specialists may create software errors as they design and develop new software or maintain existing programs.

SOFTWARE VULNERABILITY

Software errors pose a constant threat to information systems, causing untold losses in productivity and sometimes endangering people who use or depend on systems. Growing complexity and size of software programs, coupled with demands for timely delivery to markets, have contributed to an increase in software flaws or vulnerabilities. On April 29, 2015, American Airlines had to delay 40 flights due to faulty software on iPads pilots use to look at airport maps and navigational documents. The problem was fixed by having the pilots delete the malfunctioning app and reinstall it (Bajaj, 2015).

A major problem with software is the presence of hidden **bugs** or program code defects. Studies have shown that it is virtually impossible to eliminate all bugs from large programs. The main source of bugs is the complexity of decision-making code. A relatively small program of several hundred lines will contain tens of decisions leading to hundreds or even thousands of paths. Important programs within most corporations are usually much larger, containing tens of thousands or even millions of lines of code, each with many times the choices and paths of the smaller programs.

Zero defects cannot be achieved in larger programs. Complete testing simply is not possible. Fully testing programs that contain thousands of choices and millions of paths would require thousands of years. Even with rigorous testing, you would not know for sure that a piece of software was dependable until the product proved itself after much operational use.

Flaws in commercial software not only impede performance but also create security vulnerabilities that open networks to intruders. Each year security firms identify thousands of software vulnerabilities in Internet and PC software. A recent example is the Heartbleed bug, which is a flaw in OpenSSL, an open-source encryption technology that an estimated two-thirds of web servers use. Hackers could exploit the bug to access visitors' personal data as well as a site's encryption keys, which can be used to collect even more protected data.

Especially troublesome are **zero-day vulnerabilities**, which are holes in the software unknown to its creator. Hackers then exploit this security hole before the vendor becomes aware of the problem and hurries to fix it. This type of vulnerability is called zero day because the author of the software has zero days after learning about it to patch the code before it can be exploited in an attack. Sometimes security researchers spot the software holes but, more often, they remain undetected until an attack has occurred. A zero-day vulnerability played a role in the late-2014 hack at Sony Pictures Entertainment described in the chapter-ending case.

To correct software flaws once they are identified, the software vendor creates small pieces of software called **patches** to repair the flaws without disturbing the proper operation of the software. It is up to users of the software to track these vulnerabilities, test, and apply all patches. This process is called *patch management*.

Because a company's IT infrastructure is typically laden with multiple business applications, operating system installations, and other system services, maintaining patches on all devices and services a company uses is often time-consuming and costly. Malware is being created so rapidly that companies have very little time to respond between the time a vulnerability and a patch are announced and the time malicious software appears to exploit the vulnerability.

8-2 What is the business value of security and control?

Many firms are reluctant to spend heavily on security because it is not directly related to sales revenue. However, protecting information systems is so critical to the operation of the business that it deserves a second look.

Companies have very valuable information assets to protect. Systems often house confidential information about individuals' taxes, financial assets, medical records, and job performance reviews. They also can contain information on corporate operations, including trade secrets, new product development plans, and marketing strategies. Government systems may store information on weapons systems, intelligence operations, and military targets. These information assets have tremendous value, and the repercussions can be devastating if they are lost, destroyed, or placed in the wrong hands. Systems that are unable to function because of security breaches, disasters, or malfunctioning technology can have permanent impacts on a company's financial health. Some experts believe that 40 percent of all businesses will not recover from application or data losses that are not repaired within three days.

Inadequate security and control may result in serious legal liability. Businesses must protect not only their own information assets but also those of customers, employees, and business partners. Failure to do so may open the firm to costly litigation for data exposure or theft. An organization can be held liable for needless risk and harm created if the organization fails to take appropriate protective action to prevent loss of confidential information, data corruption, or breach of privacy. For example, the U.S. Federal Trade Commission sued BJ's Wholesale Club for allowing hackers to access its systems and steal credit and debit card data for fraudulent purchases. Banks that issued the cards with the stolen data sought $13 million from BJ's to compensate them for reimbursing card holders for the fraudulent purchases. A sound security and control framework that protects business information assets can thus produce a high return on investment. Strong security and control also increase employee productivity and lower operational costs.

LEGAL AND REGULATORY REQUIREMENTS FOR ELECTRONIC RECORDS MANAGEMENT

U.S. government regulations are forcing companies to take security and control more seriously by mandating the protection of data from abuse, exposure, and unauthorized access. Firms face new legal obligations for the retention and storage of electronic records as well as for privacy protection.

If you work in the health care industry, your firm will need to comply with the Health Insurance Portability and Accountability Act (HIPAA) of 1996. **HIPAA** outlines medical security and privacy rules and procedures for simplifying the administration of health care billing and automating the transfer of health care data between health care providers, payers, and plans. It requires members of the health care industry to retain patient information for six years and ensure the confidentiality of those records. It specifies privacy, security, and electronic transaction standards for health care providers handling patient information, providing penalties for breaches of medical privacy, disclosure of patient records by email, or unauthorized network access.

If you work in a firm providing financial services, your firm will need to comply with the Financial Services Modernization Act of 1999, better known as the **Gramm-Leach-Bliley Act** after its congressional sponsors. This act requires financial institutions to ensure the security and confidentiality of customer data. Data must be stored on a secure medium, and special security measures must be enforced to protect such data on storage media and during transmittal.

If you work in a publicly traded company, your company will need to comply with the Public Company Accounting Reform and Investor Protection Act of 2002, better known as the **Sarbanes-Oxley Act** after its sponsors Senator Paul Sarbanes of Maryland and Representative Michael Oxley of Ohio. This act was designed to protect investors after the financial scandals at Enron, WorldCom, and other public companies. It imposes responsibility on companies and their management to safeguard the accuracy and integrity of financial information that is used internally and released externally. One of the Learning Tracks for this chapter discusses Sarbanes-Oxley in detail.

Sarbanes-Oxley is fundamentally about ensuring that internal controls are in place to govern the creation and documentation of information in financial statements. Because information systems are used to generate, store, and transport such data, the legislation requires firms to consider information systems security and other controls required to ensure the integrity, confidentiality, and accuracy of their data. Each system application that deals with critical financial reporting data requires controls to make sure the data are accurate. Controls to secure the corporate network, prevent unauthorized access to systems and data, and ensure data integrity and availability in the event of disaster or other disruption of service are essential as well.

ELECTRONIC EVIDENCE AND COMPUTER FORENSICS

Security, control, and electronic records management have become essential for responding to legal actions. Much of the evidence today for stock fraud, embezzlement, theft of company trade secrets, computer crime, and many civil cases is in digital form. In addition to information from printed or typewritten pages, legal cases today increasingly rely on evidence represented as digital data stored on portable storage devices, CDs, and computer hard disk drives as well as in email, instant messages, and e-commerce transactions over the Internet. Email is currently the most common type of electronic evidence.

In a legal action, a firm is obligated to respond to a discovery request for access to information that may be used as evidence, and the company is required by law to produce those data. The cost of responding to a discovery request can be enormous if the company has trouble assembling the required data or the data have been corrupted or destroyed. Courts now impose severe financial and even criminal penalties for improper destruction of electronic documents.

An effective electronic document retention policy ensures that electronic documents, email, and other records are well organized, accessible, and neither retained too long nor discarded too soon. It also reflects an awareness of how to preserve potential evidence for computer forensics. **Computer forensics** is the scientific collection, examination, authentication, preservation, and analysis of data held on or retrieved from computer storage media in such a way that the information can be used as evidence in a court of law. It deals with the following problems.

- Recovering data from computers while preserving evidential integrity
- Securely storing and handling recovered electronic data
- Finding significant information in a large volume of electronic data
- Presenting the information to a court of law

Electronic evidence may reside on computer storage media in the form of computer files and as *ambient data*, which are not visible to the average user. An example might be a file that has been deleted on a PC hard drive. Data that a computer user may have deleted on computer storage media can often be recovered through various techniques. Computer forensics experts try to recover such hidden data for presentation as evidence.

An awareness of computer forensics should be incorporated into a firm's contingency planning process. The CIO, security specialists, information systems staff, and corporate legal counsel should all work together to have a plan in place that can be executed if a legal need arises. You can find out more about computer forensics in the Learning Tracks for this chapter.

8-3 What are the components of an organizational framework for security and control?

Even with the best security tools, your information systems won't be reliable and secure unless you know how and where to deploy them. You'll need to know where your company is at risk and what controls you must have in place to protect your information systems. You'll also need to develop a security policy and plans for keeping your business running if your information systems aren't operational.

INFORMATION SYSTEMS CONTROLS

Information systems controls are both manual and automated and consist of general and application controls. **General controls** govern the design, security, and use of computer programs and the security of data files in general throughout the organization's information technology infrastructure. On the whole, general controls apply to all computerized applications and consist of a combination of hardware, software, and manual procedures that create an overall control environment.

General controls include software controls, physical hardware controls, computer operations controls, data security controls, controls over the systems development process, and administrative controls. Table 8.4 describes the functions of each of these controls.

Application controls are specific controls unique to each computerized application, such as payroll or order processing. They include both automated and manual procedures that ensure that only authorized data are completely and accurately

TABLE 8.4

General Controls

Type of general control	Description
Software controls	Monitor the use of system software and prevent unauthorized access and use of software programs, system software, and computer programs.
Hardware controls	Ensure that computer hardware is physically secure and check for equipment malfunction. Organizations that are critically dependent on their computers also must make provisions for backup or continued operation to maintain constant service.
Computer operations controls	Oversee the work of the computer department to ensure that programmed procedures are consistently and correctly applied to the storage and processing of data. They include controls over the setup of computer processing jobs and backup and recovery procedures for processing that ends abnormally.
Data security controls	Ensure that valuable business data files maintained internally or by an external hosting service are not subject to unauthorized access, change, or destruction while they are in use or in storage.
Implementation controls	Audit the systems development process at various points to ensure that the process is properly controlled and managed.
Administrative controls	Formalize standards, rules, procedures, and control disciplines to ensure that the organization's general and application controls are properly executed and enforced.

processed by that application. Application controls can be classified as (1) input controls, (2) processing controls, and (3) output controls.

Input controls check data for accuracy and completeness when they enter the system. There are specific input controls for input authorization, data conversion, data editing, and error handling. *Processing controls* establish that data are complete and accurate during updating. *Output controls ensure* that the results of computer processing are accurate, complete, and properly distributed. You can find more detail about application and general controls in our Learning Tracks.

Information systems controls should not be an afterthought. They need to be incorporated into the design of a system and should consider not only how the system will perform under all possible conditions but also the behavior of organizations and people using the system.

RISK ASSESSMENT

Before your company commits resources to security and information systems controls, it must know which assets require protection and the extent to which these assets are vulnerable. A risk assessment helps answer these questions and determine the most cost-effective set of controls for protecting assets.

A **risk assessment** determines the level of risk to the firm if a specific activity or process is not properly controlled. Not all risks can be anticipated and measured, but most businesses will be able to acquire some understanding of the risks they face. Business managers working with information systems specialists should try to determine the value of information assets, points of vulnerability, the likely frequency of a problem, and the potential for damage. For example, if an event is likely to occur no more than once a year, with a maximum of a $1000 loss to the organization, it is not wise to spend $20,000 on the design and maintenance of a control to protect against that event. However, if that same event could occur at least once a day, with a potential loss of more than $300,000 a year, $100,000 spent on a control might be entirely appropriate.

INTERACTIVE SESSION: PEOPLE   Stuxnet and the Changing Face of Cyberwarfare

In July 2010, reports surfaced about a Stuxnet worm that had been targeting Iran's nuclear facilities. In November of that year, Iran's President Mahmoud Ahmadinejad publicly acknowledged that malicious software had infected Iranian nuclear facilities and disrupted the nuclear program by disabling the facilities' centrifuges. Stuxnet had earned its place in history as the first visible example of industrial cyberwarfare.

To date, Stuxnet is the most sophisticated cyberweapon ever deployed. Stuxnet's mission was to activate only computers that ran Supervisory Control and Data Acquisition (SCADA) software used in Siemens centrifuges to enrich uranium. The Windows-based worm had a "dual warhead." One part was designed to lay dormant for long periods, then speed up Iran's nuclear centrifuges so that they spun wildly out of control. Another secretly recorded what normal operations at the nuclear plant looked like and then played those recordings back to plant operators so it would appear that the centrifuges were operating normally when they were actually tearing themselves apart.

The worm's sophistication indicated the work of highly skilled professionals. Michael Assante, president and CEO at the National Board of Information Security Examiners, views Stuxnet as a weapons delivery system like the B-2 Bomber. The software program code was highly modular, so that it could be easily changed to attack different systems. Stuxnet only became active when it encountered a specific configuration of controllers, running a set of processes limited to centrifuge plants.

Over 60 percent of Stuxet-infected computers are in Iran, and digital security company Kaspersky Labs speculates that the worm was launched with nation-state support (probably from Israel and the United States) with the intention of disabling some or all of Iran's uranium enrichment program. Stuxnet wiped out about one-fifth of Iran's nuclear centrifuges by causing them to spin at too high a velocity. The damage was irreparable and is believed to have delayed Iran's ability to make nuclear arms by as much as five years. And no one is certain that the Stuxnet attacks are over. Some experts who examined the Stuxnet software code believe it contains the seeds for more versions and attacks.

According to a Tofino Security report, Stuxnet is capable of infecting even well-secured computer systems that follow industry best practices. Companies' need for interconnectivity between control systems make it nearly impossible to defend against a well-constructed, multi-pronged attack such as Stuxnet. In 2015 Kapersky's own systems were invaded by a Stuxnet derivative, which operated without detection for six months. The same malware was found on systems of diplomats involved in the negotiations with Iran over its nuclear program.

And Stuxnet is not the only cyberweapon currently at work. The Flame virus, released about five years ago, has been infecting computers in Iran, Lebanon, Sudan, Saudi Arabia, Egypt, Syria, and Israel. While researchers are still analyzing the program, the attack's main goal is espionage and information theft. Flame is able to grab images of users' computer screens, record their instant messaging chats, collect passwords, remotely turn on their microphones to record audio conversations, scan disks for specific files, and monitor their keystrokes and network traffic. The software also records Skype conversations and can turn infected computers into Bluetooth beacons that attempt to download contact information from nearby Bluetooth-enabled devices. These data, along with locally stored documents, can be sent to one of several command and control servers that are scattered around the world. The program then awaits further instructions from these servers.

Many fear the real significance of Stuxnet was that it created the foundation for many derivative malware clones and that it enlarged the universe of machines that could be destroyed. For instance, researchers have used Stuxnet-like code to corrupt the computer systems in automobiles and turn off safety devices like airbags and engine alarms.

But the more pressing worry for security experts and government officials is an act of cyberwarfare against a critical resource, such as the electric grid, financial systems, or communications systems. (In April 2009, for example, cyberspies infiltrated the U.S. electrical grid, using weak points where computers on the grid are connected to the Internet, and left behind software programs whose purpose is unclear, but which presumably could be used to disrupt the system.)

The United States has no clear strategy about how the country would respond to that level of cyberattack, and the effects of such an attack would likely be devastating. Mike McConnell, the former director of national intelligence, stated that if even a single large American bank were successfully attacked, it would have an order-of-magnitude greater impact on the global economy than the World Trade Center attacks, and that the ability to threaten the U.S.

money supply is the financial equivalent of a nuclear weapon.

Many security experts believe that U.S. cyber-security is not well-organized. Several different agencies, including the Pentagon and the National Security Agency (NSA), have their sights on being the leading agency in the ongoing efforts to combat cyberwarfare. The first headquarters designed to coordinate government cybersecurity efforts, called Cybercom, was activated in May 2010 in the hope of resolving this organizational tangle. In May 2011 President Barack Obama signed executive orders weaving cyber capabilities into U.S. military strategy, but these capabilities are still evolving.

In 2014, a virus similar to Stuxnet called Energetic Bear was found to have attacked energy companies in the United States and Europe, lending credence to fears the the energy grid is vulnerable to these kinds of attacks. It's one thing to develop a next-generation computer virus, but another one to develop methods of defending established computer systems from them. Will the United States and other nations be ready when the next Stuxnet appears?

Sources: "Hacking Cars in the Style of Stuxnet," CrySys Blog, October 28, 2015; Kim Zetter, "The U.S. Tried to Stuxnet North Korea's Nuclear Program," *Wired Magazine*, May 29, 2015; Michael Kenney, "Cyber-Terrorism in a Post-Stuxnet World," Foreign Policy Research Institute, Orbis, Winter 2015; Michael B. Kelley, "A Stuxnet-Like Virus Has Infected Hundreds of U.S. and European Energy Companies," Businessinsider.com, July 1, 2014; Brian Royer, "Stuxnet, the Nation's Power Grid, and the Law of Unintended Consequences," *Dark Reading*, March 12, 2012; Thomas Erdbrink, "Iran Confirms Attack by Virus That Collects Information," *New York Times*, May 29, 2012; Nicole Perlroth, "Virus Infects Computers Across Middle East," *New York Times*, May 28, 2012; Robert Leos, "Secure Best Practices No Proof Against Stuxnet," CSO, March 3, 2011; Lolita C. Baldor, "Pentagon Gets Cyberwar Guidelines," Associated Press, June 22, 2011; William J. Broad, John Markoff, and David E. Sanger, "Israel Tests on Worm Called Crucial in Iran Nuclear Delay," *New York Times*, January 15, 2011.

CASE STUDY QUESTIONS

1. Is cyberwarfare a serious problem? Why or why not?

2. Assess the people, organization, and technology factors that have created this problem.

3. What makes Stuxnet different from other cyberwarfare attacks? How serious a threat is this technology?

4. What solutions have been proposed for this problem? Do you think they will be effective? Why or why not?

Table 8.5 illustrates sample results of a risk assessment for an online order processing system that processes 30,000 orders per day. The likelihood of each exposure occurring over a one-year period is expressed as a percentage. The next column shows the highest and lowest possible loss that could be expected each time the exposure occurred and an average loss calculated by adding the highest and lowest figures and dividing by two. The expected annual loss for each exposure can be determined by multiplying the average loss by its probability of occurrence.

This risk assessment shows that the probability of a power failure occurring in a one-year period is 30 percent. Loss of order transactions while power is down could range from $5000 to $200,000 (averaging $102,500) for each occurrence, depending on how long processing is halted. The probability of embezzlement occurring over a yearly period is about 5 percent, with potential losses ranging from $1000 to $50,000 (and averaging $25,500) for each occurrence. User errors have a 98 percent chance of occurring over a yearly period, with losses ranging from $200 to $40,000 (and averaging $20,100) for each occurrence.

After the risks have been assessed, system builders will concentrate on the control points with the greatest vulnerability and potential for loss. In this case, controls should focus on ways to minimize the risk of power failures and user errors because anticipated annual losses are highest for these areas.

Exposure	Probability of Occurrence (%)	Loss Range/ Average ($)	Expected Annual Loss ($)
Power failure	30%	$5000–$200,000 ($102,500)	$30,750
Embezzlement	5%	$1000–$50,000 ($25,500)	$1275
User error	98%	$200–$40,000 ($20,100)	$19,698

TABLE 8.5

Online Order Processing Risk Assessment

SECURITY POLICY

After you've identified the main risks to your systems, your company will need to develop a security policy for protecting the company's assets. A **security policy** consists of statements ranking information risks, identifying acceptable security goals, and identifying the mechanisms for achieving these goals. What are the firm's most important information assets? Who generates and controls this information in the firm? What existing security policies are in place to protect the information? What level of risk is management willing to accept for each of these assets? Is it willing, for instance, to lose customer credit data once every 10 years? Or will it build a security system for credit card data that can withstand the once-in-a-hundred-year disaster? Management must estimate how much it will cost to achieve this level of acceptable risk.

The security policy drives other policies determining acceptable use of the firm's information resources and which members of the company have access to its information assets. An **acceptable use policy (AUP)** defines acceptable uses of the firm's information resources and computing equipment, including desktop and laptop computers, wireless devices, telephones, and the Internet. A good AUP defines unacceptable and acceptable actions for every user and specifies consequences for noncompliance. For example, security policy at Unilever, the giant multinational consumer goods company, requires every employee to use a company-specified device and employ a password or other method of identification when logging on to the corporate network.

Security policy also includes provisions for identity management. **Identity management** consists of business processes and software tools for identifying the valid users of a system and controlling their access to system resources. It includes policies for identifying and authorizing different categories of system users, specifying what systems or portions of systems each user is allowed to access, and the processes and technologies for authenticating users and protecting their identities.

Figure 8.3 is one example of how an identity management system might capture the access rules for different levels of users in the human resources function. It specifies what portions of a human resource database each user is permitted to access, based on the information required to perform that person's job. The database contains sensitive personal information such as employees' salaries, benefits, and medical histories.

The access rules illustrated here are for two sets of users. One set of users consists of all employees who perform clerical functions, such as inputting employee data into the system. All individuals with this type of profile can update the system but can neither read nor update sensitive fields, such as salary, medical history, or earnings data. Another profile applies to a divisional manager, who cannot update the system but who can read all employee data fields for his or her division, including medical history and salary. We provide more detail about the technologies for user authentication later on in this chapter.

DISASTER RECOVERY PLANNING AND BUSINESS

Figure 8.3
Access Rules for a
Personnel System
*These two examples
represent two security
profiles or data security
patterns that might be
found in a personnel
system. Depending on
the security profile, a
user would have certain
restrictions on access to
various systems, locations,
or data in an organization.*

SECURITY PROFILE 1

User: Personnel Dept. Clerk

Location: Division 1

Employee Identification
Codes with This Profile: 00753, 27834, 37665, 44116

Data Field Restrictions	Type of Access
All employee data for Division 1 only	Read and Update
• Medical history data	None
• Salary	None
• Pensionable earnings	None

SECURITY PROFILE 2

User: Divisional Personnel Manager

Location: Division 1

Employee Identification
Codes with This Profile: 27321

Data Field Restrictions	Type of Access
All employee data for Division 1 only	Read Only

CONTINUITY PLANNING

If you run a business, you need to plan for events, such as power outages, floods, earthquakes, or terrorist attacks, that will prevent your information systems and your business from operating. **Disaster recovery planning** devises plans for the restoration of disrupted computing and communications services. Disaster recovery plans focus primarily on the technical issues involved in keeping systems up and running, such as which files to back up and the maintenance of backup computer systems or disaster recovery services.

For example, MasterCard maintains a duplicate computer center in Kansas City, Missouri, to serve as an emergency backup to its primary computer center in St. Louis. Rather than build their own backup facilities, many firms contract with disaster recovery firms such as Comdisco Disaster Recovery Services and SunGard Availability Services. These disaster recovery firms provide hot sites housing spare computers at locations around the country where subscribing firms can run their critical applications in an emergency. For example, Champion Technologies, which supplies chemicals used in oil and gas operations, can switch its enterprise systems from Houston to a SunGard data center in Scottsdale, Arizona, in two hours.

Business continuity planning focuses on how the company can restore business operations after a disaster strikes. The business continuity plan identifies critical business processes and determines action plans for handling mission-critical functions if systems go down. For example, Deutsche Bank, which provides investment banking and asset management services in 74 countries, has a well-developed business continuity plan that it continually updates and refines. It maintains full-time teams in Singapore, Hong Kong, Japan, India, and Australia to coordinate plans addressing loss of facilities, personnel, or critical systems so that the company can continue to operate when a catastrophic event occurs. Deutsche Bank's plan distinguishes between processes critical for business survival and those critical to crisis support and is coordinated with the company's disaster recovery planning for its computer centers.

Business managers and information technology specialists need to work together on both types of plans to determine which systems and business processes are most critical to the company. They must conduct a business impact analysis to identify the firm's most critical systems and the impact a systems outage would have on the business. Management must determine the maximum amount of time the business can survive with its systems down and which parts of the business must be restored first.

THE ROLE OF AUDITING

How does management know that information systems security and controls are effective? To answer this question, organizations must conduct comprehensive and systematic audits. An **information systems audit** examines the firm's overall security environment as well as controls governing individual information systems. The auditor should trace the flow of sample transactions through the system and perform tests, using, if appropriate, automated audit software. The information systems audit may also examine data quality.

Security audits review technologies, procedures, documentation, training, and personnel. A thorough audit will even simulate an attack or disaster to test the response of the technology, information systems staff, and business employees.

The audit lists and ranks all control weaknesses and estimates the probability of their occurrence. It then assesses the financial and organizational impact of each threat. Figure 8.4 is a sample auditor's listing of control weaknesses for a loan system. It includes a section for notifying management of such weaknesses and for management's response. Management is expected to devise a plan for countering significant weaknesses in controls.

8-4 What are the most important tools and technologies for safeguarding information resources?

Businesses have an array of technologies for protecting their information resources. They include tools for managing user identities, preventing unauthorized access to systems and data, ensuring system availability, and ensuring software quality.

Function: Loans Location: Peoria, IL		Prepared by: J. Ericson Date: June 16, 2015		Received by: T. Benson Review date: June 28, 2015	
Nature of Weakness and Impact	Chance for Error/Abuse		Notification to Management		
	Yes/No	Justification	Report date	Management response	
User accounts with missing passwords	Yes	Leaves system open to unauthorized outsiders or attackers	5/10/15	Eliminate accounts without passwords	
Network configured to allow some sharing of system files	Yes	Exposes critical system files to hostile parties connected to the network	5/10/15	Ensure only required directories are shared and that they are protected with strong passwords	
Software patches can update production programs without final approval from Standards and Controls group	No	All production programs require management approval; Standards and Controls group assigns such cases to a temporary production status			

Figure 8.4
Sample Auditor's List of Control Weaknesses
This chart is a sample page from a list of control weaknesses that an auditor might find in a loan system in a local commercial bank. This form helps auditors record and evaluate control weaknesses and shows the results of discussing those weaknesses with management as well as any corrective actions management takes.

IDENTITY MANAGEMENT AND AUTHENTICATION

Midsize and large companies have complex IT infrastructures and many systems, each with its own set of users. Identity management software automates the process of keeping track of all these users and their system privileges, assigning each user a unique digital identity for accessing each system. It also includes tools for authenticating users, protecting user identities, and controlling access to system resources.

To gain access to a system, a user must be authorized and authenticated. **Authentication** refers to the ability to know that a person is who he or she claims to be. Authentication is often established by using **passwords** known only to authorized users. An end user uses a password to log on to a computer system and may also use passwords for accessing specific systems and files. However, users often forget passwords, share them, or choose poor passwords that are easy to guess, which compromises security. Password systems that are too rigorous hinder employee productivity. When employees must change complex passwords frequently, they often take shortcuts, such as choosing passwords that are easy to guess or keeping their passwords at their workstations in plain view. Passwords can also be sniffed if transmitted over a network or stolen through social engineering.

New authentication technologies, such as tokens, smart cards, and biometric authentication, overcome some of these problems. A **token** is a physical device, similar to an identification card, that is designed to prove the identity of a single user. Tokens are small gadgets that typically fit on key rings and display passcodes that change frequently. A **smart card** is a device about the size of a credit card that contains a chip formatted with access permission and other data. (Smart cards are also used in electronic payment systems.) A reader device interprets the data on the smart card and allows or denies access.

Biometric authentication uses systems that read and interpret individual human traits, such as fingerprints, irises, and voices to grant or deny access. Biometric authentication is based on the measurement of a physical or behavioral trait that makes each individual unique. It compares a person's unique characteristics, such as the fingerprints, face, or retinal image, against a stored profile of these characteristics to determine any differences between these characteristics and the stored profile. If the two profiles match, access is granted. Fingerprint and facial recognition

This smartphone has a biometric fingerprint reader for fast yet secure access to files and networks. New models of PCs and smartphones are starting to use biometric identification to authenticate users.

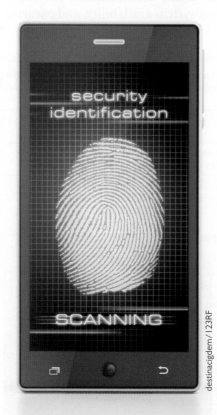

destinacigdem/123RF

technologies are just beginning to be used for security applications, with many PC laptops (and some smartphones) equipped with fingerprint identification devices and several models with built-in webcams and face recognition software.

The steady stream of incidents in which hackers have been able to access traditional passwords highlights the need for more secure means of authentication. **Two-factor authentication** increases security by validating users through a multistep process. To be authenticated, a user must provide two means of identification, one of which is typically a physical token, such as a smartcard or chip-enabled bank card, and the other of which is typically data, such as a password or personal identification number (PIN). Biometric data, such as fingerprints, iris prints, or voice prints, can also be used as one of the authenticating mechanisms. A common example of two-factor authentication is a bank card; the card itself is the physical item, and the PIN is the data that go with it.

FIREWALLS, INTRUSION DETECTION SYSTEMS, AND ANTIVIRUS SOFTWARE

Without protection against malware and intruders, connecting to the Internet would be very dangerous. Firewalls, intrusion detection systems, and antivirus software have become essential business tools.

Firewalls

Firewalls prevent unauthorized users from accessing private networks. A firewall is a combination of hardware and software that controls the flow of incoming and outgoing network traffic. It is generally placed between the organization's private internal networks and distrusted external networks, such as the Internet, although firewalls can also be used to protect one part of a company's network from the rest of the network (see Figure 8.5).

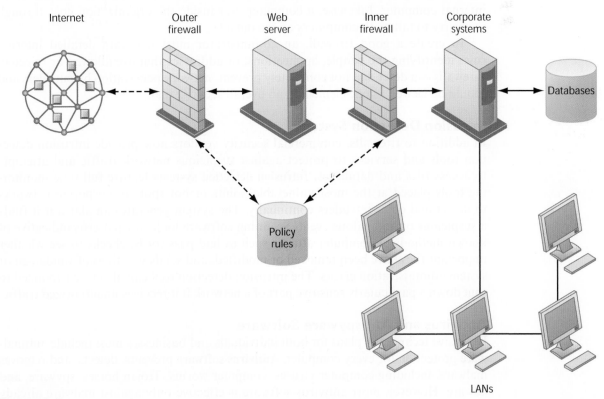

Figure 8.5

A Corporate Firewall

The firewall is placed between the firm's private network and the public Internet or another distrusted network to protect against unauthorized traffic.

The firewall acts like a gatekeeper that examines each user's credentials before it grants access to a network. The firewall identifies names, IP addresses, applications, and other characteristics of incoming traffic. It checks this information against the access rules that the network administrator has programmed into the system. The firewall prevents unauthorized communication into and out of the network.

In large organizations, the firewall often resides on a specially designated computer separate from the rest of the network, so no incoming request directly accesses private network resources. There are a number of firewall screening technologies, including static packet filtering, stateful inspection, Network Address Translation, and application proxy filtering. They are frequently used in combination to provide firewall protection.

Packet filtering examines selected fields in the headers of data packets flowing back and forth between the trusted network and the Internet, examining individual packets in isolation. This filtering technology can miss many types of attacks.

Stateful inspection provides additional security by determining whether packets are part of an ongoing dialogue between a sender and a receiver. It sets up state tables to track information over multiple packets. Packets are accepted or rejected based on whether they are part of an approved conversation or attempting to establish a legitimate connection.

Network Address Translation (NAT) can provide another layer of protection when static packet filtering and stateful inspection are employed. NAT conceals the IP addresses of the organization's internal host computer(s) to prevent sniffer programs outside the firewall from ascertaining them and using that information to penetrate internal systems.

Application proxy filtering examines the application content of packets. A proxy server stops data packets originating outside the organization, inspects them, and passes a proxy to the other side of the firewall. If a user outside the company wants to communicate with a user inside the organization, the outside user first communicates with the proxy application, and the proxy application communicates with the firm's internal computer. Likewise, a computer user inside the organization goes through the proxy to talk with computers on the outside.

To create a good firewall, an administrator must maintain detailed internal rules identifying the people, applications, or addresses that are allowed or rejected. Firewalls can deter, but not completely prevent, network penetration by outsiders and should be viewed as one element in an overall security plan.

Intrusion Detection Systems

In addition to firewalls, commercial security vendors now provide intrusion detection tools and services to protect against suspicious network traffic and attempts to access files and databases. **Intrusion detection systems** feature full-time monitoring tools placed at the most vulnerable points or hot spots of corporate networks to detect and deter intruders continually. The system generates an alarm if it finds a suspicious or anomalous event. Scanning software looks for patterns indicative of known methods of computer attacks such as bad passwords, checks to see whether important files have been removed or modified, and sends warnings of vandalism or system administration errors. The intrusion detection tool can also be customized to shut down a particularly sensitive part of a network if it receives unauthorized traffic.

Antivirus and Antispyware Software

Defensive technology plans for both individuals and businesses must include antimalware protection for every computer. **Antivirus software** prevents, detects, and removes malware, including computer viruses, computer worms, Trojan horses, spyware, and adware. However, most antivirus software is effective only against malware already known when the software was written. To remain effective, the antivirus software must be continually updated. Even then it is not always effective because some malware can evade antivirus detection. Organizations need to use additional malware detection tools for better protection.

Unified Threat Management Systems

To help businesses reduce costs and improve manageability, security vendors have combined into a single appliance various security tools, including firewalls, virtual private networks, intrusion detection systems, and web content filtering and anti-spam software. These comprehensive security management products are called **unified threat management (UTM)** systems. UTM products are available for all sizes of networks. Leading UTM vendors include Fortinet, Sophos, and Check Point, and networking vendors such as Cisco Systems and Juniper Networks provide some UTM capabilities in their products.

SECURING WIRELESS NETWORKS

The initial security standard developed for Wi-Fi, called Wired Equivalent Privacy (WEP), is not very effective because its encryption keys are relatively easy to crack. WEP provides some margin of security, however, if users remember to enable it. Corporations can further improve Wi-Fi security by using it in conjunction with virtual private network (VPN) technology when accessing internal corporate data.

In June 2004, the Wi-Fi Alliance industry trade group finalized the 802.11i specification (also referred to as Wi-Fi Protected Access 2 or WPA2) that replaces WEP with stronger security standards. Instead of the static encryption keys used in WEP, the new standard uses much longer keys that continually change, making them harder to crack.

ENCRYPTION AND PUBLIC KEY INFRASTRUCTURE

Many businesses use encryption to protect digital information that they store, physically transfer, or send over the Internet. **Encryption** is the process of transforming plain text or data into cipher text that cannot be read by anyone other than the sender and the intended receiver. Data are encrypted by using a secret numerical code, called an encryption key, that transforms plain data into cipher text. The message must be decrypted by the receiver.

Two methods for encrypting network traffic on the web are SSL and S-HTTP. **Secure Sockets Layer (SSL)** and its successor, Transport Layer Security (TLS), enable client and server computers to manage encryption and decryption activities as they communicate with each other during a secure web session. **Secure Hypertext Transfer Protocol (S-HTTP)** is another protocol used for encrypting data flowing over the Internet, but it is limited to individual messages, whereas SSL and TLS are designed to establish a secure connection between two computers.

The capability to generate secure sessions is built into Internet client browser software and servers. The client and the server negotiate what key and what level of security to use. Once a secure session is established between the client and the server, all messages in that session are encrypted.

Two methods of encryption are symmetric key encryption and public key encryption. In symmetric key encryption, the sender and receiver establish a secure Internet session by creating a single encryption key and sending it to the receiver so both the sender and receiver share the same key. The strength of the encryption key is measured by its bit length. Today, a typical key will be 56 to 256 bits long (a string of 128 binary digits) depending on the level of security desired.

The problem with all symmetric encryption schemes is that the key itself must be shared somehow among the senders and receivers, which exposes the key to outsiders who might just be able to intercept and decrypt the key. A more secure form of encryption called **public key encryption** uses two keys: one shared (or public) and one totally private as shown in Figure 8.6. The keys are mathematically related so that data encrypted with one key can be decrypted using only the other key. To send and receive messages, communicators first create separate pairs of private and public keys. The public key is kept in a directory, and the private key must be kept secret. The sender encrypts a message with the recipient's public key. On receiving the message, the recipient uses his or her private key to decrypt it.

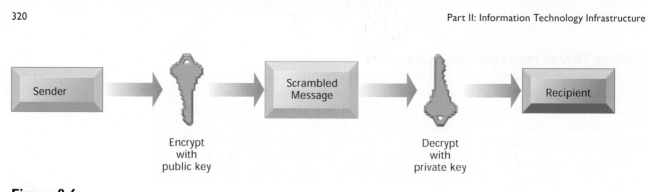

Figure 8.6
Public Key Encryption

A public key encryption system can be viewed as a series of public and private keys that lock data when they are transmitted and unlock the data when they are received. The sender locates the recipient's public key in a directory and uses it to encrypt a message. The message is sent in encrypted form over the Internet or a private network. When the encrypted message arrives, the recipient uses his or her private key to decrypt the data and read the message.

Digital certificates are data files used to establish the identity of users and electronic assets for protection of online transactions (see Figure 8.7). A digital certificate system uses a trusted third party, known as a certificate authority (CA), to validate a user's identity. There are many CAs in the United States and around the world, including Symantec, GoDaddy, and Comodo.

The CA verifies a digital certificate user's identity offline. This information is put into a CA server, which generates an encrypted digital certificate containing owner identification information and a copy of the owner's public key. The certificate authenticates that the public key belongs to the designated owner. The CA makes its own public key available either in print or perhaps on the Internet. The recipient of an encrypted message uses the CA's public key to decode the digital certificate attached to the message, verifies it was issued by the CA, and then obtains the sender's public key and identification information contained in the certificate. By using this information, the recipient can send an encrypted reply. The digital certificate system would enable, for example, a credit card user and a merchant to validate that their digital certificates were issued by an authorized and trusted third party before they exchange data. **Public key infrastructure (PKI)**, the use of public key cryptography working with a CA, is now widely used in e-commerce.

Figure 8.7
Digital Certificates

Digital certificates help establish the identity of people or electronic assets. They protect online transactions by providing secure, encrypted, online communication.

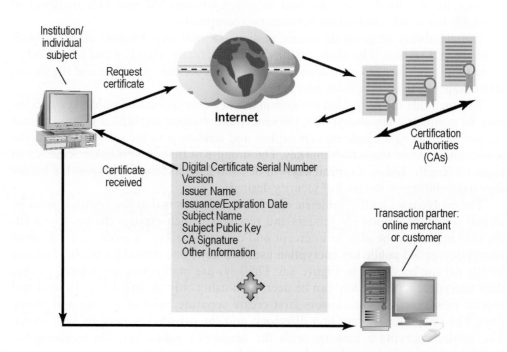

ENSURING SYSTEM AVAILABILITY

As companies increasingly rely on digital networks for revenue and operations, they need to take additional steps to ensure that their systems and applications are always available. Firms such as those in the airline and financial services industries with critical applications requiring online transaction processing have traditionally used fault-tolerant computer systems for many years to ensure 100 percent availability. In **online transaction processing**, transactions entered online are immediately processed by the computer. Multitudinous changes to databases, reporting, and requests for information occur each instant.

Fault-tolerant computer systems contain redundant hardware, software, and power supply components that create an environment that provides continuous, uninterrupted service. Fault-tolerant computers use special software routines or self-checking logic built into their circuitry to detect hardware failures and automatically switch to a backup device. Parts from these computers can be removed and repaired without disruption to the computer or downtime. **Downtime** refers to periods of time in which a system is not operational.

Controlling Network Traffic: Deep Packet Inspection

Have you ever tried to use your campus network and found that it was very slow? It may be because your fellow students are using the network to download music or watch YouTube. Bandwith-consuming applications such as file-sharing programs, Internet phone service, and online video can clog and slow down corporate networks, degrading performance. For example, Ball State University in Muncie, Indiana, found its network had slowed because a small minority of students were using P2P file-sharing programs to download movies and music.

A technology called **deep packet inspection (DPI)** helps solve this problem. DPI examines data files and sorts out low-priority online material while assigning higher priority to business-critical files. Based on the priorities established by a network's operators, it decides whether a specific data packet can continue to its destination or should be blocked or delayed while more important traffic proceeds. Using a DPI system from Allot Communications, Ball State was able to cap the amount of file-sharing traffic and assign it a much lower priority. Ball State's preferred network traffic sped up.

Security Outsourcing

Many companies, especially small businesses, lack the resources or expertise to provide a secure high-availability computing environment on their own. They can outsource many security functions to **managed security service providers (MSSPs)** that monitor network activity and perform vulnerability testing and intrusion detection. SecureWorks, BT Managed Security Solutions Group, and Symantec are leading providers of MSSP services.

SECURITY ISSUES FOR CLOUD COMPUTING AND THE MOBILE DIGITAL PLATFORM

Although cloud computing and the emerging mobile digital platform have the potential to deliver powerful benefits, they pose new challenges to system security and reliability. We now describe some of these challenges and how they should be addressed.

Security in the Cloud

When processing takes place in the cloud, accountability and responsibility for protection of sensitive data still reside with the company owning that data. Understanding how the cloud computing provider organizes its services and manages the data is critical.

Cloud computing is highly distributed. Cloud applications reside in large remote data centers and server farms that supply business services and data management for multiple corporate clients. To save money and keep costs low, cloud computing providers often distribute work to data centers around the globe where work can be accomplished most efficiently. When you use the cloud, you may not know precisely where your data are being hosted.

The dispersed nature of cloud computing makes it difficult to track unauthorized activity. Virtually all cloud providers use encryption, such as SSL, to secure the data they handle while the data are being transmitted. However, if the data are stored on devices that also store other companies' data, it's important to ensure that these stored data are encrypted as well.

Companies expect their systems to be running 24/7, but cloud providers haven't always been able to provide this level of service. On several occasions over the past few years, the cloud services of Amazon.com experienced outages that disrupted business operations for millions of users.

Cloud users need to confirm that regardless of where their data are stored, they are protected at a level that meets their corporate requirements. They should stipulate that the cloud provider store and process data in specific jurisdictions according to the privacy rules of those jurisdictions. Cloud clients should find how the cloud provider segregates their corporate data from those of other companies and ask for proof that encryption mechanisms are sound. It's also important to know how the cloud provider will respond if a disaster strikes, whether the provider will be able to restore your data completely, and how long this should take. Cloud users should also ask whether cloud providers will submit to external audits and security certifications. These kinds of controls can be written into the service level agreement (SLA) before signing with a cloud provider.

Securing Mobile Platforms

If mobile devices are performing many of the functions of computers, they need to be secured like desktops and laptops against malware, theft, accidental loss, unauthorized access, and hacking attempts.

Mobile devices accessing corporate systems and data require special protection. Companies should make sure that their corporate security policy includes mobile devices, with additional details on how mobile devices should be supported, protected, and used. They will need mobile device management tools to authorize all devices in use; to maintain accurate inventory records on all mobile devices, users, and applications; to control updates to applications; and to lock down or erase lost or stolen devices so they can't be compromised. Data loss prevention technology can identify where critical data are saved, who is accessing the data, how data are leaving the company, and where the data are going. Firms should develop guidelines stipulating approved mobile platforms and software applications as well as the required software and procedures for remote access of corporate systems. The organization's mobile security policy should forbid employees from using unsecured, consumer-based applications for transferring and storing corporate documents and files or sending such documents and files to oneself by email without encryption.

Companies should encrypt communication whenever possible. All mobile device users should be required to use the password feature found in every smartphone. Mobile security products are available from Kaspersky, Symantec, Trend Micro, and McAfee.

ENSURING SOFTWARE QUALITY

In addition to implementing effective security and controls, organizations can improve system quality and reliability by employing software metrics and rigorous software testing. Software metrics are objective assessments of the system in the form

INTERACTIVE SESSION: TECHNOLOGY   MWEB Business Hacked

You might think that Internet service providers would be among the least likely business firms to experience extensive security breaches. Think again: ISP hacking happens routinely. MWEB, launched in 1997, became South Africa's leading ISP in 1998. It has established itself as a company that provides cutting-edge network and service infrastructure and outstanding customer service. Currently, MWEB's customer base of 320,000 includes home users; small, medium, and large business customers; and corporate clients. MWEB won the ISP of the Year award at the MyBroadband Conference in Johannesburg in 2010. The award was based on the performance of its various broadband services as well as on customer satisfaction.

Its business division, MWEB Business, was founded in January 1998. MWEB Business prides itself on being a business partner that is perfectly positioned to leverage the power of Web-based technologies in all areas of an organization. MWEB Business helps companies:

- Manage business data in ways that add real value and insight to their operations.
- Integrate existing systems with the Internet so as to close the gap between technology, strategy, and the organization's bottom line.
- Develop, manage, and maintain solutions that include all aspects of Internet connectivity, Web site development and hosting, broadband and wireless applications, e-commerce, and consultancy services.
- Manage internal information among employees as well as among business partners and suppliers.

MWEB has moved forward in publicizing its plans for the South African Internet market. According to MWEB CEO Rudi Jansen, the company needs to improve the quality of their network, which is not only an MWEB problem, but also a Telkom network problem. Despite having a less-than-ideal network infrastructure, MWEB uses AVG Internet Security to offer its customers the best possible security while online. AVG Internet Security offers MWEB customers the following features:

- Identity protection for safe banking and shopping
- LinkScanner for safe surfing and searching
- WebShield for safe social networking, chatting, and downloading

- Antiphishing and antispam for a safe, uncluttered inbox
- High-speed antivirus/antispyware software with automatic updates
- An enhanced firewall

In addition, MWEB automatically protects customers against junk email and viruses that are sent via email. Its virus filter ensures that only virus-free email is delivered to clients' inboxes by automatically cleaning e-mails from recognized malware sources. MWEB advises its customers to keep their ADSL connections safe from bandwidth theft and account abuse by blocking unsolicited incoming connections to network ports commonly used by hackers.

Despite the multitude of security services offered by MWEB, a number of MWEB Business subscribers' account details were compromised when their login and password information was published on the Internet by hackers. Initial reports indicated that as many as 2,390 users of MWEB's business digital subscriber lines were affected. The company disclosed the security breach on October 25, 2010. It appears that hackers gained access to Internet Solutions' self-service management system, which MWEB Business uses to provide and manage business accounts that have not yet been migrated to the MWEB network.

Historically, MWEB Business was a reseller of Internet Solutions' Uncapped & Fixed IP ADSL services, which were provisioned and managed by MWEB using a Web-based management interface provided by Internet Solutions. All new Business ADSL services provided after April 2010, as well as the bulk of legacy services already migrated, used MWEB's internal authentication systems, which were completely unaffected by this incident.

MWEB responded quickly to the hacking incident. According to Jansen, about 1,000 clients on the Internet Solutions network needed to be migrated from the old server that was attacked by hackers. Although the network was quickly secured, most customers had recently been moved to MWEB's IPC network. MWEB also contacted these customers to reset their passwords as an added security measure. Jansen was quick to note that no personal information was lost and that none of MWEB's clients suffered any losses as their usernames and passwords had been recreated and changed. He further added that MWEB successfully repels 5,000 attacks a day.

Andre Joubert, general manager of MWEB Business, emphasized that only ADSL authentication usernames and passwords had been compromised. The integrity of the personal or private data related to the accounts remained intact, as did the access credentials for each customer's bundled onsite router. Joubert did acknowledge the seriousness of the hack, apologizing for any inconvenience the breach may have caused to MWEB's customers. As soon as the breach was identified, MWEB took immediate action to evaluate the extent of the breach and to limit any damage. In MWEB's defense, Jansen said that MWEB constantly advises its customers to be vigilant regarding their online data and security. In addition, MWEB was working closely with Internet Solutions to investigate the nature and source of the breach to ensure that it does not happen again.

The hacking of MWEB involved a small number of subscribers, but in 2015 very large ISPs are suffering massive losses of customer information. In March 2015 TalkTalk, one of the largest ISPs in the United Kingdom, was hacked and the accounts of four million subscribers compromised. Even the routers distributed by ISPs, of which there are hundreds of millions, have been found vulnerable to hackers, allowing them to direct users to rogue servers and Web sites. This includes home and business WiFi routers.

Sources: Paul Sawyers, "U.K. ISP TalkTalk Gets Hacked, the CEO Doesn't Even Know if Data Was Encrypted," Venturebeat.com, October 23, 2015; Lucian Constantin, "At Least 700,000 Routers ISPs Gave to Their Customers Are Vulnerable to Hacking," PC World, March 19, 2015; MWEB, "Hacker Trends 2014: A Frightening Report," January 31, 2014; "About MWEB," MWEB, www.mweb.co.za, accessed November 17, 2010; "Hackers Target MWEB," NewsTime, October 25, 2010, www.newstime.co.za; "MWEB Business Takes Action in 'Hacking' Incident," Moneyweb, October 25, 2010, www.moneyweb.co.za, accessed November 17, 2010.

Case contributed by Upasana Singh, University of KwaZulu-Natal

CASE STUDY QUESTIONS

1. What technology issues led to the security breach at MWEB?

2. What is the possible business impact of this security breach for both MWEB and its customers?

3. If you were an MWEB customer, would you consider MWEB's response to the security breach to be acceptable? Why or why not?

4. What should MWEB do in the future to avoid similar incidents?

of quantified measurements. Ongoing use of metrics allows the information systems department and end users to measure the performance of the system jointly and identify problems as they occur. Examples of software metrics include the number of transactions that can be processed in a specified unit of time, online response time, the number of payroll checks printed per hour, and the number of known bugs per hundred lines of program code. For metrics to be successful, they must be carefully designed, formal, objective, and used consistently.

Early, regular, and thorough testing will contribute significantly to system quality. Many view testing as a way to prove the correctness of work they have done. In fact, we know that all sizable software is riddled with errors, and we must test to uncover these errors.

Good testing begins before a software program is even written, by using a *walkthrough*—a review of a specification or design document by a small group of people carefully selected based on the skills needed for the particular objectives being tested. When developers start writing software programs, coding walkthroughs can also be used to review program code. However, code must be tested by computer runs. When errors are discovered, the source is found and eliminated through a process called *debugging*. You can find out more about the various stages of testing required to put an information system into operation in Chapter 12. Our Learning Tracks also contain descriptions of methodologies for developing software programs that contribute to software quality.

Review Summary

8-1 **Why are information systems vulnerable to destruction, error, and abuse?** Digital data are vulnerable to destruction, misuse, error, fraud, and hardware or software failures. The Internet is designed to be an open system and makes internal corporate systems more vulnerable to actions from outsiders. Hackers can unleash denial-of-service (DoS) attacks or penetrate corporate networks, causing serious system disruptions. Wi-Fi networks can easily be penetrated by intruders using sniffer programs to obtain an address to access the resources of the network. Computer viruses and worms can disable systems and websites. The dispersed nature of cloud computing makes it difficult to track unauthorized activity or to apply controls from afar. Software presents problems because software bugs may be impossible to eliminate and because software vulnerabilities can be exploited by hackers and malicious software. End users often introduce errors.

8-2 **What is the business value of security and control?** Lack of sound security and control can cause firms relying on computer systems for their core business functions to lose sales and productivity. Information assets, such as confidential employee records, trade secrets, or business plans, lose much of their value if they are revealed to outsiders or if they expose the firm to legal liability. New laws, such as HIPAA, the Sarbanes-Oxley Act, and the Gramm-Leach-Bliley Act, require companies to practice stringent electronic records management and adhere to strict standards for security, privacy, and control. Legal actions requiring electronic evidence and computer forensics also require firms to pay more attention to security and electronic records management.

8-3 **What are the components of an organizational framework for security and control?** Firms need to establish a good set of both general and application controls for their information systems. A risk assessment evaluates information assets, identifies control points and control weaknesses, and determines the most cost-effective set of controls. Firms must also develop a coherent corporate security policy and plans for continuing business operations in the event of disaster or disruption. The security policy includes policies for acceptable use and identity management. Comprehensive and systematic information systems auditing helps organizations determine the effectiveness of security and controls for their information systems.

8-4 **What are the most important tools and technologies for safeguarding information resources?** Firewalls prevent unauthorized users from accessing a private network when it is linked to the Internet. Intrusion detection systems monitor private networks for suspicious network traffic and attempts to access corporate systems. Passwords, tokens, smart cards, and biometric authentication are used to authenticate system users. Antivirus software checks computer systems for infections by viruses and worms and often eliminates the malicious software; antispyware software combats intrusive and harmful spyware programs. Encryption, the coding and scrambling of messages, is a widely used technology for securing electronic transmissions over unprotected networks. Digital certificates combined with public key encryption provide further protection of electronic transactions by authenticating a user's identity. Companies can use fault-tolerant computer systems to make sure that their information systems are always available. Use of software metrics and rigorous software testing help improve software quality and reliability.

Key Terms

Acceptable use policy (AUP), 313
Antivirus software, 318
Application controls, 310
Authentication, 316
Biometric authentication, 316
Botnet, 303
Bugs, 307
Business continuity planning, 314
Click fraud, 305
Computer crime, 303
Computer forensics, 309
Computer virus, 300
Controls, 297
Cybervandalism, 302
Cyberwarfare, 306
Deep packet inspection (DPI), 321
Denial-of-service (DoS) attack, 302
Digital certificates, 320
Disaster recovery planning, 314
Distributed denial-of-service (DDoS) attack, 303

Downtime, 321
Drive-by download, 300
Encryption, 319
Evil twin, 304
Fault-tolerant computer systems, 321
Firewall, 317
General controls, 309
Gramm-Leach-Bliley Act, 308
Hacker, 302
HIPAA, 308
Identity management, 313
Identity theft, 303
Information systems audit, 315
Intrusion detection systems, 318
Keyloggers, 302
Malware, 300
Managed security service providers (MSSPs), 321
Online transaction processing, 321
Password, 316
Patches, 307
Pharming, 304
Phishing, 304

Public key encryption, 319
Public key infrastructure (PKI), 320
Ransomware, 302
Risk assessment, 310
Sarbanes-Oxley Act, 308
Secure Hypertext Transfer Protocol (S-HTTP), 319
Secure Sockets Layer (SSL), 319
Security, 297
Security policy, 313
Smart card, 316
Sniffer, 302
Social engineering, 306
Spoofing, 302
Spyware, 302
SQL injection attack, 301
Token, 316
Trojan horse, 301
Two-factor authentication, 317
Unified threat management (UTM), 319
War driving, 299
Worms, 300
Zero-day vulnerabilities, 307

MyMISLab™

To complete the problems with the ⭐, go to EOC Discussion Questions in the MyLab.

Review Questions

8-1 Why are information systems vulnerable to destruction, error, and abuse?
- List and describe the most common threats against contemporary information systems.
- Define malware and distinguish among a virus, a worm, and a Trojan horse.
- Explain the challenges presented in securing wireless networks.
- Define computer crime. Provide two examples of crime in which computers are targets and two examples in which computers are used as instruments of crime.
- Define identity theft and phishing and explain why identity theft is such a big problem today.
- Describe the security and system reliability problems employees create.
- Define denial of service (DoS) attack, explain how it differs from a distributed denial of service (DDoS) attack, and discuss how DoS and DDoS attacks are related to the use of botnets.

8-2 What is the business value of security and control?
- Explain how security and control provide value for businesses.
- Define computer forensics and explain what it is used for.

8-3 What are the components of an organizational framework for security and control?
- Define general controls and describe each type of general control.
- Define application controls and describe each type of application control.

- Describe the function of risk assessment and explain how it is conducted for information systems.
- Define and describe the following: security policy, acceptable use policy, and identity management.
- Explain how information systems auditing promotes security and control.

8-4 What are the most important tools and technologies for safeguarding information resources?
- Name and describe three authentication methods.
- Describe the roles of firewalls, intrusion detection systems, and antivirus software in promoting security.
- Explain how encryption protects information.
- Describe the role of encryption and digital certificates in a public key infrastructure.
- Distinguish between disaster recovery planning and business continuity planning.
- Identify and describe the security problems cloud computing poses.
- Explain the actions companies should take to secure mobile platforms.

Discussion Questions

✪ 8-5 Security isn't simply a technology issue, it's a business issue. Discuss.

✪ 8-6 Who poses the biggest security threat – insiders or outsiders?

✪ 8-7 Suppose your business had an e-commerce website where it sold goods and accepted credit card payments. Discuss the major security threats to this website and their potential impact. What can be done to minimize these threats?

Hands-On MIS Projects

The projects in this section give you hands-on experience analyzing security vulnerabilities, using spreadsheet software for risk analysis, and using web tools to research security outsourcing services. Visit MyMISLab's Multimedia Library to access this chapter's Hands-On MIS Projects.

MANAGEMENT DECISION PROBLEMS

8-8 Gifty is an online e-tailer for handmade gifts. Customers can purchase either via its Web site or via a mobile app. Prepare a security analysis for this Internet-based business. What kinds of threats should it anticipate? What would be their impact on the business? What steps can it take to prevent damage to its Web sites and continuing operations?

8-9 A survey of your firm's IT infastructure has identified a number of security vulnerabilities. Review the data about these vulnerabilities, which can be found in a table in MyMISLab. Use the table to answer the following questions:
- Calculate the total number of vulnerabilities for each platform. What is the potential impact of the security problems for each computing platform on the organization?
- If you only have one information systems specialist in charge of security, which platforms should you address first in trying to eliminate these vulnerabilities? Second? Third? Last? Why?
- Identify the types of control problems these vulnerabilities illustrate and explain the measures that should be taken to solve them.

- What does your firm risk by ignoring the security vulnerabilities identified?

IMPROVING DECISION MAKING: USING SPREADSHEET SOFTWARE TO PERFORM A SECURITY RISK ASSESSMENT

Software skills: Spreadsheet formulas and charts
Business skills: Risk assessment

8-10 This project uses spreadsheet software to calculate anticipated annual losses from various security threats identified for a small company.

Mercer Paints is a paint manufacturing company located in Alabama that uses a network to link its business operations. A security risk assessment that management requested identified a number of potential exposures. These exposures, their associated probabilities, and average losses are summarized in a table, which can be found in MyMISLab. Use the table to answer the following questions:

- In addition to the potential exposures listed, identify at least three other potential threats to Mercer Paints, assign probabilities, and estimate a loss range.
- Use spreadsheet software and the risk assessment data to calculate the expected annual loss for each exposure.
- Present your findings in the form of a chart. Which control points have the greatest vulnerability? What recommendations would you make to Mercer Paints? Prepare a written report that summarizes your findings and recommendations.

IMPROVING DECISION MAKING: EVALUATING SECURITY OUTSOURCING SERVICES

Software skills: Web browser and presentation software
Business skills: Evaluating business outsourcing services

8-11 This project will help develop your Internet skills in using the web to research and evaluate security outsourcing services.

You have been asked to help your company's management decide whether to outsource security or keep the security function within the firm. Search the web to find information to help you decide whether to outsource security and to locate security outsourcing services.

- Present a brief summary of the arguments for and against outsourcing computer security for your company.
- Select two firms that offer computer security outsourcing services and compare them and their services.
- Prepare an electronic presentation for management, summarizing your findings. Your presentation should make the case of whether your company should outsource computer security. If you believe your company should outsource, the presentation should identify which security outsourcing service you selected and justify your decision.

Collaboration and Teamwork Project

Evaluating Security Software Tools

8-12 With a group of three or four students, use the web to research and evaluate security products from two competing vendors, such as for antivirus software, firewalls, or antispyware software. For each product, describe its capabilities, for what types of businesses it is best suited, and its cost to purchase and install. Which is the best product? Why? If possible, use Google Docs and Google Drive or Google Sites to brainstorm, organize, and develop a presentation of your findings for the class.

BUSINESS PROBLEM-SOLVING CASE

Information Security Threats and Policies in Europe

The IT sector is one of the key drivers of the European economy. It has been estimated that 60 percent of Europeans use the Internet regularly. Additionally, 87 percent own or have access to mobile phones. In 2015, the European broadband market was one of the largest in the world. These facts demonstrate the importance of ensuring the security and safe operation of the Internet for the well-being of the European economy. The safety and security of the Internet have been threatened in recent years as Internet-based cyber attacks have become increasingly sophisticated.

In 2007, Estonia suffered a massive cyber attack that affected the government, the banking system, media, and other services. The attack was performed using a variety of techniques, ranging from simple individual ping commands and message flooding to more sophisticated distributed denial-of-service (DDoS) attacks. Hackers coordinated the attack by using a large number of compromised servers organized in a botnet distributed around the world. A botnet is a network of autonomous malicious software agents that are under the control of a bot commander. The network is created by installing malware that exploits the vulnerabilities of Web servers, operating systems, or applications to take control of the infected computers. Once a computer is infected it becomes part of a network of thousands of "zombies," machines that are commanded to carry out the attack.

The cyber attack on Estonia started in late April 2007 and lasted for almost 3 weeks. During this period, vital parts of the Estonian Internet network had to be closed from access from outside the country, causing millions of dollars in economic losses.

At around the same time, Arsys, an important Spanish domain registration company, was also targeted by international hackers. Arsys reported that hackers had stolen codes that were then used to insert links to external servers containing malicious codes in the Web pages of some of its clients.

In 2009, an estimated 10 million computers were infected with the Conficker worm worldwide. France, the United Kingdom, and Germany were among the European countries that suffered the most infections. The French navy had to ground all military planes when it was discovered that its computer network was infected. In the United Kingdom, the worm infected computers in the Ministry of Defence, the city of Manchester's city council and police IT network, some hospitals in the city of Sheffield, and other government offices across the country. Computers in the network of the German army were also reported as infected. Once installed on a computer, Conficker is able to download and install other malware from controlled Web sites, and thus infected computers could be under full control of the hackers.

More recently, a sophisticated malware threat targeting industrial systems was detected in Germany, Norway, China, Iran, India, Indonesia, and other countries. The malware, known as Stuxnet, infected Windows PCs running the Supervisory Control and Data Acquisition (SCADA) control system from the German company Siemens. Stuxnet was propagated via USB devices. Experts estimated that up to 1,000 machines were infected on a daily basis at the peak of the infection. The malware, hidden in shortcuts to executable programs (files with extension .lnk), was executed automatically when the content of an infected USB drive was displayed. Employing this same technique, the worm was capable of installing other malware. Initially, security experts disclosed that Stuxnet was designed to steal industrial secrets from SIMATIC WinCC, a visualization and control software system from Siemens. However, data gathered later by other experts indicates that the worm was actually looking for some specific programmable logic controller (PLC) devices used in a specific industrial plant, a fact that points to the possibility that the malware was part of a well-planned act of sabotage. Even though none of the sites infected with Stuxnet suffered physical damage, the significance that such a sophisticated threat represents to the industrial resources in Europe and other parts of the world cannot be underestimated.

Europe has been the location of some large cyberattacks and data breaches in 2015. Among the targets were TalkTalk (a large ISP in the United Kingdom), J.D. Witherspoon (a pub chain), and CarphoneWarehouse. com (an online store). In each case hundreds of thousands of customers had their personal data compromised. Infrastructure is also a target in Europe. In April 2015 hackers vandalized TV5Monde in France, taking down 11 TV channels, parts of its Web site, and its social media site as well. The action was allegedly carried out by Middle Eastern terrorist groups.

To overcome the absence of cooperation among EU states, in 2004 the European Commission established the European Network and Information Security Agency (ENISA) with the goal of coordinating efforts to prevent and respond more effectively to potentially more harmful security threats. ENISA's main objectives are to secure Europe's information infrastructure, promote security standards, and educate the general public about security issues.

The European Commission has recently launched the Digital Agenda for Europe. The goal of this initiative is to define the key role that information and communication technologies will play in 2020. The initiative calls for a single, open European digital market. Another goal is that broadband speeds of 30Mbps be available to all European citizens by 2020. In terms of security, the initiative is considering the implementation of measures to protect privacy and the establishment of a well-functioning network of CERT to prevent cybercrime and respond effectively to cyber attacks.

Prior to 2015, there was no common approach to digital network breaches, hacks, or vandalism. In March 2015 the EU proposed the Network and Information Security (NIS) Directive, and in December 2015 the EU adopted this Directive. EU states agreed that most corporations and government agencies will be required to report serious cyberbreaches. The new law follows reports that many security violations are hidden from the public. The new law also sets cybersecurity standards across a wide range of government agencies such as airports, transportation centers, and government offices. For the first time, Europe has developed a coordinated approach to cyber security.

Sources: Bob Tarzey, "At Least 1 in 5 Europe Enterprises Lose Data Through Targeted Cyber Attacks," *Computer Weekly*, December 18, 2015; "Europe Agrees Response to Cyber-attacks," *BBC News*, 8 December 2015; Gunther Oettinger, "New EU Rules Agreed on Cyber Security Breaches," DW.com, December 8, 2015; Don Melvin, "Cyberattack Disables 11 French TV Channels, Takes Over Social Media Sites," Don Melvin, *CNN*, April 9, 2015; European Commission, "Network and Information Security (NIS) Directive," Digital Agenda For Europe, European Commission, March 16, 2015; "Digital Agenda for Europe," European Commission, August 2010, http://ec.europa.eu, accessed October 20, 2010; "The Cyber Raiders Hitting Estonia," *BBC News*, May 17, 2007, http://news.bbc.co.uk, accessed November 17, 2010; Robert McMillan, "Estonia Ready for the Next Cyberattack," Computerworld, April 7, 2010, www.computerworld.com, accessed November 17, 2010; "Another Cyber Attack Hits Europe," Internet Business Law Services, June 18, 2007, www.ibls.com, accessed November 17, 2010; "New Cyber Attack Hits Norway," Views and News from Norway, August 30, 2010, www.newsinenglish.no, accessed November 17, 2010; Gregg Keiser, "Is Stuxnet the 'Best' Malware Ever?" Computerworld, September 16, 2010; Robert McMillan, "Was Stuxnet Built to Attack Iran's Nuclear Program," Computerworld, September 21, 2010.

Case Study Questions

8-13 What is a botnet?

8-14 Describe some of the main points of the Network and Information Security (NIS) Directive.

8-15 Explain how a cyberattack can be carried out.

8-16 Describe some of the weaknesses exploited by malware.

Case contributed by Daniel Ortiz-Arroyo, Aalborg University.

MyMISLab

Go to the Assignments section of your MyLab to complete these writing exercises.

8-17 Describe three spoofing tactics employed in identity theft by using information systems.

8-18 Describe four reasons mobile devices used in business are difficult to secure.

Chapter 8 References

Bajaj, Vikas. "The Perils of Automated Flight." *New York Times* (April 30, 2015).

Boyle, Randall J., and Raymond R. Panko, Raymond R. *Corporate Computer Security,* 4th ed. (Upper Saddle River, NJ: Prentice-Hall, 2015.)

Breedon, John II. "Trojans Horses Gain Inside Track as Top Form of Malware," *GCN* (May 6, 2013).

Crossman, Penny. "DDoS Attacks Are Still Happening—and Getting Bigger," *Information Management* (July 29, 2014).

"Devastating Downtime: The Surprising Cost of Human Error and Unforeseen Events," *Focus Research* (October 2010).

Dey, Debabrata, Atanu Lahiri, and Guoying Zhang. "Quality Competition and Market Segmentation in the Security Software Market," *MIS Quarterly* 38, No. 2 (June 2014).

Donohue, Brian. "Malware C&C Servers Found in 184 Countries." ThreatPost.com (August 2, 2013).

FireEye. "Out of Pocket: A Comprehensive Mobile Threat Assessment of 7 Million iOS and Android Apps," (February 2015).

Galbreth, Michael R., and Mikhael Shor. "The Impact of Malicious Agents on the Enterprise Software Industry," *MIS Quarterly* 34, No. 3 (September 2010).

Grossman, Lev. "The Code," *Time* (July 21, 2014).

Hui, Kai Lung, Wendy Hui, and Wei T. Yue. "Information Security Outsourcing with System Interdependency and Mandatory Security Requirement," *Journal of Management Information Systems* 29, No. 3 (Winter 2013).

Javelin Strategy & Research. "2015 Identity Fraud Study," (March 3, 2015).

Kaplan, James, Chris Rezek, and Kara Sprague. "Protecting Information in the Cloud," *McKinsey Quarterly* (January 2013).

Karlovsky, Brian. "FireEye Names Malware's Favorite Targets, Sources," *Australian Reseller News* (March 2, 2014).

Kirk, Jeremy. "Pushdo Spamming Botnet Gains Strength Again," IDG News Service (April 20, 2015).

McAfee Labs."McAfee Labs Threats Report," (February, 2015).

Osterman Research. "The Risks of Social Media and What Can Be Done to Manage Them, *Commvault* (June 2011).

Panda Security. "Pandalabs Annual Report 2014." (2015).

Perez, Sarah, "AY Media-Owned Blogging Platform Typepad Enters Day 5 of On-And-Off DDoS Attacks," Techcrunch.com (April 21, 2014).

Ponemon Institute. "2014: A Year of Mega-Breaches," (January 2015).

Ponemon Institute. "2014 Cost of Cybercrime Study: United States,"(October 2014).

Ponemon Institute. "2014 Cost of Data Breach Study: United States," (2014).

Ponemon Institute. "The Cost of Malware Containment," (January 2015).

Reisinger, Don. "Android Security Remains a Glaring Problem: 10 Reasons Why," *eWeek* (March 2, 2014).

Ribeiro, John. "Hacker Group Targets Skype Social Media Accounts," *Computer World* (January 2, 2014).

Sadeh, Norman M. "Phish Isn't Spam," *Information Week* (June 25, 2012).

Samuel, Alexandra, "Online Security as Herd Immunity," *Harvard Business Review* (March 13, 2014).

Scharr, Jill. "Fake Instagram 'Image Viewers' Are Latest Malware Fad," *Tom's Guide* (May 8, 2014).

Schwartz, Matthew J. "Android Trojan Looks, Acts Like Windows Malware," *Information Week* (June 7, 2013).

Sengupta, Somini. "Machines That Know You without Using a Password," *New York Times* (September 10, 2013).

Solutionary. "Solutionary Security Engineering Research Team Unveils Annual Global Threat Intelligence Report," (March 12, 2013).

Spears, Janine L., and Henri Barki. "User Participation in Information Systems Security Risk Management," *MIS Quarterly* 34, No. 3 (September 2010).

Stallings, William H., and Lawrie Brown. *Computer Security: Principles and Practice*, 3rd ed. (Upper Saddle River, NJ: Prentice-Hall, 2015.)

Symantec. "State of Mobility Global Results 2013," (2013).

_____. "Symantec Internet Security Threat Report," (2015).

Temizkan, Orcun, Ram L. Kumar, Sungjune Park, and Chandrasekar Subramaniam. "Patch Release Behaviors of Software Vendors in Response to Vulnerabilities: An Empirical Analysis," *Journal of Management Information Systems* 28, No. 4 (Spring 2012).

Thompson, Jadiann. "Scam Alert: Two Clicks on Facebook Could Leak All Your Personal Info to an International Scammer," Kshb.com (April 30, 2015).

Wakida, Clayton. "Anonymous Accused of Hacking TMT Web Site," KMTV.com (April 27, 2015).

Wang, Jingguo Wang, Manish Gupta, and H. Raghav Rao. "Insider Threats in a Financial Institution: Analysis of Attack-Proneness of Information Systems Applications," *MIS Quarterly* 39, No. 1 (March 2015).

Vance, Anthony, Paul Benjamin Lowry, and Dennis Eggett. "Using Accountability to Reduce Access Policy Violations in Information Systems," *Journal of Management Information Systems* 29, No. 4 (Spring 2013).

Verizon. "2015 Data Breach Investigation Report," (2015).

Yadron, Danny. "Companies Wrestle with the Cost of Cybersecurity," *Wall Street Journal* (February 25, 2014).

Yan Chen, K., Ram Ramamurthy, and Kuang-Wei Wen. "Organizations' Information Security Policy Compliance: Stick or Carrot Approach?" *Journal of Management Information Systems* 29, No. 3 (Winter 2013).

Young, Carl S. "The Enemies of Data Security: Convenience and Collaboration," *Harvard Business Review* (February 11, 2015).

Zhao, Xia, Ling Xue, and Andrew B. Whinston. "Managing Interdependent Information Security Risks: Cyberinsurance, Managed Security Services, and Risk Pooling Arrangements," *Journal of Management Information Systems* 30, No. 1 (Summer 2013).

Key System Applications
for the Digital Age

Part III examines the core information system applications businesses are using today to improve operational excellence and decision making. These applications include enterprise systems; systems for supply chain management, customer relationship management, and knowledge management; e-commerce applications; and business intelligence systems to enhance decision making. This part answers questions such as these: How can enterprise applications improve business performance? How do firms use e-commerce to extend the reach of their businesses? How can systems improve decision making and help companies make better use of their knowledge assets?

Achieving Operational Excellence and Customer Intimacy: Enterprise Applications

LEARNING OBJECTIVES

After reading this chapter, you will be able to answer the following questions:

9-1   How do enterprise systems help businesses achieve operational excellence?

9-2   How do supply chain management systems coordinate planning, production, and logistics with suppliers?

9-3   How do customer relationship management systems help firms achieve customer intimacy?

9-4   What are the challenges that enterprise applications pose and how are enterprise applications taking advantage of new technologies?

CHAPTER CASES

Statoil Fuel and Retail Competes Using Enterprise Systems

DP World Takes Port Management to the Next Level with RFID

Unilever Unifies Globally with Enhanced ERP

Customer Relationship Management Helps Celcom Become Number One

VIDEO CASES

Case 1: Workday: Enterprise Cloud Software-as-a-Service (SaaS)

Case 2: Evolution Homecare Manages Patients with Microsoft Dynamics CRM

Instructional Video:

GSMS Protects Patients By Serializing Every Bottle of Drugs

STATOIL FUEL AND RETAIL COMPETES USING ENTERPRISE SYSTEMS

When Alimentation Couche-Tard purchased Statoil Fuel and Retail (SFR) in April 2012, it was the Canadian convenience store giant's most ambitious acquisition to date (€2.058 billion). SFR, a division of Statoil, the Norwegian State Oil Company, had been spun off from its parent in October 2010. The purchase added 2,300 retail fuel stations—most full-service with a convenience store—to its over 6,200 stores throughout North America and expanded Couche-Tard's reach to eight European countries—Norway, Sweden, Denmark, Poland, Estonia, Latvia, Lithuania, and Russia.

SFR operates in both the B2C (sales to consumers) and B2B (sales to other businesses) sectors. Fuel products including gasoline blends, diesel fuels, biofuels, and LPG (liquefied petroleum gas) generate 70 percent of its business. The full-service retail stations offer product lines that differ according to operator and location factors. Some prefer a product mix that concentrates on auto supplies and services while others focus on food-related products, beverages, and even fast-food. SFR's 12 terminals, 38 depots, and 400 road tankers provide bulk sales to commercial customers, including bus and car rental companies, road construction crews, and independent resellers.

Couche-Tard welcomed both the opportunities and the challenges of its acquisition. Immediate synergies between Couche-Tard and SFR could not completely cover the remaining expenses from SFR's split from Statoil, rebranding efforts, and the replacement of an antiquated IT infrastructure and enterprise resource planning (ERP) system. The old system used different processes in each country and market, resulting in over 5,000 custom software objects for the IT department to manage in addition to massive operational inefficiencies.

© markhall70/Fotolia

SFR needed to maximize supply chain efficiency for its three closely related value chains—the fuel value chain, the grocery value chain, and the lubricants value chain. All corporate functions that provided shared services to the value chains had to be standardized and workplace activities coordinated for its 18,500 employees. Finally, SFR managers wanted an advanced pricing method for fuel sales to maximize profits in its core low-margin business.

Oracle's JD Edwards EnterpriseOne enterprise resource planning system was chosen as the basic platform, and a Web services interface was developed within the ERP system to convert all data into a single format. This common source of master data now drives all transactions throughout the supply chains, as well as financial and other reports generated by the Oracle Business Intelligence Suite. Stock availability and average sales at each service station feed a real-time planning program that projects expected demand and feeds the data to a third-party distribution planning system. Onboard computers convey product types and quantities to tanker drivers at terminals and delivery locations. Fuel restocking, delivery, and confirmation occur automatically.

To coordinate workplace activities, Oracle Fusion Middleware integrates data management and communication across social, mobile, and cloud technologies and among multiple systems and regions. Called the "Connect Project," the software coordinates dozens of interfaces throughout the supply chain, implements a consistent fuel pricing structure, and manages multiple complicated excise taxes and regulations.

In 2014 Statoil began a migration from Oracle database software to SAP's Business Planning and Consolidation Application. Such a move is quite rare, and requires moving massive amounts of data from one system to another. As a result, in 2015 Statoil achieved financial consolidation six times faster than before, data processing speeds increased fifteen times, and opening and closing periods for work status is now eight times faster than before.

Sources: Alyn Bailey, "Statoil Fuel & Retail the World's First SAP to Oracle JD Edwards Migration," http://www.pcubed.com/bulletins, accessed January 2, 2016; Jade Vachon, "Statoil Switches from an Oracle DB to the SAP HANA Platform with SAP MaxAttention," SAP.com, February 21, 2014; "Statoil: Accelerating Planning and Financial Close Cycles with SAP® EPM powered by SAP HANA® and SAP MaxAttentionTM," dam.sap.com/28274_Statoil_BTS.htm, accessed January 2, 2016; "Our Operations," statoilfuelretail.com, accessed January 15, 2014; "Statoil Fuel & Retail," statoil.com, accessed January 15, 2014; "History," statoilfuelretail.com, accessed January 15, 2014; "From Well to Wheel," www.statoilfuelretail.com, accessed January 15, 2014; "The Fuel and Retail Market," statoil.com, accessed January 15, 2014; "Our Company," couche-tard.com, accessed January 15, 2014.

Statoil's efforts to standardize and integrate corporate functions into the supply chain and coordinate workplace activity illustrate the impact of ERP systems on supply chain management (SCM). SFR did not have a single source of business data nor uniform methods for handling many critical SCM functions. Inventory holding costs were unnecessarily high, the IT department was strained, and lack of coordination was negatively impacting workplace productivity.

The chapter-opening diagram calls attention to important points raised by this case and this chapter. All transactions throughout SFR's supply chains are now in a common and consistent format that feeds directly into SFR's reporting software. The integrated ERP environment enables real-time planning based on stock availability and average sales at each service station, and a real-time fuel value chain can now accommodate variable demand from both consumer and business customers.

Benchmarks against which to assess future results by country, terminal, or market are being developed using the advanced pricing method developed by the Connect team. On the B2B side, managers will be able to quickly assess the effects of pricing structures and even sales reps will be able to evaluate the effects of purchasing terms

Here are some questions to think about: How did SFR's lack of standardized processes affect its business operations? How were SFR's employees and supply chain

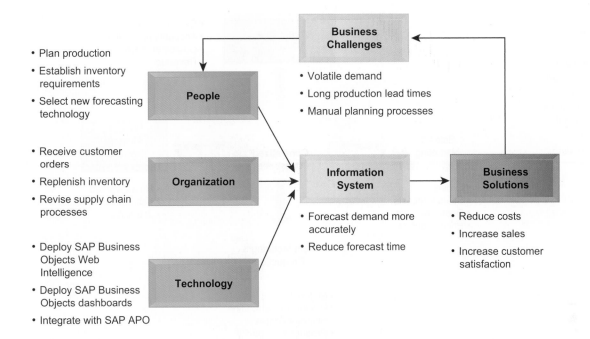

management affected by the adoption of standardized interfaces? Why did SFR retain its legacy systems instead of replacing them entirely?

9-1 How do enterprise systems help businesses achieve operational excellence?

Around the globe, companies are increasingly becoming more connected, both internally and with other companies. If you run a business, you'll want to be able to react instantaneously when a customer places a large order or when a shipment from a supplier is delayed. You may also want to know the impact of these events on every part of the business and how the business is performing at any point in time, especially if you're running a large company. Enterprise systems provide the integration to make this possible. Let's look at how they work and what they can do for the firm.

WHAT ARE ENTERPRISE SYSTEMS?

Imagine that you had to run a business based on information from tens or even hundreds of databases and systems, none of which could speak to one another? Imagine your company had 10 major product lines, each produced in separate factories and each with separate and incompatible sets of systems controlling production, warehousing, and distribution.

At the very least, your decision making would often be based on manual hardcopy reports, often out of date, and it would be difficult to understand what is happening in the business as a whole. Sales personnel might not be able to tell at the time they place an order whether the ordered items are in inventory, and manufacturing could not easily use sales data to plan for new production. You now have a good idea of why firms need a special enterprise system to integrate information.

Chapter 2 introduced enterprise systems, also known as enterprise resource planning (ERP) systems, which are based on a suite of integrated software modules and a common central database. The database collects data from many divisions and departments in a firm and from a large number of key business processes in manufacturing and production, finance and accounting, sales and marketing, and human

Figure 9.1
How Enterprise
Systems Work

*Enterprise systems feature
a set of integrated software
modules and a central
database by which business
processes and functional
areas throughout the
enterprise can share data.*

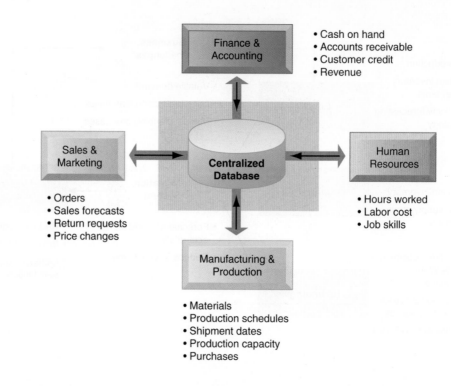

resources, making the data available for applications that support nearly all an organization's internal business activities. When new information is entered by one process, the information is made immediately available to other business processes (see Figure 9.1).

If a sales representative places an order for tire rims, for example, the system verifies the customer's credit limit, schedules the shipment, identifies the best shipping route, and reserves the necessary items from inventory. If inventory stock is insufficient to fill the order, the system schedules the manufacture of more rims, ordering the needed materials and components from suppliers. Sales and production forecasts are immediately updated. General ledger and corporate cash levels are automatically updated with the revenue and cost information from the order. Users can tap into the system and find out where that particular order is at any minute. Management can obtain information at any point in time about how the business was operating. The system can also generate enterprise-wide data for management analyses of product cost and profitability.

ENTERPRISE SOFTWARE

Enterprise software is built around thousands of predefined business processes that reflect best practices. Table 9.1 describes some of the major business processes that enterprise software supports.

Companies implementing this software first have to select the functions of the system they wish to use and then map their business processes to the predefined business processes in the software. (One of our Learning Tracks shows how SAP enterprise software handles the procurement process for a new piece of equipment.) Configuration tables provided by the software manufacturer enable the firm to tailor a particular aspect of the system to the way it does business. For example, the firm could use these tables to select whether it wants to track revenue by product line, geographical unit, or distribution channel.

If the enterprise software does not support the way the organization does business, companies can rewrite some of the software to support the way their business processes work. However, enterprise software is unusually complex, and extensive

TABLE 9.1

Business Processes Supported By Enterprise Systems

Financial and accounting processes, including general ledger, accounts payable, accounts receivable, fixed assets, cash management and forecasting, product-cost accounting, cost-center accounting, asset accounting, tax accounting, credit management, and financial reporting

Human resources processes, including personnel administration, time accounting, payroll, personnel planning and development, benefits accounting, applicant tracking, time management, compensation, workforce planning, performance management, and travel expense reporting

Manufacturing and production processes, including procurement, inventory management, purchasing, shipping, production planning, production scheduling, material requirements planning, quality control, distribution, transportation execution, and plant and equipment maintenance

Sales and marketing processes, including order processing, quotations, contracts, product configuration, pricing, billing, credit checking, incentive and commission management, and sales planning

customization may degrade system performance, compromising the information and process integration that are the main benefits of the system. If companies want to reap the maximum benefits from enterprise software, they must change the way they work to conform to the business processes defined by the software.

To implement a new enterprise system, Tasty Baking Company identified its existing business processes and then translated them into the business processes built into the SAP ERP software it had selected. To ensure that it obtained the maximum benefits from the enterprise software, Tasty Baking Company deliberately planned for customizing less than 5 percent of the system and made very few changes to the SAP software itself. It used as many tools and features that were already built into the SAP software as it could. SAP has more than 3,000 configuration tables for its enterprise software.

Leading enterprise software vendors include SAP, Oracle, IBM, Infor Global Solutions, and Microsoft. Versions of enterprise software packages are designed for small and medium-sized businesses and on-demand versions, including software services running in the cloud (see Section 9-4).

BUSINESS VALUE OF ENTERPRISE SYSTEMS

Enterprise systems provide value by both increasing operational efficiency and providing firmwide information to help managers make better decisions. Large companies with many operating units in different locations have used enterprise systems to enforce standard practices and data so that everyone does business the same way worldwide.

Coca-Cola, for instance, implemented a SAP enterprise system to standardize and coordinate important business processes in 200 countries. Lack of standard, companywide business processes prevented the company from using its worldwide buying power to obtain lower prices for raw materials and from reacting rapidly to market changes. Unilever used ERP for similar purposes, as described in the Interactive Session on Technology in Section 9-4 of this chapter.

Enterprise systems help firms respond rapidly to customer requests for information or products. Because the system integrates order, manufacturing, and delivery data, manufacturing is better informed about producing only what customers have ordered, procuring exactly the right number of components or raw materials to fill actual orders, staging production, and minimizing the time that components or finished products are in inventory.

Alcoa, the world's leading producer of aluminum and aluminum products with operations spanning 31 countries and more than 200 locations, had initially been organized around lines of business, each of which had its own set of information systems. Many of these systems were redundant and inefficient. Alcoa's costs for executing requisition-to-pay and financial processes were much higher, and its cycle times were longer than those of other companies in its industry. (Cycle time refers to the total elapsed time from the beginning to the end of a process.) The company could not operate as a single worldwide entity.

After implementing enterprise software from Oracle, Alcoa eliminated many redundant processes and systems. The enterprise system helped Alcoa reduce requisition-to-pay cycle time by verifying receipt of goods and automatically generating receipts for payment. Alcoa's accounts payable transaction processing dropped 89 percent. Alcoa was able to centralize financial and procurement activities, which helped the company reduce nearly 20 percent of its worldwide costs.

Enterprise systems provide much valuable information for improving management decision making. Corporate headquarters has access to up-to-the-minute data on sales, inventory, and production and uses this information to create more accurate sales and production forecasts. Enterprise software includes analytical tools to use data the system captures to evaluate overall organizational performance. Enterprise system data have common standardized definitions and formats that are accepted by the entire organization. Performance figures mean the same thing across the company. Enterprise systems allow senior management to find out easily at any moment how a particular organizational unit is performing, determine which products are most or least profitable, and calculate costs for the company as a whole.

For example, Alcoa's enterprise system includes functionality for global human resources management that shows correlations between investment in employee training and quality, measures the companywide costs of delivering services to employees, and measures the effectiveness of employee recruitment, compensation, and training.

9-2 How do supply chain management systems coordinate planning, production, and logistics with suppliers?

If you manage a small firm that makes a few products or sells a few services, chances are you will have a small number of suppliers. You could coordinate your supplier orders and deliveries by using just a telephone and fax machine. But if you manage a firm that produces more complex products and services, you will have hundreds of suppliers, and each of your suppliers will have its own set of suppliers. Suddenly, you will need to coordinate the activities of hundreds or even thousands of other firms to produce your products and services. Supply chain management (SCM) systems, which we introduced in Chapter 2, are an answer to the problems of supply chain complexity and scale.

THE SUPPLY CHAIN

A firm's **supply chain** is a network of organizations and business processes for procuring raw materials, transforming these materials into intermediate and finished products, and distributing the finished products to customers. It links suppliers, manufacturing plants, distribution centers, retail outlets, and customers to supply goods and services from source through consumption. Materials, information, and payments flow through the supply chain in both directions.

Goods start out as raw materials and, as they move through the supply chain, are transformed into intermediate products (also referred to as components or parts), and finally, into finished products. The finished products are shipped to distribution centers and from there to retailers and customers. Returned items flow in the reverse direction from the buyer back to the seller.

Let's look at the supply chain for Nike sneakers as an example. Nike designs, markets, and sells sneakers, socks, athletic clothing, and accessories throughout the world. Its primary suppliers are contract manufacturers with factories in China, Thailand, Indonesia, Brazil, and other countries. These companies fashion Nike's finished products.

Nike's contract suppliers do not manufacture sneakers from scratch. They obtain components for the sneakers—the laces, eyelets, uppers, and soles—from other suppliers and then assemble them into finished sneakers. These suppliers in turn have their own suppliers. For example, the suppliers of soles have suppliers for synthetic rubber, suppliers for chemicals used to melt the rubber for molding, and suppliers for the molds into which to pour the rubber. Suppliers of laces have suppliers for their thread, for dyes, and for the plastic lace tips.

Figure 9.2 provides a simplified illustration of Nike's supply chain for sneakers; it shows the flow of information and materials among suppliers, Nike, Nike's distributors, retailers, and customers. Nike's contract manufacturers are its primary suppliers. The suppliers of soles, eyelets, uppers, and laces are the secondary (Tier 2) suppliers. Suppliers to these suppliers are the tertiary (Tier 3) suppliers.

The *upstream* portion of the supply chain includes the company's suppliers, the suppliers' suppliers, and the processes for managing relationships with them. The *downstream* portion consists of the organizations and processes for distributing and delivering products to the final customers. Companies that manufacture, such as Nike's contract suppliers of sneakers, also manage their own *internal supply chain processes* for transforming materials, components, and services their suppliers furnish into finished products or intermediate products (components or parts) for their customers and for managing materials and inventory.

The supply chain illustrated in Figure 9.2 has been simplified. It only shows two contract manufacturers for sneakers and only the upstream supply chain for sneaker

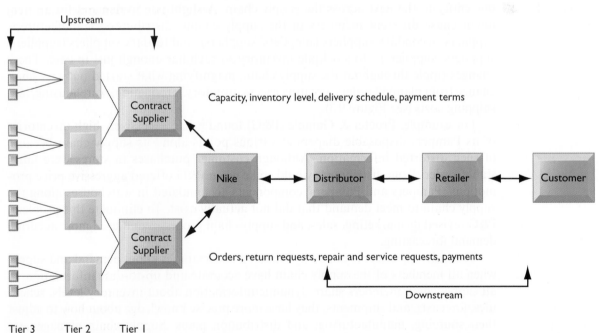

Tier 3   Tier 2   Tier 1
Suppliers   Suppliers   Suppliers

Figure 9.2
Nike's Supply Chain

This figure illustrates the major entities in Nike's supply chain and the flow of information upstream and downstream to coordinate the activities involved in buying, making, and moving a product. Shown here is a simplified supply chain, with the upstream portion focusing only on the suppliers for sneakers and sneaker soles.

soles. Nike has hundreds of contract manufacturers turning out finished sneakers, socks, and athletic clothing, each with its own set of suppliers. The upstream portion of Nike's supply chain would actually comprise thousands of entities. Nike also has numerous distributors and many thousands of retail stores where its shoes are sold, so the downstream portion of its supply chain is also large and complex.

INFORMATION SYSTEMS AND SUPPLY CHAIN MANAGEMENT

Inefficiencies in the supply chain, such as parts shortages, underused plant capacity, excessive finished goods inventory, or high transportation costs, are caused by inaccurate or untimely information. For example, manufacturers may keep too many parts in inventory because they do not know exactly when they will receive their next shipments from their suppliers. Suppliers may order too few raw materials because they do not have precise information on demand. These supply chain inefficiencies waste as much as 25 percent of a company's operating costs.

If a manufacturer had perfect information about exactly how many units of product customers wanted, when they wanted them, and when they could be produced, it would be possible to implement a highly efficient **just-in-time strategy**. Components would arrive exactly at the moment they were needed, and finished goods would be shipped as they left the assembly line.

In a supply chain, however, uncertainties arise because many events cannot be foreseen—uncertain product demand, late shipments from suppliers, defective parts or raw materials, or production process breakdowns. To satisfy customers, manufacturers often deal with such uncertainties and unforeseen events by keeping more material or products in inventory than they think they may actually need. The *safety stock* acts as a buffer for the lack of flexibility in the supply chain. Although excess inventory is expensive, low fill rates are also costly because business may be lost from canceled orders.

One recurring problem in supply chain management is the **bullwhip effect**, in which information about the demand for a product gets distorted as it passes from one entity to the next across the supply chain. A slight rise in demand for an item might cause different members in the supply chain—distributors, manufacturers, suppliers, secondary suppliers (suppliers' suppliers), and tertiary suppliers (suppliers' suppliers' suppliers)—to stockpile inventory so each has enough just in case. These changes ripple throughout the supply chain, magnifying what started out as a small change from planned orders, creating excess inventory, production, warehousing, and shipping costs (see Figure 9.3).

For example, Procter & Gamble (P&G) found it had excessively high inventories of its Pampers disposable diapers at various points along its supply chain because of such distorted information. Although customer purchases in stores were fairly stable, orders from distributors would spike when P&G offered aggressive price promotions. Pampers and Pampers' components accumulated in warehouses along the supply chain to meet demand that did not actually exist. To eliminate this problem, P&G revised its marketing, sales, and supply chain processes and used more accurate demand forecasting.

The bullwhip effect is tamed by reducing uncertainties about demand and supply when all members of the supply chain have accurate and up-to-date information. If all supply chain members share dynamic information about inventory levels, schedules, forecasts, and shipments, they have more precise knowledge about how to adjust their sourcing, manufacturing, and distribution plans. Supply chain management systems provide the kind of information that helps members of the supply chain make better purchasing and scheduling decisions.

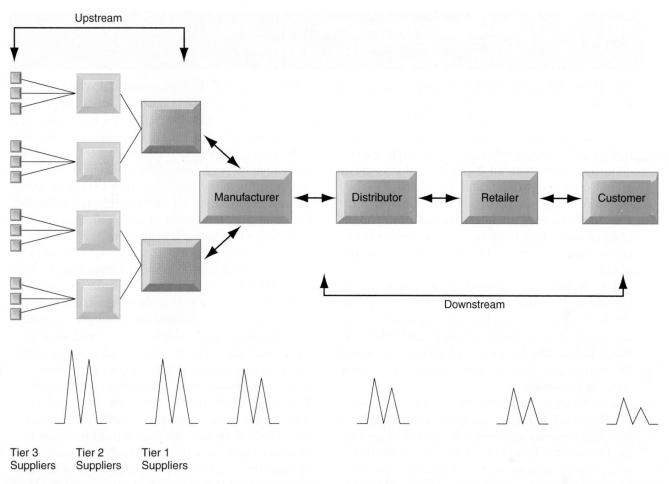

Figure 9.3
The Bullwhip Effect

Inaccurate information can cause minor fluctuations in demand for a product to be amplified as one moves further back in the supply chain. Minor fluctuations in retail sales for a product can create excess inventory for distributors, manufacturers, and suppliers.

SUPPLY CHAIN MANAGEMENT SOFTWARE

Supply chain software is classified as either software to help businesses plan their supply chains (supply chain planning) or software to help them execute the supply chain steps (supply chain execution). **Supply chain planning systems** enable the firm to model its existing supply chain, generate demand forecasts for products, and develop optimal sourcing and manufacturing plans. Such systems help companies make better decisions such as determining how much of a specific product to manufacture in a given time period; establishing inventory levels for raw materials, intermediate products, and finished goods; determining where to store finished goods; and identifying the transportation mode to use for product delivery.

For example, if a large customer places a larger order than usual or changes that order on short notice, it can have a widespread impact throughout the supply chain. Additional raw materials or a different mix of raw materials may need to be ordered from suppliers. Manufacturing may have to change job scheduling. A transportation carrier may have to reschedule deliveries. Supply chain planning software makes the necessary adjustments to production and distribution plans. Information about changes is shared among the relevant supply chain members so that their work can be coordinated. One of the most important—and complex—supply chain planning functions is **demand planning**, which determines how much product a business needs to make to satisfy all its customers' demands JDA Software, SAP, and Oracle all offer supply chain management solutions.

INTERACTIVE SESSION: ORGANIZATIONS   DP World Takes Port Management to the Next Level With RFID

DP (Dubai Ports) World has reason to be proud to have become one of the leading terminal operators in the world. Today, DP World has 65 terminals across 6 continents, and 11 new terminals are under development. The firm moved 60 million containers in 2014 (about 9 percent of global container trade), and generated $3.4 billion in revenues, an 11 percent increase over 2013. The firm employs an international professional team of more than 36,000 people to serve customers in some of the most dynamic economies in the world.

DP World has adopted a customer-centric approach to enhancing its customers' supply chains by providing quality, innovative services to effectively manage container, bulk, and other terminal cargo. The firm invests heavily in terminal infrastructures, technologies, and people to best serve its customers.

Like other global port and terminal operators, DP World helps shippers around the world address the often complex and costly challenges of managing the supply chain. One of the typical problems encountered in container terminal operations is traffic congestion at port entry points. This congestion is often due to delays introduced by lengthy procedures and paper-based logistics. In response, DP World has introduced many IT-based solutions to enhance terminal capacity utilization. These solutions include the electronic custom release of cargo, electronic data interchange (EDI) reporting, twoway digital radio communications, and the "e-token" advanced booking system.

DP World management wanted to take things a step further and decided to make the loading and unloading of containers operate on "just in time" principles to improve container turnaround. It found that radio frequency identification (RFID) technology was an effective way of increasing the efficiency of truck movements through port access gates. Today, DP World uses RFID-enabled automatic gate systems at the port terminals it operates in Dubai and Australia. According to Mohammed Al Muallem, managing director of DP World UAE, the introduction of an automated gate system would not only eliminate traffic congestion but would also help to eliminate a number of lengthy procedures, increasing productivity at the ports, and improving customer satisfaction. This will in turn increase the turnaround of shipping goods.

Prior to the RFID deployment, DP World spent several months performing proof-of-concept trials involving several competing RFID suppliers. Because of the rugged environmental conditions at the ports, DP World required that 99.5 percent of all tags be read successfully, which was a key challenge for many vendors. After extensive testing and evaluation, DP World selected Identec Solutions, a global leader in active wireless tracking solutions, as its RFID supplier.

How does the RFID tracking system work? Trucks that visit a port terminal are equipped with active RFID tags supplied by Identec Solutions that are fixed on the rear chassis. As a truck moves towards the gate, its unique tag ID number is read by an RFID reader, which is integrated with an automated gate system. At the gate, an optical character recognition (OCR) system determines if the truck is loaded with a container, identifies the ID number of the truck's container, and reads the truck license plate number as a backup identification. The system uses the supplied information to automatically issue a ticket to the driver specifying the lane the truck should proceed to in order to load or unload the container. The system can also automatically determine if the truck is on time, which is essential information for the efficient pickup and drop off of containers. As the truck leaves the gate, the RFID tag is read once again, and the driver receives a receipt for the completed transaction.

RFID has enabled DP World to increase the productivity of container handoffs, speed the entry and exit of trucks through terminal gates, and increase fuel efficiency. Victoria Rose, Regional Office Project Coordinator at DP World Sydney, maintained that RFID would improve gate efficiency through improved truck management, reducing queues and congestion around gates, and removing the number of trucks from public roads by streamlining procedures.

Identec's RFID-based solution has also enabled DP World to improve customer satisfaction by enhancing the efficiency of customers' supply chains through smoother, faster, and more effective delivery of their containers at terminal gates. The elimination of lengthy paper transactions and manual inspections at gates and the reduction in manual data input errors demonstrate DP World's customer-centric approach to delivering a superior level of service. The technology also allows transport companies to save time, increase revenues, and reduce costs.

DP World's use of RFID has also helped it to tighten security by providing better accuracy on inbound and outbound truck movements through the terminals. For instance, the system can automatically check whether a truck has a booking and whether it is authorized to enter the port.

As a next step, DP World will consider expanding its use of RFID-enabled scanning and tracking technology to further optimize supply chain flow. In the future, Rose hopes DP World will focus on investigating its use within the yard, and how data captured can be used.

In 2014, DP World was still going strong, acquiring Economic Zones World for $2.6 billion in cash. Their main goal was to acquire the Jebel Ali Free Zone, a 22-square mile plot of land near DP World's Dubai container port. DP World's RFID technologies will be essential to optimizing the use of this new acquisition.

The slowdown in world trade in 2015 is forcing DP World and others in the supply chain (including ports) to use information and communications technology (ICT) to drive further improvements in efficiency. In 2015 DP World is exploring replacing humans with robots in warehouses and yard operations, autonomous vehicles, simulation and virtual reality tools, the Internet of Things and Big Data, and advanced cybersecurity tools. These technologies will require significant investment in port facilities.

Sources: "DP World: Enhancing Commerce Through the Supply Chain," http://industry-me.com/features, accessed January 2, 2016; The Economist Intelligence Unit, "A Turning Point: The Potential Role of ICT Innovations in Ports and Logistics," DP World Report, November 2015; DP World, "Annual Report 2014," April 30, 2015; Simeon Kerr, "DP World to Buy Jebel Ali for $2.6bn from Dubai World," *Financial Times*, November 13, 2014; Dave Friedlos, "RFID Boosts DP World's Productivity in Australia," *RFID Journal*, July 27, 2009, www.rfidjournal.com/article/view/5086, accessed October 20, 2010; Rhea Wessel, "DP World Ramps Up Its Dubai Deployment," *RFID Journal*, August 13, 2009, www.rfidjournal.com/article/view/5130, accessed October 20, 2010.

CASE STUDY QUESTIONS

1. How did Identec Solutions' RFID-based technology help DP World increase the efficiency and effectiveness of its customers' supply chains?

2. Describe two improvements that resulted from implementing the Identec RFID-based solution.

3. How does the concept of supply chain execution relate to this interactive session?

4. What managerial, organizational, and technological challenges might DP World have faced in the early stages of the RFID project's deployment?

Case contributed by Faouzi Kamoun, The University of Dubai.

Supply chain execution systems manage the flow of products through distribution centers and warehouses to ensure that products are delivered to the right locations in the most efficient manner. They track the physical status of goods, the management of materials, warehouse and transportation operations, and financial information involving all parties. An example is the Warehouse Management System (WMS) that Haworth Incorporated uses. Haworth is a world-leading manufacturer and designer of office furniture, with distribution centers in four states. The WMS tracks and controls the flow of finished goods from Haworth's distribution centers to its customers. Acting on shipping plans for customer orders, the WMS directs the movement of goods based on immediate conditions for space, equipment, inventory, and personnel.

GLOBAL SUPPLY CHAINS AND THE INTERNET

Before the Internet, supply chain coordination was hampered by the difficulties of making information flow smoothly among disparate internal supply chain systems for purchasing, materials management, manufacturing, and distribution. It was also difficult to share information with external supply chain partners because the systems of suppliers, distributors, or logistics providers were based on incompatible technology platforms and standards. Enterprise and supply chain management systems enhanced with Internet technology supply some of this integration.

A manager uses a web interface to tap into suppliers' systems to determine whether inventory and production capabilities match demand for the firm's products. Business partners use web-based supply chain management tools to collaborate online on forecasts. Sales representatives access suppliers' production schedules and logistics information to monitor customers' order status.

Global Supply Chain Issues

More and more companies are entering international markets, outsourcing manufacturing operations, and obtaining supplies from other countries as well as selling abroad. Their supply chains extend across multiple countries and regions. There are additional complexities and challenges to managing a global supply chain.

Global supply chains typically span greater geographic distances and time differences than domestic supply chains and have participants from a number of countries. Performance standards may vary from region to region or from nation to nation. Supply chain management may need to reflect foreign government regulations and cultural differences.

The Internet helps companies manage many aspects of their global supply chains, including sourcing, transportation, communications, and international finance. Today's apparel industry, for example, relies heavily on outsourcing to contract manufacturers in China and other low-wage countries. Apparel companies are starting to use the web to manage their global supply chain and production issues. (Review the discussion of Li & Fung in Chapter 3.)

In addition to contract manufacturing, globalization has encouraged outsourcing warehouse management, transportation management, and related operations to third-party logistics providers, such as UPS Supply Chain Solutions and Schneider Logistics Services. These logistics services offer web-based software to give their customers a better view of their global supply chains. Customers can check a secure website to monitor inventory and shipments, helping them run their global supply chains more efficiently.

Demand-Driven Supply Chains: From Push to Pull Manufacturing and Efficient Customer Response

In addition to reducing costs, supply chain management systems facilitate efficient customer response, enabling the workings of the business to be driven more by customer demand. (We introduced efficient customer response systems in Chapter 3.)

Earlier supply chain management systems were driven by a push-based model (also known as build-to-stock). In a **push-based model**, production master schedules are based on forecasts or best guesses of demand for products, and products are pushed to customers. With new flows of information made possible by web-based tools, supply chain management more easily follows a pull-based model. In a **pull-based model**, also known as a demand-driven or build-to-order model, actual customer orders or purchases trigger events in the supply chain. Transactions to produce and deliver only what customers have ordered move up the supply chain from retailers to distributors to manufacturers and eventually to suppliers. Only products

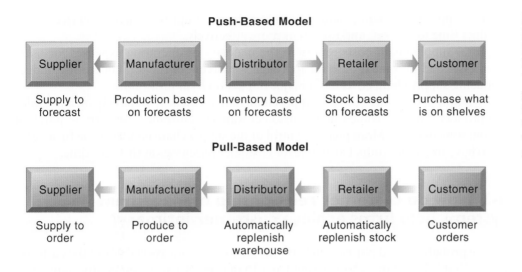

Figure 9.4
Push- versus Pull-Based Supply Chain Models
The difference between push- and pull-based models is summarized by the slogan "Make what we sell, not sell what we make."

to fulfill these orders move back down the supply chain to the retailer. Manufacturers use only actual order demand information to drive their production schedules and the procurement of components or raw materials, as illustrated in Figure 9.4. Walmart's continuous replenishment system described in Chapter 3 is an example of the pull-based model.

The Internet and Internet technology make it possible to move from sequential supply chains, where information and materials flow sequentially from company to company, to concurrent supply chains, where information flows in many directions simultaneously among members of a supply chain network. Complex supply networks of manufacturers, logistics suppliers, outsourced manufacturers, retailers, and distributors can adjust immediately to changes in schedules or orders. Ultimately, the Internet will enable a digital logistics nervous system for supply chains (see Figure 9.5).

BUSINESS VALUE OF SUPPLY CHAIN MANAGEMENT SYSTEMS

You have just seen how supply chain management systems enable firms to streamline both their internal and external supply chain processes and provide management with more accurate information about what to produce, store, and move. By implementing a networked and integrated supply chain management system, companies

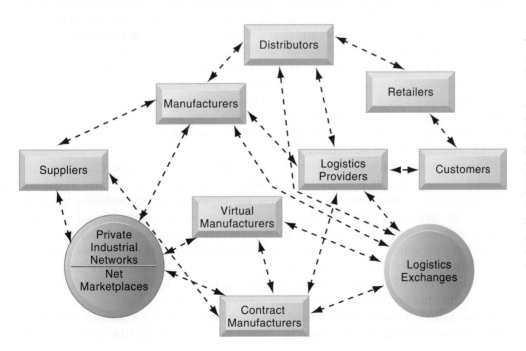

Figure 9.5
The Emerging Internet-Driven Supply Chain
The emerging Internet-driven supply chain operates like a digital logistics nervous system. It provides multidirectional communication among firms, networks of firms, and e-marketplaces so that entire networks of supply chain partners can immediately adjust inventories, orders, and capacities.

match supply to demand, reduce inventory levels, improve delivery service, speed product time to market, and use assets more effectively.

Total supply chain costs represent the majority of operating expenses for many businesses and in some industries approach 75 percent of the total operating budget. Reducing supply chain costs has a major impact on firm profitability.

In addition to reducing costs, supply chain management systems help increase sales. If a product is not available when a customer wants it, customers often try to purchase it from someone else. More precise control of the supply chain enhances the firm's ability to have the right product available for customer purchases at the right time.

9-3 How do customer relationship management systems help firms achieve customer intimacy?

You've probably heard phrases such as "the customer is always right" or "the customer comes first." Today these words ring truer than ever. Because competitive advantage based on an innovative new product or service is often very short lived, companies are realizing that their most enduring competitive strength may be their relationships with their customers. Some say that the basis of competition has switched from who sells the most products and services to who "owns" the customer and that customer relationships represent a firm's most valuable asset.

WHAT IS CUSTOMER RELATIONSHIP MANAGEMENT?

What kinds of information would you need to build and nurture strong, long-lasting relationships with customers? You'd want to know exactly who your customers are, how to contact them, whether they are costly to service and sell to, what kinds of products and services they are interested in, and how much money they spend on your company. If you could, you'd want to make sure you knew each of your customers well, as if you were running a small-town store. And you'd want to make your good customers feel special.

In a small business operating in a neighborhood, it is possible for business owners and managers to know their customers well on a personal, face-to-face basis, but in a large business operating on a metropolitan, regional, national, or even global basis, it is impossible to know your customer in this intimate way. In these kinds of businesses, there are too many customers and too many ways that customers interact with the firm (over the web, the phone, email, blogs, and in person). It becomes especially difficult to integrate information from all these sources and deal with the large number of customers.

A large business's processes for sales, service, and marketing tend to be highly compartmentalized, and these departments do not share much essential customer information. Some information on a specific customer might be stored and organized in terms of that person's account with the company. Other pieces of information about the same customer might be organized by products that were purchased. In this traditional business environment, there is no convenient way to consolidate all this information to provide a unified view of a customer across the company.

This is where customer relationship management systems help. Customer relationship management (CRM) systems, which we introduced in Chapter 2, capture and integrate customer data from all over the organization, consolidate the data, analyze the data, and then distribute the results to various systems and customer touch points across the enterprise. A **touch point** (also known as a contact point) is a method of interaction with the customer, such as telephone, email, customer service desk, conventional mail, Facebook, Twitter, website, wireless device, or retail store. Well-designed CRM systems provide a single enterprise view of customers that is useful for improving both sales and customer service (see Figure 9.6.)

Good CRM systems provide data and analytical tools for answering questions such as these: What is the value of a particular customer to the firm over his or her

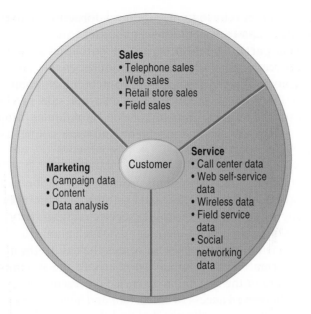

Figure 9.6
Customer Relationship
Management (CRM)
*CRM systems examine
customers from a
multifaceted perspective.
These systems use a set
of integrated applications
to address all aspects of
the customer relationship,
including customer service,
sales, and marketing.*

lifetime? Who are our most loyal customers? Who are our most profitable customers? What do these profitable customers want to buy? Firms use the answers to these questions to acquire new customers, provide better service and support to existing customers, customize their offerings more precisely to customer preferences, and provide ongoing value to retain profitable customers.

CUSTOMER RELATIONSHIP MANAGEMENT SOFTWARE

Commercial CRM software packages range from niche tools that perform limited functions, such as personalizing websites for specific customers, to large-scale enterprise applications that capture myriad interactions with customers, analyze them with sophisticated reporting tools, and link to other major enterprise applications, such as supply chain management and enterprise systems. The more comprehensive CRM packages contain modules for **partner relationship management (PRM)** and **employee relationship management (ERM)**.

PRM uses many of the same data, tools, and systems as customer relationship management to enhance collaboration between a company and its selling partners. If a company does not sell directly to customers but rather works through distributors or retailers, PRM helps these channels sell to customers directly. It provides a company and its selling partners with the ability to trade information and distribute leads and data about customers, integrating lead generation, pricing, promotions, order configurations, and availability. It also provides a firm with tools to assess its partners' performances so it can make sure its best partners receive the support they need to close more business.

ERM software deals with employee issues that are closely related to CRM, such as setting objectives, employee performance management, performance-based compensation, and employee training. Major CRM application software vendors include Oracle, SAP, Salesforce.com, and Microsoft Dynamics CRM.

Customer relationship management systems typically provide software and online tools for sales, customer service, and marketing. We briefly describe some of these capabilities.

Sales Force Automation

Sales Force Automation (SFA) Sales force automation modules in CRM systems help sales staff increase productivity by focusing sales efforts on the most profitable customers, those who are good candidates for sales and services. SFA modules provide sales prospect and contact information, product information, product configuration capabilities, and sales quote generation capabilities. Such software can assemble information about a particular customer's past purchases to help the salesperson make personalized recommendations. SFA modules enable sales, marketing, and shipping departments to share customer and prospect information easily. It increases each salesperson's efficiency by reducing the cost per sale as well as the cost of acquiring new customers and retaining old ones. SFA modules also provide capabilities for sales forecasting, territory management, and team selling.

Customer Service

Customer service modules in CRM systems provide information and tools to increase the efficiency of call centers, help desks, and customer support staff. They have capabilities for assigning and managing customer service requests.

One such capability is an appointment or advice telephone line. When a customer calls a standard phone number, the system routes the call to the correct service person, who inputs information about that customer into the system only once. When the customer's data are in the system, any service representative can handle the customer relationship. Improved access to consistent and accurate customer information helps call centers handle more calls per day and decrease the duration of each call. Thus, call centers and customer service groups achieve greater productivity, reduced transaction time, and higher quality of service at lower cost. The customer is happier because he or she spends less time on the phone restating his or her problem to customer service representatives.

CRM systems may also include web-based self-service capabilities: The company website can be set up to provide inquiring customers personalized support information as well as the option to contact customer service staff by phone for additional assistance.

Marketing

CRM systems support direct-marketing campaigns by providing capabilities for capturing prospect and customer data, for providing product and service information, for qualifying leads for targeted marketing, and for scheduling and tracking direct-marketing mailings or email (see Figure 9.7). Marketing modules also include tools for analyzing marketing and customer data, identifying profitable and unprofitable customers, designing products and services to satisfy specific customer needs and interests, and identifying opportunities for cross-selling.

Figure 9.7
How CRM Systems Support Marketing
Customer relationship management software provides a single point for users to manage and evaluate marketing campaigns across multiple channels, including email, direct mail, telephone, the web, and social media.

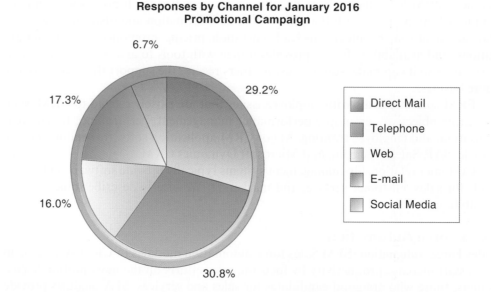

Responses by Channel for January 2016 Promotional Campaign

6.7%

29.2%

17.3%

16.0%

30.8%

Direct Mail
Telephone
Web
E-mail
Social Media

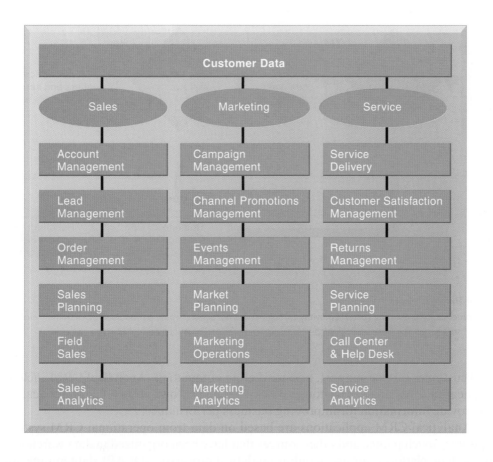

Figure 9.8
CRM Software
Capabilities
The major CRM software products support business processes in sales, service, and marketing, integrating customer information from many sources. Included is support for both the operational and analytical aspects of CRM.

Cross-selling is the marketing of complementary products to customers. (For example, in financial services, a customer with a checking account might be sold a money market account or a home improvement loan.) CRM tools also help firms manage and execute marketing campaigns at all stages, from planning to determining the rate of success for each campaign.

Figure 9.8 illustrates the most important capabilities for sales, service, and marketing processes found in major CRM software products. Like enterprise software, this software is business-process driven, incorporating hundreds of business processes thought to represent best practices in each of these areas. To achieve maximum benefit, companies need to revise and model their business processes to conform to the best-practice business processes in the CRM software.

Figure 9.9 illustrates how a best practice for increasing customer loyalty through customer service might be modeled by CRM software. Directly servicing customers provides firms with opportunities to increase customer retention by singling out profitable long-term customers for preferential treatment. CRM software can assign each customer a score based on that person's value and loyalty to the company and provide that information to help call centers route each customer's service request to agents who can best handle that customer's needs. The system would automatically provide the service agent with a detailed profile of that customer that includes his or her score for value and loyalty. The service agent would use this information to present special offers or additional service to the customer to encourage the customer to keep transacting business with the company. You will find more information on other best-practice business processes in CRM systems in our Learning Tracks.

OPERATIONAL AND ANALYTICAL CRM

All of the applications we have just described support either the operational or analytical aspects of customer relationship management. **Operational CRM** includes customer-facing applications, such as tools for sales force automation, call center

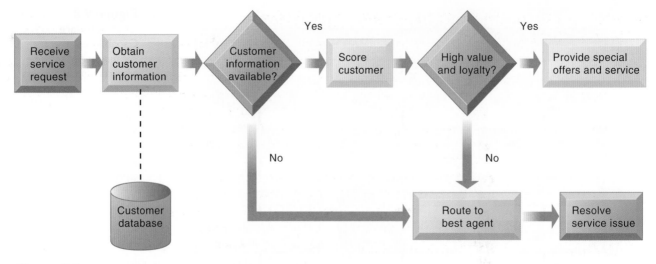

Figure 9.9
Customer Loyalty Management Process Map
This process map shows how a best practice for promoting customer loyalty through customer service would be modeled by customer relationship management software. The CRM software helps firms identify high-value customers for preferential treatment.

and customer service support, and marketing automation. **Analytical CRM** includes applications that analyze customer data generated by operational CRM applications to provide information for improving business performance.

Analytical CRM applications are based on data from operational CRM systems, customer touch points, and other sources that have been organized in data warehouses or analytic platforms for use in online analytical processing (OLAP), data mining, and other data analysis techniques (see Chapter 6). Customer data collected by the organization might be combined with data from other sources, such as customer lists for direct-marketing campaigns purchased from other companies or demographic data. Such data are analyzed to identify buying patterns, to create segments for targeted marketing, and to pinpoint profitable and unprofitable customers (see Figure 9.10).

Another important output of analytical CRM is the customer's lifetime value to the firm. **Customer lifetime value (CLTV)** is based on the relationship between the revenue produced by a specific customer, the expenses incurred in acquiring and servicing that customer, and the expected life of the relationship between the customer and the company.

Figure 9.10
Analytical CRM
Analytical CRM uses a customer data warehouse or analytic platform and tools to analyze customer data collected from the firm's customer touch points and from other sources.

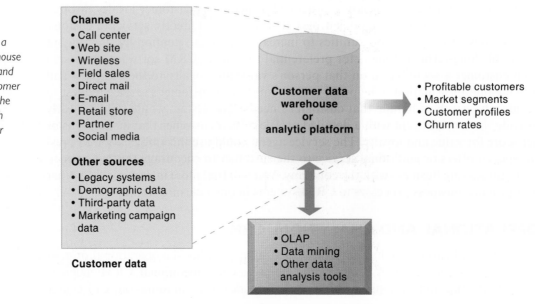

BUSINESS VALUE OF CUSTOMER RELATIONSHIP MANAGEMENT SYSTEMS

Companies with effective customer relationship management systems realize many benefits, including increased customer satisfaction, reduced direct-marketing costs, more effective marketing, and lower costs for customer acquisition and retention. Information from CRM systems increases sales revenue by identifying the most profitable customers and segments for focused marketing and cross-selling.

Customer churn is reduced as sales, service, and marketing respond better to customer needs. The **churn rate** measures the number of customers who stop using or purchasing products or services from a company. It is an important indicator of the growth or decline of a firm's customer base.

9-4 What are the challenges that enterprise applications pose and how are enterprise applications taking advantage of new technologies?

Many firms have implemented enterprise systems and systems for supply chain and customer relationship management because they are such powerful instruments for achieving operational excellence and enhancing decision making. But precisely because they are so powerful in changing the way the organization works, they are challenging to implement. Let's briefly examine some of these challenges as well as new ways of obtaining value from these systems.

ENTERPRISE APPLICATION CHALLENGES

Promises of dramatic reductions in inventory costs, order-to-delivery time, more efficient customer response, and higher product and customer profitability make enterprise systems and systems for SCM and CRM very alluring. But to obtain this value, you must clearly understand how your business has to change to use these systems effectively.

Enterprise applications involve complex pieces of software that are very expensive to purchase and implement. It might take a large Fortune 500 company several years to complete a large-scale implementation of an enterprise system or a system for SCM or CRM. According to a 2014 survey of 192 companies conducted by Panorama Consulting Solutions, the average cost of an ERP project was $2.8 million. Projects took a little longer than 16 months to complete, and 66 percent of the projects delivered 50 percent or less of the expected benefits (Panorama, 2014). Changes in project scope and additional customization work add to implementation delays and costs.

Enterprise applications require not only deep-seated technological changes but also fundamental changes in the way the business operates. Companies must make sweeping changes to their business processes to work with the software. Employees must accept new job functions and responsibilities. They must learn how to perform a new set of work activities and understand how the information they enter into the system can affect other parts of the company. This requires new organizational learning and should also be factored into ERP implementation costs.

SCM systems require multiple organizations to share information and business processes. Each participant in the system may have to change some of its processes and the way it uses information to create a system that best serves the supply chain as a whole.

Some firms experienced enormous operating problems and losses when they first implemented enterprise applications because they didn't understand how much organizational change was required. For example, Kmart had trouble getting products to store shelves when it first implemented i2 Technologies (now JDA Software) SCM software. The i2 software did not work well with Kmart's promotion-driven business model, which created sharp spikes in demand for products. Overstock.com's order tracking system went down for a full week when the company replaced a homegrown system with an Oracle enterprise system. The company rushed to implement the software and did not properly synchronize the Oracle software's process for recording customer refunds with its accounts receivable system. These problems contributed to a third-quarter loss of $14.5 million that year.

Enterprise applications also introduce switching costs. When you adopt an enterprise application from a single vendor, such as SAP, Oracle, or others, it is very costly to switch vendors, and your firm becomes dependent on the vendor to upgrade its product and maintain your installation.

Enterprise applications are based on organization-wide definitions of data. You'll need to understand exactly how your business uses its data and how the data would be organized in a CRM, SCM, or ERP. CRM systems typically require some data cleansing work.

Enterprise software vendors are addressing these problems by offering pared-down versions of their software and fast-start programs for small and medium-sized businesses and best-practice guidelines for larger companies. Companies are also achieving more flexibility by using cloud applications for functions not addressed by the basic enterprise software so that they are not constrained by a single do-it-all type of system (Drobik and Rayner, 2013).

Companies adopting enterprise applications can also save time and money by keeping customizations to a minimum. For example, Kennametal, a $3 billion metal-cutting tools company in Pennsylvania, had spent $10 million over 13 years maintaining an ERP system with more than 6400 customizations. The company replaced it with a plain-vanilla, uncustomized version of SAP enterprise software and changed its business processes to conform to the software. ACH Food Companies, described in the chapter-opening case, also moved to a vanilla ERP system as it simplified its business model.

NEXT-GENERATION ENTERPRISE APPLICATIONS

Today, enterprise application vendors are delivering more value by becoming more flexible, web-enabled, mobile, and capable of integration with other systems. Stand-alone enterprise systems, customer relationship management systems, and SCM systems are becoming a thing of the past. The major enterprise software vendors have created what they call *enterprise solutions, enterprise suites*, or e-business suites to make their CRM, SCM, and ERP systems work closely with each other and link to systems of customers and suppliers. SAP Business Suite, Oracle E-Business Suite, and Microsoft Dynamics Suite (aimed at mid-sized companies) are examples, and they now use web services and service-oriented architecture (SOA) (see Chapter 5).

SAP's next-generation enterprise applications incorporate SOA standards and can link SAP's own applications and web services developed by independent software vendors. Oracle also has included SOA and business process management capabilities in its Fusion middleware products. Businesses can use these tools to create platforms for new or improved business processes that integrate information from multiple applications.

Next-generation enterprise applications also include open source and cloud solutions as well as more functionality available on mobile platforms. Open source products such as Compiere, Apache Open for Business (OFBiz), and Openbravo do not offer as many capabilities as large commercial enterprise software but are attractive to companies such as small manufacturers because of their low cost.

For small- and medium-sized businesses, SAP offers cloud-based versions of its Business One and Business ByDesign enterprise software solutions. Cloud-based enterprise systems are also offered by smaller vendors such as NetSuite and Plex Systems, but they are not as popular as cloud-based CRM products. The undisputed global market leader in cloud-based CRM systems is Salesforce.com, with more than 100,000 customers. Salesforce.com delivers its service through Internet-connected computers or mobile devices, and it is widely used by small, medium, and large enterprises. As cloud-based products mature, more companies will be choosing to run all or part of their enterprise applications in the cloud on an as-needed basis.

Social CRM and Business Intelligence

CRM software vendors are enhancing their products to take advantage of social networking technologies. These social enhancements help firms identify new ideas more rapidly, improve team productivity, and deepen interactions with customers (see the Chapter 10 Interactive Session on People).

Employees who interact with customers through social networking sites such as Facebook and Twitter can often provide customer service functions much faster and at lower cost than by using telephone conversations or email. Customers who are active social media users increasingly want—and expect—businesses to respond to their questions and complaints through this channel.

Social CRM tools enable a business to connect customer conversations and relationships from social networking sites to CRM processes. The leading CRM vendors now offer such tools to link data from social networks into their CRM software. SAP, Salesforce.com and Oracle CRM products now feature technology to monitor, track, and analyze social media activity in Facebook, LinkedIn, Twitter, YouTube, and other sites. Business intelligence and analytics software vendors such as SAS also have capability for social media analytics (with several measures of customer engagement across a variety of social networks) along with campaign management tools for testing and optimizing both social and traditional web-based campaigns.

Salesforce.com connected its system for tracking leads in the sales process with social-listening and social-media marketing tools, enabling users to tailor their social-marketing dollars to core customers and observe the resulting comments. If an ad agency wants to run a targeted Facebook or Twitter ad, these capabilities make it possible to aim the ad specifically at people in the client's lead pipeline who are already being tracked in the CRM system. Users will be able to view tweets as they take place in real time and perhaps uncover new leads. They can also manage multiple campaigns and compare them all to figure out which ones generate the highest click-through rates and cost per click.

Business Intelligence in Enterprise Applications

Enterprise application vendors have added business intelligence features to help managers obtain more meaningful information from the massive amounts of data these systems generate. SAP now makes it possible for its enterprise applications to use HANA in-memory computing technology so that they are capable of much more rapid and complex data analysis (see the Interactive Session on Technology). Included are tools for flexible reporting, ad hoc analysis, interactive dashboards, what-if scenario analysis, and data visualization. Rather than requiring users to leave an application and launch separate reporting and analytics tools, the vendors are starting to embed analytics within the context of the application itself. They are also offering complementary analytics products such as SAP BusinessObjects and Oracle Business Intelligence Enterprise Edition.

The major enterprise application vendors offer portions of their products that work on mobile handhelds. You can find out more about this topic in our Learning Track on Wireless Applications for Customer Relationship Management, Supply Chain Management, and Healthcare.

INTERACTIVE SESSION: TECHNOLOGY   Unilever Unifies Globally with Enhanced ERP

Unilever is the third largest consumer goods company in the world behind Proctor & Gamble and Nestlé. This Anglo-Dutch multinational boasts more than 400 brands, sells its products in more than 190 countries, and employs more than 175,000 people worldwide. Unilever has operating companies and factories on every continent and subsidiaries in almost 100 countries. Twelve Unilever brands—including such recognized names as Knorr, Hellman's, Lipton, and Dove—generate revenues of more than 1 billion Euros (US $1.15 billion) each year.

Unilever is organized as two separate holding companies: Unilever PLC (public limited company), headquartered in London, United Kingdom, and Unilever N.V., headquartered in Rotterdam, The Netherlands. The two legal divisions operate as nearly as possible as a single economic entity—the Unilever Group.

To grow its business in developing and emerging markets, Unilever needed to unify its core business processes. Standardized processes were essential to manage volatile prices and changing commodity supplies effectively. However, prior to 2007, ambitious companywide goal setting such as this was not feasible. At that point, almost every business in each of the more than 190 countries in which Unilever operated functioned as an independent division.

Every transaction for each order Unilever receives, material it produces, item it ships, and invoice it issues runs through ERP systems. Ten years ago, there were 250 different ERP systems trying to do this work, which was too complicated for running a global business that was doubling its transaction volume. Unilever has been trying to consolidate and simplify its technology platform so that it would support the company operating as a single global entity. Unilever transitioned to running its worldwide business on only four instances of SAP ERP, with the ultimate goal of managing these landscapes as one global platform by 2015.

With transactions slated to reach the 60,000 per minute worldwide, Unilever sought additional tools to increase transaction processing speed. At the end of 2012, the company started to use SAP HANA in-memory computing tools for some key SAP ERP applications. SAP HANA is very well suited for performing real-time analytics and processing extremely large numbers of transactions very rapidly (see Chapter 6).

Using HANA reduced the number of days to produce the month-end close from three to just one. HANA also made it easier for Unilever to input raw material costs and quickly calculate product price. Understanding its margins—the percent profit after all costs have been deducted—helped Unilever analyze ways to improve them.

Unilever's enterprise data warehouse (EDW) system extracts, transforms, and integrates ERP transaction data with external data for use in reporting and data analysis. A profitability analysis accelerator analyzes reams of financial data and outputs valuable statistics about cost and profit drivers. By mid-2013, the SAP CO-PA (Controlling Profitability Analysis) HANA Accelerator had been added to all four Unilever regional ERP centers. Profitability Analysis (CO-PA) is a module of SAP ERP software that allows users to report sales and profit data by using different customized characteristics (such as customer, country, product) and key figures (such as number of units, price, cost, etc.). The HANA Accelerator works with a firm's existing SAP CO-PA system. Transactions remain in the ERP system, but queries are processed using HANA. SAP CO-PA Accelerator makes is possible for firms to perform real-time profitability reporting on large data volumes; conduct instant analysis of profitability data at any level of granularity, aggregation, and dimension; and run cost allocations at significantly faster processing times.

Cost Center assessment time was reduced 39 percent, pushing this data into CO-PA in 6.7 hours rather than 11 hours and speeding profitability reporting. Overall, controlling and profitability reports were produced ten times more quickly. The Material Ledger Accelerator reduced run time for period-end closing reports by 66 percent, and cost reduction opportunities were identified by the Overall Equipment Effectiveness (OEE) Management platform. Four and a half billion records for General Ledger line items and more than 400 million controlling and profitability analysis records are now run through the CO-PA Accelerator.

Next, SAP Cash Forecasting was added to SAP ERP Financials to maximize the use of working capital and cash. Product Cost Planning was incorporated to help Unilever plan the costs for materials independently from orders; set prices for materials, operations, production lines, and processes; analyze the costs of manufactured materials; and assess product profitability. The time to analyze the approximately 150 million records produced each month was halved, and product cost forecasts could be generated in 30 seconds, down from seven minutes.

Unilever wanted to maximize product availability on store shelves during new product launches and promotional campaigns. Since trade promotion processes drive a significant portion of its sales, Global ERP Vice President Marc Béchet wanted to enhance the speed and efficiency with which they could be planned, budgeted, and executed and in how stock was allocated. Previously, Unilever used a process in which stock was sequentially assigned to orders as they were received. There was no mechanism for assigning limited stock between customers running a promotion and those who were not. Using HANA-accelerated trade promotion management tools, different inventory matching scenarios are instantly available. Allocation options can be compared and the most profitable chosen. Inventory shortfalls can be handled while safeguarding current promotions to the maximum extent possible. Plans are now underway to add in-memory technology to the rest of the SAP Business Suite.

By significantly cutting the time it takes to calculate product costs, the HANA in-memory database accelerators fast-track raw material sourcing decisions and pricing analysis. Unilever estimates that time spent tracking raw materials has declined by 80 percent. Without the ERP enhancements Unilever devised and implemented, the company would have had a difficult time tracking the 10,000 home and personal care products that use the 2000 chemicals that must be reduced to meet the European Union's REACH (Registration, Evaluation, Authorization and Restriction of Chemicals) regulations and its own more stringent sustainability goals. Consolidation of its ERP platforms and the transaction and processing speed of the HANA platform are the keys to improved performance, reporting, and scalability that will enable Unilever to fulfill its ambitious growth, social impact, and environmental goals.

Sources: "Doing Things Differently to Make a Big Difference in the World," SAP.com, accessed January 19, 2015; "Unilever: SAP HANA," www.accenture.com, accessed January 19, 2015; "Our Compass Strategy," www.unilever.com, accessed January 20, 2015; and Ken Murphy, "Unilever Goes Global with a Transformative SAP HANA Project," *SAP insiderPROFILES*, July 1, 2013.

CASE STUDY QUESTIONS

1. Identify the problem facing Unilever in this case. What people, organization, and technology factors were responsible for this problem?

2. How is enterprise resource planning related to Unilever's business strategy? How did consolidating ERP systems support Unilever's business strategy?

3. Why was using SAP HANA so helpful?

4. How effective was the solution the company chose?

5. How did Unilever's new systems improve operations and management decision making? Give two examples.

Review Summary

9-1 **How do enterprise systems help businesses achieve operational excellence?** Enterprise software is based on a suite of integrated software modules and a common central database. The database collects data from and feeds the data into numerous applications that can support nearly all of an organization's internal business activities. When one process enters new information, the information is made available immediately to other business processes.

Enterprise systems support organizational centralization by enforcing uniform data standards and business processes throughout the company and a single unified technology platform. The firm-wide data that enterprise systems generate help managers evaluate organizational performance.

9-2 **How do supply chain management systems coordinate planning, production, and logistics with suppliers?** Supply chain management (SCM) systems automate the flow of information among members of the supply chain so they can use it to make better decisions about when and how much to purchase, produce, or ship. More accurate information from supply chain management systems reduces uncertainty and the impact of the bullwhip effect.

Supply chain management software includes software for supply chain planning and for supply chain execution. Internet technology facilitates the management of global supply chains by providing the connectivity for organizations in different countries to share supply chain information. Improved communication among supply chain members also facilitates efficient customer response and movement toward a demand-driven model.

9-3 **How do customer relationship management systems help firms achieve customer intimacy?** Customer relationship management (CRM) systems integrate and automate customer-facing processes in sales, marketing, and customer service, providing an enterprise-wide view of customers. Companies can use this customer knowledge when they interact with customers to provide them with better service or sell new products and services. These systems also identify profitable or unprofitable customers or opportunities to reduce the churn rate.

The major customer relationship management software packages provide capabilities for both operational CRM and analytical CRM. They often include modules for managing relationships with selling partners (partner relationship management) and for employee relationship management.

9-4 **What are the challenges that enterprise applications pose and how are enterprise applications taking advantage of new technologies?** Enterprise applications are difficult to implement. They require extensive organizational change, large new software investments, and careful assessment of how these systems will enhance organizational performance. Enterprise applications cannot provide value if they are implemented atop flawed processes or if firms do not know how to use these systems to measure performance improvements. Employees require training to prepare for new procedures and roles. Attention to data management is essential.

Enterprise applications are now more flexible, web-enabled, and capable of integration with other systems, using web services and service-oriented architecture (SOA). They also have open source and on-demand versions and can run in cloud infrastructures or on mobile platforms. CRM software has added social networking capabilities to enhance internal collaboration, deepen interactions with customers, and use data from social networking sites. Open source, mobile, and cloud versions of some of these products are becoming available.

Key Terms

Analytical CRM, 352
Bullwhip effect, 342
Churn rate, 353
Cross-selling, 351
Customer lifetime value (CLTV), 352
Demand planning, 343
Employee relationship management (ERM), 349

Enterprise software, 338
Just-in-time strategy, 342
Operational CRM, 351
Partner relationship management (PRM), 349
Pull-based model, 346
Push-based model, 346
Sales Force Automation (SFA), 349

Social CRM, 355
Supply chain, 340
Supply chain execution systems, 345
Supply chain planning systems, 343
Touch point, 348

MyMISLab™

To complete the problems with the ⭐, go to EOC Discussion Questions in the MyLab.

Review Questions

9-1 How do enterprise systems help businesses achieve operational excellence?
- Define an enterprise system and explain how enterprise software works.
- List the business processes supported by enterprise systems.

9-2 How do supply chain management systems coordinate planning, production, and logistics with suppliers?
- Define a supply chain and identify each of its components.
- Describe some of the issues that arise with supply chains and explain what causes them.
- Define and compare supply chain planning systems and supply chain execution systems.
- Describe the challenges of global supply chains and how Internet technology can help companies manage them better.
- Distinguish between a push-based and a pull-based model of supply chain management and explain how contemporary supply chain management systems facilitate a pull-based model.

9-3 How do customer relationship management systems help firms achieve customer intimacy?
- Define customer relationship management and explain why customer relationships are so important today.
- Describe how partner relationship management (PRM) and employee relationship management (ERM) are related to customer relationship management (CRM).
- Describe the tools and capabilities of customer relationship management software for sales, marketing, and customer service.
- Explain the business value of customer relationship management systems.

9-4 What are the challenges that enterprise applications pose and how are enterprise applications taking advantage of new technologies?
- List and describe the challenges enterprise applications pose.
- Explain how these challenges can be addressed.
- How are enterprise applications taking advantage of SOA, web services, open source software, and wireless technology?
- Describe how business intelligence features are being used in enterprise applications.

Discussion Questions

⭐9-5 Supply chain management is less about managing the physical movement of goods and more about managing information. Discuss the implications of this statement.

⭐9-6 If a company wants to implement an enterprise application, it had better do its homework. Discuss the implications of this statement.

⭐9-7 What advantages does a firm gain by implementing a social CRM application?

Hands-On MIS Projects

The projects in this section give you hands-on experience analyzing business process integration, suggesting supply chain management and customer relationship management applications, using database software to manage customer service requests, and evaluating supply chain management business services. Visit MyMISLab's Multimedia Library to access this chapter's Hands-On MIS Projects,

MANAGEMENT DECISION PROBLEMS

9-8 Mercedes-Benz Retail Group UK Ltd, with a network of 18 retail sites, nine used car sites, and seven smart centers across London, Birmingham and Manchester, wanted to learn more about its customers. How could CRM and PRM systems help solve this problem?

9-9 Office Depot is a global supplier of office supply products and services in 59 countries. The company tries to offer a wider range of office supplies at lower cost than other retailers by using just-in-time replenishment and tight inventory control systems. It uses information from a demand forecasting system and point-of-sale data to replenish its inventory in its 2,200 retail stores around the world. Explain how these systems help Office Depot minimize costs and any other benefits they provide. Identify and describe other supply chain management applications that would be especially helpful to Office Depot.

IMPROVING DECISION MAKING: USING DATABASE SOFTWARE TO MANAGE CUSTOMER SERVICE REQUESTS

Software skills: Database design; querying and reporting
Business skills: Customer service analysis

9-10 In this exercise, you'll use database software to develop an application that tracks customer service requests and analyzes customer data to identify customers meriting priority treatment.

Prime Service is a large service company that provides maintenance and repair services for close to 1200 commercial businesses in New York, New Jersey, and Connecticut. Its customers include businesses of all sizes. Customers with service needs call into its customer service department with requests for repairing heating ducts, broken windows, leaky roofs, broken water pipes, and other problems. The company assigns each request a number and writes down the service request number, the identification number of the customer account, the date of the request, the type of equipment requiring repair, and a brief description of the problem. The service requests are handled on a first-come-first-served basis. After the service work has been completed, Prime calculates the cost of the work, enters the price on the service request form, and bills the client. This arrangement treats the most important and profitable clients—those with accounts of more than $70,000—no differently from its clients with small accounts. Management would like to find a way to provide its best customers with better service. It would also like to know which types of service problems occur most frequently so that it can make sure it has adequate resources to address them.

Prime Service has a small database with client account information, which can be found in MyMISLab™. Use database software to design a solution that would enable Prime's customer service representatives to identify the most important customers so that they could receive priority service. Your solution will require more than one table. Populate your database with at least 10 service requests. Create several reports that would be of interest to management, such as a list of the highest—and lowest—priority accounts and a report showing the most frequently occurring service problems. Create a report listing service calls that customer service representatives should respond to first on a specific date.

ACHIEVING OPERATIONAL EXCELLENCE: EVALUATING SUPPLY CHAIN MANAGEMENT SERVICES

Software skills: Web browser and presentation software
Business skills: Evaluating supply chain management services

9-11 Third party logistics providers provide transportation, consolidation, forwarding and customs brokerage, warehousing, fulfillment, distribution and virtually any logistics and trade-related services that their international customers need. In this project, you'll use the Web to research and evaluate two of these business services. Investigate the Web sites of two companies, U.K-based Exel and Swiss-based Kuehne & Nagel, to see how these companies' services can be used for supply chain management. Then respond to the following questions:

- What supply chain processes can each of these companies support for its clients?
- How can customers use the websites of each company to help them with supply chain management?
- Compare the supply chain management services these companies provide. Which company would you select to help your firm manage its supply chain? Why?

Collaboration and Teamwork Project

Analyzing Enterprise Application Vendors

9-12 With a group of three or four students, use the web to research and evaluate the products of two vendors of enterprise application software. You could compare, for example, the SAP and Oracle enterprise systems, the supply chain management systems from JDA Software and SAP, or the customer relationship management systems of Oracle and Salesforce.com. Use what you have learned from these companies' websites to compare the software products you have selected in terms of business functions supported, technology platforms, cost, and ease of use. Which vendor would you select? Why? Would you select the same vendor for a small business (50–300 employees) as well as for a large one? If possible use Google Docs and Google Drive or Google Sites to brainstorm, organize, and develop a presentation of your findings for the class.

BUSINESS PROBLEM-SOLVING CASE

Customer Relationship Management Helps Celcom Become Number One

Celcom Axiata Berhad (Celcom) is the oldest mobile telecommunications company in Malaysia and its largest, with a reputation for quality and reliability that is unrivaled in that country. Nevertheless, maintaining its competitive edge has been a struggle. In 2006, Celcom dropped to third place among Malaysian cellular providers and posted losses. Since then, management has worked feverishly to turn the company around, and Celcom has regained the top spot in its market. To do this required major changes in the business, including a new CEO, changes to corporate culture, and new technology and business processes for managing the customer experience.

To become number one in the Malaysian market again, Celcom's senior management knew that the company had to build better networks and market more aggressively, but the real key to success lay in improving the customer experience. According to Suresh Sidhu, Celcom's chief corporate and operations officer, there will always be a competitor who can beat you on price, or even out-innovate you. However, it's much harder for a competitor to disrupt a strong, positive relationship with customers. Celcom believes it's the market's best differentiator.

The Malaysia telecommunications market is quite mature, so there are few opportunities to acquire new customers. Customer retention is essential, as is luring customers away from competitors. Malaysia's customer base of 14 million is large and diverse, which requires multiple approaches to interacting with them. Older customers prefer in-person service from Celcom dealers or retail outlets, whereas sophisticated young urban users prefer to do business online. All want reliable mobile service.

Companies such as Skype, Google, and Netflix provide services that companies access over a variety of networks and devices, which can disrupt traditional telecommunications billing models. For Celom to be number one in data services, it would have to build enterprise systems that would be able to collaborate with these new players.

Celcom was unable to address these challenges because it had a siloed information technology architecture and business processes that could not provide a complete view of customers. For instance, customer data from one system such as billing were not easily available to other systems such as inventory. This is a common problem for mobile providers because carriers have traditionally counted customers by looking at SIM (subscriber identity modules in mobile phones) IDs. However many customers have multiple devices and SIMs for personal and work uses. Celcom needed systems that could identify and serve each customer rather than that person's SIMs. Otherwise, Celcom service representatives would waste valuable company and customer time making sense of a customer's multiple SIM IDs scattered among various records in the system. The company wanted to be able to see a customer as a specific person, not a SIM or a number.

For Celcom, customers included not only mobile users but also its dealers and resellers. Celcom has nearly 30,000 channel partners who provide many in-person customer services, such as handset sales and activation. Any change in technology and business processes would need to improve the customer experience for Celcom's partners as well as for the company itself.

Celcom's solution involved changes to the company's technology, processes, and people. At the core is an Oracle-based business support system (BSS) that consolidated customer records, centralized inventory management, and sped up business processes. This system consolidates customer information into a single view of the customer to improve customer service across online, call center, and retail channels. The Oracle implementation included new customer portal sites and retail stores as well as an Oracle Siebel call center system and Oracle inventory management and Communications Order and Service Management applications.

Celcom's chief sales and commercial officer Eric Chong was co-chairman along with Sidhu of the BSS transformation. They kicked off the project by asking two questions: What do Celcom's business users need from BSS? What experiences should BSS deliver to Celcom's customers? The BSS project team asked approximately 700 Celcom employees in customer service, retail, marketing, and other divisions to list the top ten experiences that users and dealers wanted, such as fast activation, less paperwork, and always having the most popular phones in stock. The BSS transformation team then developed technical and business process requirements based on these Top 10 lists and then compared offerings from several vendors.

Celcom chose Oracle as the primary technology provider for the new customer experience management system. The company wanted the most complete suite of customer relationship management (CRM) tools that would support multichannel and cross-channel marketing efforts. Oracle seemed the best fit and had the most functionality built-in without requiring additional modifications. Celcom enlisted Accenture consultants to manage the implementation and EMC for storage technology. BT Group assisted with network deployment and ongoing network support.

Celcom's transformation plan entailed retaining some of Celcom's existing systems, and the Celcom team liked Oracle Communications' modularity and interoperability as well as its cross-channel capabilities. Oracle Communications is a cross-channel product suite that provides a variety of services, including broadband data, wireless data, and mobile voice services. It helps communications services providers such as Celcom manage and integrate customer interactions across multiple channels to improve customer support, reduce problem resolution time, customize marketing to narrow market segments, and expedite time-to-market for new products and services. Celcom understood the importance of cross-channel customer experiences and wanted to use this to differentiate itself from its competitors. Celcom's systems solution enables customer interactions to traverse its retail shop, online shops, call center, and partner/dealer channels seamlessly.

BSS provides a single customer record, regardless of how many services (mobile, landline, and data) and devices a customer purchases, that is populated with data from various touchpoints. By consolidating customer data into a unified customer record, Celcom can offer tailored promotion offers in real time that fit a customer's individual history. Celcom's holistic view of a customer includes family relationships, which has special significance when marketing in Asia. The company can see every aspect of service each customer uses, which makes cross-marketing and up-selling more efficient.

Celcom completed the BSS implementation in just 18 months. Celcom replaced 17 systems with one seven-module Oracle system. Oracle Communications Consulting experts played a crucial role in helping Celcom meet its customer satisfaction goals by providing strong program governance, advising about best practice approaches and working with Celcom to improve deployment speed, enhance its customer experience, and reduce operational costs.

Celcom officials explicitly tried to get employees invested in the new system to ensure that it aligned with the business. The company enlisted project directors from both business and IT departments. Representatives from sales and marketing chaired the technology selection committees to ensure that people outside of IT were making the case for the project. Top management, including sales and marketing department heads and Celcom's CEO, are part of a steering committee for customer experience management that meets every two weeks.

A group of business advocates was charged with championing the causes most important to the business staff. Their connections to business departments also helped expedite funding for the project and obtain review and approval of project plans and specifications.

In addition, Celcom also replaced some telecommunications technical terms with ones that were more easily understood by nontechnical users. For example, business support systems (which included applications for customer-facing business operations) were renamed the Best Sales and Service (BSS) platform. BSS conveyed the key objectives of Celcom's business and technology transformation better.

Celcom's integrated systems make it possible for call center representatives to respond much more rapidly to customer queries. In the past, customer agents needed to toggle between two and five screens to do their work. Now they work with just a single screen, which increases efficiency. Sidhu estimates that using fewer screens cuts average call-handling time by 15 to 20 percent.

BSS includes a new tablet-based app for Celcom dealers that makes signing a customer up for a new mobile phone completely paperless. New-phone activation time has been cut from two hours to two minutes. Fewer activations require manual follow-up. Celcom dealers and customers are happier.

Celcom's dealers used to be paid once a month. With BSS, they can be paid twice a month and even more frequently in the future. Chong believes that just being able to pay dealers more frequently will enable Celcom to take market share from competitors.

Inventory of mobile handsets at Celcom facilities and dealer stores is now centralized and managed using BSS. Dealers can see what Celcom has in stock, and Celcom inventory managers can monitor the stock on dealer shelves. More detailed inventory control helps Celcom move more products because it can ship fast-selling units to dealers before shortages occur or have marketers target promotions in regions where the company wants to move specific products. This would have been impossible before. Salespeople are beginning to use big data collected in BSS to manage sales by region better.

Celcom now can provide a single consolidated product catalog, which helps it get products out faster to the market—another way the new system will help Celcom achieve its goal of becoming number one. Celcom is now much closer to achieving its brand vision, pleasing its customers and exceeding their expectations.

Sources: Jessica Sirkin, "Oracle Implementation at Celcom Brings IT, Business Together," searchoracle.com, accessed January 17, 2015; www.celcom.com, accessed January 18, 2015; Fred Sandsmark, "Customers First," *Profit Magazine*, May 2014; and Oracle Corporation, "Celcom Transforms Its Customer Experience with Industry Leading Oracle Communications Suite," March 31, 2014.

Case Study Questions

9-13 What was the problem at Celcom that was described this case? What people, organization, and technology factors contributed to this problem?

9-14 What was Celcom's business strategy and what was the role of customer relationship management in that strategy?

9-15 Describe Celcom's solution to its problem. What people, organization, and technology issues did the solution have to address?

9-16 How effective was this solution? How did it affect the way Celcom ran its business and its business performance?

9-17 Describe two operational activities and two business decisions that were improved by Celcom's new CRM capabilities.

MyMISLab

Go to the Assignments section of your MyLab to complete these writing exercises.

9-18 What are three reasons a company would want to implement an enterprise resource planning (ERP) system and two reasons it might not want to do so.

9-19 What are the sources of data for analytical CRM systems? Provide three examples of outputs from analytical CRM systems.

Chapter 9 References

"Social and Mobile CRM Boost Productivity by 26.4 Percent," *DestinationCRM* (March 8, 2012).

Bozarth, Cecil, and Robert B. Handfield. *Introduction to Operations and Supply Chain Management*, 3e. (Upper Saddle River, NJ: Prentice-Hall, 2013.)

Carew, Joanne. "Most Companies Failing at CRM," *IT Web Business* (February 14, 2013).

Cole, Brenda. "Cloud ERP Users Say Up, Up and Away," *Business Information* (February 2014).

D'Avanzo, Robert, Hans von Lewinski, and Luk N. Van Wassenhove. "The Link Between Supply Chain and Financial Performance," *Supply Chain Management Review* (November 1, 2003).

Davenport, Thomas H. *Mission Critical: Realizing the Promise of Enterprise Systems*. (Boston: Harvard Business School Press, 2000.)

Davenport, Thomas H., Leandro Dalle Mule, and John Lucke. "Know What Your Customers Want Before They Do," *Harvard Business Review* (December 2011).

Drobik, Alexander, and Nigel Rayner. "Develop a Strategic Road Map for Postmodern ERP in 2013 and Beyond," *Gartner Inc.* (July 2013).

Essex, David. "Tomorrow's ERP Raises New Hopes, Fears," *Business Information* (February 2014).

Hitt, Lorin, D. J. Wu, and Xiaoge Zhou. "Investment in Enterprise Resource Planning: Business Impact and Productivity Measures," *Journal of Management Information Systems* 19, No. 1 (Summer 2002).

IBM Institute for Business Value. "Customer Analytics Pay Off," IBM Corporation (2011).

Kanaracus, Chris. "ERP Software Project Woes Continue to Mount, Survey Says," *IT World* (February 20, 2013).

Kimberling, Eric. "5 Lessons from Successful CRM Implementations," Paarama-consulting.com (January 28, 2015).

Klein, Richard, and Arun Rai. "Interfirm Strategic Information Flows in Logistics Supply Chain Relationships," *MIS Quarterly* 33, No. 4 (December 2009).

Laudon, Kenneth C. "The Promise and Potential of Enterprise Systems and Industrial Networks," Working paper, The Concours Group. Copyright Kenneth C. Laudon (1999).

Lee, Hau, L., V. Padmanabhan, and Seugin Whang. "The Bullwhip Effect in Supply Chains," *Sloan Management Review* (Spring 1997).

Liang, Huigang, Nilesh Sharaf, Quing Hu, and Yajiong Xue. "Assimilation of Enterprise Systems: The Effect of Institutional Pressures and the Mediating Role of Top Management," *MIS Quarterly* 31, No. 1 (March 2007).

Maklan, Stan, Simon Knox, and Joe Peppard. "When CRM Fails," *MIT Sloan Management Review* 52, No. 4 (Summer 2011).

Malik, Yogesh, Alex Niemeyer, and Brian Ruwadi. "Building the Supply Chain of the Future." *McKinsey Quarterly* (January 2011).

Mehta, Krishna. "Best Practices for Developing a Customer Lifetime Value Program," *Information Management* (July 28, 2011).

Morrison, Tod. "Custom ERP No Longer in Vogue," *Business Information* (February 2014).

Maurno, Dann Anthony. "The New Word on ERP," *CFO Magazine* (July 25, 2014).

Novet, Jordan. "New Salesforce.com Features Meld Social Media, Marketing, and CRM," *Gigaom* (April 23, 2013).

Oracle Corporation. "Alcoa Implements Oracle Solution 20% Below Projected Cost, Eliminates 43 Legacy Systems." www.oracle.com, accessed August 21, 2005.

Panorama Consulting Solutions. "2014 ERP Report," (2014).

Rai, Arun, Paul A. Pavlou, Ghiyoung Im, and Steve Du. "Interfirm IT Capability Profiles and Communications for Cocreating Relational Value: Evidence from the Logistics Industry," *MIS Quarterly* 36, No. 1 (March 2012).

Rai, Arun, Ravi Patnayakuni, and Nainika Seth. "Firm Performance Impacts of Digitally Enabled Supply Chain Integration Capabilities," *MIS Quarterly* 30, No. 2 (June 2006).

Ranganathan, C., and Carol V. Brown. "ERP Investments and the Market Value of Firms: Toward an Understanding of Influential ERP Project Variables," *Information Systems Research* 17, No. 2 (June 2006).

Sarker, Supreteek, Saonee Sarker, Arvin Sahaym, and Bjørn-Andersen. "Exploring Value Cocreation in Relationships Between an ERP Vendor and its Partners: A Revelatory Case Study," *MIS Quarterly* 36, No. 1 (March 2012).

Seldon, Peter B., Cheryl Calvert, and Song Yang. "A Multi-Project Model of Key Factors Affecting Organizational Benefits from Enterprise Systems," *MIS Quarterly 34,* No. 2 (June 2010).

Strong, Diane M., and Olga Volkoff. "Understanding Organization-Enterprise System Fit: A Path to Theorizing the Information Technology Artifact," *MIS Quarterly* 34, No. 4 (December 2010).

SupplyChainBrain. "Trends in Enterprise Resource Planning Cloud Technology." (February 25, 2015).

Sykes, Tracy Ann, Viswanath Venkatesh, and Jonathan L. Johnson. "Enterprise System Implementation and Employee Job Performance: Understanding the Role of Advice Networks." *MIS Quarterly* 38, No. 1 (March 2014).

Tian, Feng, and Sean Xin Xu. "How Do Enterprise Resource Planning Systems Affect Firm Risk? Post-Implementation Impact," *MIS Quarterly* 39, No. 1 (March 2015).

"Top 5 Reasons ERP Implementations Fail and What You Can Do About It," Ziff Davis (2013).

"Trends in Enterprise Resource Planning Cloud Technology," *SupplyChainBrain* (February 25, 2015).

Wong, Christina W.Y., Lai, Kee-Hung, and Cheng, T.C.E. "Value of Information Integration to Supply Chain Management: Roles of Internal and External Contingencies," *Journal of Management Information Systems* 28, No. 3 (Winter 2012).

E-Commerce: Digital Markets, Digital Goods

CHAPTER 10

LEARNING OBJECTIVES

After reading this chapter, you will be able to answer the following questions:

10-1 What are the unique features of e-commerce, digital markets, and digital goods?

10-2 What are the principal e-commerce business and revenue models?

10-3 How has e-commerce transformed marketing?

10-4 How has e-commerce affected business-to-business transactions?

10-5 What is the role of m-commerce in business and what are the most important m-commerce applications?

10-6 What issues must be addressed when building an e-commerce presence?

CHAPTER CASES

Uber Storms Europe: Europe Strikes Back

Getting Social with Customers

Can Instacart Deliver?

Walmart and Amazon Duke It Out for E-commerce Supremacy

VIDEO CASES

Case 1: Groupon: Deals Galore

Case 2: Etsy: A Marketplace and Community

Case 3: Ford Manufacturing Supply Chain: B2B Marketplace

Uber, the so-called "ride hailing service" (otherwise known as a taxi service) is headquartered in San Francisco and was founded in 2009 by Travis Kalanick and Garrett Camp. Uber is the posterchild (along with Airbnb) for the on-demand economy, a place where independent contractors respond to online requests for service. Uber's various services for transporting people rely on a smartphone app to hail a ride provided by an independent contractor (drivers) who are not employees of the company. Drivers are self-employed, and not under the direct control of Uber as employees would be. They may or may not be licensed or trained. The drivers supply their own car, pay for the gas and maintenance, insurance, and even their own cell phones. They take a cut of the fare, which used to be 20 percent or less, but in 2016 is moving to 25 percent. Voila: a taxi company with no taxis or employees, and an Internet platform for hooking up cars with people looking for a ride. One more thing: Uber provides rides for 30 to 50 percent less than regulated taxis, and also changes its fares depending on demand. It's called "surge pricing."

By 2016, Uber had more than 162,000 drivers working in 200 cities and 55 countries generating revenue of $10 billion and earnings (after paying its drivers) of $2 billion. More than 100,000 people use Uber on a regular basis. However, Uber's over-the-top success has created its own set of challenges.

Uber has taken many American cities by storm and largely succeeded. Not that there hasn't been plenty of opposition from local taxi businesses who have paid hundreds of thousands of dollars in many cities for official medallions licensing them to pick up and transport passengers. Local governments have also resisted Uber fearing the loss of tax revenue and threats to public safety and health posed by unskilled and uninsured drivers whose cars may not pass inspection. Nevertheless, in most cases, Uber has prevailed over local opposition based

© FocusTechnology/Alamy

in part on public support for more and better taxi service using mobile technology and support from Uber drivers who see the company as providing opportunity for a decent living. Uber has been very successful in using social media and online marketing campaigns to organize opposition to local politicians who oppose it. The result is that Uber has not been banned from any U.S. city, although in some cities like New York Uber is required to obtain a license to operate, and drivers and cars need to be certified by the city. In 2016, there are now 60,000 Uber drivers in New York City, and 30,000 taxi drivers. The price of an official taxi medallion has fallen from $1.3 million in 2013 to $640,000 in 2016, down 50 percent in a few years. The largest taxi cab owner in the United States, with thousands of cars and drivers working for him, declared that "Uber was the nastiest, most morally corrupt company ever."

In Europe Uber has generated much stronger opposition, and some outright bans in certain cities. In 2014 a Berlin court banned some of Uber's services following complaints from the Berlin Taxi Association that the service did not comply with local licensing rule. A court in Brussels outlawed Uber because it did not have the correct approvals. The EU commissioner in charge of Europe's Digital Agenda criticized such moves as anti-technology and simply protecting a taxi cartel from competition. In November 2015 courts in Frankfurt re-instated one of the most severe legal restrictions on Uber in the world for failure to train drivers and insure cars. Uber's pricing is one unspoken cause of resistance to its services: Uber's fares are typically 30 percent less than local taxis. The company withdrew its UberPop service in Frankfurt but is allowed to operate its UberBlack and UberTaxi services because they use licensed drivers.

Meanwhile, in Paris 2015, investigators raided Uber's offices as part of an investigation into the legality of Uber services in France. In 2014 France passed legislation that requires all drivers carrying paying passengers to have a license and insurance. Most UberPop drivers in Europe have neither. Uber has also pulled out of Hamburg, Dusseldorf, and Amsterdam. In Paris and Madrid opposition has often been violent. London is considering changes in its regulations that would disrupt Uber. Uber has run up against a different culture than it faces in the United States. As one taxi driver in Germany explained, "It's not part of our German culture to flaunt the laws and regulations, and not treat Uber drivers like employees but rather as contractors with no rights."

Sources: Mark Scottman, "Uber's No-Holds-Barred Expansion Strategy Fizzles in Germany," *New York Times*, January 3, 2016; Simon Van Zuylen-Wood , "The Struggles of New York City's Taxi King," Bloomberg. com,   August 27, 2015; Melissa Eddymarch, "An Uber Service Is Banned in Germany Again," *New York Times*, March 18, 2015; Mark Scott, "Uber Faces Rebukes in Europe," *New York Times*, April 17, 2014.

Uber exemplifies two major trends in e-commerce today. This e-commerce business is powered by the near-ubiquitous use of mobile smartphones, and it is one of so-called on-demand companies such as Lyft (Uber's primary competitor), Airbnb (rooms for rent), Handy and Homejoy (both part-time household helpers), Instacart (grocery shoppers), and Washio (clothes washing). These on-demand firms don't sell goods; instead, they have built a platform by which people who want a service—such as a taxi—can find a provider to fill the demand. On-demand firms are currently considered the hottest business model in e-commerce, and they are disrupting major industries.

The chapter-opening diagram calls attention to important points this case and this chapter raise. The business challenge facing Uber is how to create a profitable company based on a new, on-demand business model. Uber's management decided to base its business on the use of smartphones and apps that link buyers and sellers of taxi transportation services. The business earns revenue by charging users' credit cards for fares and giving a percentage of each fare to the driver, and it can charge prices that vary dynamically with demand. Uber has a lower cost structure than traditional cab companies because it does not have to pay employee wages or benefits,

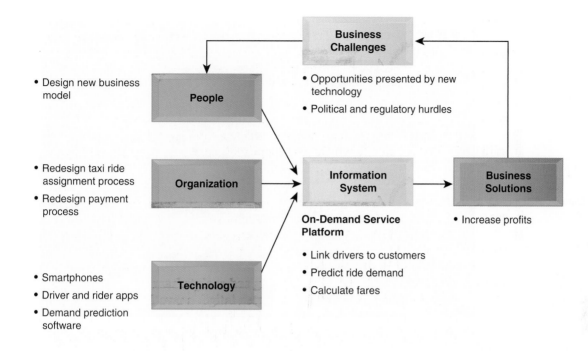

auto insurance, fuel, and licensing fees. Participating drivers pay for their own cars, fuel, and insurance. Under certain conditions, if demand is high, Uber can be more expensive than taxis, but it has disrupted the taxi industry because it offers a reliable, fast, convenient alternative to traditional taxi companies that book rides using the telephone, a central dispatcher using antiquated radio communications, or potential customers standing on street corners trying to hail a cab. Uber's growth is skyrocketing, but the company has to contend with many competitors and political and regulatory opposition from workers and the industries it is disrupting. It is still too early to tell whether Uber and other on-demand businesses will succeed.

Here are some questions to think about: Do you think Uber's business model is viable? Why or why not? How do you feel about using Uber to secure a taxi ride?

10-1 What are the unique features of e-commerce, digital markets, and digital goods?

In 2016, purchasing goods and services online by using smartphones, tablets, and desktop computer will be ubiquitous. In 2015, an estimated 205 million Americans went shopping online, and 171 million purchased something online, as did millions of others worldwide. Although most purchases still take place through traditional channels, e-commerce continues to grow rapidly and to transform the way many companies do business. In 2015, e-commerce consumer sales of goods, services, and content reached $530 billion, about 10 percent of total retail sales of $4.8 trillion, and they are growing at 14 percent annually (compared to 3.5 percent for traditional retailers) (eMarketer, 2015a). In just the past five years, e-commerce has expanded from the desktop and home computer to mobile devices, from an isolated activity to a new social commerce, and from a Fortune 1000 commerce with a national audience to local merchants and consumers whose location is known to mobile devices. At the top 100 e-commerce retail sites, more than half of online shoppers arrive from their smartphones, although most continue to purchase using a PC or tablet. The key words for understanding this new e-commerce in 2016 will be "social, mobile, local."

Figure 10.1
The Growth of
E-Commerce

*Retail e-commerce
revenues grew 15–25
percent per year until the
recession of 2008–2009,
when they slowed
measurably. In 2015,
e-commerce revenues
grew at an estimated 14
percent annually.*

Sources: Based on Data
for retail 2013-2018
based on: eMarketer
chart, "US Retail Ecom-
merce Sales, 2013-2019),"
February 5, 2015; Data for
travel 2013-2019 based
on eMarketer chart: "US
Digital Travel Metrics,
2013-2019", May 1, 2015;
Data for digital content
based on various sources
and author estimates.

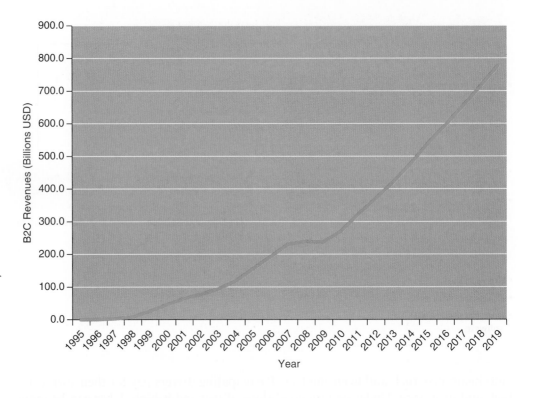

E-COMMERCE TODAY

E-commerce refers to the use of the Internet and the web to transact business. More formally, e-commerce is about digitally enabled commercial transactions between and among organizations and individuals. For the most part, this refers to transactions that occur over the Internet and the web. Commercial transactions involve the exchange of value (e.g., money) across organizational or individual boundaries in return for products and services.

E-commerce began in 1995 when one of the first Internet portals, Netscape.com, accepted the first ads from major corporations and popularized the idea that the web could be used as a new medium for advertising and sales. No one envisioned at the time what would turn out to be an exponential growth curve for e-commerce retail sales, which doubled and tripled in the early years. E-commerce grew at double-digit rates until the recession of 2008–2009, when growth slowed to a crawl, and revenues flattened (see Figure 10.1), not bad considering that traditional retail sales were shrinking by 5 percent annually. Since then, offline retail sales have increased only a few percentage points a year, whereas online e-commerce has been a stellar success.

The very rapid growth in e-commerce in the early years created a market bubble in e-commerce stocks. Like all bubbles, the dot-com bubble burst (in March 2001). A large number of e-commerce companies failed during this process. Yet for many others, such as Amazon, eBay, Expedia, and Google, the results have been more positive: soaring revenues, fine-tuned business models that produce profits and rising stock prices. By 2006, e-commerce revenues returned to solid growth, and have continued to be the fastest growing form of retail trade in the United States, Europe, and Asia.

- Online consumer sales grew to an estimated $531 billion in 2015, an increase of more than 14 percent over 2014 (including travel services and digital downloads), with 171 million people purchasing online and an additional 35 million shopping and gathering information but not purchasing (eMarketer, 2015b).
- The number of individuals of all ages online in the United States expanded to 260 million in 2015, up from 147 million in 2004. In the world, more than 3.1 billion people are now connected to the Internet. Growth in the overall Internet population has spurred growth in e-commerce (Internet World Stats, 2015).

- Approximately 91 million households had broadband access to the Internet in 2015, representing about 75 percent of all households.
- About 193 million Americans now access the Internet by using a smartphone such as an iPhone, Android, Microsoft, or BlackBerry. Mobile e-commerce has begun a rapid growth based on apps, ringtones, downloaded entertainment, and location-based services. Mobile commerce added up to about $128 billion in 2015 (a 40 percent increase over the previous year). In a few years, mobile phones will be the most common Internet access device. Currently, 75 percent of all mobile phone users access the Internet by using their phones.
- B2B e-commerce (use of the Internet for business-to-business commerce and collaboration among business partners) expanded to more than $6.3 trillion. Table 10.1 highlights these new e-commerce developments.

THE NEW E-COMMERCE: SOCIAL, MOBILE, LOCAL

One of the biggest changes is the extent to which e-commerce has become more social, mobile, and local. Online marketing once consisted largely of creating a corporate website, buying display ads on Yahoo, purchasing ad words on Google, and sending email messages. The workhorse of online marketing was the display ad. It still is, but it's increasingly being replaced by video ads, which are far more effective. Display ads from the very beginning of the Internet were based on television ads, where brand messages were flashed before millions of users who were not expected to respond immediately, ask questions, or make observations. If the ads did not work, the solution was often to repeat the ad. The primary measure of success was how many eyeballs (unique visitors) a website produced and how many impressions a marketing campaign generated. (An impression was one ad shown to one person.) Both of these measures were carryovers from the world of television, which measures marketing in terms of audience size and ad views.

From Eyeballs to Conversations

After 2007, all this changed with the rapid growth of Facebook and other social sites, the explosive growth of smartphones beginning with Apple iPhone, and the growing interest in local marketing. What's different about the new world of social-mobile-local e-commerce are the dual and related concepts of conversations and engagement. Marketing in this new period is based on firms engaging in multiple online conversations with their customers, potential customers, and even critics. Your brand is being talked about on the web and social media (that's the conversation part), and marketing your firm, building, and restoring your brands requires you to locate, identify, and participate in these conversations. Social marketing means all things social: listening, discussing, interacting, empathizing, and engaging. The emphasis in online marketing has shifted from a focus on eyeballs to a focus on participating in customer-oriented conversations. In this sense, social marketing is not simply a new ad channel but a collection of technology-based tools for communicating with shoppers.

In the past, firms could tightly control their brand messaging and lead consumers down a funnel of cues that ended in a purchase. That is not true of social marketing. Consumer purchase decisions are increasingly driven by the conversations, choices, tastes, and opinions of their social network. Social marketing is all about firms participating in and shaping this social process.

From the Desktop to the Smartphone

Traditional online marketing (browser-based, search and display ads [increasingly video ads], email, and games) still constitutes the majority (55 percent) of all online marketing ($58 billion), but it's growing much more slowly than social-mobile-local marketing. The marketing dollars are following customers and shoppers from the PC to mobile devices.

TABLE 10.1

The Growth of E-Commerce

Business Transformation

E-commerce remains the fastest growing form of commerce when compared to physical retail stores, services, and entertainment. Social, mobile, and local commerce have become the fastest growing forms of e-commerce.

The breadth of e-commerce offerings grows, especially in the services economy of social networking, travel, entertainment, retail apparel, jewelry, appliances, and home furnishings.

The online demographics of shoppers broaden to match that of ordinary shoppers.

Pure e-commerce business models are refined further to achieve higher levels of profitability, whereas traditional retail brands, such as Walmart, Sears, JCPenney, L.L.Bean, and Macy's, use e-commerce to retain their dominant retail positions. In 2015, Walmart, the world's largest retailer, has decided to get serious about e-commerce and take on Amazon with a more than $1 billion investment in its e-commerce efforts (see the chapter-ending case study).

Small businesses and entrepreneurs continue to flood the e-commerce marketplace, often riding on the infrastructures created by industry giants, such as Amazon, Apple, and Google, and increasingly taking advantage of cloud-based computing resources.

Mobile e-commerce has taken off in the United States with location-based services and entertainment downloads, including e-books, movies, music, and television shows. Mobile e-commerce will generate over $127 billion in 2015.

Technology Foundations

Wireless Internet connections (Wi-Fi, WiMax, and 4G smartphones) grow rapidly.

Powerful smartphones and tablet computers provide access to music, web surfing, and entertainment as well as voice communication. Podcasting and streaming take off as media for distribution of video, radio, and user-generated content.

Mobile devices expand to include wearable computers such as Apple Watch and Fitbit trackers.

The Internet broadband foundation becomes stronger in households and businesses as transmission prices fall. More than 91 million households had broadband cable or DSL access to the Internet in 2015, about 75 percent of all households in the United States (eMarketer, 2015c).

Social networking apps and sites such as Facebook, Google +, Twitter, LinkedIn, Instagram, and others seek to become a major new platform for e-commerce, marketing, and advertising. Facebook has 1.44 billion users worldwide, and 157 million in the United States (Facebook, 2015).

Internet-based models of computing, such as smartphone apps, cloud computing, software-as-a-service (SaaS), and database software greatly reduce the cost of e-commerce websites.

New Business Models Emerge

More than 60 percent of the Internet population has joined an online social network, created blogs, and shared photos and music. Together, these sites create an online audience as large as that of television that is attractive to marketers. In 2015, social networking accounts for an estimated 28 percent of online time. Social sites have become the primary gateway to the Internet in news, music, and, increasingly, products.

The traditional advertising industry is disrupted as online advertising grows twice as fast as TV and print advertising; Google, Yahoo, and Facebook display nearly 1 trillion ads a year.

On-demand service e-commerce sites such as Uber and Airbnb extend the market creator business model to new areas of economy.

Newspapers and other traditional media adopt online, interactive models but are losing advertising revenues to the online players despite gaining online readers. The *New York Times* adopts a paywall for its online edition and succeeds in capturing 950,000 subscribers, growing at 20 percent annually. Book publishing thrives because of the growth in e-books and the continuing appeal of traditional books.

Online entertainment business models offering television, movies, music, and games grow with cooperation among the major copyright owners in Hollywood and New York and with Internet distributors such as Apple, Amazon, Google, YouTube, and Facebook.

Social, mobile, and local e-commerce are connected. As mobile devices become more powerful, they are more useful for accessing Facebook and other social sites. As mobile devices become more widely adopted, customers can use them to find local merchants, and merchants can use them to alert customers in their neighborhood of special offers.

WHY E-COMMERCE IS DIFFERENT

Why has e-commerce grown so rapidly? The answer lies in the unique nature of the Internet and the web. Simply put, the Internet and e-commerce technologies are much richer and more powerful than previous technology revolutions such as radio, television, and the telephone. Table 10.2 describes the unique features of the Internet and web as a commercial medium. Let's explore each of these unique features in more detail.

Ubiquity

In traditional commerce, a marketplace is a physical place, such as a retail store, that you visit to transact business. E-commerce is ubiquitous, meaning that it is available

TABLE 10.2

Eight Unique Features of E-Commerce Technology

E-commerce technology dimension	Business significance
Ubiquity. Internet/web technology is available everywhere: at work, at home, and elsewhere by desktop and mobile devices. Mobile devices extend service to local areas and merchants.	The marketplace is extended beyond traditional boundaries and is removed from a temporal and geographic location. Marketspace is created; shopping can take place anytime, anywhere. Customer convenience is enhanced, and shopping costs are reduced.
Global Reach. The technology reaches across national boundaries, around the earth.	Commerce is enabled across cultural and national boundaries seamlessly and without modification. The marketspace includes, potentially, billions of consumers and millions of businesses worldwide.
Universal Standards. There is one set of technology standards, namely Internet standards.	With one set of technical standards across the globe, disparate computer systems can easily communicate with each other.
Richness. Video, audio, and text messages are possible.	Video, audio, and text marketing messages are integrated into a single marketing message and consumer experience.
Interactivity. The technology works through interaction with the user.	Consumers are engaged in a dialog that dynamically adjusts the experience to the individual and makes the consumer a participant in the process of delivering goods to the market.
Information Density. The technology reduces information costs and raises quality.	Information processing, storage, and communication costs drop dramatically, whereas currency, accuracy, and timeliness improve greatly. Information becomes plentiful, cheap, and more accurate.
Personalization/Customization. The technology allows personalized messages to be delivered to individuals as well as to groups.	Personalization of marketing messages and customization of products and services are based on individual characteristics.
Social Technology. The technology supports content generation and social networking.	New Internet social and business models enable user content creation and distribution and support social networks.

just about everywhere all the time. It makes it possible to shop from your desktop, at home, at work, or even from your car, using smartphones. The result is called a **marketspace**—a marketplace extended beyond traditional boundaries and removed from a temporal and geographic location.

From a consumer point of view, ubiquity reduces **transaction costs**—the costs of participating in a market. To transact business, it is no longer necessary for you to spend time or money traveling to a market, and much less mental effort is required to make a purchase.

Global Reach

E-commerce technology permits commercial transactions to cross cultural and national boundaries far more conveniently and cost effectively than is true in traditional commerce. As a result, the potential market size for e-commerce merchants is roughly equal to the size of the world's online population (estimated to be more than 2 billion).

In contrast, most traditional commerce is local or regional—it involves local merchants or national merchants with local outlets. Television, radio stations, and newspapers, for instance, are primarily local and regional institutions with limited, but powerful, national networks that can attract a national audience but not easily cross national boundaries to a global audience.

Universal Standards

One strikingly unusual feature of e-commerce technologies is that the technical standards of the Internet and, therefore, the technical standards for conducting e-commerce are universal standards. All nations around the world share them and enable any computer to link with any other computer regardless of the technology platform each is using. In contrast, most traditional commerce technologies differ from one nation to the next. For instance, television and radio standards differ around the world, as does cellular telephone technology.

The universal technical standards of the Internet and e-commerce greatly lower **market entry costs**—the cost merchants must pay simply to bring their goods to market. At the same time, for consumers, universal standards reduce **search costs**—the effort required to find suitable products.

Richness

Information **richness** refers to the complexity and content of a message. Traditional markets, national sales forces, and small retail stores have great richness; they can provide personal, face-to-face service, using aural and visual cues when making a sale. The richness of traditional markets makes them powerful selling or commercial environments. Prior to the development of the web, there was a trade-off between richness and reach; the larger the audience reached, the less rich the message. The web makes it possible to deliver rich messages with text, audio, and video simultaneously to large numbers of people.

Interactivity

Unlike any of the commercial technologies of the twentieth century, with the possible exception of the telephone, e-commerce technologies are interactive, meaning they allow for two-way communication between merchant and consumer. Television, for instance, cannot ask viewers any questions or enter conversations with them, and it cannot request customer information to be entered on a form. In contrast, all these activities are possible on an e-commerce website. Interactivity allows an online merchant to engage a consumer in ways similar to a face-to-face experience but on a massive, global scale.

Information Density

The Internet and the web vastly increase **information density**—the total amount and quality of information available to all market participants, consumers, and merchants alike. E-commerce technologies reduce information collection, storage, processing, and communication costs while greatly increasing the currency, accuracy, and timeliness of information.

Information density in e-commerce markets make prices and costs more transparent. **Price transparency** refers to the ease with which consumers can find out the variety of prices in a market; **cost transparency** refers to the ability of consumers to discover the actual costs merchants pay for products.

There are advantages for merchants as well. Online merchants can discover much more about consumers than in the past. This allows merchants to segment the market into groups that are willing to pay different prices and permits the merchants to engage in **price discrimination**—selling the same goods, or nearly the same goods, to different targeted groups at different prices. For instance, an online merchant can discover a consumer's avid interest in expensive, exotic vacations and then pitch high-end vacation plans to that consumer at a premium price, knowing this person is willing to pay extra for such a vacation. At the same time, the online merchant can pitch the same vacation plan at a lower price to a more price-sensitive consumer. Information density also helps merchants differentiate their products in terms of cost, brand, and quality.

Personalization/Customization

E-commerce technologies permit **personalization**. Merchants can target their marketing messages to specific individuals by adjusting the message to a person's clickstream behavior, name, interests, and past purchases. The technology also permits **customization**—changing the delivered product or service based on a user's preferences or prior behavior. Given the interactive nature of e-commerce technology, much information about the consumer can be gathered in the marketplace at the moment of purchase. With the increase in information density, a great deal of information about the consumer's past purchases and behavior can be stored and used by online merchants.

The result is a level of personalization and customization unthinkable with traditional commerce technologies. For instance, you may be able to shape what you see on television by selecting a channel, but you cannot change the content of the channel you have chosen. In contrast, *Wall Street Journal Online* allows you to select the type of news stories you want to see first and gives you the opportunity to be alerted when certain events happen.

Social Technology: User Content Generation and Social Networking

In contrast to previous technologies, the Internet and e-commerce technologies have evolved to be much more social by allowing users to create and share with their friends (and a larger worldwide community) content in the form of text, videos, music, or photos. By using these forms of communication, users can create new social networks and strengthen existing ones.

All previous mass media in modern history, including the printing press, use a broadcast model (one-to-many) in which content is created in a central location by experts (professional writers, editors, directors, and producers), and audiences are concentrated in huge numbers to consume a standardized product. The new Internet and e-commerce empower users to create and distribute content on a large scale and permit users to program their own content consumption. The Internet provides a unique many-to-many model of mass communications.

KEY CONCEPTS IN E-COMMERCE: DIGITAL MARKETS AND DIGITAL GOODS IN A GLOBAL MARKETPLACE

The location, timing, and revenue models of business are based in some part on the cost and distribution of information. The Internet has created a digital marketplace where millions of people all over the world can exchange massive amounts of information directly, instantly, and free. As a result, the Internet has changed the way companies conduct business and increased their global reach.

The Internet reduces information asymmetry. An **information asymmetry** exists when one party in a transaction has more information that is important for the transaction than the other party. That information helps determine their relative bargaining power. In digital markets, consumers and suppliers can see the prices being charged for goods, and in that sense, digital markets are said to be more transparent than traditional markets.

For example, before automobile retailing sites appeared on the web, there was significant information asymmetry between auto dealers and customers. Only the auto dealers knew the manufacturers' prices, and it was difficult for consumers to shop around for the best price. Auto dealers' profit margins depended on this asymmetry of information. Today's consumers have access to a legion of websites providing competitive pricing information, and three-fourths of U.S. auto buyers use the Internet to shop around for the best deal. Thus, the web has reduced the information asymmetry surrounding an auto purchase. The Internet has also helped businesses seeking to purchase from other businesses reduce information asymmetries and locate better prices and terms.

Digital markets are very flexible and efficient because they operate with reduced search and transaction costs, lower **menu costs** (merchants' costs of changing prices), greater price discrimination, and the ability to change prices dynamically based on market conditions. In **dynamic pricing**, the price of a product varies depending on the demand characteristics of the customer or the supply situation of the seller. For instance, online retailers from Amazon to Walmart change prices on many products based on time of day, demand for the product, and users' prior visits to their sites. Using big data analytics, some online firms can adjust prices at the individual level based on behavioral targeting parameters such as whether the consumer is a price haggler (who will receive a lower price offer) versus a person who accepts offered prices and does not search for lower prices. Prices can also vary by zip code, with higher prices set for poor sections of a community. Uber, along with other ride services, uses surge pricing to adjust prices of a ride based on demand (which always rises during storms and major conventions).

These new digital markets can either reduce or increase switching costs, depending on the nature of the product or service being sold, and they might cause some extra delay in gratification due to shipping times. Unlike a physical market, you can't immediately consume a product such as clothing purchased over the web (although immediate consumption is possible with digital music downloads and other digital products.)

Digital markets provide many opportunities to sell directly to the consumer, bypassing intermediaries such as distributors or retail outlets. Eliminating intermediaries in the distribution channel can significantly lower purchase transaction costs. To pay for all the steps in a traditional distribution channel, a product may have to be priced as high as 135 percent of its original cost to manufacture.

Figure 10.2 illustrates how much savings result from eliminating each of these layers in the distribution process. By selling directly to consumers or reducing the number of intermediaries, companies can raise profits while charging lower prices. The removal of organizations or business process layers responsible for intermediary steps in a value chain is called **disintermediation**. E-commerce has also given rise to a completely new set of new intermediaries such as Amazon, eBay, PayPal, and Blue Nile. Therefore, disintermediation differs from one industry to another.

Disintermediation is affecting the market for services. Airlines and hotels operating their own reservation sites online earn more per ticket because they have eliminated travel agents as intermediaries. Table 10.3 summarizes the differences between digital markets and traditional markets.

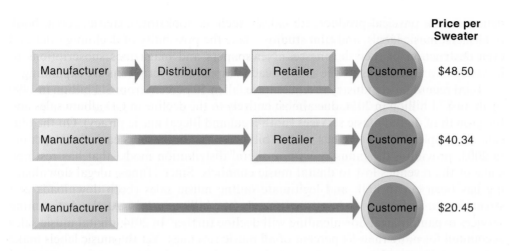

Price per Sweater

Manufacturer	Distributor	Retailer	Customer	$48.50
Manufacturer		Retailer	Customer	$40.34
Manufacturer			Customer	$20.45

Figure 10.2
The Benefits of Disintermediation to the Consumer
The typical distribution channel has several intermediary layers, each of which adds to the final cost of a product, such as a sweater. Removing layers lowers the final cost to the customer.

Digital Goods

The Internet digital marketplace has greatly expanded sales of **digital goods**—goods that can be delivered over a digital network. Music tracks, video, Hollywood movies, software, newspapers, magazines, and books can all be expressed, stored, delivered, and sold as purely digital products. For the most part, digital goods are intellectual property, which is defined as "works of the mind." Intellectual property is protected from misappropriation by copyright, patent, and trade secret laws (see Chapter 4). Today, all these products are delivered as digital streams or downloads while their physical counterparts decline in sales.

In general, for digital goods, the marginal cost of producing another unit is about zero (it costs nothing to make a copy of a music file). However, the cost of producing the original first unit is relatively high—in fact, it is nearly the total cost of the product because there are few other costs of inventory and distribution. Costs of delivery over the Internet are very low, marketing costs often remain the same, and pricing can be highly variable. On the Internet, the merchant can change prices as often as desired because of low menu costs.

The impact of the Internet on the market for these kinds of digital goods is nothing short of revolutionary, and we see the results around us every day. Businesses

TABLE 10.3

Digital Markets Compared to Traditional Markets

	Digital markets	Traditional markets
Information asymmetry	Asymmetry reduced	Asymmetry high
Search costs	Low	High
Transaction costs	Low (sometimes virtually nothing)	High (time, travel)
Delayed gratification	High (or lower in the case of a digital good)	Lower: purchase now
Menu costs	Low	High
Dynamic pricing	Low cost, instant	High cost, delayed
Price discrimination	Low cost, instant	High cost, delayed
Market segmentation	Low cost, moderate precision	High cost, less precision
Switching costs	Higher/lower (depending on product characteristics)	High
Network effects	Strong	Weaker
Disintermediation	More possible/likely	Less possible/unlikely

dependent on physical products for sales—such as bookstores, music stores, book publishers, music labels, and film studios—face the possibility of declining sales and even destruction of their businesses. Newspapers and magazines subscriptions to hard copies are declining, while online readership and subscriptions are expanding.

Total record label industry revenues have fallen 50 percent from $14 billion in 1999 to about $7.1 billion in 2014, due almost entirely to the decline in CD album sales and the growth of digital music services (both legal and illegal music piracy). On the plus side, the Apple iTunes Store has sold 35 billion songs for 99 cents each since opening in 2003, providing the industry with a digital distribution model that has restored some of the revenues lost to digital music channels. Since iTunes, illegal downloading has been cut in half, and legitimate online music sales (both downloads and streaming) are estimated to be approximately $4.5 billion in 2015. As cloud streaming services expand, illegal downloading will decline further. In 2014, digital music sales accounted for more than 64 percent of all music revenues. Yet the music labels make only about 32 cents from a single track download and only .003 cents for a streamed track (with the hope that sales of downloaded tracks or CDs will result). Although the record labels make revenue from ownership of the song (both words and music), the artists who perform the music make virtually nothing from streamed music.

Hollywood has not been similarly disrupted by digital distribution platforms, in part because it is more difficult to download high-quality, pirated copies of full-length movies. To avoid the fate of the music industry, Hollywood has struck lucrative distribution deals with Netflix, Google, Hulu, Amazon, and Apple, making it convenient to download and pay for high-quality movies and television series. These arrangements are not enough to compensate entirely for the loss in DVD sales, which fell 50 percent from 2006 to 2014, although this is changing rapidly as online distributors such as Netflix pay millions for high-quality Hollywood content. In 2015, for the first time, consumers will view more and pay more for web-based movie downloads, rentals, and streams than for DVDs or related physical products. As with television series, the demand for feature-length Hollywood movies appears to be expanding in part because of the growth of smartphones and tablets, making it easier to watch movies in more locations. In addition, the surprising resurgence of music videos, led by the VEVO website, is attracting millions of younger viewers on smartphones and tablets.

Online movies began a growth spurt in 2010 as broadband services spread throughout the country. In 2015, about 112 million Internet users are expected to view movies, about one-half of the adult Internet audience. Although this rapid growth will not continue forever, there is little doubt that the Internet is becoming a movie distribution and television channel that rivals cable television, and someday may replace cable television entirely. Table 10.4 describes digital goods and how they differ from traditional physical goods.

TABLE 10.4

How the Internet Changes the Markets for Digital Goods

	Digital goods	Traditional goods
Marginal cost/unit	Zero	Greater than zero, high
Cost of production	High (most of the cost)	Variable
Copying cost	Approximately zero	Greater than zero, high
Distributed delivery cost	Low	High
Inventory cost	Low	High
Marketing cost	Variable	Variable
Pricing	More variable (bundling, random pricing games)	Fixed, based on unit costs

10-2 What are the principal e-commerce business and revenue models?

E-commerce has grown from a few advertisements on early web portals in 1995 to more than 9 percent of all retail sales in 2015 (an estimated $531 billion), surpassing the mail-order catalog business. E-commerce is a fascinating combination of business models and new information technologies. Let's start with a basic understanding of the types of e-commerce and then describe e-commerce business and revenue models.

TYPES OF E-COMMERCE

There are many ways to classify electronic commerce transactions—one is by looking at the nature of the participants. The three major electronic commerce categories are business-to-consumer (B2C) e-commerce, business-to-business (B2B) e-commerce, and consumer-to-consumer (C2C) e-commerce.

- **Business-to-consumer (B2C)** electronic commerce involves retailing products and services to individual shoppers. BarnesandNoble.com, which sells books, software, and music to individual consumers, is an example of B2C e-commerce.
- **Business-to-business (B2B)** electronic commerce involves sales of goods and services among businesses. Elemica's website for buying and selling chemicals and energy is an example of B2B e-commerce.
- **Consumer-to-consumer (C2C)** electronic commerce involves consumers selling directly to consumers. For example, eBay, the giant web auction site, enables people to sell their goods to other consumers by auctioning their merchandise off to the highest bidder or for a fixed price. Craigslist is the most widely used platform consumers use to buy from and sell directly to others.

Another way of classifying electronic commerce transactions is in terms of the platforms participants use in a transaction. Until recently, most e-commerce transactions took place using a personal computer connected to the Internet over wired networks. Several wireless mobile alternatives have emerged: smartphones, tablet computers such as iPads, dedicated e-readers such as the Kindle, and smartphones and small tablet computers using Wi-Fi wireless networks. The use of handheld wireless devices for purchasing goods and services from any location is termed **mobile commerce** or **m-commerce**. All three types of e-commerce transactions can take place using m-commerce technology, which we discuss in detail in Section 10.3.

E-COMMERCE BUSINESS MODELS

Changes in the economics of information described earlier have created the conditions for entirely new business models to appear, while destroying older business models. Table 10.5 describes some of the most important Internet business models that have emerged. All, in one way or another, use the Internet (including apps on mobile devices) to add extra value to existing products and services or to provide the foundation for new products and services.

Portal

Portals are gateways to the web and are often defined as those sites that users set as their home page. Some definitions of a portal include search engines such as Google and Bing even if few make these sites their home page. Portals such as Yahoo, Facebook, MSN, and AOL offer powerful web search tools as well as an integrated package of content and services such as news, email, instant messaging, maps, calendars, shopping, music downloads, video streaming, and more all in one place. The portal business model now provides a destination site where users start their web searching and linger to read news, find entertainment, meet other people, and, of course, be exposed to advertising, which provides the revenues to support the portal.

TABLE 10.5

Internet Business Models

Category	Description	Examples
E-tailer	Sells physical products directly to consumers or to individual businesses.	Amazon Blue Nile
Transaction broker	Saves users money and time by processing online sales transactions and generating a fee each time a transaction occurs.	ETrade.com Expedia
Market creator	Provides a digital environment where buyers and sellers can meet, search for products, display products, and establish prices for those products; can serve consumers or B2B e-commerce, generating revenue from transaction fees.	eBay Priceline.com Exostar Elemica
Content provider	Creates revenue by providing digital content, such as news, music, photos, or video, over the web. The customer may pay to access the content, or revenue may be generated by selling advertising space.	WSJ.com GettyImages.com iTunes.com Games.com
Community provider	Provides an online meeting place where people with similar interests can communicate and find useful information.	Facebook Google+ Twitter
Portal	Provides initial point of entry to the web along with specialized content and other services.	Yahoo Bing Google
Service provider	Provides applications such as photo sharing, video sharing, and user-generated content as services; provides other services such as online data storage and backup.	Google Apps Photobucket.com Dropbox

Facebook is a very different kind of portal based on social networking. Portals generate revenue primarily by attracting very large audiences, charging advertisers for display ad placement (similar to traditional newspapers), collecting referral fees for steering customers to other sites, and charging for premium services. In 2015, portals (not including Google or Bing) generated an estimated $27 billion in display ad revenues. Although there are hundreds of portal/search engine sites, the top four portals (Yahoo, Facebook, MSN, and AOL) gather more than 95 percent of the Internet portal traffic because of their superior brand recognition (eMarketer, 2015db).

E-tailer

Online retail stores, often called **e-tailers**, come in all sizes, from giant Amazon with 2014 revenues of more than $89 billion, to tiny local stores that have websites. An e-tailer is similar to the typical bricks-and-mortar storefront, except that customers only need to connect to the Internet to check their inventory and place an order. Altogether, online retail (the sale of physical goods online) generated about $340 billion in revenues in 2015. The value proposition of e-tailers is to provide convenient, low-cost shopping 24/7; large selections; and consumer choice. Some e-tailers, such as Walmart.com or Staples.com, referred to as bricks-and-clicks, are subsidiaries or divisions of existing physical stores and carry the same products. Others, however, operate only in the virtual world, without any ties to physical locations. Amazon,

BlueNile.com, and Drugstore.com are examples of this type of e-tailer. Several other variations of e-tailers—such as online versions of direct-mail catalogs, online malls, and manufacturer-direct online sales—also exist.

Content Provider

Although e-commerce began as a retail product channel, it has increasingly become a global content channel. *Content* is defined broadly to include all forms of intellectual property. **Intellectual property** refers to tangible and intangible products of the mind for which the creator claims a property right. Content providers distribute information content—such as digital video, music, photos, text, and artwork—over the web. The value proposition of online content providers is that consumers can conveniently find a wide range of content online and purchase this content inexpensively to be played or viewed on multiple computer devices or smartphones.

Providers do not have to be the creators of the content (although sometimes they are, like Disney.com) and are more likely to be Internet-based distributors of content produced and created by others. For example, Apple sells music tracks at its iTunes Store, but it does not create or commission new music.

The phenomenal popularity of the iTunes Store, and Apple's Internet-connected devices such as the iPhone, iPod, and iPad, have enabled new forms of digital content delivery from podcasting to mobile streaming. **Podcasting** is a method of publishing audio or video broadcasts through the Internet, allowing subscribing users to download audio or video files onto their personal computers, smartphones, tablets, or portable music players. **Streaming** is a publishing method for music and video files that flows a continuous stream of content to a user's device without being stored locally on the device.

Estimates vary, but total online content was around $22 billion in 2015, one of the fastest growing e-commerce segments, growing at an estimated 20 percent annual rate.

Transaction Broker

Sites that process transactions for consumers normally handled in person, by phone, or by mail are transaction brokers. The largest industries using this model are financial services and travel services. The online transaction broker's primary value propositions are savings of money and time and providing an extraordinary inventory of financial products and travel packages in a single location. Online stock brokers and travel booking services charge fees that are considerably less than traditional versions of these services. Fidelity Financial Services and Expedia are the largest online financial and travel service firms based on a transaction broker model.

Market Creator

Market creators build a digital environment in which buyers and sellers can meet, display products, search for products, and establish prices. The value proposition of online market creators is that they provide a platform where sellers can easily display their wares and purchasers can buy directly from sellers. Online auction markets such as eBay and Priceline are good examples of the market creator business model. Another example is Amazon's Merchants platform (and similar programs at eBay), where merchants are allowed to set up stores on Amazon's website and sell goods at fixed prices to consumers. The so-called on-demand economy (mistakenly referred to often as the sharing economy), exemplified by Uber (described in the chapter-opening case) and Airbnb, is based on the idea of a market creator building a digital platform where supply meets demand; for instance, spare auto or room rental capacity finds individuals who want transportation or lodging. Crowdsource funding markets such as Kickstarter.com and Mosaic Inc. bring together private equity investors and entrepreneurs in a funding marketplace. Both are examples of B2B financial market places.

Service Provider

Whereas e-tailers sell products online, service providers offer services online. Photo sharing and online sites for data backup and storage all use a service provider business model. Software is no longer a physical product with a CD in a box but, increasingly, software-as-a-service (SaaS) that you subscribe to online rather than purchase from a retailer, such as Office 365. Google has led the way in developing online software service applications such as Google Apps, Google Sites, Gmail, and online data storage services. Salesforce.com is a major provider of cloud-based software for customer management (see Chapter 5).

Community Provider (Social Networks)

Community providers are sites that create a digital online environment where people with similar interests can transact (buy and sell goods); share interests, photos, videos; communicate with like-minded people; receive interest-related information; and even play out fantasies by adopting online personalities called *avatars*. Social networking sites Facebook, Google+, Tumblr, Instagram, LinkedIn, and Twitter and hundreds of other smaller, niche sites such as Sportsvite all offer users community-building tools and services. Social networking sites have been the fastest-growing websites in recent years, often doubling their audience size in a year.

E-COMMERCE REVENUE MODELS

A firm's **revenue model** describes how the firm will earn revenue, generate profits, and produce a superior return on investment. Although many e-commerce revenue models have been developed, most companies rely on one, or some combination, of the following six revenue models: advertising, sales, subscription, free/freemium, transaction fee, and affiliate.

Advertising Revenue Model

In the **advertising revenue model**, a website generates revenue by attracting a large audience of visitors who can then be exposed to advertisements. The advertising model is the most widely used revenue model in e-commerce, and arguably, without advertising revenues, the web would be a vastly different experience from what it is now because people would be asked to pay for access to content. Content on the web—everything from news to videos and opinions—is free to visitors because advertisers pay the production and distribution costs in return for the right to expose visitors to ads. Companies spent an estimated $58 billion on online advertising in 2015, (in the form of a paid message on a website, paid search listing, video, app, game, or other online medium, such as instant messaging). About $28 billion of this involved spending for mobile ads, the fastest-growing ad platform. In the past five years, advertisers have increased online spending and cut outlays on traditional channels such as radio and newspapers. In 2015, online advertising grew at 15 percent and constitute about 37 percent of all advertising in the United States. (eMarketer, 2014d).

Websites with the largest viewership or that attract a highly specialized, differentiated viewership and are able to retain user attention (stickiness) can charge higher advertising rates. Yahoo, for instance, derives nearly all its revenue from display ads (banner ads), video ads, and, to less extent, search engine text ads. Ninety-five percent of Google's revenue derives from advertising, including selling keywords (AdWord), selling ad spaces (AdSense), and selling display ad spaces to advertisers (DoubleClick). Facebook displayed one-third of the trillion display ads shown on all sites in 2015. Facebook's users spend an average of over 6 hours a week on the site, far longer than any of the other portal sites. In contrast, Americans spend an average of five hours watching television each day.

Sales Revenue Model

In the **sales revenue model**, companies derive revenue by selling goods, information, or services to customers. Companies such as Amazon (which sells books, music, and other products), LLBean.com, and Gap.com all have sales revenue models. Content providers make money by charging for downloads of entire files such as music tracks (iTunes Store) or books or for downloading music and/or video streams (Hulu.com TV shows). Apple has pioneered and strengthened the acceptance of micropayments. **Micropayment systems** provide content providers with a cost-effective method for processing high volumes of very small monetary transactions (anywhere from 25 cents to $5.00 per transaction). The largest micropayment system on the web is Apple's iTunes Store, which has more than 800 million credit customers worldwide who purchase individual music tracks for 99 cents and feature length movies for various prices. A Learning Track is available with more detail on micropayment and other e-commerce payment systems, including Bitcoin.

Subscription Revenue Model

In the **subscription revenue model**, a website offering content or services charges a subscription fee for access to some or all of its offerings on an ongoing basis. Content providers often use this revenue model. For instance, the online version of *Consumer Reports* provides access to premium content, such as detailed ratings, reviews, and recommendations, only to subscribers, who have a choice of paying a $6.95 monthly subscription fee or a $30.00 annual fee. Netflix is one of the most successful subscriber sites with more that 50 million customers worldwide in 2015. The *New York Times* had about 1.1 million online paid subscribers, and the *Wall Street Journal* about 900,000 in 2015. To be successful, the subscription model requires the content to be perceived as differentiated, having high added value, and not readily available elsewhere or easily replicated. Companies successfully offering content or services online on a subscription basis include Match.com and eHarmony (dating services), Ancestry.com and Genealogy.com (genealogy research), and Microsoft Xbox Live.

Free/Freemium Revenue Model

In the **free/freemium revenue model**, firms offer basic services or content for free and charge a premium for advanced or special features. For example, Google offers free applications but charges for premium services. Pandora, the subscription radio service, offers a free service with limited play time and advertising and a premium service with unlimited play. Spotify music service also uses a freemium business model. The idea is to attract very large audiences with free services and then convert some of this audience to pay a subscription for premium services. One problem with this model is converting people from being free loaders into paying customers. "Free" can be a powerful model for losing money. None of the freemium music streaming sites have earned a profit to date. Nevertheless, they are finding that free service with ad revenue is more profitable than the paid subscriber part of their business.

Transaction Fee Revenue Model

In the **transaction fee revenue model**, a company receives a fee for enabling or executing a transaction. For example, eBay provides an online auction marketplace and receives a small transaction fee from a seller if the seller is successful in selling an item. E*Trade, an online stockbroker, receives transaction fees each time it executes a stock transaction on behalf of a customer. The transaction revenue model enjoys wide acceptance in part because the true cost of using the platform is not immediately apparent to the user.

Affiliate Revenue Model

In the **affiliate revenue model**, websites (called *affiliate websites*) send visitors to other websites in return for a referral fee or percentage of the revenue from any resulting sales. Referral fees are also referred to as lead generation fees. For example, MyPoints makes money by connecting companies to potential customers by offering special deals to its members. When members take advantage of an offer and make a purchase, they earn points they can redeem for free products and services, and MyPoints receives a referral fee. Community feedback sites such as Epinions and Yelp receive much of their revenue from steering potential customers to websites where they make a purchase. Amazon uses affiliates that steer business to the Amazon website by placing the Amazon logo on their blogs. Personal blogs often contain display ads as part of affiliate programs. Some bloggers are paid directly by manufacturers, or receive free products, for speaking highly of products and providing links to sales channels.

10-3 How has e-commerce transformed marketing?

Although e-commerce and the Internet have changed entire industries and enabled new business models, no industry has been more affected than marketing and marketing communications.

The Internet provides marketers with new ways of identifying and communicating with millions of potential customers at costs far lower than traditional media, including search engine marketing, data mining, recommender systems, and targeted email. The Internet enables **long tail marketing**. Before the Internet, reaching a large audience was very expensive, and marketers had to focus on attracting the largest number of consumers with popular hit products, whether music, Hollywood movies, books, or cars. In contrast, the Internet allows marketers to find potential customers inexpensively for products where demand is very low. For instance, the Internet makes it possible to sell independent music profitably to very small audiences. There's always some demand for almost any product. Put a string of such long tail sales together and you have a profitable business.

The Internet also provides new ways—often instantaneous and spontaneous—to gather information from customers, adjust product offerings, and increase customer value. Table 10.6 describes the leading marketing and advertising formats used in e-commerce.

BEHAVIORAL TARGETING

Many e-commerce marketing firms use **behavioral targeting** techniques to increase the effectiveness of banners, rich media, and video ads. Behavioral targeting refers to tracking the clickstreams (history of clicking behavior) of individuals on thousands of websites to understand their interests and intentions and expose them to advertisements that are uniquely suited to their online behavior. Marketers and most researchers believe this more precise understanding of the customer leads to more efficient marketing (the firm pays for ads only to those shoppers who are most interested in their products) and larger sales and revenues. Unfortunately, behavioral targeting of millions of web users also leads to the invasion of personal privacy without user consent. When consumers lose trust in their web experience, they tend not to purchase anything. Backlash is growing against the aggressive uses of personal information as consumers seek out safer havens for purchasing and messaging. SnapChat offers disappearing messages, and even Facebook has retreated by making its default for new posts "for friends only."

Popular websites have hundreds of beacon programs on their home pages, which collect data about visitors' behavior and report that behavior to their databases. There the information is often sold to data brokers, firms that collect billions of data elements on every U.S. consumer and household, frequently combining online with offline purchase information. The data brokers in turn sell this information to advertisers who want to place ads on web pages. A recent Federal Trade Commission

Marketing format	2014 revenue	Description
Search engine	$23	Text ads targeted at precisely what the customer is looking for at the moment of shopping and purchasing. Sales oriented.
Display ads	$22.2	Banner ads (pop-ups and leave-behinds) with interactive features; increasingly behaviorally targeted to individual web activity. Brand development and sales. Includes blog display ads.
Video	$5.8	Fastest-growing format, engaging and entertaining; behaviorally targeted, interactive. Branding and sales.
Classified	$3.0	Job, real estate, and services ads; interactive, rich media, and personalized to user searches. Sales and branding.
Rich media	$3.7	Animations, games, and puzzles. Interactive, targeted, and entertaining. Branding orientation.
Lead generation	$2	Marketing firms that gather sales and marketing leads online and then sell them to online marketers for a variety of campaign types. Sales or branding orientation.
Sponsorships	$1.7	Online games, puzzles, contests, and coupon sites sponsored by firms to promote products. Sales orientation.
Email	$.25	Effective, targeted marketing tool with interactive and rich media potential. Sales oriented.

TABLE 10.6

Online Marketing and Advertising Formats (Billions)

report about nine data brokers found that one data broker's database had information on 1.4 billion consumer transactions and more than 700 billion aggregated data elements. Another data broker had 3,000 data measures for nearly every consumer in the United States. (FTC, 2014).

Behavioral targeting takes place at two levels: at individual websites or from within apps and on various advertising networks that track users across thousands of websites. All websites collect data on visitor browser activity and store it in a database. They have tools to record the site that users visited prior to coming to the website, where these users go when they leave that site, the type of operating system they use, browser information, and even some location data. They also record the specific pages visited on the particular site, the time spent on each page of the site, the types of pages visited, and what the visitors purchased (see Figure 10.3). Firms analyze this information about customer interests and behavior to develop precise profiles of existing and potential customers. In addition, most major websites have hundreds of tracking programs on their home pages, which track your clickstream behavior across the web by following you from site to site and re-target ads to you by showing you the same ads on different sites. The leading online advertising networks are Google's DoubleClick, Yahoo's RightMedia, and AOL's Ad Network. Ad networks represent publishers who have space to sell and advertisers who want to market online. The lubricant of this trade is information about millions of web shoppers, which helps advertisers target their ads to precisely the groups and individuals they desire.

This information enables firms to understand how well their website is working, create unique personalized web pages that display content or ads for products or services of special interest to each user, improve the customer's experience, and create additional value through a better understanding of the shopper (see Figure 10.4).

Figure 10.3
Website Visitor Tracking
E-commerce websites and advertising platforms like Google's DoubleClick have tools to track a shopper's every step through an on-line store and then across the web as shoppers move from site to site. Close examination of customer behavior at a website selling women's clothing shows what the store might learn at each step and what actions it could take to increase sales.

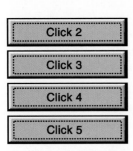

The shopper clicks on the home page. The store can tell that the shopper arrived from the Yahoo! portal at 2:30 PM (which might help determine staffing for customer service centers) and how long she lingered on the home page (which might indicate trouble navigating the site). Tracking beacons load cookies on the shopper's browser to follow her across the Web.

The shopper clicks on blouses, clicks to select a woman's white blouse, then clicks to view the same item in pink. The shopper clicks to select this item in a size 10 in pink and clicks to place it in her shopping cart. This information can help the store determine which sizes and colors are most popular. If the visitor moves to a different site, ads for pink blouses will appear from the same or different vendor.

From the shopping cart page, the shopper clicks to close the browser to leave the Web site without purchasing the blouse. This action could indicate the shopper changed her mind or that she had a problem with the Web site's checkout and payment process. Such behavior might signal that the Web site was not well designed.

By using personalization technology to modify the web pages presented to each customer, marketers achieve some of the benefits of using individual salespeople at dramatically lower costs. For instance, General Motors will show a Chevrolet banner ad to women emphasizing safety and utility, whereas men will receive ads emphasizing power and ruggedness.

What if you are a large national advertising company with many clients trying to reach millions of consumers? What if you were a large global manufacturer trying to reach potential consumers for your products? With millions of websites, working with each one would be impractical. Advertising networks solve this problem by creating a network of several thousand of the most popular websites millions of

Figure 10.4
Website Personalization
Firms can create unique personalized web pages that display content or ads for products or services of special interest to individual users, improving the customer experience and creating additional value.

User ⟷ Web site

Based on your portfolio and recent market trends, here are some recommendations.

Welcome back, Steve P. Munson.
Check out these recommended titles: One Minute Manager
Leading Change
Results-Based Leadership

Sarah,
Here are the items you want to bid on: Halogen reading lamp
Portable reading lamp
LED book reading lamp

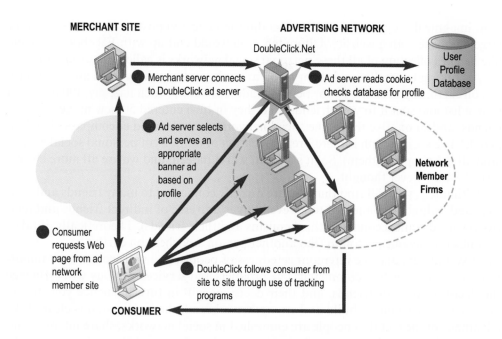

Figure 10.5

How an Advertising Network Such as Doubleclick Works

Advertising networks and their use of tracking programs have become controversial among privacy advocates because of their ability to track individual consumers across the Internet.

people visit, tracking the behavior of these users across the entire network, building profiles of each user, and then selling these profiles to advertisers. Popular websites download dozens of web tracking cookies, bugs, and beacons, which report user online behavior to remote servers without the users' knowledge. Looking for young, single consumers with college degrees, living in the Northeast, in the 18- to 34-age range who are interested in purchasing a European car? Not a problem. Advertising networks can identify and deliver thousands of people who fit this profile and expose them to ads for European cars as they move from one website to another. Estimates vary, but behaviorally targeted ads are generally 10 times more likely to produce a consumer response than a randomly chosen banner or video ad (see Figure 10.5). So-called advertising exchanges use this same technology to auction access to people with very specific profiles to advertisers in a few milliseconds. In 2015, about 25 percent of online display ads are targeted, and the rest depend on the context of the pages shoppers visit—the estimated demographics of visitors, or so-called blast-and-scatter advertising—which is placed randomly on any available page with minimal targeting, such as time of day or season.

Two-thirds (68 percent) of Internet users disapprove of search engines and websites tracking their online behavior to aim targeted ads at them. Twenty-eight percent of those surveyed approve of behavioral targeting because they believe it produces more relevant ads and information. A majority of Americans want a Do Not Track option in browsers that will stop websites from collecting information about their online behavior. More than 50 percent are very concerned about the wealth of personal data online; 86 percent have taken steps to mask their online behavior; 25 percent of web users use ad-blocking software. Next to hackers, Americans try to avoid advertisers pursuing them while online, and 64 percent block cookies to make tracking more difficult (Pew Internet, 2015a; 2015b).

SOCIAL E-COMMERCE AND SOCIAL NETWORK MARKETING

Social e-commerce is commerce based on the idea of the digital **social graph**, a mapping of all significant online social relationships. The social graph is synonymous with the idea of a social network used to describe offline relationships. You can map your own social graph (network) by drawing lines from yourself to the ten closest people you know. If they know one another, draw lines between these people. If you are ambitious, ask these 10 friends to list and draw in the names of the 10 people closest to them. What emerges from this exercise is a preliminary map of your social network.

Now imagine if everyone on the Internet did the same and posted the results to a very large database with a website. Ultimately, you would end up with Facebook or a site like it. The collection of all these personal social networks is called the *social graph*.

According to small world theory, you are only six links away from any other person on earth. If you entered your personal address book, which has, say, 100 names in it, in a list and sent it to your friends, and they in turn entered 50 new names of their friends, and so on, five times, the social network created would encompass 31 billion people! The social graph is therefore a collection of millions of personal social graphs (and all the people in them). So, it's a small world indeed, and we are all more closely linked than we ever thought.

Ultimately, you will find that you are directly connected to many friends and relatives and indirectly connected to an even larger universe of indirect friends and relatives (your distant second and third cousins and their friends). Theoretically, it takes six links for any one person to find another person anywhere on earth.

If you understand the interconnectedness of people, you will see just how important this concept is to e-commerce: The products and services you buy will influence the decisions of your friends, and their decisions will in turn influence you. If you are a marketer trying to build and strengthen a brand, the implication is clear: Take advantage of the fact that people are enmeshed in social networks, share interests and values, and communicate and influence one another. As a marketer, your target audience is not a million isolated people watching a TV show but the social network of people who watch the show and the viewers' personal networks. Table 10.7 describes the features of social commerce that are driving its growth.

In 2015, one of the fastest-growing media for branding and marketing is social media. Companies spent $9.6 billion using social networks such as Facebook to reach millions of consumers who spend hours a day on the Facebook site. Facebook accounts for 90 percent of all social marketing in the United States. Expenditures

TABLE 10.7

Features Of Social Commerce

Social commerce feature	Description
Newsfeed	A stream of notifications from friends, and advertisers, that social users find on their home pages.
Timelines	A stream of photos and events in the past that create a personal history for users, one that can be shared with friends.
Social sign-on	Websites allow users to sign into their sites through their social network pages on Facebook or another social site. This allows websites to receive valuable social profile information from Facebook and use it in their own marketing efforts.
Collaborative shopping	An environment where consumers can share their shopping experiences with one another by viewing products, chatting, or texting. Friends can chat online about brands, products, and services.
Network notification	An environment where consumers can share their approval (or disapproval) of products, services, or content or share their geo-location, perhaps a restaurant or club, with friends. Facebook's ubiquitous Like button is an example, as is Twitter's tweets and followers.
Social search (recommendations)	An environment where consumers can ask their friends for advice on purchases of products, services, and content. Although Google can help you find things, social search can help you evaluate the quality of things by listening to the evaluations of your friends or their friends. For instance, Amazon's social recommender system can use your Facebook social profile to recommend products.

for social media marketing are much smaller than for television, magazines, and even newspapers, but this will change in the future. Social networks in the offline world are collections of people who voluntarily communicate with one another over an extended period of time. Online social networks, such as Facebook, LinkedIn, Twitter, Tumblr, and Google+, along with other sites with social components, are websites that enable users to communicate with one another, form group and individual relationships, and share interests, values, and ideas. Individuals establish online profiles with text and photos, creating an online profile of how they want others to see them, and then invite their friends to link to their profile. The network grows by word of mouth and through email links. Facebook, with 150 million U.S. monthly visitors, receives most of the public attention given to social networking, but the other top four social sites are also growing, though at slower rates than in the past. Facebook user growth has slowed in the United States. LinkedIn growth slowed in 2014 to 40 percent, and it had 93 million visitors a month in 2015. Twitter grew to reach 284 million active users, with stronger offshore growth than in the United States. The social blogging site Tumblr reached 23 million people a month; and Pinterest hit the top 50 websites with 26 million. According to ComScore, about 28 percent of the total time spent online in the United States was spent on social network sites, and it is the most common online activity. (ComScore, 2014). The fastest growing smartphone applications are social network apps; nearly half of smartphone users visit social sites daily. More than 60 percent of all visits to Facebook in 2015 came from smartphones.

At **social shopping** sites such as Pinterest and Kaboodle, you can swap shopping ideas with friends. Facebook offers the Like button and Google the +1 button to let your friends know you admire a product, service, or content and, in some cases, purchase something online. (Facebook processes around 50 million Likes a day, or 1.5 billion a year.) Online communities are also ideal venues to employ viral marketing techniques. Online viral marketing is like traditional word-of-mouth marketing except that the word can spread across an online community at the speed of light and go much further geographically than a small network of friends.

The Wisdom of Crowds

Creating sites where thousands, even millions, of people can interact offers business firms new ways to market and advertise and to discover who likes (or hates) their products. In a phenomenon called the **wisdom of crowds**, some argue that large numbers of people can make better decisions about a wide range of topics or products than a single person or even a small committee of experts.

Obviously, this is not always the case, but it can happen in interesting ways. In marketing, the wisdom of crowds concept suggests that firms should consult with thousands of their customers first as a way of establishing a relationship with them and, second, to understand better how their products and services are used and appreciated (or rejected). Actively soliciting the comments of your customers builds trust and sends the message to your customers that you care what they are thinking and that you need their advice.

Beyond merely soliciting advice, firms can be actively helped in solving some business problems by using **crowdsourcing**. For instance, in 2012, BMW launched a crowdsourcing project to enlist the aid of customers in designing an urban vehicle for 2025. Kickstarter.com is arguably one of the most famous e-commerce crowdfunding sites where visitors invest in start-up companies. Other examples include Caterpillar working with customers to design better machinery, IKEA for designing furniture, and Pepsico using Super Bowl viewers to build an online video (Wethinq, 2014).

Marketing through social media is still in its early stages, and companies are experimenting in hopes of finding a winning formula. Social interactions and customer sentiment are not always easy to manage, presenting new challenges for companies eager to protect their brands. The Interactive Session on People provides specific examples of companies' social marketing efforts by using Facebook and Twitter.

INTERACTIVE SESSION: PEOPLE   Getting Social with Customers

Businesses of all sizes are finding Facebook, Twitter, and other social media to be powerful tools for engaging customers, amplifying product messages, discovering trends and influencers, building brand awareness, and taking action on customer requests and recommendations. Half of all Twitter users recommend products in their tweets.

About 1.4 billion people use Facebook, and more than 30 million businesses have active brand pages enabling users to interact with the brand through blogs, comment pages, contests, and offerings on the brand page. The Like button gives users a chance to share with their social network their feelings about content and other objects they are viewing and websites they are visiting. With Like buttons on millions of websites, Facebook can track user behavior on other sites and then sell this information to marketers. Facebook also sells display ads to firms that show up in the right column of users' homepages and in most other pages in the Facebook interface such as Photos and Apps.

New Haven, Connecticut's Karaoke Heroes bar was started in 2012, and half of its new customers come through Facebook. Karaoke Heroes is the only karaoke bar in the state of Connecticut, and the only superhero-themed karaoke bar in North America. Its customers include college students from the New Haven area as well as hardcore karaoke and superhero fans, middle-aged couples out for a date night, and Korean and Chinese families that come in to do karaoke in the bar's private rooms.

Owner Andrew Lebwohl and his wife design Facebook ads to appeal to people most interested in karaoke and superheroes and can experiment with different Facebook ads for different audiences without spending a great deal of money. For example, ads can target Connecticut residents who are interested in superheroes, mothers of young children interested in hosting parties during the weekend, or people who speak Mandarin or Spanish to let them know about the bar's music in those languages. When Karaoke Heroes runs special events, it can advertise the bar as an event space.

Twitter has developed many new offerings to interested advertisers, such as Promoted Tweets and Promoted Trends. These features give advertisers the ability to have their tweets displayed more prominently when Twitter users search for certain keywords. Many big advertisers are using Twitter's Vine service, which allows users to share short, repeating videos with a mobile-phone app or post them on other platforms such as Facebook.

In addition to monitoring people's chatter on Twitter, Facebook, and other social media, some companies are using sentiment analysis (see Chapter 6) to probe more deeply into their likes and dislikes. For example, during the 2014 Golden Globe Awards, thousands of women watching the ceremony tweeted detailed comments about Hayden Panettiere and Kelly Osborne's slicked-back hairdos. Almost instantaneously, the Twitter feeds of these women received instructions from L'Oréal Paris showing them how to capture various red-carpet looks at home, along with promotions and special deals for L'Oréal products. L'Oreal had worked with Poptip, a real-time market research company to analyze what conversations about hairstyling connected to Golden Globe hashtags and other key phrases were appearing on Twitter. When the Golden Globe red-carpet events began, Poptip's software looked for similar chatter and analyzed which conversations were genuine discussions from the appropriate demographic. Poptip determined that the target audience was captivated by slicked-back hairdos, and L'Oréal sponsored tweets to land in those Twitter conversations.

TomTom, a company that offers digital navigation and mapping products and services, has been using social media to enhance its product-development process. Like other companies, TomTom closely monitors social media conversations as part of its effort to evaluate performance in marketing and customer service. During this process, a company analyst discovered that users posting on a UK forum were focused on connectivity problems and channeled this information to TomTom's product-development teams. The product-development teams then worked directly and in real time with customers to resolve these problems. Social media helped TomTom improve its processes for research and development (R&D) and product development. TomTom now interacts directly with its driving community for ideas on design and product features as well as to troubleshoot new offerings quickly.

Still, the results of a social presence can be unpredictable and not always beneficial, as a number of companies have learned. Social media provided a platform for angry backlash against Starbucks in March 2015 for its Race Together campaign. Starbucks has taken on sensitive social issues before, and it launched the campaign to encourage conversation with its customers about race relations. Critics hammered Starbucks on social media for trying to capitalize on racial tensions in the United States.

Companies everywhere have rushed to create Facebook pages and Twitter accounts, but many still don't understand how to make effective use of these social media tools. Although large companies have learned how to stand out on social networks and get lots of help from sites such as Facebook and Twitter, most local business owners remain stumped by social marketing. This is especially true in the auto industry. Car manufacturers, including Hyundai and Ford Motor, have embraced social media and spend tens of millions of dollars on sophisticated marketing campaigns. Yet many of their local dealers barely maintain a Facebook page, and those that do report little or no gains in sales from going social.

Traditional marketing is all about creating and delivering a message using communication that is primarily one-way. Social media marketing is all about two-way communication and interaction. It enables businesses to receive an immediate response to a message—and to react and change the message, if necessary. Many companies still don't understand that difference.

Sources: Vindu Goel, "The Gap Between Auto Dealers and Social Media," *New York Times*, April 9, 2015; Dennis Nishi, "The Secret to a Perfect Six-Second Video," *Wall Street Journal*, January 26, 2015; Ben DiPetro, "The Morning Risk Report: Takeaways from Starbucks' Race Relations Gambit," *Wall Street Journal*, March 24, 2015; Martin Harrysson, Estelle Métayer, and Hugo Sarrazin, "The Strength of 'WeakSignals'," *McKinsey Quarterly*, February 2014; Katherine Rosman and Elizabeth Dwoskin, "Marketers Want to Know What You Really Mean Online," *Wall Street Journal*, March 23, 2014; "How Karaoke Heroes Builds Awareness of its 'Super' Business," Facebook for Business, July 1, 2014; and Ashley Smith, "Social Media for Businesses Begs for More Listening and Less Marketing," SearchCRM.com, January 22, 2013.

CASE STUDY QUESTIONS

1. Assess the people, organization, and technology issues for using social media to engage with customers.

2. What are the advantages and disadvantages of using social media for advertising, brand building, market research, and customer service?

3. Give some examples of business decisions in this case study that were facilitated by using social media to interact with customers.

4. Should all companies use Facebook and Twitter for customer service and marketing? Why or why not? What kinds of companies are best suited to use these platforms?

10-4 How has e-commerce affected business-to-business transactions?

The trade between business firms (business-to-business commerce, or B2B) represents a huge marketplace. The total amount of B2B trade in the United States in 2015 is estimated to be about $14.6 trillion, with B2B e-commerce (online B2B) contributing about $6.2 trillion of that amount (U.S. Bureau of the Census, 2015; authors' estimates). By 2019, B2B e-commerce is expected to grow to about $8.6 trillion in the United States. The process of conducting trade among business firms is complex and requires significant human intervention; therefore, it consumes significant resources. Some firms estimate that each corporate purchase order for support products costs them, on average, at least $100 in administrative overhead. Administrative overhead includes processing paper, approving purchase decisions, spending time using the telephone and fax machines to search for products and arrange for purchases, arranging for shipping, and receiving the goods. Across the economy, this adds up to trillions of dollars annually spent for procurement processes that could be automated. If even just a portion of inter-firm trade were automated, and parts of the entire procurement process were assisted by the Internet, literally trillions of dollars might be released for more productive uses, consumer prices potentially would fall, productivity would increase, and the economic wealth of the nation would expand.

This is the promise of B2B e-commerce. The challenge of B2B e-commerce is changing existing patterns and systems of procurement and designing and implementing new Internet-based B2B solutions.

ELECTRONIC DATA INTERCHANGE (EDI)

B2B e-commerce refers to the commercial transactions that occur among business firms. Increasingly, these transactions are flowing through a variety of Internet-enabled mechanisms. About 80 percent of online B2B e-commerce is still based on proprietary systems for **electronic data interchange (EDI)**. EDI enables the computer-to-computer exchange between two organizations of standard transactions such as invoices, bills of lading, shipment schedules, or purchase orders. Transactions are automatically transmitted from one information system to another through a network, eliminating the printing and handling of paper at one end and the inputting of data at the other. Each major industry in the United States and much of the rest of the world has EDI standards that define the structure and information fields of electronic documents for that industry.

EDI originally automated the exchange of documents such as purchase orders, invoices, and shipping notices. Although many companies still use EDI for document automation, firms engaged in just-in-time inventory replenishment and continuous production use EDI as a system for continuous replenishment. Suppliers have online access to selected parts of the purchasing firm's production and delivery schedules and automatically ship materials and goods to meet prespecified targets without intervention by firm purchasing agents (see Figure 10.6).

Although many organizations still use private networks for EDI, they are increasingly web-enabled because Internet technology provides a much more flexible and low-cost platform for linking to other firms. Businesses can extend digital technology to a wider range of activities and broaden their circle of trading partners.

Procurement, for example, involves not only purchasing goods and materials but also sourcing, negotiating with suppliers, paying for goods, and making delivery arrangements. Businesses can now use the Internet to locate the lowest-cost supplier, search online catalogs of supplier products, negotiate with suppliers, place orders, make payments, and arrange transportation. They are not limited to partners linked by traditional EDI networks.

NEW WAYS OF B2B BUYING AND SELLING

The Internet and web technology enable businesses to create electronic storefronts for selling to other businesses using the same techniques as used for B2C commerce. Alternatively, businesses can use Internet technology to create extranets or electronic marketplaces for linking to other businesses for purchase and sale transactions.

Private industrial networks typically consist of a large firm using a secure website to link to its suppliers and other key business partners (see Figure 10.7). The buyer owns the network, and it permits the firm and designated suppliers, distributors,

Figure 10.6
Electronic Data Interchange (EDI)
Companies use EDI to automate transactions for B2B e-commerce and continuous inventory replenishment. Suppliers can automatically send data about shipments to purchasing firms. The purchasing firms can use EDI to provide production and inventory requirements and payment data to suppliers.

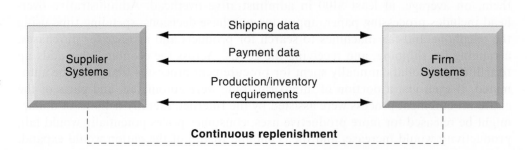

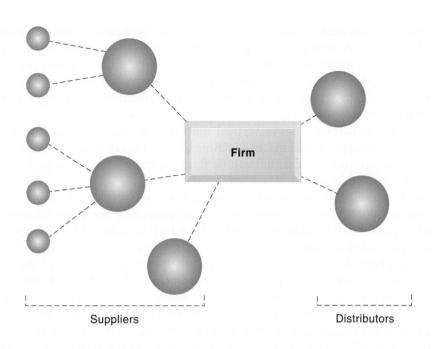

Figure 10.7
A Private Industrial Network
A private industrial network, also known as a private exchange, links a firm to its suppliers, distributors, and other key business partners for efficient supply chain management and other collaborative commerce activities.

Suppliers   Distributors

and other business partners to share product design and development, marketing, production scheduling, inventory management, and unstructured communication, including graphics and email. Another term for a private industrial network is a **private exchange**.

An example is VW Group Supply, which links the Volkswagen Group and its suppliers. VW Group Supply handles 90 percent of all global purchasing for Volkswagen, including all automotive and parts components.

Net marketplaces, which are sometimes called e-hubs, provide a single, digital marketplace based on Internet technology for many buyers and sellers (see Figure 10.8). They are industry-owned or operate as independent intermediaries between buyers and sellers. Net marketplaces generate revenue from purchase and sale transactions and other services provided to clients. Participants in Net marketplaces can establish prices through online negotiations, auctions, or requests for quotations, or they can use fixed prices.

There are many types of Net marketplaces and ways of classifying them. Some sell direct goods and some sell indirect goods. **Direct goods** are goods used in a

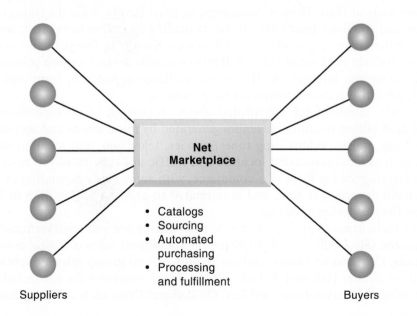

Figure 10.8
A Net Marketplace
Net marketplaces are online marketplaces where multiple buyers can purchase from multiple sellers.

Suppliers   Buyers

production process, such as sheet steel for auto body production. **Indirect goods** are all other goods not directly involved in the production process, such as office supplies or products for maintenance and repair. Some Net marketplaces support contractual purchasing based on long-term relationships with designated suppliers, and others support short-term spot purchasing, where goods are purchased based on immediate needs, often from many suppliers.

Some Net marketplaces serve vertical markets for specific industries, such as automobiles, telecommunications, or machine tools, whereas others serve horizontal markets for goods and services that can be found in many industries, such as office equipment or transportation.

Exostar is an example of an industry-owned Net marketplace, focusing on long-term contract purchasing relationships and on providing common networks and computing platforms for reducing supply chain inefficiencies. This aerospace and defense industry-sponsored Net marketplace was founded jointly by BAE Systems, Boeing, Lockheed Martin, Raytheon, and Rolls-Royce plc to connect these companies to their suppliers and facilitate collaboration. More than 100,000 trading partners in the commercial, military, and government sectors use Exostar's sourcing, e-procurement, and collaboration tools for both direct and indirect goods.

Exchanges are independently owned third-party Net marketplaces that connect thousands of suppliers and buyers for spot purchasing. Many exchanges provide vertical markets for a single industry, such as food, electronics, or industrial equipment, and they primarily deal with direct inputs. For example, Go2Paper enables a spot market for paper, board, and craft among buyers and sellers in the paper industries from more than 75 countries.

Exchanges proliferated during the early years of e-commerce, but many have failed. Suppliers were reluctant to participate because the exchanges encouraged competitive bidding that drove prices down and did not offer any long-term relationships with buyers or services to make lowering prices worthwhile. Many essential direct purchases are not conducted on a spot basis because they require contracts and consideration of issues such as delivery timing, customization, and quality of products.

10-5 What is the role of m-commerce in business, and what are the most important m-commerce applications?

Walk down the street in any major metropolitan area and count how many people are pecking away at their iPhones, Samsungs, or BlackBerrys. Ride the trains or fly the planes, and you'll see your fellow travelers reading an online newspaper, watching a video on their phone, or reading a novel on their Kindle. In five years, the majority of Internet users in the United States will rely on mobile devices as their primary device for accessing the Internet. As the mobile audience expands in leaps and bounds, mobile advertising and m-commerce have taken off.

In 2015, m-commerce constituted about 26 percent of all e-commerce, with about $128 billion in annual revenues generated by retail goods and services, apps, advertising, music, videos, ring tones, movies, television, and location-based services such as local restaurant locators and traffic updates. However, m-commerce is the fastest-growing form of e-commerce, with some areas expanding at a rate of 50 percent or more per year, and is estimated to grow to $246 billion in 2019 (see Figure 10.9) (eMarketer, 2015e).

The main areas of growth in mobile e-commerce are mass market retailing such as Amazon ($16.8 billion) and Apple (about $14 billion); sales of digital content such as music, TV shows and movies (about $6 billion); and in-app sales to mobile devices (about $9 billion) (Internet Retailer, 2015). These estimates do not include mobile advertising or location-based services. On-demand firms such as Uber (described in

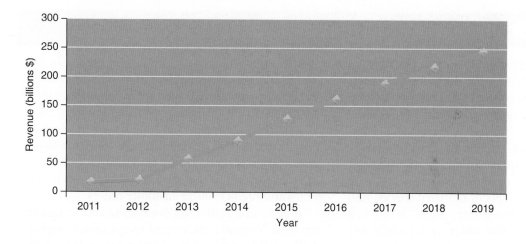

Figure 10.9
Consolidated Mobile
Commerce Revenues
*Mobile e-commerce is
the fastest growing type
of B2C e-commerce
and represented about
26 percent of all
e-commerce in 2015.*

Sources: Data from
e-Marketer chart,
"US Retail Mcommerce
Sales, 2013-2019,"
May 2015.

the chapter-opening case) and Airbnb are location-based services, but they are certainly examples of mobile commerce as well.

LOCATION-BASED SERVICES AND APPLICATIONS

Location-based services include geosocial, geoadvertising, and geoinformation services. Seventy-four percent of smartphone owners use location-based services. What ties these activities together and is the foundation for mobile commerce is the global positioning system (GPS)–enabled map services available on smartphones. A **geosocial service** can tell you where your friends are meeting. **Geoadvertising services** can tell you where to find the nearest Italian restaurant, and **geoinformation services** can tell you the price of a house you are looking at or about special exhibits at a museum you are passing. In 2015, the fastest-growing and most popular location-based services are on-demand economy firms such as Uber, Lyft, Airbnb, Instacart (see the Interactive Session on Organizations), and hundreds more that provide services to users in local areas and are based on the user's location (or, in the case of Airbnb, the user's intended travel location).

Wikitude.com is an example of a geoinformation service. Wikitude is an augmented reality application that overlays information such as videos, photos, and reviews on your smartphone screen based on your GPS position. Using information from more than 800,000 points of interest available on Wikipedia, plus thousands of other local sites, the Wikitude browser overlays information about points of interest you are viewing, and displays that information on your smartphone screen, superimposed on a map or photograph that you just snapped. For example, users can point their smartphone cameras toward mountains from a tour bus and see the names and heights of the mountains displayed on the screen. Wikitude.me also allows users to geo-tag the world around them and then submit the tags to Wikitude to share content with other users.

Foursquare, Loopt, and new offerings by Facebook and Google are examples of geosocial services. Geosocial services help you find friends, or your friends to find you, by checking in to the service, announcing your presence in a restaurant or other place. Your friends are instantly notified. About 20 percent of smartphone owners use geosocial services.

Foursquare provides a location-based social networking service to 55 million registered individual users, who may connect with friends, update their location, and provide reviews and tips for enjoying a location. Points are awarded for checking in at designated venues. Users choose to post their check-ins on their accounts on Twitter, Facebook, or both. Users also earn badges by checking in at locations with certain tags, for check-in frequency, or for the time of check-in. More than 500,000 local merchants worldwide use the merchant platform for marketing.

Connecting people to local merchants in the form of geoadvertising is the economic foundation for mobile commerce. Mobile advertising reached $17.7 billion in

INTERACTIVE SESSION: ORGANIZATIONS   Can Instacart Deliver?

The online grocery store Webvan was perhaps the most well-known flop of the dot-com boom. Its 2001 failure led many pundits and investors to conclude that the online grocery business model was untenable.

However, Webvan's downfall was due mainly to pursuing a first-mover advantage strategy. It paid over $1 billion to build huge distribution warehouses, bought fleets of delivery trucks, and invested heavily in marketing. Then, it offered free deliveries on any size order, at virtually any hour, at prices that trumped its brick-and-mortar competitors. This was not a formula for generating profits.

In recent years other companies are testing the waters again for online grocery sales. FreshDirect in New York City has succeeded by combining fresh local produce, organic and kosher items, and custom-prepared meals with standard grocery store fare. Established brick-and-mortar firms including Albertson's, Safeway and Peapod.com (the online entity for both Stop & Shop and Giant) took over as pure play online firms perished.

The newest entrant, Instacart bypasses the expenses of warehousing and transportation altogether by using a legion of independent contractors. These personal shoppers receive orders via the Instacart smartphone app, fill them from grocery store aisles, and use their own vehicles to deliver them to customers' doors. Like fellow "sharing economy" firm Uber, Instacart minimizes labor costs by requiring its personal shoppers to pay for their own auto and health insurance and Social Security contributions. Purportedly paid between $15 and $30.00 an hour, depending on how quickly they can fill and deliver an order, most Instacart shoppers work part-time on flexible schedules.

Instacart co-founder and CEO, Apoorva Mehta believes Instacart's competitive advantage is twofold. First, customers are not limited to a single vendor and can combine items from multiple stores on one order, so product selection is truly customized. (Instacart uses special software that can track inventory across multiple supermarkets.) And since personal shoppers are on call around the clock, customers neither have to order many hours in advance of delivery nor wait for a delivery window. In fact, customers can have their grocery list filled and delivered in under an hour!

Instacart's app provides a detailed map of each local establishment including store aisle contents. The customer's grocery list, compiled using exten-sive drop-down menus either on the website or in the app, is organized by merchant and aisle to provide maximum order fulfillment efficiency. Inventory is tracked for all of Instacart-affiliated merchants. As a personal shopper skims an aisle, bedecked in a bright green T-shirt flaunting the Instacart logo, items can be selected for different orders placed at different times. The software can also plan delivery routes and predict future customer orders.

iPhone users can even connect to the Instacart app from Yummly, the largest recipe search engine in the world, and have the ingredients delivered in time for dinner. The Instacart app is integrated with Google Now cards so that Android users can place orders for either delivery or pickup using a token generated within the app.

Instacart's core competencies thus dictate its target market: the price-insensitive, convenience shopper. At first, item prices were marked up (20 percent in one sampling) and a $3.99 delivery fee charged. An Amazon Prime-like service called Instacart Express requires a certain volume of business and a $99.00 yearly fee in exchange for free delivery. One of Webvan's big mistakes was pursuing a mass-market strategy. It was never going to be able to turn a profit by providing quality and selection at rock-bottom prices—with free delivery to boot. Instacart is instead catering to shoppers who are willing to pay a premium to have both quality and selection.

By mid-2015 Instacart had 200 employees and 4,000 personal shoppers in New York, Los Angeles, San Francisco, San Jose, Washington DC, Chicago, Boston, Austin, Seattle, Philadelphia, Atlanta, Boulder, Denver, Houston, and Portland, Oregon. It continues to grow. Grocery purveyors, from large chains such as Costco, BJ's Wholesale Club, Safeway, Kroger, Super Fresh, Trader Joe's and Whole Foods to local specialty shops, such as Erewhon Organic Grocer & Café in LA, Marczyk Fine Foods in Denver, and Green Zebra in Portland, are now welcoming Instacart as a way to expand their customer bases ahead of the full national roll-out of Amazon subsidiary Amazon Fresh.

Instacart's 2014 revenue grew more than ten times over 2013, with fourth quarter sales doubling. While many analysts predict that matching the bargain basement prices of Amazon and Walmart is unavoidable, Instacart is instead modifying its business model. Partnerships with Petco and Tomlinson's Pet Supplies in Austin, Texas, hint of additional product areas on the horizon, while Mehta speculates that expansion into general logistics is conceivable.

Many of Instacart's grocery store partners now set their own prices, paying Instacart a cut of each order. This has freed Instacart of the burden of markups, protected it from the vagaries of variable food prices, and provided a more stable profit structure. Retailers have been willing to pay Instacart in the hope of gaining more business, because Instacart enables a single store to serve people across a larger geographic area. Affiliated retailers are reporting gains, although the numbers are small. Nilam Ganenthiran, head of Business Development and Strategy, maintains that different types of agreements have been reached, declining to specify whether partners are outsourcing their e-commerce to Instacart for a monthly fee, or if they are charged per item purchased, per order placed, or per customer serviced.

With national chains achieving just 1 to 2 percent margins on grocery delivery, the Instacart model of layering labor on top of the existing grocery infrastructure

is still unproven. According to a *Wall Street Journal* analysis, an order of 15 common items such as frozen peas, milk, cereal and fresh fruit costing about $68 from a San Francisco Safeway store would produce a profit of only $1.50 for Instacart. If the order were smaller by one 28-ouce jar of peanut butter, Instacart would break even, and a smaller order could push it into the red. Without price concessions from participating merchants, can Instacart attract enough customers? *And* maintain a pay scale that ensures the topnotch customer service demanded by its target market? *And* still make a profit? And can retailers' sales gains from Instacart be sustained? Instacart may be a great idea, but it's a very big bet.

Sources: Brad Stone, "Instacart Rings Up $220 Million More for its Grocery Delivery Service," by Brad Stone, Bloomberg Business, January 13, 2015; Carmel DeAmicis, "On the Way to $220M in Funding, Instacart Quietly Changed Its Business Model,"gigaom.com, January 14, 2015; Seth Fiegerman, "Instacart Bags $220 Billion to Expand Beyond Grocery Delivery," mashable.com, January 13, 2015; Farhad Manjoo, "Instacart's Bet on Online Grocery Shopping, New York Times, April 29, 2015 and "Grocery Deliveries in the Sharing Economy," New York Times, May 21, 2014; and "Instacart," crunchbase.com; accessed February 4, 2015.

CASE STUDY QUESTIONS

1. Analyze Instacart using the value chain and competitive forces models. What competitive forces does the company have to deal with? What is its value proposition?

2. Explain how Instacart's business model works. How does the company generate revenue?

3. What is the role of information technology in Instacart's business model?

4. Is Instacart's model for selling online groceries viable? Why or why not?

2014, up 83 percent from 2013. Geoadvertising sends ads to users based on their GPS locations. Smartphones report their locations back to Google and Apple. Merchants buy access to these consumers when they come within range of a merchant. For instance, Kiehl Stores, a cosmetics retailer, sent special offers and announcements to customers who came within 100 yards of their store.

OTHER MOBILE COMMERCE SERVICES

Banks and credit card companies have developed services that let customers manage their accounts from their mobile devices. JPMorgan Chase and Bank of America customers can use their cell phones to check account balances, transfer funds, and pay bills. Apple Pay for the iPhone 6 and Apple Watch, along with other Android and Windows smartphone models, allows users to charge items to their credit card accounts with a swipe of their phone. (See our Learning Track on mobile payment systems.)

The mobile advertising market is the fastest growing online ad platform, racking up $28 billion in ad revenue in 2015 and growing at 47 percent annually. Ads eventually move to where the eyeballs are, and increasingly that means mobile phones and, to less extent, tablets. Google is the largest mobile advertising market, posting about

$10 billion in mobile ads, with Facebook number two with $4.9 billion. Yahoo displays ads on its mobile home page for companies such as Pepsico, Procter & Gamble, Hilton, Nissan, and Intel. Google is displaying ads linked to cell phone searches by users of the mobile version of its search engine; Microsoft offers banner and text advertising on its MSN Mobile portal in the United States. Ads are embedded in games, videos, and other mobile applications.

Shopkick is a mobile application that enables retailers such as Best Buy, Sports Authority, and Macy's to offer coupons to people when they walk into their stores. The Shopkick app automatically recognizes when the user has entered a partner retail store and offers a new virtual currency called kickbucks, which can be redeemed for Facebook credits, iTunes gift cards, travel vouchers, DVDs, or immediate cashback rewards at any of the partner stores.

Fifty-five percent of online retailers now have m-commerce websites—simplified versions of their websites that enable shoppers to use cell phones to shop and place orders. Clothing retailers Lilly Pulitzer and Armani Exchange, Home Depot, Amazon, Walmart, and 1-800-Flowers are among those companies with apps for m-commerce sales.

10-6 What issues must be addressed when building an e-commerce presence?

Building a successful e-commerce presence requires a keen understanding of business, technology, and social issues as well as a systematic approach. Today, an e-commerce presence is not just a corporate website, but also includes a social network site on Facebook, a Twitter feed, and smartphone apps where customers can access your services. Developing and coordinating all these customer venues can be difficult. A complete treatment of the topic is beyond the scope of this text, and students should consult books devoted to just this topic (Laudon and Traver, 2016). The two most important management challenges in building a successful e-commerce presence are (1) developing a clear understanding of your business objectives and (2) knowing how to choose the right technology to achieve those objectives.

DEVELOP AN E-COMMERCE PRESENCE MAP

E-commerce has moved from being a PC-centric activity on the web to a mobile and tablet-based activity. Currently, a majority of Internet users in the United States use smartphones and tablets to shop for goods and services, look up prices, enjoy entertainment, and access social sites, less so to make purchases. Your potential customers use these various devices at different times during the day and involve themselves in different conversations, depending what they are doing—touching base with friends, tweeting, or reading a blog. Each of these is a touch point where you can meet the customer, and you have to think about how you develop a presence in these different virtual places. Figure 10.10 provides a roadmap to the platforms and related activities you will need to think about when developing your e-commerce presence.

Figure 10.10 illustrates four kinds of e-commerce presence: websites, email, social media, and offline media. You must address different platforms for each of these types. For instance, in the case of website presence, there are three platforms: traditional desktop, tablets, and smartphones, each with different capabilities. Moreover, for each type of e-commerce presence, there are related activities you will need to consider. For instance, in the case of websites, you will want to engage in search engine marketing, display ads, affiliate programs, and sponsorships. Offline media, the fourth type of e-commerce presence, is included here because many firms use multiplatform or integrated marketing by which print ads refer customers to websites.

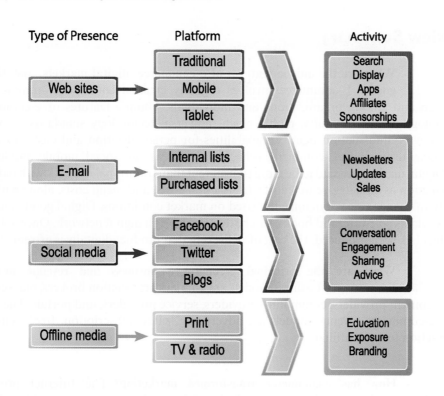

Figure 10.10
E-commerce Presence
Map
An e-commerce presence requires firms to consider the four types of presence, with specific platforms and activities associated with each.

DEVELOP A TIMELINE: MILESTONES

Where would you like to be a year from now? It's very helpful for you to have a rough idea of the time frame for developing your e-commerce presence when you begin. You should break your project down into a small number of phases that could be completed within a specified time. Table 10.8 illustrates a one-year timeline for the development of an e-commerce presence for a start-up company devoted to fashions for teenagers. You can also find more detail about developing an e-commerce website in the Learning Tracks for this chapter.

TABLE 10.8

E-Commerce Presence
Timeline

Phase	Activity	Milestone
Phase 1: Planning	Envision web presence; determine personnel.	Web mission statement
Phase 2: Website development	Acquire content; develop a site design; arrange for hosting the site.	Website plan
Phase 3: Web Implementation	Develop keywords and metatags; focus on search engine optimization; identify potential sponsors.	A functional website
Phase 4: Social media plan	Identify appropriate social platforms and content for your products and services.	A social media plan
Phase 5: Social media implementation	Develop Facebook, Twitter, and Pinterest presence.	Functioning social media presence
Phase 6: Mobile plan	Develop a mobile plan; consider options for porting your website to smartphones.	A mobile media plan

Review Summary

10-1 **What are the unique features of e-commerce, digital markets, and digital goods?** E-commerce involves digitally enabled commercial transactions between and among organizations and individuals. Unique features of e-commerce technology include ubiquity, global reach, universal technology standards, richness, interactivity, information density, capabilities for personalization and customization, and social technology. E-commerce is becoming increasingly social, mobile, and local.

Digital markets are said to be more transparent than traditional markets, with reduced information asymmetry, search costs, transaction costs, and menu costs, along with the ability to change prices dynamically based on market conditions. Digital goods, such as music, video, software, and books, can be delivered over a digital network. Once a digital product has been produced, the cost of delivering that product digitally is extremely low.

10-2 **What are the principal e-commerce business and revenue models?** E-commerce business models are e-tailers, transaction brokers, market creators, content providers, community providers, service providers, and portals. The principal e-commerce revenue models are advertising, sales, subscription, free/freemium, transaction fee, and affiliate.

10-3 **How has e-commerce transformed marketing?** The Internet provides marketers with new ways of identifying and communicating with millions of potential customers at costs far lower than traditional media. Crowdsourcing using the wisdom of crowds helps companies learn from customers to improve product offerings and increase customer value. Behavioral targeting techniques increase the effectiveness of banner, rich media, and video ads. Social commerce uses social networks and social network sites to improve targeting of products and services.

10-4 **How has e-commerce affected business-to-business transactions?** B2B e-commerce generates efficiencies by enabling companies to locate suppliers, solicit bids, place orders, and track shipments in transit electronically. Net marketplaces provide a single, digital marketplace for many buyers and sellers. Private industrial networks link a firm with its suppliers and other strategic business partners to develop highly efficient and responsive supply chains.

10-5 **What is the role of m-commerce in business, and what are the most important m-commerce applications?** M-commerce is especially well suited for location-based applications such as finding local hotels and restaurants, monitoring local traffic and weather, and providing personalized location-based marketing. Mobile phones and handhelds are being used for mobile bill payment, banking, securities trading, transportation schedule updates, and downloads of digital content such as music, games, and video clips. M-commerce requires wireless portals and special digital payment systems that can handle micropayments. The GPS capabilities of smartphones make geoadvertising, geosocial, and geoinformation services possible.

10-6 **What issues must be addressed when building an e-commerce presence?** Building a successful e-commerce presence requires a clear understanding of the business objectives to be achieved and selection of the right platforms, activities, and timeline to achieve those objectives. An e-commerce presence includes not only a corporate website but also a presence on Facebook, Twitter, and other social networking sites and smartphone apps.

Key Terms

Advertising revenue model, 382

Affiliate revenue model, 383

Behavioral targeting, 384

Business-to-business (B2B), 379

Business-to-consumer (B2C), 379

Community providers, 382

Consumer-to-consumer (C2C), 379

Cost transparency, 375

Crowdsourcing, 389

Customization, 375

Digital goods, 377

Direct goods, 393

Disintermediation, 376

Dynamic pricing, 376

Electronic data interchange (EDI), 392

E-tailer, 380

Exchanges, 394

Free/freemium revenue model, 383

Geoadvertising services, 395

Geoinformation services, 395

Geosocial services, 395

Indirect goods, 394

Information asymmetry, 376

Information density, 374

Intellectual property, 381

Location-based services, 395

Long tail marketing, 384

Market creator, 381

Market entry costs, 374

Marketspace, 374

Menu costs, 376

Micropayment systems, 383

Mobile commerce (m-commerce), 379

Net marketplaces, 393

Personalization, 375

Podcasting, 381

Price discrimination, 375

Price transparency, 375

Private exchange, 393

Private industrial networks, 392

Revenue model, 382

Richness, 374

Sales revenue model, 383

Search costs, 374

Social graph, 387

Social shopping, 389

Streaming, 381

Subscription revenue model, 383

Transaction costs, 374

Transaction fee revenue model, 383

Wisdom of crowds, 389

MyMISLab™

To complete the problems with the ⭐, go to EOC Discussion Questions in the MyLab.

Review Questions

10-1 What are the unique features of e-commerce, digital markets, and digital goods?

- Name and describe four business trends and three technology trends shaping e-commerce today.
- List and describe the eight unique features of e-commerce.
- Explain how e-commerce has become more social, mobile, and local.

10-2 What are the principal e-commerce business and revenue models?

- Summarize the three main types of e-commerce.
- Name and describe the principal e-commerce business models.
- Name and describe the e-commerce revenue models.

10-3 How has e-commerce transformed marketing?

- Explain how social networking and the wisdom of crowds help companies improve their marketing.
- Define behavioral targeting and explain how it works at individual websites and on advertising networks.
- Define the social graph and explain how it is used in e-commerce marketing.

10-4 How has e-commerce affected business-to-business transactions?

- Explain how Internet technology supports business-to-business electronic commerce.
- Define and describe exchanges and explain how they differ from Net marketplaces.

10-5 What is the role of m-commerce in business, and what are the most important m-commerce applications?
- List and describe important types of m-commerce services and applications.
- Describe common location-based services and applications.

10-6 What issues must be addressed when building an e-commerce presence?
- List and describe the four types of e-commerce presence.

Discussion Questions

⭐ 10-7 How does the Internet change consumer and supplier relationships?

⭐ 10-8 The mobile platform may not make desktop PCs obsolete, but corporations will have to change their business models to adjust to this shift. Do you agree? Why or why not?

⭐ 10-9 How have social technologies changed e-commerce?

Hands-On MIS Projects

The projects in this section give you hands-on experience developing e-commerce strategies for businesses, using spreadsheet software to research the profitability of an e-commerce company and using web tools to research and evaluate e-commerce hosting services. Visit MyMISLab's Multimedia Library to access this chapter's Hands-On MIS Projects.

MANAGEMENT DECISION PROBLEMS

10-10 Columbiana is a small, independent island in the Caribbean that has many historical buildings, forts, and other sites along with rain forests and striking mountains. A few first-class hotels and several dozen less expensive accommodations lie along its beautiful white-sand beaches. The major airlines have regular flights to Columbiana, as do several small airlines. Columbiana's government wants to increase tourism and develop new markets for the country's tropical agricultural products. How can a web presence help? What Internet business model would be appropriate? What functions should the website perform?

10-11 Explore the Web sites of the following companies: Eurosparkle, Promod, Kingfisher plc, and ebookers.com. Determine which of these Web sites would benefit most from adding a company-sponsored blog to the Web site. List the business benefits of the blog. Specify the intended audience for the blog. Decide who in the company should author the blog, and select some topics for the blog.

IMPROVING DECISION MAKING: USING SPREADSHEET SOFTWARE TO ANALYZE A DOT-COM BUSINESS

Software skills: Spreadsheet downloading, formatting, and formulas
Business skills: Financial statement analysis

10-12 Pick one e-commerce company on the Internet—for example, Ashford, Yahoo, or Priceline. Study the web pages that describe the company and explain its purpose and structure. Use the web to find articles that comment on the company. Then visit the Securities and Exchange Commission's website at www. sec.gov to access the company's 10-K (annual report) form showing income statements and balance sheets. Select only the sections of the 10-K form containing the desired portions of financial statements that you need to examine and download them into your spreadsheet. (MyMISLab provides more detailed instructions on how to download this 10-K data into a spreadsheet.) Create simplified spreadsheets of the company's balance sheets and income statements for the past three years.

- Is the company a dot-com success, borderline business, or failure? What information provides the basis of your decision? Why? When answering these questions, pay special attention to the company's three-year trends in revenues, costs of sales, gross margins, operating expenses, and net margins.
- Prepare an overhead presentation (with a minimum of five slides), including appropriate spreadsheets or charts, and present your work to your professor and classmates.

ACHIEVING OPERATIONAL EXCELLENCE: EVALUATING E-COMMERCE HOSTING SERVICES

Software skills: Web browser software
Business skills: Evaluating e-commerce hosting services

10-13 This project will help develop your Internet skills in evaluating commercial services for hosting an e-commerce site for a small start-up company.

You would like to set up a website to sell towels, linens, pottery, and tableware from Portugal and are examining services for hosting small business Internet storefronts. Your website should be able to take secure credit card payments and calculate shipping costs and taxes. Initially, you would like to display photos and descriptions of 40 products. Visit Verio Europe, Host Europe, and iPage and compare the range of e-commerce hosting services they offer to small businesses, their capabilities, and their costs. Examine the tools they provide for creating an e-commerce site. Compare these services and decide which you would use if you were actually establishing a web store. Write a brief report indicating your choice and explaining the strengths and weaknesses of each service.

Collaboration and Teamwork Project

Performing a Competitive Analysis of E-Commerce Sites

10-14 Form a group with three or four of your classmates. Select two businesses that are competitors in the same industry and that use their websites for electronic commerce. Visit these websites. You might compare, for example, the websites for Pandora and Spotify, Amazon and BarnesandNoble.com, or E*Trade and Scottrade. Prepare an evaluation of each business's website in terms of its functions, user friendliness, and ability to support the company's business strategy. Which website does a better job? Why? Can you make some recommendations to improve these websites? If possible, use Google Docs and Google Drive or Google Sites to brainstorm, organize, and develop a presentation of your findings for the class.

BUSINESS PROBLEM-SOLVING CASE

Walmart and Amazon Duke It Out for E-Commerce Supremacy

Walmart is the world's largest and most successful retailer, with $487.5 billion in 2014 sales and nearly 11,000 stores worldwide, including more than 4,000 in the United States. Walmart has 2.2 million employees and ranks first on the Fortune 500 list of companies. Walmart had such a large and powerful selling machine that it really didn't have any serious competitors—until now.

Today, Walmart's greatest threat is Amazon.com, often called the Walmart of the web. Amazon sells not only books but just about everything else people want to buy—DVDs, video, and music streaming downloads, software, video games, electronics, apparel, furniture, food, toys, and jewelry. The company also produces consumer electronics, notably the Amazon Kindle e-book reader and Kindle Fire tablet and Amazon Fire smartphone. No other online retailer can match Amazon's breadth of selection; low prices; and fast, reliable shipping.

For many years, Amazon has been the world's largest e-commerce retailer with the world's largest and most powerful online selling machine. Moreover, Amazon has changed the habits and expectations of consumers in ways to which Walmart and other retailers must adapt. Instead of a push model, by which merchandisers have a large degree of control of what items they stock and sell, retailers must adapt to a pull model, by which shoppers are more empowered than ever. According to Brian Yarbrough, a retail analyst at Edward Jones in St. Louis, Amazon and online retailing is probably the biggest disrupter of retail since Walmart itself.

Walmart was founded as a traditional, off-line, physical store in 1962, and that's still what it does best. However, it is being forced to compete in e-commerce as well. Six or seven years ago, only one-fourth of all Walmart customers shopped at Amazon.com, according to data from researcher Kantar Retail. Today, however, half of Walmart customers say they've shopped at both retailers. Online competition and the profits to be reaped from e-commerce have become too tough to ignore.

Walmart's traditional customers—who are primarily bargain hunters making less than $50,000 per year—are becoming more comfortable using technology. More-affluent customers who started shopping at Walmart during the recession are returning to Amazon as their finances improve. Amazon has started stocking merchandise categories that Walmart traditionally sold, such as vacuum bags, diapers, and apparel, and its revenue is growing much faster than Walmart's. In 2014, Amazon had sales of nearly $89 billion.

If more people want to do even some of their shopping online, Amazon has some clear-cut advantages. It has created a recognizable and highly successful brand in online retailing. The company has developed extensive warehousing facilities and an extremely efficient distribution network specifically designed for web shopping. Its premium shipping service, Amazon Prime, provides fast, free two-day shipping at an affordable fixed annual subscription price ($99 per year), often considered to be a weak point for online retailers. According to the *Wall Street Journal*, Amazon's shipping costs are lower than Walmart's, ranging from $3 to $4 per package, while Walmart's online shipping can run $5 to $7 per parcel. Walmart's massive supply chain needs to support more than 4000 physical stores worldwide, which Amazon doesn't have to worry about. Shipping costs can make a big difference for a store like Walmart, where popular purchases tend to be low-cost items such as $10 packs of underwear. It makes no sense for Walmart to create a duplicate supply chain for e-commerce.

However, Walmart is no pushover. It is an even larger and more recognizable brand than Amazon. Consumers associate Walmart with the lowest price, which Walmart has the flexibility to offer on any given item because of its size. The company can lose money selling a hot product at extremely low margins and expect to make money on the strength of the large quantities of other items it sells. Walmart also has a significant physical presence, and its stores provide the instant gratification of shopping, buying an item, and taking it home immediately as opposed to waiting when ordering from Amazon. Two-thirds of the U.S. population is within five miles of a Walmart store, according to company management.

Walmart has steadily increased its investment in its online business, spending between $1.2 billion and $1.5 billion annually in 2015 and the next few years on e-commerce, including fulfillment centers and technology. Walmart's e-commerce business now employs about 2,500 people. Walmart has constructed one of the world's largest private cloud computing centers, which provides the computing horsepower for Walmart to increase the number of items available for sale on Walmart.com from 1 million three years ago to 10 million today. In spring 2015, the company opened four new fulfillment centers around the country, each of which is more than 1 million square feet. To counter Amazon further, Walmart is preparing to introduce its own version of a free delivery service for premium customers similar to Amazon Prime.

New technology will also give Walmart more expertise in improving the product recommendations for web visitors to Walmart.com, using smartphones as a marketing channel, and personalizing the shopping experience. Walmart has been steadily adding new applications to its mobile and online shopping channels and is expanding its integration with social networks such as Pinterest.

A Pay With Cash program enables the 25 percent of Walmart customers who don't have credit cards or bank accounts to order their products online and then pay for them in cash at their nearest Walmart store. Walmart's online and digital development division, @WalmartLabs, acquired the recipe technology start-up Yumprint to expand its online grocery delivery services. Management hopes that Yumprint will help Walmart customers make shopping lists more easily from recipes they find in Yumprint before they shop. The company also hired former eBay executive Jamie Iannone to manage the integration of the Sam's Club's website with Walmart's global e-commerce unit.

Walmart is also trying to improve links among its store inventory, website, and mobile phone apps so that more customers can order online and pick up their purchases at stores. Shoppers can order items online and pick them up from lockers in local stores without waiting in line. Walmart's lockers are similar to Amazon's recent deal with Staples and 7-Eleven to do the same. The idea is to be able to offer Walmart products anywhere a consumer prefers to shop, whether that's online, in stores, or on the phone.

The company is rethinking its in-store experience to draw more people into its stores. More than half of Walmart customers own smartphones. Walmart has designed its mobile app to maximize Walmart's advantage over Amazon: its physical locations. About 140 million people visit a Walmart store each week. The company started testing the app's in-store mode, which detects when a customer is in a physical store. When the mode is activated, customers can check their wish lists, locate items of interest in the store, and see local promotions. The app's Scan & Go feature lets customers scan items as they shop so they can move quickly through self-checkout.

Shoppers can add items to their lists by voice or by scanning bar codes.

The Walmart website uses software to monitor prices at competing retailers in real time and lower its online prices if necessary. The company is also doubling inventory sold from third-party retailers in its online marketplace and tracking patterns in search and social media data to help it select more trendy products. This strikes directly at Amazon's third-party marketplace, which accounts for a significant revenue stream for Amazon. In addition, Walmart is expanding its online offerings to include upscale items such as $146 Nike sunglasses and wine refrigerators costing more than $2,500 to attract customers who never set foot in a Walmart store.

Walmart's commitment to e-commerce is not designed to replicate Amazon's business model. Instead, CEO Doug McMillon is crafting a strategy that gives consumers the best of both worlds— an omnichannel approach to retailing. Walmart's management believes the company's advantage is that it is not a pure-play e-commerce retailer and that customers want some real interaction with physical stores as well as digital contact. Walmart will sell vigorously through the web and in its physical stores, retaining its hallmark everyday low prices and wide product assortment in both channels and using its large network of stores as distribution points. Walmart will closely integrate online shopping and fulfillment with its physical stores so that customers can shop however they want, whether it's ordering on their mobile phones for home delivery, through in-store pickup, or by wandering down the aisles of a Walmart superstore. Walmart is aiming to be the world's biggest omnichannel retailer.

Amazon is working on expanding its selection of goods to be as exhaustive as Walmart's. Amazon has allowed third-party sellers to sell goods through its website for a number of years, and it has dramatically expanded product selection through acquisitions such as its 2009 purchase of online shoe-shopping site Zappos.com to give Amazon an edge in footwear.

On June 18, 2014, Amazon announced its own Fire Phone to provide a better mobile platform for selling its products and services online. Users can scroll through web or book pages just by tilting the device or quickly navigate menus, access shortcuts, and view notifications. Mayday is a 24-hour customer support service for users of Amazon's devices, offering one-tap access to Amazon customer service agents who can talk to phone users by video chat and take over the screen on their devices to show them exactly how to do something. To date, the Fire Phone has not lived up to expectations.

Amazon continues to build more fulfillment centers closer to urban centers and expand its same-day delivery services, and it has a supply chain optimized for online commerce that Walmart just can't match. Nevertheless, Walmart has thousands of stores in almost every neighborhood that Amazon won't ever be able to replicate. The winner of this epic struggle will be which company leverages its advantage better. Walmart's technology initiative looks promising, but it still has work to do before its local stores are anything more than local stores. Can Walmart successfully move to an omnichannel strategy and successfully compete in e-commerce?

Sources: Hiroko Tabuchi, "Walmart, Lagging in Online Sales, Is Strengthening E-Commerce," *New York Times*, June 5, 2015; Brian O'Keefe, "The Man Who's Reinventing Walmart," *Fortune*, June 4, 2015; Edward Teach, "Walmart's Next Move," *CFO, Magazine*, May 14, 2015; Nathan Layne, "Wal-Mart Eyes Amazon in Potentially Costly E-Commerce Battle," Reuters, May 20, 2015; Anna Rose Welch, "Walmart, Sam's Club Amp Up Online Shopping Experiences," *Integrated Solutions for Retailers*, February 28, 2014; Donna Tam, "Walmart: Amazon Image Recognition a 'Shiny Object'," CNET, February 6, 2014; Claire Cain Miller and Stephanie Clifford, "To Catch Up, Walmart Moves to Amazon Turf," *New York Times*, October 19, 2013; Claire Cain Miller, "Wal-Mart Introduces Lockers as It Battles Amazon in E-Commerce," *New York Times*, March 27, 2013; and Evan Schuman, "Amazon's Supply Chain Kicking the SKUs Out of Walmart's," *StorefrontBacktalk*, June 19, 2013.

Case Study Questions

10-15 Analyze Walmart and Amazon.com, using the competitive forces and value chain models.

10-16 Compare Walmart's and Amazon's business models and business strategies.

10-17 What role does information technology play in each of these businesses? How is it helping them refine their business strategies?

10-18 Will Walmart be successful against Amazon.com? Explain your answer.

MyMISLab

Go to the Assignments section of your MyLab to complete these writing exercises.

10-19 Describe the six features of social commerce. Provide an example for each feature, describing how a business could use that feature for selling to consumers online.

10-20 List and describe the main activities involved in building an e-commerce presence.

Chapter 10 References

Adomavicius, Gediminas, Jesse Bockstedt, and Shawn P. Curley. "Bundling Effects on Variety Seeking for Digital Information Goods," *Journal of Management Information Systems* 31, No. 4 (Spring 2015).

Brynjolfsson, Erik, Yu Hu, and Michael D. Smith. "Consumer Surplus in the Digital Economy: Estimating the Value of Increased Product Variety at Online Booksellers," *Management Science* 49, No. 11 (November 2003).

Brynjolfsson, Erik, Yu Jeffrey Hu, and Mohammad S. Rahman. "Competing in the Age of Multichannel Retailing," *MIT Sloan Management Review* (May 2013).

Butler, Brian S., Patrick J. Bateman, Peter H. Gray, and E. Ilana Diamant. "An Attraction-Selection-Attrition Theory of Online Community Size and Resilience," *MIS Quarterly* 38, No. 3 (September 2014).

Chandlee, Blake and Gerald C. (Jerry) Kane. "How Facebook Is Delivering Personalization on a Whole New Scale," *MIT Sloan Management Review* 55, No. 4 (August 5, 2014).

Chen, Jianquing, and Jan Stallaert. "An Economic Analysis of Online Advertising Using Behavioral Targeting," *MIS Quarterly* 38, No. 2 (June 2014).

comScore Inc. "ComScore 2013 US Digital Future in Focus," [Nick Mulligan]. (April 2, 2014).

Dewan, Sanjeev, and Jui Ramaprasad. "Anxious or Angry? Effects of Discrete Emotions on the Perceived Helpfulness of Online Reviews," *MIS Quarterly* 38, No. 1 (March 2014).

eMarketer, "U.S. Retail Ecommerce Sales, 2013–2019 (billions, % change, and% of total retail sales)," (June 2015a).

eMarketer. "U.S. Digital Shoppers and Buyers, 2013–2019 (millions and % of Internet users), (June 2015b).

eMarketer, "Fixed Broadband Households (millions, % of households), United States, 2013–2019," (February 2015c).

eMarketer, "U.S. Ad Spending: 2015 Complete Forecast," (March 2015d).

eMarketer, "U.S. Retail Mcommerce Sales, 2013–2019," (May 2015e).

Federal Trade Commission, "Data Brokers: A Call for Transparency and Accountability," Federal Trade Commission, May 2014.

Fang, Yulin, Israr Qureshi, Heshan Sun, Patrick McCole, Elaine Ramsey, and Kai H. Lim. "Trust, Satisfaction, and Online Repurchase Intention: The Moderating Role of Perceived Effectiveness of E-Commerce Institutional Mechanisms," *MIS Quarterly* 38, No. 2 (June 2014).

Gast, Arne, and Michele Zanini. "The Social Side of Strategy," *McKinsey Quarterly* (May 2012).

Ghoshal, Abhijeet, Subodha Kumar, and Vijay *Mookerjee.* " Impact of Recommender System on Competition Between Personalizing and Non-Personalizing Firms," *Journal of Management Information Systems* 31, No. 4 (Spring 2015).

Gupta, Sunil. "For Mobile Devices, Think Apps, Not Ads," *Harvard Business Review* (March 2013).

Hinz, Oliver, Il-Horn Hann, and Martin Spann. "Price Discrimination in E-Commerce? An Examination of Dynamic Pricing in Name-Your-Own Price Markets," *MIS Quarterly* 35, No. 1 (March 2011).

Hoofnagle, Chris Jay, Jennifer M. Urban, and Su Li. "Privacy and Modern Advertising: Most U.S. Internet Users Want 'Do Not Track' to Stop Collection of Data About Their Online Activities." Berkeley Consumer Privacy Survey, BCLT Research Paper, October 8, 2012.

Howe, Heff. *Crowdsourcing: Why the Power of the Crowd Is Driving the Future of Business.* (New York: Random House, 2008.)

Internet Retailer. "Mobile Commerce Top 400 2015," (2015).

Internet World Stats. "Internet Users in the World," Internetworldstats.com (2015).

Kumar, V., and Rohan Mirchandan. "Increasing the ROI of Social Media Marketing," *MIT Sloan Management Review* 54, No. 1 (Fall 2012).

Laudon, Kenneth C., and Carol Guercio Traver. *E-Commerce: Business, Technology, Society*, 12th edition. (Upper Saddle River, NJ: Prentice-Hall, 2016.)

Liu, Charles Zhechao, Yoris A. Au, and Hoon Seok Choi. Effects of Freemium Strategy in the Mobile App Market: An Empirical Study of Google Play," *Journal of Management Information Systems* 31, No. 3 (Winter 2014).

Oestreicher-Singer, Gal, and Arun Sundararajan. "Recommendation Networks and the Long Tail of Electronic Commerce," *MIS Quarterly* 36, No. 1 (March 2012).

Orlikowski, Wanda, and Susan V. Scott. "The Algorithm and the Crowd: Considering the Materiality of Service Innovation." *MIS Quarterly* 39, No.1 (March 2015).

Ou, Carol Xiaojuan, Paul A. Pavlou, and Robert M. Davison. "Swift Guanxi in Online Marketplaces: The Role of Computer-Mediated Communication Technologies," *MIS Quarterly* 38, No. 1 (March 2014).

Pew Internet and American Life Project. "Americans' Attitudes About Privacy, Security, and Surveillance," (May 20, 2015a).

Pew Internet and American Life Project. "Americans' Privacy Strategies Post-Snowden," (March 16, 2015b).

Rigby, Darrell K. "Digital Physical Mashups," *Harvard Business Review* (September 2014).

Schulze, Christian, Lisa Schöler, and Bernd Skier. "Customizing Social Media Marketing," *MIT Sloan Management Review* (Winter 2015).

Shuk, Ying Ho, and David Bodoff. "The Effects of Web Personalization on User Attitude and Behavior: An Integration of the Elaboration Likelihood Model and Consumer Search Theory," *MIS Quarterly* 38, No. 2 (June 2014).

Urban, Glen L., and Fareena Sultan. "The Case for 'Benevolent' Mobile Apps," *MIT Sloan Management Review* (Winter 2015).

U.S. Bureau of the Census. "E-Stats. 2014," http://www.census.gov/econ/index.html (May 22, 2014).

Wethinq.com. "36 Great Examples of Crowdsourcing," November 2014.

Yin, Dezhi, Samuel D. Bond, and Han Zhang. "Anxious or Angry? Effects of Discrete Emotions on the Perceived Helpfulness of Online Reviews," *MIS Quarterly* 38, No. 2 (June 2014).

Improving Decision Making and Managing Knowledge

CHAPTER 11

LEARNING OBJECTIVES

After reading this chapter, you will be able to answer the following questions.

11-1 What are the different types of decisions, and how does the decision-making process work?

11-2 How do business intelligence and business analytics support decision making?

11-3 What are the business benefits of using intelligent techniques in decision making and knowledge management?

11-4 What types of systems are used for enterprise-wide knowledge management and knowledge work, and how do they provide value for businesses?

CHAPTER CASES

Fiat: Real Time Management With Business Intelligence

America's Cup: The Tension Between Technology and Human Decision Makers

Facial Recognition Systems: Another Threat to Privacy?

Knowledge Management and Collaboration at Tata Consulting Services

VIDEO CASES

Case 1: How IBM's Watson Became a Jeopardy Champion

Case 2: Alfresco: Open Source Document Management and Collaboration

Case 3: FreshDirect Uses Business Intelligence to Manage Its Online Grocery

Case 4: Business Intelligence Helps the Cincinnati Zoo

Instructional Video:

Analyzing Big Data: IBM Watson After Jeopardy

FIAT: REAL TIME MANAGEMENT WITH BUSINESS INTELLIGENCE

Few industries have experienced as much disruption due to the financial meltdown of 2007–2009 as the auto industry. Global production peaked in 2007 when 53 million cars were produced, but fell to 47 million two years later at the height of the global financial recession. Two large American firms, General Motors and Chrysler, required a financial bail out of €5.6 billion from the United States government. After filing for bankruptcy in 2009, Chrysler found a buyer in Fiat Automobiles S.p.A., who eventually purchased majority control by 2011, and has since attempted to purchase all the shares from the Canadian government and employee unions in 2013. In 2015 global auto production zoomed to 92 million cars.

Fiat was one of the global automotive companies to weather the financial storm of 2008–2011 without significant government intervention. The 114-year-old automaker is based in Turin, Italy, and is Italy's largest auto manufacturer, with 9 percent of the European market. Its second largest market is Brazil, where it has been the market leader for a decade. The combined Chrysler Fiat company has nearly 228,000 employees, 158 plants, and 77 R&D centers. Fiat's 2014 revenue approached €96 billion and the company produced 4.6 million vehicles. In 2014, Fiat Chrysler moved its headquarters to the United Kingdom and was listed on the New York Stock Exchange, indicating a strong move towards becoming a more global company.

Fiat faced several information system challenges resulting from its global expansion, and in particular its purchase of Chrysler. In the past, Fiat global production centers adopted their own database systems to manage their business, and these legacy systems evolved independently over many years. Even enterprise systems from a single vendor differed by country and market, making compatibility

© Vladimir Kramin/Fotolia

and reporting a challenge for executives. This meant that executives in Turin could not receive timely and complete information on the firm's key business processes and financial performance. A good deal of management decision making relied on manual spreadsheets using data from different systems, and this led to errors in the data. With Chrysler, Fiat inherited another set of enterprise systems. All business functions were impacted, from supply management and production to marketing and finance.

Fiat decided it needed a new system that could provide near real-time information on its operations across the globe to integrate control and reporting, data definitions, pricing, and marketing campaigns for new vehicles. Working with Oracle's Hyperion in-memory database and Exalytics software and the consulting firm TechEdge SpA, Fiat set out to build an enterprise performance management system with significant business intelligence capabilities based on current data from the divisions.

The new system allows Fiat managers to analyze automobile production across divisions, including the motors used and vehicle options. In turn this enables executives to define the costs and budgets of production worldwide. Manual work with spreadsheets has been greatly reduced. Using Oracle's Hyperion Planning system, Fiat managers are able to achieve transparency in sales, build more accurate planning models, and respond to changes in markets. This translates into real-time decision-making. In 2015 Fiat built a global financial management system and customer relationship management system based on its new IT system capabilities.

Oracle's Hyperion Financial Management provided an integrated platform for managing government reporting requirements and the ability to trace and audit assembly and sales by providing a detailed view of dealer sales to final customers. For marketing, the new system enabled Fiat managers to simulate sales volumes and costs, and compared marketing expenditures in each market to sales results. An important element of the new system is making data and information more understandable by creating performance dashboards for managers that reflect their needs as decision makers.

Sources: "Global Vehicle Production Forecast from 2012 to 2017," Statista.com, accessed January 9, 2016; "For Fiat, Big Investment in Oracle Business Analytics Yields Big Returns," http://www.oracle.com/us/dm/ oracleandfiat, December 20, 2015; "Fiat Brazil Transforms Customer Care with Oracle CX Suite," Focus on Automotive at Oracle World, Rainfocus.com, October 26, 2015; Tommaso Ebhardt and Daniele Lepido, "Fiat Says Ciao to Italy as Merger with Chrysler Ends Era," Bloomberg.com, August 1, 2014; Technology Reply, "Competitive Analysis: Second Generation Business Intelligence for Competitive Advantage," October 2013; "Fiat Group Automobiles Aligns Operational Decisions with Strategy by Using End-to-End Enterprise Performance Management System," *Oracle Magazine*, September 2013; David Baum, "Dashboard View: As Fiat Maneuvers Beyond Italy, New Analytics Help Steer Managers in the Right Direction, *Oracle Magazine*, May 2013.

The experiences of Fiat provide an excellent of example of the challenges that businesses face when increasing their scope of operations and moving towards a truly global business. The existing legacy systems at Fiat made it very difficult to coordinate supply chain, production, financial, and marketing decisions on a global basis. Existing systems could not provide real-time data to central management in Turin, and did not have the analytical power to analyze the data from these legacy systems. In this traditional climate, management had a difficult time responding to changes in local conditions, and discovering potential synergies among their divisions.

The chapter-opening diagram calls attention to important points raised by this case and this chapter. To operate efficiently on a global scale, firms need more timely and accurate data to make intelligent decisions. They also need sophisticated analytic packages that can make sense of the data, provide capsule summaries to management, and provide interfaces that managers can easily use. With these systems, managers are able to see where production bottlenecks occur, understand how their various divisions can cooperate by sharing parts and designs, and respond to changes in demand and avoid excess inventories. Better decision making using business intelligence makes companies like Fiat more profitable.

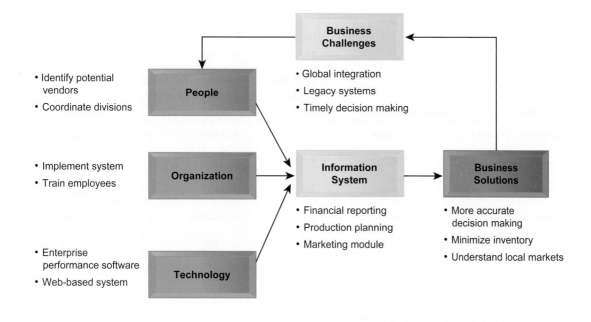

Here are some questions to think about: Why is it important that global performance management be delivered using Web-based technologies rather than traditional software running on corporate servers and PCs? What people and organizational difficulties do you think firms will face when implementing these global systems? Do firms become too dependent on database firms like Oracle?

11-1 What are the different types of decisions, and how does the decision-making process work?

One of the main contributions of information systems has been to improve decision making for both individuals and groups. Decision making in businesses used to be limited to management. Today, lower-level employees are responsible for some of these decisions as information systems make information available to lower levels of the business. However, what do we mean by better decision making? How does decision making take place in businesses and other organizations? Let's take a closer look.

BUSINESS VALUE OF IMPROVED DECISION MAKING

What does it mean to the business to be able to make a better decision? What is the monetary value to the business of improved decision making? Table 11.1 measures the monetary value of improved decision making for a small U.S. manufacturing firm with $280 million in annual revenue and 140 employees. The firm has identified a number of key decisions where new system investments might improve the quality of decision making. The table provides selected estimates of annual value (in the form of cost savings or increased revenue) from improved decision making in selected areas of the business.

We can see from Table 11.1 that decisions are made at all levels of the firm and that some of these decisions are common, routine, and numerous. Although the value of improving any single decision may be small, improving hundreds of thousands of small decisions adds up to a large annual value for the business.

TABLE 11.1

Business Value of Enhanced Decision Making

Example Decision Value	Decision Maker	Number of Annual Decisions	Estimated Value to Firm of a Single Improved Decision	Annual
Allocate support to most-valuable customers	Accounts manager	12	$100,000	$1,200,000
Predict call center daily demand	Call center management	4	$150,000	$600,000
Decide parts inventory levels daily	Inventory manager	365	$5,000	$1,825,000
Identify competitive bids from major suppliers	Senior management	1	$2,000,000	$2,000,000
Schedule production to fill orders	Manufacturing manager	150	$10,000	$1,500,000
Allocate labor to complete a job	Production floor manager	100	$4,000	$400,000

TYPES OF DECISIONS

Chapter 2 showed that there are different levels in an organization. Each of these levels has different information requirements for decision support and responsibility for different types of decisions (see Figure 11.1). Decisions are classified as structured, semistructured, and unstructured.

Unstructured decisions are those in which the decision maker must provide judgment, evaluation, and insight to solve the problem. Each of these decisions is novel, important, and not routine, and there is no well-understood or agreed-on procedure for making them.

Structured decisions, by contrast, are repetitive and routine, and they involve a definite procedure for handling them so that they do not have to be treated each time as if they were new. Many decisions have elements of both types and are **semistructured decisions**, when only part of the problem has a clear-cut answer provided by an accepted procedure. In general, structured decisions are more prevalent at lower organizational levels, whereas unstructured problems are more common at higher levels of the firm.

Senior executives face many unstructured decision situations, such as establishing the firm's 5-year or 10-year goals or deciding new markets to enter. Answering the

Figure 11.1
Information Requirements of Key Decision-Making Groups in a Firm
Senior managers, middle managers, operational managers, and employees have different types of decisions and information requirements.

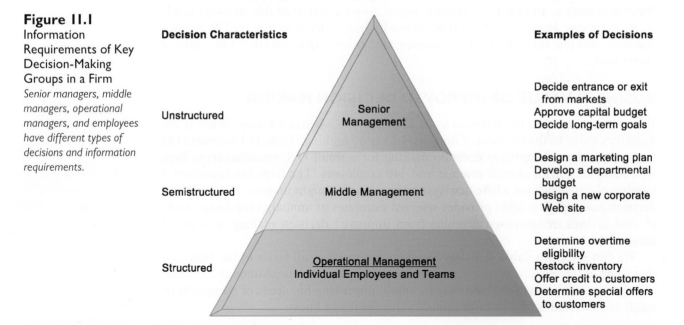

question, "Should we enter a new market?" would require access to news, government reports, and industry views as well as high-level summaries of firm performance. However, the answer would also require senior managers to use their own best judgment and poll other managers for their opinions.

Middle management faces more structured decision scenarios, but their decisions may include unstructured components. A typical middle-level management decision might be, "Why is the reported order fulfillment showing a decline over the past six months at a distribution center in Minneapolis?" This middle manager could obtain a report from the firm's enterprise system or distribution management system on order activity and operational efficiency at the Minneapolis distribution center. This is the structured part of the decision, but before arriving at an answer, this middle manager will have to interview employees and gather more unstructured information from external sources about local economic conditions or sales trends.

Operational management and rank-and-file employees tend to make more structured decisions. For example, a supervisor on an assembly line has to decide whether an hourly paid worker is entitled to overtime pay. If the employee worked more than eight hours on a particular day, the supervisor would routinely grant overtime pay for any time beyond eight hours that was clocked on that day.

A sales account representative often has to make decisions about extending credit to customers by consulting the firm's customer database that contains credit information. If the customer met the firm's specific criteria for granting credit, the account representative would grant that customer credit to make a purchase. In both instances, the decisions are highly structured and routinely made thousands of times each day in most large firms. The answer has been programmed into the firm's payroll and accounts receivable systems.

THE DECISION-MAKING PROCESS

Making a decision is a multistep process. Simon (1960) described four stages in decision making: intelligence, design, choice, and implementation (see Figure 11.2). These stages correspond to the four steps in problem solving used throughout this book.

Intelligence consists of discovering, identifying, and understanding the problems occurring in the organization—why the problem exists, where, and what effects it is having on the firm. **Design** involves identifying and exploring various solutions to the problem. **Choice** consists of choosing among solution alternatives. **Implementation** involves making the chosen alternative work and continuing to monitor how well the solution is working.

What happens if the solution you have chosen does not work? Figure 11.2 shows that you can return to an earlier stage in the decision-making process and repeat it if necessary. For instance, in the face of declining sales, a sales management team may decide to pay the sales force a higher commission for making more sales to spur on the sales effort. If this does not increase sales, managers would need to investigate whether the problem stems from poor product design, inadequate customer support, or a host of other causes that call for a different solution.

HIGH-VELOCITY AUTOMATED DECISION MAKING

Today, many decisions organizations make are not made by managers or any humans. For instance, when you enter a query in Google's search engine, Google's computer system has to decide which URLs to display in about half a second on average (500 milliseconds). High-frequency trading programs at electronic stock exchanges in the United States execute their trades in under 30 milliseconds. Humans are eliminated from the decision chain because they are too slow.

In these high-speed automated decisions, the intelligence, design, choice, and implementation parts of the decision-making process are captured by computer algorithms that precisely define the steps to be followed to produce a decision. The people who wrote the software identified the problem, designed a method for finding

Figure 11.2
Stages in Decision
Making
*The decision-making
process can be broken
down into four stages.*

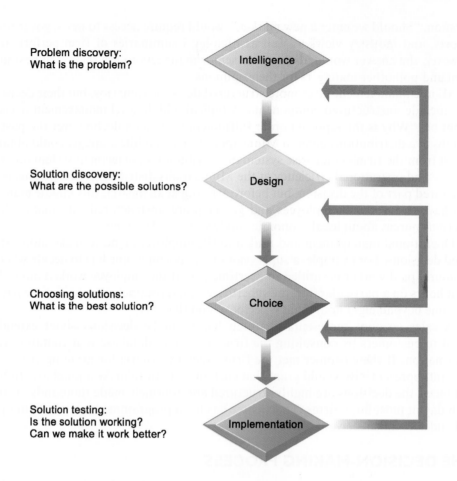

Problem discovery:
What is the problem? → Intelligence

Solution discovery:
What are the possible solutions? → Design

Choosing solutions:
What is the best solution? → Choice

Solution testing:
Is the solution working?
Can we make it work better? → Implementation

a solution, defined a range of acceptable solutions, and implemented the solution. In these situations, organizations are making decisions faster than managers can monitor or control, and great care needs to be taken to ensure the proper operation of these systems to prevent significant harm.

QUALITY OF DECISIONS AND DECISION MAKING

How can you tell whether a decision has become better or the decision-making process improved? Accuracy is one important dimension of quality; in general, we think decisions are better if they accurately reflect the real-world data. Speed is another dimension; we tend to think that the decision-making process should be efficient, even speedy. For instance, when you apply for car insurance, you want the insurance firm to make a fast and accurate decision. However, there are many other dimensions of quality in decisions and the decision-making process to consider. Which is important for you will depend on the business firm where you work, the various parties involved in the decision, and your own personal values. Table 11.2 describes some quality dimensions for decision making. When we describe how systems "improve decisions and the decision-making process" in this chapter, we are referencing the dimensions in this table.

11-2 How do business intelligence and business analytics support decision making?

Chapter 2 introduced you to different kinds of systems for supporting the levels and types of decisions we have just described. The foundation for all of these systems is a business intelligence and business analytics infrastructure that supplies data and the analytic tools for supporting decision making.

TABLE 11.2

Qualities of Decisions
and the Decision-Making
Process

Quality Dimension	Description
Accuracy	Decision reflects reality
Comprehensiveness	Decision reflects a full consideration of the facts and circumstances
Fairness	Decision faithfully reflects the concerns and interests of affected parties
Speed (efficiency)	Decision making is efficient with respect to time and other resources, including the time and resources of affected parties, such as customers
Coherence	Decision reflects a rational process that can be explained to others and made understandable
Due process	Decision is the result of a known process and can be appealed to a higher authority

WHAT IS BUSINESS INTELLIGENCE?

"Business intelligence" (BI) is a term hardware and software vendors and information technology consultants use to describe the infrastructure for warehousing, integrating, reporting, and analyzing data that come from the business environment. The foundation infrastructure collects, stores, cleans, and makes available relevant data to managers. Think databases, data warehouses, data marts, Hadoop, and analytic platforms, which we described in Chapter 6. "Business analytics" (BA) is also a vendor-defined term; it focuses more on tools and techniques for analyzing and understanding data. Think OLAP (online analytical processing), statistics, models, and data mining, which we also introduced in Chapter 6.

BI and analytics are essentially about integrating all the information streams a firm produces into a single, coherent enterprise-wide set of data and then using modeling, statistical analysis, and data mining tools to make sense out of all these data so managers can make better decisions and better plans. The German World Cup soccer team described in the chapter-opening case is using BI and analytics to make some very fine-grained decisions about how to improve team and player performance.

It is important to remember that BI and analytics are products defined by technology vendors and consulting firms. The largest five providers of these products are SAP, Oracle, IBM, SAS, and Microsoft. A number of BI and BA products now have cloud and mobile versions.

THE BUSINESS INTELLIGENCE ENVIRONMENT

Figure 11.3 gives an overview of a BI environment, highlighting the kinds of hardware, software, and management capabilities that the major vendors offer and that firms develop over time. There are six elements in this BI environment:

Data from the business environment: Businesses must deal with both structured and unstructured data from many sources, including big data. The data need to be integrated and organized so that they can be analyzed and used by human decision makers.

Business intelligence infrastructure: The underlying foundation of BI is a powerful database system that captures all the relevant data to operate the business. The data may be stored in transactional databases or combined and integrated into an enterprise data warehouse, series of interrelated data marts, or analytic platforms.

Figure 11.3
Business Intelligence
and Analytics for
Decision Support
*Business intelligence and
analytics require a strong
database foundation, a
set of analytic tools, and
an involved management
team that can ask intelligent questions and analyze
data.*

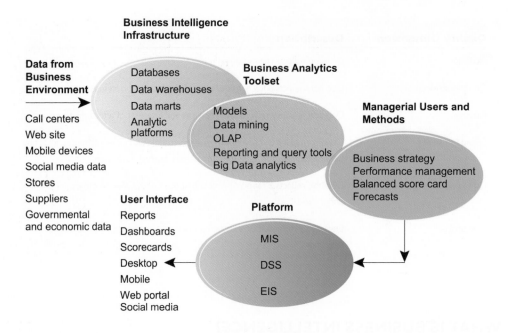

Business analytics toolset: A set of software tools is used to analyze data and produce reports, respond to questions managers pose, and track the progress of the business by using key indicators of performance.

Managerial users and methods: BI hardware and software are only as intelligent as the human beings who use them. Managers impose order on the analysis of data by using a variety of managerial methods that define strategic business goals and specify how progress will be measured. These include business performance management and balanced scorecard approaches that focus on key performance indicators, with special attention to competitors.

Delivery platform—MIS, DSS, ESS: The results from BI and analytics are delivered to managers and employees in a variety of ways, depending on what they need to know to perform their job. MIS, decision-support systems (DSS), and executive support systems (ESS), which we introduced in Chapter 2, deliver information and knowledge to different people and levels in the firm—operational employees, middle managers, and senior executives. In the past, these systems could not easily share data and operated as independent systems. Today, business intelligence and analytics tools can integrate all this information and bring it to managers' desktops or mobile platforms.

User interface: Business people often learn quicker from a visual representation of data than from a dry report with columns and rows of information. Today's business analytics software suites feature **data visualization** tools, such as rich graphs, charts, dashboards, and maps. They also can deliver reports on mobile phones and tablets as well as on the firm's web portal. BA software is adding capabilities to post information on Twitter, Facebook, or internal social media to support decision making in an online group setting rather than in a face-to-face meeting.

BUSINESS INTELLIGENCE AND ANALYTICS CAPABILITIES

BI and analytics promise to deliver correct, nearly real-time information to decision makers, and the analytic tools help them quickly understand the information and take action. There are five analytic functionalities that BI systems deliver to achieve these ends:

Production reports: These are predefined reports based on industry-specific requirements (see Table 11.3).

Business Functional Area	Production Reports
Sales	Sales forecasts, sales team performance, cross selling, sales cycle times
Service/Call Center	Customer satisfaction, service cost, resolution rates, churn rates
Marketing	Campaign effectiveness, loyalty and attrition, market basket analysis
Procurement and Support	Direct and indirect spending, off-contract purchases, supplier performance
Supply Chain	Backlog, fulfillment status, order cycle time, bill of materials analysis
Financials	General ledger, accounts receivable and payable, cash flow, profitability
Human Resources	Employee productivity, compensation, workforce demographics, retention

TABLE 11.3

Examples of Predefined Business Intelligence Production Reports

Parameterized reports: Users enter several parameters to filter data and isolate impacts of parameters. For instance, you might want to enter region and time of day to understand how sales of a product vary by region and time. If you were Starbucks, you might find that customers in the eastern United States buy most of their coffee in the morning, whereas in the northwest customers buy coffee throughout the day. This finding might lead to different marketing and ad campaigns in each region. (See the discussion of pivot tables later in this section.)

Dashboards/scorecards: These are visual tools for presenting performance data users define.

Ad hoc query/search/ report creation: This allows users to create their own reports based on queries and searches.

Drill down: This is the ability to move from a high-level summary to a more detailed view.

Forecasts, scenarios, models: These include capabilities for linear forecasting, what-if scenario analysis, and data analysis, using standard statistical tools.

Predictive Analytics

An important capability of BI analytics is the ability to model future events and behaviors, such as the probability that a customer will respond to an offer to purchase a product. **Predictive analytics** use statistical analysis, data mining techniques, historical data, and assumptions about future conditions to predict future trends and behavior patterns. Variables that can be measured to predict future behavior are identified. For example, an insurance company might use variables such as age, gender, and driving record as predictors of driving safety when issuing auto insurance policies. A collection of such predictors is combined into a predictive model for forecasting future probabilities with an acceptable level of reliability.

FedEx has been using predictive analytics to develop models that predict how customers will respond to price changes and new services, which customers are most at risk of switching to competitors, and how much revenue will be generated by new storefront or drop-box locations. The accuracy rate of FedEx's predictive analytics system ranges from 65 to 90 percent.

Predictive analytics are being incorporated into numerous BI applications for sales, marketing, finance, fraud detection, and health care. One of the best-known applications is credit scoring, which is used throughout the financial services industry. When you apply for a new credit card, scoring models process your credit history, loan application, and purchase data to determine your likelihood of making future credit payments on time. Health care insurers have been analyzing data for years to identify which patients are most likely to generate high costs.

Many companies employ predictive analytics to predict response to direct marketing campaigns. By identifying customers less likely to respond, companies can lower their marketing and sales costs by bypassing this group and focusing their resources on customers who have been identified as more promising. For instance, the U.S. division of The Body Shop International PLC used predictive analytics and its database of catalog, web, and retail store customers to identify customers who were more likely to make catalog purchases. That information helped the company build more precise and targeted mailing lists for its catalogs, improving the response rate for catalog mailings and catalog revenues.

Big Data Analytics

Predictive analytics are starting to use big data from both private and public sectors, including data from social media, customer transactions, and output from sensors and machines. In e-commerce, many online retailers have capabilities for making personalized online product recommendations to their website visitors to help stimulate purchases and guide their decisions about what merchandise to stock. However, most of these product recommendations are based on the behaviors of similar groups of customers, such as those with incomes under $50,000 or whose ages are between 18 and 25. Now some firms are starting to analyze the tremendous quantities of online and in-store customer data they collect along with social media data to make these recommendations more individualized. These efforts are translating into higher customer spending and retention rates. Table 11.4 provides examples of companies using big data analytics.

In the public sector, big-data analytics are driving the movement toward smart cities, which make intensive use of digital technology and data stores to make better decisions about running cities and serving their residents. Public recordkeeping has produced warehouses full of property transfers, tax records, corporate filings, environmental compliance audits, restaurant inspections, building maintenance reports, mass transit appraisals, crime data, health department stats, public education records,

TABLE 11.4		
What Big Data Analytics Can Do	**Organization**	**Big Data Capabilities**
	Bank of America	Able to analyze all of its 50 million customers at once to understand each customer across all channels and interactions and present consistent, finely customized offers. Can determine which of its customers has a credit card or a mortgage loan that could benefit from refinancing at a competitor. When the customer visits BofA online, calls a call center, or visits a branch, that information is available for an online app or sales associate to present BofA's competing offer.
	Vestas Wind Systems	Improves wind turbine placement for optimal energy output by using IBM BigInsights software and an IBM Firestorm supercomputer to analyze 2.8 petabytes of structured and unstructured data such as weather reports, tidal phases, geospatial and sensor data, satellite images, deforestation maps, and weather modeling research. The analysis, which used to take weeks, can now be completed in less than one hour.
	Hunch.com	Analyzes massive database with data from customer purchases, social networks, and signals from around the web to produce a taste graph that maps users with their predicted affinity to products, services, and websites. The taste graph includes predictions about 500 million people, 200 million objects (videos, gadgets, books), and 30 billion connections between people and objects. Helps eBay develop more finely customized recommendations on items to offer. Hunch was acquired by eBay where it is used to target marketing campaigns.
	Actian	Provides Fidelity National Information Services and other financial companies with platforms to run fraud analytics against 440,000 ATMs, supporting 95 million cards and more than 2 million point-of-sale locations.

utility reviews, and more. Municipalities are adding more data captured through sensors, location data from mobile phones, and targeted smartphone apps. Predictive modeling programs now inform public policy decisions on utility management, transportation operation, health care delivery, and public safety. What's more, the ability to evaluate how changes in one service affect the operation and delivery of other services enables holistic problem solving that could only be dreamed of a generation ago.

Operational Intelligence and Analytics

Many decisions deal with how to run the business on a day-to-day basis. These are largely operational decisions, and this type of business activity monitoring is called **operational intelligence**. Another example of operational intelligence is the use of data generated by sensors on trucks, trailers, and intermodal containers owned by Schneider National, one of North America's largest truckload, logistics, and intermodal services providers. The sensors monitor location, driving behaviors, fuel levels, and whether a trailer or container is loaded or empty. Data from fuel tank sensors help Schneider identify the optimal location at which a driver should stop for fuel based on how much is left in the tank, the truck's destination, and fuel prices en route. General Electric Company (GE) is using myriad sensors to collect data about heat, vibrations, and pressure inside a massive steam-driven GE generator capable of powering 750,000 homes. These sensor data are analyzed along with data on fuel costs, local weather, demand for power, and alternative supplies of electricity to determine the optimal generator performance for the conditions of the moment (Davenport, 2014).

The Internet of Things is creating huge streams of data from web activities, smartphones, sensors, gauges, and monitoring devices that can be used for operational intelligence about activities inside and outside the organization. Software for operational intelligence and analytics enables organizations to analyze these streams of big data as they are generated in real time. Companies can set trigger alerts on events or have them fed into live dashboards to help managers with their decisions. For example, Schneider's sensors capture hard braking in a moving truck and relay the data to corporate headquarters, where the data are tracked in dashboards monitoring safety metrics. The event initiates a conversation between the driver and that person's supervisor.

Another example of operational intelligence is the use of real-time data in the 34th America's Cup race, as described in the "Interactive Session on Technology" section. As you read this case, try to determine the extent to which information technology was able to replace human decision makers.

Location Analytics and Geographic Information Systems

Big-data analytics include **location analytics**, the ability to gain business insight from the location (geographic) component of data, including location data from mobile phones, output from sensors or scanning devices, and data from maps. For example, location analytics might help a marketer determine which people to target with mobile ads about nearby restaurants and stores or quantify the impact of mobile ads on in-store visits. Location analytics would help a utility company identify, view, and measure outages and their associated costs as related to customer location to help prioritize marketing, system upgrades, and customer service efforts. UPS's package tracking and delivery routing systems, described in Chapter 1 use location analytics, as does an application Starbucks uses to determine where to open new stores. (The system identifies geographic locations that will produce a high sales-to-investment ratio and per-store sales volume.)

The Starbucks and utility company applications are examples of **geographic information systems (GIS)**. GIS provide tools to help decision makers visualize problems that benefit from mapping. GIS software ties location data about the distribution of people or other resources to points, lines, and areas on a map. Some GIS have

INTERACTIVE SESSION: TECHNOLOGY — America's Cup: The Tension Between Technology and Human Decision Makers

On September 25, 2013, Oracle Team USA pulled off one of the greatest comebacks in organized sports by winning the last race of the 34th America's Cup Race on breezy San Francisco Bay. Oracle was down 8–1 to its archrival New Zealand in the previous week after losing seven races in a row. Looked like a rout but then a miracle: Oracle won seven races in a row and, in a winner-take-all finale, Oracle beat Team New Zealand by 44 seconds over the 12-mile racecourse. Both Team USA and Team New Zealand were the highest of high-tech boats ever to leave a designer's computer screen.

In earlier days, America's Cup races were typically among single-hulled sailboats in the 70-foot range that looked like sailboats in the local yacht club, just more so: a single long, narrow hull and a really tall mast to hold the sails up. They might get up to 10 miles an hour on the racecourse.

In 2010 software billionaire Larry Ellison, founder of Oracle, changed all that by spending over $300 million on a new kind of Cup racer: a three-hulled catamaran made of carbon fiber and having what looked like an aircraft wing instead of a mast with sails. The boat, *BMW Oracle USA*, beat its Swiss contender *Alinghi* to win the 33rd America's Cup, That meant Ellison could set the boat design and rules for the 34th race.

The 2013 boats were 72-foot, twin-hull catamarans dubbed AC72s, capable of more than 50 miles per hour, among the fastest sailboats ever built. The AC72 used small hydrofoils underneath the hulls that provided over 12,000 pounds of lift, bringing the boats out of the water completely and flying them like airplanes. In the end, it was unclear to seasoned sailors worldwide whether the AC72 was really a sailboat at all but, rather, more aptly called a sailing machine.

The 34th America's Cup campaign cost Ellison $100 million. The new boats were also capable of going completely out of control, usually by digging their bows into the water and then flipping. Controlling this wickedly sleek sailing machine requires a lightning-fast collection of massive amounts of data, powerful data management, rapid real-time data analysis, quick decision making, and immediate measurement of the results— in short, all the information technologies (ITs) needed by a modern business firm. When you can perform all these tasks thousands of times in an hour, you can improve your performance incrementally and gain an overwhelming advantage over less IT-savvy opponents on race day.

For Team USA, this meant using 250 sensors on the wing, hull, and rudder to gather real-time data on pressure, angles, loads, and strains to monitor the effectiveness of each adjustment. The sensors track 4,000 variables 10 times a second, producing 90 million data points an hour. The sensors are wired to an onboard server that processes the information and sends it out on a wireless network to crew member wrist displays. Managing all these data is Oracle Database 11g data management software. The data are also wirelessly transferred to a tender ship running Oracle 11g for near real-time analysis, using a family of formulas (called *velocity prediction formulas*) geared to understanding what makes the boat go fast. Oracle's Application Express presentation graphics summarize the millions of data points and present the boat managers with charts that make sense of the information. The data are also sent to Oracle's Austin data center for more in-depth analysis, using powerful data analysis tools, For the first time in history, it seemed possible to leave sailing to computer hardware and software.

Each Team USA crew member wore a small mobile, handheld computer on his wrist to display data about the key performance variables customized for that person's responsibilities, such as the load balance on a specific rope or the current aerodynamic performance of the wing sail. The captain's and tactician's sunglasses displayed their data. In this way, each crew member received the data he needed instantly to perform his job. The crew was trained to sail like pilots looking at instruments rather than like sailors looking at the boat and sea for clues. Professional and amateur sailors across the world wondered whether the technology had transformed sailing into something else, something akin to flying drones from a desk.

So why did Team USA lose seven races in a row, and how was Oracle able to pull out a victory? After the seventh loss, skipper James Spithill called for a one-day time-out allowed by the rules. Team USA was losing the upwind legs of all the races where Team New Zealand had the edge. The sailors and engineers disagreed about the solution. The engineers called for boat modifications; the sailors called for more attention to sailing and less attention to monitoring their wrist computers. In training for the races, the sailors were told to listen to the engineers who had the best technology to predict boat speeds. The engineers' software program told them to sail Team USA as close as possible to wind on the upwind legs (about 45 degrees to the wind), but the sailors' observations of the actual races suggested New Zealand was winning because it sailed 5 degrees off the wind at about 50 degrees, sailing a longer but faster upwind course. The difference was seconds per mile, which, all other things being equal, adds up to victory in a 12-mile race. The sailors claimed the engineers' software was just wrong.

In the end, Team USA pursued both solutions. Multiple small changes were made in the boat hull and underwater foils and on the racecourse. Spithill and his team stopped looking so much at their wrist computer screens and started to act like sailors on a racecourse rather than drone pilots in an office. Team USA won every upwind leg of the last eight races. The engineers admitted their software models were not providing accurate advice.

The next America's Cup race will take place in 2017 in Bermuda. Competing boats will range from 45 to 50 feet with more advanced technology and design than ever, and the role of technology versus human decision makers will be put to the test again.

Sources: Herve Guilbaud, "America's Cup to Feature Six or Seven Yachts," Coutts, *Agence France-Presse*, April 10, 2015; "New Class Will Astonish," www.oracle-team-usa.americascup.com/en, April 1, 2015; Stu Wood, "Against the Wind, One of the Greatest Comebacks in Sports History," *Wall Street Journal*, Feb. 28, 2014; Stu Wood, "America's Cup: Resolving the Tension Between Man and Technology," *Wall Street Journal*, March 3, 2014; Christopher Carey, "Oracle Completes Voyage to History, Winning America's Cup," *New York Times*, September 25, 2013; Christopher Carey, "After Comeback for the Ages, a Last Dash for America's Cup," *New York Times*, September 25, 2013; and Joe Schneider, "Team New Zealand Gets Last Shot at America's Cup as Costs Surge," *Bloomberg News*, Feb. 7, 2013.

CASE STUDY QUESTIONS

1. How did information technology change the way America's Cup boats were managed and sailed?

2. How did information technology impact decision making at Team USA?

3. How much was technology responsible for Team USA's America's Cup victory? Explain your answer.

modeling capabilities for changing the data and automatically revising business scenarios. GIS might be used to help state and local governments calculate response times to natural disasters and other emergencies, to help banks identify the best locations for new branches or ATM terminals, or to help police forces pinpoint locations with the highest incidence of crime.

The U.S. Centers for Disease Control and Prevention created a GIS for identifying the stroke hospitalization rate per 1000 Medicare beneficiaries age 65 and older in various parts of the United States. The small yellow triangles designate primary stroke care centers.

Source: U.S. Centers for Disease Control and Prevention

BUSINESS INTELLIGENCE USERS

Figure 11.4 shows that more than 80 percent of the audience for BI consists of casual users. Senior executives tend use BI to monitor firm activities by using visual interfaces such as dashboards and scorecards. Middle managers and analysts are much more likely to be immersed in the data and software, entering queries and slicing and dicing the data along different dimensions. Operational employees will, along with customers and suppliers, be looking mostly at prepackaged reports.

Support for Semistructured Decisions

Many BI prepackaged production reports are MIS reports supporting structured decision making for operational and middle managers. We described operational and middle management, and the systems they use, in Chapter 2. However, some managers are super users and keen business analysts who want to create their own reports; they use more sophisticated analytics and models to find patterns in data, to model alternative business scenarios, or to test specific hypotheses. DSS are the BI delivery platform for this category of users, with the ability to support semistructured decision making.

DSS rely more heavily on modeling than MIS, using mathematical or analytical models to perform what-if or other kinds of analysis. What-if analysis, working forward from known or assumed conditions, allows the user to vary certain values to test results to predict outcomes if changes occur in those values. What happens if we raise product prices by 5 percent or increase the advertising budget by $1 million? **Sensitivity analysis** models ask what-if questions repeatedly to predict a range of outcomes when one or more variables are changed multiple times (see Figure 11.5). Backward sensitivity analysis helps decision makers with goal seeking: If I want to sell 1 million product units next year, how much must I reduce the price of the product?

Chapter 6 described multidimensional data analysis and OLAP as one of the key business intelligence technologies. Spreadsheets have a similar feature for multidimensional analysis, called a **pivot table**, which super-user managers and analysts employ to identify and understand patterns in business information that may be useful for semistructured decision making.

Figure 11.6 illustrates a Microsoft Excel pivot table that examines a large list of order transactions for a company selling online management training videos and books. It shows the relationship between two dimensions: the sales region and the source of contact (web banner ad or email) for each customer order. It answers the question of whether the source of the customer makes a difference in addition to region. The pivot table in this figure shows that most customers come from the West and that banner advertising produces most of the customers in all the regions.

Figure 11.4
Business Intelligence Users
Casual users are consumers of BI output, whereas intense power users are the producers of reports, new analyses, models, and forecasts.

Power Users: Producers (20% of employees)	Capabilities	Casual Users: Consumers (80% of employees)
IT developers	Production reports	Customers/Suppliers Operational employees
Super users	Parameterized reports	Senior managers
Business analysts	Dashboards/Scorecards	
	Ad hoc queries; Drill down Search/OLAP	Managers/Staff
Analytical modelers	Forecasts; What-if analysis; statistical models	Business analysts

		Variable Cost per Unit				
Total fixed costs	19000					
Variable cost per unit	3					
Average sales price	17					
Contribution margin	14					
Break-even point	1357					

			Variable Cost per Unit			
Sales	1357	2	3	4	5	6
Price	14	1583	1727	1900	2111	2375
	15	1462	1583	1727	1900	2111
	16	1357	1462	1583	1727	1900
	17	1267	1357	1462	1583	1727
	18	1188	1267	1357	1462	1583

Figure II.5
Sensitivity Analysis
This table displays the results of a sensitivity analysis of the effect of changing the sales price of a necktie and the cost per unit on the product's break-even point. It answers the question, "What happens to the break-even point if the sales price and the cost to make each unit increase or decrease?"

One of the Hands-on MIS projects for this chapter asks you to use a pivot table to find answers to a number of other questions by using the same list of transactions for the online training company as we used in this discussion. The complete Excel file for these transactions is available in MyMISLab™. We have a Learning Track on creating pivot tables by using Excel.

In the past, much of this modeling was done with spreadsheets and small stand-alone databases. Today these capabilities are incorporated into large enterprise BI systems, and they can analyze data from large corporate databases. BI analytics include tools for intensive modeling. Such capabilities help Progressive Insurance identify the best customers for its products. Using widely available insurance industry data, Progressive defines small groups of customers, or cells, such as motorcycle riders aged 30 or older with college educations, credit scores over a certain level, and no accidents. For each cell, Progressive performs a regression analysis to identify factors

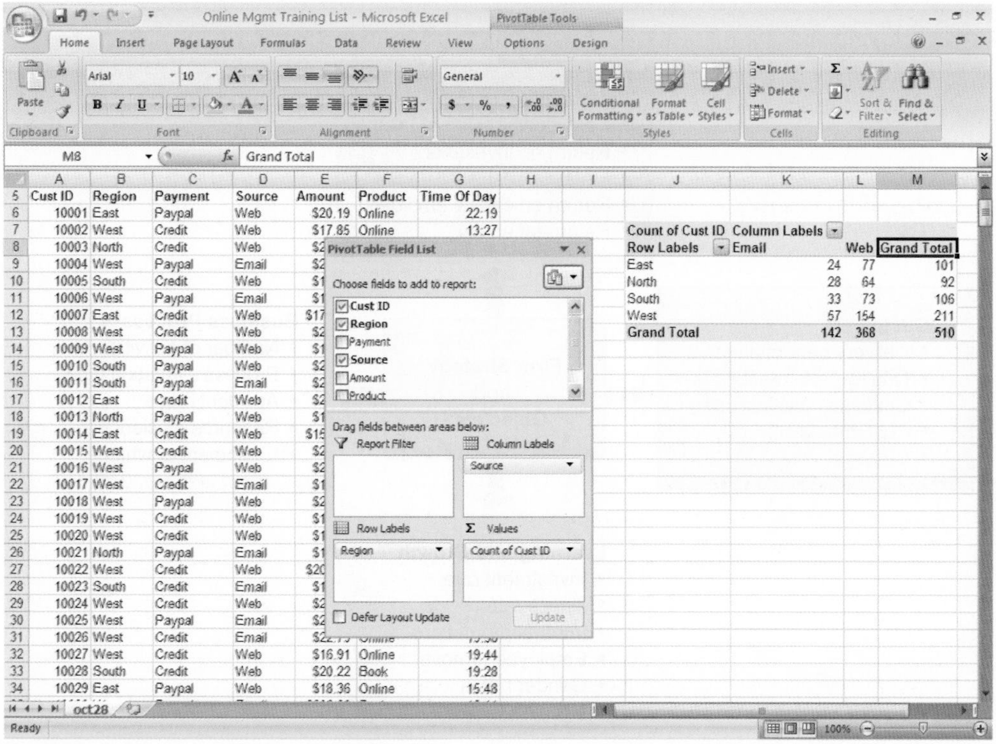

Figure II.6
A Pivot Table That Examines Customer Regional Distribution and Advertising Source
In this pivot table, we can examine where an online training company's customers come from in terms of region and advertising source.
Source: Microsoft Excel, Microsoft Corporation. Used by permission.

most closely correlated with the insurance losses that are typical for this group. It then sets prices for each cell and uses simulation software to test whether this pricing arrangement will enable the company to make a profit. These analytic techniques make it possible for Progressive to insure customers profitably in traditionally high-risk categories that other insurers would have rejected.

Decision Support for Senior Management: The Balanced Scorecard and Enterprise Performance Management

BI delivered in the form of ESS helps senior executives focus on the most important performance information that affects the overall profitability and success of the firm. Currently, the leading methodology for understanding this important information a firm's executives needs is called the **balanced scorecard method** (Kaplan and Norton, 1992, 2004). The balanced scorecard is a framework for operationalizing a firm's strategic plan by focusing on measurable outcomes of four dimensions of firm performance: financial, business process, customer, and learning and growth (see Figure 11.7).

Performance of each dimension is measured using **key performance indicators (KPIs)**, which are the measures proposed by senior management for understanding how well the firm is performing along any given dimension. For instance, one key indicator of how well an online retail firm is meeting its customer performance objectives is the average length of time required to deliver a package to a consumer. If your firm is a bank, one KPI of business process performance is the length of time required to perform a basic function such as creating a new customer account.

The balanced scorecard framework is thought to be balanced because it causes managers to focus on more than just financial performance. In this view, financial performance is past history—the result of past actions—and managers should focus on the things they can influence today, such as business process efficiency, customer satisfaction, and employee training. Once consultants and senior executives develop a scorecard, the next step is automating a flow of information to executives and other managers for each of the key performance indicators.

Figure 11.7
The Balanced
Scorecard Framework
In the balanced scorecard framework, the firm's strategic objectives are operationalized along four dimensions: financial, business process, customer, and learning and growth. Each dimension is measured, using several KPIs.

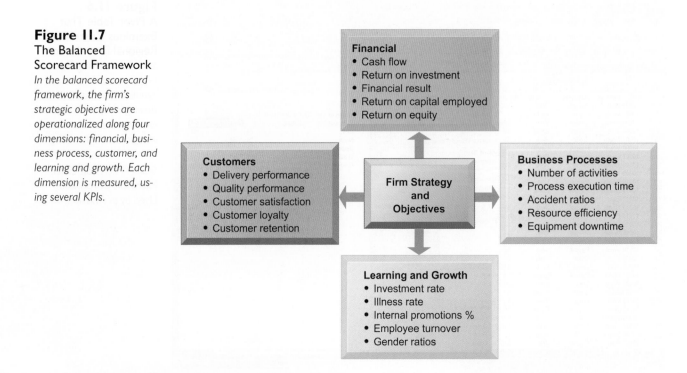

Another closely related management methodology is **business performance management (BPM)**. Originally defined by an industry group in 2004 (led by the same companies that sell enterprise and database systems, such as Oracle, SAP, and IBM), BPM attempts to translate a firm's strategies (e.g., differentiation, low-cost producer, market share growth, and scope of operation) systematically into operational targets. Once the strategies and targets are identified, a set of key performance indicators is developed to measure progress toward the targets. The firm's performance is then measured with information drawn from the firm's enterprise database systems.

Corporate data for contemporary ESS are supplied by the firm's existing enterprise applications (enterprise resource planning, supply chain management, and customer relationship management). ESS also provide access to news services, financial market databases, economic information, and whatever other external data senior executives require. ESS have significant **drill-down** capabilities if managers need more detailed views of data.

Well-designed ESS help senior executives monitor organizational performance, track activities of competitors, recognize changing market conditions, and identify problems and opportunities. Employees lower down in the corporate hierarchy also use these systems to monitor and measure business performance in their areas of responsibility. For these and other business intelligence systems to be truly useful, the information must be actionable—readily available and easy to use when making decisions. If users have difficulty identifying critical metrics within the reports they receive, employee productivity and business performance will suffer.

GROUP DECISION-SUPPORT SYSTEMS

The systems we have just described focus primarily on helping you make a decision acting alone. However, what if you are part of a team and need to make a decision as a group? You would use a special category of systems called group decision-support systems for this purpose.

Group decision-support systems (GDSS) are interactive computer-based systems that facilitate the solution of unstructured problems by a set of decision makers working together as a group in the same location or in different locations. Originally, GDSS required dedicated conference rooms with special hardware and software tools to facilitate group decision making. But today GDSS capabilities have evolved along with the power of desktop PCs, the explosion of mobile computing in the form of smartphones and tablets, and the rapid expansion of bandwidth on WiFi and cellular networks. Dedicated rooms for collaboration can be replaced with much less expensive and flexible virtual collaboration rooms which can connect mobile employees with colleagues in the office sitting at desktops in a high quality video and audio environment. We introduced some of these contemporary collaboration environments in Chapter 2.

Cisco's Collaboration Meeting Rooms Hybrid (CMR) allows groups of employees to meet using any device, via WebEx video software, which does not require any special network connections, special displays, or complex software. The software to run CMR can be hosted on company servers, or in the cloud. This allows even customers to participate in group meetings. The meetings can be scheduled by employees whenever needed. CMR can handle up to 500 participants in a meeting, but that is quite rare.

Skype began deploying a similar cloud-based collaboration environment called Skype for Business to support online meetings, sharing of documents, audio, and video. Skype for Business is integrated into Microsoft Office 365, which will make Skype for Business available to all customers who use Office 365. In this sense, high end collaboration and decision support capabilities will become a very common part of office life in the near future.

11-3 What are the business benefits of using intelligent techniques in decision making and knowledge management?

Decision making is also enhanced by intelligent techniques and knowledge management systems. **Intelligent techniques** consist of expert systems, case-based reasoning, genetic algorithms, neural networks, fuzzy logic, and intelligent agents. These techniques are based on **artificial intelligence (AI)** technology, which consists of computer-based systems (both hardware and software) that attempt to emulate human behavior and thought patterns. Intelligent techniques aid decision makers by capturing individual and collective knowledge, discovering patterns and behaviors in very large quantities of data, and generating solutions to problems that are too large and complex for human beings to solve on their own.

Knowledge management systems, which we introduced in Chapter 2, and knowledge work systems provide tools for knowledge discovery, communication, and collaboration that make knowledge more easily available to decision makers and integrate it into the business processes of the firm.

EXPERT SYSTEMS

What if employees in your firm had to make decisions that required some special knowledge, such as how to formulate a fast-drying sealing compound or how to diagnose and repair a malfunctioning diesel engine, but all the people with that expertise had left the firm? Expert systems are one type of decision-making aid that could help you out. An **expert system** captures human expertise in a limited domain of knowledge as a set of rules in a software system that can be used by others in the organization. These systems typically perform a limited number of tasks that can be performed by professionals in a few minutes or hours, such as diagnosing a malfunctioning machine or determining whether to grant credit for a loan. They are useful in decision-making situations when expertise is expensive or in short supply.

How Expert Systems Work

Human knowledge must be modeled or represented in a form that a computer can process. Expert systems model human knowledge as a set of rules that collectively are called the **knowledge base**. Expert systems can have from 200 to as many as 10,000 of these rules, depending on the complexity of the decision-making problem. These rules are much more interconnected and nested than in a traditional software program (see Figure 11.8).

The strategy used to search through the collection of rules and formulate conclusions is called the **inference engine**. The inference engine works by searching through the rules and firing those rules that are triggered by facts the user gathers and enters.

Expert systems provide businesses with an array of benefits, including improved decisions, reduced errors, reduced costs, reduced training time, and improved quality and service. For example, Con-way Inc. built an expert system called Line-haul to automate and optimize planning of overnight shipment routes for its nationwide freight-trucking business. The expert system captures the business rules that dispatchers follow when assigning drivers, trucks, and trailers to transport 50,000 shipments of heavy freight each night across 25 U.S. states and Canada and when plotting their routes. Line-haul uses data on daily customer shipment requests, available drivers, trucks, trailer space, and weight, stored in an Oracle database. The expert system uses thousands of rules and 100,000 lines of program code written in C++ to crunch the numbers and create optimum routing plans for 95 percent of daily freight shipments. Con-way dispatchers tweak the routing plan the expert system provides and relay final routing specifications to field personnel responsible for

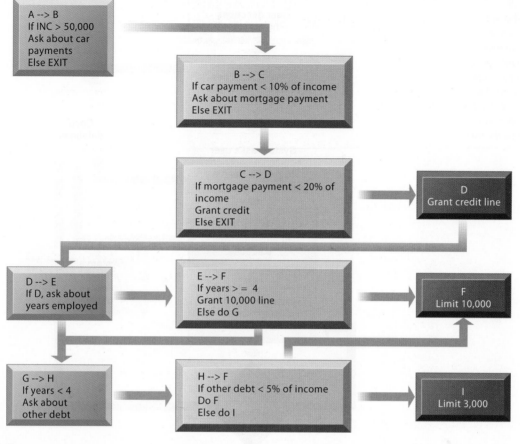

Figure 11.8
Rules in an Expert System

An expert system contains a set of rules to be followed when used. The rules are interconnected, the number of outcomes is known in advance and is limited, there are multiple paths to the same outcome, and the system can consider multiple rules at a single time. The rules illustrated are for a simple credit-granting expert system.

packing the trailers for their nighttime runs. Con-way recouped its $3 million investment in the system within two years by reducing the number of drivers, packing more freight per trailer, and reducing damage from rehandling. The system also reduces dispatchers' arduous nightly tasks.

Although expert systems lack the robust and general intelligence of human beings, they can provide benefits to organizations if their limitations are well understood. Only certain classes of problems can be solved using expert systems. Virtually all successful expert systems deal with problems of classification in which there are relatively few alternative outcomes and in which these possible outcomes are all known in advance. Expert systems are much less useful for dealing with unstructured problems that managers typically encounter.

CASE-BASED REASONING

Expert systems primarily capture the knowledge of individual experts, but organizations also have collective knowledge and expertise that they have built up over the years. This organizational knowledge can be captured and stored using case-based reasoning. In **case-based reasoning (CBR)**, knowledge and past experiences of human specialists are represented as cases and stored in a database for later retrieval when the user encounters a new case with similar parameters. The system searches for stored cases with problem characteristics similar to the new one, finds the closest fit, and applies the solutions of the old case to the new case. Successful solutions are

Figure 11.9
How Case-Based
Reasoning Works
*Case-based reasoning
represents knowledge as
a database of past cases
and their solutions. The
system uses a six-step process to generate solutions
to new problems the user
encounters.*

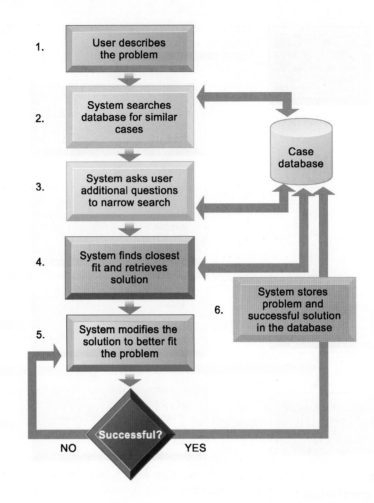

tagged to the new case and both are stored together with the other cases in the knowledge base. Unsuccessful solutions also are appended to the case database along with
explanations of why the solutions did not work (see Figure 11.9).

You'll find CBR in diagnostic systems in medicine or customer support where
users can retrieve past cases whose characteristics are similar to the new case. The
system suggests a solution or diagnosis based on the best-matching retrieved case.

FUZZY LOGIC SYSTEMS

Most people do not think in terms of traditional IF-THEN rules or precise numbers.
Humans tend to categorize things imprecisely, using rules for making decisions that
may have many shades of meaning. For example, a man or a woman may be *strong*
or *intelligent*. A company may be *large, medium*, or *small* in size. Temperature may be
hot, cold, cool, or *warm*. These categories represent a range of values.

Fuzzy logic is a rule-based technology that represents such imprecision by creating rules that use approximate or subjective values. It describes a particular phenomenon or process linguistically and then represents that description in a small number
of flexible rules.

Let's look at the way fuzzy logic would represent various temperatures in a computer application to control room temperature automatically. The terms (known
as *membership functions*) are imprecisely defined so that, for example, in Figure
11.10, cool is between 45 degrees and 70 degrees, although the temperature is most
clearly cool between about 60 degrees and 67 degrees. Note that *cool* is overlapped
by *cold* or *norm*. To control the room environment using this logic, the programmer
would develop similarly imprecise definitions for humidity and other factors, such
as outdoor wind and temperature. The rules might include one that says, "If the

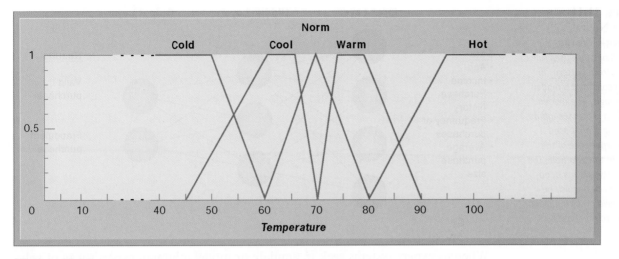

Figure 11.10
Fuzzy Logic for Temperature Control
The membership functions for the input called "temperature" are in the logic of the thermostat to control the room temperature. Membership functions help translate linguistic expressions, such as warm, into numbers that the computer can manipulate.

temperature is *cool* or *cold* and the humidity is low while the outdoor wind is high and the outdoor temperature is low, raise the heat and humidity in the room." The computer would combine the membership function readings in a weighted manner and, using all the rules, raise and lower the temperature and humidity.

Fuzzy logic provides solutions to problems requiring expertise that is difficult to represent in the form of crisp IF-THEN rules. In Japan, Sendai's subway system uses fuzzy logic controls to accelerate so smoothly that standing passengers need not hold on. Fuzzy logic allows incremental changes in inputs to produce smooth changes in outputs instead of discontinuous ones, making it useful for consumer electronics and engineering applications.

NEURAL NETWORKS

Neural networks are used for solving complex, poorly understood problems for which large amounts of data have been collected. They find patterns and relationships in massive amounts of data that would be too complicated and difficult for a human being to analyze. Neural networks discover this knowledge by using hardware and software that parallel the processing patterns of the biological or human brain. Neural networks learn patterns from large quantities of data by sifting through data, searching for relationships, building models, and correcting over and over again the model's own mistakes.

A neural network has a large number of sensing and processing nodes that continuously interact with each other. Figure 11.11 represents one type of neural network comprising an input layer, a hidden processing layer, and an output layer. Humans train the network by feeding it a set of training data for which the inputs produce a known set of outputs or conclusions. This helps the computer learn the correct solution by example. As the computer is fed more data, each case is compared with the known outcome. If it differs, a correction is calculated and applied to the nodes in the hidden processing layer. These steps are repeated until a condition, such as corrections being less than a certain amount, is reached. The neural network in Figure 11.11 has learned how to identify a fraudulent credit card purchase. In addition, self-organizing neural networks can be trained by exposing them to large amounts of data and allowing them to discover the patterns and relationships in the data.

Figure 11.11
How a Neural
Network Works
A neural network uses rules it learns from patterns in data to construct a hidden layer of logic. The hidden layer then processes inputs, classifying them based on the experience of the model. In this example, the neural network has been trained to distinguish between valid and fraudulent credit card purchases.

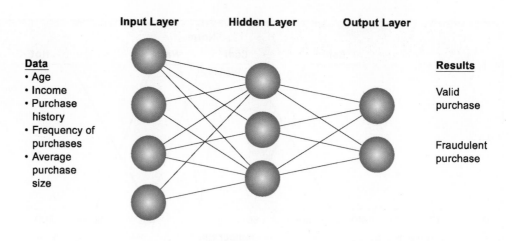

Input Layer   **Hidden Layer**   **Output Layer**

<u>Data</u>
- Age
- Income
- Purchase history
- Frequency of purchases
- Average purchase size

<u>Results</u>

Valid purchase

Fraudulent purchase

Whereas expert systems seek to emulate or model a human expert's way of solving problems, neural network builders claim that they do not program solutions and do not aim to solve specific problems. Instead, neural network designers seek to put intelligence into the hardware in the form of a generalized capability to learn. In contrast, the expert system is highly specific to a given problem and cannot be retrained easily.

Neural network applications in medicine, science, and business address problems in pattern classification, prediction, financial analysis, and control and optimization. In medicine, neural network applications are used for screening patients for coronary artery disease, for diagnosing patients with epilepsy and Alzheimer's disease, and for performing pattern recognition of pathology images. The financial industry uses neural networks to discern patterns in vast pools of data that might help investment firms predict the performance of equities, corporate bond ratings, or corporate bankruptcies. Visa International uses a neural network to help detect credit card fraud by monitoring all Visa transactions for sudden changes in the buying patterns of cardholders. The Interactive Session on People describes neural network applications for facial recognition and their potential impact on privacy.

There are puzzling aspects of neural networks. Unlike expert systems, which typically provide explanations for their solutions, neural networks cannot always explain why they arrived at a particular solution. They may not perform well if their training covers too little or too much data. In most current applications, neural networks are best used as aids to human decision makers instead of substitutes for them.

GENETIC ALGORITHMS

Genetic algorithms are useful for finding the optimal solution for a specific problem by examining a very large number of alternative solutions for that problem. They are based on techniques inspired by evolutionary biology such as inheritance, mutation, selection, and crossover (recombination).

A genetic algorithm works by representing a solution as a string of 0s and 1s. The genetic algorithm searches a population of randomly generated strings of binary digits to identify the right string representing the best possible solution for the problem. As solutions alter and combine, the worst ones are discarded and the better ones survive to go on to produce even better solutions.

In Figure 11.12, each string corresponds to one of the variables in the problem. One applies a test for fitness, ranking the strings in the population according to their level of desirability as possible solutions. After the initial population is evaluated for fitness, the algorithm then produces the next generation of strings, consisting of strings that survived the fitness test plus offspring strings produced from mating pairs of strings, and tests their fitness. The process continues until a solution is reached.

INTERACTIVE SESSION: PEOPLE   Facial Recognition Systems: Another Threat to Privacy?

Are you on Facebook? Do you worry about how much Facebook knows about you? Well, as much as it knows now, it's about to know much more. Facebook has been investing heavily in artificial intelligence (AI) technology to identify your face uniquely and track your behavior more precisely.

Facebook's facial recognition tool, called *DeepFace*, is nearly as accurate as the human brain in recognizing a face. DeepFace can compare two photos and state with 97.25 percent accuracy whether the photos show the same face. Humans are able to perform the same task with 97.53 percent accuracy.

DeepFace was developed by Facebook's AI research group in Menlo Park, California, and is based on an advanced deep learning neural network. Deep learning looks at a huge body of data, including human faces, and tries to develop a high-level abstraction of a human face by looking for recurring patterns (cheeks, eyebrow, etc.). The DeepFace neural network consists of nine layers of neurons. Its learning process has created 120 million connections (synapses) between those neurons, using four million photos of faces.

Once the learning process is complete, every image fed into the system passes through the synapses in a different way, producing a unique fingerprint among the layers of neurons. For example, a neuron might ask whether a particular face has a heavy brow. If so, one synapse would be followed; if no, another path would be taken.

DeepFace soon will be ready for commercial use, most likely to help Facebook improve the accuracy of Facebook.com's existing facial recognition capabilities to ensure that every photo of you on Facebook is connected to your account. (Facebook has one of the largest facial databases in the world for its photo tagging service.) DeepFace might also be used for real-world facial tracking, for example to monitor someone's shopping habits as that person moves from physical store to store. Facebook could profit handsomely from the detailed behavioral tracking data collected through DeepFace.

Facebook is one of many organizations using facial recognition systems, and neural networks are one of several techniques for this purpose. The Oregon Department of Motor Vehicles (DMV) uses facial recognition software to ensure that driver licenses, instruction permits, and ID cards are not issued under false names In Pinellas County, Florida, police can capture a 3D video

and upload it to an image gallery for comparison to identify people with prior criminal records or outstanding warrants.

Whatever the technology foundation, facial recognition systems are raising alarm among privacy advocates, who are worried about the far-reaching use of people's facial photos without their knowledge or consent. Although police departments and DMVs have strict limits on the use of their facial recognition software, casinos are beginning to faceprint their visitors to identify high rollers to pamper, and some Japanese grocery stores now use face-matching to identify shoplifters.

Dr. Joseph J. Atick, one of the pioneers of facial recognition technology, is at the forefront of these concerns. Atick is in favor of facial recognition for specific purposes such as law and immigration enforcement, motor vehicle department authentication, and airport entry, but he warns about its use for mass surveillance. Atick has been encouraging companies to adopt policies that safeguard the retention and reuse of facial data, stipulating that it cannot be matched, shared, or sold without permission.

Facial analysis has progressed beyond scrutinizing static features. Frame-by-frame analysis can isolate involuntary millisecond-long expressions, revealing private sentiments. Although these insights can drive productive endeavors, they are fraught with privacy implications. For example, do you want the person conducting your job interview to be able to review a videotape, identify fleeting moments of confusion or indecision, and decide against hiring you? People might try to use the software to determine whether their spouse was lying, police might read the emotions of crowds, or employers might use it to monitor workers or job applicants secretly. In addition to revealing people's emotions without their consent, these facial recognition tools might misinterpret people's feelings.

Psychologist Paul Eckman studied these fleeting microexpressions that surface when people are attempting to suppress an emotion and devised the Facial Action Coding System (FACS). Forty-three facial muscles control seven primary expressions—happiness, sadness, fear, anger, disgust, contempt, and surprise. Combinations of other basic muscle movements signal more advanced emotions such as frustration and confusion. People, and now computer programs, can be trained to recognize the universal spontaneous micromovements that divulge peoples' true feelings—narrowed eyelids, raised eyebrows, wrinkled forehead, scrunched nose, flared nostrils, or tensed lips.

Ekman has served as an advisor to Emotient, a San Diego startup whose software can recognize emotions from a database of microexpressions that happen in a fraction of a second. Emotient has worked with Honda Motor Co. and Procter & Gamble Co. to gauge people's emotions as they try out products. Emotient is confident that the ability to gauge customer emotions objectively and accurately will give retailers more tools to increase sales. Ekman says he is torn between the potential power of all this data and the need to ensure that it is used responsibly without infringing on personal privacy.

Although facial expression analysis will likely never be an exact science, academics, business people, and, certainly, government agencies are

intrigued by its possible applications. Online learning could be improved using webcams that perceive confusion in a student's expression and trigger additional tutoring sessions. Cameras could sense when a trucker is exhausted and prevent him from falling asleep at the wheel. When voice and gesture analysis and gaze tracking can be combined with facial expression analysis, the possibilities will explode, along with the privacy implications.

Sources: Elizabeth Dwoskin and Evelyn M. Rusli, "The Software That Unmasks Your Hidden Emotions," *Wall Street Journal*, January 28, 2015, www.emotient.com, accessed April 10, 2015; Sebastian Anthony, "Facebook's facial recognition software is now as accurate as the human brain, but what now?" *ExtremeTech*, March 19, 2014; Natasha Singer, "Never Forgetting a Face," *New York Times*, May 17, 2014; Ingrid Lunden, "Emotient Raises $6M For Facial Expression Recognition Tech, Debuts Google Glass Sentiment Analysis App," techcrunch.com, March 6, 2014; and Anne Eisenberg, "When Algorithms Grow Accustomed to Your Face," *New York Times*, November 30, 2013.

CASE STUDY QUESTIONS

1. What are some of the benefits of using facial recognition technology? Describe some current and future applications of this technology.

2. How does facial recognition technology threaten the protection of individual privacy? Give several examples.

3. Would you like DeepFace to track your activities on Facebook and in the physical world? Why or why not?

		Length	Width	Weight	Fitness
1 1 0 1 1 0	1	Long	Wide	Light	55
1 0 1 0 0 0	2	Short	Narrow	Heavy	49
0 0 0 1 0 1	3	Long	Narrow	Heavy	36
1 0 1 1 0 1	4	Short	Medium	Light	61
0 1 0 1 0 1	5	Long	Medium	Very light	74
A population of chromosomes			**Decoding of chromosomes**		**Evaluation of chromosomes**

Figure 11.12
The Components of a Genetic Algorithm
This example illustrates an initial population of chromosomes, each representing a different solution. The genetic algorithm uses an iterative process to refine the initial solutions so that the better ones, those with the higher fitness, are more likely to emerge as the best solution.

Genetic algorithms are used to solve problems that are very dynamic and complex, involving hundreds or thousands of variables or formulas. The problem must be one whose range of possible solutions can be represented genetically and criteria can be established for evaluating fitness. Genetic algorithms expedite the solution because they can evaluate many solution alternatives quickly to find the best one. For example, General Electric engineers used genetic algorithms to help optimize the design for jet turbine aircraft engines, in which each design change required changes in up to 100 variables. The supply chain management software from JDA Software uses genetic algorithms to optimize production-scheduling models, incorporating hundreds of thousands of details about customer orders, material and resource availability, manufacturing and distribution capability, and delivery dates.

INTELLIGENT AGENTS

Intelligent agent technology helps businesses and decision makers navigate through large amounts of data to locate and act on information they consider important. **Intelligent agents** are software programs that work in the background without direct human intervention to carry out specific, repetitive, and predictable tasks for an individual user, business process, or software application. The agent uses a limited built-in or learned knowledge base to accomplish tasks or make decisions on the user's behalf, such as deleting junk email, scheduling appointments, or finding the cheapest airfare to California.

There are many intelligent agent applications today in operating systems, application software, email systems, mobile computing software, and network tools. Of special interest to business are intelligent agents that search for information on the Internet. Chapter 7 describes how intelligent agent shopping bots help consumers find products they want and assist them in comparing prices and other features.

Although some intelligent agents are programmed to follow a simple set of rules, others are capable of learning from experience and adjusting their behavior. Siri, an application on Apple's iPhone and iPad, is an example. Siri uses voice recognition technology to answer questions, make recommendations, and perform actions. The software adapts to the user's individual preferences over time and personalizes results, performing tasks such as getting directions, scheduling appointments, and sending messages.

Procter & Gamble (P&G) used intelligent agent technology to make its supply chain more efficient (see Figure 11.13). It modeled a complex supply chain as a group of semiautonomous agents representing individual supply chain components such as trucks, production facilities, distributors, and retail stores. The behavior of each agent is programmed to follow rules that mimic actual behavior, such as "order an item when it is out of stock." Simulations using the agents enable the company to perform what-if analyses on inventory levels, in-store stockouts, and transportation costs.

Using intelligent agent models, P&G discovered that trucks should often be dispatched before being fully loaded. Although transportation costs would be higher using partially loaded trucks, the simulation showed that retail store stockouts would occur less often, thus reducing the number of lost sales, which would more than make up for the higher distribution costs. Agent-based modeling has saved P&G $300 million annually on an investment of less than 1 percent of that amount.

Although artificial intelligence technology plays an important role in contemporary knowledge management, it still does not exhibit the breadth, complexity, and originality of human intelligence. Computer scientists and neurologists alike have come to realize how sophisticated our brains actually are and how complicated certain tasks, such as recognizing language, identifying objects, and making informed decisions, can be for computers. The chapter-ending case study on IBM's Watson deals with these issues.

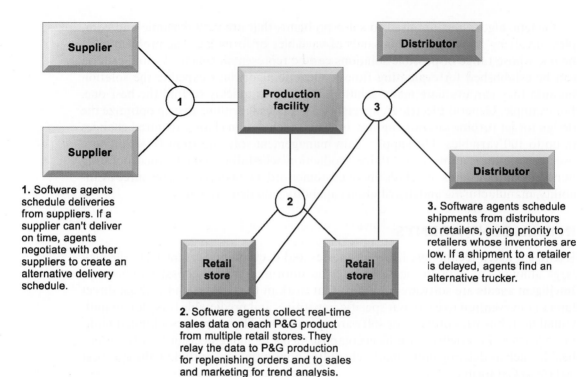

Figure 11.13
Intelligent Agents in P&G's Supply Chain Network
Intelligent agents are helping Procter & Gamble shorten the replenishment cycles for products such as a box of Tide.

11-4 What types of systems are used for enterprise-wide knowledge management and knowledge work, and how do they provide value for businesses?

Systems for knowledge management improve the quality and usage of knowledge used in the decision-making process. **Knowledge management** refers to the set of business processes developed in an organization to create, store, transfer, and apply knowledge. Knowledge management increases the ability of the organization to learn from its environment and to incorporate knowledge into its business processes and decision making.

Knowledge that is not shared and applied to the problems facing firms and managers does not add any value to the business. Knowing how to do things effectively and efficiently in ways that other organizations cannot duplicate is a major source of profit and competitive advantage. Businesses will operate less effectively and efficiently if this unique knowledge is not available for decision making and ongoing operations. There are two major types of knowledge management systems: enterprise-wide knowledge management systems and knowledge work systems.

ENTERPRISE-WIDE KNOWLEDGE MANAGEMENT SYSTEMS

Firms must deal with at least three kinds of knowledge. Some knowledge exists within the firm in the form of structured text documents (reports and presentations). Decision makers also need knowledge that is semistructured, such as email, voice mail, chat room exchanges, videos, digital pictures, brochures, or bulletin board postings. In still other cases, there is no formal or digital information of any kind, and the knowledge resides in the heads of employees. Much of this knowledge is **tacit knowledge** and is rarely written down.

Enterprise-wide knowledge management systems deal with all three types of knowledge. Enterprise-wide knowledge management systems are general-purpose, firm-wide systems that collect, store, distribute, and apply digital content and knowledge. These systems include capabilities for searching for information, storing both structured and unstructured data, and locating employee expertise within the firm. They also include supporting technologies such as portals, search engines, collaboration and social business tools, and learning management systems.

Enterprise Content Management Systems

Businesses today need to organize and manage both structured and semistructured knowledge assets. **Structured knowledge** is explicit knowledge that exists in formal documents as well as in formal rules that organizations derive by observing experts and their decision-making behaviors. Nevertheless, according to experts, at least 80 percent of an organization's business content is semistructured or unstructured—information in folders, messages, memos, proposals, emails, graphics, electronic slide presentations, and even videos created in different formats and stored in many locations.

Enterprise content management (ECM) systems help organizations manage both types of information. They have capabilities for knowledge capture, storage, retrieval, distribution, and preservation to help firms improve their business processes and decisions. Such systems include corporate repositories of documents, reports, presentations, and best practices as well as capabilities for collecting and organizing semistructured knowledge such as email (see Figure 11.14). Major ECM systems also enable users to access external sources of information, such as news feeds and research, and to communicate by email, chat/instant messaging, discussion groups, and videoconferencing. They are starting to incorporate blogs, wikis, and other enterprise social networking tools.

A key problem in managing knowledge is the creation of an appropriate classification scheme to organize information into meaningful categories. Once the categories for classifying knowledge have been created, each knowledge object needs to be tagged, or classified, so that it can be easily retrieved. ECM systems have capabilities for tagging, interfacing with corporate databases where the documents are stored, and creating an enterprise portal environment for employees to use when searching for corporate knowledge. Open Text, EMC Documentum, IBM, and Oracle are leading vendors of enterprise content management software.

The city of Calgary in Alberta, Canada, adopted OpenText Content Suite Platform to help its 15,000 employees manage and share the many kinds of documents required to provide essential services to citizens. Once a workspace is established in Content Server, the system automatically classifies documents, including graphic content, according to record type; retention requirements; and who in the

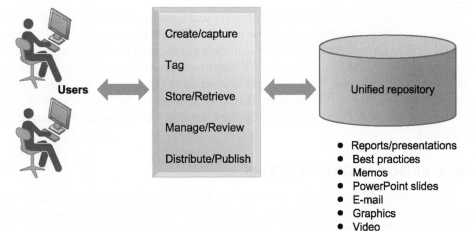

Figure II.14
An Enterprise Content Management System
An enterprise content management system has capabilities for classifying, organizing, and managing structured and semistructured knowledge and making it available throughout the enterprise.

organization is responsible for the document. Content created by one workgroup is easily accessible by other workgroups. Content Suite helped the city establish a strong records management program that supports groups with different needs.

Firms in publishing, advertising, broadcasting, and entertainment have special needs for storing and managing unstructured digital data such as photographs, graphic images, video, and audio content. **Digital asset management systems** help them classify, store, and distribute these digital objects.

Locating and Sharing Expertise

Some of the knowledge businesses need is not in the form of a digital document but, instead, resides in the memory of individual experts in the firm. Contemporary enterprise content management systems, along with the systems for collaboration and social business introduced in Chapter 2, have capabilities for locating experts and tapping their knowledge. These include online directories of corporate experts and their profiles, with details about their job experience, projects, publications, and educational degrees, and repositories of expert-generated content. Specialized search tools make it easier for employees to find the appropriate expert in a company.

For knowledge resources outside the firm, social networking and social business tools enable users to bookmark web pages of interest, tag these bookmarks with keywords, and share the tags and web page links with other people. These bookmarks are often public on sites such as Delicious and Reddit, but some can be saved privately and shared only with specified people or groups.

Learning Management Systems

Companies need ways to keep track of and manage employee learning and to integrate it more fully into their knowledge management and other corporate systems. **Learning management systems (LMS)** provide tools for the management, delivery, tracking, and assessment of various types of employee learning and training.

Contemporary LMS support multiple modes of learning, including CD-ROM, downloadable videos, web-based classes, live instruction in classes or online, and group learning in online forums and chat sessions. LMS consolidate mixed-media training, automate the selection and administration of courses, assemble and deliver learning content, and measure learning effectiveness.

CVM Solutions, LLC (CVM) uses Digitec's Knowledge Direct learning management system to provide training about how to manage suppliers for clients such as Procter & Gamble, Colgate-Palmolive, and Delta Airlines. Knowledge Direct provides a portal for accessing course content online along with hands-free administration features such as student registration and assessment tools, built-in Help and Contact Support, automatic email triggers to remind users of courses or deadlines, automatic email acknowledgement of course completions, and web-based reporting for accessed courses.

Businesses run their own learning management systems, but they are also turning to publicly available **massive open online courses (MOOCs)** to educate their employees. A MOOC is an online course made available via the web to very large numbers of participants. For example, in March 2013, employees from General Electric, Johnson & Johnson, Samsung, and Walmart were among more than 90,000 learners from 143 countries enrolled in Foundations for Business Strategy, a MOOC offered through the Coursera online learning platform by the University of Virginia's Darden School of Business.

KNOWLEDGE WORK SYSTEMS

The enterprise-wide knowledge systems we have just described provide a wide range of capabilities many, if not all, the workers and groups use in an organization. Firms also have specialized systems for knowledge workers to help them create

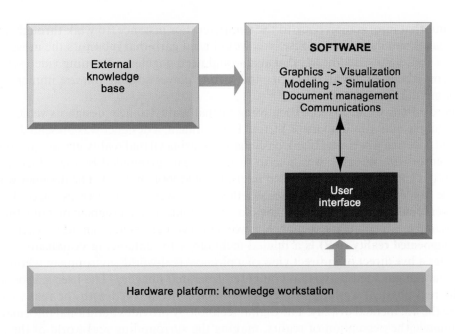

Figure 11.15
Requirements of Knowledge Work Systems
Knowledge work systems require strong links to external knowledge bases in addition to specialized hardware and software.

new knowledge for improving the firm's business processes and decision making. **Knowledge work systems (KWS)** are specialized systems for engineers, scientists, and other knowledge workers that are designed to promote the creation of knowledge and ensure that new knowledge and technical expertise are properly integrated into the business.

Requirements of Knowledge Work Systems

Knowledge work systems give knowledge workers the specialized tools they need, such as powerful graphics, analytical tools, and communications and document management. These systems require great computing power to handle the sophisticated graphics or complex calculations necessary for such knowledge workers as scientific researchers, product designers, and financial analysts. Because knowledge workers are so focused on knowledge in the external world, these systems also must give the worker quick and easy access to external databases. They typically feature user-friendly interfaces that enable users to perform needed tasks without having to spend a lot of time learning how to use the computer. Figure 11.15 summarizes the requirements of knowledge work systems.

Knowledge workstations often are designed and optimized for the specific tasks to be performed. Design engineers need graphics with enough power to handle three-dimensional CAD systems. However, financial analysts are more interested in access to a myriad of external databases and technology for efficiently storing and accessing massive amounts of financial data.

Examples of Knowledge Work Systems

Major knowledge work applications include CAD systems (which we introduced in Chapter 3), virtual reality systems for simulation and modeling, and financial workstations.

Contemporary CAD systems are capable of generating realistic-looking three-dimensional graphic designs that can be rotated and viewed from all sides. The CAD software produces design specifications for manufacturing, reducing both errors and production time. **Virtual reality systems** use interactive graphics software to create computer-generated simulations that are so close to reality that users almost believe they are participating in a real-world situation. In many virtual reality systems, the user dons special clothing, headgear, and equipment, depending on the application. The clothing contains sensors that record the user's movements and immediately

transmit that information back to the computer. For instance, to walk through a virtual reality simulation of a house, you would need garb that monitors the movement of your feet, hands, and head. You also would need goggles containing video screens and, sometimes, audio attachments and feeling gloves so that you are immersed in the computer feedback.

Ford Motor Company has been using virtual reality to help design its vehicles. In one example of Ford's Immersive Virtual Environment, a designer was presented with a car seat, steering wheel, and blank dashboard. Wearing virtual reality glasses and gloves with sensors, the designer was able to sit in the seat surrounded by the vehicle's 3-D design to experience how a proposed interior would look and feel. The designer would be able to identify blind spots or see whether knobs were in an awkward place. Ford's designers could also use this technology to see the impact of a design on manufacturing. For example, is a bolt that assembly line workers need to tighten too hard to reach?

Augmented reality (AR) is a related technology for enhancing visualization. AR provides a live direct or indirect view of a physical real-world environment whose elements are augmented by virtual computer-generated imagery. The user is grounded in the real physical world, and the virtual images are merged with the real view to create the augmented display. The digital technology provides additional information to enhance the perception of reality, making the surrounding real world of the user more interactive and meaningful. The yellow first-down markers shown on televised football games are examples of AR, as are medical procedures such as image-guided surgery, by which data acquired from computerized tomography (CT) and magnetic resonance imaging (MRI) scans or from ultrasound imaging are superimposed on the patient in the operating room. Virtual reality applications developed for the web use a standard called **Virtual Reality Modeling Language (VRML)**. VRML is a set of specifications for interactive, three-dimensional modeling on the World Wide Web that organizes multiple media types, including animation, images, and audio, to put users in a simulated real-world environment. VRML is platform independent, operates over a desktop computer, and requires little bandwidth.

DuPont, the Wilmington, Delaware, chemical company, created a VRML application called HyperPlant, which enables users to access three-dimensional data over the Internet using web-browser software. Engineers can go through three-dimensional models as if they were physically walking through a plant, viewing objects at eye level. This level of detail reduces the number of mistakes they make during construction of oil rigs, oil plants, and other structures.

The financial industry is using specialized **investment workstations** to leverage the knowledge and time of its brokers, traders, and portfolio managers. Firms such as Merrill Lynch and UBS Financial Services have installed investment workstations that integrate a wide range of data from both internal and external sources, including contact management data, real-time and historical market data, and research reports. Previously, financial professionals had to spend considerable time accessing data from separate systems and piecing together the information they needed. By providing one-stop information faster and with fewer errors, the workstations streamline the entire investment process from stock selection to updating client records.

Review Summary

11-1 **What are the different types of decisions, and how does the decision-making process work?** Decisions may be structured, semistructured, or unstructured, with structured decisions clustering at the operational level of the organization and unstructured decisions at the strategic level. Decision making can be performed by individuals or groups and includes employees as well as operational, middle, and senior managers. There are four stages in decision making: intelligence, design, choice, and implementation.

11-2 **How do business intelligence and business analytics support decision making?** Business intelligence and analytics promise to deliver correct, nearly real-time information to decision makers, and the analytic tools help them quickly understand the information and take action. A business intelligence environment consists of data from the business environment, the BI infrastructure, a BA toolset, managerial users and methods, a BI delivery platform (MIS, DSS, or ESS), and the user interface. There are six analytic functionalities that BI systems deliver to achieve these ends: predefined production reports, parameterized reports, dashboards and scorecards, ad hoc queries and searches, the ability to drill down to detailed views of data, and the ability to model scenarios and create forecasts. BI analytics are starting to handle big data. Predictive analytics, location analytics, and operational intelligence are important analytic capabilities.

Management information systems (MIS) producing prepackaged production reports are typically used to support operational and middle management, whose decision making is fairly structured. For making unstructured decisions, analysts and super users employ decision-support systems (DSS) with powerful analytics and modeling tools, including spreadsheets and pivot tables. Senior executives making unstructured decisions use dashboards and visual interfaces displaying key performance information affecting the overall profitability, success, and strategy of the firm. The balanced scorecard and business performance management are two methodologies used in designing executive support systems (ESS).

Group decision-support systems (GDSS) help people meeting in a group arrive at decisions more efficiently. GDSS feature special conference room facilities where participants contribute their ideas using networked computers and software tools for organizing ideas, gathering information, ranking and setting priorities, and documenting meeting sessions.

11-3 **What are the business benefits of using intelligent techniques in decision making and knowledge management?** Expert systems capture tacit knowledge from a limited domain of human expertise and express that knowledge in the form of rules. The strategy to search through the knowledge base is called the inference engine. Case-based reasoning represents organizational knowledge as a database of cases that can be continually expanded and refined.

Fuzzy logic is a software technology for expressing knowledge in the form of rules that use approximate or subjective values. Neural networks consist of hardware and software that attempt to mimic the thought processes of the human brain. Neural networks are notable for their ability to learn without programming and to recognize patterns in massive amounts of data.

Genetic algorithms develop solutions to particular problems using genetically based processes, such as fitness, crossover, and mutation. Intelligent agents are software programs with built-in or learned knowledge bases that carry out specific, repetitive, and predictable tasks for an individual user, business process, or software application.

11-4 **What types of systems are used for enterprise-wide knowledge management and knowledge work, and how do they provide value for businesses?** Enterprise content management systems feature databases and tools for organizing and storing structured documents and semistructured knowledge such as email or rich media. Often these systems include group collaboration and social tools, portals to simplify information access, search tools, and tools for classifying information based on a taxonomy that is appropriate for the organization. Learning management systems provide tools for the management, delivery, tracking, and assessment of various types of employee learning and training.

Knowledge work systems (KWS) support the creation of new knowledge and its integration into the organization. KWS require easy access to an external knowledge base; powerful computer hardware that can support software with intensive graphics, analysis, document management, and communications capabilities; and a user-friendly interface.

Key Terms

Artificial intelligence (AI), 426
Augmented reality, 438
Balanced scorecard method, 424
Business performance management (BPM), 424
Case-based reasoning (CBR), 427
Choice, 413
Data visualization, 416
Design, 413
Digital asset management systems, 436
Drill down, 425
Enterprise content management systems, 435
Enterprise-wide knowledge management systems, 435
Expert system, 426
Fuzzy logic, 428

Genetic algorithms, 430
Geographic information systems (GIS), 419
Group decision-support systems (GDSS), 425
Implementation, 413
Inference engine, 426
Intelligence, 413
Intelligent agents, 433
Intelligent techniques, 426
Investment workstations, 438
Key performance indicators (KPIs), 424
Knowledge base, 426
Knowledge management, 434
Knowledge work systems (KWS), 437
Learning management system (LMS), 436

Location analytics, 419
Massive open online course (MOOC), 436
Neural networks, 429
Operational intelligence, 419
Pivot table, 422
Predictive analytics, 417
Semistructured decisions, 412
Sensitivity analysis, 422
Structured decisions, 412
Structured knowledge, 435
Tacit knowledge, 434
Unstructured decisions, 412
Virtual Reality Modeling Language (VRML), 438
Virtual reality systems, 437

MyMISLab™

To complete the problems with the ⭐, go to EOC Discussion Questions in the MyLab..

Review Questions

11-1 What are the different types of decisions and how does the decision-making process work?
  • List and describe the different decision-making levels and groups in organizations and their decision-making requirements.
  • Distinguish among an unstructured, semistructured, and structured decision.
  • Explain how you can determine the quality of decisions and decision making.
  • Explain how you might handle a situation in which a decision does not work.

11-2 How do BI and business analytics support decision making?
  • Define and describe business intelligence and business analytics.
  • List and describe the elements of a BI environment.
  • List and describe the analytic functionalities BI systems provide.
  • Define predictive analytics and location analytics and give two examples of each.
  • List each of the types of BI users and describe the kinds of systems that provide decision support for each type of user.
  • Describe Big Data analytics and provide 2 examples.
  • Define and describe the balanced scorecard method and business performance management.

11-3 What are the business benefits of using intelligent techniques in decision making and knowledge management?
  • Define an expert system, describe how it works, and explain its value to business.
  • Define case-based reasoning and explain how it differs from an expert system.
  • Define a neural network and describe how it works and how it benefits businesses.

- Define and describe fuzzy logic, genetic algorithms, and intelligent agents. Explain how each works and the kinds of problems for which each is suited.

11-4 What types of systems are used for enterprise-wide knowledge management and knowledge work, and how do they provide value for businesses?
- Define knowledge management and explain its value to businesses.
- Define and describe the various types of enterprise-wide knowledge systems and explain how they provide value for businesses.
- Provide examples of collaboration tools and learning management systems.
- Describe how the following systems support knowledge work: computer-aided design (CAD), virtual reality, and investment workstations.

Discussion Questions

⊗ 11-5 Why is the balanced scorecard method a leading methodology for understanding the most important information needed a firm's executives? How is related to business performance management?.

⊗ 11-6 Describe various ways that knowledge management systems could help firms with sales and marketing or with manufacturing and production.

⊗ 11-7 How much can business intelligence and business analytics help companies refine their business strategy? Explain your answer.

Hands-On MIS Projects

The projects in this section give you hands-on experience designing a knowledge portal, identifying opportunities for business intelligence, using a spreadsheet pivot table to analyze sales data, and using intelligent agents to research products for sale on the web. Visit MyMISLab's Multimedia Library to access this chapter's Hands-On MIS Projects.

MANAGEMENT DECISION PROBLEMS

11-8 British Pharma Corporation is headquartered in London but has research sites in Germany, France, Switzerland, and Australia. Research and development of new pharmaceuticals is key to ongoing profits, and British Pharma researches and tests thousands of possible drugs. The company's researchers need to share information with others within and outside the company, including the the World Health Organization, and the International Federation of Pharmaceutical Manufacturers & Associations. Also critical is access to health information sites, such as the and to industry conferences and professional journals. Design a knowledge portal for British Pharma's researchers. Include in your design specifications relevant internal systems and databases, external sources of information, and internal and external communication and collaboration tools. Design a home page for your portal.

11-9 Applebee's is the largest casual dining chain in the world, with over 1,800 locations in 21 countries throughout the world. The menu features beef, chicken, and pork items, as well as burgers, pasta, and seafood. Applebee's CEO wants to make the restaurant more profitable by developing menus that are tastier and contain more items that customers want and are willing to pay for despite rising costs for gasoline and agricultural products. How might business intelligence help management implement this strategy? What pieces of data would Applebee's need to collect? What kinds of reports would be useful to help management make decisions on how to improve menus and profitability?

IMPROVING DECISION MAKING: USING PIVOT TABLES TO ANALYZE SALES DATA

Software skills: Pivot tables
Business skills: Analyzing sales data

11-10   This project gives you an opportunity to learn how to use Excel's PivotTable functionality to analyze a database or data list. Use the data file for Online Management Training Inc. described earlier in the chapter. This is a list of the sales transactions at OMT for one day. You can find this spreadsheet file at MyMISLab. Use Excel's PivotTable to help you answer the following questions:

- Where are the average purchases higher? The answer might tell managers where to focus marketing and sales resources or pitch different messages to different regions.

- What form of payment is the most common? The answer could be used to emphasize in advertising the most preferred means of payment.

- Are there any times of day when purchases are most common? Do people buy products while at work (likely during the day) or at home (likely in the evening)?

- What's the relationship among region, type of product purchased, and average sales price?

    We provide instructions on how to use Excel PivotTables in our Learning Tracks.

IMPROVING DECISION MAKING: USING INTELLIGENT AGENTS FOR COMPARISON SHOPPING

Software skills: Web browser and shopping bot software
Business skills: Product evaluation and selection

11-11   This project will give you experience using shopping bots to search online for products, find product information, and find the best prices and vendors. Select a digital camera you might want to purchase, such as the Canon PowerShot S120 or the Olympus TG-4. Visit MySimon (www.mysimon.com), BizRate.com (www.bizrate.com), and Google Shopping to do price comparisons for you. Evaluate these shopping sites in terms of their ease of use, number of offerings, speed in obtaining information, thoroughness of information offered about the product and seller, and price selection. Which site or sites would you use and why? Which camera would you select and why? How helpful were these sites in making your decision?

Collaboration and Teamwork Project

Analyzing MOOCs for College Degree Programs

11-12   With three or four of your classmates, research the issue of whether MOOCs can and should be used by university students pursuing a college degree. Search the web for articles and findings about the appropriateness of MOOCs for college degree programs. Can students learn effectively with MOOCs? Should universities provide MOOC courses for college credit? What are the pros and cons? If possible, use Google Docs and Google Drive or Google Sites to brainstorm, organize, and develop a presentation of your findings for the class.

BUSINESS PROBLEM-SOLVING CASE

Knowledge Management and Collaboration at Tata Consulting Services

Tata Consultancy Services (TCS) is an IT-services, business-solutions, and outsourcing organization that offers a portfolio of IT and IT-enabled services to clients all over the globe in horizontal, vertical, and geographical domains. A part of the Tata Group, India's largest industrial conglomerate, TCS has over 108,000 IT consultants in 47 countries.

The concept of knowledge management (KM) was introduced in TCS in 1995 and a dedicated KM team called "Corporate GroupWare" was formed in 1998. This group launched the KM-pilot in mid-1999, which was implemented subsequently by a team comprising the steering committee, corporate GroupWare implanters, branch champions, application owners, and the infrastructure group.

At that time, KM in TCS covered nearly every function, from quality assurance to HR management. While its 50 offices in India were linked through dedicated communication lines, overseas offices were connected through the Net and the Lotus Notes Domino Servers. The employees could access the knowledge repository that resided on the corporate and branch servers through the intranet with a browser front-end or a Notes client. The knowledge repository, also called KBases, contained a wide range of information about processes, line of business, line of technology, and projects.

Though the formal KM efforts started in TCS in the late 1990s, the informal, closely knit communities of practices (CoPs) had existed at TCS since the 1980s, when it had around a thousand employees. The earliest "group" was based on the migration of technologies. Later, teams were formed for mainframe, Unix, and databases. The groups, consisting of one or two experts in their respective fields, began formal documentation practices with the members writing down the best practices. Recollecting the group practices in the initial days, K. Ananth Krishnan, a technology consultant at that time, recounted that in the mid-1980s, problems and solutions were documented and there were over 1,500 case studies dealing with mainframes. Similarly, 40 case studies dealing with overall system quality were reviewed as early as 1993.

The next step was to create process asset libraries (PALs). These contained information related to technology, processes, and case studies for project leaders, which were made available to all development centers through the intranet.

Then Ultimatix, a Web-based electronic knowledge management (EKM) portal, which made the knowledge globally available, was developed. The PAL library and KBases, which were hosted on the intranet, were merged with Ultimatix, which had sub-portals for a quality management system, software productivity improvement, training materials, and tools information. There were EKM administrators for each practice and subject group with defined responsibilities, such as editing the documents and approving them for publication. Commenting on the success of CoP, Krishnan maintained that between January 2003 and June 2003, CoP members had exchanged around 10,000 document transactions relating to the industry practices and 21,000 service practices via Ultimatix. The telecom CoP alone had 6,000 transactions, excluding the intranet-based community activities.

To encourage employee conversations, TCS took considerable care in the architecture of its development centers located across the country. Reflecting on the new design of one of its development centers in Sholinganallur, Chennai, CFO S. Mahalingam commented that the center is made up of modules, each dedicated to one particular technology or a client or an industry practice. These structures lead to garden terraces where employees gather during their break for informal conversations and to brainstorm the solutions to many problems.

TCS also launched a number of training programs such as the Initial Learning Program, targeted at new employees; the Continuous Learning Program for experienced employees; and the Leadership Development Program for employees with more than five years' experience. The integrated competency and learning management systems (iCALMS) that was deployed globally across all TCS offices promoted a culture of learning and growth in the organization. Equipped with data about competency definitions, role definitions, and online/classroom learning objectives, it helped the consultants to enhance their skills in a customized manner. To gain cross-industry experience, TCS regularly rotated people across various functions and within other Tata Group companies. Employees were also encouraged to join outside bodies like the IEEE and to go in for certifications.

Knowmax, a knowledge management system, developed using Microsoft sharepoint portal server in 2007, gave TCS consultants access to nearly 40 years of experience and best practices, arranged by type of engagement, the technology in use, and customer requirements. It supported more than 60 knowledge assets and was accessible via Ultimatix to all TCS associates. Any associate could contribute to the K-Bank and knowledge officers were made responsible for maintaining the quality of content.

To maintain the work–life balance of its employees, TCS initiated Propel sessions, which brought together employees with similar interests to conduct various activities such as reading books. Held every quarter through conferences and camps, this initiative also spurred knowledge transfer among the employees. The knowledge sharing at the project level was done through the LiveMeeting application, where all the project meetings were recorded and stored in the project repository. Team members who missed the meeting or any new members in the team could listen to the recorded sessions, and this enabled them to catch up with the rest of the team. Furthermore, Knowledge Transition sessions conducted weekly by a subject matter expert helped the team to learn from the experience of the experts. A "Tip of the Day" mail, comprising technical, conceptual, or human skills tips, was also shared within the organization almost daily.

Though Ultimatix, launched in 2002, digitized the entire organization from end to end and improved the business processes' efficiency, it still couldn't tap the knowledge of employees effectively. To improve collaboration among employees, Project Infinity was launched in 2007; this involved a number of technologies including IBM's Sametime, QuickPlace, Lotus Domino Collaboration tools, Avaya VOIP telephony, and Polycom IP videoconferencing.

As a result of adopting Infinity, collaboration of overseas and local offices improved as instant messaging (IM) got rid of cultural and pronunciation differences that could occur on the phone. Furthermore, corporate communications were able to run a 24-hour internal news broadcast to all TCS offices in the world. In addition, travel and telecommunications costs were reduced by 40 percent and 6 percent respectively.

In 2015, TCS remained India's largest software exporter, and became the first company to surpass $90 billion in market capitalization. In 2015, TCS continued to report solid financial figures, generating $15.5 billion in revenue with over 319,000 employees. Clearly knowledge management tools are a key strategic resource at TCS, and are the source of new services that the company can market to other firms seeking knowledge management systems. The future for TCS continues to look bright going forward.

Sources: TCS, "Case Study: A Global Professional Services Firm Successfully Optimizes Its Knowledge Management Function and Accrues Cost Savings Worth USD 400,000," Tata Consulting Services, TCS.com, 2015; Jolly Marikan, "Case Study: Knowledge Management and Collaboration at Tata Consulting Services," Jollymarikan.blogspot.com, October 12, 2015; N. Hainisani, "Knowledge Management and Collaboration at TATA Consulting Services," Malaysian Graduate School of Entrepreneurship and Business, University of Malaysia Kelantan, May 15, 2015; "Strong Customer Additions, Holistic Growth Helps TCS Take Market Leadership in FY15," press release, TCS, April 16, 2015; Dhanya Thoppil, "Tata Consultancy Services Manages Its Size to Stay Agile," *Wall Street Journal*, July 27, 2014; Sankaranarayanan G., "Building Communities, the TCS Way," expressitpeople.com, September 2003; Kavita Kaur, "Give and Take," india-today.com, January 2000; Sunil Shah, "Network Wonder: Collaborative Tools Help TCS Grow," cio.com, July 2007; Shivani Shinde, "TCS Sees Synergy in Gen X Tools," rediff.com, July 2008.

Case Study Questions

11-13 Analyze the knowledge management efforts at TCS using the knowledge management value chain model. Which tools or activities were used for managing tacit knowledge and which ones are used for explicit knowledge?

11-14 Describe the growth of knowledge management systems at TCS. How have these systems helped TCS in its business?

11-15 Describe the collaboration tools used at TCS. What benefits did TCS reap from these tools?

11-16 How did Web 2.0 tools help TCS to manage knowledge and collaboration among its employees?

Case contributed by Neerja Sethi and Vijay Sethi, Nanyang Technological University

MyMISLab

Go to the Assignments section of your MyLab to complete these writing exercises.

11-17 Give three examples of data used in location analytics and explain how each can help businesses.

11-18 How do each of the following types of systems acquire and represent knowledge: Expert system, case-based reasoning, neural network?

Chapter 11 References

Alavi, Maryam, and Dorothy Leidner. "Knowledge Management and Knowledge Management Systems: Conceptual Foundations and Research Issues," *MIS Quarterly* 25, No. 1 (March 2001).

Althuizen, Niek, and Berend Wierenga. "Supporting Creative Problem Solving with a Case-Based Reasoning System." *Journal of Management Information Systems* 31, No. 1 (Summer 2014).

Bhandari, Rishi, Marc Singer, and Hiek van der Scheer. "Using Marketing Analytics to Drive Superior Growth." McKinsey & Co. (June 2014).

Breuer, Peter, Jessica Moulton, and Robert Turtle. "Applying Advanced Analytics in Consumer Companies," McKinsey & Company (May 2013).

Bloomberg News, "The Return of Artificial Intelligence," (February 4, 2015).

Burns, Ed. "Customer Data Analysis Turns Info Crude Oil into Business Fuel," Searchbusinessanalytics.techtarget.com, accessed January 2, 2015.

Burtka, Michael. "Genetic Algorithms," *The Stern Information Systems Review* 1, No. 1 (Spring 1993).

Davenport, Thomas H. "Big Data at Work: Dispelling the Myths, Uncovering the Opportunities." *Harvard Business Review* (2014).

Davenport, Thomas H., Jeanne Harris, and Robert Morison. *Analytics at Work: Smarter Decisions, Better Results*. (Boston: Harvard Business Press, 2010.)

Dennis, Alan R., Jay E. Aronson, William G. Henriger, and Edward D. Walker III. "Structuring Time and Task in Electronic Brainstorming," *MIS Quarterly* 23, No. 1 (March 1999).

Dhar, Vasant, and Roger Stein. *Intelligent Decision Support Methods: The Science of Knowledge Work*. (Upper Saddle River, NJ: Prentice-Hall, 1997.)

Fisher, Lauren T. "Data Management Platforms: Using Big Data to Power Marketing Performance," *eMarketer* (May 2013).

Grau, Jeffrey. "How Retailers Are Leveraging 'Big Data' to Personalize Ecommerce," *eMarketer* (May 2012).

Holland, John H. "Genetic Algorithms," *Scientific American* (July 1992).

Hurst, Cameron, with Michael S. Hopkins and Leslie Brokaw. "Matchmaking with Math: How Analytics

Beats Intuition to Win Customers," *MIT Sloan Management Review* 52, No. 2 (Winter 2011).

Ihrig, Martin, and Ian MacMillan. "Managing Your Mission-Critical Knowledge," *Harvard Business Review* (January–February 2015).

King, William R., Peter V. Marks, Jr., and Scott McCoy. "The Most Important Issues in Knowledge Management," *Communications of the ACM* 45, No.9 (September 2002).

Kiron, David, Pamela Kirk Prentice, and Renee Boucher Ferguson, "Raising the Bar with Analytics." *MIT Sloan Management Review* (Winter 2014).

LaValle, Steve, Eric Lesser, Rebecca Shockley, Michael S. Hopkins, and Nina Kruschwitz. "Big Data, Analytics, and the Path from Insights to Value," *MIT Sloan Management Review* 52, No. 2 (Winter 2011).

Malone, Thomas. "Rethinking Knowledge Work: A Strategic Approach," *McKinsey Quarterly* (February 2011).

Mankins, Michael C., and Lori Sherer. "Creating Value Through Advanced Analytics," Bain and Company (2015).

Marchand, Donald A., and Joe Peppard. "Why IT Fumbles Analytics," *Harvard Business Review* (January-February 2013).

Markoff, John. "How Many Computers to Identify a Cat? 16,000," *New York Times* (June 26, 2012).

Markoff, John. "Innovators of Intelligence Look to Past," *New York Times* (December 15, 2014).

McKnight, William. "Predictive Analytics: Beyond the Predictions," *Information Management* (July/August 2011).

Murphy, Chris. "4 Ways Ford Is Exploring Next-Gen Car Tech," *Information Week* (July 27, 2012).

Nichols, Wes. "Advertising Analytics 2.0," *Harvard Business Review* (March 2013).

Nunamaker, Jay, Robert O. Briggs, Daniel D. Mittleman, Douglas R. Vogel, and Pierre A. Balthazard. "Lessons from a Dozen Years of Group Support Systems Research: A Discussion of Lab and Field Findings," *Journal of Management Information Systems* 13, No. 3 (Winter 1997).

Nurmohamed, Zafrin, Nabeel Gillani, and Michael Lenox "A New Use for MOOCs: Real-World Problem Solving," *Harvard Business Review* (July 14, 2013).

Pugh, Katrina, and Lawrence Prusak. "Designing Effective Knowledge Networks," *MIT Sloan Management Review* (Fall 2013).

Ransbotham, Sam, David Kiron, and Pamela Kirk Prentice. "Minding the Analytics Gap," *MIT Sloan Management Review* (Spring 2015).

Rosman, Katherine. "Augmented Reality Finally Starts to Gain Traction," *Wall Street Journal* (March 3, 2014).

Samuelson, Douglas A., and Charles M. Macal. "Agent-Based Simulation," *OR/MS Today* (August 2006).

Simon, H. A. *The New Science of Management Decision.* (New York: Harper & Row, 1960.)

"The New Science of Sales Performance," *Harvard Business Review Analytic Services* (March 5, 2015).

Ukelson, Jacob. "Trends in Knowledge Work," *Information Management* (May/June 2011).

Viaene, Stijn, and Annabel Van den Bunder. "The Secrets to Managing Business Analytics Projects," *Sloan Management Review* 52, No. 1 (Fall 2011).

Wang, Yinglei, Darren B. Meister, and Peter H. Gray. "Social Influence and Knowledge Management Systems Use: Evidence from Panel Data." *MIS Quarterly* 37, No. 1 (March 2013).

Wheatley, Malcolm. "Data-Driven Location Choices Drive Latest Starbucks Surge," *Data Informed* (January 10, 2013).

Zadeh, Lotfi A. "The Calculus of Fuzzy If/Then Rules," *AI Expert* (March 1992).

Building and Managing Systems

PART IV

12 Building Information Systems and Managing Projects

Part IV shows how to use the knowledge acquired in earlier chapters to analyze and design information system solutions to business problems. This part answers questions such as these: How can I develop a solution to an information system problem that provides genuine business benefits? How can the firm adjust to the changes introduced by the new system solution? What alternative approaches are available for building system solutions?

Building Information Systems and Managing Projects

CHAPTER 12

LEARNING OBJECTIVES

After reading this chapter, you will be able to answer the following questions:

12-1 What are the core problem-solving steps for developing new information systems?

12-2 What are the alternative methods for building information systems?

12-3 What are the principal methodologies for modeling and designing systems?

12-4 How should information systems projects be selected and managed?

CHAPTER CASES

Girl Scout Cookie Sales Go Digital

Analytics Help the Cincinnati Zoo Know Its Customers

Britain's National Health Service Jettisons Choose and Book System

A Shaky Start for Healthcare.gov

VIDEO CASES

Case 1: IBM: BPM in a Service-Oriented Architecture

Case 2: IBM Helps the City of Madrid with Real-Time BPM Software

Instructional Videos:

BPM: Business Process Management Customer Story

Workflow Management Visualized

GIRL SCOUT COOKIE SALES GO DIGITAL

Thin Mints, Samoas, and Trefoils may be fun to eat, but selling Girl Scout cookies is a serious business. Girl Scout cookie sales bring in about $800 million annually. Cookie sales are a major source of funding for the Girl Scouts and an opportunity for the 2.3 million girls who do the selling to develop valuable sales and money management skills. However, collecting, counting, and organizing the annual avalanche of cookie orders has become a tremendous challenge.

The Girl Scouts' traditional cookie-ordering process has been heavily manual. During the peak sales period in January, each Girl Scout would enter her sales on an individual order card and turn the card in to the troop leader when she was finished. The troop leader would transfer the information to a five-part form and give this form to a community volunteer who tabulated the orders. From there, the order data passed to a regional council headquarters, where they would be batched into final orders for the manufacturer. (Little Brownie Bakers in Louisville, Kentucky, and ABC Bakers in Richmond, Virginia, are the two licensed suppliers for Girl Scout Cookies.) It might take weeks or months for customers to receive the cookies they ordered.

The paperwork was overwhelming. Order transactions changed hands too many times, creating many opportunities for error. All the added columns, multiple prices per box, and calculations had to be made by different people, all on a deadline.

The Girl Scouts are trying to use information technology to improve this process. For example, the Patriots' Trail Girl Scout Council, representing 65 communities and 18,000 Girl Scouts in the greater Boston area, used Intuit's hosted QuickBase for Corporate WorkGroups to document, manage, and organize

© Rob Hainer/Shutterstock

cookie sales and deliveries, including online entry of cookie orders over the web and electronic transmission of orders to ABC Bakers. Other regional Girl Scout councils have also moved to a QuickBase system. ABC Bakers and Little Brownie Bakers have their own order management systems for Girl Scout cookies.

Girl Scouts of the USA decided that instead of relying on all these disparate systems, it should develop a single nationwide digital solution for Girl Scout cookie sales for all Girl Scouts to use if they chose. Working with Accenture consultants and Hybris e-commerce specialists, Girl Scouts of the USA developed the Digital Cookie system. The system includes capabilities for individual Girl Scouts to create their own personalized websites for taking cookie orders and a mobile app for cookie sales that runs on iOS and Android smartphones and tablets. The Hybris Commerce Suite provides a single system for managing product content, commerce operations, and multiple sales channels (including the web and mobile devices) to create a unified and consistent cross-channel experience for customers.

A scout with a mobile device would contact a potential customer, meet the customer in person, and help him or her fill out an online order form on the mobile device. The customer would enter his or her credit card information. A scout using her own personal website would contact the customer in person or via phone or e-mail. The customer would be provided with information on how to access that particular scout's personal website and use the website to enter order and payment information online. Customer credit card payment data can be entered directly online. Both options perform the required order calculations and eliminate the need for paper order forms.

The Digital Cookie websites and apps are available only to Girl Scouts. Customers must purchase cookies through an individual Girl Scout or troop, but there is a mobile app for customers to locate where Girl Scout cookies are being sold nearby. Cookies can be shipped directly to customers' homes for an additional fee, sometimes as quickly as three to five business days. Alternatively, scouts can still deliver the cookies to your door. Digital Cookie is optional. If a Girl Scout or troop wants to use the traditional paper order forms, they can do so. The system has been designed so that the Girl Scouts themselves are still the ones making the cookie sales.

Clearly, Digital Cookie is helping the Girl Scouts dramatically reduce paperwork, errors, and order processing time as well as develop strong technology, business, and social skills for the twenty-first century workforce.

Sources: Joanna Stern, "Girl Scouts Use New App for Cookie Sales" and "How to Order Girl Scout Cookies Online," *Wall Street Journal*, January 6, 2015; Emanuella Grinberg, "What Girl Scouts Can Learn from Online Cookie Sales," CNN, January 18, 2015; Chris Hauk, "CES 2015: Girl Scouts Cookie Ordering Goes High Tech," *MacTrast*, January 6, 2015; "Girl Scouts Bring Digital Cookie to the 2015 International Consumer Electronics Show," *PR Newswire*, December 17, 2014; and "Girl Scout Cookies Go Digital," *PR Newswire*, December 1, 2014.

The experience of the Girl Scouts illustrates some of the steps required to design and build new information systems. It also illustrates some of the benefits of a new system solution. The Girl Scouts had an outdated manual, paper-based system for processing cookie orders that was excessively time-consuming and error ridden. The Girl Scouts tried several alternative solutions before opting for a new online and mobile ordering system. In this chapter, we will examine the Girl Scouts' search for a system solution as we describe each step of building a new information system by using the problem-solving process.

Here are some questions to think about: Compare the traditional Girl Scout cookie-ordering process with the Digital Cookie online ordering process using the web and the process using a mobile device. Diagram each of these processes.

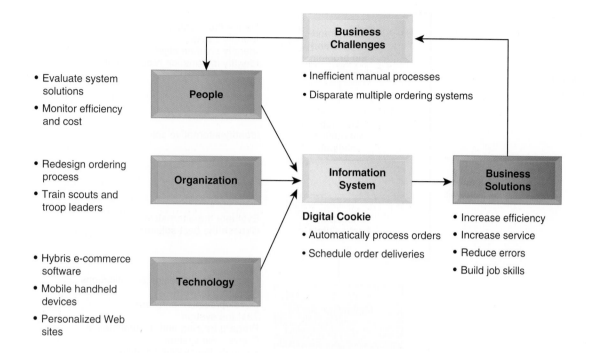

- Evaluate system solutions
- Monitor efficiency and cost

- Redesign ordering process
- Train scouts and troop leaders

- Hybris e-commerce software
- Mobile handheld devices
- Personalized Web sites

Business Challenges
- Inefficient manual processes
- Disparate multiple ordering systems

People

Organization

Technology

Information System

Digital Cookie
- Automatically process orders
- Schedule order deliveries

Business Solutions
- Increase efficiency
- Increase service
- Reduce errors
- Build job skills

12-1 What are the core problem-solving steps for developing new information systems?

We have already described the problem-solving process and how it helps us analyze and understand the role of information systems in business. This problem-solving process is especially valuable when we need to build new systems. A new information system is built as a solution to a problem or set of problems the organization perceives it is facing. The problem may be one in which managers and employees believe that the business is not performing as well as expected, or it may come from the realization that the organization should take advantage of new opportunities to perform more effectively.

Let's apply this problem-solving process to system building. Figure 12.1 illustrates the four steps we would need to take: (1) define and understand the problem, (2) develop alternative solutions, (3) choose the best solution, and (4) implement the solution.

Before a problem can be solved, it first must be properly defined. Members of the organization must agree that a problem actually exists and that it is serious. The problem must be investigated so that it can be better understood. Next comes a period of devising alternative solutions, then one of evaluating each alternative and selecting the best solution. The final stage is one of implementing the solution, in which a detailed design for the solution is specified, translated into a physical system, tested, introduced to the organization, and further refined as it is used over time.

In the information systems world, we have a special name for these activities. Figure 12.1 shows that the first three problem-solving steps, when we identify the problem, gather information, devise alternative solutions, and make a decision about the best solution, are called **systems analysis**.

DEFINING AND UNDERSTANDING THE PROBLEM

Defining the problem may take some work because various members of the company may have different ideas about the nature of the problem and its severity. What caused the problem? Why is it still around? Why wasn't it solved long ago? Systems analysts typically gather facts about existing systems and problems by examining

Figure 12.1
Developing an
Information System
Solution

*Developing an information
system solution is based
on the problem-solving
process.*

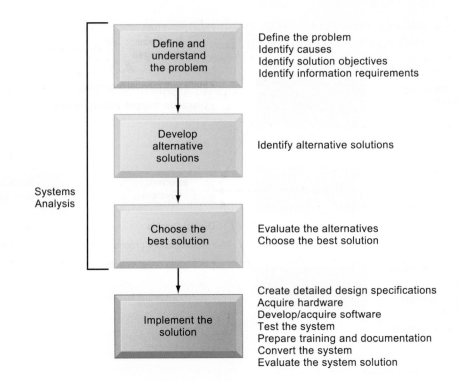

documents, work papers, procedures, and system operations and by interviewing key users of the system.

Information systems problems in the business world typically result from a combination of people, organization, and technology factors. When identifying a key issue or problem, ask what kind of problem it is: Is it a people problem, an organizational problem, a technology problem, or a combination of these? What people, organizational, and technological factors contributed to the problem?

Once the problem has been defined and analyzed, it is possible to make some decisions about what should and can be done. What are the objectives of a solution to the problem? Is the firm's objective to reduce costs, increase sales, or improve relationships with customers, suppliers, or employees? Do managers have sufficient information for decision making? What information is required to achieve these objectives?

At the most basic level, the **information requirements** of a new system identify who needs what information, where, when, and how. Requirements analysis carefully defines the objectives of the new or modified system and develops a detailed description of the functions that the new system must perform. A system designed around the wrong set of requirements will either have to be discarded because of poor performance or will need to undergo major modifications. Section 12-2 describes alternative approaches to eliciting requirements that help minimize this problem.

Let's return to our opening case about the Girl Scouts. The problem here is that the traditional ordering process for Girl Scout cookies has been heavily manual and time-consuming. Cookie ordering is extremely inefficient with high error rates and volunteers spending excessive time organizing orders and deliveries. Customers must pay in cash and wait weeks or months to receive their orders. This process is ripe for improvement with information technology. Tools for creating personalized e-commerce sales platforms on mobile devices and the web are readily available.

Organizationally, the Girl Scouts is a nationwide volunteer organization using cookie sales as the primary source of revenue. The Girl Scout cookie-ordering process requires many steps and coordination of multiple groups—individual Girl Scouts, volunteers, the council office, the cookie manufacturing factory, and delivery companies. The Girl Scout organization is also somewhat decentralized, with regional councils retaining the profits from cookie sales and deciding how to use them. Regional councils also have the power to decide whether to use automated tools.

The objectives of a solution for the Girl Scouts would be to reduce the amount of time, effort, and errors in the cookie-ordering process while providing an easier way to order cookies. Developing young women's leadership and business skills remains a high priority with the Girl Scouts, so the solution should ensure that scouts can still interact with customers and remain the primary sales channel for Girl Scout cookies.

Information requirements for the solution include the ability to take orders instantly and total and organize order transactions rapidly for transmittal to ABC Bakers or Little Brownie Bakers; the ability to track orders by type of cookie, troop, and individual Girl Scout; and the ability to schedule direct cookie deliveries to customers or bulk deliveries to individual Girl Scouts.

DEVELOPING ALTERNATIVE SOLUTIONS

What alternative solutions are possible for achieving these objectives and meeting these information requirements? The systems analysis lays out the most likely paths to follow given the nature of the problem. Some possible solutions do not require an information system solution but instead call for an adjustment in management, additional training, or refinement of existing organizational procedures. Some, however, do require modifications of the firm's existing information systems or an entirely new information system.

EVALUATING AND CHOOSING SOLUTIONS

The systems analysis includes a **feasibility study** to determine whether each proposed solution is feasible, or achievable, from financial, technical, and organizational standpoints. The feasibility study establishes whether each alternative solution is a good investment, whether the technology needed for the system is available and can be handled by the firm's information systems staff, and whether the organization is capable of accommodating the changes the system introduces.

A written systems proposal report describes the costs and benefits and advantages and disadvantages of each alternative solution. Which solution is best in a financial sense? Which works best for the organization? The systems analysis will detail the costs and benefits of each alternative and the changes that the organization will have to make to use the solution effectively. We provide a detailed discussion of how to determine the business value of systems and manage change in the following section. On the basis of this report, management will select what it believes is the best solution for the company.

The Girl Scouts had three alternative solutions. One was to maintain the status quo, a mixture of manual processes and multiple computerized order management systems that regional Girl Scout councils and licensed Girl Scout cookie baking companies used. The Girl Scouts of the USA did not favor this alternative because it was an uneven one. Some Girl Scout regional councils had their own automated ordering systems or access to the ABC and Little Brownies order management systems. Others were tied to the old manual processes. Girl Scout leadership worried that girls and their families versed in information technology would have an unfair advantage over those without such knowledge. The Girl Scouts wanted and needed a solution that was more uniform and capable of levelling the playing field.

A second alternative was to create a single standard digital system for ordering Girl Scout cookies online that would bypass individual Girl Scouts. Customers would be able to order Girl Scout cookies on their own online much as they would place a book order on Amazon.com. The Girl Scout leadership rejected this solution because it ran counter to the mission and goals of the organization, which were to develop members' leadership and interpersonal skills and to nurture the essential 5 Skills of goal setting, decision making, money management, people skills, and business ethics. Allowing customers to order cookies on their own would prevent the scouts from acquiring the valuable business and managerial skills that were among the main reasons for the organization's existence.

The third alternative was to develop a standard digital cookie ordering system for use nationwide that automates cookie ordering but still relies on individual Girl Scouts as the principal sales channel. Cookie customers would still have to place their orders with an individual Girl Scout or troop—they could not order online on their own. Nevertheless, they could take advantage of new online capabilities for locating cookie sellers, selecting cookies, paying by credit card, and arranging for cookie shipment directly to their homes. Use of the Digital Cookie system would be voluntary because some families and regional councils lacking access to computers or mobile devices would want to use the old manual order-taking system. This last alternative was the most feasible for the Girl Scouts.

IMPLEMENTING THE SOLUTION

The first step in implementing a system solution is to create detailed design specifications. **Systems design** shows how the chosen solution should be realized. The system design is the model or blueprint for an information system solution and consists of all the specifications that will deliver the functions identified during systems analysis. These specifications should address all the technical, organizational, and people components of the system solution.

Table 12.1 shows some of the design specifications for the Girl Scouts' new Digital Cookie system, which were based on information requirements for the solution that was selected. These design specifications apply to both the web and mobile app platforms.

Completing Implementation

In the final steps of implementing a system solution, the following activities would be performed:

- *Hardware selection and acquisition.* System builders select appropriate hardware for the application. They would either purchase the necessary computers and networking hardware or lease them from a technology provider.
- *Software development and programming.* Software is custom programmed in-house or purchased from an external source such as an outsourcing vendor, an application software package vendor, or a software service provider. Individual Girl Scouts can use their own computers and mobile devices. The core ordering system and databases are maintained on remote servers accessed through the Internet. These servers are in private data centers, which may be hosted for the Girl Scouts or maintained by their own IT department. Consultants from Accenture and Hybris helped the Girl Scouts develop the software for the system and Web site, most likely using Hybris e-commerce software tools.
- *Testing.* The system is thoroughly tested to ensure that it produces the right results. The **testing process** requires detailed testing of individual computer programs, called **unit testing** as well as **system testing**, which tests the performance of the information system as a whole. **Acceptance testing** provides the final certification that the system is ready to be used in a production setting. Information systems tests are evaluated by users and reviewed by management. When all parties are satisfied that the new system meets their standards, the system is formally accepted for installation.

The systems development team works with users to devise a systematic test plan. The **test plan** includes all the preparations for the series of tests we have just described. Figure 12.2 shows a sample from a test plan that might have been used for the Girl

Output	Online reports	**TABLE 12.1**
	Hard-copy reports (web version)	Design Specifications for
	Online queries	the Digital Cookie System
	Order transactions for baking companies	
Input	Order data entry screen	
	Girl Scout data entry screen	
	Customer data entry screen	
Database	Database with cookie order file, Girl Scout file, troop file, regional council file, customer file	
Processing	Calculate order totals by type of cookie and number of boxes	
	Transmit orders to baking companies	
	Track orders by customer	
	Track orders by troop and individual Girl Scout	
	Schedule deliveries or pickups	
	Update Girl Scout and customer data for address changes	
Manual procedures	Girl Scouts contact customers by phone, email, door-to-door, cookie sales booths	
	Girl Scouts deliver cookies to customers requesting this option	
Security and controls	Online passwords	
	Only authorized Girl Scouts and troops can access Digital Cookie	
	Parent must sign off on individual Girl Scout's site before it goes live	
	Girl Scout's site can only list the scout's first name	
Conversion	Input Girl Scout and troop data	
	Input customer data	
	Input bakery data	
	Test system	
Training and documentation	System guide for users	
	Online practice demonstration	
	Online training sessions and tutorials	

Scout cookie system. The condition being tested is online access of the system by an authorized user.

- *Training and documentation.* End users and information system specialists require training so that they will be able to use the new system. Detailed **documentation** showing how the system works from both a technical and end-user standpoint must be prepared.

The Digital Cookie System features hardcopy training manuals and online tutorials to help Girl Scouts and their leaders learn how to use the system.

- *Conversion* is the process of changing from the old to the new system. There are four main conversion strategies: the parallel strategy, the direct cutover strategy, the pilot study strategy, and the phased approach strategy.

In a **parallel strategy**, both the old system and its potential replacement are run together for a time until everyone is assured that the new one functions correctly. The

Figure 12.2
A Sample Test Plan for the Girl Scout Digital Cookie System

When developing a test plan, it is imperative to include the various conditions to be tested, the requirements for each condition tested, and the expected results. Test plans require input from both end users and information systems specialists. Illustrated here is a test case for accessing the mobile Android app by an authorized Girl Scout user.

Test Case Number: GS02-010

Prepared by: A. Patterson   **Date:** February 19, 2016

Objective: This subtest checks for an authorized user accessing the system.

Platform: Android

Procedure Description:
Select Sign In
Select Username
Enter Username
Select Password
Enter Password
Select Submit

Expected Result:
When user selects Sign In, the Sign In menu appears
When user selects User Name, the cursor moves to the User Name field
When user enters that person's system user name the user name appears on the screen
When user selects Password, the cursor moves to the Password field.
When user enters that person's password, the password appears on the screen as asterisks
When user selects Submit, the system verifies the entered data and allows the user to access the system
When user enters an incorrect (or unauthorized) username or password, the error message "Wrong User Name or Password" appears

Test Results:
All OK

old system remains available as a backup in case of problems. The **direct cutover strategy** replaces the old system entirely with the new system on an appointed day, carrying the risk that there is no system to fall back on if problems arise. The **pilot study** strategy introduces a new system to only a limited area of the organization, such as a single department or operating unit. Once this pilot version is working smoothly, it is installed throughout the rest of the organization. A **phased approach** introduces the system in stages (such as first introducing the modules for ordering Girl Scout cookies and then introducing the modules for transmitting orders and instructions to the cookie factory and shipper).

- *Production and maintenance.* After the new system is installed and conversion is complete, the system is said to be in **production**. During this stage, users and technical specialists review the solution to determine how well it has met its original objectives and to decide whether any revisions or modifications are in order. Changes in hardware, software, documentation, or procedures to a production system to correct errors, meet new requirements, or improve processing efficiency are termed **maintenance**.

The Girl Scouts continue to refine their Digital Cookie system. Future versions of Digital Cookie will see improvements in the user interface and user experience for both scouts and customers.

Managing the Change

Developing a new information systems solution is not merely a matter of installing hardware and software. The business must also deal with the organizational changes that the new solution will bring about—new information, new business processes, and perhaps new reporting relationships and decision-making power. A very well-designed solution may not work unless it is introduced to the organization very carefully. The process of planning change in an organization so that it is implemented in an orderly and effective manner is so critical to the success or failure of information system solutions that we devote Section 12-4 to a detailed discussion of this topic.

To manage the transition from the old system to the new Digital Cookie system, the Girl Scouts would have to inform troop leaders and volunteers about changes in cookie-ordering procedures, provide training, and provide resources for answering any questions that arose as scouts, parents, and administrators started using the system. They would need to work with ABC Bakers, Little Brownie Bakers, and their shippers on new procedures for transmitting and delivering orders.

12-2 What are the alternative methods for building information systems?

There are alternative methods for building systems, by using the basic problem-solving model we have just described. These alternative methods include the traditional systems life cycle, prototyping, end-user development, application software packages, and outsourcing.

TRADITIONAL SYSTEMS DEVELOPMENT LIFE CYCLE

The **systems development life cycle (SDLC)** is the oldest method for building information systems. The life cycle methodology is a phased approach to building a system, dividing systems development into a series of formal stages, as illustrated in Figure 12.3. Although systems builders can go back and forth among stages in the life cycle, the systems life cycle is predominantly a waterfall approach in which tasks in one stage are completed before work for the next stage begins.

This approach maintains a very formal division of labor between end users and information systems specialists. Technical specialists, such as system analysts and programmers, are responsible for much of the systems analysis, design, and implementation work; end users are limited to providing information requirements and reviewing the technical staff's work. The life cycle also emphasizes formal specifications and paperwork, so many documents are generated during the course of a systems project.

The systems life cycle is still used for building large, complex systems that require rigorous and formal requirements analysis, predefined specifications, and tight controls over the systems-building process. However, this approach is also

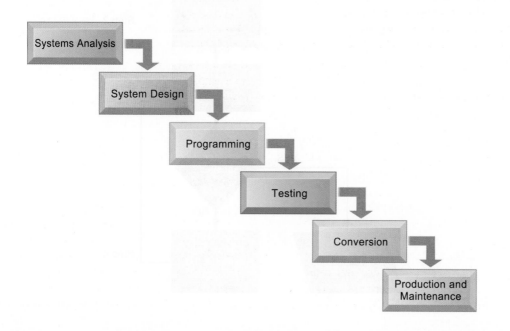

Figure 12.3
The Traditional Systems Development Life Cycle
The systems development life cycle partitions systems development into formal stages, with each stage requiring completion before the next stage can begin.

time-consuming and expensive to use. Tasks in one stage are supposed to be completed before work for the next stage begins. Activities can be repeated, but volumes of new documents must be generated and steps retraced if requirements and specifications need to be revised. This encourages freezing of specifications relatively early in the development process. The life cycle approach is also not suitable for many small desktop systems and apps, which tend to be less structured and more individualized.

PROTOTYPING

Prototyping consists of building an experimental system rapidly and inexpensively for end users to evaluate. The prototype is a working version of an information system or part of the system, but it is intended as only a preliminary model. Users interact with the prototype to get a better idea of their information requirements, refining the prototype multiple times. When the design is finalized, the prototype will be converted to a polished production system. Figure 12.4 shows a four-step model of the prototyping process.

Step 1: *Identify the user's basic requirements.* The system designer (usually an information systems specialist) works with the user only long enough to capture the user's basic information needs.

Step 2: *Develop an initial prototype.* The system designer creates a working prototype quickly, using tools for rapidly generating software.

Step 3: *Use the prototype.* The user is encouraged to work with the system to determine whether the prototype meets his or her needs and to suggest improvements for the prototype.

Step 4: *Revise and enhance the prototype.* The system builder notes all changes the user requests and refines the prototype accordingly. After the prototype has been revised, the cycle returns to Step 3. Steps 3 and 4 are repeated until the user is satisfied.

   Prototyping is especially useful in designing an information system's user interface. Because prototyping encourages intense end-user involvement throughout the systems development process, it is more likely to produce systems that fulfill user requirements.

Figure 12.4
The Prototyping Process
The process of developing a prototype consists of four steps. Because a prototype can be developed quickly and inexpensively, systems builders can go through several iterations, repeating steps 3 and 4, to refine and enhance the prototype before arriving at the final operational one.

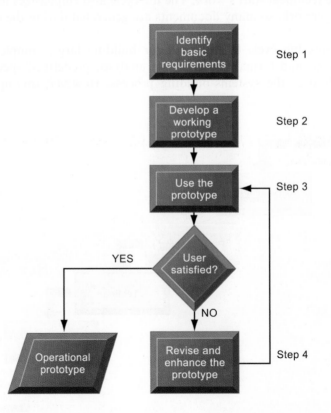

However, rapid prototyping may gloss over essential steps in systems development, such as thorough testing and documentation. If the completed prototype works reasonably well, management may not see the need to build a polished production system. Some hastily constructed systems do not easily accommodate large quantities of data or a large number of users in a production environment.

END-USER DEVELOPMENT

End-user development allows end users, with little or no formal assistance from technical specialists, to create simple information systems, reducing the time and steps required to produce a finished application. Using user-friendly query, reporting, website development, graphics, and PC software tools, end users can access data, create reports, and develop simple applications on their own with little or no help from professional systems analysts or programmers.

For example, Yellow Pages (YP), a digital media and marketing solutions company serving 260,000 small and medium-sized Canadian businesses, used Information Builders WebFOCUS to build a user-friendly analytics application that helps customers measure return on their advertising dollars and track the success of their campaigns. The system, called YP Analytics, features a user-friendly dashboard to track interactions and measure key performance indicators focused on return on investment (ROI) and revenue. YP Analytics users can track important metrics such as visitors, visits, page views, and interactions/clicks as well as calls, in-shop walk-ins, digital contacts, and other performance indicators, and they can customize the outputs they want (Information Builders, 2015).

On the whole, end-user-developed systems are completed more rapidly than those developed with conventional programming tools. Allowing users to specify their own business needs improves requirements gathering and often leads to a higher level of user involvement and satisfaction with the system. However, end-user development tools still cannot replace conventional tools for some business applications because they cannot easily handle the processing of large numbers of transactions or applications with extensive procedural logic and updating requirements.

End-user development also poses organizational risks because systems are created rapidly, without a formal development methodology, testing, and documentation. To help organizations maximize the benefits of end-user applications development, management should require cost justification of end-user information system projects and establish hardware, software, and quality standards for user-developed applications.

PURCHASING SOLUTIONS: APPLICATION SOFTWARE PACKAGES AND OUTSOURCING

As you learned in Chapter 5, the software for most systems today is not developed in-house but is purchased from external sources. Firms may choose to purchase a software package from a commercial vendor, rent the software from a service provider, or outsource the development work to another firm. Selection of the software or software service is often based on a **Request for Proposal (RFP)**, which is a detailed list of questions submitted to external vendors to see how well they meet the requirements for the proposed system.

Application Software Packages

Most new information systems today are built using an application software package or preprogrammed software components. Many applications are common to all business organizations—for example, payroll, accounts receivable, general ledger, or inventory control. For such universal functions with standard processes that do not change a great deal over time, a generalized system will fulfill the requirements of many organizations.

If a software package can fulfill most of an organization's requirements, the company does not have to write its own software. The company saves time and money by using the prewritten, predesigned, pretested software programs from the package.

Many packages include capabilities for customization to meet unique requirements not addressed by the packaged software. **Customization** features allow a software package to be modified to meet an organization's unique requirements without destroying the integrity of the packaged software. However, if extensive customization is required, additional programming and customization work may become so expensive and time-consuming that it negates many of the advantages of software packages. If the package cannot be customized, the organization will have to adapt to the package and change its procedures.

Outsourcing

If a firm does not want to use its internal resources to build or operate information systems, it can outsource the work to an external organization that specializes in providing these services. Software service providers, which we describe in Chapter 5, are one form of outsourcing. Subscribing companies use the software and computer hardware of the service provider as the technical platform for their systems. In another form of outsourcing, a company hires an external vendor to design and create the software for its system, but that company operates the system on its own computers. The Girl Scouts outsourced software development for the Digital Cookie System to Accenture and Hybris.

The outsourcing vendor might be domestic or in another country. Domestic outsourcing is driven primarily by the fact that outsourcing firms possess skills, resources, and assets that their clients do not have. Installing a new supply chain management system in a very large company might require hiring an additional 30 to 50 people with specific expertise in supply chain management software. Rather than hire permanent new employees and then release them after the new system is built, it makes more sense, and is often less expensive, to outsource this work for a 12-month period.

In the case of offshore outsourcing, the decision tends to be driven by cost. A skilled programmer in India or Russia earns about U.S. $10,000 to $20,000 per year, compared to $65,000 to $100,000 per year for a comparable programmer in the United States. The Internet and low-cost communications technology have drastically reduced the expense and difficulty of coordinating the work of global teams in faraway locations. In addition to cost savings, many offshore outsourcing firms offer world-class technology assets and skills. For example, leading companies such as Hilton, NBC, Fox News, and Yahoo have outsourced website design and development work to India-based Profit By Outsourcing. Profit By Outsourcing provides expertise in areas such as custom programmed content management, e-commerce solutions, mobile application development, and application development using Java, Adobe Flash, and Adobe Flex, that is not available internally in most companies. However, wage inflation outside the United States has eroded some of these advantages, and some jobs have moved back to the United States.

There is a very strong chance that at some point in your career, you'll be working with offshore outsourcers or global teams. Your firm is most likely to benefit from outsourcing if it takes the time to evaluate all the risks and make sure outsourcing is appropriate for its particular needs. Any company that outsources its applications must thoroughly understand the project, including its requirements, method of implementation, source of expected benefits, cost components, and metrics for measuring performance. And it must comply with the legal requirements of the H-1B program of the Department of Labor.

Many firms underestimate costs for identifying and evaluating vendors of information technology services, for transitioning to a new vendor, for improving internal software development methods to match those of outsourcing vendors, and for monitoring vendors to make sure they are fulfilling their contractual obligations. Outsourcing

TOTAL COST OF OFFSHORE OUTSOURCING				
Cost of outsourcing contract			$10,000,000	
Hidden Costs	Best Case	Additional Cost ($)	Worst Case	Additional Cost ($)
1. Vendor selection	0.2%	20,000	2%	200,000
2. Transition costs	2%	200,000	3%	300,000
3. Layoffs & retention	3%	300,000	5%	500,000
4. Lost productivity/cultural issues	3%	300,000	27%	2,700,000
5. Improving development processes	1%	100,000	10%	1,000,000
6. Managing the contract	6%	600,000	10%	1,000,000
Total additional costs		**1,520,000**		**5,700,000**
	Outstanding Contract ($)	Additional Cost ($)	Total Cost ($)	Additional Cost
Total cost of outsourcing (TCO) best case	10,000,000	1,520,000	11,520,000	15.2%
Total cost of outsourcing (TCO) worst case	10,000,000	5,700,000	15,700,000	57.0%

Figure 12.5
Total Cost of Offshore Outsourcing
If a firm spends $10 million on offshore outsourcing contracts, that company will actually spend 15.2 percent in extra costs even in the best-case scenario. In the worst-case scenario, when there is a dramatic drop in productivity along with exceptionally high transition and layoff costs, a firm can expect to pay up to 57 percent in extra costs on top of the $10 million outlay for an offshore contract.

offshore incurs additional costs for coping with cultural differences that drain productivity and dealing with human resources issues, such as terminating or relocating domestic employees. These hidden costs undercut some of the anticipated benefits from outsourcing. Firms should be especially cautious when using an outsourcer to develop or operate applications that give some type of competitive advantage.

Figure 12.5 shows best- and worst-case scenarios for the total cost of an offshore outsourcing project. It shows how much hidden costs affect the total project cost. The best case reflects the lowest estimates for additional costs, and the worst case reflects the highest estimates for these costs. As you can see, hidden costs increase the total cost of an offshore outsourcing project by an extra 15 to 57 percent. Even with these extra costs, many firms will benefit from offshore outsourcing if they manage the work well.

MOBILE APPLICATION DEVELOPMENT: DESIGNING FOR A MULTI-SCREEN WORLD

Today, employees and customers expect, and even demand, to be able to use a mobile device of their choice to obtain information or perform a transaction anywhere and at any time. To meet these needs, companies will need to develop mobile websites, mobile apps, and native apps as well as traditional information systems.

Once an organization decides to develop mobile apps, it has to make some important choices, including the technology it will use to implement these apps (whether to write a native app or mobile web app) and what to do about a mobile website. A **mobile website** is a version of a regular website that is scaled down in content and navigation for easy access and search on a small mobile screen. (Access Amazon's website from your computer and then from your smartphone to see the difference from a regular website.)

A **mobile web app** is an Internet-enabled app with specific functionality for mobile devices. Users access mobile web apps through their mobile device's web browser. The web app resides primarily on a server, is accessed through the Internet, and doesn't need to be installed on the device. The same application can be used by most devices that can surf the web, regardless of their brand.

A **native app** is a stand-alone application designed to run on a specific platform and device. The native app is installed directly on a mobile device. Native apps can connect to the Internet to download and upload data, and they can operate on these data even when not connected to the Internet. For example, an e-book reading app such as Kindle software can download a book from the Internet, disconnect from the Internet, and present the book for reading. Native mobile apps provide fast performance and a high degree of reliability. They can also take advantage of a mobile device's particular capabilities, such as its camera or touch features. However, native apps are expensive to develop because multiple versions of an app must be programmed for different mobile operating systems and hardware.

Developing applications for mobile platforms is quite different from development for PCs and their much larger screens. The reduced size of mobile devices makes using fingers and multi-touch gestures much easier than typing and using keyboards. Mobile apps need to be optimized for the specific tasks they are to perform. They should not try to carry out too many tasks, and they should be designed for usability. The user experience for mobile interaction is fundamentally different from using a desktop or laptop PC. Saving resources—bandwidth, screen space, memory, processing, data entry, and user gestures—is a top priority.

When a full website created for the desktop shrinks to the size of a smartphone screen, it is difficult for the user to navigate through the site. The user must continually zoom in and out and scroll to find relevant material. Therefore, companies need to design websites specifically for mobile interfaces and create multiple mobile sites to meet the needs of smartphones, tablets, and desktop browsers. This equates to at least three sites with separate content, maintenance, and costs. Currently, websites know what device you are using because your browser will send this information to the server when you log on. Based on this information, the server will deliver the appropriate screen.

One solution to the problem of having multiple websites is to use **responsive web design**. Responsive web design enables websites to change layouts automatically according to the visitor's screen resolution, whether on a desktop, laptop, tablet, or smartphone. Responsive design uses tools such as flexible grid-based layouts, flexible images, and media queries to optimize the design for different viewing contexts. This eliminates the need for separate design and development work for each new device. HTML5, which we introduced in Chapter 5, is also used for mobile application development because it can support cross-platform mobile applications

RAPID APPLICATION DEVELOPMENT FOR E-BUSINESS

Technologies and business conditions are changing so rapidly that agility and scalability have become critical elements of system solutions. Companies are adopting shorter, more informal development processes for many of their e-commerce and e-business applications, processes that provide fast solutions that do not disrupt their core transaction processing systems and organizational databases. In addition to using software packages, application service providers, and other outsourcing services, they are relying more heavily on fast-cycle techniques, such as joint application design, prototypes, and reusable standardized software components that can be assembled into a complete set of services for e-commerce and e-business.

The term **rapid application development (RAD)** refers to the process of creating workable systems in a very short period of time. RAD includes the use of visual programming and other tools for building graphical user interfaces, iterative prototyping of key system elements, the automation of program code generation, and close teamwork among end users and information systems specialists. Simple systems often can be assembled from prebuilt components (see Section 12-3). The process does not have to be sequential, and key parts of development can occur simultaneously.

Sometimes a technique called **joint application design (JAD)** will be used to accelerate the generation of information requirements and to develop the initial systems design. JAD brings end users and information systems specialists together in an interactive session to discuss the system's design. Properly prepared and facilitated, JAD sessions can significantly speed up the design phase and involve users at an intense level.

INTERACTIVE SESSION: TECHNOLOGY   Analytics Help the Cincinnati Zoo Know Its Customers

Founded in 1873, the Cincinnati Zoo & Botanical Garden is one of the world's top-rated zoological institutions, and the second oldest zoo in the United States. It is also one of the nation's most popular attractions, a Top 10 Zagat-rated Zoo, and a *Parents Magazine* Top Zoo for Children. The Zoo's 71-acre site is home to more than 500 animal and 3,000 plant species. About 1.3 million people visit it each year.

Although the Zoo is a nonprofit organization partially subsidized by Hamilton County, more than two-thirds of its $26 million annual budget is paid from fundraising efforts, and the remainder comes from admission fees, food, and gifts. To increase revenue and improve performance, the Zoo's senior management team embarked on a comprehensive review of its operations. The review found that management had limited knowledge and understanding of what was actually happening in the Zoo on a day-to-day basis, other than how many people visited every day and the Zoo's total revenue.

Who is coming to the Zoo? How often do they come? What do they do and what do they buy? Management had no idea. Each of the Zoo's four income streams—admissions, membership, retail, and food service—had different point-of-sale platforms, and the food service business, which brings in $4 million a year, still relied on manual cash registers. Management had to sift through paper receipts just to understand daily sales totals.

The Zoo had compiled a spreadsheet that collected visitors' zip codes, hoping to use the data for geographic and demographic analysis. If the data could be combined with insight into visitor activity at the Zoo—what attractions they visited, what they ate and drank, and what they bought at the gift shops—the information would be extremely valuable for marketing.

To achieve this, however, the Zoo needed to change its information systems to focus more on analytics and data management. The Zoo replaced its four legacy point-of-sale systems with a single platform—Galaxy POS from Gateway Ticketing Systems. It then enlisted IBM and BrightStar Partners (a consulting firm partnering with IBM) to build a centralized data warehouse and implement IBM Cognos Business Intelligence to provide real-time analytics and reporting.

Like all outdoor attractions, the Zoo's business is highly weather-dependent. On rainy days, attendance falls off sharply, often leaving the Zoo overstaffed and overstocked. If the weather is unusually hot, sales of certain items such as ice cream and bottled water are likely to rise, and the Zoo may run out of these items.

The Zoo now feeds weather forecast data from the U.S. National Oceanic and Atmospheric Administration (NOAA) Web site into its business intelligence system. By comparing current forecasts to historic attendance and sales data during similar weather conditions, the Zoo is able to make more accurate decisions about labor scheduling and inventory planning.

As visitors scan their membership cards at the Zoo's entrance, exit, attractions, restaurants, and stores, or use the Zoo's Loyalty Rewards card, the Zoo's system captures these data and analyzes them to determine usage and spending patterns down to the individual customer level. This information helps the Zoo segment visitors based on their spending and visitation behaviors and use this information to target marketing and promotions specifically for each customer segment.

One customer segment the Zoo identified consisted of people who spent nothing other than the price of admissions during their visit. If each of these people spent $20 on their next visit to the Zoo, the Zoo would take in an extra $260,000, which is almost 1 percent of its entire budget. The Zoo used its customer information to devise a direct mail marketing campaign in which this type of visitor would be offered a discount for some of the Zoo's restaurants and gift shops. Loyal customers are also rewarded with targeted marketing and recognition programs.

Instead of sending a special offer to its entire mailing list, the Zoo is able to tailor campaigns more precisely to smaller groups of people, increasing its chances of identifying the people who were most likely to respond to its mailings. More targeted marketing helped the Zoo cut $40,000 from its annual marketing budget.

Management had observed that food sales tend to trail off significantly after 3 p.m. each day, and started closing some of the Zoo's food outlets at that time. But more detailed data analysis showed that a big spike in soft-serve ice cream sales occurs during the last hour before the Zoo closes. As a result, the Zoo's soft-serve ice cream outlets are open for the entire day.

The Zoo's Beer Hut concession features six different brands, which are typically rotated based on sales volume and the seasons. With IBM analytics, management can now instantly identify which beer is selling best, on what day, and at what time to make sure inventory meets demand. Previously, it took 7 to 14 days to get this information, which required hiring part-time staff to sift through register tapes.

In 2015 the Zoo's data base was used by graduate students at the University of Cincinnati to model and predict attendance on a weekly, daily, and hourly basis. The Zoo's ability to make better decisions about operations has led to dramatic improvements in sales. After deploying its business intelligence solution, the Zoo achieved a 30.7 percent increase in food sales and a 5.9 percent increase in retail sales compared to the same period a year earlier.

Other zoos across the country have taken note of the Cincinnati Zoo's success, including the Point Defiance Zoo in Tacoma, Washington. Point Defiance's online ticket sales increased by 700 per-

cent in 2013, but management had no idea how or why the increase had occurred. After consulting with the Cincinnati Zoo, Point Defiance purchased IBM Cognos 10.2. With more customizability in ticket offers and promotions, and more granular data available on customer demographics, the zoo has been able to sustain its record attendance through 2015.

Sources: "2014–2015 Annual Report," Cincinnati Zoo & Botanical Garden, April 2015; Anila Chebrolu, "Zoo Visitor Prediction," University of Cincinnati, Lindner College of Business, MS-Business Analytics Program, July 2015; Charith Acharya, "Forecasting Daily Attendance at the Cincinnati Zoo and Botanical Gardens," University of Cincinnati, Lindner College of Business, MS-Business Analytics Program, July 2015; "Amy Lee, "Tacoma Zoo Taps IBM Cognos for Analytics Push," Cruxialcio.com, June 18, 2014; Justin Kern, "Analytics: Coming to a Zoo, Museum, or Park Near You," Information Management, August 28, 2012; IBM Corporation, "Cincinnati Zoo Improves Customer Experience and Enhances Performance," 2011; Nucleus Research, "IBM ROI Case Study: Cincinnati Zoo," July 2011; and www.cincinnatizoo.org, accessed May 26, 2012.

CASE STUDY QUESTIONS

1. What management, organization, and technology factors were behind the Cincinnati Zoo losing opportunities to increase revenue?

2. Why was replacing legacy point-of-sale systems and implementing a data warehouse essential to an information system solution?

3. How did the Cincinnati Zoo benefit from business intelligence? How did it enhance operational performance and decision making? What role was played by predictive analytics?

4. Visit the IBM Cognos Web site and describe the business intelligence tools that would be the most useful for the Cincinnati Zoo.

12-3 What are the principal methodologies for modeling and designing systems?

We have just described alternative methods for building systems. There are also alternative methodologies for modeling and designing systems. The two most prominent are structured methodologies and object-oriented development.

STRUCTURED METHODOLOGIES

Structured methodologies have been used to document, analyze, and design information systems since the 1970s. **Structured** refers to the fact that the techniques are step by step, with each step building on the previous one. Structured methodologies are top-down, progressing from the highest, most abstract level to the lowest level of detail—from the general to the specific.

Structured development methods are process-oriented, focusing primarily on modeling the processes, or actions, that capture, store, manipulate, and distribute data as the data flow through a system. These methods separate data from processes. A separate programming procedure must be written every time someone wants to take an action on a particular piece of data. The procedures act on data that the program passes to them.

The primary tool for representing a system's component processes and the flow of data between them is the **data flow diagram (DFD)**. The DFD offers a logical graphic model of information flow, partitioning a system into modules that show manageable levels of detail. It rigorously specifies the processes or transformations that occur within each module and the interfaces that exist between them.

Figure 12.6 shows a simple data flow diagram for a mail-in university course registration system. The rounded boxes represent processes, which portray the transformation of data. The square box represents an external entity, which is an originator or receiver of information located outside the boundaries of the system being modeled. The open rectangles represent data stores, which are either manual or automated inventories of data. The arrows represent data flows, which show the movement between processes, external entities, and data stores. They always contain packets of data with the name or content of each data flow listed beside the arrow.

This DFD shows that students submit registration forms with their names, identification numbers, and the numbers of the courses they wish to take. In Process 1.0, the system verifies that each course selected is still open by referencing the university's course file. The file distinguishes courses that are open from those that have been canceled or filled. Process 1.0 then determines which of the student's selections can be accepted or rejected. Process 2.0 enrolls the student in the courses for which he or she has been accepted. It updates the university's course file with the student's name and identification number and recalculates the class size. If maximum enrollment has been reached, the course number is flagged as closed. Process 2.0 also updates the university's student master file with information about new students or changes in address. Process 3.0 then sends each student applicant a confirmation-of-registration letter listing the courses for which he or she is registered and noting the course selections that could not be fulfilled.

Through leveled DFDs, a complex process can be broken down into successive levels of detail. An entire system can be divided into subsystems with a high-level data flow diagram. Each subsystem, in turn, can be divided into additional

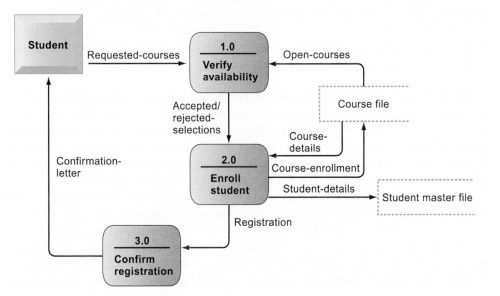

Figure 12.6
Data Flow Diagram for Mail-in University Registration System
The system has three processes: Verify availability (1.0), enroll student (2.0), and confirm registration (3.0). The name and content of each of the data flows appear adjacent to each arrow. There is one external entity in this system: the student. There are two data stores: the student master file and the course file.

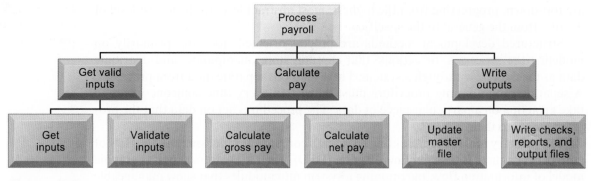

Figure 12.7
High-Level Structure Chart for a Payroll System
This structure chart shows the highest or most abstract level of design for a payroll system, providing an overview of the entire system.

subsystems with lower-level DFDs, and the lower-level subsystems can be broken down again until the lowest level of detail has been reached. **Process specifications** describe the transformation occurring within the lowest level of the DFDs, showing the logic for each process.

In structured methodology, software design is modeled using hierarchical structure charts. The **structure chart** is a top-down chart, showing each level of design, its relationship to other levels, and its place in the overall design structure. The design first considers the main function of a program or system, then breaks this function into subfunctions, and decomposes each subfunction until the lowest level of detail has been reached. Figure 12.7 shows a high-level structure chart for a payroll system. If a design has too many levels to fit onto one structure chart, it can be broken down further on more detailed structure charts. A structure chart may document one program, one system (a set of programs), or part of one program.

OBJECT-ORIENTED DEVELOPMENT

Structured methods treat data and processes as logically separate entities, whereas in the real world such separation seems unnatural. **Object-oriented development** addresses these issues. Object-oriented development uses the object, which we introduced in Chapter 5, as the basic unit of systems analysis and design. An object combines data and the specific processes that operate on those data. Data encapsulated in an object can be accessed and modified only by the operations, or methods, associated with that object. Instead of passing data to procedures, programs send a message for an object to perform an operation that is already embedded in it. The system is modeled as a collection of objects and the relationships among them. Because processing logic resides within objects rather than in separate software programs, objects must collaborate with each other to make the system work.

Object-oriented modeling is based on the concepts of *class* and *inheritance*. Objects belonging to a certain class, or general categories of similar objects, have the features of that class. Classes of objects in turn inherit all the structure and behaviors of a more general class and then add variables and behaviors unique to each object. New classes of objects are created by choosing an existing class and specifying how the new class differs from the existing class, instead of starting from scratch each time.

We can see how class and inheritance work in Figure 12.8, which illustrates the relationships among classes concerning employees and how they are paid. Employee is the common ancestor, or superclass, for the other three classes. Salaried, Hourly, and Temporary are subclasses of Employee. The class name is in the top compartment, the attributes for each class are in the middle portion of each box, and the list of operations is in the bottom portion of each box. The features that all employees

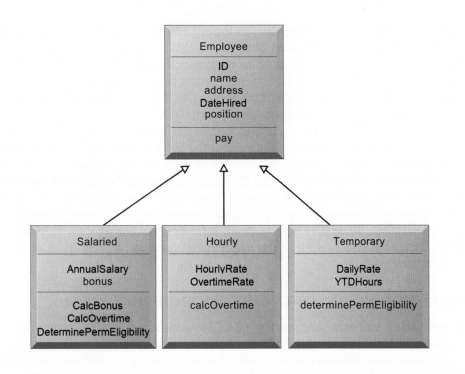

Figure 12.8
Class and Inheritance
This figure illustrates how classes inherit the common features of their superclass.

share (ID, name, address, date hired, position, and pay) are stored in the Employee superclass, whereas each subclass stores features that are specific to that particular type of employee. Specific to Hourly employees, for example, are their hourly rates and overtime rates. A solid line from the subclass to the superclass is a generalization path showing that the subclasses Salaried, Hourly, and Temporary have common features that can be generalized into the superclass Employee.

Object-oriented development is more iterative and incremental than traditional structured development. During systems analysis, systems builders document the functional requirements of the system, specifying its most important properties and what the proposed system must do. Interactions between the system and its users are analyzed to identify objects, which include both data and processes. The object-oriented design phase describes how the objects will behave and how they will interact with one another. Similar objects are grouped to form a class, and classes are grouped into hierarchies in which a subclass inherits the attributes and methods from its superclass.

The information system is implemented by translating the design into program code, reusing classes that are already available in a library of reusable software objects and adding new ones created during the object-oriented design phase. Implementation may also involve the creation of an object-oriented database. The resulting system must be thoroughly tested and evaluated.

Because objects are reusable, object-oriented development could reduce the time and cost of writing software if organizations reuse software objects that have already been created as building blocks for other applications. New systems can be created by using some existing objects, changing others, and adding a few new objects.

Component-Based Development, Web Services, and Cloud-Based Development

To expedite software creation further, groups of objects have been assembled into software components for common functions, such as a graphical user interface or online ordering capability, and these components can be combined to create large-scale business applications. This approach to software development is called **component-based development**. Businesses are using component-based development to create their e-commerce applications by combining commercially available components for shopping carts, user authentication, search engines, and catalogs with pieces of software for their own unique business requirements.

Chapter 5 introduced web services as loosely coupled, reusable software components based on Extensible Markup Language (XML) and other open protocols and standards that enable one application to communicate with another with no custom programming required. In addition to supporting internal and external integration of systems, web services provide nonproprietary tools for building new information system applications or enhancing existing systems.

Platform as a service (PaaS), introduced in the Chapter 5 discussion of cloud computing, also holds considerable potential for helping system developers quickly write and test customer- or employee-facing web applications. These online development environments come from a range of vendors, including Oracle, IBM, Salesforce. com (Force.com), and Microsoft (Azure). These platforms automate tasks such as setting up a newly composed application as a web service or linking to other applications and services. Some also offer a cloud infrastructure service, or links to cloud vendors such as Amazon, so that developers can launch what they build in a cloud infrastructure.

COMPUTER-AIDED SOFTWARE ENGINEERING (CASE)

Computer-aided software engineering (CASE)—sometimes called computer-aided systems engineering—provides software tools to automate the methodologies we have just described to reduce the amount of repetitive work in systems development. CASE tools provide automated graphics facilities for producing charts and diagrams, screen and report generators, data dictionaries, extensive reporting facilities, analysis and checking tools, code generators, and documentation generators. CASE tools also contain features for validating design diagrams and specifications.

CASE tools facilitate clear documentation and coordination of team development efforts. Team members can share their work by accessing each other's files to review or modify what has been done. Modest productivity benefits are achieved if the tools are used properly. Many CASE tools are PC based with powerful graphical capabilities.

12-4 How should information systems projects be selected and managed?

Your company might have developed what appears to be an excellent system solution. Yet when the system is in use, it does not work properly or it doesn't deliver the benefits that were promised. If this occurs, your firm is not alone. There is a very high failure rate among information systems projects because they have not been properly managed. A joint study by McKinsey and Oxford University found that large software projects on average run 66 percent over budget and 33 percent over schedule. As many as 17 percent of projects run over so badly that they can threaten the existence of the company (Chandrasekaran et al., 2014). Firms may have incorrectly assessed the business value of the new system or were unable to manage the organizational change the new technology required. That's why it's essential to know how to manage information systems projects and the reasons they succeed or fail.

The Interactive Session on Organizations provides an example of a problem-ridden information systems project. As you read this case, try to determine why this project was not successful and the role of project management in the outcome.

PROJECT MANAGEMENT OBJECTIVES

A **project** is a planned series of related activities for achieving a specific business objective. Information systems projects include the development of new information systems, enhancement of existing systems, or projects for replacing or upgrading the firm's information technology (IT) infrastructure.

INTERACTIVE SESSION: ORGANIZATIONS Britain's National Health Service Jettisons Choose and Book System

When senior cardiologist Duncan Dymond complained in 2010 that patients were arriving at his hospital at incorrect times and, far worse, in need of a different specialist, it was neither the beginning nor the end of problems with the Choose and Book system. Installed in 2004 as part of a £200 million IT modernization of Great Britain's National Health Service (NHS), the patient booking system was supposed to enable patients to select a hospital for an outpatient appointment from a range of options, primarily with the help and direction of their general practitioner (GP). A letter with a referral number and a secure code was then generated so that the patient could either go online or call a central booking service to confirm the appointment. Initial contact could also occur directly through the national appointments line or at the HealthSpace website. The goals were threefold: to speed up the referral process, eliminate costly paperwork, and encourage patient participation to stem losses of up to £225 million annually from 1.6 million patient no-shows.

Implementation was sluggish and plagued with glitches. One early problem was that many hospital Patient Administration Systems (PAS) and GP clinical computer systems were not compatible. Choose and Book served as the liaison between the two systems; thus, both had to be compliant. The objective to book 90 percent of all referrals by December 2006 was never met. Four years later, even though Choose and Book had been installed in 94 percent of all GP surgeries, it was used to book just 54 percent of appointments. Even a three-year £100 million incentive program to encourage physician adoption failed to sway doctors who had witnessed patients unnecessarily travelling to distant hospitals and referral letters rebuffed when patients sought confirmation.

Designers also focused on building provider choice into the service. This turned out to be a solution in search of a problem. According to the NHS Alliance, a coalition of health care providers, managers, and patients dedicated to improving care and providing a voice to patients, the ability to choose physicians and facilities from a wide range of options was never a chief concern. Instead, patients were looking for swift referrals to their local hospital. In rural areas, choice was considerably limited anyway, and older patients, in particular, simply found the array of choices confusing, difficult to navigate, and time-consuming to select.

Although many doctors were fans, system misfires created a significant population of disgruntled caregivers who refused to use Choose and Book. Glitches included appointment letters gone astray, last-minute cancellations, costs incurred for phone calls to the booking line in some locations, and treatment delays due to lack of visit categorization—either urgent or routine—not incorporated because cases requiring immediate treatment bypassed the queuing system.

By 2014, Choose and Book's cost had ballooned to £356 million. It did provide reliable referrals for more than half of first-time outpatients and was used—at least to some degree—by more than 90 percent of providers. However, when a study by the Public Accounts Committee (PAC) reported that use by both doctors and patients had dropped and that waiting times for elective care had shown no improvement, Choose and Book's days were numbered. The system had never been able to function optimally because not all available outpatient appointments were listed. Members of Parliament (MPs) were fatigued by nearly a decade of patchwork fixes and frustrated that projected annual savings of up to £51 million had never materialized.

The discrete replacement of Choose and Book by a new system of unstipulated—and perhaps greater—cost underscores both the mission and the challenges of NHS. Launched in 1948, the comprehensive health system is funded by tax dollars and administered by the Department of Health (DH). All British citizens are afforded care from their first newborn exam to their end-of-life care, with many services free of charge. NHS England covers 53 million citizens. Another 10.2 million people are covered by NHS divisions in Northern Ireland, Wales, and Scotland.

The most pressing and urgent challenge NHS faces is the often lengthy waiting time to receive care, which can sometimes yield dire consequences. Health care for all, regardless of wealth, is a core value of British society. A 2013 Commonwealth Fund study of national health care systems ranked NHS first for quality of care, safety, coordination of care, patient-centered care, and cost. On timeliness of care, the UK ranked third.

With timeliness of care the overriding goal, NHS planned to launch in England a new e-Referral Service in spring 2015. Director of Strategic Systems and Technology, Beverley Bryant, expects significantly reduced paperwork and fewer data errors, along with an accelerated referral process because patients monitor and manage their own hospital appointments. Several ideas to encourage adoption are being explored, including making physician participation mandatory and developing an incentive program that incorporates penalties as well as rewards. The goal is to improve upon or eliminate the flaws of Choose and Book—for example, moving away from the hybrid electronic/paper environment that has proved burdensome for hospitals. The switch to all digital will occur by 2019.

The new system uses an open platform and a set of APIs, both of which provide more flexibility to integrate with other systems than the restrictive proprietary system Choose and Book employed. What's more, these changes should reduce operating costs. After a decade of technological advances,

updates would have been necessary even if Choose and Book had been a resounding success. The new e-Referrals system must trump Choose and Book's record of booking 40,000 referrals every day, ensure that all appointment slots are available, and shuttle citizens to their appointments at a quicker pace, all while ensuring that existing health care inequalities are not exacerbated.

Sources: Warwick Ashford, "NHS to Scrap £356m o\Outpatient Booking System," ComputerWeekly.com, May 12, 2014, www.chooseandbook.nhs .uk, accessed February 22, 2015; Toby Helm and Dennis Campbell, "NHS Hit by New Tech Failure as It Scraps Patient Booking System," *The Observer*, May 10, 2014; "About the National Health Service (NHS)," nhs.uk/NHSEngland, accessed August 10, 2014; Caroline Baldwin, "New NHS e-Referral Service to Use Agile and Open Technologies," ComputerWeekly.com, May 13, 2014; "NHS e-Referral Service Vision," systems.hscic.gov.uk, accessed August 10, 2014; "NHS to Stop Choose and Book Outpatient Appointments System and Replace It with New IT System," *UK News*, May 11, 2014; and Mark Gould, "Claims That NHS Choose and Book System Puts Choice Before Quality," *The Guardian*, March 23, 2010.

CASE STUDY QUESTIONS

1. Clarify and describe the problems of the NHS Choose and Book System. What people, organization, and technology factors were responsible for those problems?

2. To what extent was Choose and Book a failure? Explain your answer.

3. What was the economic and social impact of Choose and Book?

4. Describe the steps that should have been taken to make Choose and Book more successful.

Project management refers to the application of knowledge, skills, tools, and techniques to achieve specific targets within specified budget and time constraints. Project management activities include planning the work, assessing risk, estimating resources required to accomplish the work, organizing the work, acquiring human and material resources, assigning tasks, directing activities, controlling project execution, reporting progress, and analyzing the results. As in other areas of business, project management for information systems must deal with five major variables: scope, time, cost, quality, and risk.

Scope defines what work is or is not included in a project. For example, the scope of a project for a new order processing system might include new modules for inputting orders and transmitting them to production and accounting but not any changes to related accounts receivable, manufacturing, distribution, or inventory control systems. Project management defines all the work required to complete a project successfully and should ensure that the scope of a project does not expand beyond what was originally intended.

Time is the amount of time required to complete the project. Project management typically establishes the amount of time required to complete major components of a project. Each of these components is further broken down into activities and tasks. Project management tries to determine the time required to complete each task and establish a schedule for completing the work.

Cost is based on the time to complete a project multiplied by the daily cost of human resources required to complete the project. Information systems project costs also include the cost of hardware, software, and work space. Project management develops a budget for the project and monitors ongoing project expenses.

Quality is an indicator of how well the result of a project satisfies the objectives management specified. The quality of information systems projects usually boils down to improved organizational performance and decision making. Quality also considers the accuracy and timeliness of information the new system produces and ease of use.

Risk refers to potential problems that would threaten the success of a project. These potential problems might prevent a project from achieving its objectives by increasing time and cost, lowering the quality of project outputs, or preventing the project from being completed altogether. We discuss the most important risk factors for information systems projects later in this section.

SELECTING PROJECTS: MAKING THE BUSINESS CASE FOR A NEW SYSTEM

Companies typically are presented with many projects for solving problems and improving performance. There are far more ideas for systems projects than there are resources. You will need to select the projects that promise the greatest benefit to the business.

Determining Project Costs and Benefits

As we pointed out earlier, the systems analysis includes an assessment of the economic feasibility of each alternative solution—whether each solution represents a good investment for the company. To identify the information systems projects that will deliver the most business value, you'll need to identify their costs and benefits and how they relate to the firm's information systems plan.

Table 12.2 lists some of the more common costs and benefits of systems. **Tangible benefits** can be quantified and assigned a monetary value. **Intangible benefits**, such as

TABLE 12.2

Costs and Benefits of Information Systems

Implementation Costs	Intangible Benefits
Hardware	Improved asset usage
Telecommunications	Improved resource control
Software	Improved organizational planning
Personnel costs	Increased organizational flexibility
Operational Costs	More timely information
Computer processing time	More information
Maintenance	Increased organizational learning
Operating staff	Legal requirements attained
User time	Enhanced employee goodwill
Ongoing training costs	Increased job satisfaction
Facility costs	Improved decision making
	Improved operations
Tangible Benefits	Higher client satisfaction
Increased productivity	Better corporate image
Lower operational costs	
Reduced workforce	
Lower computer expenses	
Lower outside vendor costs	
Lower clerical and professional costs	
Reduced rate of growth in expenses	
Reduced facility costs	
Increased sales	

more efficient customer service or enhanced decision making, cannot be immediately quantified. Yet systems that produce mainly intangible benefits may still be good investments if they produce quantifiable gains in the long run.

To determine the benefits of a particular solution, you'll need to calculate all its costs and all its benefits. Obviously, a solution whose costs exceed benefits should be rejected, but even if the benefits outweigh the costs, some additional financial analysis is required to determine whether the investment represents a good return on the firm's invested capital. Capital budgeting methods, such as net present value, internal rate of return (IRR), or accounting rate of return on investment (ROI), would typically be employed to evaluate the proposed information system solution as an investment. You can find out more about how these capital budgeting methods are used to justify information system investments in our Learning Tracks.

Some of the tangible benefits the Girl Scouts obtained were increased productivity and lower operational costs resulting from streamlining the ordering process and reducing errors. Intangible benefits included customer satisfaction, more timely information, and improved operations.

The Information Systems Plan

An **information systems plan** shows how specific information systems fit into a company's overall business plan and business strategy. Table 12.3 lists the major components of such a plan. The plan contains a statement of corporate goals and specifies how information technology will help the business attain these goals. The report shows how general goals will be achieved by specific systems projects. It identifies specific target dates and milestones that can be used later to evaluate the plan's progress in terms of how many objectives were actually attained in the time frame specified in the plan. The plan indicates the key management decisions concerning hardware acquisition; telecommunications; centralization/decentralization of authority, data, and hardware; and required organizational change.

The plan should describe organizational changes, including management and employee training requirements; changes in business processes; and changes in authority, structure, or management practice. When you are making the business case for a new information system project, you show how the proposed system fits into that plan.

Portfolio Analysis and Scoring Models

Once you have determined the overall direction of systems development, **portfolio analysis** will help you evaluate alternative system projects. Portfolio analysis inventories all of the firm's information systems projects and assets, including infrastructure, outsourcing contracts, and licenses. This portfolio of information systems investments can be described as having a certain profile of risk and benefit to the firm (see Figure 12.9), similar to a financial portfolio. Each information systems project carries its own set of risks and benefits. Firms try to improve the return on their information system portfolios by balancing the risk and return from their systems investments.

Obviously, you begin first by focusing on systems of high benefit and low risk. These promise early returns and low risks. Second, high-benefit, high-risk systems should be examined; low-benefit, high-risk systems should be totally avoided; and low-benefit, low-risk systems should be reexamined for the possibility of rebuilding and replacing them with more desirable systems having higher benefits. By using portfolio analysis, management can determine the optimal mix of investment risk and reward for their firms, balancing riskier, high-reward projects with safer, lower-reward ones.

Another method for evaluating alternative system solutions is a **scoring model**. Scoring models give alternative systems a single score based on the extent to which they meet selected objectives. Table 12.4 shows part of a simple scoring model that the Girl Scouts could have used in evaluating new system solutions (Alternatives 2 and 3

TABLE 12.3

Information Systems Plan

1. Purpose of the Plan

Overview of plan contents

Current business organization and future organization

Key business processes

Management strategy

2. Strategic Business Plan Rationale

Current situation

Current business organization

Changing environments

Major goals of the business plan

Firm's strategic plan

3. Current Systems

Major systems supporting business functions and processes

Current infrastructure capabilities

    Hardware

    Software

    Database

    Telecommunications and the Internet

Difficulties meeting business requirements

Anticipated future demands

4. New Developments

New system projects

    Project descriptions

    Business rationale

    Applications' role in strategy

New infrastructure capabilities required

    Hardware

    Software

    Database

    Telecommunications and the Internet

5. Management Strategy

    Acquisition plans

    Milestones and timing

    Organizational realignment

    Internal reorganization

    Management controls

    Major training initiatives

    Personnel strategy

6. Implementation of the Plan

    Anticipated difficulties in implementation

    Progress reports

7. Budget Requirements

    Requirements

    Potential savings

    Financing

    Acquisition cycle

Figure 12.9
A System Portfolio
Companies should examine their portfolio of projects in terms of potential benefits and likely risks. Certain kinds of projects should be avoided altogether and others developed rapidly. There is no ideal mix. Companies in different industries have different in-formation systems needs.

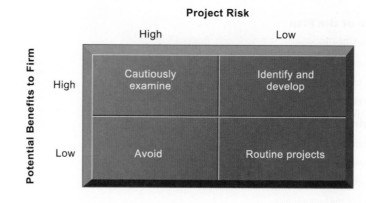

described earlier). The first column lists the criteria that decision makers use to evaluate the systems. Table 12.4 shows that the Girl Scouts attach the most importance to capabilities for sales order processing, ease of use, ability to support individual Girl Scouts taking orders, and web access from multiple locations. The second column in Table 12.4 lists the weights that decision makers attached to the decision criteria. Columns 3 and 5 show the percentage of requirements for each function that each alternative system solution meets. Each alternative's score is calculated by multiplying the percentage of requirements met for each function by the weight attached to that function. Solution Alternative 3 has the highest total score.

MANAGING PROJECT RISK AND SYSTEM-RELATED CHANGE

Some systems development projects are more likely to run into problems or to suffer delays because they carry a much higher level of risk than others. The level of project risk is influenced by project size, project structure, and the level of technical expertise of the information systems staff and project team. The larger the project—as indicated by the dollars spent, project team size, and how many parts of the organization will be affected by the new system—the greater the risk. Very large-scale systems projects have a failure rate that is 50 to 75 percent higher than that for other projects because such projects are complex and difficult to control. Risks are also higher for systems whose information requirements are not clear and straightforward or the project team must master new technology.

Implementation and Change Management

Dealing with these project risks requires an understanding of the implementation process and change management. A broader definition of **implementation** refers to all the organizational activities working toward the adoption and management of an innovation, such as a new information system. Successful implementation requires a high level of user involvement in a project and management support.

If users are heavily involved in the development of a system, they have more opportunities to mold the system according to their priorities and business requirements and to control the outcome. They also are more likely to react positively to the completed system because they have been active participants in the change process.

The relationship between end users and information systems specialists has traditionally been a problem area for information systems implementation efforts because of differing backgrounds, interests, and priorities. These differences create a **user–designer communications gap**. Information systems specialists often have a highly technical orientation to problem solving, focusing on technical solutions in which hardware and software efficiency is optimized at the expense of ease of use or organizational effectiveness. End users prefer systems that are oriented toward solving business problems or facilitating organizational tasks. Often the orientations of both groups are so at odds that they appear to speak in different tongues. These differences are illustrated in Table 12.5.

Example of a Scoring Model for the Girl Scouts Cookie System

Criteria	Weight	Alternative 2 (%)	Alternative 2 Score	Alternative 3 (%)	Alternative 3 Score
1.1 Order processing					
1.2 Online order entry	5	67	335	83	415
1.3 Order tracking by customer	5	81	405	75	375
1.4 Order tracking by individual Girl Scout	5	30	150	80	400
Total order processing			890		1190
2.1 Ease of use					
2.2 Web access from multiple platforms	5	55	275	92	460
2.3 Short training time	4	79	316	85	340
2.4 User-friendly online screens and data entry	4	65	260	87	348
Total ease of use			851		1,148
3.1 Costs					
3.2 Software costs	3	51	153	65	195
3.3 Hardware (server) costs	4	57	228	90	360
3.4 Maintenance and support costs	4	42	168	89	356
Total costs			549		911
Grand Total			2290		3249

If an information systems project has the backing and commitment of management at various levels, it is more likely to receive higher priority from both users and the technical information systems staff. Management backing also ensures that a systems project receives sufficient funding and resources to be successful. Furthermore, to be enforced effectively, all the changes in work habits and procedures and any organizational realignments associated with a new system depend on management backing. According to the Project Management Institute, having executive sponsors who are actively engaged is the leading factor in project success (Project Management Institute, 2014).

Controlling Risk Factors

There are strategies you can follow to deal with project risk and increase the chances of a successful system solution. If the new system involves challenging and complex technology, you can recruit project leaders with strong technical and administrative experience. Outsourcing or using external consultants are options if your firm does not have staff with the required technical skills or expertise.

User Concerns	Designer Concerns
Will the system deliver the information I need for my work?	What demands will this system put on our servers?
Can we access the data on our iPhones, tablets, and PCs?	What kind of programming demands will this place on our group?
What new procedures do we need to enter data into the system?	Where will the data be stored? What's the most efficient way to store them?
How will the operation of the system change employees' daily routines?	What technologies should we use to secure the data?

Large projects benefit from appropriate use of **formal planning and control tools** for documenting and monitoring project plans. The two most commonly used methods for documenting project plans are Gantt charts and PERT charts. A **Gantt chart** lists project activities and their corresponding start and completion dates. The Gantt chart visually represents the timing and duration of different tasks in a development project as well as their human resource requirements (see Figure 12.10). It shows each task as a horizontal bar whose length is proportional to the time required to complete it.

Although Gantt charts show when project activities begin and end, they don't depict task dependencies, how one task is affected if another is behind schedule or how tasks should be ordered. That is when **PERT charts** are useful. PERT stands for Program Evaluation and Review Technique, a methodology the U.S. Navy developed during the 1950s to manage the Polaris submarine missile program. A PERT chart graphically depicts project tasks and their interrelationships. The PERT chart lists the specific activities that make up a project and the activities that must be completed before a specific activity can start, as illustrated in Figure 12.11.

The PERT chart portrays a project as a network diagram consisting of numbered nodes (either circles or rectangles) representing project tasks. Each node is numbered and shows the task, its duration, the starting date, and the completion date. The direction of the arrows on the lines indicates the sequence of tasks and shows which activities must be completed before the commencement of another activity. In Figure 12.11, the tasks in nodes 2, 3, and 4 do not depend on each other and can be undertaken simultaneously, but each depends on completion of the first task.

Project Management Software

Commercial software tools are available to automate the creation of Gantt and PERT charts and facilitate the project management process. Project management software typically features capabilities for defining and ordering tasks, assigning resources to tasks, establishing starting and ending dates for tasks, tracking progress, and facilitating modifications to tasks and resources. The most widely used project management tool today is Microsoft Project. We should also point out that these traditional project management tools are being supplemented with some of the social business tools described in Chapter 2. For example, projects might use collaborative, shared workspaces, where project tasks are updated in real time or let activity streams inform team members of events taking place on a project as they occur.

Overcoming User Resistance

You can overcome user resistance by promoting user participation (to elicit commitment as well as improve design), by making user education and training easily available, and by providing better incentives for users who cooperate. End users can become active members of the project team, take on leadership roles, and take charge of system installation and training.

HRIS COMBINED PLAN–HR

Task schedule (Da = person-days, Who = responsible initials). Timeline columns span 2015 (Oct–Dec), 2016 (Jan–Dec), and 2017 (Jan–Mar).

DATA ADMINISTRATION SECURITY

Task	Da	Who
QMF security review/setup	20	EF TP
Security orientation	2	EF JA
QMF security maintenance	35	TP GL
Data entry sec. profiles	4	EF TP
Data entry sec. views est.	12	EF TP
Data entry security profiles	65	EF TP

DATA DICTIONARY

Task	Da	Who
Orientation sessions	1	EF
Data dictionary design	32	EFWV
DD prod. coordn-query	20	GL
DD prod. coordn-live	40	EF GL
Data dictionary cleanup	35	EF GL
Data dictionary maint.	35	EF GL

PROCEDURES REVISION
DESIGN PREP

Task	Da	Who
Work flows (old)	10	PK JL
Payroll data flows	31	JL PK
HRIS P/R model	11	PK JL
P/R interface orient. mtg.	6	PK JL
P/R interface coordn. 1	15	PK
P/R interface coordn. 2	8	PK
Benefits interfaces (old)	5	JL
Benefits interfaces (new flow)	8	JL
Benefits communication strategy	3	PK JL
New work flow model	15	PK JL
Posn. data entry flowsc	14	WV JL

RESOURCE SUMMARY

Columns: 2015 (Oct Nov Dec), 2016 (Jan Feb Mar Apr May Jun Jul Aug Sep Oct Nov Dec), 2017 (Jan Feb Mar)

Name	Rate	Who	Oct	Nov	Dec	Jan	Feb	Mar	Apr	May	Jun	Jul	Aug	Sep	Oct	Nov	Dec	Jan	Feb	Mar
Edith Farrell	5.0	EF	2	21	24	24	23	22	22	27	34	34	29	26	28	19	14			
Woody Vinton	5.0	WV	5	17	20	19	12	10	14	10	2							4	3	
Charles Pierce	5.0	CP		5	11	20	13	9	10	7	6	8	4	4	4	4	4			
Ted Leurs	5.0	TL		12	17	17	19	17	14	12	15	16	2	1	1	1	1			
Toni Cox	5.0	TC	1	11	10	11	11	12	19	19	21	21	21	17	17	12	9			
Patricia Knopp	5.0	PC	7	23	30	34	27	25	15	24	25	16	11	13	17	10	3	3	2	
Jane Lawton	5.0	JL	1	9	16	21	19	21	21	20	17	15	14	12	14	8	5			
David Holloway	5.0	DH	4	4	5	5	5	2	7	5	4	16	2							
Diane O'Neill	5.0	DO	6	14	17	16	13	11	9	4										
Joan Albert	5.0	JA	5	6			7	6	2	1				5	5	1				
Marie Marcus	5.0	MM	15	7	2	1	1													
Don Stevens	5.0	DS	4	4	5	4	5	1												
Casual	5.0	CASL		3	4	3			4	7	9	5	3	2						
Kathy Mendez	5.0	KM		1	5	16	20	19	22	19	20	18	20	11	2					
Anna Borden	5.0	AB					9	10	16	15	11	12	19	10	7	1				
Gail Loring	5.0	GL		3	6	5	9	10	17	18	17	10	13	10	10	7	17			
UNASSIGNED	0.0	X											9		236	225	230	14	13	
Co-op	5.0	CO		6	4					2	3	4	4	2	4	16		216	178	
Casual	5.0	CAUL									3	3	3							
TOTAL DAYS			49	147	176	196	194	174	193	195	190	181	140	125	358	288	284	237	196	12

Figure 12.10
A Gantt Chart

The Gantt chart in this figure shows the task, person-days, and initials of each responsible person as well as the start and finish dates for each task. The resource summary provides a good manager with the total person-days for each month and for each person working on the project to manage the project successfully. The project described here is a data administration project.

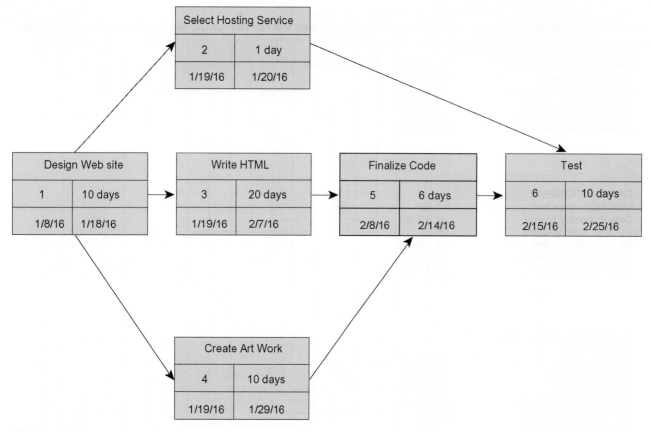

Figure 12.11
A PERT Chart
This is a simplified PERT chart for creating a small website. It shows the ordering of project tasks and the relationship of a task with preceding and succeeding tasks.

You should pay special attention to areas where users interface with the system, with sensitivity to ergonomics issues. **Ergonomics** refers to the interaction of people and machines in the work environment. It considers the design of jobs, health issues, and the end-user interface of information systems. For instance, if a system has a series of complicated online data entry screens that are extremely difficult or time-consuming to work with, users will reject the system if it increases their workload or level of job stress.

Users will be more cooperative if organizational problems are solved prior to introducing the new system. In addition to procedural changes, transformations in job functions, organizational structure, power relationships, and behavior should be identified during systems analysis, using an **organizational impact analysis**.

Review Summary

12-1 **What are the core problem-solving steps for developing new information systems?** The core problem-solving steps for developing new information systems are: (1) define and understand the problem, (2) develop alternative solutions, (3) evaluate and choose the solution, and (4) implement the solution. The third step includes an assessment of the technical, financial, and organizational feasibility of each alternative. The fourth step entails finalizing design specifications, acquiring hardware and software, testing, providing training and documentation, conversion, and evaluating the system solution once it is in production.

12-2 **What are the alternative methods for building information systems?** The systems life cycle requires information systems to be developed in formal stages. The stages must proceed sequentially and have defined outputs; each requires formal approval before the next stage can commence. The system life cycle is rigid and costly but nevertheless useful for large projects.

Prototyping consists of building an experimental system rapidly and inexpensively for end users to interact with and evaluate. The prototype is refined and enhanced until users are satisfied that it includes all their requirements and can be used as a template to create the final system. End-user-developed systems can be created rapidly and informally using user-friendly software tools. End-user development can improve requirements determination and reduce application backlog.

Application software packages eliminate the need for writing software programs when developing an information system. Application software packages are helpful if a firm does not have the internal information systems staff or financial resources to custom-develop a system.

Outsourcing consists of using an external vendor to build (or operate) a firm's information systems. If it is properly managed, outsourcing can save application development costs or enable firms to develop applications without an internal information systems staff.

Rapid application design, joint application design (JAD), cloud-based platforms, and reusable software components (including web services) can be used to speed up the system's development process. Mobile application development must address multiple platforms, small screen sizes, and the need to conserve resources.

12-3 **What are the principal methodologies for modeling and designing systems?** The two principal methodologies for modeling and designing information systems are structured methodologies and object-oriented development. Structured methodologies focus on modeling processes and data separately. The data flow diagram is the principal tool for structured analysis, and the structure chart is the principal tool for representing structured software design. Object-oriented development models a system as a collection of objects that combine processes and data.

12-4 **How should information systems projects be selected and managed?** To determine whether an information system project is a good investment, one must calculate its costs and benefits. Tangible benefits are quantifiable, and intangible benefits cannot be immediately quantified but may provide quantifiable benefits in the future. Benefits that exceed costs should then be analyzed using capital budgeting methods to make sure they represent a good return on the firm's invested capital.

Organizations should develop information systems plans that describe how information technology supports the company's overall business plan and strategy. Portfolio analysis and scoring models can be used to evaluate alternative information systems projects. Information systems projects and the entire implementation process should be managed as planned organizational change using an organizational impact analysis. Management support and control of the implementation process are essential, as are mechanisms for dealing with the level of risk in each new systems project. Project risks are influenced by project size, project structure, and the level of technical expertise of the information systems staff and project team. Formal planning and control tools (including Gantt and PERT charts) track the resource allocations and specific project activities. Users can be encouraged to take active roles in systems development and become involved in installation and training.

Key Terms

Acceptance testing, 454

Component-based development, 467

Computer-aided software engineering (CASE), 468

Customization, 460

Data flow diagram (DFD), 465

Direct cutover strategy, 456

Documentation, 455

End-user development, 459

Ergonomics, 478

Feasibility study, 453

Formal planning and control tools, 476

Gantt chart, 476

Implementation, 474

Information requirements, 452

Information systems plan, 472

Intangible benefits, 471

Joint application design (JAD), 462

Maintenance, 456

Mobile web app, 461

Mobile website, 461

Native app, 461

Object-oriented development, 466

Organizational impact analysis, 478

Parallel strategy, 455

PERT charts, 476

Phased approach, 456

Pilot study, 456

Portfolio analysis, 472

Process specifications, 466

Production, 456

Project, 468

Project management, 470

Prototyping, 458

Rapid application development (RAD), 462

Request for Proposal (RFP), 459

Responsive web design, 462

Scope, 470

Scoring model, 472

Structure chart, 466

Structured, 464

System testing, 454

Systems analysis, 451

Systems design, 454

Systems development life cycle (SDLC), 457

Tangible benefits, 471

Test plan, 454

Testing process, 454

Unit testing, 454

User–designer communications gap, 474

MyMISLab™

To complete the problems with the ★, go to EOC Discussion Questions in the MyLab.

Review Questions

12-1 What are the core problem-solving steps for developing new information systems?
- List and describe the problem-solving steps for building a new system.
- Define information requirements and explain why they are important for developing a system solution.
- List the various types of design specifications required for a new information system.
- Explain why managing change is an important part of developing a new information system.
- Describe the roles of documentation, conversion, production, and maintenance in systems development.

12-2 What are the alternative methods for building information systems?
- Define the traditional systems life cycle and describe its advantages and disadvantages for systems building.
- Define information system prototyping and describe its benefits and limitations. List and describe the steps in the prototyping process.
- Define end-user development and explain its advantages and disadvantages.
- Describe the advantages and disadvantages of developing information systems based on application software packages.
- Define outsourcing. Describe the circumstances in which it should be used for building information systems. List and describe the hidden costs of offshore software outsourcing.
- Explain how businesses can rapidly develop e-business applications.
- Explain the differences between mobile Web sites, mobile Web apps, and native apps.

12-3 What are the principal methodologies for modeling and designing systems?
- Compare object-oriented and traditional structured approaches for modeling and designing systems.

12-4 How should information systems projects be selected and managed?
- Explain the difference between tangible and intangible benefits.
- List six tangible benefits and six intangible benefits.
- List and describe the major components of an information systems plan.
- Define a project and describe the five major variables of project management and their effects.
- Explain the importance of implementation for managing the organizational change surrounding a new information system.
- Define the user–designer communications gap and explain the kinds of implementation problems it creates.
- Describe ways that firms can overcome user resistance to new project implementations.
- List and describe the factors that influence project risk and describe strategies for minimizing project risks.

Discussion Questions

✪ 12-5 Evaluating an information systems' worth can be a difficult task. What are some ways to do this

✪ 12-6 What are some of the ways a firm overcome user resistance to new project implementations?

✪ 12-7 Why is building a system a form of organizational problem-solving?

Hands-On MIS Projects

The projects in this section give you hands-on experience evaluating information systems projects, designing a customer system for auto sales, and analyzing website information requirements. Visit MyMISLab's Multimedia Library to access this chapter's Hands-On MIS Projects.

MANAGEMENT DECISION PROBLEMS

12-8 The Warm and Toasty Heating Oil Company in Glasgow, Scotland used to deliver heating oil by sending trucks that printed out a ticket with the number of gallons of oil delivered that was placed on customers' doorsteps. Customers received their oil delivery bills in the mail two weeks later. The company recently revised its oil delivery and billing system so that oil truck drivers can calculate and print out a complete bill for each delivery and leave customers with the bill and a return envelope at the time the delivery takes place. Evaluate the business impact of the new system and the people and organizational changes required to implement the new technology.

12-9 Caterpillar is the world's leading maker of earth-moving machinery and supplier of agricultural equipment. The software for its Dealer Business System (DBS), which it licenses to its dealers to help them run their businesses, is becoming outdated. Senior management wants its dealers to use a hosted version of the software supported by Accenture consultants so Caterpillar can concentrate on its core business. The system had become a de facto standard for doing business with the company. The majority of the Cat dealers in North America use some version of DBS, as do about half of the Cat dealers in the rest of the world. Before Caterpillar turns the product over to Accenture, what factors and issues should it consider? What questions should it ask? What questions should its dealers ask?

IMPROVING DECISION MAKING: USING DATABASE SOFTWARE TO DESIGN A CUSTOMER SYSTEM FOR AUTO SALES

Software skills: Database design, querying, reporting, and forms
Business skills: Sales lead and customer analysis

12-10 This project requires you to perform a systems analysis and then design a system solution using database software.

Ace Auto Dealers specializes in selling new vehicles from Subaru in Portland, Oregon. The company advertises in local newspapers and is listed as an authorized dealer on the Subaru website and other major websites for auto buyers. The company benefits from a good local word-of-mouth reputation and name recognition.

Ace does not believe it has enough information about its customers. It cannot easily determine which prospects have made auto purchases, nor can it identify which customer touch points have produced the greatest number of sales leads or actual sales so it can focus advertising and marketing more on the channels that generate the most revenue. Are purchasers discovering Ace from newspaper ads, from word of mouth, or from the web?

Prepare a systems analysis report detailing Ace's problem and a system solution that can be implemented using PC database management software. Then use database software to develop a simple system solution. In MyMISLab™, you will find more information about Ace and its information requirements to help you develop the solution.

ACHIEVING OPERATIONAL EXCELLENCE: ANALYZING WEBSITE DESIGN AND INFORMATION REQUIREMENTS

Software skills: Web browser software
Business skills: Information requirements analysis, website design

12-11 Visit the website of your choice and explore it thoroughly. Prepare a report analyzing the various functions provided by that website and its information requirements. Your report should answer these questions: What functions does the website perform? What data does it use? What are its inputs, outputs, and processes? What are some of its other design specifications? Does the website link to any internal systems or systems of other organizations? What value does this website provide the firm?

Collaboration and Teamwork Project

Preparing Website Design Specifications

12-12 With three or four of your classmates, select a system described in this text that uses the web. Review the website for the system you select. Use what you have learned from the website and the description in this book to prepare a report describing some of the design specifications for the system you select. If possible, use Google Docs and Google Drive or Google Sites to brainstorm, organize, and develop a presentation of your findings for the class.

BUSINESS PROBLEM-SOLVING CASE

A Shaky Start for Healthcare.gov

The Patient Protection and Affordable Care Act, often called Obamacare, is considered the centerpiece of President Barack Obama's legacy. Essential to Obama's health care reform plan is Healthcare.gov, a health insurance exchange website that facilitates the sale of private health insurance plans to U.S. residents, assists people eligible to sign up for Medicaid, and has a separate marketplace for small businesses.

The site allows users to compare prices on health insurance plans in their states, to enroll in a plan they choose, and to find out whether they qualify for government health care subsidies. Users must sign up and create their own specific account first, providing some personal information, to receive detailed information about available health care plans in their area.

Healthcare.gov was launched on October 1, 2013, as promised, but visitors quickly encountered numerous technical problems. Software that assigned digital identities to enrollees and ensured that they saw only their own personal data was overwhelmed. Customers encountered cryptic error messages and could not log on to create accounts. Many users received quotes that were incorrect because the feature used prices based on just two age groups. It was estimated that only 1 percent of interested consumers were able to enroll through the site for the first week of operations, and many applications sent to insurers contained erroneous information. Thousands of enrollees for HealthCare.gov—at least one in five at the height of the problems—received inaccurate assignments to Medicaid or to private health plans. Some people were wrongly denied coverage.

Insurers received enrollment files from the federal exchange that were incomplete or inaccurate, as many as one in ten. The information includes who is enrolling and what subsidies they may receive. Some insurers reported being deluged with phone calls from people who believed they had signed up for a particular health plan, only to find that the company had no record of the enrollment. Enrollment problems with insurers persisted into November.

U.S. chief technology officer Todd Park stated on October 6 that Healthcare.gov's glitches were caused by an unexpectedly high volume of users. Between 50,000 and 60,000 had been expected, but the site had to handle 250,000 simultaneous users.

More than 8.1 million people visited Healthcare.gov between October 1, 2013, and October 4, 2013.

White House officials later admitted that Healthcare.gov's problems were not just caused by high traffic volume but also by software and system design issues. Stress tests performed by contractors a day before the launch date revealed that the site slowed substantially with only 1100 simultaneous users, far fewer than the 50,000 to 60,000 that were anticipated. Technical experts found out that the site was riddled with hardware and software defects, amounting to more than 600 items that needed to be fixed.

A major contributor to these problems was the part of the system's design that required users to create individual accounts before shopping for health insurance. This meant that before users could shop for coverage, they must input personal data that would be exchanged among separate computer systems built or run by multiple vendors, including CGI Group, developer of Healthcare.gov, Quality Software Services, and credit-checker Experian PLC. If any part of this web of systems failed to work properly, users would be blocked from entering the exchange marketplace. A bottleneck had been created where these systems interacted with a software component called Oracle Identity Manager supplied by Oracle Corporation that was embedded in the government's identity-checking system. This problem might have been averted if the system allowed users to browse plans without first going through the complex registration process.

Problems, including pull-down menus that only worked intermittently and excruciatingly long wait times, persisted into the third week of operations. For some weeks in October, the site was down 60 percent of the time.

What happened to Healthcare.gov is another example of IT project management gone awry, which often happens with large technology projects, especially those for the U.S. federal government. There was no single leader overseeing the Healthcare.gov implementation. The U.S. Centers for Medicare and Medicaid Services (CMS) coordinated the development effort. However, CMS had a siloed management structure, and no single unit was designated to take charge of the entire project.

CMS parceled out the work for building and implementing the Healthcare.gov system to a number of outside contractors. The front end of the website (including the user interface) was developed by the start-up Development Seed. The back end (where all the heavy-duty processing of enrollment data and transactions with insurers takes place) was contracted to CGI Federal, a subsidiary of the Canadian multinational CGI Group, which received $231 million for the project. CGI then subcontracted much of its work to other companies. This is common in large government projects. Functions relating to digital identity authentication were contracted to Experian, the global information services company noted for its credit-checking expertise.

CMS set deadlines for the contractors, who were expected to attend meetings to hammer out the details of the specifications for the website, but the computer specialists skipped some of those sessions. Contractors for different parts of the system barely communicated with each other.

Some IT experts also criticized CMS's decision to use database software from a company called MarkLogic, which handles data management differently from more mainstream database management systems of companies such as IBM and Oracle. Work proceeded more slowly because so few people were familiar with MarkLogic, and MarkLogic continued to perform below expectations after the Healthcare.gov website was launched.

The website had not been thoroughly tested before it went live, so a number of software and hardware defects had not been detected. Testing of the system by insurers had been scheduled for July but didn't begin until the third week in September. CMS was responsible for user-testing the system during the final weeks.

Technology experts also faulted Healthcare.gov's developers for trying to go live with all parts of a large and very complex system all at once. It would have been better to roll out system functions gradually. CGI believed that a full-function Healthcare.gov with all the anticipated bells and whistles was an unrealistic target. Given the time required to complete and test the software, it was impossible to launch a full-function exchange by October 1, but government officials insisted that October 1 was not negotiable and had become impatient with CGI's pattern of excuses for missed deadlines. The Obama administration kept on modifying regulations and policies until summer 2013, which meant that contractors had to deal with changing requirements.

The Healthcare.gov enrollment system is very complex. It connects to other federal computer networks, including the Social Security Administration (SSA), Internal Revenue Service (IRS), Veterans

Affairs (VA), Office of Personnel Management, and the Peace Corps. It has to verify a considerable amount of personal information, including income and immigration status.

Vital components were never secured. There was insufficient access to a data center to prevent the website from crashing. No backup system for a website crash was created. The interaction between the data center where the information is stored and the system was so poorly configured that it had to be redesigned.

CMS had several warnings between March and July that the project was going off-track but didn't seek deep White House involvement or change the leadership structure, according to officials, congressional aides, and emails from the period. An administration report noted that inadequate management oversight and coordination among technical teams prevented real-time decision making and efficient responses to address the issues with the site.

The consulting firm McKinsey & Co. detailed the project's potential risks in a presentation between March 28 and April 8 to the top CMS official, Marilyn Tavenner, to Health and Human Services Secretary Kathleen Sebelius, and to White House Chief Technology Officer Todd Park. McKinsey's report anticipated many of the site's pitfalls and urged the administration to name a single project leader to streamline decision-making. It also emphasized the importance of White House support for CMS to meet the October 1 launch date. Nevertheless, according to documents from the period and officials, the White House's minimal involvement in the project's details didn't change after the McKinsey report.

The White House assembled experts from government and industry who worked frantically to fix the system. The Obama administration appointed contractor Quality Software Services Inc. (QSSI) to coordinate the work involved in fixing the website. QSSI had worked earlier on the website's back-end. In January 2014, Accenture replaced CGI Group as the website's lead contractor.

Work on fixing the website continued through October and November 2013, and the website appeared to be working more smoothly. For the vast majority of users, Healthcare.gov was working more than 90 percent of the time. Response time (the time required for a web page to load) was reduced from eight seconds to less than one. The incidence of error messages preventing people from using the site went from 6 percent down to .75 percent, but by November 30, only 137,000 people had signed up for private health insurance, far fewer than the government had forecast. Healthcare.gov's problems also forced the Obama administration to delay by one year an online exchange for small business.

Reuters reported in mid-October 2013 that the total cost of building Healthcare.gov using contractors had tripled from an initial estimate of $93.7 million to about $292 million. Overall cost for building the website reached $500 million by October 2013. As of February 2014, the government had committed to paying $800 million for contracts for the site, and the full amount spent to date is still unknown.

By early 2014, Healthcare.gov was working much better but was not problem-free. Then HealthCare .gov went down shortly after midnight March 30, 2014, and remained unusable until a day later. Some of the hundreds of thousands of Americans trying to sign up for health care at the last minute of the enrollment period were unable to do so. Nevertheless, 8 million people signed up for health care that year.

Kathleen Sebelius resigned as Secretary for Health and Human Services on April 10, 2014, replaced by Sylvia Mathews Burwell on June 9 of that year. On July 30, 2014, the U.S. Government Accountability Office (GAO) released a nonpartisan study finding that the Healthcare.gov website was developed without effective planning or oversight practices. These findings were supported by another report issued by the Inspector General of the Department of Health and Human Services in January 2015. The Inspector General's investigation found that the federal government failed to probe fully the past performance of CGI before awarding its contract and had neglected to put a cap on contractor billings.

After a bumpy debut, HealthCare.gov appeared in 2015 to be running smoothly. There have been a few minor, short-lived technical glitches. The Obama administration was able to boast that enrollment of 11 million people in health care plans for 2015 surpassed the president's goals.

Sources: Louise Radnofsky, "Poor Oversight, Work Marred Health Care Site's Launch," *Wall Street Journal*, January 20, 2015; Alex Barinka,"Healthcare.gov Bug Plagues Obamacare Just before Deadline," *Bloomberg*, February 14, 2015; Amy Nordrum, "Obama's Healthcare.gov Website Isn't Consumer-Friendly Enough, Experts Say," *International Business Times*, February 18, 2015; Spencer E. Ante and Louise Radnofsky, "New Technical Woes Hobble Health-Insurance Sign-Ups at Zero Hour," *Wall Street Journal*, March 31, 2014; "How HealthCare.gov Was Supposed to Work and How It Didn't," *New York Times*, December 2, 2013; Sheryl Gay Stolberg and Michael D. Shear, "Inside the Race to Rescue a Health Care Site, and Obama," *New York Times*, November 30, 2013; Gautham Nagesh, "Health Website Problems Weren't Flagged in Time," *Wall Street Journal*, December 2, 2013; Christopher Weaver and Louise Radnofsky, "Healthcare.gov's Flaws Found, Fixes Eyed," *Wall Street Journal*, October 10, 2013, and "Federal Health Site Stymied by Lack of Direction," *Wall Street Journal*, October 28, 2013; and Eric Lipton, Jan Austen, and Sharon LaFraniere, "Tension and Flaws before Health Website Crash," *New York Times*, November 22, 2013.

Case Study Questions

12-13 Why was the Healthcare.gov project so important?

12-14 Evaluate the key risk factors in this project.

12-15 Classify and describe the problems this project encountered. What people, organization, and technology factors were responsible for these problems?

12-16 What were the economic, political, and social impacts of Healthcare.gov's botched implementation?

12-17 Describe the steps that should have been taken to prevent a negative outcome in this project.

MyMISLab

Go to the Assignments section of your MyLab to complete these writing exercises.

12-18 Describe four system conversion strategies.

12-19 Compare the two major types of planning and control tools.

Chapter 12 References

Appan, Radha, and Glenn J. Browne. "The Impact of Analyst-Induced Misinformation on the Requirements Elicitation Process," *MIS Quarterly* 36, No. 1 (March 2012).

Armstrong, Deborah J., and Bill C. Hardgrove. "Understanding Mindshift Learning: The Transition to Object-Oriented Development," *MIS Quarterly* 31, No. 3 (September 2007).

Bloch, Michael, Sen Blumberg, and Jurgen Laartz. "Delivering Large-Scale IT Projects on Time, on Budget, and on Value," *McKinsey Quarterly* (October 2012).

Cecez-Kecmanovic, Dubravka, Karlheinz Kautz, and Rebecca Abrahall, "Reframing Success and Failure of Information Systems: A Performative Perspective," *MIS Quarterly* 38, No. 2 (June 2014).

Chandrasekaran, Sriram, Sauri Gudlavalleti, and Sanjay Kaniyar. "Achieving Success in Large Complex Software Projects," *McKinsey Quarterly* (July 2014).

Debane, Francine, Katya Defossez, and Mark McMillan. "Developing Talent for Large IT Projects," *McKinsey Quarterly* (August 2014).

Feeny, David, Mary Lacity, and Leslie P. Willcocks. "Taking the Measure of Outsourcing Providers," *MIT Sloan Management Review* 46, No. 3 (Spring 2005).

Flyvbjerg, Bent, and Alexander Budzier. "Why Your IT Project May Be Riskier Than You Think," *Harvard Business Review* (September 2011).

Gefen, David, and Erarn Carmel. "Is the World Really Flat? A Look at Offshoring in an Online Programming Marketplace," *MIS Quarterly* 32, No. 2 (June 2008).

Hahn, Eugene D., Jonathan P. Doh, and Kraiwinee Bunyaratavej. "The Evolution of Risk in Information Systems Offshoring: The Impact of Home Country Risk, Firm Learning, and Competitive Dynamics," *MIS Quarterly* 33, No. 3 (September 2009).

Han, Kunsoo, and Sunil Mithas. "Information Technology Outsourcing and Non-IT Operating Costs: An Empirical Investigation," *MIS Quarterly* 37, No. 1 (March 2013).

Hoffer, Jeffrey, Joey George, and Joseph Valacich. *Modern Systems Analysis and Design*, 7th ed. (Upper Saddle River, NJ: Prentice-Hall, 2014.)

Information Builders. "Yellow Pages Uses WebFOCUS to Demonstrate ROI to Advertisers," www.informationbuilders.com, accessed March 30, 2015.

Keil, Mark, H. Jeff Smith, Charalambos L. Iacovou, and Ronald L. Thompson. "The Pitfalls of Project Status Reporting," *MIT Sloan Management Review* 55, No. 3 (Spring 2014).

Kendall, Kenneth E., and Julie E. Kendall. *Systems Analysis and Design,* 9th ed. (Upper Saddle River, NJ: Prentice-Hall, 2013.)

Kim, Hee Woo, and Atreyi Kankanhalli. "Investigating User Resistance to Information Systems Implementation: A Status Quo Bias Perspective," *MIS Quarterly* 33, No. 3 (September 2009).

Kloppenborg, Timothy J. and Debbie Tesch. "How Executive Sponsors Influence Project Success," *MIT Sloan Management Review* (Spring 2015).

Kotlarsky, Julia, Harry Scarbrough, and Ilan Oshri. "Coordinating Expertise across Knowledge Boundaries in Offshore-Outsourcing Projects: The Role of Codification," *MIS Quarterly* 38 No. 2 (June 2014).

Lapointe, Liette, and Suzanne Rivard. "A Multilevel Model of Resistance to Information Technology Implementation," *MIS Quarterly* 29, No. 3 (September 2005).

Levina, Natalia, and Jeanne W. Ross. "From the Vendor's Perspective: Exploring the Value Proposition in Information Technology Outsourcing," *MIS Quarterly* 27, No. 3 (September 2003).

Majchrzak, Ann, Cynthia M. Beath, and Ricardo A. Lim. "Managing Client Dialogues during Information Systems Design to Facilitate Client Learning," *MIS Quarterly* 29, No. 4 (December 2005).

McCafferty, Dennis. "What Dooms IT Projects," *Baseline* (June 10, 2010).

McDougall, Paul. "Outsourcing's New Reality: Choice Beats Costs." *Information Week* (August 29, 2012).

McGrath, Rita. "Six Problems Facing Large Government IT Projects (and Their Solutions)," *Harvard Business Review* Online (October 10, 2008).

Nelson, H. James, Deborah J. Armstrong, and Kay M. Nelson. Patterns of Transition: The Shift from Traditional to Object-Oriented Development," *Journal of Management Information Systems* 25, No. 4 (Spring 2009).

Overby, Stephanie. "The Hidden Costs of Offshore Outsourcing," *CIO Magazine* (September 1, 2003).

Polites, Greta L., and Elena Karahanna. "Shackled to the Status Quo: The Inhibiting Effects of Incumbent System Habit, Switching Costs, and Inertia on New System Acceptance," *MIS Quarterly* 36, No. 1 (March 2012).

Project Management Institute and Boston Consulting Group. "Executive Sponsor Engagement: Top Driver of Project and Program Success," Newtown Square, Pennsylvania: PMI/BCG (October 2014).

Ryan, Sherry D., David A. Harrison, and Lawrence L Schkade. "Information Technology Investment Decisions: When Do Cost and Benefits in the Social Subsystem Matter?" *Journal of Management Information Systems* 19, No. 2 (Fall 2002).

Schwalbe, Kathy. *Information Technology Project Management*, 7th ed. Cengage (2014).

Sharma, Rajeev, and Philip Yetton. "The Contingent Effects of Training, Technical Complexity, and Task Interdependence on Successful Information Systems Implementation," *MIS Quarterly 31*, No. 2 (June 2007).

Sircar, Sumit, Sridhar P. Nerur, and Radhakanta Mahapatra. "Revolution or Evolution? A Comparison of Object-Oriented and Structured Systems Development Methods," *MIS Quarterly* 25, No. 4 (December 2001).

Whitaker, Jonathan, Sunil Mithas, and M. S. Krishnan. "Organizational Learning and Capabilities for Onshore and Offshore Business Process Outsourcing," *Journal of Management Information Systems* 27, No. 3 (Winter 2011).

Glossary

3-D printing: Uses machines to make solid objects, layer by layer, from specifications in a digital file. Also known as additive manufacturing.

3G networks: High-speed cellular networks based on packet-switched technology, enabling users to transmit video, graphics, and other rich media in addition to voice.

4G networks: Ultra high–speed wireless networks that are entirely packet switched, with speeds between 1 Mbps and 1 Gbps.

acceptable use policy (AUP): Defines acceptable uses of the firm's information resources and computing equipment, including desktop and laptop computers, wireless devices, telephones, and the Internet, and specifies consequences for noncompliance.

acceptance testing: Provides the final certification that the system is ready to be used in a production setting.

accountability: The mechanisms for assessing responsibility for decisions made and actions taken.

advertising revenue model: website generating revenue by attracting a large audience.

affiliate revenue model: E-commerce revenue mode in which websites are paid as affiliates for sending their visitors to other sites in return for a referral fee.

agile development: Rapid delivery of working software by breaking a large project into a series of small subprojects that are completed in short periods of time using iteration and continuous feedback.

analytic platform: Preconfigured hardware-software system that is specifically designed for high-speed analysis of large data sets.

analytical CRM: Customer relationship management applications dealing with the analysis of customer data to provide information for improving business performance.

Android: Open source operating system for mobile devices Google and the Open Handset Alliance developed; currently the most popular smartphone operating system worldwide.

antivirus software: Software designed to detect, and often eliminate, computer viruses from an information system.

application controls: Specific controls unique to each computerized application that ensure that only authorized data are completely and accurately processed by that application.

application proxy filtering: Firewall screening technology that uses a proxy server to inspect and transmit data packets flowing into and out of the organization so that all the organization's internal applications communicate with the outside by using a proxy application.

application server: Software that handles all application operations between browser-based computers and a company's back-end business applications or databases.

application software: Programs written for a specific application to perform functions specified by end users.

apps: Small pieces of software that run on the Internet, on a computer, or on a mobile phone and are generally delivered over the Internet.

artificial intelligence (AI): The effort to develop computer-based systems that can behave like humans, with the ability to learn languages, accomplish physical tasks, use a perceptual apparatus, and emulate human expertise and decision making.

attributes: Pieces of information describing a particular entity.

augmented reality: Technology for enhancing visualization that provides a live view of a physical world environment whose elements are augmented by virtual computer-generated imagery.

authentication: The ability of each party in a transaction to ascertain the identity of the other party.

authorization management systems: Systems for allowing each user access only to those portions of a system or the web that person is permitted to enter, based on information established by a set of access rules.

authorization policies: Determine differing levels of access to information assets for different levels of users in an organization.

autonomic computing: Effort to develop systems that can manage themselves without user intervention.

backbone: Part of a network handling the major traffic and providing the primary path for traffic flowing to or from other networks.

balanced scorecard method: Framework for operationalizing a firm's strategic plan by focusing on measurable financial, business process, customer, and learning and growth outcomes of firm performance.

bandwidth: The capacity of a communications channel as measured by the difference between the highest and lowest frequencies that can be transmitted by that channel.

banner ad: A graphic display on a web page used for advertising. The banner is linked to the advertiser's website so that a person clicking it will be transported to the advertiser's website.

behavioral targeting: Tracking the click-streams (history of clicking behavior) of individuals across multiple websites for the purpose of understanding their interests and intentions and exposing them to advertisements that are uniquely suited to their interests.

benchmarking: Setting strict standards for products, services, or activities and measuring organizational performance against those standards.

best practices: The most successful solutions or problem-solving methods that have been developed by a specific organization or industry.

big data: Data sets with volumes so huge that they are beyond the ability of typical relational DBMS to capture, store, and analyze. The data are often unstructured or semi-structured.

biometric authentication: Technology for authenticating system users that compares a person's unique characteristics, such as fingerprints, face, or retinal image, against a stored set profile of these characteristics.

bit: A binary digit representing the smallest unit of data in a computer system. It can only have one of two states, representing 0 or 1.

blog: Popular term for weblog, designating an informal yet structured website where individuals can publish stories, opinions, and links to other websites of interest.

blogosphere: The totality of blog-related websites.

Bluetooth: Standard for wireless personal area networks that can transmit up to 722 Kbps within a 10-meter area.

botnet: A group of computers that have been infected with bot malware without users' knowledge, enabling a hacker to use the amassed resources of the computers to launch distributed denial-of-service attacks, phishing campaigns, or spam.

broadband: High-speed transmission technology; also designates a single communications medium that can transmit multiple channels of data simultaneously.

bugs: Software program code defects.

bullwhip effect: Distortion of information about the demand for a product as it passes from one entity to the next across the supply chain.

business continuity planning: Planning that focuses on how the company can restore business operations after a disaster strikes.

business intelligence (BI): Applications and technologies to help users make better business decisions.

business model: An abstraction of what an enterprise is and how the enterprise delivers a product or service, showing how the enterprise creates wealth.

business performance management: Methodology for measuring firm performance by using key performance indicators based on the firm's strategies.

business process management: Tools and methodologies for continuously improving and managing business processes.

business process reengineering (BPR): The radical redesign of business processes to maximize the benefits of information technology.

business processes: The unique ways in which organizations coordinate and organize work activities, information, and knowledge to produce a product or service.

business strategy: Set of activities and decisions that determine the products and services the firm produces, the industries in which the firm competes, firm competitors, suppliers, and customers, and the firm's long-term goals.

business: A formal organization whose aim is to produce products or provide services for a profit.

business-to-business (B2B) electronic commerce: Electronic sales of goods and services among businesses.

business-to-consumer (B2C) electronic commerce: Electronic retailing of products and services directly to individual consumers.

BYOD: Allowing employees to use their personal mobile devices in the workplace.

C: A powerful programming language with tight control and efficiency of execution, portable across different microprocessors and used primarily with PCs.

cable Internet connections: Using digital cable coaxial lines to deliver high-speed Internet access to homes and businesses.

call center: An organizational department responsible for handling customer service issues by telephone and other channels.

campus area network (CAN): An interconnected set of local area networks in a limited geographical area such as a college or corporate campus.

capacity planning: The process of predicting when a computer hardware system becomes saturated to ensure that adequate computing resources are available for work of different priorities and that the firm has enough computing power for its current and future needs.

carpal tunnel syndrome (CTS): Type of RSI in which pressure on the median nerve through the wrist's bony carpal tunnel structure produces pain.

case-based reasoning (CBR): Artificial intelligence technology that represents knowledge as a database of cases and solutions.

CD-ROM (compact disk read-only memory): Read-only optical disk storage used for imaging, reference, and database applications with massive amounts of unchanging data and for multimedia.

CD-RW (CD-ReWritable): Optical disk storage that can be rewritten many times by users.

cellular telephones (cell phones): A device that transmits voice or data, using radio waves to communicate with radio antennas placed within adjacent geographic areas called cells.

centralized processing: Processing that is accomplished by one large central computer.

change agent: In the context of implementation, the individual acting as the catalyst during the change process to ensure successful organizational adaptation to a new system or innovation.

change management: Giving proper consideration to the impact of organizational change associated with a new system or alteration of an existing system.

chat: Live, interactive conversations over a public network.

chief data officer (CDO): Individual responsible for enterprise-wide governance and usage of information to maximize the value the organization can realize from its data.

chief information officer (CIO): Senior manager in charge of the information systems function in the firm.

chief knowledge officer (CKO): Responsible for the firm's knowledge management program.

chief privacy officer (CPO): Responsible for ensuring that the company complies with existing data privacy laws.

chief security officer (CSO): Heads a formal security function for the organization and is responsible for enforcing the firm's security policy.

choice: Simon's third stage of decision making, when the individual selects among the various solution alternatives.

Chrome OS: Google's lightweight operating system for cloud computing using a web-connected computer or mobile device.

churn rate: Measurement of the number of customers who stop using or purchasing products or services from a company; used as an indicator of the growth or decline of a firm's customer base.

click fraud: Fraudulently clicking an online ad in pay-per-click advertising to generate an improper charge per click.

clickstream tracking: Tracking data about customer activities at websites and storing them in a log.

client/server computing: A model for computing that splits processing between clients and servers on a network, assigning functions to the machine most able to perform the function.

client: The user point of entry for the required function in client/server computing; normally a desktop computer, workstation, or laptop computer.

cloud computing: Model of computing that provides access to a shared pool of computing resources over a network, often the Internet.

coaxial cable: A transmission medium consisting of thickly insulated copper wire; can transmit large volumes of data quickly.

collaboration: Working with others to achieve shared and explicit goals.

collaborative filtering: Tracking users' movements on a website, comparing the information gleaned about a user's behavior against data about

other customers with similar interests to predict what the user would like to see next.

community provider: Website business model that creates a digital online environment in which people with similar interests can transact; share interests, photos, and videos; and receive interest-related information.

competitive forces model: Model used to describe the interaction of external influences, specifically threats and opportunities, that affect an organization's strategy and ability to compete.

component-based development: Building large software systems by combining preexisting software components.

computer abuse: The commission of acts involving a computer that may not be illegal but are considered unethical.

computer crime: The commission of illegal acts through the use of a computer or against a computer system.

computer forensics: The scientific collection, examination, authentication, preservation, and analysis of data held on or retrieved from computer storage media in such a way that the information can be used as evidence in a court of law.

computer hardware: Physical equipment used for input, processing, and output activities in an information system.

computer literacy: Knowledge about information technology, focusing on understanding of how computer-based technologies work.

computer software: Detailed, preprogrammed instructions that control and coordinate the work of computer hardware components in an information system.

computer virus: Rogue software program that attaches itself to other software programs or data files and activates, often causing hardware and software malfunctions.

computer vision syndrome (CVS): Eyestrain condition related to computer display screen use; symptoms include headaches, blurred vision, and dry and irritated eyes.

computer-aided design (CAD) system: Information system that automates the creation and revision of designs by using sophisticated graphics software.

computer-aided software engineering (CASE): Automation of step-by-step methodologies for software and systems development to reduce the amount of repetitive work the developer needs to perform.

consumerization of IT: New information technology originating in the consumer market that spreads to business organizations.

consumer-to-consumer (C2C) electronic commerce: Consumers selling goods and services electronically to other consumers.

controls: All of the methods, policies, and procedures that ensure protection of the organization's assets, accuracy and reliability of its records, and operational adherence to management standards.

conversion: The process of changing from the old system to the new system.

cookies: Tiny files deposited on a computer hard drive when an individual visits certain websites; used to identify the visitor and track visits to the website.

copyright: A statutory grant that protects creators of intellectual property against copying by others for any purpose during the life of the author plus an additional 70 years after the author's death.

core competency: Activity at which a firm excels as a world-class leader.

cost transparency: The ability of consumers to discover the actual costs merchants pay for products.

cost–benefit ratio: A method for calculating the returns from a capital expenditure by dividing total benefits by total costs.

critical thinking: Sustained suspension of judgment with an awareness of multiple perspectives and alternatives.

cross-selling: Marketing complementary products to customers.

crowdsourcing: Using large Internet audiences for advice, market feedback, new ideas, and solutions to business problems; related to the wisdom-of-crowds theory.

culture: Fundamental set of assumptions, values, and ways of doing things that has been accepted by most members of an organization.

customer lifetime value (CLTV): Difference between revenues produced by a specific customer and the expenses for acquiring and servicing that customer minus the cost of promotional marketing over the lifetime of the customer relationship, expressed in today's dollars.

customer relationship management (CRM) systems: Information systems that track all the ways in which a company interacts with its customers and analyze these interactions to optimize revenue, profitability, customer satisfaction, and customer retention.

customization: In e-commerce, changing a delivered product or service based on a user's preferences or prior behavior.

customization: The modification of a software package to meet an organization's unique requirements without destroying the package software's integrity.

cyberlocker: Online file-sharing service that allows users to upload files to a secure online storage site from which the files can be synchronized and shared with others.

cybervandalism: Intentional disruption, defacement, or even destruction of a website or corporate information system.

cyberwarfare: State-sponsored activity designed to cripple and defeat another state or nation by damaging or disrupting its computers or networks.

cycle time: The total elapsed time from the beginning of a process to its end.

data administration: A special organizational function for managing the organization's data resources, concerned with information policy, data planning, maintenance of data dictionaries, and data quality standards.

data center: Facility housing computer systems and associated components, such as telecommunications, storage and security systems, and backup power supplies.

data cleansing: Activities for detecting and correcting data in a database or file that are incorrect, incomplete, improperly formatted, or redundant. Also known as data scrubbing.

data definition: Specifies the structure of the content of a database.

data dictionary: An automated or manual tool for storing and organizing information about the data maintained in a database.

data flow diagram (DFD): Primary tool for structured analysis that graphically illustrates a system's component process and the flow of data between them.

data management software: Software used for creating and manipulating lists, creating files and databases to store data, and combining information for reports.

data management technology: Software governing the organization of data on physical storage media.

data manipulation language: A language associated with a database management system that end users and programmers use to manipulate data in the database.

data mart: A small data warehouse containing only a portion of the organization's data for a specified function or population of users.

data mining: Analysis of large pools of data to find patterns and rules that can be used to guide decision making and predict future behavior.

data quality audit: A survey and/or sample of files to determine accuracy and completeness of data in an information system.

data visualization: Technology for helping users see patterns and relationships in large amounts of data by presenting the data in graphical form.

data warehouse: A database, with reporting and query tools, that stores current and historical data extracted from various operational systems and consolidated for management reporting and analysis.

data workers: People such as secretaries or bookkeepers who process the organization's paperwork.

data: Streams of raw facts representing events occurring in organizations or the physical environment before they have been organized and arranged into a form that people can understand and use.

database administration: Refers to the more technical and operational aspects of managing data, including physical database design and maintenance.

database management system (DBMS): Special software to create and maintain a database and enable individual business applications to extract the data they need without having to create separate files or data definitions in their computer programs.

database server: A computer in a client/server environment that is responsible for running a DBMS to process SQL statements and perform database management tasks.

database: A group of related files.

decision-support systems (DSS): Information systems at the organization's management level that combine data and sophisticated analytical models or data analysis tools to support semistructured and unstructured decision making.

deep packet inspection (DPI): Technology for managing network traffic by examining data packets, sorting out low-priority data from higher priority business-critical data, and sending packets in order of priority.

demand planning: Determining how much product a business needs to make to satisfy all its customers' demands.

denial of service (DoS) attack: Flooding a network server or web server with false communications or requests for services to crash the network.

Descartes' rule of change: A principle that states that if an action cannot be taken repeatedly, then it is not right to be taken at any time.

design: Simon's second stage of decision making, when the individual conceives of possible alternative solutions to a problem.

digital asset management systems: Classify, store, and distribute digital objects such as photographs, graphic images, video, and audio content.

digital certificates: Attachments to an electronic message to verify the identity of the sender and provide the receiver with the means to encode a reply.

digital checking: Systems that extend the functionality of existing checking accounts so they can be used for online shopping payments.

digital dashboard: Displays all of a firm's key performance indicators as graphs and charts on a single screen to provide one-page overview of all the critical measurements necessary to make key executive decisions.

digital divide: Large disparities in access to computers and the Internet among different social groups and different locations.

digital goods: Goods that can be delivered over a digital network.

digital market: A marketplace that is created by computer and communication technologies that link many buyers and sellers.

Digital Millennium Copyright Act (DMCA): Adjusts copyright laws to the Internet Age by making it illegal to make, distribute, or use devices that circumvent technology-based protections of copyrighted materials.

digital signature: A digital code that can be attached to an electronically transmitted message to identify its contents and the sender uniquely.

digital subscriber line (DSL): A group of technologies providing high-capacity transmission over existing copper telephone lines.

digital video disk (DVD): High-capacity optical storage medium that can store full-length videos and large amounts of data.

direct cutover strategy: A risky conversion approach by which the new system completely replaces the old one on an appointed day.

disaster recovery planning: Planning for the restoration of computing and communications services after they have been disrupted.

disintermediation: The removal of organizations or business process layers responsible for certain intermediary steps in a value chain.

disruptive technologies: Technologies with disruptive impact on industries and businesses, rendering existing products, services, and business models obsolete.

distributed denial-of-service (DDoS) attack: Attack that uses numerous computers to inundate and overwhelm a network from numerous launch points.

distributed processing: The distribution of computer processing work among multiple computers linked by a communications network.

documentation: Descriptions of how an information system works from either a technical or end-user standpoint.

Domain Name System (DNS): A hierarchical system of servers maintaining a database enabling the conversion of domain names to their numeric IP addresses.

domain name: English-like name that corresponds to the unique 32-bit numeric Internet Protocol (IP) address for each computer connected to the Internet.

domestic exporter: Form of business organization characterized by heavy centralization of corporate activities in the home country of origin.

downtime: Period of time in which an information system is not operational.

drill down: The ability to move from summary data to increasingly granular levels of detail.

drive-by download: Malware that comes with a downloaded file a user unintentionally opens.

due process: A process by which laws are well-known and understood and provide an ability to appeal to higher authorities to ensure that laws are applied correctly.

dynamic pricing: Pricing of items based on real-time interactions between buyers and sellers that determine what an item is worth at any particular moment.

efficient customer response system: System that directly links consumer behavior to distribution, production, and supply chains.

e-government: Use of the Internet and related technologies to enable government and public sector agencies' relationships with citizens, businesses, and other arms of government digitally.

electronic business (e-business): The use of the Internet and digital technology to execute all the business processes in the enterprise; includes e-commerce as well as processes for the internal management of the firm and coordination with suppliers and other business partners.

electronic commerce (e-commerce): The process of buying and selling goods and services electronically, involving transactions by using the Internet, networks, and other digital technologies.

electronic data interchange (EDI): The direct computer-to-computer exchange between two organizations of standard business transactions, such as orders, shipment instructions, or payments.

electronic mail (email): The computer-to-computer exchange of messages.

electronic records management (ERM): Policies, procedures, and tools for managing the retention, destruction, and storage of electronic records.

employee relationship management (ERM): Software dealing with employee issues that are closely related to CRM, such as setting objectives, employee performance management, performance-based compensation, and employee training.

encryption: The coding and scrambling of messages to prevent them from being read or accessed without authorization.

end users: Representatives of departments outside the information systems group for whom applications are developed.

end-user development: The development of information systems by end users with little or no formal assistance from technical specialists.

end-user interface: The part of an information system through which the end user interacts with the system, such as online screens and commands.

enterprise applications: Systems that can coordinate activities, decisions, and knowledge across many functions, levels, and business units in a firm; include enterprise systems, supply chain management systems, customer relationship management systems, and knowledge management systems.

enterprise content management systems: Systems that help organizations manage structured and semistructured knowledge, providing corporate repositories of documents, reports, presentations, and best practices and capabilities for collecting and organizing email and graphic objects.

enterprise systems: Integrated, enterprise-wide information systems that coordinate key internal processes of the firm. Also known as enterprise resource planning (ERP).

enterprise-wide knowledge management systems: General-purpose, firm-wide systems that collect, store, distribute, and apply digital content and knowledge.

entity: A person, place, thing, or event about which information must be kept.

entity-relationship diagram: A methodology for documenting databases illustrating the relationship between various entities in the database.

ergonomics: The interaction of people and machines in the work environment, including the design of jobs, health issues, and the end-user interface of information systems.

e-tailer: Online retail stores from the giant Amazon to tiny local stores that have websites where retail goods are sold.

Ethernet: The dominant LAN standard at the physical network level, specifying the physical medium to carry signals between computers; access control rules; and a standardized set of bits to carry data over the system.

ethical no-free-lunch" rule: Assumption that all tangible and intangible objects are owned by someone else, unless there is a specific declaration otherwise, and that the creator wants compensation for this work.

ethics: Principles of right and wrong that can be used by individuals acting as free moral agents to make choices to guide their behavior.

evil twins: Wireless networks that pretend to be legitimate Wi-Fi networks to entice participants to log on and reveal passwords or credit card numbers.

exchanges: Third-party Net marketplaces that are primarily transaction oriented and that connect many buyers and suppliers for spot purchasing.

executive support systems (ESS): Information systems at the organization's strategic level designed to address unstructured decision making through advanced graphics and communications.

expert systems: Knowledge-intensive computer programs that capture the expertise of a human in limited domains of knowledge.

Extensible Markup Language (XML): A more powerful and flexible markup language than hypertext markup language (HTML) for web pages, allowing data to be manipulated by the computer.

extranets: Private intranets that are accessible to authorized outsiders.

Fair Information Practices (FIP): A set of principles originally set forth in 1973 that governs the collection and use of information about individuals and forms the basis of most U.S. and European privacy laws.

fault-tolerant computer systems: Systems that contain extra hardware, software, and power supply components that can back a system up and keep it running to prevent system failure.

feasibility study: As part of the systems analysis process, the way to determine whether the solution is achievable, given the organization's resources and constraints.

feedback: Output that is returned to the appropriate members of the organization to help them evaluate or correct input.

fiber-optic cable: A fast, light, and durable transmission medium consisting of thin strands of clear glass fiber bound into cables. Data are transmitted as light pulses.

field: A grouping of characters into a word, a group of words, or a complete number, such as a person's name or age.

file transfer protocol (FTP): Tool for retrieving and transferring files from a remote computer.

firewalls: Hardware and software placed between an organization's internal network and an external network to prevent outsiders from invading private networks.

foreign key: Field in a database table that enables users to find related information in another database table.

formal planning and control tools: Tools to improve project management by listing the specific activities that make up a project, their duration, and the sequence and timing of tasks.

franchiser: Form of business organization in which a product is created, designed, financed, and initially produced in the home country, but for product-specific reasons relies heavily on foreign personnel for further production, marketing, and human resources.

free/freemium revenue model: E-commerce revenue mode in which a firm offers free basic services or content while charging a premium for advanced or high-value features.

fuzzy logic: Rule-based AI that tolerates imprecision by using nonspecific terms called membership functions to solve problems.

Gantt chart: Chart that visually represents the timing, duration, and human resource requirements of project tasks, with each task represented as a horizontal bar whose length is proportional to the time required to complete it.

general controls: Overall control environment governing the design, security, and use of computer programs and the security of data files in general throughout the organization's information technology infrastructure.

genetic algorithms: Problem-solving methods that promote the evolution of solutions to specified problems using the model of living organisms adapting to their environment.

geoadvertising services: Delivering ads to users based on their GPS location.

geographic information systems (GIS): Systems with software that can analyze and display data using digitized maps to enhance planning and decision-making.

geoinformation services: Information on local places and things based on the GPS position of the user.

geosocial services: Social networking based on the GPS location of users.

gigabyte: Approximately one billion bytes.

Google Apps: Google's cloud-based productivity suite for businesses.

Golden Rule: Putting oneself in the place of others as the object of a decision.

Gramm-Leach-Bliley Act: Requires financial institutions to ensure the security and confidentiality of customer data.

graphical user interface (GUI): The part of an operating system users interact with that uses graphic icons and the computer mouse to issue commands and make selections.

green computing: Practices and technologies for producing, using, and disposing of computers and associated devices to minimize impact on the environment.

grid computing: Applying the resources of many computers in a network to a single problem.

group decision-support system (GDSS): An interactive computer-based system to facilitate the solution to unstructured problems by a set of decision makers working together as a group.

hacker: A person who gains unauthorized access to a computer network for profit, criminal mischief, or personal pleasure.

Hadoop: Open-source software framework that enables distributed parallel processing of huge amounts of data across many inexpensive computers.

hertz: Measure of frequency of electrical impulses per second, with 1 hertz (Hz) equivalent to 1 cycle per second.

HIPAA: Law outlining medical security and privacy rules and procedures for simplifying the administration of health care billing and automating the transfer of health care data between health care providers, payers, and plans.

home page: A World Wide Web text and graphical screen display that welcomes the user and explains the organization that has established the page.

hotspots: Specific geographic locations in which an access point provides public Wi-Fi network service.

HTML5: Next evolution of HTML, which will make it possible to embed images, video, and audio directly into a document without using add-on software.

hubs: Very simple devices that connect network components, sending a packet of data to all other connected devices.

hybrid cloud: Computing model by which firms use both their own IT infrastructure and public cloud computing services.

Hypertext Markup Language (HTML): Page description language for creating web pages and other hypermedia documents.

Hypertext Transport Protocol (HTTP): The communications standard that transfers pages on the web. Defines how messages are formatted and transmitted.

identity management: Business processes and software tools for identifying the valid users of a system and controlling their access to system resources.

identity theft: Theft of key pieces of personal information, such as credit card or Social Security numbers, to obtain merchandise and services in the name of the victim or to obtain false credentials.

Immanuel Kant's categorical imperative: A principle that states that if an action is not right for everyone to take, it is not right for anyone.

implementation: All the organizational activities surrounding the adoption, management, and regular reuse of an innovation, such as a new information system.

implementation: Simon's final stage of decision-making, when the individual puts the decision into effect and reports on the progress of the solution.

inference engine: The strategy used to search through the rule base in an expert system; can be forward or backward chaining.

information appliance: Device that has been customized to perform a few specialized computing tasks well with minimal user effort.

information asymmetry: Situation when the relative bargaining power of two parties in a transaction is determined by one party in the transaction possessing more information essential to the transaction than the other party.

information density: The total amount and quality of information available to all market participants, consumers, and merchants.

information policy: Formal rules governing the maintenance, distribution, and use of information in an organization.

information requirements: A detailed statement of the information needs that a new system must satisfy; identifies who needs what information and when, where, and how the information is needed.

information rights: The rights that individuals and organizations have with respect to information that pertains to them.

information system: Interrelated components working together to collect, process, store, and disseminate information to support decision making, coordination, control, analysis, and visualization in an organization.

Information systems audit: Identifies all the controls that govern individual information systems and assesses their effectiveness.

information systems department: The formal organizational unit that is responsible for the information systems function in the organization.

information systems literacy: Broad-based understanding of information systems that includes behavioral knowledge about organizations and individuals by using information systems as well as technical knowledge about computers.

information systems managers: Leaders of the various specialists in the information systems department.

information systems plan: A road map indicating the direction of systems development: the rationale, the current situation, the management strategy, the implementation plan, and the budget.

information technology (IT): All the hardware and software technologies that a firm needs to use to achieve its business objectives.

information technology (IT) infrastructure: Computer hardware, software, data, storage technology, and networks providing a portfolio of shared IT resources for the organization.

information: Data that have been shaped into a form that is meaningful and useful to human beings.

informed consent: Consent given with knowledge of all the facts needed to make a rational decision.

in-memory computing: Technology for very rapid analysis and processing of large quantities of data by storing the data in the computer's main memory rather than in secondary storage.

input devices: Device that gathers data and converts them into electronic form for use by the computer.

input: The capture or collection of raw data from within the organization or from its external environment for processing in an information system.

instant messaging: Chat service that allows participants to create their own private chat channels so that a person can be alerted whenever someone on his or her private list is online to initiate a chat session with that particular individual.

intangible benefits: Benefits that are not easily quantified; they include more efficient customer service or enhanced decision making.

intellectual property: Intangible property created by individuals or corporations that is subject to protections under trade secret, copyright, and patent law.

intelligence: The first of Simon's four stages of decision making, when the individual collects information to identify problems occurring in the organization.

intelligent agents: Software programs that use a built-in or learned knowledge base to carry out specific, repetitive, and predictable tasks for an individual user, business process, or software application.

intelligent techniques: Technologies that aid decision makers by capturing individual and collective knowledge, discovering patterns and behaviors in very large quantities of data, and generating solutions to problems that are too large and complex for human beings to solve on their own.

Internet Protocol (IP) address: Four-part numeric address indicating a unique computer location on the Internet.

Internet service provider (ISP): A commercial organization with a permanent connection to the Internet that sells temporary connections to subscribers.

Internet telephony: Technologies that use the Internet Protocol's packet-switched connections for voice service.

Internet: Global network of networks using universal standards to connect millions of networks.

Internet2: Research network with new protocols and transmission speeds that provides an infrastructure for supporting high-bandwidth Internet applications.

Internet of Things: Pervasive web in which each object or machine has a unique identity and is able to use the Internet to link with other machines or send data; also known as the industrial Internet.

internetworking: The linking of separate networks, each of which retains its own identity, into an interconnected network.

interorganizational system: Information systems that automate the flow of information across organizational boundaries and link a company to its customers, distributors, or suppliers.

intranets: Internal networks based on Internet and World Wide Web technology and standards.

intrusion detection systems: Tools to monitor the most vulnerable points in a network to detect and deter unauthorized intruders.

investment workstations: Powerful desktop computers for financial specialists; optimized to access and manipulate massive amounts of financial data.

iOS: Operating system for the Apple iPad, iPhone, and iPod Touch.

IPv6: New IP addressing system using 128-bit IP addresses. Stands for Internet Protocol version 6.

IT governance: Strategy and policies for using information technology within an organization, specifying the decision rights and accountabilities to ensure that information technology supports the organization's strategies and objectives.

Java: An operating system–independent, processor-independent, object-oriented programming language that has become a leading interactive programming environment for the web.

Joint application design (JAD): Process to accelerate the generation of information requirements by having end users and information systems specialists work together in intensive interactive design sessions.

just-in-time strategy: Scheduling system for minimizing inventory by having components arrive exactly at the moment they are needed and finished goods shipped as soon as they leave the assembly line.

key field: A field in a record that uniquely identifies instances of that record so that it can be retrieved, updated, or sorted.

key loggers: Spyware that records every keystroke made on a computer.

key performance indicators (KPIs): Measures proposed by senior management for understanding how well the firm is performing along specified dimensions.

knowledge base: Model of human knowledge that expert systems use.

knowledge management systems (KMS): Systems that support the creation, capture, storage, and dissemination of firm expertise and knowledge.

knowledge management: The set of processes developed in an organization to create, gather, store, maintain, and disseminate the firm's knowledge.

knowledge work systems (KWS): Information systems that aid knowledge workers in the creation and integration of new knowledge in the organization.

knowledge workers: People such as engineers or architects who design products or services and create knowledge for the organization.

learning management system (LMS): Tools for the management, delivery, tracking, and assessment of various types of employee learning.

legacy systems: Systems that have been in existence for a long time and that continue to be used to avoid the high cost of replacing or redesigning them.

liability: Laws that permit individuals to recover the damages done to them by other actors, systems, or organizations.

Linux: Reliable and compactly designed operating system that is an open-source offshoot of UNIX, can run on many hardware platforms, and is available free or at very low cost.

local area network (LAN): A telecommunications network that requires its own dedicated channels and that encompasses a limited distance, usually one building or several buildings in close proximity.

location-based services: GPS map services available on smartphones.

location analytics: Ability to gain insight from the location (geographic) component of data, including location data from mobile phones, output from sensors or scanning devices, and data from maps.

long tail marketing: Ability of firms to market goods profitably to very small online audiences, largely because of the lower costs of reaching very small market segments.

magnetic disk: A secondary storage medium in which data are stored by means of magnetized spots on a hard or floppy disk.

magnetic tape: Inexpensive, older secondary-storage medium in which large volumes of information are stored sequentially by means of magnetized and nonmagnetized spots on tape.

mainframe: Largest category of computer, used for major business processing.

maintenance: Changes in hardware, software, documentation, or procedures to a production system to correct errors, meet new requirements, or improve processing efficiency.

malware: Malicious software programs such as computer viruses, worms, and Trojan horses.

managed security service providers (MSSPs): Companies that provide security management services for subscribing clients.

management information systems (MIS): Specific category of information system providing reports on organizational performance to help middle management monitor and control the business.

management information systems (MIS): The study of information systems, focusing on their use in business and management.

market creator: E-commerce business model in which firms provide a digital online environment where buyers and sellers can meet, search for products, and engage in transactions.

market entry costs: The cost merchants must pay simply to bring their goods to market.

marketspace: A marketplace extended beyond traditional boundaries and removed from a temporal and geographic location.

mashups: Composite software applications that depend on high-speed networks, universal communication standards, and open source code and are intended to be greater than the sum of their parts.

mass customization: The capacity to offer individually tailored products or services on a large scale.

massive open online course (MOOC): Online course made available on the web to very large numbers of participants.

menu prices: Merchants' costs of changing prices.

metropolitan area network (MAN): Network that spans a metropolitan area, usually a city and its major suburbs. Its geographic scope falls between a WAN and a LAN.

microblogging: Blogging featuring very short posts such as those using Twitter.

microbrowser: Web browser software with a small file size that can work with low-memory constraints, tiny screens of handheld wireless devices, and low bandwidth of wireless networks.

micropayment systems: Systems that facilitate payment for a very small sum of money, often less than $10.

microprocessor: Very large-scale, integrated circuit technology that integrates the computer's memory, logic, and control on a single chip.

Microsoft Office 365: Hosted cloud version of Office productivity and collaboration tools as a subscription service.

microwave: A high-volume, long-distance, point-to-point transmission in which high-frequency radio signals are transmitted through the atmosphere from one terrestrial transmission station to another.

middle management: People in the middle of the organizational hierarchy who are responsible for carrying out the plans and goals of senior management.

middleware: Software that connects two disparate applications, allowing them to communicate with each other and to exchange data.

midrange computers: Middle-size computers that are capable of supporting the computing needs of smaller organizations or of managing networks of other computers.

minicomputers: iddle-range computers used in systems for universities, factories, or research laboratories.

mobile commerce (m-commerce): The use of wireless devices, such as cell phones or handheld digital information appliances, to conduct both business-to-consumer and business-to-business e-commerce transactions over the Internet.

mobile device management: Software that monitors, manages, and secures mobile devices the organization is using.

mobile web app: Application residing on a server and accessed through the mobile web browser built into a smartphone or tablet computer.

mobile website: Version of a regular website that is scaled down in content and navigation for easy access and search on a small mobile screen.

model: An abstract representation that illustrates the components or relationships of a phenomenon.

modem: A device for translating a computer's digital signals into analog form or for translating analog signals back into digital form for reception by a computer.

mouse: Handheld input device with point-and-click capabilities that is connected to the computer by either a a cable or a direct USB port.

MP3 (MPEG3): Standard for compressing audio files for transfer over the Internet.

multicore processor: Integrated circuit to which two or more processors have been attached for enhanced performance, reduced power consumption and more efficient simultaneous processing of multiple tasks.

multinational: Form of business organization that concentrates financial management and control out of a central home base while decentralizing production, sales, and marketing.

multitouch: Interface that features the use of one or more finger gestures to manipulate lists or objects on a screen without using a mouse or keyboard.

nanotechnology: Technology that builds structures and processes based on the manipulation of individual atoms and molecules.

native app: Stand-alone application specifically designed to run on a mobile platform.

natural languages: Nonprocedural languages that enable users to communicate with the computer by using conversational commands resembling human speech.

net marketplaces: Digital marketplaces based on Internet technology linking many buyers to many sellers.

netbook: Small, low-cost, lightweight subnotebooks optimized for wireless communication and Internet access.

network address translation (NAT): Conceals the IP addresses of the organization's internal host computer(s) to prevent sniffer programs outside the firewall from ascertaining them and using that information to penetrate internal systems.

network economics: Model of strategic systems at the industry level based on the concept of a network when adding another participant entails zero marginal costs but can create much larger marginal gains.

network operating system (NOS): Special software that routes and manages communications on the network and coordinates network resources.

network: The linking of two or more computers to share data or resources such as a printer.

networking and telecommunications technology: Physical devices and software that link various pieces of hardware and transfer data from one physical location to another.

neural networks: Hardware or software that attempts to emulate the processing patterns of the biological brain.

nonobvious relationship awareness (NORA): Technology that can find obscure connections between people or other entities by analyzing information from many sources to correlate relationships.

nonrelational database management system: Database management system for working with large quantities of structured and unstructured data that would be difficult to analyze with a relational model.

normalization: The process of creating small, stable data structures from complex groups of data when designing a relational database.

n-tier client/server architecture: Client/server arrangement that balances the work of the entire network over multiple levels of servers.

object: Software building block that combines data and the procedures acting on the data.

object-oriented development: Approach to systems development that uses the object as the basic unit of systems analysis and design. The system is modeled as a collection of objects and the relationship between them.

offshore software outsourcing: Outsourcing systems development work or maintenance of existing systems to external vendors in another country.

on-demand computing: Firms off-loading peak demand for computing power to remote, large-scale data processing centers, investing just enough to handle average processing loads and paying for only as much additional computing power as they need. Also called utility computing.

online analytical processing (OLAP): Capability for manipulating and analyzing large volumes of data from multiple perspectives.

online transaction processing: Transaction processing mode in which transactions entered online are immediately processed by the computer.

open source software: Software that provides free access to its program code, allowing users to modify the program code to make improvements or fix errors.

operating system: The system software that manages and controls the activities of the computer.

operational CRM: Customer-facing applications, such as sales force automation, call center and customer service support, and marketing automation.

operational intelligence: Business analytics that deliver insight into data, streaming events, and business operations.

operational management: People who monitor the day-to-day activities of the organization.

opt-in: Model of informed consent permitting prohibiting an organization from collecting any personal information unless the individual specifically takes action to approve information collection and use.

opt-out: Model of informed consent permitting the collection of personal information until the consumer specifically requests the data not to be collected.

organizational impact analysis: Study of the way a proposed system will affect organizational structure, attitudes, decision making, and operations.

output device: Device that displays data after they have been processed.

output: The distribution of processed information to the people who will use it or to the activities for which it will be used.

outsourcing: The practice of contracting computer center operations, telecommunications networks, or applications development to external vendors.

packet filtering: Examines selected fields in the headers of data packets flowing back and forth between the trusted network and the Internet.

packet switching: Technology that breaks messages into small, fixed bundles of data and routes them in the most economical way through any available communications channel.

parallel processing: Type of processing in which more than one instruction can be processed at a time by breaking down a problem into smaller parts and processing them simultaneously with multiple processors.

parallel strategy: A safe and conservative conversion approach in which both the old system and its potential replacement are run together for a time until everyone is assured that the new one functions correctly.

partner relationship management (PRM): Automation of the firm's relationships with its selling partners using customer data and analytical tools to improve coordination and customer sales.

password: Secret word or string of characters for authenticating users so they can access a resource such as a computer system.

patches: Small pieces of software that repair flaws in programs without disturbing the proper operation of the software.

patent: A legal document that grants the owner an exclusive monopoly on the ideas behind an invention for 17 years; designed to ensure that inventors of new machines or methods are rewarded for their labor while making available widespread use of their inventions.

peer-to-peer: Network architecture that gives equal power to all computers on the network; used primarily in small networks.

people perspective: Consideration of the firm's management, as well as employees, as individuals and their interrelationships in workgroups.

personal computer (PC): Small desktop or portable computer.

personal-area networks (PANs): Computer networks used for communication among digital devices (including telephones and PDAs) that are close to one person.

personalization: Ability of merchants to target their marketing messages to specific individuals by adjusting the message to a person's name, interests, and past purchases.

PERT chart: A chart that graphically depicts project tasks and their interrelationships, showing the specific activities that must be completed before others can start.

pharming: Phishing technique that redirects users to a bogus web page, even when the individual types the correct web page address into his or her browser.

phased approach: Introduces the new system in stages either by functions or by organizational units.

phishing: A form of spoofing involving setting up fake websites or sending email messages that look like those of legitimate businesses to ask users for confidential personal data.

pilot study: A strategy to introduce the new system to a limited area of the organization until it proves to be fully functional; only then can the conversion to the new system across the entire organization take place.

pivot table: Spreadsheet tool for reorganizing and summarizing two or more dimensions of data in a tabular format.

podcasting: Method of publishing audio broadcasts through the Internet, allowing subscribing users to download audio files to their personal computers, smartphones, or portable music players.

pop-up ads: Ads that open automatically and do not disappear until the user clicks them.

portal: Web interface for presenting integrated personalized content from a variety of sources. Also refers to a website service that provides an initial point of entry to the web.

portfolio analysis: An analysis of the portfolio of potential applications within a firm to determine the risks and benefits and to select among alternatives for information systems.

predictive analytics: Use of data mining techniques, historical data, and assumptions about future conditions to predict outcomes of events.

predictive search: Part of a search algorithm that predicts what a user query is looking for as it is entered, based on popular searches.

presentation graphics: Software to create professional-quality graphics presentations that can incorporate charts, sound, animation, photos, and video clips.

price discrimination: Selling the same goods, or nearly the same goods, to different targeted groups at different prices.

price transparency: The ease with which consumers can find out the variety of prices in a market.

primary activities: Activities most directly related to the production and distribution of a firm's products or services.

primary key: Unique identifier for all the information in any row of a database table.

privacy: The claim of individuals to be left alone, free from surveillance or interference from other individuals, organizations, or the state.

private cloud: Proprietary network or data center that ties together servers, storage, networks, data, and applications as a set of virtualized services that users inside a company share.

private exchange: Another term for a private industrial network.

private industrial networks: Web-enabled networks linking systems of multiple firms in an industry for the coordination of trans-organizational business processes.

process specifications: Specifications that describe the logic of the processes occurring within the lowest levels of a data flow diagram.

processing: The conversion, manipulation, and analysis of raw input into a form that is more meaningful to humans.

procurement: Sourcing goods and materials, negotiating with suppliers, paying for goods, and making delivery arrangements.

product differentiation: Competitive strategy for creating brand loyalty by developing new and unique products and services that are not easily duplicated by competitors.

production or service workers: People who actually produce the products or services of the organization.

production: The stage after the new system is installed and the conversion is complete; during this time, the system is reviewed by users and technical specialists to determine how well it has met its original goals.

profiling: The use of computers to combine data from multiple sources and create electronic dossiers of detailed information on individuals.

program: Series of instructions for the computer.

programmers: Highly trained technical specialists who write computer software instructions.

programming: The process of translating the system specifications prepared during the design stage into program code.

project management: Application of knowledge, skills, tools, and techniques to achieve specific targets within specified budget and time constraints.

project portfolio management software: Software that helps organizations evaluate and manage portfolios of projects and dependencies among them.

project: A planned series of related activities for achieving a specific business objective.

protocol: A set of rules and procedures that govern transmission between the components in a network.

prototyping: The process of building an experimental system quickly and inexpensively for demonstration and evaluation so that users can better determine information requirements.

Public cloud: Cloud maintained by an external service provider, accessed through the Internet, and available to the general public.

public key encryption: Encryption using two keys: one shared (or public) and one private.

public key infrastructure (PKI): System for creating public and private keys by using a certificate authority (CA) and digital certificates for authentication.

pull-based model: Supply chain driven by actual customer orders or purchases so that members of the supply chain produce and deliver only what customers have ordered.

pure-play: Business models based purely on the Internet.

push-based model: Supply chain driven by master production schedules based on forecasts or best guesses of demand for products; products are pushed to customers.

quality: Product or service's conformance to specifications and standards.

quantum computing: Use of principles of quantum physics to represent data and perform operations on the data, with the ability to be in many states at once and to perform many computations simultaneously.

query languages: Software tools that provide immediate online answers to requests for information that are not predefined.

radio frequency identification (RFID): Technology using tiny tags with embedded microchips containing data about an item and its location to transmit short-distance radio signals to special RFID readers that then pass the data on to a computer for processing.

ransomware: malware that extorts money from users by taking control of their computers or displaying annoying pop-up messages

Rapid application development (RAD): Process for developing systems in a very short time period by using prototyping, user-friendly tools, and close teamwork among users and systems specialists.

rationalization of procedures: The streamlining of standard operating procedures, eliminating obvious bottlenecks, so that automation makes operating procedures more efficient.

reach: Measurement of how many people a business can connect with and how many products it can offer those people.

records: Groups of related fields.

referential integrity: Rules to ensure that relationships between coupled database tables remain consistent.

relational database: A type of logical database model that treats data as if they were stored in two-dimensional tables. It can relate data stored in one table to data in another as long as the two tables share a common data element.

repetitive stress injury (RSI): Occupational disease that occurs when muscle groups are forced through repetitive actions with high-impact loads or thousands of repetitions with low-impact loads.

Request for Proposal (RFP): A detailed list of questions submitted to vendors of software or other services to determine how well the vendor's product can meet the organization's specific requirements.

responsibility: Accepting the potential costs, duties, and obligations for the decisions one makes.

responsive web design: Ability of a website to change screen resolution and image size automatically as a user switches to devices of different sizes, such as a laptop, tablet computer, or smartphone. Eliminates the need for separate design and development work for each new device.

revenue model: Description of how a firm will earn revenue, generate profits, and produce a return on investment.

richness: Measurement of the depth and detail of information that a business can supply to the customer as well as information the business collects about the customer.

ringtones: Digitized snippets of music that play on mobile phones when a user receives or places a call.

risk assessment: Determining the potential frequency of the occurrence of a problem and the potential damage if the problem were to occur. Used to determine the cost/benefit of a control.

risk aversion principle: Principle that one should take the action that produces the least harm or incurs the least cost.

router: Specialized communications processor that forwards packets of data from one network to another network.

RSS: Technology using aggregator software to pull content from websites and feed it automatically to subscribers' computers.

SaaS (software as a service): Services for delivering and providing access to software remotely as a web-based service.

safe harbor: Private, self-regulating policy and enforcement mechanism that meets the objectives of government regulations but does not involve government regulation or enforcement.

sales revenue model: Selling goods, information, or services to customers as the main source of revenue for a company.

Sarbanes-Oxley Act: Law passed in 2002 that imposes responsibility on companies and their management to protect investors by safeguarding the accuracy and integrity of financial information that is used internally and released externally.

satellites: Machines that orbit the earth and serve as relay stations for transmitting microwave signals over very long distances.

scalability: The ability of a computer, product, or system to expand to serve a larger number of users without breaking down.

Scope: Defines what work is or is not included in a project.

scoring model: A quick method for deciding among alternative systems based on a system of ratings for selected objectives.

search costs: The time and money spent locating a suitable product and determining the best price for that product.

search engine marketing: Use of search engines to deliver sponsored links, for which advertisers have paid, in search engine results.

Search engine optimization (SEO): Process of changing a website's content, layout, and format to increase the site's ranking on popular search engines and to generate more site visitors.

search engines: Tools for locating specific sites or information on the Internet.

secondary storage: Relatively long-term, nonvolatile storage of data outside the CPU and primary storage.

Secure Hypertext Transfer Protocol (S-HTTP): Protocol used for encrypting data flowing over the Internet; limited to individual messages.

Secure Sockets Layer (SSL): Enables client and server computers to manage encryption and decryption activities as they communicate with each other during a secure web session.

security policy: Statements ranking information risks, identifying acceptable security goals, and identifying the mechanisms for achieving these goals.

security: Policies, procedures, and technical measures used to prevent unauthorized access, alteration, theft, or physical damage to information systems.

semantic search: Search technology capable of understanding human language and behavior.

semantic web: Ways of making the web more intelligent, with machine-facilitated understanding of information so that searches can be more intuitive and effective; executed using intelligent software agents.

semistructured decisions: Decisions in which only part of the problem has a clear-cut answer provided by an accepted procedure.

semistructured knowledge: Information in the form of less structured objects such as email, chat room exchanges, videos, graphics, brochures, or bulletin boards.

senior management: People occupying the topmost hierarchy, who are responsible for making long-range decisions, in an organization.

sensitivity analysis: Models that ask what-if questions repeatedly to determine the impact of changes in one or more factors on the outcomes.

sensors: Devices that collect data directly from the environment for input in a computer system.

sentiment analysis: Mining text comments in an email message, blog, or other social media.

server: Computer specifically optimized to provide software and other resources to other computers over a network.

service-level agreement (SLA): Formal contract between customers and their service providers that defines the specific responsibilities of the service provider and the level of service the customer expects.

service-oriented architecture (SOA): Software architecture of a firm built on a collection of software programs that communicate with each other to perform assigned tasks to create a working software application.

shopping bots: Software with varying levels of built-in intelligence to help electronic commerce shoppers locate and evaluate products or service they might wish to purchase.

six sigma: A specific measure of quality, representing 3.4 defects per million opportunities; used to designate a set of methodologies and techniques for improving quality and reducing costs.

smart card: A credit-card-size plastic card that stores digital information and can be used for electronic payments in place of cash.

smartphones: Wireless phones with voice, messaging, scheduling, email, and Internet capabilities.

sniffer: A type of eavesdropping program that monitors information traveling over a network.

social business: Use of social networking platforms, including Facebook, Twitter, and internal corporate social tools, to engage employees, customers, and suppliers.

social CRM: Tools enabling a business to link customer conversations, data, and relationships from social networking sites to CRM processes.

social engineering: Tricking people into revealing their passwords by pretending to be legitimate users or members of a company in need of information.

social graph: Map of all significant online social relationships, comparable to a social network describing offline relationships.

social networking: Online community for expanding users' business or social contacts through their mutual business or personal connections.

social search: Effort to provide more relevant and trustworthy search results based on a person's network of social contacts.

social shopping: Use of websites featuring user-created web pages to share knowledge about items of interest to other shoppers.

software localization: Process of converting software to operate in a second language.

software package: A prewritten, precoded, commercially available set of programs that eliminates the need to write software programs for certain functions.

software-defined networking (SDN): Using a central control program separate from network devices to manage the flow of data on a network.

solid state drive (SSD): Storage device that stores data on an array of semiconductor memory organized as a disk drive.

spam: Unsolicited commercial email.

spamming: A form of abuse in which thousands and even hundreds of thousands of unsolicited email and electronic messages are sent out, creating a nuisance for both businesses and individual users.

spoofing: Tricking or deceiving computer systems or other computer users by hiding one's identity or faking the identity of another user on the Internet.

spreadsheet: Software displaying data in a grid of columns and rows, with the capability of easily recalculating numerical data.

spyware: Technology that aids in gathering information about a person or organization without their knowledge.

SQL injection attack: Attack against a website that takes advantage of vulnerabilities in poorly coded SQL applications to introduce malicious program code into a company's systems and networks.

stateful inspection: Provides additional security by determining whether packets are part of an ongoing dialogue between a sender and a receiver.

storage area networks (SAN): High-speed networks dedicated to storage that connect different kinds of storage devices, such as tape libraries and disk arrays, so multiple servers can share them.

strategic information system: Information system that changes the goals, operations, products, services, or environmental relationships of an organization to help gain a competitive advantage.

structure chart: System documentation showing each level of design, the relationship among the levels, and the overall place in the design structure; can document one program, one system, or part of one program.

structured decisions: Decisions that are repetitive, routine, and have a definite procedure for handling them.

structured knowledge: Knowledge in the form of structured documents and reports.

Structured Query Language (SQL): The standard data manipulation language for relational database management systems.

structured: Refers to the fact that techniques are carefully drawn up, step by step, with each step building on a previous one.

subscription revenue model: Website charging a subscription fee for access to some or all of its content or services on an ongoing basis.

supercomputer: Highly sophisticated and powerful computer that can perform very complex computations extremely rapidly.

supply chain execution systems: Systems to manage the flow of products through distribution centers and warehouses to ensure that products are delivered to the right locations in the most efficient manner.

supply chain management (SCM) systems: Information systems that automate the flow of information between a firm and its suppliers to optimize the planning, sourcing, manufacturing, and delivery of products and services.

supply chain planning systems: Systems that enable a firm to generate demand forecasts for a product and develop sourcing and manufacturing plans for that product.

supply chain: Network of organizations and business processes for procuring materials, transforming raw materials into intermediate and finished products, and distributing the finished products to customers.

support activities: Activities that make the delivery of a firm's primary activities possible; consist of the organization's infrastructure, human resources, technology, and procurement.

switch: Device to connect network components that has more intelligence than a hub and can filter and forward data to a specified destination.

switching costs: The expense a customer or company incurs in lost time and expenditure of resources when changing from one supplier or system to a competing supplier or system.

system software: Generalized programs that manage the computer's resources, such as the central processor, communications links, and peripheral devices.

system testing: Tests the functioning of the information system as a whole to determine whether discrete modules will function together as planned.

systems analysis: The analysis of a problem that the organization will try to solve with an information system.

systems analysts: Specialists who translate business problems and requirements into information requirements and systems, acting as liaison between the information systems department and the rest of the organization.

systems design: Details how a system will meet the information requirements as determined by the systems analysis.

systems development life cycle (SDLC): A traditional methodology for developing an information system that partitions the systems development process into formal stages that must be completed sequentially with a very formal division of labor between end users and information systems specialists.

systems development: The activities that go into producing an information systems solution to an organizational problem or opportunity.

systems integration: Ensuring that a new infrastructure works with a firm's older systems and that the new elements of the infrastructure work with one another.

T lines: High-speed data lines leased from communications providers, such as T-1 lines (with a transmission capacity of 1.544 Mbps).

tablet computer: Mobile handheld computer that is larger than a mobile phone and operated primarily by touching a flat screen

tacit knowledge: Expertise and experience of organizational members that has not been formally documented.

tangible benefits: Benefits that can be quantified and assigned a monetary value; they include lower operational costs and increased cash flows.

taxonomy: Method of classifying things according to a predetermined system.

teams: Formal groups whose members collaborate to achieve specific goals.

technostress: Stress induced by computer use; symptoms include aggravation, hostility toward humans, impatience, and enervation.

telepresence: Technology that allows a person to give the appearance of being present at a location other than his or her true physical location.

terabyte: Approximately one trillion bytes.

test plan: Plan prepared by the development team in conjunction with the users; it includes all the preparations for the series of tests to be performed on the system.

testing: The exhaustive and thorough process that determines whether the system produces the desired results under known conditions.

text mining: Discovery of patterns and relationships from large sets of unstructured data.

token: Physical device, similar to an identification card, that is designed to prove the identity of a single user.

Total cost of ownership (TCO): Designates the total cost of owning technology resources, including initial purchase costs, the cost of hardware and software upgrades, maintenance, technical support, and training.

Total quality management (TQM): A concept that makes quality control a responsibility to be shared by all people in an organization.

touch point: Method of firm interaction with a customer, such as telephone, email, customer service desk, conventional mail, or point of purchase.

touch screen: Device that allows users to enter limited amounts of data by touching the surface of a sensitized video display monitor with a finger or a pointer.

trade secret: Any intellectual work or product used for a business purpose that can be classified as belonging to that business, provided it is not based on information in the public domain.

transaction fee revenue model: E-commerce revenue model in which the firm receives a fee for enabling or executing transactions.

transaction processing systems (TPS): Computerized systems that perform and record the daily routine transactions necessary to conduct the business; they serve the organization's operational level.

Transmission Control Protocol/Internet Protocol (TCP/IP): Dominant model for achieving connectivity among different networks. Provides a universally agreed-on method for breaking up digital messages into packets, routing them to the proper addresses, and then reassembling them into coherent messages.

transnational: Truly global form of business organization where value-added activities are managed from a global perspective without reference to national borders, optimizing sources of supply and demand and local competitive advantage.

Trojan horse: A software program that appears legitimate but contains a second hidden function that may cause damage.

tuples: Rows or records in a relational database.

twisted wire: A transmission medium consisting of pairs of twisted copper wires; used to transmit analog phone conversations but can be used for data transmission.

two-factor authentication: Validating user identity with two means of identification, one of which is typically a physical token, and the other of which is typically data.

unified communications: Integrates disparate channels for voice communications, data communications, instant messaging, email, and electronic conferencing into a single experience by which users can seamlessly switch back and forth between different communication modes.

unified threat management (UTM): Comprehensive security management tool that combines multiple security tools, including firewalls, virtual private networks, intrusion detection systems, and web content filtering and anti-spam software.

Uniform Resource Locator (URL): The address of a specific resource on the Internet.

unit testing: The process of testing each program separately in the system; sometimes called program testing.

UNIX: Operating system for all types of computers, which is machine independent and supports multiuser processing, multitasking, and networking; used in high-end workstations and servers.

unstructured decisions: Nonroutine decisions in which the decision maker must provide judgment, evaluation, and insights in the problem definition; there is no agreed-upon procedure for making such decisions.

up-selling: Marketing higher-value products or services to new or existing customers.

user interface: The part of the information system through which the end user interacts with the system; type of hardware and the series of on-screen commands and responses required for a user to work with the system.

user–designer communications gap: The difference in backgrounds, interests, and priorities that impede communication and problem solving among end users and information systems specialists.

utilitarian principle: Principle that assumes one can put values in rank order and understand the consequences of various courses of action.

value chain model: Model that highlights the primary or support activities that add a margin of value to a firm's products or services where information systems can best be applied to achieve a competitive advantage.

value web: Customer-driven network of independent firms who use information technology to coordinate their value chains to produce a product or service collectively for a market.

virtual company: A company that uses networks to link people, assets, and ideas, enabling it to ally with other companies to create and distribute products and services without being limited by traditional organizational boundaries or physical locations.

virtual private network (VPN): A secure connection between two points across the Internet to transmit corporate data. Provides a low-cost alternative to a private network.

Virtual Reality Modeling Language (VRML): A set of specifications for interactive three-dimensional modeling on the World Wide Web.

virtual reality systems: Interactive graphics software and hardware that create computer-generated simulations that provide sensations that emulate real-world activities.

virtual world: Computer-based simulated environment intended for its users to inhabit and interact through graphical representations called avatars.

virtualization: Presenting a set of computing resources so that they can all be accessed in ways that are not restricted by physical configuration or geographic location.

visual programming language: Allows users to manipulate graphic or iconic elements to create programs.

visual web: Refers to web linking visual sites such as Pinterest where pictures replace text documents and where users search on pictures and visual characteristics.

Voice over IP (VoIP): Facilities for managing the delivery of voice information using the Internet Protocol (IP).

war driving: An eavesdropping technique in which eavesdroppers drive by buildings or park outside and try to intercept wireless network traffic.

wearable computer: Small wearable computing device such as a smartwatch, smartglasses, or activity tracker.

Web 2.0: Second-generation, interactive Internet-based services that enable people to collaborate, share information, and create new services online, including mashups, blogs, RSS, and wikis.

Web 3.0: Future vision of the web when all digital information is woven together with intelligent search capabilities.

web beacons: Tiny objects invisibly embedded in email messages and web pages that are designed to monitor the behavior of the user visiting a website or sending email.

web browsers: Easy-to-use software tool for accessing the World Wide Web and the Internet.

web hosting service: Company with large web server computers to maintain the websites of fee-paying subscribers.

Web mining: Discovery and analysis of useful patterns and information from the World Wide Web.

web server: Software that manages requests for web pages on the computer where they are stored and delivers the page to the user's computer.

web services: Set of universal standards using Internet technology for integrating different applications from different sources without time-consuming custom coding. Used for linking systems of different organizations or for linking disparate systems within the same organization.

website: All of the World Wide Web pages maintained by an organization or an individual.

wide area networks (WANs): Telecommunications networks that span a large geographical distance. May consist of a variety of cable, satellite, and microwave technologies.

Wi-Fi: Standards for wireless fidelity and refers to the 802.11 family of wireless networking standards.

wiki: Collaborative website where visitors can add, delete, or modify content on the site, including the work of previous authors.

WiMax: Popular term for IEEE Standard 802.16 for wireless networking over a range of up to 31 miles with a data transfer rate of up to 75 Mbps. Stands for Worldwide

Interoperability for Microwave Access.

Windows 10: Most recent Microsoft client operating system.

wireless sensor networks (WSNs): Networks of interconnected wireless devices with built-in processing, storage, and radio frequency sensors and antennas that are embedded in the physical environment to provide measurements of many points over large spaces.

wisdom of crowds: Belief that large numbers of people can make better decisions about a wide range of topics and products than a single person or even a small committee of experts.

word processing software: Software for electronically creating, editing, formatting, and printing documents.

workflow management: The process of streamlining business procedures so that documents can be moved easily and efficiently from one location to another.

workstation: Desktop computer with powerful graphics and mathematical capabilities and the ability to perform several complicated tasks at once.

World Wide Web: A system with universally accepted standards for storing, retrieving, formatting, and displaying information in a networked environment.

worms: Independent software programs that propagate themselves to disrupt the operation of computer networks or destroy data and other programs.

zero-day vulnerabilities: Security vulnerabilities in software, unknown to the creator, that hackers can exploit before the vendor becomes aware of the problem.

Index

Name Index

Atick, Joseph J., 431

Balter, Gary, 134
Béchet, Marc, 357
Blake, Frank, 61
Boire, Ron, 133
Brin, Sergey, 274
Bryant, Beverley, 469–470
Brynjolfsson, Erik, 162–163
Burwell, Sylvia Burwell, 485

Carey, Matt, 61
Casey, Jim, 45
Chong, Eric, 362, 363
Cohen, Steven, 140

Deming, W. Edwards, 121
Dymond, Duncan, 469

Eckman, Paul, 431–432
Ellison, Larry, 90

Filo, David, 273–274
Ford, Bill, 109
Ford, Henry, 83
Friedman, Thomas, 34, 36

Ganenthiran, Nilam, 397
Gates, Bill, 83
Goelman, Aitan, 312
Gonzales, Albert, 305
Gupta, Rajat, 140

Holifield, Mark, 61, 62
Howes, Rick, 254

Iannone, Jamie, 405
Ingham, Don, 134

Jobs, Steve, 83
Jones, Kevin, 90
Juran, Joseph, 121

Kalanick, Travis, 367
Kant, Immanuel, 147
Keen, Bill, 463

Lamonica, Sam, 213
Lampert, Edward, 133
Lebwohl, Andrew, 390
Lezon, Joe, 464

Martinez, Arthur, 132
McAfee, Andrew P., 162–163
McGinley, Matt, 133
McMillon, Doug, 405
Mehta, Apoorva, 396

Obama, Barack, 266

Olson, Cliff, 191
Orwell, George, 160
Osborne, Kelly, 390
Oxley, Michael, 308

Page, Larry, 274
Panettiere, Hayden, 390
Park, Todd, 483, 484
Porter, Michael E., 105–107

Ryan, Claude, 45

Sarao, Navinder, 311–312
Sarbanes, Paul, 308
Sebelius, Kathleen, 484, 485
Sidhu, Suresh, 362
Simon, Herbert, 413
Soards, Susan, 464
Spithill, James, 420

Tavenner, Marilyn, 484

Wahid, Mohamed, 60–61
Wheeler, Tom, 266

Yang, Jerry, 273–274

Zuckerberg, Mark, 170, 292

Organizations Index

ABC Bakers, 449–450
Aberdeen Group, 212
Accenture, 311, 363, 450, 454, 460
Actian, 418
Adobe, 34, 87, 198, 200, 300, 460
Advanced Micro Design (AMD), 36
Airbnb, 368, 372, 381, 395
Ajax Boiler, 270
Albertson's, 396
Alcoa, 340
Alex and Ani, 463–464
Alimentation Couche-Tard, 335–336
Allot Communications, 321
Alta Vista, 118
Amazon, 37, 105, 110, 111, 112, 126, 128, 151, 157, 159, 160, 185, 190, 192, 219, 230, 266, 370, 372, 376, 378, 380, 381, 383, 384, 388, 394, 396, 398, 404–406
Amazon.com, 115, 121, 132, 152, 304, 322
Amazon Web Services, 190, 191, 192, 193, 230
American Airlines, 306–307
American Bar Association (ABA), 148
American Library Association, 266

American Management Association, 270
American Medical Association, 148
American Trucking Association, 235
American Water, 232–233
Ancestry.com, 383
Angkasa Library, 290–291
Annenberg School of Communication, 172
Ann Taylor, 117
AOL, 379, 385
Apache Software Foundation, 233, 273
Applebee's, 441
Apple Inc., 33, 34, 37–38, 39, 83, 87, 105, 108, 110, 111, 118, 119, 151, 155–156, 157, 160, 170, 189, 193, 194, 195, 202, 323, 372, 378, 381, 394, 433
Armani Exchange, 398
Aruba Networks, 213
Arxan Technologies, 323
Association for Computing Machinery (ACM), 148
Association of Information Technology Professionals (AITP), 148
AT&T, 118, 255, 262, 267, 280
Automotive Resources International® (ARI®), 235–236

BAE Systems, 217–218, 394
Ball State University, 321
Bank of America (BofA), 116, 140, 397, 418
Barclays, 140
Barnes & Noble, 126, 233
BASF, 65-67
Bayer Material Science, 90
BCBGMAXAXRIAGROUP, 323
Bell, 38
Bell Laboratories, 196
Best Buy, 398
Bing, 276, 379, 380
BJ's Wholesale Club, 308, 396
BlackLocus, 61
Blockbuster, 118
Blue Nile, 376, 380, 381
BMW, 389
Body Shop International PLC, 418
Boeing Corporation, 132, 394
BT Group, 363
BT Managed Security Solutions Group, 321
Buffalo Bills, 187
Bureau of Labor Statistics, 53

Cablevision, 255, 271
Caesars Entertainment, 239
Cass Information systems, 213
Catapult Sports, 187
Caterpillar Corporation, 120, 389,

481–482
Celcom Axiata Berhad, 362–364
Cenoric Projects, 323
CenterPoint Properties, 271–272
CGI Federal, 484
CGI Group, 483, 484
Champion Technologies, 314
Charles Schwab, 239
Check Point Technologies, 319
Chicago Mercantile Exchange, 311
ChoicePoint, 143
Christian Coalition, 266
Cincinnati Zoo, 463–464
CIRRUS, 39
Cisco Systems, 87, 231, 319
Citibank, 39, 118
Citigroup, 140
CloudHarmony, 192
Coca-Cola, 339
Colgate-Palmolive, 436
Colloquy, 132
Comcast, 153, 255, 266
Comdisco Disaster Recovery Services, 314
Commodity Futures Trading Commission (CFTC), 311
Comodo, 320
ComScore, 389
Continental AG, 253–254
Con-way Inc., 426–427
Copyright Office, 155
Costco, 396
Countrywide Financial, 116, 140
Covestro, 90–91
Crowne Plaza Hotels & Resorts, 463
CTIA, 267
CVM Solutions, LLC, 436

Darden School of Business, 436
Dassault Systemes, 218, 254
DEC, 118
Decisive Analytics, 323
Dell, 197
Delta Airlines, 122, 436
Demand Foresight, 61
Deutsche Bank, 314
Development Seed, 484
Digitec, 436
Disney.com, 381
Dollar General Corporation, 58
Dollar Rent-a-Car, 201
DoubleClick, 143, 152, 153, 382, 385, 386
Dow Chemical, 36
Dow Jones Industrial Average, 311
Drugstore.com, 381
Dubai Ports World, 344–345
DuPont, 438

E*Trade Financial, 197, 383
EarthLink, 262

Subject Index

BUSINESS CASES AND INTERACTIVE SESSIONS

Here are some of the business firms you will find described in the cases and Interactive Sessions of this book:

Chapter 1: Business Information Systems in Your Career

Rugby Football Union Tries Big Data
The Mobile Pocket Office
UPS Competes Globally with Information Technology
Mashaweer: On-Demand Personal Services in the Gulf

Chapter 2: Global E-Business and Collaboration

Social Business at BASF
Schiphol International Hub to Become Faultless: Truth or Dare?
Is Social Business Working Out?
Modernization of NTUC Income

Chapter 3: Achieving Competitive Advantage with Information Systems

Should T.J. Maxx Sell Online?
Automakers Become Software Companies
Identifying Market Niches in the Age of Big Data
Will Technology Save Sears?

Chapter 4: Ethical and Social Issues in Information Systems

Content Pirates Sail the Web
Monitoring in the Workplace
Big Data Gets Personal: Behavioral Targeting
Facebook Privacy: What Privacy?

Chapter 5: IT Infrastructure: Hardware and Software

Toyota Motor Europe Reaches for the Cloud
The Greening of the Data Center
Cloud Computing Is the Future
The Risks and Benefits of BYOD

Chapter 6: Foundations of Business Intelligence: Databases and Information Management

BAE Systems
American Water Keeps Data Flowing
Driving ARI Fleet Management with Real-Time Analytics
Lego's Enterprise Software Spurs Growth

Chapter 7: Telecommunications, the Internet and Wireless Technology

RFID and Wireless Technology Speed Up Production at Continental Tires

The Battle over Net Neutrality

Monitoring Employees on Networks: Unethical or Good Business?

RFID Propels the Angkasa Library Management System

Chapter 8: Securing Information Systems

MiniDuke Exposes EU Cybersecurity Gaps

Stuxnet and the Changing Face of Cyberwarfare

MWEB Business Hacked

Information Security Threats and Policies in Europe

Chapter 9: Achieving Operational Excellence and Customer Intimacy: Enterprise Applications

Statoil Fuel and Retail Competes Using Enterprise Systems

DP World Takes Port Management to the Next Level with RFID

Unilever Unifies Globally with Enhanced ERP

Customer Relationship Management Helps Celcom Become Number One

Chapter 10: E-Commerce: Digital Markets, Digital Goods

Uber Storms Europe: Europe Strikes Back

Getting Social with Customers

Can Instacart Deliver?

Walmart and Amazon Duke It Out for E-commerce Supremacy

Chapter 11: Improving Decision Making and Managing Knowledge

Fiat: Real Time Management With Business Intelligence

America's Cup: The Tension Between Technology and Human Decision Makers

Facial Recognition Systems: Another Threat to Privacy?

Knowledge Management and Collaboration at Tata Consulting Services

Chapter 12: Building Information Systems and Managing Projects

Girl Scout Cookie Sales Go Digital

Analytics Help the Cincinnati Zoo Know Its Customers

Britain's National Health Service Jettisons Choose and Book System

A Shaky Start for Healthcare.Gov